THE

New York Yankee

ENCYCLOPEDIA

THE
New York Yankee
ENCYCLOPEDIA

HARVEY FROMMER

A MOUNTAIN LION BOOK

MACMILLAN • USA

Macmillan
A Simon & Schuster Macmillan Company
1633 Broadway
New York, N.Y. 10019

Library of Congress Cataloging-in-Publication Data
Frommer, Harvey.
     The New York Yankee encyclopedia: the complete record of
Yankee baseball including the 1996 world championship season/ by Harvey
Frommer.
          p.   cm.
     "A Mountain Lion book."
     Includes index.
     ISBN 0-02-861511-5
       1. New York Yankees (Baseball team) —History I. Title.
GV875.N4F76   1996   97-7455
796.357'67'097471—dc21   CIP

ISBN: 0-02-861511-5

Manufactured in the United States of America

10 9 8 7 6 5 4 3 2 1

Contents

Acknowledgments

Many people were very helpful in providing guidance, access, information, materials, and memories. Thanks to Randy Voorhees and John Monteleone of Mountain Lion, Greg Mazzola of the New York Yankees, Dean Al Schlazer of Miami-Dade Community College, my agent Don Congdon, and the interviewees who graciously gave of their time to provide memories and perceptions for this book.

Roger Harris, as always, came through with access to his vast archival collection of facts, figures, and memorabilia.

Editor Ken Samelson of Macmillan was a steady force and a knowledgeable voice.

And Arthur Richman of the Yankees, a true mensch and a guy who knows the score, was invaluable.

Introduction

The heritage is there, complete and unchallenged: Reggie hitting home runs into the October nights, the Babe blasting the ball, the Mick ripping the tape measure shots, Gehrig playing through 2,130 games when it mattered a great deal and when it mattered not at all, Eddie Lopat throwing the junk balls, Don Larsen soft tossing the Perfect Game, Billy Martin coming back as manager, coming back as manager, coming back as manager.

When Casey jawed and juggled, when Joe McCarthy pushed the buttons, when Miller Huggins molded, when DiMag hit in 56 straight, when Maris hit 61, when Bucky Dent hit the tin in Fenway, when Chris Chambliss hit it out, when the Yankees won five straight world championships.

The 34 pennants and the 23 World Championships, the standing-room-only crowds, the Ballantine Blasts, the White Owl Wallops and the Holy Cows, the Subway Series, Five O'Clock Lightning, Murderer's Row and the Bronx Bombers, the Springfield Rifle, the Big Cat, the Bull, the Scooter, Yogi, Goofy, the Goose, Moose, Old Reliable, Donnie Baseball, Iron Horse, Ellie, Slick, King Kong, Bulldog, the Yankee Clipper and Joltin' Joe, the Sultan of Swat, the Boss, Pride of the Yankees, Mr. October and Mr. May, the Oklahoma Kid and the Commerce Comet, Sailor Bob, the Almighty Tired Man, Billy Ball, Blind Ryne, the Count, Puff, Pepi, the Battle of Broadway, Superchief, The House That Ruth Built.

"Close games make me nervous."

"Yankee Stadium was a mistake, not mine, but the Giants."

"I never woulda done it without my players."

"I'd rather be lucky than good."

"There is a silent torch that we all carried for Donnie."

"If I'da known I was going to live this long I woulda taken better care of myself."

"If all I am entitled to is an asterisk, it will be all right with me."

"I consider myself the luckiest man on the face of the earth."

"It's great to be young and a Yankee."

The heritage is there, complete and unchallenged.

ONE

THE Greatest Franchise OF ALL

*T*he most fabled franchise in all of sports had the most modest of beginnings.

On April 30, 1903, 16,294 people jammed into Hilltop Park for the Opening Day of the New York Highlanders, the brand-new American League franchise. Many had arrived via the new subway station at 168th Street. Each fan received a little American flag courtesy of American League president Ban Johnson.

Located on Broadway and Ft. Washington Avenue between 165th and 168th streets in Washington Heights, the new ballpark was 10 blocks north of the Polo Grounds. To create it, more than $200,000 was expended carving 12,000 cubic yards of rock out of solid ramparts. Then, in six weeks, at a cost of $15,000, the hastily constructed wooden ballpark rose on the roughly cleared site. The playing field surface was dirt on rock, dirt on dirt, uneven, lumpy, bumpy, and badly pitted in spots. There was a gigantic and unsightly roped-off hollow in right field. A hastily decided on grounds rule mandated the awarding of a double to a player who hit a ball past the ropes. That June, a fence would be erected in front of the hollow; any player hitting a ball over that fence would be credited with a home run. The park's dimensions were gargantuan: left field was 365 feet, center field a monstrous 542 feet, and right field was 400 feet.

Ticket prices were 50 cents for a seat in the single-deck, covered wooden grandstand that extended from first base to third base. It cost 75 cents to sit in the bleachers that reached to the right-field corner. Those who paid a dollar watched the game from a box. Those who sat in the upper seats behind home plate were afforded a splendid view of the Palisades in New Jersey and the Hudson River, just two blocks to the west of the ballpark.

At 3:00 P.M. players from the Highlanders and Washington Senators marched from the outfield to home plate. They stood at attention as the 69th Regiment band played the "Washington Post March" and then the "Star Spangled Banner." Ban Johnson threw out the first ball; a short speech was delivered by umpire Tom Connolly. And then the cry of "Play ball" was heard. When the day was done, the home team had a 6–2 victory. The fans of the Highlanders were happy.

Happier still was Ban Johnson. For two years his upstart league had been involved in a war of lawsuits, bitterness, and backbiting with the established National League. One of the provisions of a peace agreement was the transfer of the Baltimore Orioles franchise to New York, the largest city in the United States.

The franchise was purchased for $18,000 in cash by well-known gambler Frank Farrell and former New York City chief of police William S. "Big Bill" Devery, who bragged that he had never read a book. Farrell and Devery owned hundreds of pool rooms and nearly as many politicians, and they knew their way around town.

Nothing associated with the new franchise was ever clear-cut. Devery and Farrell were the owners, but their sordid reputations convinced Ban Johnson that it would be wiser at the start to keep them backstage. Front stage was Joseph W. Gordon, dealer in coal, ex-state assemblyman, ex-president of the New York Metropolitans of the American Association. He was installed as the figurehead president of the new team.

(Preceding page)
Between 1925 and 1934, Babe Ruth and Lou Gehrig hit 772 home runs for the Yankees, the highest combined total by teammates in American League history.

Hilltop Park, at 168th Street and Broadway, was the Highlanders' home field from 1903-12.

The formal name for the park was the New York American League Ball Park. But since it was situated at the highest point in Manhattan, it was dubbed Hilltop Park. The official name for the team was the New York Americans. But because of its lofty location, fans and sportswriters used the nickname Hilltoppers. Others preferred Highlanders because of the elevated playing site and because club president Gordon's name was reminiscent of the Gordon Highlanders, the fabled British army unit. Other names employed to describe the new American League entry included Hill Dwellers, Porch Climbers, Burglars, and Cliffmen.

Since many of the players on the Highlanders hailed from New York, New Jersey, and Pennsylvania, the team had a decidedly local flavor. It also had a patchwork look, with seven first-year performers and an assortment of other players whose roots were with 11 teams.

But there was some name recognition that came from two former National League stars—Wee Willie Keeler, 31, of "hit 'em where they ain't" fame, and ace spitballer "Happy Jack" Chesbro. The 5-4 Keeler brought to the Highlanders his 30½-inch bat, shortest in major league history, a .373 lifetime batting average, and all kinds of superstitions.

The Sporting News offered this mangled prose about Keeler: "He swears by the teeth of his mask-carved horse chestnut, that he always carries with him as a talisman that he invariably dreams of it the night before when he is going to boot one—muff an easy fly ball, that is to say, in the meadow on the morrow. 'All of us fellows in the outworks have got just so many of them in

Player-manager Clark Griffith pitched in 25 games during the Highlanders' first season. Here Griffith (far right) is shown smoking a cigar as owner of the Washington Senators.

a season to drop and there's no use trying to buck against fate.'"

Another name on the new team was pilot-manager Clark Griffith. Made an offer he could not refuse by Johnson to give up employment as player-manager of the Chicago White Sox and pilot the new AL team, the "Old Fox" was then 33 years old and past his prime as a pitcher. Some also said he was past his prime as a manager.

Overall, that first season the Highlanders fared fairly well. They won 72 games, finishing in fourth place, 17 games out of first, and 211,808 came out to see them play. Wee Willie Keeler, in the first of his seven seasons with the team, batted .318. Chesbro posted a 21–15 mark. And player-manager Clark Griffith pitched in 25 games and surprised many by winning 14 of them.

In 1904, Keeler, whose salary was $10,000—highest in the American League—batted .343, second in the circuit. But it was Chesbro who had a season of seasons, winning 41 games, a modern major league record.

And the 30-year-old hurler was on the mound to pitch the first game of a doubleheader on the final day of the season against Boston. The Highlanders had a good shot at the pennant. Fans were stacked up in the outfield 10 and 20 deep. There were 25,584 present, the largest attendance in Hilltop Park history.

The score was tied 2–2 as the ninth inning got under way. Boston's Lou Criger singled. He was sacrificed to second. A groundout moved him on to third base. Then Chesbro put too much on a spitter. Catcher Jack Kleinow couldn't handle it. The wild pitch gave Boston a 3–2 win. The Highlanders won the nightcap of the doubleheader but it was too little, too late. They finished one and a half games behind Boston. It would be the closest the franchise would come to winning a pennant in its first 18 years of existence.

The Chesbro wild pitch was a disappointing way for the Highlanders to end the 1904 season, but they did win 20 more games than the season before, double their first season's attendance, and make strides in the standings. There was progress. The same could not be said for Hilltop Park.

A slum of a ball park right off the bat, Hilltop became more and more ramshackle as time passed by. It was a home improvement hobbyist's dream but a nightmare for players and fans. At first players dressed in their hotels, since there was not even a clubhouse. That came later. Installed in deep center field, it was a poor man's version of the one in the Polo Grounds. Parking space was minimal, too, until lots were set up in 1906 inside the grounds behind the grandstand for carriages and cars.

There were so many complaints about the condition of Hilltop Park that Farrell and Devery talked about moving into a park location on 225th Street in Manhattan. They talked about creating a floating ballpark in the Harlem River. They did a lot of talking.

But it was all talk.

There was also a promise by the Highlander owners that there would be no advertising in the ballpark. That promise lasted until 1907, when boards in the outfield were plastered with advertisements for Morocco cigarettes at 15 cents a package, Regal shoes, and F.C. Rye. Joseph Gordon, too, only lasted until 1907.

Farrell fired him, stating: "I decided that I should get some of the glory. I had put up the money and done a lot of work." Farrell did get more attention, but the biggest attention-getter arrived in 1909. It was a Bull Durham tobacco sign shaped like a bull and positioned in right-center field that was twice the size of the fence.

Farrell was just one in a long line that moved on and off the team. In 1907, a utility player named Branch Rickey appeared in 52 games, batting .182. One of his dubious distinctions took place on June 28. Catching that day, he watched in dismay as 13 Senators stole bases.

In 1908 Clark Griffith was out as manager. Shortstop Norman Arthur Elberfeld, also known as "The Tabasco Kid," was in. The kid managed a 27–71 record and gave way to George Stallings in 1909, the final season for Wee Willie Keeler. It was reported that Stallings paid the rent for an apartment just outside of Hilltop Park. There he stationed a "spy" with binoculars, who allegedly picked up the opposition's signals and, using a mirror, relayed the signs to Yankee batters. The cloak-and-dagger work notwithstanding, Stallings was gone as manager in 1910, succeeded by first baseman Hal Chase.

Stallings had accused Chase of throwing games, but no one seemed to listen or to care. Chase won 10 of the 14 games he managed, closing out the

First baseman Hal Chase took over as manager at the end of the 1910 season, despite rumors that he threw games. In 1911, New York dropped to sixth place and Chase was replaced by Harry Wolverton.

In 1913, the New York Yankees moved their home field to the Polo Grounds, a site already occupied by the New York Giants. This spurred a great rivalry between the Yanks and Giants for many years.

1910 season. His 1911 player-manager salary was about $6,000—one of the top salaries in the American League. The team dropped to sixth place, four notches below their finish of the season before.

It was exit Chase and enter cigar-smoking Harry Wolverton in 1912. Disaster time. Wolverton presided over a sorry team that won just 50 games, lost 102, and finished in last place. It was probably the worst team in the history of the Yankees. One of the few bright spots of that era was the pitcher they called the "Father of the Emory Ball." In 1910, rookie right-hander Russ Ford posted a 26–6 record with 8 shutouts. He followed that up with 22 wins in his sophomore season.

Highlander changes in managers and playing personnel were echoed by tinkering with the team's uniform, which at the start was black with an *N* and a *Y* on the jersey front. By 1909, the Yankee monogram was placed on the uniform jersey's left sleeve and the front of the cap. Two years later "NEW YORK" was spelled out in arched capital letters on the jersey front.

By 1912, the Highlanders were frequently being referred to as Yankees in newspapers. *The New York Times* noted: "The Yankees presented a natty appearance in their new uniforms of white with black pinstripes." The Yankee nickname was coined by Jim Price, sports editor of the *New York Press.* He, like other journalists, had complained that Highlanders was too long a name to squeeze into newspaper headlines. It was said that the red, white, and blue flags that adorned Hilltop Park gave Price the idea for the Yankee name.

Through the first decade of the New York American League franchise's history, change was the only constant. But Devery and Farrell outdid themselves in 1913. Everything was changed.

For the 1913 season the Highlanders–Hilltoppers officially changed their name to the New York Yankees. That was one change. Another was the abandoning of Hilltop Park. The last game played there was on October 5, 1912. The rotting facility would be razed in 1914. Still another change was the switching of their spring-training site. The franchise had trained in places like Hot Springs, Arkansas, and Macon, Georgia. In 1913, the Yankees trained in Bermuda, making them the first team to train outside the United States.

Perhaps the most significant change was the home field. The Yankees became tenants at the Polo Grounds of the Giants, who had won three pennants in a row. It was kind of a quid pro quo arrangement. Back in 1911, there was a major fire at the Polo Grounds and John McGraw's team had played at Hilltop Park from April 15 to May 30.

There was still another change. A new manager was in place for the Yankees in 1913—Frank Chance of Tinker to Evers to Chance fame. Signed for $40,000 a year for three years, Chance was the highest-paid manager to that point in time. Many beanings had concluded Chance's playing career, but he was a big name, a successful one, a keen baseball mind. "The Peerless Leader" had averaged 100 or more wins in eight years as manager and piloted the Cubs to five pennants and two World Championships in five seasons.

Devery and Farrell reasoned that even if Chance couldn't lead their team to that many wins, at least he might help stir up some positive press and take away some of the headlines from John J. McGraw.

There really was not much chance of that for Chance. The 1913 Yankees had but four holdovers from the last-place Wolverton club. One writer moaned: "Chance was handed about as poor a lot of ballplayers as any man ever undertook to make into a ball club."

On Opening Day in Washington on April 10, 1913, the Yankees played their first game using their new nickname. The first ball was thrown out by President Woodrow Wilson. After allowing an unearned run in the first inning, Walter Johnson muffled the Yankee bats. The Senators won the game, 2–1. And from that day on all through the season bodies kept coming and going.

Forty-five different players wore the Yankee uniform that 1913 campaign, including seven catchers. One of those who was sent packing was Hal Chase. Chance was convinced that Chase, potentially one of the premier performers in the American League but a man "with a corkscrew mind," was throwing games. And the fierce and firmly honest manager traded him to the White Sox for journeyman Rollie Zeider and first baseman Babe Borton.

Zeider suffered from corns. Bortin suffered from a lack of talent. The trade infuriated Yankee fans, the New York press, and Devery and Farrell. "Chance traded Chase for a bunion and an onion," was the line all over the Big Apple. With the bunion and onion and others like them around, the Yankees were mediocre verging on horrible. They finished the season next to last in the standings, ERA, and batting average, and tied for last in fielding.

But it got even worse in 1914. Openmouthed in their negative feelings about Chance, the Yankee owners were closefisted in their willingness to spend any money to improve the team. Chance had many arguments with Devery that 1914 season. In one of them he lunged at the 250-pound co-owner, attempting to punch him out. Cooler heads intervened.

With the Yankees languishing in sixth place, sporting the lowest batting average in the majors, the "Peerless Leader" realized the team didn't have a ghost of a chance to go anywhere. So he decided to go somewhere. With two weeks left in the season he packed it in and went home to his California ranch. Baseball, he said, was behind him.

The new pilot was 23-year-old shortstop Roger Peckinpaugh, still the holder of the record as the youngest manager in the history of major league baseball. "The Yankees," he recalled, "were what we used to call a 'joy club.' Lots of joy and lots of losing. Nobody thought we could win and most of the time we didn't. But it didn't seem to bother the boys too much. They would start singing songs in the infield right in the middle of a game."

The blues were the only songs Farrell and Devery were singing. Their team wound up in the second division for the fourth consecutive time in 1914. Attendance was less than 360,000 each of those seasons. One of the few bright spots in the 1914 season was the 74 bases stolen by third baseman Fritz Maisel, still a record for the franchise.

But the disasters on the playing field were being echoed off the field for Farrell and Devery. With their team a shambles and their varied business forays fizzling, the co-owners, who had begun as friends, now barely spoke to each other. And when they talked, it was never in a whisper and often with much profanity and rancor. It was no secret that they were anxious to get out of baseball.

Anxious to get into baseball were Col. Jacob Ruppert, 47, and Capt. Tillinghast L'Hommedieu Huston, 45. Both men were season box holders at the Polo Grounds and fans of the New York Giants. Ruppert was a

New York Giant manager John McGraw (left) had no problem with a new team using his park as a home field. It was a decision that he would later regret.

Col. Jacob Ruppert knew more about beer than baseball when he co-purchased the Yankees in 1915 for $460,000. In fact, he was a Giant fan at heart. However, his competitive spirit and generous bank account is what helped turn the Yankee organization into a winner.

former congressman, a venture capitalist, and the owner of Ruppert Brewery—one of the largest in the world. Huston made a fortune bringing the sewerage system and harbor of Cuba into the modern age.

What the two men had in common was money, organizational talent, and a love of baseball. They had wanted to buy the Giants, but their friend John McGraw informed them the team was not for sale. "I think the Yankees might be," he said.

Oddly enough, Ruppert had only seen the Yankees play twice. Once was when the Tigers came to town. He wanted to see Ty Cobb. Another time was for a Washington game. He wanted to see Walter Johnson.

On January 11, 1915, Ruppert and Huston paid the $460,000 price and became co-owners of the New York Yankees, a franchise that had a 12-year record of 861–937 and an average attendance of just 345,000 each season. Devery and Farrell split the purchase price, went their separate ways, and never spoke to each other again.

A competitive and driven man, and an envious one too, Ruppert was irked that the Giants had won five pennants and one World Championship and that the Brooklyn National League team had won four pennants. His Yankees had won nothing.

When he had investigated the possibilities of purchasing the Yankees, he remarked in exasperation, "I never saw such a mixed up business in my life—contracts, liabilities, notes, obligations of all sorts. There were times when it looked so bad no man would want to put a penny into it."

Realizing the work that lay ahead for the team he called "an orphan ball club, without a home of its own, without players of outstanding ability, without prestige," Ruppert started out with some organizational changes. He named himself president of the team. Then he appointed Harry Sparrow as business manager. Sparrow had organized the world tour of the Giants and White Sox the previous winter. He knew how to get things done.

Peckinpaugh was returned to full-time duty as a player and in his place as manager was 39-year-old Wild Bill Donovan. His claim to fame was a pennant won managing Providence in the International League, where he had a rookie named Babe Ruth.

One of the immediate and obvious changes in the Yankees was the first-class style that Ruppert and Huston initiated. The team stayed at good hotels, enjoyed restful hours in railroad sleeping cars, and sported freshly laundered uniforms day after day.

One change Ruppert was unable to effect was to rename the team the "Knickerbockers" after his best-selling beer. The 13 managing editors of New York City newspapers were not too enamored of the idea. So the Yankees name remained. And Ruppert vowed that he would find another way to make the team pay for itself—by winning on the baseball field.

"I want to win," Ruppert said. "Every day I want to win 10–0. Close games make me nervous."

The first couple of years he and Huston were very nervous as they lost almost as much money as they had paid to buy the Yankees. But they made it clear to all they were ready, willing, and anxious to spend whatever it took to get a winner.

Wally Pipp was purchased from Detroit for the waiver price. Pitcher Bob

Shawkey was plucked from Philadelphia for $18,000. The Yankees finished the 1915 season in fifth place.

Philadelphia's Frank "Home Run" Baker had retired from baseball at age 28 after the end of the 1914 season and gone back to the farm. The best third baseman in the majors was burnt out. But Bill Donovan thought there were still some sparks burning. The Yankees paid $37,500 to Connie Mack for permission to talk Baker out of retirement.

Donovan succeeded, and the Yanks got themselves a bargain. Fiery, professional, and a draw at the gate, Baker hit 10 home runs in 1916. Pipp led the league with a dozen roundtrippers. Shawkey posted 24 wins. And the Yankees moved up to fourth place, their first time out of the second division since 1910.

But 1917 saw a reversal in the team's fortunes, especially for Wild Bill Donovan. The season began with Huston bringing army drill sergeants to spring training in Macon, Georgia. Yankees were all over the field presenting arms with Louisville Sluggers. Huston left for France to present arms with the real thing. And the season got under way. It ended for the Yankees rather quickly—they never had a shot at the first division and wound up in sixth place with an anemic team batting average of .239 and a drop in attendance of more than 100,000. Wally Pipp did lead the majors in home runs for the second straight season, but that mattered little to Ruppert. It was a toss-up as to what bothered him more, the sixth-place finish or the attendance drop. Changes, the beer baron knew, had to be made. Wild Bill Donovan was out.

The ninth manager in the franchise's 16-year history was in place as the 1918 season was launched. Miller Huggins was his name. And although he was only a little wisp of a man, whose claim to fame was that he had guided the St. Louis Cardinals to a 346–415 record the past five seasons, Hug would be on the scene for the next dozen seasons and become the first great manager in Yankee history.

Yet at the start the odds of the 39-year-old Huggins even becoming the field boss of the Yankees were very long. New York newspapermen and fans were against his being hired, claiming he had never won a pennant, that he was a National Leaguer, and that he was replacing popular Bill Donovan.

More important, Til Huston had gone off to World War I and was stationed at an army base in France when the signing of Huggins was announced. He was furious. His choice for the new Yankee manager was one of his cronies, Brooklyn's rotund pilot, Wilbert Robinson. Huston fired off letters and cablegrams blasting Ruppert and Huggins. Peace was finally reached between the two Yankee owners, but their relationship was never the same again.

With all these negatives swirling around him and knowing full well that *the* manager in New York City was John J. McGraw, Miller Huggins went to work. The 1918 Yankees, shy 11 men who were in the service in that season shortened by the war, finished in fourth place. When the season ended, Huston and Ruppert went to work.

They sent four players plus $50,000 to the Red Sox and acquired outfielder Duffy Lewis and pitchers Ernie Shore and Dutch Leonard. The deal came about through the friendship of Huston and Boston owner Harry

Earle Combs was referred to as "The Waiter." Combs would simply get on base and wait for Ruth and Gehrig to knock him in.

Frazee. It was just the beginning of the Boston to New York shuttle of players and cash, especially cash.

In July 1919 submarine-ball hurler Carl Mays came over for pitchers Alan Russell and Bob McGraw and, more important, $40,000. Roger Peckinpaugh, still on the scene as the first great Yankee shortstop and one of the greatest at his position in major league history, batted .306. Signs of things to come that season were Bob Shawkey's 20 wins and the league-leading 45 home runs hit by the Yanks. Finishing in third place, setting a new attendance record as 619,000 came out to see them play, the Yankees' .617 winning percentage was the best in its history to that point.

But Jake Ruppert was still not happy. He asked Miller Huggins: "What do you need to win it all?"

The answer was "Babe Ruth."

THE RUTH/GEHRIG ERA

Babe Ruth and Lou Gehrig, the most famous one-two punch in baseball history, played together as Yankees full-time from 1925 to 1934. In that momentous decade there were three World Championships, four first-place finishes, and four second-place finishes.

There were many moments at Yankee Stadium when fans jumped to their feet roaring at the mighty power of the two sluggers. There were so many times when Ruth or Gehrig or both slugged the ball in the direction of the right-center-field bleachers that they were dubbed "Ruthsville" and "Gehrigsville." Those bleachers were separated from the field of play by a 10-foot chicken-wire fence. And many an outfielder, like the little Dutch boy sticking his finger in the dike, stuck his finger into that chicken-wire fence, watching a shot by Ruth or Gehrig land in the old wooden bleachers.

Stars spangled the Yankees in the '20s and '30s—Earle Combs, Tony Lazzeri, Lefty Gomez, Red Rolfe, Bill Dickey, Bob Meusel . . . but Babe Ruth and Lou Gehrig were the stars of stars—the driving power, the explosive force, the Bronx Bombers.

They were called the "Home Run Twins." But they were as opposite as fire and ice, as different as night and day. Nothing bothered Ruth, nothing. Many things bothered the shy Gehrig, who went out of his way to avoid the press. Ruth went out of his way to be in the limelight.

The Babe had sipped beer and chewed tobacco before he was seven years old. In his prime he feasted on a quart of chocolate ice cream and many pickled eels between games of a doubleheader. He was a man of the moment and of his time.

Gehrig lived in an apartment with his parents until he was 31 years old. He even did the dishes. A mama's boy, a young man who dreamed of building a home for his parents in the suburbs, Gehrig was frugal to the point of stinginess. He left 10-cent tips. The expansive Ruth lived wherever he pleased, did whatever pleased him. A big tipper, disrespectful of authority, the Babe was the Sultan of Swat, the reigning royalty of the baseball scene of his time.

Gehrig had a retentive memory for names and faces. Ruth never remembered a name. He also never remembered to flush the toilet. Gehrig, it was said, not only flushed but also put the toilet seat down.

(Opposite)
The Yankees captured their first pennant in 1921, but lost to the Giants in a hard-fought World Series.

The American League Champions 1921

PIPP   WARD   FERGUSON   McNALLY

HARPER   MAYS   SHAWKEY   HOYT   QUINN

COLLINS   PIERCEY   PECKINPAUGH   SCHANG   HOFMANN

RUTH   MILLER   R. MEUSEL   ROTH   FEWSTER

MITCHELL   ROGERS   BAKER   HAWKS   DEVOMER

G is for Gehrig,
The Pride of the Stadium;
His record is pure gold,
His courage, pure radium.
—Ogden Nash

Queried about off-season plans, Gehrig indicated in his tenor voice that he was anxious to get his body conditioned by playing basketball. Ruth, on the other hand, said, "I ain't doing nothin' except you know what."

The two would play poker on the long train rides from city to city. Five card stud. And Gehrig would envy the careless way the Babe tossed his money around. "Ruth would bet like the devil," recalled former *New York Times* sportswriter John Drebinger. "He would be taking wild gambles. Gehrig would be sitting across the aisle watching him. The Babe would be throwing his dough around in his fine style and Lou would look at him and say: 'My God, isn't that wonderful.'"

Gehrig's alma mater was Columbia University, Ivy League. Ruth's roots were at St. Mary's in Baltimore, an upscale reform school. The Babe was homely, oddly put together. Gehrig was a dimpled Adonis. His body was like that of a weight lifter. He had suits altered to fit his powerful physique. Constantly exercising, Gehrig was fond of staring at his image in a mirror as he flexed his biceps.

Gehrig's swing was parallel and hard. Some of his liners were like blue bullets—shots knocked infielders down. Possessed of superb eyesight, Ruth swung the heaviest bat of his time. His swings were up, up, and away. He hit Ruthian blasts—baseballs that traveled a country mile.

The back-to-back power the dynamic pair generated was mind-boggling. Seventy-four times they homered in the same game, 19 times in the same inning. In the World Series of 1926, 1927, 1928, and 1932 with Ruth and Gehrig doing their thing—combining for a batting average of .415, 47 RBIs, and 18 homers—the Yankees won 15 of the 19 games played, including a dozen straight.

Ruth was in his fourth season as a Yankee in 1923 when the 20-year-old Gehrig came up, played in 13 games, and batted .423. The youngster hero-worshiped Ruth, and the Babe had a certain fondness for Gehrig.

When he became the regular first baseman in 1925, Gehrig batted sixth in the Yankee order. Bob Meusel was ahead of him. Ruth was ahead of everyone as the cleanup hitter. Sam Gray of Philadelphia was the first pitcher to feel the home run power of Ruth and Gehrig. They got him for solo shots in the fourth inning on September 10.

Throughout most of the 1926 season Gehrig batted in the cleanup spot behind Ruth. He had 20 home runs, 107 RBIs, 135 runs scored. It was the first of a record 13 straight seasons that Gehrig scored and drove in 100 or more runs in a career where he averaged 141 RBIs a season.

In 1927, Gehrig hit full-time behind the Babe for the second straight year. Both Yankees loved it. Like two siege guns, they hit on American League pitching throughout the season, combining for a .365 average and 270 RBIs.

Fame's spotlight was all over Babe Ruth in 1927 because of the record-breaking 60 home runs he produced. "I'm not a headline guy and we may as well face it," said Gehrig, accepting his role. "I'm just the guy who is in there every day, the fellow who follows the Babe in the batting order. When Babe's turn at bat is over, whether he strikes out or belts a home run, the fans are still talking about him when I come up."

But fans and others did a lot of talking about the Iron Horse. No less an authority than Jimmie Foxx said: "Actually, Lou was a more dangerous hitter than Ruth." Gehrig actually had a better 1927 season than the Babe did, leading the league in RBIs and doubles. As late as September 1, Gehrig was ahead of Ruth 46–43 in the home run race. The Yankee first baseman wound up with 47 home runs—only the second player up to then to slug that many in a season. Gehrig's 175 RBIs broke Ruth's mark of 171, set in 1921. It was a remarkable accomplishment considering that at least 60 times Gehrig batted with no baserunners to drive in. Ruth's home runs wiped the bases clean.

In 1928, the Ruth and Gehrig show was in full stride. An especially explosive moment took place on May 29 at Yankee Stadium. The two sluggers touched up Washington pitchers Milt Gaston and Lloyd Brown for four home runs—all solo shots. Gehrig homered in the third off Gaston, in the fourth inning off Brown. Ruth rocked Brown for homers in innings four and seven. Ruth hit 54 home runs that 1928 season, the fourth time he reached that number in the decade. The Iron Horse's .374 batting average made the headlines in 1928, but the real eye-popping statistic of that Yankee season was the combined 397 RBIs recorded by Ruth, Gehrig, and Meusel, the 142 RBIs of both Gehrig and Ruth, tying them for the American League lead.

Winning their sixth pennant of the decade that 1928 season, the Yankees and especially Ruth and Gehrig went to work in the World Series against St. Louis. Ruth batted .625 with three home runs in game four; Gehrig batted .545 and pounded four home runs in the Series. The Yankees won the World Championship in four straight, stretching their string of World Series game victories to eight.

The Bronx Bombers of Ruth and Gehrig headed into the 1929 season with two straight seasons of 100 or more wins, with three straight pennants, and with two consecutive World Championships. The chant of "Break Up the Yankees" was heard. In spring training numbers were placed on the backs of Yankee uniforms, making the team the first to do so on a continuous basis. The numbers were based on the position of players in the batting order. Babe Ruth wore number 3, Gehrig number 4. It added up to a lucky "7."

That 1929 season Ruth clubbed 46 homers, batted .345, and drove in 154 runs. Gehrig had 35 homers and 126 RBIs. R&G once again were one-two in the home run race. The Yankee immortals also received a lot of help from their teammates. Tony Lazzeri drove in more than 100 runs and batted .354. Earle Combs lashed out 202 hits and hit .345. Despite these offensive efforts, it was a disappointing year for the Yankees. Their top pitchers, Waite Hoyt and Herb Pennock, managed a combined 19–20 record. Talented but new players on the left side of the infield and at catcher affected the team's rhythm. And the biggest blow was the death in late season of Miller Huggins. The Philadelphia Athletics came of age and won the first in a string of three pennants.

While Yankee pennant domination was short-circuited, the pulverizing power generated by Ruth and Gehrig showed the baseball world that the duo were still doing their thing in 1930. The Babe homered nine times in one week in May, and led the league in slugging, home runs, and walks.

You're a hero one day and a bum the next.
—Babe Ruth

Despite a combined 99 home runs and 382 RBIs from Babe Ruth, Lou Gehrig, and Tony Lazzeri, the Yanks failed to win the American League pennant in 1929. The Philadelphia Athletics earned their first of three consecutive titles.

———————

(Opposite)
The Yankees avenged their 1926 World Series loss to St. Louis by sweeping the Cardinals two years later.

Gehrig racked 41 homers, drove in 174 runs, and batted .379. The Yankees as a team batted a league-leading .309. Scoring 1,062 runs, slugging at a .488 percentage, the Yankees led the league in every offensive category except doubles and stolen bases. But the pitching was subpar. Only Red Ruffing and George Pipgras won as many as 15 games. A third-place finish, 16 games off the pace, ended Bob Shawkey's Yankee managing career.

All through their years together it was Gehrig who was always in Ruth's shadow. Perhaps that was part of the motivation for his playing day after day through 2,130 games, pushing himself to be in the lineup. It was partly an act of vanity, partly loyalty to the team and the game, partly his desire to make himself unique and to get out of Ruth's shadow.

The Babe did not approve of the streak. Gehrig, Ruth said, was shortening his career playing every day. The Yankee first baseman's retort was that it was his duty and job to play every day. That was what he was getting paid to do. It was a not-too-subtle jab at the Sultan of Swat's downtime on the job.

Although the Yankees had a new manager in Joe McCarthy in 1931, Ruth and Gehrig kept doing their same old thing—bashing American League pitchers. Ruth was second in batting average. Gehrig finished fifth. Ruth led all batters in slugging percentage, home runs per time at bat, and walks. Gehrig was runner-up to Ruth in all those categories. The Iron Horse was number one in RBIs, runs scored, and total bases. Ruth was close behind him. They tied for the league lead with 46 home runs. Both scored well over 100 runs. Ruth had 163 RBIs. Gehrig came out of the Bambino's shadow, driving in an American League record 184 runs.

Yankees *vs.* Cardinals

Souvenir ~ Program

MILLER J. HUGGINS
New York Yankees

BILL McKECHNIE
St. Louis Cardinals

Worlds Championship Series, 1928

Yankee Stadium ~ New York
Price **25** cents

After a Ruth home run (as shown here against the Athletics in 1932), pitchers had the unfortunate task of facing Gehrig.

In 1932, Ruth and Gehrig again torqued the dynamo that was the Yankees. The team scored more than a thousand runs for the third straight season. The Babe and the Iron Horse accounted for 258 of those runs. They were still doing their thing on the baseball field, but their personal relationship was becoming more and more frayed.

In their years together Gehrig had gone from Ruth's errand boy to his biggest fan and then to his adversary. "The big guy," Gehrig said of Ruth, "has a big loose mouth. He pops off too much about a lot of things."

In 1933, Babe Ruth was down in all offensive categories but still hit 34 homers and notched 103 RBIs. Gehrig was now the main Yankee bomber. He hammered 32 homers, collected 139 RBIs, and scored 138 runs.

Popular with teammates, who affectionately dubbed him "Biscuit Pants," Gehrig was truly the pride of his Yankee teammates. Ruth was more of a pain. The years of waving his check around on paydays for all to see, of playing practical jokes on players, of bullying, all had wore thin, as had the familiar newspaper headline: "It was the Ruth, the whole Ruth and nothing but the Ruth at the Yankee Stadium yesterday."

The final year Ruth and Gehrig played together as Yankees was 1934.

It was also a time the two stars rarely spoke to each other. Gehrig's mother allegedly made some unkind comment about Ruth's wife, and the Babe supposedly had some nasty things to say about Mrs. Gehrig. On June 3, 1934, Ruth and Gehrig both homered for the last time in a game.

Although 1934 was the end of the line for the Babe as a Yankee, Gehrig was still very much at the top of his form. He played on in the "House That

Ruth Built," batted .363, hit a career-high 49 home runs, drove in 165 runs, and won the Triple Crown in 1934. He would play on as the "Pride of the Yankees" to 1939, and then, sapped by disease, he would have to call it a career.

Other Yankees would come on the scene—superstars, flamboyant types, highly skilled performers. But no Yankee era would ever approach the style and power of the time of the handsome, heroic Gehrig and the boisterous, brawny Ruth.

THE DIMAGGIO ERA

Though Ruth's star began to fade during his final season with the Yankees in 1934, Gehrig's shined brighter than ever as he won the Triple Crown.

In the 11 seasons before Joe DiMaggio arrived on the scene, the Yankees won only four pennants. In Joe Dee's 13 seasons with the Bronx Bombers, they won 10 pennants.

Throughout his time the Yankees had all kinds of stars, but it was Joltin' Joe who carried the Yankees on his back. Bone chips on his heel, ulcers, muscle tears and pulls, a personal life skewered by the pressures of a divorce—all of these he coped with. And his example was the example for his Yankee teammates.

"When people ask who was the greatest ballplayer—Babe Ruth stands out above everyone else because he made the national pastime what it is," Yankee official and longtime observer of the baseball scene Arthur Richman explains, "but I have to pick DiMaggio. If you needed that base hit in the ninth inning—he was the man you wanted out there."

DiMaggio was a star from the moment he joined the Yankees in 1936. Lou Gehrig had an MVP season, but the focus was on the rookie with the jet-black hair. Gehrig was the "Pride of the Yankees," but Joe DiMaggio was the Yankee with the most pride. "There is always some kid who may be seeing me for the first or last time," DiMaggio said. "I owe him my best." Working constantly to improve his great natural skills, DiMag made all of those around him better.

"We played a doubleheader in Washington," former Yankee hurler Eddie Lopat recalled. "We won the first game. The second ended after 10 innings in a 3–3 tie. Yogi Berra didn't catch the second game. Charlie Silvera caught, and when he walked up to the plate, he was like a battleship in a canoe. He came up three times with the bases loaded and made out three times. You know Yogi, three times with the bases loaded, something would have popped. After the second game, DiMag was in the clubhouse about to fall down. He was so exhausted from the heat and the strain of playing both games. Yogi was jumping around.

"What in the world are you so happy about?" DiMag asked Yogi.

"We didn't do so bad today," Yogi said.

"You're 21 years old, and you can't catch a double header," DiMag lit into him. You could hear a pin drop. Then two or three other fellows started with Yogi. The next few years, Yogi caught 152–153 games a season. He was afraid to ask Stengel to get out."

Throughout the 1948 season DiMaggio played with highly painful calcium deposit bone chips in his right heel. "Each time I took a step on the field it was like someone was driving an ice pick into my head," he said. But Joltin'

You saw Joe DiMaggio standing out there and you knew you had a pretty damn good chance to win the baseball game.
—Tommy Henrich

Joe still batted .320 in 1948 and led the league in homers and runs batted in. Only his fielding showed the effects of the bone chips. He made 13 errors and fielded .972, his worst year in the field in a decade.

"I think," DiMaggio said, "I overworked every nerve in my body making it to that last game."

The 1948 Yankees finished two and a half games behind the pennant-winning Indians. There were many who knew that had DiMag been at full strength it would have been a different story.

It was a different story in 1949, DiMaggio's "comeback year." Wearing orthopedic shoes without spikes, DiMag had missed 66 games and gone eight months since his last American League at bat when he took the field for his first game of the '49 season at Fenway Park on June 28. His Yankee teammates had performed quite well during his absence and were in first place. But the Red Sox were closing in, having won 10 of their last 11 games.

In game one, in his first at bat, DiMaggio showed off that classic swing and singled. He homered in his second at bat. In the bottom of the ninth, the Yankee Clipper effortlessly snared a Ted Williams bid for an extra-base hit. The Yankees defeated Boston, 5–4. In game two, DiMaggio hit a pair of two-run homers, pushing the Yankees to a 9–7 come-from-behind win. In game three, the Yankees clung to a 3–2 lead after seven innings. A three-run homer off the light tower by DiMag settled matters. The Yanks won, 6–3, sweeping the Sox in the series.

Even Red Sox fanatics stood up and cheered the great Yankee. DiMaggio said they were "the most satisfying days of my life." In the three-game series, DiMaggio batted .455, with nine RBIs and four home runs. "But what he meant to the team you'll never find in the statistics," former Yankee hurler Eddie Lopat said. "He was the real leader of the club."

DiMaggio played in 76 games in 1949, batted .346 with 14 home runs and 67 RBIs. On the field and in the clubhouse he pushed the Yankees to the first of five straight pennants and World Championships.

For a dozen seasons, "When Joe walked in the lights flickered," according to clubhouse man Pete Sheehy. But as DiMaggio began the 1951 season, the spotlight was dimming. Time, age, and injuries had taken their toll.

When DiMaggio told reporters that 1951 would be his final season, he added, "There's always some kid coming up. They'll find somebody." In 1951, Mickey Mantle played right field alongside DiMaggio. When a ball was hit to the outfield, DiMag would wave his hand, telling Mantle where to go. "And all of a sudden," Casey Stengel said, "here would come the ball and he'd catch it and everybody would say what a smart young outfielder. He knows exactly where to play."

No player in baseball history placed his stamp on a franchise and an era so deeply as did Joseph Paul DiMaggio. Dedicated to the game, to the Yankees, to the fans, Number 5 was one of a kind.

"It wasn't the records," he said, "the Hall of Fame. It was none of that. I was most proud that I was a Yankee."

The Streak

On May 15, 1941, a Joe DiMaggio single in the first inning off Edgar Smith drove in Phil Rizzuto. But a bad throw by the Yankee center fielder attracted much more attention than his first-inning hit. The fans at the Stadium, miffed by the ineptitude of the Yanks, booed the team at the conclusion of each inning. The new double-play combination of Jerry Coleman and Phil Rizzuto appeared unsteady, and it seemed to some they would never last in the major leagues. Both were taken out of the game before its conclusion as the White Sox racked the Yankees, 13–1.

On May 24, Joe DiMaggio, hitless in three at bats, came to the plate in the seventh inning against the Red Sox. Few were aware that he had managed a hit in every game since his first-inning single on May 15 off Edgar Smith. Measuring out an Earl Johnson pitch, DiMaggio singled home two runs. The Yanks defeated the Red Sox. The streak was at a modest 10 straight games. And there were those who made the point that in 1933, DiMaggio, with the San Francisco Seals, batted safely in 61 straight games.

On June 1, the closemouthed DiMaggio notched hits in both games of a doubleheader against Cleveland. The streak was at 18. The death of Lou Gehrig the next day overshadowed the single and double DiMag racked off Bob Feller to move the streak to 19. Only 10 games away was the all-time New York Yankees record shared by Roger Peckinpaugh and Earle Combs. But George Sisler's American League mark of 41 seemed out of reach.

"That's when I became conscious of the streak," DiMaggio said, "when the writers started talking about the records I could break. But at that stage I didn't think too much about it."

On June 8, DiMaggio hit safely in both games of a doubleheader against the St. Louis Browns to tie and break his own previous 23-game hitting streak set in 1940. Two days later the streak was at 25 straight—and the nation had caught the fever.

Joe DiMaggio versus Bob Feller on June 14 was a highly publicized matchup: A third-inning single off Feller pushed DiMaggio past Babe Ruth's 1921 record of 26 games. The 26-year-old DiMaggio was positioned but two games away from the all-time Yankee consecutive-game mark.

On June 17, DiMag hit a ground ball that bounced off the shoulder of shortstop Luke Appling. It was declared a hit by scorer Dan Daniel. There was some controversy. But the streak moved to 30 games—one beyond the all-time Yankee record. A nation eager to turn away from news of World War II was elated. News programs and songs were interrupted on the radio: "The streak is alive! The streak is alive!"

A very private person, Joseph Paul DiMaggio became the most talked-about athlete in America. On the streets, traffic stopped when he walked by. Fans milled about him asking for autographs. He was bothered constantly in restaurants. At the ballparks, reporters kept asking the same question: "Joe, how many games straight do you think you can hit in?"

Day after day, DiMaggio would step into the batter's box and stub his right toe into the dirt in back of his left heel. It was almost a dance step. His feet were spaced wide apart, with the weight of his frame on his left leg. Erect, almost in a military position, Joe Dee would hold his bat at the end, poise it on his right shoulder, primed for action. He would look out at the pitcher from deep in the batter's box and assume a stance that almost crowded the plate. Intent, organized, DiMag was ready. Waiting in the batter's box, he seemed to be able to hit the ball right out of the catcher's mitt.

You know, Yankee Stadium center field is real deep. They didn't know Joe [DiMaggio] could go back that far for a high fly ball until I pitched. The only time I saw his face was in the clubhouse.
—Lefty Gomez

DiMaggio's seemingly effortless swing produced 361 lifetime homers and countless hits in the clutch. Once he decided to take the lumber off his shoulder, he rarely missed as he struck out only 369 times in 6,821 lifetime at bats.

On June 21, the Yankee Clipper singled off Dizzy Trout of the Detroit Tigers. The streak was at 34—one game more than the 1922 record set by Rogers Hornsby. Throughout the streak, two of the most interested observers were Joe's brother Dom, Boston Red Sox center fielder, and Ted Williams, the Yankee star's rival for American League accolades.

But "Ted really rooted for Joe," recalled Dom DiMaggio. "They were rivals, but they had great admiration for each other. As a great hitter himself, Ted could appreciate what Joe was accomplishing."

Game after game, Williams, playing left field for the Red Sox, received information about Joe DiMaggio's streak from the scoreboard operator at Fenway Park. And Williams would yell to Dom DiMaggio, playing in the outfield next to him: "Joe's got another." On July 1, Joe DiMaggio tied the 43-year-old record of Wee Willie Keeler by hitting safely in both games of a doubleheader against the Red Sox. The next day DiMag was hungering to reach 45 straight games—a new major league record. Stationed in center field was Dom DiMaggio, Joe's scheduled dinner guest that evening.

In his first at bat Joe Dee mashed a Dick Newsome pitch; the long drive was caught by Stan Spence. In his second at bat, DiMaggio poled the ball to center field. Racing at top speed as soon as he heard the crack of the bat against the ball, Dom dramatically snared the ball, robbing his brother of an extra-base hit.

"It was one of the best Dom ever made," Joe said, "but at that moment the only thing on my mind was to withdraw the dinner invitation I had extended to my brother." In his third at bat of the game, with two teammates on base, DiMaggio belted the ball into the seats for one of the 15 home runs he would record during his fabled streak. The home run gave him the record—the only player in history to hit in 45 straight games.

The next night the New York center fielder and the Boston center fielder dined on steak and spaghetti. "You know, Joe," Dom said, "I couldn't have gone another inch for the ball you hit that I caught. But I'm glad you have the record."

A single on July 5 moved the streak to 46. The next day DiMaggio lashed out six hits in a doubleheader. The streak was now at 48. On July 8, DiMaggio played in the All-Star Game. It was a time for relaxing and socializing. But even in that midsummer baseball parenthesis, there was still magic in DiMaggio's bat. He hit safely in the All-Star Game. Of course, it was not counted in the official record. But it was a special moment.

"I doubled," DiMag noted, "and Dom drove me in with a single." It was the first time the DiMaggio brothers combined in an All-Star Game to produce a run.

The streak was still alive in mid-July. People stayed up past their normal bedtimes to find out how Joe was doing. Radio announcers described how the Yankee Clipper managed to keep the consecutive-game hitting streak going.

On July 16, the Yankees arrived in Cleveland to start a series with the Indians inside the cavernous open spaces of Municipal Stadium. Wherever Joe DiMaggio and the Yankees went, crowds cheered him and rivals talked boldly of stopping the streak. The memory of the challenges, the breaks that kept the streak alive would always be with DiMaggio.

Before game 40, Johnny Babich of Philadelphia, who had beaten the Yankees five times the season before, announced that he was not going to give the Yankee Clipper anything good to hit, that he would be pitching around DiMaggio. A Babich pitch outside the strike zone was swung at by DiMag and slammed back through the legs of the pitcher. "Babich looked like he saw a ghost," said DiMaggio, savoring the double he recorded off a pitch that should have been called a ball.

Between games of a doubleheader on June 29 in Washington, the Yankee Clipper had experienced panic. In the first game his double off Dutch Leonard tied George Sisler's record of 41 straight games. But the bat that tied the record was stolen between games. "Move over, Sisler, here comes DiMag," the crowd screamed throughout that second game.

Hitless in his first three at bats, DiMaggio recalled that he had loaned a bat to Tommy Heinrich awhile back. Joe Dee reclaimed it and used it to lash a solid single. The crowd chanted, "42! 42! 42!"

The memory of the tenuous moments of the streak was very much with DiMaggio as the Bronx Bombers faced Cleveland. The Indians were managed by Roger Peckinpaugh, former coholder of the Yankees' batting-streak mark. A first-inning single on the night of July 16 off Al Milnar extended the streak to 56 straight games.

On the night of July 17, swelled by an advance sale of 40,000 seats, 67,468 crammed into Municipal Stadium, the largest night-game attendance to that time in history. Veteran southpaw Al Smith was the Cleveland starter.

DiMaggio had taken a cab to the ballpark with Lefty Gomez. "I got a feel-

DiMaggio was constantly in the spotlight during his incredible 56-game hitting streak.

SIDELIGHTS

OF THE STREAK

Games
53 day,
3 night,
29 at Yankee Stadium,
27 road games

At Bats
223 official

Batting Average
.408

Runs
56

Hits
91

Doubles
16

Triples
4

Home runs
15

RBIs
55

Strikeouts
7

Walks
21

Hit by Pitch
2

Bunts
0

ing," the driver said, "that if you don't get a hit the first time up, they're going to stop you tonight."

Gomez was furious. "What the hell are you trying to do, trying to jinx him?"

The gentlemanly DiMaggio tipped the driver and said "Well, if it is, it is."

As DiMag came to bat for the first time in the game, Indian third baseman Ken Keltner stationed himself deep, almost to the edge of the outfield grass. It was as if Keltner were daring DiMag to bunt—something he had not done during the entire streak. DiMaggio drove a 1–0 pitch past the third-base bag. A lunging, leaping Keltner backhanded the ball and fired it to first base. DiMag was out. Gomez screamed in the dugout, "Damn cabdriver"—or words to that effect.

In the fourth inning, DiMag walked. He came up in the seventh, straining to push the streak to 57. A deafening din filled Municipal Stadium. Smith pitched. DiMag slapped the ball to third and took off flat out for first base. A deft backhanded pickup and a strong throw by Keltner and DiMag was denied again.

In the eighth inning DiMaggio came up with the bases loaded, one out. On the mound was Jim Bagby, Jr., a right-handed relief pitcher who had replaced the left-handed Smith. The stadium rocked with noise. Most rooted for a hit.

Stoical, DiMaggio ran the count to 1–1. Then he slammed the ball on the ground to shortstop Lou Boudreau. It came up on a tricky hop. Boudreau gloved it at shoulder level, flipped to Ray Mack at second for one out; the pivot throw to first base doubled up DiMaggio. The play ended the inning for the Yanks and the streak for Joe DiMaggio.

The Yankees defeated Cleveland that day, 4-3, but in the dressing room after the game there was an atmosphere of defeat. DiMaggio, hitless for the first time in two months, was calm as he smoked a cigarette and answered questions.

"I can't say I'm glad it's over," he said. "Of course, I wanted it to go on as long as I could. Now that the streak's over, I just want to go out there and keep helping to win ballgames."

In that streak there were 15 home runs, 4 triples, 16 doubles, 55 RBIs, and 56 runs scored. DiMaggio batted .408 from May 15 to July 17, collecting 91 hits in 223 at bats. The Yankees won 41 games during the streak.

Linked forever with the streak is Ken Keltner. "I'm glad that I was part of it all," he said. "To me it was just another game and we were losing and I hated to lose. I made a couple of great plays against the greatest ballplayer I ever saw. He didn't only hit. He threw and he caught, and I don't think I ever saw him make a mistake. It wasn't Joe's day. He didn't show any emotion. You couldn't tell whether he was going good or bad—he kept that same face all the time. Both plays that I made, they were one way or the other—if I didn't catch the ball, it's a base hit for Joe. Unfortunately for him, the ball stuck in the glove and I was able to get it out and straighten up and threw him out by a half a step both times. There are no hard feelings."

With the streak ended, DiMaggio began another one. He hit in 16 straight games to flesh out one of the epic examples of sustained excellence in all the history of baseball—hitting safely in 72 out of 73 games.

The Yankee Clipper concluded the 1941 season with a .357 batting average. He led the league with 125 RBIs. Half of his 30 home runs came during the streak, as did 91 of his 193 hits.

"You can talk all you want about Hornsby's .424 average and Hack Wilson's 190 RBIs," said Ted Williams, whose .400 season was dwarfed by the hype and hoopla over the streak. "But when DiMaggio hit in those 56 consecutive games, he put a line in the record book. It's one that will never be changed."

DiMaggio hit safely against 63 right-handed pitchers and 28 left-handed hurlers.

The Yankees record during the streak: won 41, lost 13, tied 2, .759 winning percentage.

THE MANTLE ERA

"When Mickey came to bat," Phil Rizzuto said, "all the ushers stopped."

"As long as I knew him—about 30 years," Bobby Murcer said, "he never realized the impact he had on people's lives."

Gene Michael, his teammate in 1968, admitted it took half a season before he worked up the nerve to ask Mickey Mantle to pose with him for a photo. "That's how much I and so many others were in awe of him."

"I played with him for nine years," Tony Kubek said. "He was as great a player as any who ever lived. I marveled at how hard he hit and how fast he ran. He was one of the warmest human beings I ever met."

"He was a god among his teammates," Jim Bouton said. " I remember on payday when the traveling secretary brought our checks to the clubhouse, guys would wave the checks and say, 'Thanks, Mick.'"

Mickey Mantle's managers included Casey Stengel, Ralph Houk, Yogi Berra, Johnny Keane, and Houk again. In 1951, he was called "Golden Boy," and "the husky blond with the speed of a deer." During his first three years as a Yankee there were three World Championships. His teammates included Jerry Coleman, Joe Collins, Joe DiMaggio, Johnny Mize, Vic Raschi, Eddie Lopat, and Allie Reynolds. Then there were Roger Maris, Tony Kubek, Elston Howard, Johnny Blanchard, Ralph Terry, and always Whitey Ford.

A last link to the 1950s, a time of glory for the Yankees, a time the team won 955 games and lost 582, for a .621 percentage, Mantle played on with a new group of Yankees in the 1960s—Joe Pepitone, Tom Tresh, Phil Linz, Mel Stottlemyre, Jim Bouton, Clete Boyer.

In his last three seasons, in which he had teammates like Horace Clarke, Roy White, Jake Gibbs, Bill Robinson, and Stan Bahnsen, the Yankees stumbled to tenth-, ninth-, and fifth-place finishes. Told he had 15 game-winning hits in 1967, he smiled. "I didn't think we won that many games." Publicly, he joked about the dark years. Privately, he suffered. The sight of Mantle in the bathroom in the dugout sobbing in frustration at those losing Yankee seasons in the late '60s was too much for teammates to bear.

The faces changed and the fortunes of the Yankees ebbed and flowed, but Mickey Mantle, playing in the media capital of the world through 18 summers, getting those very strong hands and forearms to generate the power, was the constant, the most famous figure in all of baseball. He was the Commerce Comet that lit up New York. In his time, just as Babe Ruth and Joe DiMaggio had been, the Mick was the Yankees.

Mantle took part in many locker-room celebrations as he won 12 pennants and seven World Series titles during his reign with the Yankees.

Mantle combined power and speed to become the most dominant player in baseball during the 1950s. Here he's shown hitting one of his major league record 18 home runs in the World Series.

From 1954 to 1958, Mantle batted .300, .306, .353, .365, and .304 and averaged more than 38 homers and more than 100 RBIs a season. Mickey Mantle led the Yankees to 12 pennants and 7 World Championships. Only twice between 1951 and 1964 did the Yankees fail to play in the World Series with Mantle on the scene.

In those years he went from a callow youth to a pouting pinup superstar who fans booed when he struck out or when he pulled up short on a fly ball and wouldn't leave his feet. But he was protecting his brittle knees. Then, ironically, when the interloper Roger Maris came along and heard the boos, Mantle lightened up and became the favorite.

Mantle said his biggest thrills were a grand slam against the Brooklyn Dodgers in the 1953 World Series, breaking Babe Ruth's World Series record with his 16th home run in the Fall Classic, and a ninth-inning home run off knuckleballer Barney Schultz in game three of the 1964 World Series against St. Louis, giving the Yankees a 2–1 victory.

And there were all the other marker times: the home run providing Don Larsen with the only run he needed, and the catch to save the Perfect Game in 1956, the three home runs and .400 batting average against Pittsburgh in the 1960 World Series, the 536 home runs, placing him second only to Babe Ruth as a Yankee, the home run trots that were as famous as the Babe's.

"You could tell it was the Mick's trot," Bobby Murcer said. "Nobody could duplicate that." He went around the bases on his heels, head down, almost shy. But rounding third and coming home, his head was always up.

His peak years were 1956–57 and 1961–62. Between 1955 and 1964, Mantle was first or second in the Most Valuable Player voting half a dozen times. The Mantle Yankees won pennants more consistently than any other team, including the Yankees of Ruth-Gehrig and those of DiMaggio. Mantle was the Most Valuable Player in 1956, 1957, and 1962. Ralph Houk said of him, "As Mantle goes, so go the Yankees."

In 1965, with his body subjected to the wear and tear of over 2,000 games, Mantle was still a superstar. "But Johnny Keane didn't give him that much respect," noted Pedro Ramos. "He didn't know if he was in the lineup from day to day." Keane would put the likes of Ross Moschitto into the game. Mantle would be running to the outfield to take up his position. And then he would have to make a U-turn as Moschitto or someone else was sent out to take his place.

It was no doubt moments like that which prompted Mantle to remark: "I was sitting here the other day and I tried to remember what it was like to hit a home run and win a game. And I couldn't remember. It was like the whole thing happened to somebody else."

On September 19, 1968, Mantle faced Detroit's Denny McLain, a 30-game winner. The Tigers had clinched the pennant two nights before.

Mantle's humble home run trot became as recognizable as the tape-measure homers he would hit to circle the bases

My dad played in Chicago and Cleveland. But I thought that being a Yankee would be the greatest thing a fellow could do.
—Tom Tresh

McLain knew that Mantle was tied with Jimmie Foxx for third place on the all-time home-run list at 534.

"He was my idol," McLain said. He wanted the Mick to hit one out and grooved a pitch. Catcher Jim Price told the Mick what to expect. Mantle swung—home run!

The next day at Yankee Stadium, Mickey Mantle homered off Jim Lonborg of the Red Sox. It was number 536 for his career—the last home run.

Then, like Gehrig and DiMag before him, the Mick retired at age 36. He finished with a combined 3,400 walks and strikeouts and joked: "I mustn't have been so hot. I spent seven years without even hitting the ball."

But, oh, when he did hit the ball, he carried the Yankees on his back. He once said he wanted the inscription on his tombstone to read, "A Great Teammate."

He was all of that and a lot more.

THE DARK YEARS: 1965–75

"The biggest thing that happened to me in my career was going to the Yankees," Pedro Ramos recalled. "After all the years of pitching against them, I joined them in Kansas City. I put on the pinstripes and looked in the mirror—and said, 'Man, I'm a Yankee.' I wanted that so bad. I helped them win the pennant in '64. I had seven saves and one win. It only made me sad that I could not pitch in the World Series. They got my contract too late."

Putting together an 11-game winning streak, the Yankees won the 1964 pennant, their 13th in the past 15 seasons, their 15th in 18 seasons. Despite Jim Bouton's two wins and Bobby Richardson's 13 hits in the World Series against St. Louis, the Yankees lost to the Cardinals in seven games. Despite managing the Yankees to the best record in baseball in 1964 (99–63, .611), despite bringing them to within a game of the World Championship, Yogi Berra was fired after the Series loss.

"Yogi was still one of the guys coming off the field," Pedro Ramos said. "To be a manager is tough 'cause you're used to playing with all those guys. He won the pennant. He did the job. But it's tough to manage guys who you played with the year before.

"Johnny Keane came in and replaced Yogi as manager in 1965," Ramos said. "He was a hell of a nice guy, serious. Very religious. But he was not the right manager for the Yankees those years. He didn't talk much to the players. He kept to himself."

The 1965 Yankees included a starting rotation of Mel Stottlemyre, Whitey Ford, Al Downing, and Jim Bouton. The relievers were Ramos, Hal Reniff, Pete Mikkelsen, and Steve Hamilton. Joe Pepitone was at first base, Bobby Richardson at second, and Tony Kubek backed up by Phil Linz at the shortstop position. Clete Boyer was the third baseman. The outfield featured Tom Tresh in left field, Mickey Mantle in center, and Hector Lopez and Roger Maris sharing right field. Elston Howard did the catching.

On paper it was still a formidable roster. "We just didn't have that great superstar," Linz said, "that continued on from Ruth to DiMag to Mantle. The talent that came up in those early '60s was Joe Pepitone, Tommy Tresh, who averaged 21 homers a year from 1961 to 1967 and was MVP in two leagues, Al Downing, who was great, and Jim Bouton, who was a terrific prospect."

"I figured with Stottlemyre, myself, and Downing," Jim Bouton said, "that we were never going to be beat. That we were going to go on forever."

That was the general feeling. There were very few who foresaw the dark and down years that lay ahead. But the success of the team was built on a hollow surface. Mickey Mantle and Whitey Ford were on the decline. They, like other Yankees, were getting old all at once. The 1965 free-agent draft closed out the Yankee monopoly on being able to sign anyone they wanted. And like the crumbling stadium the team played in, the Yankee farm system was decaying. The top four Yankee farm teams finished last in 1963.

One of the few bright spots for the 1965 Yankees was Ramos, who relieved 65 times, saved 19 and won 5. But Tony Kubek, racked by an aching back, batted but .218. He retired after the season. Elston Howard, troubled by a damaged elbow, saw his batting average drop 80 points to .233. The 1965 Yankees won 77, lost 85, and finished in sixth place, 25 games out of first.

Things got much worse in 1966. After the Yankees lost 16 of their first 20 games, Johnny Keane was fired. Ralph Houk returned. "Ralph came in when things weren't going good," Ramos said. "He was for the players. He was there to try and straighten things out."

But it was too late. "Everybody was in a bad mood," said Jim Bouton. "Everybody was rubbing each other the wrong way." Among the starters, only Fritz Peterson won more games than he lost. Stottlemyre took the elevator ride from a 20-win season to a 20-defeat year. Yankee attendance dropped below 1.2 million. It had not been that low since World War II. The Yankees were flat last, in tenth place—their first last-place finish since 1912. Pedro Ramos had given the Yankees two terrific seasons of relief pitching. He was traded to the Phillies at season's end. Bobby Richardson retired.

Mediocrity, glumness, and despair pervaded the fire-sale atmosphere. In December 1966, Roger Maris was traded to St. Louis for run-of-the-mill third baseman Charley Smith. Like Maris, Elston Howard, Clete Boyer, and Johnny Blanchard all were sent packing with the Yankees receiving very little in return. Hobbled and hurting, Mantle played statuelike at first base. Joe Pepitone became the new center fielder. Nothing helped. The Yankees finished ninth in 1967. Whitey Ford retired during the season.

Regular catcher Jake Gibbs batted .213 in 1968, a point below the team average. The Yankees finished fifth in 1968—the fourth straight second-division finish for the team. Mantle, who hung around too long, who batted .254 with a total of 84 home runs in his final four seasons—the last two played at first base—packed it in after the 1968 season. The 1969 Yankees, playing in a city lit up by the dramatics of the Miracle Mets, finished 28½ games out of first place. Only Mel Stottlemyre seemed to remind people of the good old days: He posted a 20–14 season.

Some said the only real high points of those dark years were a fresh paint job on the House That Ruth Built in 1966 and Mickey Mantle Day at the Stadium in 1969. The Mick's Number 7 was retired, and he rode around the baselines sitting in a golf cart.

There were many low points. On December 2, 1971, Stan Bahnsen was traded to the White Sox for third baseman Rich McKinney. Hyped as the

The Yanks fell on hard times during the late 1960s and traded away several names from their glory years, such as third baseman Clete Boyer.

George Steinbrenner bought the Yankees from CBS in 1973, and shocked the baseball world when he signed pitcher Catfish Hunter for a record $3.5 million for five years beginning in 1975.

future franchise player, McKinney couldn't throw and couldn't hit. He lasted 37 games, batting just .215. Bahnsen went on to win 39 games for the White Sox in two seasons.

A year later Fritz Peterson and Mike Kekich traded "lifestyles" and moved in with each other's families and pets. It was a very un-Yankeelike thing to do. Even Babe Ruth would have disapproved.

The 1970 Yankees finished in second place. "I know old Yankee purists must have been thinking that celebrating second place was really bush," said Rookie of the Year Thurman Munson, who batted .302, "but we enjoyed it." The second-place finish looks good in the record book. In actuality, the Yankees finished a distant 15 games off the pace. For that achievement Ralph Houk won the Manager of the Year award. The 1970 Yankees had an infield of first baseman Danny Cater, shortstop Gene Michael, third baseman Jerry Kenney, and second baseman Horace Clarke. A symbol of the dark years, Clarke was a Yankee from 1965 to 1974. He was adequately mediocre.

There were three straight fourth-place finishes that included an exciting 1972 campaign. Contending for the pennant for the first time since 1964, the Yanks stumbled in the frenetic race in mid-September and wound up in fourth place.

The pushing away of the darkness for the fabled franchise that had lost its way began in 1973. There was new ownership headed by George Steinbrenner. There was a veteran baseball man running things. Gabe Paul, a man with 40 years of experience as a major league executive, replaced Mike Burke. "Build a winner," Steinbrenner told Paul.

On hand were several players who formed the foundation that Paul would build on. In November of 1972 the Yankees had acquired Graig Nettles for four nondescript players. Roy White was a solid outfielder. Mel Stottlemyre was a throwback to the talented Yankee pitchers of the past. There was also the young Thurman Munson and the irrepressible Sparky Lyle.

In December of 1973 Lou Piniella was acquired from Kansas City for Lindy McDaniel. Then on April 26, 1974, in what was billed as the "Friday Night Massacre," Gabe Paul, also known as "Dial-a-Deal," came into the Yankee clubhouse. He was smiling. He had shipped Fritz Peterson, Steve Kline, Fred Beene, and Tom Buskey—half the pitching staff—to Cleveland. In return the Yankee received first baseman Chris Chambliss and pitchers Dick Tidrow and Cecil Upshaw. Then Elliot Maddox was brought in from Texas. When Horace Clarke was sold to San Diego on May 31, 1974, only nine players remained from the Yankee roster of the previous season.

The Yankees in 1974 had a new manager. Bill Virdon took over for Houk, who had resigned after almost eight seasons of running the show. The Major had been garrulous, a communicator. Virdon, it was said, could go for weeks without talking to players. It was also said it was because he had nothing to say. The Yanks also had a new home—Shea Stadium, while Yankee Stadium was being refurbished.

With all the changes, with all the controversy, the Yankees, winning 20 of 31 games from September 1 on, went down to the final week of the 1974 season before being eliminated from the race. They finished in second place,

two games behind the division-champion Baltimore Orioles. But it was plain to all that the Yanks were coming.

In the off-season Oklahoma-bred Bobby Murcer was traded to the San Francisco Giants for Bobby Bonds, just another of the moves Paul made to restructure the roster, not yet championship caliber but highly competitive.

In December 1974 the Yankees signed Catfish Hunter to a record $3.5 million for five years. Starting pitchers in 1975 included Hunter, Doc Medich, Pat Dobson, Rudy May, and Larry Gura. The relievers were Sparky Lyle, Dick Tidrow, and Tippy Martinez. The regulars were Chris Chambliss 1b, Sandy Alomar 2b, Jim Mason/Fred Stanley ss, Graig Nettles 3b. The out-fielders were Elliot Maddox, Bobby Bonds, and Roy White. Thurman Munson was a fixture behind the plate. Ed Herrmann and Ron Blomberg were the designated hitters.

Bill Virdon had won the Manager of the Year award in 1974. After 104 games of the 1975 season, he was expendable. It was not that he was managing poorly. It was just that Steinbrenner had always had a gleam in his eye for Billy Martin, more his type of man. Number One returned to the Yankees as manager at an odd time and place—Old-Timers' Day at Shea Stadium.

The 1975 Yankees finished third, behind Baltimore and first place Boston. But the dark years were over. The rest of the 1970s would see the New York Yankees return to the top of the hill.

New York received a spark in 1970 from a young catcher named Thurman Munson. Munson won the Rookie of the Year award in '70, and was the foundation for great Yankee teams in years to come.

Bill Virdon was hired as the new Yankee skipper in 1974 and won the Manager of the Year award in his first campaign. He was fired in 1975, however, and replaced by former Yankee second baseman Billy Martin.

THE BRONX ZOO: 1976–80

Many moments of accomplishment characterized the New York Yankee experience in the late 1970s. The team won its first World Championship since 1962. Reggie Jackson smacked three home runs on three consecutive pitches in game six of the 1977 World Series. Tremendous talent was spread thick all over the roster.

But sadly, all the positives were sometimes obscured by players coming and going, like the 47 different ones who wore pinstripes in 1979—a Yankees record—the fights, the feuds, the bickering in public and private, the craziness and crassness engaged in by players, managers, and executives, especially Billy Martin, Reggie Jackson, and George Steinbrenner.

That time started with a thousand protesters massed across the street from the new Yankee Stadium on Opening Day 1976. They were angry that renovations and refurbishments had cost New York City approximately $100 million—four times the price originally announced. Fury and anger were in the air.

Fury and anger were in the air again on May 20, 1976—Boston versus New York. Sox catcher Carlton Fisk and Lou Piniella got into it after a collision at home plate. That triggered all kinds of hand-to-hand skirmishes. Boston's Bill Lee got the worst of things. He was smashed in the face by Mickey Rivers. Then Nettles lifted him up and threw him down on his pitching shoulder.

Eleven days later the Yankees traveled to Fenway Park. "If any fans come over the top of the dugout," Billy Martin told his team, "pick up your bats and be ready to take them apart, I'll be right with you."

Martin's various personalities featured the field general, the tough soldier, the kindly father figure, the cruel despot, the racist, the drunk, the street fighter, and the brilliant field tactician. He was also a chronic pathological liar.

There were times when the Yankee manager would spit out the most profane language at a player and then turn around and send flowers to that player's wife. Racist and anti-Semitic slurs came out of Martin's alcoholic fog and so did handouts of hundreds of dollars. He made appointments, and then when writers showed up he claimed the appointment was supposed to be on a different day or at a different time, that it was inconvenient to talk.

Part of Martin's problem was that he was drinking more and enjoying it less. He also had a highly tenuous relationship with George Steinbrenner and his "Seven Commandments," announced criteria for judging the embattled manager:

Billy Martin brought nearly as many problems as solutions to the Yankee dugout. But more importantly to New York fans, he brought home a pennant in 1976.

1. Does he win?

2. Does he work hard enough?

3. Is he emotionally equipped to lead the men?

4. Is he organized?

5. Is he prepared?

6. Does he understand human nature?

7. Is he honorable?

Altercations between the two included dialogue like:

GEORGE STEINBRENNER: What's wrong with the team, Billy?

BILLY MARTIN: You're the problem. We don't leak stories or do things like that. That's unlike any Yankee I ever saw in my life.

The Yankee owner's calls down to the dugout with directions for Martin and Steinbrenner's tips on tactics made the excitable manager fume. There were a couple of times Number One became so furious and out of control that he ripped the phone off the dugout wall.

Then there was the Minnesota hotel "Marshmallow King" incident after the 1979 World Series. As the story goes, a salesman of marshmallows goaded Martin into a fight and Billy's answer was to give the guy a split lip. The tag line was Billy saying: "How in the hell did I get into this?" That cost Martin his job as manager—for a while.

Brandishing the whip with such phrases as, "They know what the bottom line is," Steinbrenner employed private detectives to monitor the movements

Reggie Jackson often feuded with Martin and Steinbrenner during his years with the Yankees. But when a big game was on the line (shown here after hitting a two-run homer in game six of the 1978 World Series), he let his bat do the talking.

and behavior of players. He also peered through binoculars to check the length of players' hair and issued edicts for trips to the barber if he didn't like what he saw. All his actions did were to stir up things even more, exacerabating the atmosphere in the Bronx Zoo.

Reggie Jackson was one of the most hyper of the Yankees of that time. He kept wishing to be traded and finally became an ex-Yankee. But while he was on the scene, Reggie was caught many times in the relentless glare of the media's eye. One of the more famous moments took place when he and Billy Martin had a physical confrontation on national television.

The Jackson–Martin–Steinbrenner game of chicken and insults reached its apex when Number One snapped, "One's a born liar, the other's convicted," and then recanted with the words, "I didn't mean it about George. How he came into it I don't know, I meant it about the other guy."

Even the opposition got into the verbal dirt throwing. Feeling the sting of the Yankees and their highly involved fans in games played in the 1978 World Series at Yankee Stadium, Dodger outfielder Rick Monday griped: "I don't like this town. I don't like this park. I don't understand these people. I don't understand their existence."

Then there was the 1978 Welcome Home Luncheon. Five Yankee players were fined for not showing up. But the five did not include Willie Randolph, who was one of the real constants of that time, a serene presence amidst all the turmoil. Randolph, in his phrase, "was out of Brownsville, Brooklyn, only 21 years old when I came to the Yankees out of the Pirates chain in 1976." He went on to play more games at second base than any other player in Yankee history—consistent, reliable, a class individual.

The same could not be said in all honesty about backup catcher Cliff Johnson and relief pitcher Goose Gossage. The two excitable men had a clubhouse contretemps. The Goose tore ligaments in his thumb and missed three months of pitching.

Enter Jim Kaat as sort of the replacement for Gossage. "I came over from the Phillies. Bob Lemon was managing and Billy took over not too long afterwards." The public perception of the Yankees might have been that they were a team of cliques and confrontation. Kaat has a different point of view. "My fondest memories," Kaat said, "are of the camaraderie that existed on that team, particularly Catfish Hunter, Oscar Gamble, Reggie Jackson, Lou Piniella. Some of the bus trips and the bantering that went on among players were really pleasant."

By 1980, as the Yankees came up against Kansas City in the playoffs for the league championship, only four players remained from two seasons before. The Royals swept the Yankees in three. In the second game third-base coach Mike Ferraro sent Willie Randolph home. He was out on a very close play. An enraged Steinbrenner went public with his demands that Don Zimmer replace Ferraro as coach. Yankee manager Dick Howser balked, claiming he should be the one to decide on his coaches. That ended it for Howser. Gene Michael, the eighth manager employed by Steinbrenner in seven years, replaced Howser, who had won 103 games.

It was truly a zoo in the Bronx.

THE ERA OF AGONY: 1981–91

Willie Randolph is thrown out at the plate in a 3-2 loss during the 1980 American League Championship Series. After losing three consecutive playoff series to the Yanks in 1976, 1977, and 1978, the Kansas City Royals finally got the best of New York in '80.

Just from a managerial point of view, what took place with the Yankees from 1981 to 1991 appears to be a misprint. Gene Michael was replaced by Bob Lemon who was replaced by Gene Michael who was replaced by Clyde King who was replaced by Billy Martin who was replaced by Yogi Berra who was replaced by Billy Martin who was replaced by Lou Piniella who was replaced by Billy Martin who was replaced by Lou Piniella who was replaced by Dallas Green who was replaced by Bucky Dent who was replaced by Stump Merrill.

The front-office door also kept revolving. The parade included Cedric Tallis, Gene Michael, Bill Bergesch, Murray Cook, Clyde King, Woody Woodward, Lou Piniella, Syd Thrift, and Gene Michael one more time.

Prime prospects were given away for relatively little, then went on to star with other teams. The long list includes Greg Gagne, Doug Drabek, Tim Burke, Fred McGriff, Scott McGregor, and Jose Rijo. Free agents, and trade acquisitions with few exceptions, were overall dismal disappointments and very un-Yankee types. That list includes Bill Castro, Don Baylor, Steve Kemp,

Many felt by signing free agent Dave Winfield and pairing him with the power-hitting Jackson, the Yanks would have a dynamic duo that could be mentioned in the same breath as Ruth-Gehrig and Mantle-Maris. Jackson left for California though, and only played with Winfield for one season.

Bob Shirley, Dale Murray, Phil Niekro, Ed Whitson, Joe Niekro, Butch Wynegar, Al Holland, Rod Scurry, Claudell Washington, Lenn Sakata, Gary Ward, Wayne Tolleson, Bob Shirley, Jack Clark, John Candelaria, Jose Cruz, Steve Sax, Dave LaPoint, Andy Hawkins, Jamie Quirk, Pascual Perez, Mel Hall, Damaso Garcia, Tim Leary, and Steve Farr.

Winning more games in the 1980s than any other team in baseball, the Yankees also led the majors in that period with a merry-go-round of players, managers, batting instructors, and pitching coaches coming and going, going and coming.

Yet, even with all that whirlwind activity, there were not too many positives on the playing field. Steinbrenner's charges managed a first- and a sixth-place finish in the split season of 1981. Four times the Yankees finished fifth, two times second and third, once fourth, and once seventh. It was roller-coaster time.

On November 21, 1980, Gene Michael was in place as the 25th manager in Yankee history. Ten days before Christmas of 1980, Dave Winfield signed a 10-year, $23-million contract. Visions of the powerfully built Winfield bracket-

ed with the flamboyant Reggie Jackson in the Yankee lineup promised a mini-Murderer's Row for some time to come. It didn't work out quite that way. The two played only one season together as Yankees.

The 1981 season was the time of the players' strike. Major league ballparks were empty from June 12 to August 9, wiping out 714 games from the schedule. A split-season format pitted the winner of the first half of the schedule against the winner of the second half of the season in the playoffs. In a way the Yankees also had a managerial split season, with Gene Michael (48–34) yielding to Bob Lemon (11–14).

Edging past Milwaukee in the American League East playoff, the Yankees came up against Oakland in the ALCS. It was "Billy Ball" (Billy Martin) versus "Bobby Ball" (Bob Lemon). Martin bragged: "We'll beat Steinbrenner's tail like a drum."

But it was Martin who was beaten, badly. The Yankees won the first game, 3–1, at the Stadium. They won the next game 13–3. Fans screamed "Goodbye, Billy." The Yankees took the next game in Oakland and had a sweep of the A's and their 33rd pennant. The biggest headlines coming out of the quick series were reports of what had transpired in an Oakland restaurant. Graig Nettles decked Jackson. It seemed that several of Reggie's "guests" were a little bit disrespectful to Nettles's wife.

The World Series matchup was the Dodgers of Los Angeles versus the favored Yankees. The team from the Bronx featured three superb southpaws in Dave Righetti, Ron Guidry, and Tommy John, the power of Reggie Jackson and Dave Winfield, Bob Watson, and a strong supporting cast led by Lou Piniella and Willie Randolph.

Graig Nettles was only the sixth player in Yankee history to be named team captain. He was traded two seasons later, however, for Dennis Rasmussen and minor leaguer Darin Cloninger.

35

Steve Kemp was just one of a long list of free-agent signings that didn't live up to the Yankees' expectations in the 1980s. After many successful years with the Tigers and White Sox, Kemp signed with New York in 1983 and hit just .241 with 12 homers.

At the age of 24, Dave Righetti pitched a no-hitter and went 14-8 on the mound in 1983. Desperately in need of relief pitching, the Yanks made him a closer in 1984.

The Yankees won the first two games. Gift victories in the next two games came the Dodger way via Yankee errors. LA then beat Guidry in game five. That set the stage for the most controversial moment in the Series.

In game six in the bottom of the fourth inning with the scored tied, 1–1, Lemon surprised almost everyone by sending Bobby Murcer up to pinch-hit for Tommy John. Murcer flew out. Two Yankee baserunners were stranded.

"I hope you have someone who can hold them," a disgusted John snapped at Lemon as the Dodgers came to bat. The Yankee manager didn't have anyone. Los Angeles hammered George Frazier, who lost a record three Series games, Ron Davis, and Rick Reuschel for three runs in the fifth and four runs in the sixth. The Dodgers won the game and their first World Championship in 16 years.

Enraged, George Steinbrenner called a news conference and apologized for his team's play. He was especially piqued at Dave Winfield, who managed just one hit in 22 attempts. A statement was distributed in the Yankee Stadium press box:

> *I want to sincerely apologize to the people of New York and to the fans of the New York Yankees everywhere for the performance of the Yankee team in the World Series. I also want to assure you that we will be at work immediately to prepare for 1982.*

"I don't have to apologize to anybody," snapped Reggie Jackson, who had missed the first three games of the Series with injuries. "I played my best." His best would now be given to California. On January 22, 1982, Reggie signed for five years with the Angels.

What happened in that 1981 World Series set the tone for the era of agony that was 1981–91 in the Bronx. And although talented and dedicated professional players like Don Mattingly, Dave Winfield, Willie Randolph, Rickey Henderson, Dave Righetti, and Ron Guidry were on the scene through most of those years, something always seemed to be lacking. The Yankees of that time just could not get it done.

The 1982 edition saw various personalities come and go, strange moves on and off the field. With the loss of Jackson, Steinbrenner wheeled and dealed. Outfielder Dave Collins was signed as a free agent. Shortstop Roy Smalley was acquired even though the Yankees had Bucky Dent. Ken Griffey came over from the Reds.

When Collins joined the Yankees, he wanted to meet another newcomer, catcher Juan Espino. He was told that the player was there but had just been shipped off to Columbus. The shuttle back and forth to the Yankee Triple-A team in Ohio became a kind of not-so-inside joke. Nineteen players at one time or another rode the shuttle in 1982. Pitcher Dave LaRoche alone made the trip four times. Dave Righetti never made the shuttle, but during the era of agony he was shuttled back and forth from starter to reliever so many times that it affected his orientation, not to say anything about his pitching effectiveness.

That 1982 season Graig Nettles became Yankee captain, the sixth in the history of the franchise. Bob Lemon yielded to Gene Michael, who was replaced by Clyde King. None of the managerial changes did much good. The team had many down times during the '82 season. One of the worst was an August doubleheader at the Stadium. The Yankees lost the first game, 1–0. They were humiliated in the second game, 14–2. George Frazier, the goat of the 1981 Series, took one for the team, his head hung low on the mound. Bob Sheppard made the announcement that fans could attend any other home game for free. That was their reward for sitting through the Yankee debacle that August afternoon. The Yankees finished the season in fifth place, 16 games out.

And then along came Billy! Incredibly, for the third time in eight years, Billy Martin was again part of the New York scene, managing the Yankees in 1983. More hyper than ever, Martin led the Yankees to 9 wins in the 20 games they played in April. Then things got worse. By the middle of May the team was sixth in the standings. He did rally the troops to finish third at season's end. But that was the end of him for the moment as manager of the Yankees. A highlight of the '83 season for the Yanks was a no-hitter pitched on a 95-degree Fourth of July by Dave Righetti.

In 1964, as a first-year manager, Yogi Berra had led the Yankees to the World Series. Now, two decades later, George Steinbrenner brought him back to win a World Championship. Billy Martin was kicked upstairs to keep an eye on things, and hovered about, waiting in the wings.

The 1984 Yankees posted an 87–75 record. They finished 17 games off the pace in third place. Berra had not won a championship, but he had given a full-time job at first base to Don Mattingly, a homegrown Yankee who had spent the '83 season with Martin in charge of things riding the New York–Columbus shuttle. "Donnie Baseball" won the batting title and became the first Yankee in 22 years to record 200 hits.

Adding speedster Rickey Henderson to a lineup that included Mattingly, Winfield, and Don Baylor, the 1985 Yankees looked very good on paper. But the team got off to a disappointing 6–10 start. On April 25, 1985, with the season 17 games old for the Yankees, everything old was new again. Billy Martin replaced Yogi Berra as manager. Despite the MVP season of Don Mattingly, the 22-win season of Ron Guidry, the 20-plus home run totals for Mattingly, Winfield, Henderson, and Baylor, it was another close-but-no-cigar season. The Yankees fell two games shy of Toronto in the American League East.

Hitting instructor Lou Piniella took over for Martin in 1986. The Yankees finished in second place. The next year they were in first place more than any other team. But that mattered little in that star-crossed decade. They finished fourth. Injuries to Willie Randolph and especially Rickey Henderson wreaked havoc. The fleet Henderson had hit 52 homers in 1985–86 as well as leading the league in runs scored and stolen bases. Too much offense was lost with him out of the lineup.

In 1986, Piniella had replaced Martin. Now in 1988 it was Billy's time again—his fifth time as manager of the New York Yankees. Martin lasted only until June 23. Piniella was brought back to replace the beleaguered Billy the Kid. It was like a soap opera. As the decade came to an end, the Yankees sank to two fifth-place finishes. Dallas Green replaced Lou Piniella. On August 18, 1989, Bucky Dent replaced Dallas Green.

Rickey Henderson added speed to the Yanks, and his 326 steals is a team record.

Don Mattingly was the backbone of the New York Yankees during the 1980s. His best season came in 1985, when he batted .324 with 35 home runs and 145 RBIs. It was the second of six straight seasons which he batted over .300.

Bucky Dent finished out the 1989 season as the Yankee skipper. In 1990, he only made it through 49 games as an 18-31 record was not enough to keep George Steinbrenner happy.

Bucky Dent managed the Yankees for 89 games and then on June 6, 1990, he was gone, replaced by Stump Merrill, a potbellied, old-school type. "Here we have a fellow who doesn't come with a hell of a lot of glamour," Steinbrenner said. "For the first five years I knew him, I kept calling him 'Lump.' He was madder than hell." Stump Merrill lasted through the 1991 season—a campaign in which the Yankees won four more games than the year before and finished fifth.

The New York Yankees of 1981–91 and their fans suffered through a true era of agony. They won a lot of games and frustrated a lot of people. They were living proof that managers are indeed hired to be fired, that everything old is new again, that the best-laid plans often go astray, that you can't tell the players (and sometimes the owners) without a scorecard.

THE 1990s

George Steinbrenner, in exile, the first owner in the history of the American League to be removed by disciplinary action, watched his 1990 Yankees finish out the season in seventh place, 21 games off the pace. Their .414 winning percentage was their lowest since 1913. One of the highlights of the 1990 season was the no-hitter hurled by Andy Hawkins. But he lost the game, 4–0. It sort of figured, the way the Yankee luck was going.

Stump Merrill lasted through the 1991 season—a campaign in which the Yankees posted a 71–91 record, winning four more games than the year before, and finished fifth. In 1992, career Yankee Buck Showalter became manager. The pitching staff was racked as starter Pascual Perez and relief pitcher Steve Howe were suspended with drug charges swirling about them. The Yankees stumbled through their fourth straight losing season—10 games under .500. Not since 1912–15 had the Yankees posted such a string of losing seasons.

But the 1993 season created a lot of excitement in the Bronx. Attendance at the Stadium was 2,416,942, the best since 1987. "You measure the value of a ballplayer," Steinbrenner had remarked, "by how many fannies he puts in the seats."

There was a lot of value connected to the players on the '93 team. The Yankees won 88 games. Nine times they were tied for first. They finished in second place and were hooked up in a tight battle with Toronto for the American League East title until late September. Free agent Jimmy Key won 18 games, and Jim Abbott tossed a no-hitter on September 4. After four straight losing seasons things were looking up. Surprisingly, Steinbrenner was low-key about it all. There were those who even were so bold as to say that perhaps the Boss was mellowing.

Buck Showalter began the 1994 season as Yankee manager—his third straight campaign. Only Billy Martin had lasted that long in one stretch during Steinbrenner's time as owner. That 1994 season the Yankees boasted the best hitter in Paul O'Neill and the best pitcher in Jimmy Key. The team posted a 70–43 record, the best in the American League. Then the baseball strike aborted everything.

Don Mattingly said: "We have failed the fans. I understand and sympathize with what they are experiencing. We felt that this year's team had the chemistry, dedication, talent, and work ethic to win it all. Unfortunately, we will never know how far we would have gone."

"It's a very terrible day," Steinbrenner said. "We were doing so well and it looked like we were going to win our division."

The New York Yankees didn't win their division in 1994. They didn't win it in 1995 either. But as a wild-card team they made the postseason for the first time since 1981, the longest drought in franchise history. Guiding the fortunes of the highest-payroll team in baseball was Buck Showalter in his fourth straight year as Yankee skipper, the longest consecutive tenure of any pilot in Steinbrenner's regime. In the playoffs, there were two Yankee wins over Seattle at the Stadium. Then the teams traveled west. In a stunning extra-inning come-from-behind victory in game five, the Mariners swept the Yankees in Seattle.

The sweep swept out Buck Showalter, who became the second manager in the 23-year tenure of Steinbrenner as principal owner who voluntarily exited. The other was Ralph Houk. In 1996 there was a new general manager, Bob Watson, the team's 15th in 23 seasons. There was also a new manager, Joe Torre, making a total of 20 in Steinbrenner's time, factoring in the multiple terms of four managers.

Under Torre, the Yankees won their first division title in 15 years. Following playoff victories over Texas and Baltimore, the Yanks advanced to the World Series, where they defeated the defending champion Atlanta Braves. For the 23rd time in their history, the New York Yankees were World Champions.

Cecil Fielder was a key pickup for the Yankees in 1996, hitting 13 home runs down the stretch, and three more in the postseason.

TWO

THE
Great
Yankee
TEAMS

1927: MURDERER'S ROW

For the Yankees the 1926 season was just the reverse of their sorry 1925 seventh-place finish. Taking advantage of every opportunity on the field, winning 16 straight games in May, the Yankees won the pennant. Their World Series matchup against the St. Louis Cardinals had a touch of poignancy. Player-manager Rogers Hornsby led the Redbirds; many claimed it was Miller Huggins who had transformed Hornsby into a star when he managed him in St. Louis.

In the seventh inning of the seventh game, grizzled Grover Cleveland Alexander faced Yankee rookie Tony Lazzeri. There were two outs. The bases were loaded. The Cardinals were leading 3–2. The 39-year-old Alexander had hurled complete-game victories in the second and sixth games. But there was talk of his not being up to the task, of his being hung over from a night of merriment following his win the day before.

Breaking off a big curve, Alexander fanned Lazzeri. Alexander was up to the task. The game moved to the ninth inning. The "big son of a bitch," in Alexander's phrase, Babe Ruth, came to bat. There were two outs. The Babe walked and then, in a shocker, was out attempting to steal second base.

Despite the loss to the Cardinals, the Yankees in one season had vaulted from seventh place to within a stride of being World Champions. But there were many who doubted the Yankees had the right stuff to win it all in 1927.

Grantland Rice, writing in *The New York Times*, picked them to finish in second place, behind Philadelphia. His was not a minority view. There were doubts about how much the 32-year-old Ruth had left. His storied 1921 season of 59 home runs had taken place a half dozen seasons before. Even the Sultan of Swat did not think he could break his own record.

"To do that," he said, "you've got to start early, and the pitchers have got to pitch to you. I don't start early and the pitchers haven't really pitched to me in four seasons. I get more bad balls to hit than any other six men—and fewer good ones."

There were many doubts about the Yankee hurlers. "The staff," Huggins announced in spring training, "has reached the stage where I must gamble." The over-30 staff included "Sailor Bob" Shawkey, 37, Urban Shocker, 37, Dutch Ruether, 33, and Herb Pennock, 33. Waite Hoyt, 28, was the young arm of the grizzled crew.

Thirty-year-old rookie Wilcy Moore had a scouting report that read: "He can't pitch. And anyway, he says he's 30, but he must be 40." But Moore's 20–1 record in the Piedmont League tempted Ed Barrow into taking a gamble. The Yankee general manager paid the $3,500 purchase price for the part-time Oklahoma dirt farmer whose bread-and-butter pitch was a sidearm sinker.

There were also doubts about the Yankee turnover in personnel. Moore and three other players who would play key roles on the 1927 Yankees were brand new to the team. Four other players had arrived the year before. Eleven of the 18 players on the roster had three years of tenure or less.

Even Miller Huggins hedged his bets: "It will be a closer race this time. Six clubs with almost equal chance must be considered contenders."

(Preceding page)
The "M&M" boys—Roger Maris and Mickey Mantle— staged a thrilling home run race during the '61 season. Mantle, weakened by illness, faded in September while Maris went on to set the single-season home run record with 61. Together, the two Bronx Bombers totaled 115 of the Yankees 240 home runs in 1961.

Breaking camp at their St. Petersburg, Florida, spring-training site on March 31, the Yankees barnstormed north with the St. Louis Cardinals. The teams split eight games. Two exhibition game wins over Brooklyn at Ebbets Field set the stage for the Yankees' season opener.

A *New York World* account brings back the moment—April 12, 1927, Opening Day at Yankee Stadium. "By game time the vast structure was packed solid. Rows of men were standing in back of the seats and along the runways. Such a crowd had never seen a baseball game or any other kind of game in New York." The managers—diminutive Miller Huggins and tall, patrician Connie Mack—posed for photographs. The Seventh Regiment Band entertained the throng of 65,000, which included 1,000 with passes and 9,000 invited guests. In columns of four, the Yankees and the Philadelphia Athletics marched out to the outfield. The National Anthem was played. New York City's flamboyant mayor Jimmy Walker presented Babe Ruth with a three-foot-high silver loving cup and then threw out the first ball. The starting batteries were announced over a megaphone.

This was the Yankee Opening Day lineup:

Earle Combs cf

Mark Koenig ss

Babe Ruth rf

Lou Gehrig 1b

Bob Meusel lf

Tony Lazzeri 2b

Joe Dugan 3b

Johnny Grabowski c

Waite Hoyt p

Mark Koenig went 5–5, and a four-run fifth and a four-run sixth gave the Yankees an 8–3 win over Lefty Grove and the Athletics. And the first of their 110 victories was in the record book. For all practical purposes the 1927 season was over the day it began for the New York Yankees and their American League rivals. In first place, the Yankees would remain there day in and day out throughout that entire season.

The second game of the series was a 10–4 romp over the A's. The third game was tied at 9–9 in the 10th inning when it was called because of darkness. The Yankees won the fourth game, 6–3. Philadelphia had seven players who would be Hall of Famers, a team that would bat .303 and win 91 games. But exiting the Big Apple after being swept, they were just happy to get out of town.

On April 17, Easter Sunday, Lou Gehrig hit his first and second home runs of the season as the Yankees racked the Red Sox, 14–2. On May 15, the lead was nine games. By the end of May the Yankees had won 23 of 33 games and Babe Ruth had hammered 16 home runs.

Ritual and routine were part of the scene. Waite Hoyt would only pitch warm-ups to his starting catcher. Joe Dugan always scratched out a mark at third base. Wilcy Moore would only throw his first warm-up pitch to Eddie Bennett, a hunchbacked orphan who was the Yankee batboy and good-luck charm throughout the 1920s and early 1930s. And before each game Babe

It's great to be young and a Yankee.
—Waite Hoyt

———

(Over)
The 1927 Yankees won 110 games, winning the American League pennant by 19 games, and swept the Pittsburgh Pirates in the World Series.

The "Home Run Twins," Lou Gehrig (47) and Babe Ruth (60), combined to smash an incredible 107 home runs during the 1927 season. Ruth hit an astonishing 32 homers on the road and Gehrig went on to win MVP honors.

Ruth would only warm up with a catcher. Fred Hofmann had the job from 1920 to 1924; Benny Bengough took the Babe's tosses from 1925 to 1930. After each home run, the Sultan of Swat would put a notch on one of his bats. But when he hit his 21st home run off Cleveland's George "the Bull" Uhle on June 12, the 21st notch split his bat—and that was the end of his whittling.

On June 24, the Yankees had a 44–17 record. The lead was 10 games over Philadelphia. The Bronx Bombers went 21–6 in June. That set up the fireworks for a Fourth of July doubleheader at Yankee Stadium against Washington, a team that had won 10 straight and was gaining confidence. If there was anything Murderer's Row specialized in, it was destroying the confidence of opponents.

The Yankees pounded out a 12–1 victory in game one. Then they really got to work in the nightcap, humbling the Senators 21–1. Gehrig homered in each game. The Yankee lead was 11 games. "Those fellows not only beat you," moaned Senator first baseman Joe Judge, "they tear your heart out. I wish the season was over."

The Yankees never felt that way. They were having too much fun. "We had a good bunch of ballplayers on that club," George Pipgras recalled, "a good bunch of fellows. They were all friends. There were no cliques. We all got along real good."

The team's theme song was "Roll Out the Barrel." And it was one sung many times—with gusto. Thrashing the opposition became the order of the day. The St. Louis Browns especially felt the fury, losing 21 in a row to the Bronx Bombers.

"We'd just go out there and hit," recalled Mark Koenig. "We never had to bunt much. We never had anybody that stole a lot of bases. It was just hitting away."

At five o'clock the blowing of a whistle at a factory near Yankee Stadium signaled the end of the workday. For the Yankees the sound of the whistle accentuated what they were doing to the opposition on the field. It was called "Five O'clock Lightning."

George Pipgras, who was known as "the Danish Viking," replaced Ruether in the rotation the fifth starter. "When we got to the ballpark," Pipgras recalled, "we knew we were going to win. That's all there was to it. We weren't cocky. I wouldn't call it confidence either. We just knew. Like when you go to sleep, you know the sun is going to come up in the morning."

Almost 25 percent of all the American League home runs in 1927 would be hit by Ruth and Gehrig. Newspapers referred to the Yankees as Babe Ruth, Lou Gehrig, and Company. But the "Company" was something special, something devastating.

Combs and Koenig batted one-two in the powerful lineup. They were the table setters. When Earle Combs first reported to the Yankees, he bragged to Miller Huggins, "They call me the Mail Carrier," a reference to his base-stealing accomplishments in the minors.

"Up here," Huggins shot back, "we're going to call you the Waiter. When you get on first base you just wait for Ruth or Gehrig or one of the other fellows to send you the rest of the way around."

A sharp contrast to the flashy and the dour personalities on the team, Combs was a Bible-reading churchgoer who neither smoked nor drank nor cursed. "No one ever accused him of being out on a drinking party," Ruth pointed out, "and you'd laugh at the words he'd use for cussing. He came from a strict mountaineer family. But Earle was all man and a great competitor."

"I never went in much for liquor," Combs admitted. "Some of the boys on those Huggins clubs could not understand how a Kentuckian did not drink. One of them came to me in 1925 and said, 'Combs, if you expect to stay on this club you had better learn to drink.'"

The "Kentucky Colonel" was a graceful and fleet performer whose 411 putouts would top all American League outfielders in 1927. His 331 total bases would place him third in the league behind Ruth and Gehrig.

Tony Lazzeri was purchased by the Yankees after hitting 60 home runs and driving in 222 runs for Salt Lake City. In 1927, he was in the second of what would be a dozen solid seasons as a Yankee second baseman. Born in 1903 in San Francisco, Lazzeri carried the memory of his growing-up years with him: "I was a pretty tough kid," he said. "The neighborhood wasn't one in which a boy was likely to grow up a sissy, for it was fight or get licked, and I never got licked."

"Poosh 'em up" Tony Lazzeri turning a double play for the Yankees.

The son of a blacksmith, Lazzeri's strong wrists helped him become the main right-handed power hitter on the '27 team. He was a magnet for Italian fans at Yankee Stadium, who would scream out, "Poosh 'em up, Tony," urging him to hit home runs. Lazzeri seemed aloof to some. He really was not, but he was an epileptic, and almost painfully quiet.

Another native of San Francisco, shortstop Mark Koenig was in his third season as a Yankee. He did lead the league in errors in 1927, but he had exceptional range and made the big plays.

The 30-year-old "Jumping Joe" Dugan was peerless at third base. His nickname came from the early years in his career when he "jumped" the last-place Philadelphia Athletics, discouraged by their losing ways. He also "jumped" when he developed a longing to just go home. The fans and opposition would taunt him with "I wanna go home," shouted repeatedly. Not surprisingly, Dugan lost his "Jumping Joe" habits when he joined the Yankees. Dugan was part of the Babe's inner circle, and it was he who coined the nickname "Jidge" for Ruth. Many of Ruth's nights out were spent in the company of the free-spirited third baseman, who always sat next to him in the Yankee dugout.

But Dugan did have one complaint: "It's always the same. Combs walks. Koenig singles. Ruth hits one out of the park. Gehrig doubles. Lazzeri triples. Then Dugan goes down on the dirt on his can."

Bob Meusel was another who was close to the Babe, always there to do Ruth's bidding. They called him "Long Bob," and "Silent Bob," and other, earthier names because of his aloofness. On that most colorful team, Meusel was a muted presence. "His attitude," Huggins said, "is just plain indifference."

"He's learning to say hello," sportswriter Frank Graham said of Meusel when he was approaching the end of his career, "just when it's time to say good-bye."

A talented all-around performer, Meusel batted in the order between Gehrig and Lazzeri. He hit .337 in 1927. But it was his arm, baseball's best, that they all talked about. "I never saw a better thrower," Casey Stengel said. "He had lightnin' on the ball." And Joe Dugan said, "Meusel could hit a dime at 100 yards and flatten it against a wall." From 1920 to 1929, Babe Ruth was the only Yankee to have more RBIs than Meusel.

The regular left fielder at Yankee Stadium, when the team took to the road Meusel generally switched places with the Babe and played right field. Ruth had lost a ball in the sun in his first year as an outfielder in 1918, and just would not play the sun field. So to help the Yankees and to "save" Ruth's eyes, Meusel did what he did.

Some claimed that the only weak spot on the team was the catching. Yet the threesome who shared the duties—Pat Collins (.275), Johnny Grabowski (.277), and Benny Bengough (.247)—did all right. Collins, who Ruth called "Horse Nose," played more than the other backstops and chipped in with seven home runs.

Waite Hoyt uttered the now-famous quip, "The secret of success as a pitcher lies in getting a job with the New York Yankees." It was a not-too-backhanded reference to the belief that any pitcher could win backed by the hitting of Murderer's Row.

That belief prompted Miller Huggins to always seem to be saying something positive about his undervalued staff. Wilcy Moore got a healthy dose of Huggins's hyperbole. "He is cool as a cake of ice," the little Yankee pilot said. "He has splendid control and a deceptive delivery. He is always ready as nonchalantly as if he was going up to pitch to batters in practice."

Moore posted a 19–7 record. His gaudy 13–3 mark in relief made him the first great Yankee relief pitcher. He had the lowest ERA and the most shutouts in the league. An old wrist injury enabled him to throw a potent sidearm sinkerball that befuddled batters. He teamed with Waite Hoyt, George Pipgras, Urban Shocker, Dutch Ruether, and Herb Pennock to give the Yankees outstanding pitching.

Herb Pennock, dubbed the "Knight of Kennett Square," had attended the finest prep schools, was a horticulturist, and bred red silver foxes at his spacious country home near Kennett Square, Pennsylvania. He and Walter Johnson were the only hurlers who would not throw at a batter. A control pitcher, he was stylish and graceful. Though Pennock was almost completely opposite to the Babe in all ways, Pennock and Ruth were nevertheless close friends from their time as teammates on the Red Sox. Pennock would

As a starter and reliever, Wilcy Moore won 19 games for the 1927 Yankees. Moore led the league in ERA (2.28) and saves (13). A notoriously poor hitter, Moore won a $100 bet with Babe Ruth by getting 6 hits in 75 at-bats during the 1927 season. Moore used the money to buy two mules for his farm. He named one mule "Babe" and the other "Ruth."

Pitcher Urban Shocker won 18 games for the 1927 Yankees despite a heart condition that would claim his life the following year. Shocker's "out pitch" was the spitball, which he continued to throw as one of seven pitchers who were exempt from a league rule banning the pitch.

take Ruth along with him on fox hunts. That 1927 season Pennock would notch a 19–8 record and a .704 winning percentage.

Urban Shocker, one of seven "grandfathered" legal spitball pitchers, who was to die the following year, suffered all through that '27 season from a heart condition that was kept secret from his fellow Yankees. Despite his medical problems, Shocker posted an 18–6 record and a .750 winning percentage.

An artist, singer, and writer, one of the most sophisticated players of his era, Waite Hoyt was the ace of the '27 team. He won 22 of 29 decisions, leading the league in wins and winning percentage.

Walter Henry Ruether, better known as "Dutch," was picked up via the waiver route from the Senators in August of 1926. The veteran was the fourth starter for Murderer's Row until he was replaced in midseason by the hard-throwing rookie George Pipgras (10–3, .769). The 1927 season was Ruether's last, and he went out in style with a 13–6 record.

Orchestrating the collection of superb talent, the odd assortment of personalities, was Miller Huggins, "It was the only team in history that did not need the breaks," he said. That might have been true, but Hug hedged his bets all season long by keeping up his rituals. He sent only Mike Gazella to the bullpen to deliver a message. He slid over on the bench when Ruth was up and sat next to the player he had been next to when the Babe had last homered.

"Huggins was almost like a schoolmaster in the dugout," Waite Hoyt noted. "There was no goofing off. You watched the game and you kept track not only of the score and the number of outs, but of the count on the batter. At any moment Hug might ask you what the situation was. Hug was not a man to keep a fellow around if the man didn't measure up in character and willingness to play. 'Let him go lose for someone else,' Hug would say, and ship the man down the river."

But the little pilot had no shipping to do in 1927. The Yankees went through the entire season without a single change in their 18-player roster. Different players took turns strutting their stuff. There was a three-triple day by Combs, a three-home run day by Lazzeri, another one by Gehrig, and the first home run (by Ruth) to be hit out of the expanded Comiskey Park.

"One of the things that inadvertently meshed," Waite Hoyt said, "was the personalities of the fellows playing on that club. We all got along. We had inordinate pride in ourselves as a unit. It was a team that didn't often beat itself."

"It was murder," said Ruth. "We never even worried five or six runs behind. Wham! Wham! Wham! And wham! No matter who was pitching."

On July 9, the Yankees demolished Detroit, 19–7. Ruth collected his 28th and 29th home runs. On July 24, the Yankees led the second-place Senators by 13 games. By the end of July, a month in which the Yankees posted a 24–7 record, the lead was 15 games. The team's winning percentage was a gaudy .730. The only real suspense was the battle between Ruth and Gehrig, the "home run twins."

The back-to-back power generated by Ruth and Gehrig in their careers together in the Yankees' lineup was just mind-boggling. Seventy-four times they homered in the same game. The first time was on September 10, 1925, off Philadelphia's Sam Gray. The last time was on June 3, 1934, off Merritt Cain of Philadelphia.

On August 15, Gehrig was ahead 38–36 in the home run race with the Babe. But there were to be just nine more home runs by Gehrig the rest of the season. He admitted that he was so worried about his mother's health that he "couldn't see straight." After each home game he would rush to the hospital to be by her side.

Ruth had another obsession—shattering his own home run record. He played on with a passion, smashing 24 homers in his last 42 games. The Sultan of Swat swatted his 40th home run on August 22, a day the Yankees lost their fourth straight game for the first time that momentous season. The Tigers won their 13th straight. But the Yankee lead was impregnable; they still led Detroit by 12½ games.

By August 31, the lead over the second-place Athletics had stretched to 17 games. Ruth's lead over Gehrig in the home run race was two. That set the stage for Ruth's September surge—17 home runs in his last 29 games. One of them was on September 2—number 44, the 400th of Ruth's career. On September 6, he hit three home runs in a doubleheader at Fenway Park. He pounded numbers 48 and 49 the next day.

On September 9, 1927, the Babe didn't hit any home runs, but the day belonged to another Yankee anyway. It was "Tony Lazzeri Day" at the Stadium. And thousands of his compadres came out to honor the Yankee second baseman.

Two days later the spotlight was again on the Babe: He ripped home run number 50. Numbers 51 and 52 came in a doubleheader sweep over Cleveland on September 13 that clinched the pennant for the Yankees.

On September 27, the Yankees defeated the Athletics, 7–4. Both Ruth and Gehrig homered off Lefty Grove. Ruth's shot was a grand slam. On September 29, at Yankee Stadium, Ruth smashed home runs off two different Washington pitchers in a 15–4 Yankee rout. The second home run tied his old record of 59.

On September 30, Tom Zachary was on the mound for the Senators. "I had made up my mind," Zachary said, "that I wasn't going to give him a good pitch to hit." The pitches might not have been good, but the Babe made do.

In his first two at bats, Ruth singled and scored. The game moved to the bottom of the eighth—the Yankees and Senators were tied, 2–2. Ruth strolled to the plate questing for number 60. Number 59 had been hit with the bat Ruth called "Black Betsy." His other bats were the ash blond "Big Bertha" and the reddish-colored "Beautiful Bella." He was carrying "Beautiful Bella."

Koenig had tripled and was on third base. There was one out. Why the Senators didn't intentionally walk Ruth to attempt to set up a double play remains a moot point. A fastball—strike one. A high pitch—ball one. Zachary tried to move the Babe off the plate with his next pitch. "I don't say it was the best curve I ever threw, but it was as good as any I ever threw."

Ruth lunged, reached for the ball, and pulled it. The ball was fair by about 10 feet. It landed in the first row of the bleachers near the right-field foul pole. It was number 60, Ruth's fourth home run in three days. The 8,000 in attendance cheered the Babe as he slow-trotted out the epic home

What visions burn, what dreams possess him, seeker of the night. The packed stands of the stadium, the bleachers sweltering with their unshaded hordes, the faultless velvet of the diamond. The mounting roar of eighty thousand voices and Gehrig coming to bat.
—Thomas Wolfe

Babe Ruth watches his 60th home run of the 1927 season sail over the right-field fence. The Sultan of Swat hit his record-breaking round-tripper against Tom Zachary of the Washington Senators. During the post-game celebration Ruth boasted, "Now let's see some other son of a bitch match that." It took 34 years and a 162-game season before someone could.

run, touching each base carefully, doffing his cap several times to acknowledge the cheers.

Gehrig was the first to congratulate the Babe as he stepped on home plate. A double line of Yankees formed a kind of honor guard as he made his way into the dugout. When he came out to take his fielding position in right field in the top of the ninth inning, his fans in "Ruthville" waved handkerchiefs and cheered.

Later, a chagrined Zachary said, "If I'd a known it was gone be a famous record, I'd a stuck it in his ear."

Later, a jubilant Ruth bellowed, "Now let's see some other son of a bitch match that."

Home run number 60 was the whipped cream on the cake for the 1927 Yankees, just part of the arithmetic giving them bragging rights to the title of greatest team of all time. The Bronx Bombers completed their domination of the American League with a 110–44 record, winning the pennant by 19 games. Not only had they played through a grueling major league schedule, but almost always when there were open dates the team played exhibition games across America in little towns and villages.

Babe Ruth was a colossus. He batted .356, drove in 164 runs, slugged for an astounding .772 percentage. He scored the most runs, drew the most walks, accumulated the most total bases, recorded the highest on-base and slugging percentages, outhomered every other major league team except for the Giants, Cubs, and Cardinals. Thirty-two of the record 60 home runs were hit on the road—a major league record.

Lou Gehrig batted .373, drove in 175 runs, and was the second player to that time to hit at least 47 home runs. The Yankee first baseman led the league in RBIs and doubles. He recorded 447 total bases and a slugging percentage of .765, second only to Ruth. The Iron Horse was voted the American League Most Valuable Player. As a former winner, Ruth was not eligible for the honor.

Earle Combs batted .356 and led the league in hits and in triples. Tony Lazzeri finished at .309 with 102 RBIs, and Bob Meusel recorded 103 RBIs to go with his .337 average.

Pounding 158 home runs, batting .307 as a team, recording an astonishing all-time best slugging percentage of .489, the Yankees averaged 6.5 runs a game, scoring 975 runs. They topped the league in batting average, walks, hits, and triples. In short, the Yankees led the American League in every offensive category except doubles and stolen bases.

Five Yankees batted .300 or better. Of the eight American Leaguers who drove in 100 or more runs, four of those were Yankees. The pitching staff led the league in shutouts and its ERA (3.20) was almost a run below the American League average. That staff had the pitchers with the four best winning percentages in the league.

The favored Yankees faced off in the World Series against a Pittsburgh team that had batted .305 during the season. It was reported that Gehrig hit 10 home runs in batting practice. Then Ruth stepped in and hit 10 more. Then, for good measure, he hit an 11th that rocketed out of spacious Forbes Field as Pirate players gaped at the man who had hit six more home runs during the season than their entire team.

"Okay, sonnies," G. H. Ruth snarled, "if any of you want my autograph, go out there and get those balls and I'll sign them for you."

Waite Hoyt went up against the Pirates' 19-game winner Ray Kremer in game one. The Yankees won, 5–4. Urban Shocker was expected to start the second game, but George Pipgras took the mound instead. The Pirates saw only three curveballs all day as Pipgras fired his live fastball pitch after pitch, going the distance in the 6–2 Yankee victory. Herb Pennock had a perfect game to the eighth inning in game three and wound up with a three-hitter. The Yankees won, 8–1. Game four was a 3–3 tie in the bottom of the ninth. The Yanks had the bases loaded. A wild pitch. Earle Combs scored from third base. The sweep was completed.

"If the two teams had played a hundred games," recalled a member of that Pittsburgh team, "I honestly think the Yankees would have won them all. That's how intimidated we were." And Pirate manager Joe Bush chipped in with, "Am I glad it's over. Nobody was killed and we're all safe and sound."

For Ruth, it was just another four games in another World Series. He drove in seven runs, homered twice, and batted .400. Shortstop Mark Koenig chipped in with a .500 batting average, and Wilcy Moore surrendered just one run in 10 2/3 innings.

"Everything meshed for us," Koenig said, "the personalities, the manager, the luck, everything that 1927 season."

The $6,595.38 biweekly checks made out to G. H. Ruth by the Manufacturers Trust Company, Yorkville Branch Office, 1511 Third Avenue, New York, N.Y., added up to the record $70,000 the Sultan of Swat earned for the season. He made more money than the rest of the starting lineup combined. But Ruth and the others on that awesome team were not exactly overpaid.

The second-highest salary went to Combs at $19,500. Pennock was next at $17,500. Shocker was paid $13,500 and Meusel $500 less. Dugan earned $12,000; Hoyt received the same amount after getting a thousand-dollar bonus for winning 20 games.

The average salary was about $8,000, which was what Gehrig, Bengough, and Lazzeri were paid. The Yankee second baseman also was provided with round-trip fare to California for his wife and himself. Mark Koenig's salary was $7,000. Pipgras and Durst made $4,500 each. The lowest salary on the team was the $2,400 paid to backup third baseman Julie Wera.

And the fun-loving Wilcy Moore, one of the biggest bargains, earned $2,500, just $100 more than Wera. However, he did manage to pick up some extra cash. Part of it was a $5,000 bonus—part of his contract for lasting the season. And he pocketed another $100 that came in handy.

In spring training Ruth bet Moore $100 that he would not get more than three hits all season. A notoriously weak hitter, Moore somehow managed to get six hits in 75 at bats. Ruth paid off his debt and Moore purchased two mules for his farm. One he named Babe; the other he named Ruth.

With the historic season concluded, Ruth and Gehrig headed pickup teams called the "Bustin' Babes" and the "Larrupin' Lous." More than 220,000 came out to see them play 21 games on 20 ballfields from Trenton, New Jersey, all the way to California. In some locales schools were closed or classes were let out early so that children (and their teachers) could partake

The Waner brothers, Lloyd ("Little Poison") and Paul ("Big Poison") manned left and right fields for the Pittsburgh Pirates during the 1927 World Series matchup with the Yankees. Though both fashioned Hall of Fame careers, they and their teammates were dispatched in four games by the powerful New Yorkers.

of the excitement. More than half the games were stopped when fans broke out onto the field seeking autographs. It was estimated that the two Yankees signed more than 5,000 baseballs on that barnstorming junket.

Ruth and Gehrig pitched to each other game after game, the Iron Horse batted .618—two points higher than the Sultan of Swat. But the Babe hit 20 home runs—7 more than Gehrig.

But the Pride of the Yankees, who lived that 1927 season in a modest apartment with his mother and father on West 133rd Street, had no complaints. He saw America. And he earned more money for that tour than the Yankees paid him for the entire 1927 season.

Batting Practice: 1927 World Series

The Pirates were an old-fashioned team, almost a throwback kind of team that used bunting, running, base stealing, and singles as a major part of their offense. Two of their major weapons were the Waner brothers, Paul and Lloyd. The elder Waner had won the National League MVP award and was in his second full major league season. Lloyd was a rookie who batted .355 in 1927. There were many Pirate fans who bet that the Waners collectively would hit for a higher average in the World Series than Ruth and Gehrig. Pittsburgh also had Pie Traynor, one of the greatest third basemen in the history of the game, who learned how to hit using broom handles and flailing away against corncobs on his family farm in Oklahoma.

Miller Huggins elected to have the Yankees take batting practice first at Forbes Field. He also made sure to tell Waite Hoyt to "make it look good, but just lay it in there." And he told Ruth and Gehrig and Meusel and company, "See those upper bleachers. I want to see how many of those nice unblemished balls you can drop into those stands."

The mashers of Murderer's Row followed orders. Open mouthed, the Pirates watched the show of intimidation, of power and force. "I've never seen anything like that," one Buc moaned. "Do they do that all the time?"

Pirate manager Donie Bush had hoped to spend time going over the weaknesses of the Yankees in a pregame meeting. Instead, all he could say to his team was, "Let's go out on the field."

The Yankees swept the Pirates in four—the first sweep by an American League team in World Series history up to then. The only consolations for Pittsburgh fans were the swiftness of defeat and the fact that the Waner brothers had collectively but just barely hit for a higher average in the Series than Ruth and Gehrig.

Some said the Yankee batting-practice fireworks that preceded the Series and the sweep that followed scared and jinxed the Pirates. That may or may not be true. But it was not until 1960 that Pittsburgh finally returned to the World Series.

1932: McCarthy's Payback

The Yankees of 1932 began spring training in St. Petersburg, Florida. They were in their third year of residence at the Don CeSar Hotel, 21 miles west of Tampa on the Gulf of Mexico. Col. Jake Ruppert always sought to have the

Yankees' experience be first class, and the deal with the Don CeSar was definitely first class, kept the Yankees away from the "flesh pots" of St. Petersburg, and was also a bargain.

Room rates were eight dollars per person, double occupancy, and that included meals. The Yankee owner also received assurances that his players would be served steak for breakfast plus unlimited quantities of milk each morning.

Babe Ruth was the only Yankee who did not stay at the Don CeSar—he preferred the high life in St. Pete. The only mainstays left from the 1927 Murderer's Row were Ruth, Gehrig, Lazzeri, Combs, Pipgras, and Pennock. Gone were Waite Hoyt, Mark Koenig, and Bob Meusel. In Meusel's place in left field, in his third season as a Yankee, was Ben Chapman. The swift southerner led the league in stolen bases from 1931 to 1933.

New Yankees included first-year pitcher Johnny Allen and rookie shortstop Frank Crosetti. Off a .343 season with the Pacific Coast League San Francisco Seals, Crosetti was purchased for $75,000, a lot of money in that Depression time. The "Crow" would be a fixture until 1968 as player and coach and would appear in 122 Series games.

With Crosetti and third baseman Joe Sewell, the left side of the Yankee infield was strengthened for 1932. Just 5-6 and 155 pounds, Sewell swung a 40-ounce bat, dubbed "Black Betsy," that he rubbed with a bone and plug tobacco. He claimed the reason he hardly ever struck out was all the time spent as a youth swinging a bat at bottle caps and rocks.

"I would pick up the ball," Sewell said, "from the time it left the pitcher's hand and I could actually see the seams as the ball was coming to the plate." He would strike out just three times in 503 at bats in 1932.

Southpaw Vernon Gomez was purchased in 1930 from the San Francisco Seals for $35,000. A breath of free spiritedness on a starkly businesslike team, Gomez bragged that he owed his success to clean living and a fast outfield and relief pitcher Johnny Murphy.

He could have also added Herb Pennock and Joe McCarthy to the list. The veteran Pennock was not too thrilled to see the rookie at first. The proud-as-a-peacock Pennock even refused at first to shake hands with Gomez. Then he did an about-face and became a personal tutor to the brash young man.

"If you were to cut that bird's head open," Yankee coach Charley O'Leary said, "the weaknesses of every batter in the league would spill out." Pennock served up to Gomez more than two decades of pitching insights. Then Joe McCarthy did a little fine-tuning, switching Gomez into a straight overhand delivery from the sidearm style he was used to.

Known as "El Goofo" and "Goofy," Gomez was known for his wild antics and self-deprecating humor. Chinning on the dugout roof, watching airplanes fly by, and talking an unsuspecting victim's ear off were a few of his specialties. He especially enjoyed explaining his "go fer" or gopher ball: "This is a special delivery of mine. I throw the ball and then the batter swings and then it will go for three or four bases."

Bill Dickey, who grew up in Louisiana, was so bland and somber that he was characterized by a writer of the time as "the man nobody knows." In his third year as a regular catcher, the left-handed hitter was already rounding into the Hall of Fame form that would see him hit .300 or better 11 times and catch 100 or more games for 13 straight years. Dickey roomed with Gehrig.

"We were very good buddies," Dickey noted. "In fact, I'd say we were more like brothers." Both quiet men reserved the evenings for reading and engaging in the challenge of honeymoon bridge.

Charles Herbert Ruffing, better known as "Red," had come to the Yankees in a trade with the Red Sox in 1930. The price was $50,000 and Cedric Durst. With Boston, Ruffing twice led the league in losses. With the Yankees, he would be a completely different pitcher, one of the greats in Yankee history. He employed a great fastball together with a sharp breaking curve to post a 231–124 record in 15 Yankee seasons. Despite the loss of four toes on his left foot in a mine accident, Ruffing was a superb all-around athlete and one of the best fielding and hitting pitchers ever.

With this retooled cast, Joe McCarthy was starting his second full season as manager. In 1931, the Yankees had finished in second place. It had been five years since the team had won a World Championship.

Colonel Ruppert, whose idea of a wonderful day at the ballpark was any time the Yankees scored 11 runs in the first inning and then slowly pulled away, had snapped at McCarthy in 1931: "I will stand for your finishing second because you are new to the league, but I warn you, McCarthy, I don't like finishing second."

"Colonel," McCarthy responded, "neither do I."

Opening Day of the 1932 season at Yankee Stadium saw Lefty versus Lefty—Grove versus Gomez. The 55,452 went home satisfied. The Yankees won, 8–3, hitting five home runs, including one by the Babe, who had lost 12 pounds from a battle with the flu and described himself as "as weak as a cat."

The Yankees were anything but weak. They thundered out of the gate slamming 20 home runs in their first eight games. Winning 10 of 13 games in April, 18 of 26 in May, and losing just five games in June, the Bronx Bombers had a 48–19 record going into July. And just like the weather, they were just warming up.

The Philadelphia Athletics, the highest-paid team in baseball to that time, had won three straight pennants. They had Jimmie Foxx, who would hit 58 home runs and drive in a league-leading 169 runs. They had Lefty Grove, who would be the American League ERA leader. They had a solid team, but they never had a chance against the '32 Yankees.

On May 16, the Yankee pitching rotation of Allen, Pipgras, Ruffing, and Gomez recorded its fourth straight shutout. Fourteen days later a plaque honoring Miller Huggins was unveiled at Yankee Stadium—the first of many that would pay homage to Yankee greats.

On June 3, Lou Gehrig became the first American Leaguer to hit four home runs in one game in a Yankee slugfest win over Philadelphia, 20–13. In the first inning and then again in the fifth inning he homered into the left-center field seats. His fourth- and seventh-inning shots climbed over the wall in right field. George Earnshaw, who had won more than 20 games for three straight seasons, was the victim of Gehrig's first three roundtrippers. Connie Mack mercifully put Roy Mahaffey in to replace Earnshaw.

"Connie Mack always liked Roy," Earnshaw recalled, "so he brought him in to cool Gehrig off. Boy, he sure did cool him off." Gehrig's fourth homer was off Mahaffey. In the ninth inning he just missed a fifth homer when Al Simmons made a one-handed snare of a booming shot a few steps from the deepest point of the ballpark in center field.

It was an epic home run performance. But once again Lou Gehrig was forced off center stage by another New York City baseball legend. John McGraw retired that day after 31 years as manager of the New York Giants. Gehrig's giant feat was overshadowed by extensive newspaper coverage of McGraw's decision to call it quits.

On June 5, Danny MacFayden, just another in a long line of reborn retreads from the Red Sox, was picked up by the Yankees for two pitchers and $50,000. He was 1–10 with the Sox; he would be 7–5 with the Yanks. On July 9, Ben Chapman smacked three home runs in the second game of a doubleheader against Detroit. Two of them were inside-the-park jobs. That 1932 season Chapman would score more than 100 runs, drive in more than a hundred, and steal a league-leading 38 bases.

Scoring runs in bunches, the Yankees posted a 23–5 record in August. But McCarthy never allowed them to let up. "A ballplayer," he said, "has only two hours of concentrated work every day with occasional days off. If he cannot attend to business with the high pay and the working hours so pleasant, something is wrong with him and he ought to move on."

There were no hot dogs or peanuts in the Yankee dugout. All players except for the starting pitcher had to show up for breakfast in jackets and ties before 8:30 A.M. For McCarthy, baseball was part business, part sport, all obsession. His only focus during the season was the game. He permitted himself no diversions, no hobbies, no distractions. His single-minded pursuit of excellence was transmitted to his team: There was a toughness about the 1932 Yankees, a kind of swagger.

Only Babe Ruth, the man who lusted for the job McCarthy held, didn't fit the mold. Still the game's greatest star, Ruth was virtually isolated on a team filled with what McCarthy called his "solid citizens." But the two distinctive personalities somehow coexisted, driven by their mutual obsession—winning.

For McCarthy, the future would be filled with winning. For Ruth, the future would see him winding down. All the years of not taking care of his body, all the times of wild abandon showed. Ruth, in his 18th major league season, was an old 38-year-old. Throughout that 1932 season McCarthy never hesitated to use the "caddies" Sammy Byrd ("Babe Ruth's Legs") or Myril Hoag to run for Ruth or replace him in late innings of games when the Yankees were ahead. The two utility players were also called on when the Babe was fighting off one ache or pain or another. For one two-week stretch, Ruth was out of the lineup because of torn leg muscles. He played in only 133 games in 1932, down a dozen games from the year before.

But he was still Babe Ruth, still a mighty force, and his 41 home runs that season led the parade of half a dozen Yankees who recorded at least 10

Pitcher Danny MacFayden, shown here as a Cincinnati Red, was an important pick-up for the '32 Yanks. Saddled with a 1-10 record with the lowly Red Sox, MacFayden joined the Yankees via trade and won an important seven games for the New Yorkers.

Yankee outfielder Sam Byrd became known as "Babe Ruth's Legs" during the 1932 season. Manager Joe McCarthy frequently used Byrd to "caddie" for the 38-year-old Ruth as a pinch-runner or defensive replacement in the outfield.

Outfielder Ben Chapman led the American League in stolen bases (38) during the 1932 season.

home runs: Gehrig (34), Dickey (15), Lazzeri (15), Sewell (11), and Chapman (10).

But even with all that power the Yankees, for the first time in a decade, did not lead the league in home runs. The Athletics, with 173, finished 13 homers ahead. The margin came mainly from Philadelphia's Jimmie Foxx, who pounded 58 roundtrippers—17 more than Ruth.

Still, the '32 Yankees were a wrecking crew. They scored over a thousand runs and led the league for the third year in a row in that category. No American League team drew more walks or drove in more runs. McCarthy's club went through the entire season without being shut out. That was a claim to fame that even the 1927 team could not make. At Yankee Stadium, McCarthy's team was nearly invincible. The multiple-run-scoring innings thrilled the fans and the Yankees won 62 of 77 games.

And with Red Ruffing on the scene there was always another bat handy. The star hurler was so good with the wood that McCarthy didn't hesitate to use him as a pinch-hitter. Ruffing had more than 200 career pinch-hit at bats, and he even came in to hit for the likes of Joe Sewell, Frank Crosetti, and Bill Dickey. Eight times he batted over .300.

One of Ruffing's most extraordinary moments both on the mound and in the batter's box took place on August 13, 1932, in a game against the Senators. Pounding what would be one of his 36 career home runs, he broke a scoreless tie in the tenth, giving himself and the Yankees a victory.

Ruffing was just one of the strong arms on a remarkable pitching staff that led the league in ERA, strikeouts, shutouts, and complete games; he was 18–7. Twenty-eight-year-old rookie Johnny Allen was 17–4. Pipgras won 16 of 25 decisions. Herb Pennock, still sporting that flowing motion and fidgety movement on the mound, still on the scene at 38, was 9–5. The skinny Gomez, 21–9 as a rookie, improved on that mark, going 24–7 in 1932. And Joseph Vincent McCarthy became the first manager to win a pennant in both leagues when the Bronx Bombers won their 100th game on September 11 and clinched the flag.

In the World Series, the Yankees matched up against the Chicago Cubs. The teams had never met before in a World Series, but it would be a Series to remember, a bitter grudge match. McCarthy, fired in 1930 as manager of Chicago, lusted for payback. The Yankees, especially Babe Ruth, were infuriated by the way the Cubs had treated Mark Koenig. The former Yankee shortstop had batted .353 over the final 33 games to help the Cubs clinch their pennant. Yet they voted him only a half World Series share.

"Hey, Mark," the Babe shouted as the Series opened, "why do you associate with a bunch of cheapskates like that? They're all a bunch of lousy bums." That started the taunting off and it got worse as the Series moved on.

McCarthy's favorite player, Lou Gehrig, hit a two-run homer to pace the Yankee 12–6 opening-game victory; his three hits and two runs scored insured the 5–2 win in the second game. In those first two games, 9 of the 10 Yankees that Cub pitchers walked were able to score. That fired up the atmosphere even more.

The Series shifted to Chicago on October 1. At the Edgewater Beach hotel, Ruth and his wife Claire were spat upon and cursed by Cubs faithful. The mighty Ruth was not a man to trifle with, let alone disrespect. He was flaming with fury when he got to Wrigley Field.

During batting practice Ruth screamed at the Cubs, "Hey, you damn bums, you won't be seeing Yankee Stadium again this year. This is going to be all over Sunday—four straight."

Chicago players lashed back with a stream of epithets. Generally, opponents called Ruth "monkey" and "monk." This day was reserved for earthier terms. Even the Chicago trainer got his licks in: "If I had you, I'd hitch you to a wagon, you potbelly." For the Babe that might have been the unkindest cut of all.

There were 49,986—many of them diehard Cub fans—and Democratic presidential candidate Franklin D. Roosevelt on hand. Ruth stepped into the batter's box and battered nine shots into the bleachers. "You know I'd play for half my salary if I could hit in this dump all the time," he bellowed.

The game got under way. Lemons rolled out onto the field. A stream of profanity was unleashed from the Cub dugout. Waving white towels greeted Ruth as he came to bat in the first inning. The Babe answered with his bat, blasting a three-run homer into the bleachers in right-center field. When he took up his outfield position as the Cubs came to bat, Chicago fans showered him with fruit and vegetables and other projectiles. All he did was smile.

In the bottom of the fourth inning the Babe tried to come up with a low liner stroked by Chicago shortstop Billy Jurges. Ruth muffed the play, to the delight of the fans, who didn't hold anything back in letting him know how they felt. The Bambino simply doffed his cap in a good-natured gesture, unfazed by the booing and tumult.

Up at bat in the fifth inning, Ruth gave the choke sign to the Chicago dugout. Right-hander Charlie Root got a strike across the heart of the plate. Ruth, as the account goes, raised one big finger and yelled, "Strike one!"

Another fastball strike. Ruth, as the story continues, raised two fingers and bellowed, "Strike two!"

Then, as the story goes, the 38-year-old superstar stepped out of the batter's box and pointed. Some said he pointed to the Chicago bench. Some said he pointed at Root. Some said he pointed to the center-field bleachers. Some said he did not point.

"He didn't point," said Billy Herman, "don't kid yourself." If he'd pointed do you think Root would've thrown him a strike to hit? I'll tell you what he would've done. Remember he was ahead on the count. Right—you guessed it. Ruth would've been sitting in the dirt, maybe rubbing himself where it hurt."

"I know the true story," said Bill Dickey. "I was in the on-deck circle with Gehrig at the time, but I'm gonna hold my tongue. I used to get into arguments with Gabby Hartnett. He'd say, 'Ruth did not point.' And I'd say, 'Oh, yes, he did, Gabby.' And he'd get so mad at me he couldn't see. Let's leave it just at that."

"To tell the truth," McCarthy said, "I didn't see him point anywhere at all. But maybe I turned my head for a moment."

"The Babe pointed out to right field," said George Pipgras, who pitched and won that game, "and that's where he hit the ball."

"I was there," said Sewell. "I saw it. I don't care what anybody says. He called it."

Chicago Cubs pitcher Charlie Root. Root became famous for giving up Babe Ruth's "called shot" home run during game three of the 1932 World Series.

"He never called it," Cub pitcher Burleigh Grimes insisted. "Forget it."

"The nerve of the big monkey," Gehrig exclaimed, "calling his shot and getting away with it."

The count was 2–2 when Babe swung that mighty swing of his, and the ball jumped off his bat, high and deep. Johnny Moore, the Chicago center fielder, started back, then stopped. The ball vanished just at the angle created by the scoreboard and the right-field bleachers, 436 feet from home plate.

"As I hit the ball," Ruth would say later, "every muscle in my system, every sense I had, told me that I had never hit a better one, that as long as I lived nothing would ever feel as good as this one."

For the Chicago fans it was an emotional roller coaster of a time. In an instant their loathing of the big Yankee had turned to admiration. They were on their feet cheering and applauding as he rounded the bases with those little mincing steps of his. He punctuated the touching of each base with a special curse for each Cub infielder for good measure. When he reached third base, he paused. Then he bent from the waist in a mocking bow to the enemy dugout. Then he made his way across home plate.

It was the 15th and final World Series home run of Babe Ruth's career, the longest home run ever hit to that point in time in Wrigley Field. In that same game Gehrig also hit two home runs, one right after what has gone down in history as the "Called Shot." The Iron Horse actually hit three homers in the series to Ruth's two, had nine hits while Ruth had five, batted .529 to Ruth's .333. But Ruth stole the spotlight from Gehrig, as he always did.

"I'm not a headline guy," Gehrig acknowledged. "I knew as long as I was following Ruth up to the plate I could have stood on my head and no one would have known the difference."

That night after the game a letter from Commissioner Landis was delivered to Joe McCarthy. "The judge," Joe Sewell recalled, "said that from then on any player using profanity would be fined five hundred dollars. The next day McCarthy read us the letter in the clubhouse before the game. And do you know, you could've heard a pin drop. We sat there on the bench like mummies. But our bats made a lot of noise."

The bats that especially made a lot of noise the next day belonged to Tony Lazzeri and Earle Combs. Lazzeri homered twice, Combs once. The Yankees stroked 19 hits to thrash the Cubs, 13–6. For the Yankees it was their third straight World Series sweep.

George Herman Ruth reveled in the controversy, savored all the hype and hoopla. At times he denied that he "called the shot." Other times he claimed the credit for it. Through the decades the debate has raged: Did he or did he not call the home run? "I didn't exactly point to any spot like the flagpole," the Babe said. "Anyway I didn't mean to. I just sorta waved at the whole fence. All I wanted to do was give that thing a ride. Outta the park. Anywhere."

Four years after the event, he was still being quoted. This retrospective was supplied by a Detroit sportswriter. ("Ooogly googly" performed the role of bleeped out commentary.)

"Every time I went to the bat the Cubs on the bench would yell 'Oogly googly.' It's all part of the game, but this particular inning when I went to bat there was a whole chorus of oogly googlies. The first pitch was a pretty good strike, and I didn't kick. But the second was outside and I turned around to beef about it. As I said, Gabby Hartnett said 'Oogly googly.' That kinda burned me and I said 'All right, you bums, I'm gonna knock this one a mile.' I guess I pointed, too.

"The next pitch was a fast one and I got a hold of it. Before I started to first base, I pointed to Gabby Hartnett and said right back to him, 'Oogly googly.' It was the first time I ever knew him not to have an answer. He didn't say a word."

Babe Ruth rips at a pitch during the second game of the 1932 World Series. In game three, Ruth would smack two homers, the second being his famous "called shot" off Cubs pitcher Charlie Root. It would be the Babe's 15th, and final, World Series homer.

GEHRIG AND THE 1932 WORLD SERIES

It was the World Series remembered for Babe Ruth's "Called Shot."

But the 1932 World Series was really the Lou Gehrig show.

The Yankees easily disposed of the Chicago Cubs in the first two games at the Stadium, 12–6, 5–2. One of Lou Gehrig's five hits in those games was a home run.

In game three at Wrigley Field, Babe Ruth blasted a three-run homer into the bleachers in right-center field. Gehrig homered into the same spot

Babe Ruth and his second wife, Claire. During the 1932 World Series against the Chicago Cubs, Mrs. Ruth was cursed and spat at by the Cubs faithful.

two innings later. The game was tied, 4–4, in the fifth inning when Ruth pulled off what went down in history as the "Called Shot"—a homer off Charlie Root. Crossing the plate, the Babe allegedly winked at Gehrig: "You do the same thing."

Root's first offering to Gehrig was a knockdown pitch. The Iron Horse showed no emotion. He simply collected himself, brushed off his uniform, and got back in. Then Gehrig took the next pitch deep, deep into the temporary bleachers that had been set up in right field. It was his third home run in the series. The Yankees won the game, 7–5, and the next day they clobbered the Cubs, 11–6.

Ruth and Gehrig's final totals that 1932 World Series were:

	Ruth	**Gehrig**
hits	5	9
average	.333	.529
home runs	2	3
runs scored	6	9
RBIs	6	8

It was quite a performance for Gehrig, who said, "I'm just a guy who's in there every day. The fellow who follows the Babe in the batting order."

1936: THE WINDOW BREAKERS

After their sweep of the Cubs in the 1932 World Series, the Yankees weren't able to get back to the Fall Classic. In 1933, they finished in second place, seven games behind the talented Washington Senators. In 1934 and 1935, they wound up in second place behind the powerful Detroit Tigers.

"Second-place Joe," the old nickname for Joseph Vincent McCarthy from his days as manager of the Cubs, was brought out of mothballs. He detested the nickname, detested finishing second.

As the Yankees prepared for the 1936 season, they were a team stamped by the personality of the man they called "Marse Joe." Earle Combs had retired. Babe Ruth, too, belonged to Yankee history.

The greatest slugger of them all, who a dozen times led the American League in home runs, who had all those moments of "them coming out in groves" to see him strut his stuff, was shipped to the other league, to Boston.

"McCarthy and Ruth barely spoke to each other," reserve pitcher Burleigh Grimes noted. "Babe wanted to manage and he didn't particularly care for Joe. There wasn't a hell of a lot Joe could do about Ruth. Christ, the man was an institution."

In Grimes's view Ruth was an institution. Joe McCarthy used stronger language in private to describe the Babe. As 1936 began he was just elated that his big headache was gone. But he did pay G. H. Ruth a fitting tribute.

"He was a great team player. There was always one thing you could count on—his desire to help the team win."

On the scene now were others with a strong desire to help the team win. They were players with muted dispositions, with dedicated detachment, with pride in their accomplishments, with egos sublimated to a team effort.

Lou Gehrig, the Pride of the Yankees, was still there. The year before, he had been appointed captain. Going into the 1936 season, the Iron Horse had played in 1,600 straight games. He was the personification of all McCarthy preached—the work ethic, not beating yourself, doing everything possible for the team. On the scene were Red Rolfe, George Selkirk, Bill Dickey, Frank Crosetti, Tony Lazzeri, Red Ruffing, Lefty Gomez. And waiting in the wings was Joe DiMaggio.

The season began for the Yankees on April 14 in Washington. President Franklin Delano Roosevelt threw out the first ball, and the Senators eked out a 1–0 win. It was a muted start for the team that would be a powerhouse all though that 1936 campaign. But things would get better, much better.

The Yankees won 10 of the 15 games they played in April. Eddie Brannick, the secretary of the Giants, attended one of those games at Yankee Stadium. His team was on the road. The Yankees roughed up the opposition in a one-sided victory.

"What do you think of them?" Brannick was asked.

"Window breakers," was his response.

In 1933, Joseph Paul DiMaggio, son of a fisherman, had hit in 61 straight games for San Francisco of the Pacific Coast League. The following year he injured his left knee exiting from a taxicab. To some he was damaged goods. For the Yankees he was pure gold.

Three of the 1936 Window Breakers: Joe DiMaggio, Lou Gehrig, and Bill Dickey.

"Getting him," George Weiss said on many occasions, "was the greatest thing I ever did for the Yankees." The price for the man they would call the Yankee Clipper was $25,000 and five minor leaguers. The deal also stipulated that DiMaggio could play one more season for the Seals. He gave the citizens of San Francisco something to remember him by. His 1935 stats included a .398 average, 270 hits, and 154 RBIs.

DiMaggio set out by car from San Francisco to the Yankees spring-training site in St. Petersburg with Tony Lazzeri and Frank Crosetti. The trio reached Utah. Lazzeri turned to DiMaggio. "Would you like to take over and drive?"

"I don't drive." It was reported that those were the only words uttered by DiMaggio in that three-day cross-country trek.

On March 2, 1936, DiMaggio finally reported to spring training. Red Ruffing greeted him with, "So you're the great DiMaggio?"

In the minor leagues DiMag had been known as "Dead Pan Joe." Watching him perform in spring training, Yankee owner Ruppert agreed with the assessment. "He seems to be very hard to get acquainted with."

Driving a car and engaging in small talk were not things DiMaggio could do with any degree of ease. Baseball was another matter. In spring training he rapped out a dozen hits in his first 20 at bats.

Then he suffered the "hot foot" heard all over New York City. Left unattended in a diathermy machine, he burned his foot. The accident delayed the much-ballyhooed rookie's debut for 16 games.

On May 3, 1936, DiMaggio, wearing Number 9, played in his first game, a 14–5 whacking of the St. Louis Browns. He notched a triple and two singles and scored three times. Four days later he showed off his throwing arm, gunning down Pete Fox of Detroit to preserve a 6–5 Yankee win. Three days later he recorded his first home run—a 400-foot-plus shot at Yankee Stadium off George Turbeville of the Philadelphia Athletics. It was the first of his 361 career home runs. And it came on the day the Yankees took over first place, where they would remain for the rest of the season. That was how he started, and he never let up.

Success for DiMaggio seemed to come easy. And along with it came the kudos, the adulation. He was fast becoming the toast of New York. Ed Barrow decided it was time for a fatherly chat. The Yankee executive took DiMaggio aside and explained how important it was to take things in stride, to not get emotionally caught up in success.

"Don't worry about me, Mr. Barrow," DiMaggio replied. "I never get excited."

The exterior view of DiMaggio reflected placidity, discipline, calm. Only the inner circle saw the legs scraped and raw from hard slides or diving catches. Only those in the clubhouse saw him sit for a half hour or more before his locker as if in a hypnotic trance after the Yankees had lost or when he thought he had played beneath his extraordinarily high standards.

Realizing what furies drove his prize rookie, Joe McCarthy paired the somber DiMaggio with the hyperactive Lefty Gomez. Roommates on the road, they were the original odd couple. "We were opposites," Gomez said. "I talked all the time and Joe never talked at all. He was always relaxed. And how that feller could sleep. Joe became a big star almost as soon as he joined the Yankees," said Gomez.

"The man I felt sorry for was Lou Gehrig. He had always played behind Ruth, and finally Ruth quit and he had it all to himself in 1935. Now Joe comes along. Lou had another big year, but Joe was the rookie sensation, so he got all the attention. The relationship between Joe and Lou was very good. They never had a cross word that I know of. They were both quiet fellows and they got along. But it just seemed a shame that Lou never got the attention he deserved. He didn't seem to care—but maybe he did. Anyway I always felt a bit sorry for him because of it."

On May 24, the Yankees, and especially Tony Lazzeri, showed why they were being called "Window Breakers." Playing against the Athletics in Shibe Park, Lazzeri hit two grand-slam home runs, a bases-empty homer, and a triple—15 total bases—to torque a 25–2 ravaging. The feat gave Lazzeri seven home runs in four games. And he was the eighth-place hitter in the Yankee lineup. The fact that Ben Chapman reached base seven straight times in that game was overshadowed by the Lazzeri barrage.

The Yankees went 20–8 in May with DiMaggio playing left field. On June 14, the Yankees were in first place by a few games when they announced that outfielder Ben Chapman had been traded to Washington for outfielder Jake Powell. Chapman was a lifetime .300 hitter, but McCarthy disliked his often surly, sometimes out-of-control personality. Powell, however, was not too laid back either.

On his first road trip with the Yankees, Powell administered a hotfoot to one of his new colleagues in the train station in Boston. "You're with the Yankees now," McCarthy admonished him. "We don't do those kinds of things."

With Powell in his place and in place, McCarthy would be able to make the move he had planned all season. "I started DiMaggio in left field," McCarthy explained, "and then I moved him to right field for a while. I wanted to make sure he was comfortable before I put him in center field." On August 8, the Yankee Clipper took over in center field, where he would preside until 1951, except for three years during the Second World War.

The Yankees were not only presiding over the American League, they were punishing it. In June, they were busting out all over. On the 17th, they swept a doubleheader from Cleveland, 15–4, 12–2, pounding out 19 hits in each game. The first game was won by Red Ruffing, who chipped in with two homers and a pair of singles.

The team batting average on June 21 was .310—the best in baseball. And the 71 homers in 58 games looked like a misprint. Four of the American League's 10 leading batters that day were:

(2) Lou Gehrig		.395
(4) Red Rolfe		.370
(5) Bill Dickey		.365
(9) Joe DiMaggio		.356

On June 24, *The New York Times* reported on a game in Chicago: "With Colonel Jacob Ruppert in town for a brewer's convention viewing the spectacle and wearing at the same time the best smile . . . the Yankees today put on a gorgeous show for the edification of their employer." It was mainly the Joe DiMaggio show. He recorded his seventh and eighth home runs of the

The "Yankee Clipper," Joe DiMaggio, made his major league debut for the Yanks during the '36 season. Always smooth and graceful on a baseball diamond, Joe D. was shy, almost withdrawn, and had some difficulty adjusting to the hot New York spotlight cast upon him by the fans and media.

Hall of Famer Charles "Red" Ruffing won 273 games in his career, 20 of them for the Yankees in 1936. Ruffing was just as devastating at the plate as he was on the mound. He hit .300 or better 8 times as a pitcher! And only two pitchers, Wes Farrell (38) and Bob Lemon (37), ever hit more home runs than Ruffing (36).

season, capping a Yankee 10-run fifth inning. He also collected two doubles. His two homers in the same inning tied a record shared by just four other players. Crosetti, Powell, and Dickey also homered as the Yankees crushed the White Sox, 18–11.

And even when the starting pitchers faltered, the Yankees found ways to win, usually with a combination of the long ball and good relief pitching. Such was the case on June 25. Right-hander Bump Hadley was routed, but southpaw Ted Kleinhans and the bespectacled Johnny Broaca checked Chicago in relief. Behind home runs by Gehrig, Dickey, and Rolfe, the Yanks nudged the White Sox, 7–6.

By the end of June, operating with machinelike precision, the Yankees had a 47–22 record, a 9½ game lead. Lou Gehrig was batting .400. Through the batting order there was more power, more versatility, more talent than even the 1927 Murderer's Row possessed. American League pitchers had to face (final batting averages):

Crosetti	.288
Rolfe	.319
DiMaggio	.323
Gehrig	.354
Dickey	.362
Selkirk	.308
Powell	.306
Lazzeri	.287

The fixed infield was steady day in and day out. Gehrig was solid as a rock at first base. The keystone combination of Lazzeri and Crosetti could "turn two" with the best of them and break the hearts of opposing batters in the process. At third in his third season, Robert "Red" Rolfe out of Pennock, New Hampshire, was quiet, disciplined, and highly skilled. The Dartmouth-educated athlete played for a decade for the Yankees, personifying the McCarthy way.

The outfielders—DiMaggio in center, Powell in left, and George Selkirk, nicknamed "Twinkletoes" because of his odd way of running—all could run and throw and make the right decisions.

The powerful Bill Dickey was behind the plate. Perhaps the greatest catcher of all time, he functioned like another manager on the field. His actions were an instant barometer of the ebb and flow of Yankee pitching. Dickey intuitively knew the needs of the different hurlers and meshed his pitch calls and catching style to fit those needs.

The Yankees were pitching rich. The staff led the league in saves, ERA, and strikeouts. Red Ruffing posted a 20–12 record, the first of his four straight 20-win seasons. Another in the long line of "steals" from the Red Sox, Ruffing came to the Yankees in 1930.

Although Lefty Gomez had an up-and-down year in 1936, he still won 13 of 20 decisions. The pitching staff was also helped greatly by two shrewd trades. Monte Pearson, acquired from Cleveland, was 19–7 and had the best winning percentage in the league. Irving Darius "Bump" Hadley came over from Washington and was 14–4. The team's fourth starter, Johnny Broaca, in his third season with the Yankees, won 12 of 19 decisions. Pat Malone had nine saves and a 12–4 record. "Fordham Johnny" Murphy was 9–3 with five saves.

When they weren't breaking windows there was one player or another who stepped up to make winning possible. On August 28 in a rare start, Murphy pitched the second game of a doubleheader against the Tigers. The Yankees had clobbered Detroit in the first game, 14–5. Murphy rapped out five singles—two of them in the second inning when the Yankees scored 11 runs—to destroy Detroit, 19–4.

Posting a 21–8 record in August, the Yankees not only were window breakers, they just broke the hearts of the competition. The runs scored in bunches, the power that coursed up and down the mighty lineup, the relentless pressure on opposing pitchers all became trademarks of that 1936 team. A doubleheader sweep of the Indians on September 9 clinched the pennant for the Yankees—the earliest date ever. The Bombers won 102 games and the pennant by 19½ games over second-place Detroit.

The only real oddball moment in that marvelous 1936 season for the Yankees was provided by pitcher Johnny Broaca. A former star pitcher for Yale, Broaca announced in September that he would no longer be a Yankee, that he was leaving baseball to concentrate on a boxing career. His dream was to one day fight for the heavyweight championship. The Yankees had another championship on their mind that they wanted to fight for—the World Championship.

They matched up against the Giants in the 1936 World Series—the first Subway Series since 1923. On paper the Yankees seemed invincible. Their collective and individual accomplishments gave them bragging rights as one of the greatest teams of all time.

Helped by DiMaggio in the lineup, Gehrig had a career year. He smashed a league-leading 49 home runs (14 of them against Cleveland), batted .354, and drove in 152 runs. The Iron Horse also led the league in slugging percentage, runs scored, and walks.

Five players had more than 100 runs batted in: Gehrig (152), DiMaggio (125), Lazzeri (109), Dickey (107), and Selkirk (107). In addition to Gehrig, five other Yankees batted .300 or better, paced by Dickey at .362—best ever for a season for a catcher. DiMaggio wound up at .323 with 29 home runs. Red Rolfe recorded a .319 average and scored 116 runs. George Selkirk batted .308; Jake Powell hit .306.

The only starters who did not hit over .300 were Lazzeri and Crosetti, but they managed 29 home runs between them. The Yankees batted .300 and hit more home runs (182) and scored more runs (1,065) than any other team in the American League.

The New York Giants had an ace in Carl Hubbell, who had posted a 26–6 record in the regular season and had won 16 in a row. But even with "King Carl" at the ready no one gave the Giants much of a chance.

On September 30, game one got under way at the Polo Grounds. It was Carl Hubbell versus Red Ruffing. The Giant star spun his screwball to near perfection in that game, which was played in a steady rain. Spacing seven

Johnny Broaca won 12 games in 1936, but didn't appear in the World Series.

Outfielder Jake Powell was the product of another shrewd Yankees trade. Acquired from the Washington Senators during the middle of the 1936 season (for Ben Chapman), Powell went on to bat .306 for the Yankees. Powell saved his best for last, though. He led all batters in the World Series with a .455 average. Sadly, Powell died in 1948 at the young age of 40.

hits, Hub beat the McCarthy men, 6–1. The sole Yankee run came on George Selkirk's homer—the only fly ball Hubbell allowed in the game. The defeat snapped the Yankees' 12-game World Series winning streak.

Game two saw President Franklin D. Roosevelt in the stands and Yankee power on parade. A grand slam by Tony Lazzeri was the big blow in a seven-run third inning. Every Yankee had at least one hit and scored at least one run as five Giant pitchers felt the sting of the 18–4 romp. And it seemed the Yankees could have kept on scoring into the night as they underscored their ravaging of the Giants in the ninth inning with six runs—three of them coming in on a Bill Dickey homer. There was no mercy.

But mercifully the end came when Joe DiMaggio made the play of the day for the final out in the ninth inning. Racing back, turning one way and then the other, he snared a 480-foot shot off the bat of Hank Leiber just in front of the clubhouse steps in the Polo Grounds. Then DiMag and the other Yankees stood in place as the convertible carrying Franklin D. Roosevelt drove across the field to take the president out of the ballpark. As the automobile passed by DiMag, FDR waved to Joe D.

Before a record crowd of 64,842 at the Stadium, the Yankees eked out a 2–1 win in game three. Frank Crosetti had the game-winning RBI in the eighth inning, a liner off the glove of Freddie Fitzsimmons.

Behind the pitching of Monte Pearson and the hitting of Gehrig, the Yanks defeated Carl Hubbell and won game four, 5–2. This time there were 66,669 at the Stadium—a new World Series record for the second straight day.

Game five pitted Red Ruffing against Prince Hal Schumacher. It was a languid day at Yankee Stadium. The Giants drew first blood in a three-run first inning. The Yankees came back. The game moved to the tenth, tied at 4–4, with Pat Malone pitching in relief, a double by Jo-Jo Moore, a bunt, and a Bill Terry fly ball to DiMaggio gave the Giants a run. Schumacher closed down the Yankees in the bottom of the tenth, and Giant fans celebrated the 5–4 triumph.

It would be a short-lived celebration, for the next day in game six at the Polo Grounds the Yankees erupted for a 13–5 victory. A two-run home run by Jake Powell, the leading hitter in the Series at .455, highlighted the seven-run Yankee ninth. Gomez picked up his second victory of the Series.

The New York Yankees had won their first World Series without Ruth. No longer "Second-place Joe," the stone-jawed McCarthy had won the big one and was magnanimous in victory.

Monte Pearson, acquired from Cleveland after the 1935 season, won 19 games for the '36 Yanks and added a complete game victory in game four of the World Series, the first of four consecutive Fall Classics in which Pearson would boast a record of 1-0. Pearson's lifetime World Series ERA (1.01) is seventh best all-time and his winning percentage (1.000) can never be bested.

Red Rolfe, show here sliding into third base during the 1936 World Series, was the quintessential "steady" performer for the Yankees 1936 club. Rolfe hit .319 for the season, .400 in the World Series and led all American League third basemen in fielding (.957).

(Opposite)
After defeating the Giants in the 1936 World Series, the Yankees repeated the feat a year later.

"The Giants are a much better team than people give them credit for," McCarthy said. "They gave us a whale of a battle." Those were kind words but not exactly true. The Bronx Bombers outscored the Giants 43–23 and batted .302 as a team.

"That club," said Giant manager Bill Terry, "has everything. They're the toughest club I've ever faced. I've always heard that one player could make the difference between a losing team and a winner, and I never believed it. Now I know it's true."

That one player, Joe DiMaggio, batted .346 and showed his whole repertoire in the field. He would be on the scene for 13 seasons and play in 10 World Series. For the Yankees, getting Babe Ruth was called the biggest steal of the century. For the Yankees, then, getting Joe DiMaggio for $25,000 and five anonymous minor leaguers had to be the biggest steal of all time.

After the Series ended, McCarthy recalled, "Somebody came up to me and said my club was so good it don't look like anybody was going to beat us for a long time. I'll tell you, that fellow knew what he was talking about."

Yankee Stadium was the House That Ruth Built. But now it belonged to Joe DiMaggio and Lou Gehrig. That 1936 season the Bronx Bombers began a string of four straight pennants and World Championships.

70

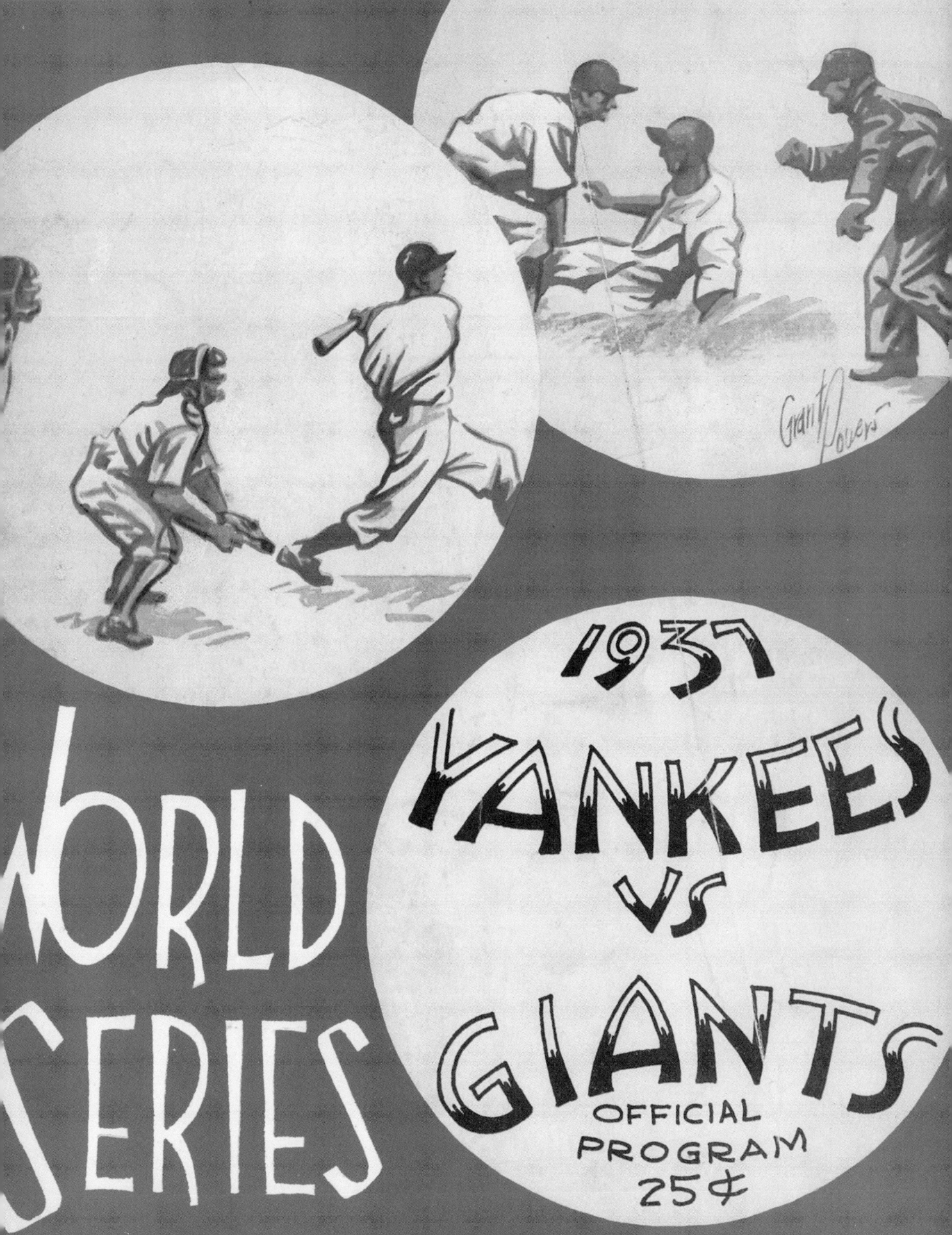

WORLD SERIES

1937
YANKEES
VS
GIANTS
OFFICIAL
PROGRAM
25¢

Johnny Kucks, a 23-year-old pitcher in only his second major-league season, won 18 games for the '56 Yanks. Kucks finished his outstanding season in style, firing a three-hit complete-game shutout in game seven of the Series vs. the cross-town Dodgers.

1956: THE LAST SUBWAY SERIES

In the months leading up to the 1956 baseball season, the talk in New York City was all about what had happened in the 1955 World Series. Losers to the Yankees in 1941, 1947, 1949, 1952, and 1953, the Dodgers of Brooklyn had finally done it—beaten the Yankees in the 1955 Fall Classic. It was the first World Series triumph for the Dodgers, the first World Series loss for the Yankees since 1942.

And as major league teams left their spring-training sites and headed north, it was the Yankees "Waiting till Next Year," planning on another pennant, looking forward to meeting the Dodgers once again in the World Series.

Reporters asked Mickey Mantle if he thought he had a shot at breaking Babe Ruth's home run record. "I think that this year," the Mick responded, "I'd rather lead the league in home runs, runs batted in, and hitting—and that's my goal."

The 1956 baseball season got under way on April 17 with President Dwight D. Eisenhower throwing out the first ball for the fourth straight time. A baseball fan, and especially a Mickey Mantle fan, Ike remained through all nine innings. The Yankees roughed up the Senators, 10–4. Batting left-handed, Mickey Mantle slammed two tape-measure home runs off Camilo Pascual. That was the tip off to the kind of year he was going to have.

With Mantle acting as siege gun, with Whitey Ford in his fifth season anchoring a practically unknown and definitely unheralded young pitching staff that included Johnny Kucks, Tom Sturdivant, and Don Larsen, the Yankees won seven of their first eight games. And they just kept on winning.

The pressure they put on the other American League teams was relentless. And the line "Rooting for the Yankees is like rooting for General Motors" was a not-too-oblique criticism of the team's machinelike winning ways.

"Why is everyone mad at us?" Casey Stengel asked. "What do they expect us to do? Roll over and play dead? Draw up a chair and sit by the roadside until the rest catch up? If you ran a delicatessen store, you would want it to be the best delicatessen store, wouldn't you? Well, that's how I feel about the Yankees."

On May 18, in a 10-inning 8–7 Yankee win over Chicago, Mantle homered for the third time in his career from both sides of the plate, eclipsing a mark set by outfielder Jim Russell. Six days later, a zoned-in Mantle was unstoppable. Rapping out five hits in five at bats, the Mick pushed his batting average to a gaudy .421 in an 11–4 Yankee stomping of the Tigers.

Throughout that 1956 season for Mantle it was mountain after mountain that he climbed, feat after feat that he racked up. Yankee fans were ecstatic; opposition fans were envious. On Memorial Day at Yankee Stadium in the first game of a doubleheader against Washington, batting left-handed, Mantle came to bat with two men on base in the fifth inning against Pedro Ramos.

"One of our guys," Ramos said, "was the victim of a knockdown pitch the previous inning, so Mickey knew I'd knock him down. I thought I'd fool him

and lay one right over, knowing he'd be ready to hit the dirt. Well, he forgot about the knockdown and was just standing there."

"Ramos threw me a perfect, hard fastball," Mantle said, "right over the middle of the plate. I swung as hard as I've ever swung and as soon as it left the bat I knew it was fair, and I also knew it was the longest ball I'd ever hit."

The ball was still soaring when it banged off the copper filigree facade of the upper stands in right field—379 feet from home plate, 118 feet above the level of the field. No one had ever hit a home run out of Yankee Stadium, but Mantle came within 18 inches of accomplishing that feat.

"I was glad the ball hit the roof," Ramos recalled, "because if it didn't it would have traveled another six miles."

"I didn't believe it myself," said Mantle. "Even when I saw it I couldn't believe it." The gargantuan nature of the blow dwarfed the fact that the homer was Mantle's 20th. It was the first time in baseball history that any player ever hit that many home runs before June. They didn't call Mantle "Mr. May," but they might just as well have.

Casey Stengel, his one-man fan club, remarked in June: "A tree-mendous ballplayer—don't matter what ballpark he is in either. One of those shots he hit in Washington might be travlin' yet except it strikes a tree outside the

The Mick. The 1956 season may have been Mantle's finest, as he led the league in home runs (52), RBIs (130), and batting average (.353) to win the Triple Crown. Teammate Elston Howard said of the oft-injured Mantle, "On two legs Mickey Mantle would have been the greatest player who ever lived."

Shown here after singling in the 1956 World Series, 40-year-old Hall of Famer Enos "Country" Slaughter hit .289 as a part-time outfielder for the '56 Yankees. Most famous for his "mad dash" from first to home in the deciding seventh game of the 1946 World Series, Slaughter hit .350 in the '56 Series against the Dodgers. There have been few to play major league baseball who were as competitive as Slaughter.

park. They tell me the only other feller which hit that tree was Ruth. He shook some kids out of the tree when the ball landed.

"Everybody admires Mick but the umpires," Casey continued. "Mantle does not swing at many bad pitches any longer. When Ted Williams lets a pitch go by the umpires give him credit for having a great eye and he gets the benefit of the doubt. Mantle does not."

The New York Times on June 20 reported: "Mickey Mantle continued his one man reign of terror against American League pitchers with his 26th and 27th home runs."

Both were shots into the upper deck at Briggs Stadium in Detroit. The roundtrippers powered the Yankees to their seventh straight win that day and put Mantle 18 games ahead of Babe Ruth's 60 home run pace of 1927. Ruth had 27 homers in 78 games; Mantle had his 27 in 60 games. All but six of Mantle's were hit left-handed, but that was because he had fewer opportunities to bat right-handed.

The talk was all about the power of the "Oklahoma Kid," Mickey Mantle. But the finesse of Whitey Ford was another big reason the 1956 Yankees were on track for another pennant. For "Whitey and Mickey" and the rest of the Yankees at the top of their form, 1956 was a magical season. A half dozen of them were selected to the All-Star team: Berra, Kucks, Mantle, Martin, McDougald, and Ford.

"I don't care what the situation was," Mantle said of Ford, "how high the stakes were—the bases could be loaded, the pennant riding on every pitch, it never bothered Whitey. He pitched his game. Cool. Crafty. Nerves of steel."

On July 20, Whitey Ford fanned a half-dozen Kansas City batters in succession. If Mantle wasn't doing it to the competition, Ford was.

Stengel called Ford "my banty rooster. He'd stick out his chest and walk out to the mound against any of those pitchers."

Ford was the banty rooster. But Mantle was Stengel's "big fella," and America's pinup boy. On July 1, he homered right-handed and left-handed—for the fourth time in his career. On August 23 against Chicago, he showed off the whole package—home run, triple, bunt single. Two days later his home run total was 44, despite a gimpy knee.

"On two legs Mickey Mantle would have been the greatest player who ever lived," Elston Howard noted. "The man hit all those home runs and did everything else on one leg."

There was a gathering of the clan at Yankee Stadium on August 25—Old-Timers' Day at Yankee Stadium. One of the few down moments of the season took place. Phil Rizzuto, 38, was given his unconditional release to make room on the roster for veteran outfielder Enos Slaughter, purchased from Kansas City.

For the man they called "Country," it was his second tour of duty with the Yankees. "I came back on a Saturday night. We played Detroit a doubleheader on Sunday. I went 5 for 9 and we beat them. I really felt my return to the Yankees had something to do with their winning the pennant in 1956."

With the old Cardinal on the Yankee roster, Stengel had even more maneuvering room. And even though Slaughter replaced Yankee legend Rizzuto, the move enabled the Yankees to retool their infield. Billy Martin came out of two years of military service and took over at second base. Gil

McDougald was shifted to shortstop, replacing Rizzuto. The realigned infield with Andy Carey at third base and Moose Skowron at first base would see the Yankees turn a league-leading 214 double plays in 1956.

The double play and especially the long ball were hallmarks of the 1956 Yankees.

Day after day, one Yankee or another took his turn in the home run barrage on American League pitchers. On September 11, Yogi Berra hammered his 236th career home run, tying him with Gabby Hartnett for most career home runs by a catcher. It was the 177th homer of the season for the Yankees.

Seven days later, on September 18, Mantle became only the eighth player to hit 50 home runs. It was his 171st career homer—a shot into the upper deck at Comiskey Park. "Seats were flying around for five minutes," rasped Stengel. The Yankees nipped the White Sox, 3–2, and clinched their 22nd pennant, Casey's seventh.

On September 21, Mantle slugged another monster home run—this one traveled 480 feet—just a foot from the top of the bleachers at Fenway Park. His three hits in that game put him neck and neck with Ted Williams in the battle for the batting title.

At season's end Mantle wound up with a .353 average and the batting title. "I think Ted was kind of upset about losing the title," Mantle said. "Of course, I got a couple of bunt hits to protect my average."

Williams was more than upset. He was annoyed and snapped, "If I could run like him I'd hit .400 every year."

The season the 24-year-old Mickey Mantle put together in 1956 was unsurpassed by anyone in the 1950s. It was also one of the greatest years any player ever had in the history of the game. Mantle's spectacular stats—a .353 average, 52 home runs, 130 RBIs—gave him the Triple Crown, the first by a Yankee since Gehrig accomplished that feat in 1934. The Mick also led the league in runs scored (132), slugging percentage (.705), and total bases (376). Mantle's major league-leading slugging percentage was the highest ever by a switch-hitter in a season, as were his 376 total bases and 130 runs batted in.

Whitey Ford registered his best season to that point, winding up with a 19–6 record and a league-leading winning percentage and ERA. The slick left-hander would have been a 20-game winner, but he had the bad luck to be in the wrong place at the wrong time on the final day of the season. On that day rookie pitcher Charlie Beamon of Baltimore tossed a four-hit shutout to nip Ford and the Yankees, 1–0.

The Bronx Bombers scored more runs, hit more home runs (190), and slugged the ball at a higher percentage than any other American League team. Bill Skowron and Gil McDougald batted over .300. Yogi Berra slammed 30 home runs and drove in 105 runs. Former Marine Hank Bauer and Bill Skowron combined for 49 home runs.

Whitey Ford was the ace but the pitching staff had plenty of depth. Johnny Kucks won 18 games. Tom Sturdivant won 16 games. Don Larsen was 11–5 and Bob Turley was 8–4. The Yankees won 97 games and had no difficulty winning the pennant and finishing nine games ahead of Cleveland. The Indians had a trio of 20-game winners, but they scored 145 fewer runs

Most ballgames are lost, not won.
—Casey Stengel

The 1956 New York Yankees. First row: Whitey Ford, Billy Martin, Bill Hunter, Tom Carroll, Bill Dickey, coach; Frank Crosetti, coach; Casey Stengel, manager; Jim Turner, coach; Yogi Berra, Irv Noren, Charlie Silvera, Gil McDougald. Second row: Gus Mauch, trainer; Enos Slaughter, Bob Cerv, Jerry Coleman, Bill Skowron, Elston Howard, Bob Turley, Sonny Dixon, George Wilson, Rip Coleman, Don Larsen. Third row: Tom Sturdivant, Norm Siebern, Andy Carey, Tommy Byrne, Bob Grim, Mickey Mantle, Hank Bauer, Mickey McDermott, Tom Morgan, Johnny Kucks, Joe Collins. Bat boys: Eddie Carr, William Loperfido.

than the Yankees.

"You just kind of took it for granted around the Yankees," Ford said, "that there was always going to be baseball in October."

And the fans of New York City baseball in that era took if for granted that there would be a Subway Series. In 1956, it was Dodgers versus Yankees, their fourth Fall Classic encounter in five years, their sixth Fall Classic confrontation since 1947. Only this time it was the Yankees who were looking for revenge against "Dem Bums."

"The thing that made the Subway Series so wonderful," former Dodger center fielder Duke Snider recalled, "was that a team would bring thousands of its fans across town to the other team's ballpark. In most Series, your away game is in enemy territory. Here you had your fans with you all the time. It was great for the players and the fans. Those Series really made New York fans feel a part of baseball forever."

Although they just squeaked by the powerful Milwaukee Braves to win the pennant on the final day of the season, the Dodgers were a potent adversary. Left-handed slugger Duke Snider led the National League in homers and slugging percentage. Other big Brooklyn bats included Gil Hodges, who hit 32 home runs, and Carl Furillo and Roy Campanella, who combined for 41 more. Jackie Robinson, though winding down, was still a force. Don Newcombe's 27 wins topped the National League.

On October 2, game one saw a matchup of 39-year-old former New York Giant pitcher Sal Maglie against Whitey Ford at Ebbets Field. That Mickey Mantle watcher, President Dwight D. Eisenhower, was in attendance. The swarthy Maglie fanned 10 and spaced 9 hits, hurling the Dodgers to a 6–3 win. Home runs by Jackie Robinson and Gil Hodges sparked the Brooklyn attack. The defeat of Ford had Dodger fans crowing: "See, even da good left-ies get rooned at Ebbets Field."

The second game of the Series was delayed by rain, but when it was played on October 5, the Dodgers triumphed again, coming from six runs down to outlast the Yankees, 13–8, in a marathon 3 hours and 26 minutes. Stengel had starters and relievers coming and going—Don Larsen, Johnny Kucks, Tommy Byrne, Tom Sturdivant, Tom Morgan, Bob Turley, and Mickey McDermott all saw action. The headline in the *New York Daily News* read "Murder at Ebbets Field." Berra's second-inning bases-loaded homer off Don Newcombe gave him the distinction of being the only player in World Series history to hit a grand slam in a losing cause.

Elation was the operative emotion for the fans of "Dem Bums." But Casey Stengel, like ol' man river, kept his spirits high and his syntax scrambled and everybody guessing about who he would be using as starting pitchers in the Series. "It may be McDermott," Casey explained, "if it ain't Kucks. But then that Ford he wants a chance to win another, but it could be Sturdivant or maybe Larsen, and I'm even thinking of giving Turley a chance if it ain't McDermott or Ford, if I don't use Coleman."

With the Dodgers leading the Series 2–0, there were those who were saying that Brooklyn was heading to its second straight World Championship. The Series switched to the Stadium on October 6, and for a time it seemed the Dodgers were really going to make it two straight titles. But Enos Slaughter, who would bat .350 in the Series, rapped a three-run homer to save the day and probably the Series for the Yankees, who won the game, 5–3.

The Bronx Bombers tied the Series the next day in game four as Tom Sturdivant spaced six hits. Mantle and Bauer homered to supply the power in the 6–2 win.

The fifth game was played on October 8, before 64,519. Sal Maglie was on the mound again for the Dodgers. But Maglie, the Dodgers, the Yankees, the season—all were forgotten that day. Don Larsen was king of the universe. The Yankee right-hander pitched the only perfect game in World Series history as the Yanks won, 2–0.

The next day at Ebbets Field it was Clem Labine versus Bob Turley, another no-windup specialist. The Dodgers eked out a 1–0 triumph in 10 innings. The winning run scored when Slaughter misplayed a Jackie Robinson fly ball and Jim Gilliam scored from second base. And there was another unhappy losing pitcher—only this one wanted to talk. "I pitched the greatest game I ever pitched in my life," Turley said, "and I still got beat."

On October 10, the Yankees won their first World Series in three years. They romped, 9–0, behind the three-hit pitching of 23-year-old sophomore Johnny Kucks. An Elston Howard home run, two two-run homers by Berra, and a Bill Skowron grand slam torqued the Yankee power.

Casey Stengel had his sixth World Championship, and the Yankees had their 17th. And no one knew it then, but never again would there be a World Series played between the Brooklyn Dodgers and the New York Yankees.

In an 11-year career with the Cleveland Indians and Brooklyn Dodgers, Dale Mitchell accumulated over 1,200 hits for a gaudy lifetime batting average of .312. But he's best remembered for his last career at-bat, when he didn't get a hit. Mitchell suffered the indignity of being the last out of Don Larsen's game five Perfect Game in the 1956 Series. Appearing as a pinch-hitter, Mitchell took a disputed called third strike to end the game.

Roger Maris, shown here in 1959 as a Kansas City Athletic, was brought to the Yankees via trade following the '59 season. Maris took New York by storm, winning the Most Valuable Award in his first two seasons as a Yankee.

1961: THE M&M BOYS

In 1958 the New York Giants and Brooklyn Dodgers had defected to California, sending shock waves throughout the baseball world. In the fall of 1960 two other fixtures were no longer on the New York City baseball scene: Casey Stengel, 70, and General Manager George Weiss, 66, belonged to the Yankee past.

And even those who hated the Yankees were taken aback by the insensitive and abrupt discharge of the two legends. Arthur Daley of *The New York Times* expressed the feelings of many: "Competence has ceased to be the measuring rod in the Yankee scheme of things. It can be over-ruled and neglected by the date on a man's birth certificate."

The garrulous Stengel, who said, "I couldn't be a yes-man. I never was and never will be," and the closemouthed Weiss were an odd couple. But they had been the two most responsible for creating the New York Yankee dynasty. Ironically, the last trade made by the man they called "Lonesome George" brought Roger Maris to the Yankees. And ironically, on November 2, 1960, the day Weiss cried in public when he was involuntarily retired, the powerfully built outfielder won the American League Most Valuable Player award.

The new pecking order on the Yankees saw Ralph Houk installed as manager and Roy Hamey in place as general manager. Houk's résumé included much success managing in the Yankee minor league system, coaching with the big club, and a short stint as interim manager in 1959 when Stengel was ill. Hamey had 36 years in baseball in various capacities, his last as assistant general manager to Weiss, a four-time pick by *The Sporting News* as Executive of the Year.

Ralph Houk knew full well that he was stepping where few men would have dared to tread. He was being asked to manage the Yankees, a team stamped by the personality and accomplishments of the highly personal Casey Stengel. Houk also knew he was hired to win the World Series and nothing else would suffice. For most other men the pressure would have been unbearable. But Ralph Houk was not like most other men. He was used to pressure and used to leading.

During World War II, he was an army major and earned a Silver Star in the Battle of the Bulge for "exposing himself" to enemy fire. That phrase did not tell the full story. Houk's clothing was literally shredded by German machine-gunners.

Where Casey had juggled lineups, played around with pitching rotations, and castigated players, Houk would play one lineup, stay with a set pitching rotation, and work on establishing rapport with his players.

A couple of early moves made by the likable man they called "the Major" involved Yogi Berra and Mickey Mantle. Houk prevailed on Yogi to shift to left field and platoon with Hector Lopez. That move enabled Houk to install Elston Howard as the regular catcher. It was a move that paid off big.

The rookie Yankee manager also told 11-year veteran Mickey Mantle that he was the club leader and convinced him that hitting cleanup would help him and the team. Mantle had batted third all of his career, but he, like Berra, agreed to the shift. That was also a move that paid off big, especially for Roger Maris. That entire 1961 season he did not draw an intentional walk. He was always pitched to because Mantle came up right after him.

The typical 1961 Houk batting order was a blend of speed and power, especially power.

Bobby Richardson and Tony Kubek, known as the "Bobbsey twins," a reference to their solid-citizen ways and good-guy behavior, batted one-two and were steady day in and day out. They were the table setters in the lineup. Collectively, they manufactured 343 hits, which made for a lot of table setting. As the keystone combination at second and short they helped the Yankee infield turn most of its 180 double plays.

Roger Maris batted third in the powerful lineup. In 1959, he had collected 16 home runs for the Kansas City Athletics. The following season he was traded to the New York Yankees. A loner, sometimes, surly and moody, Maris thought of himself as the odd man out in Yankee pinstripes. But the left-handed pull hitter was ideally suited to the inviting environment of the right field stands at Yankee Stadium—an area that had once been known as "Ruthville." In his first Yankee season, in 1960, Maris led the league in RBIs (112) and hit 39 home runs. He also won the Most Valuable Player award.

In 1956, Mickey Mantle had 52 home runs, and there was talk that he was the heir apparent to break the home run mark of 60 set by Babe Ruth. In 1960, the Mick hammered 40 home runs. Back-to-back in the batting order, Maris and Mantle gave the Yankees the most potent one-two punch in baseball.

The fifth through eighth positions in the order featured such talent as Yogi Berra, Elston Howard, Bill Skowron, and Clete Boyer. Reserves like Hector Lopez, Bob Cerv, and Johnny Blanchard would have been starters on most teams.

Even with this array of talent poised and ready, the Yankees got off to a bland 18–15 start, hitting just 34 home runs in those first 33 games. The pitching was searching for a rhythm and a rotation. Art Ditmar was erratic and Bob Turley had elbow problems. The 26-year-old Maris did not hit his first home run until game 16 on April 26. He was stuck in a deep slump until the middle of May, managing just four home runs and a .210 average. There was so much concern about his lack of production that he was sent to an eye doctor.

The only real bright spots for the Yankees were Mantle, with 10 home runs, Elston Howard, who was hitting for a very high average, and Whitey Ford. Under Stengel, the stylish southpaw generally started a game once a week. Houk plugged the man Elston Howard dubbed "Chairman of the Board" into the rotation, allowing him to start every fourth day. And Ford thrived on the extra work. He was off to a 4–1 start and went 8–0 in June.

Perhaps it was the sight of the Red Sox at Fenway Park or the weather warming up. Whatever it was, May 30 saw the Yankees slam seven homers and romp 12–3 over the Sox. Mantle, Maris, and Skowron each had a pair of homers. The victory seemed not only to snap the Yanks out of their lethargy, but also to jump-start the home run race between Mantle and Maris. It was like Babe Ruth and Lou Gehrig and 1927 all over again, maybe better.

As the season moved into June, Mantle had 14 home runs, Maris had 12. Going head to head over the next eight weeks, Mantle slugged 25 more home runs while Maris recorded 28 more. Both were on a pace to break

Outfielder Bob Cerv made three different stops in New York during his career. During the 1961 season, Cerv shared a Queens apartment with fellow Yankee outfielders Maris and Mantle. He managed a .278 lifetime average in 12 big league seasons.

Slick-fielding Yankee third baseman Clete Boyer. Many baseball purists swear Boyer was the defensive equal of Hall of Famer Brooks Robinson. Boyer's brothers, Ken and Cloyd, were also major leaguers.

Ruth's 60 home run mark. At ballparks all over the American League, fans flocked to see the new "home run twins." The 1961 Yankees would draw 1,946,292—a new road record.

Media scrutiny was unrelenting. Photographers insisted on pairing Mantle and Maris in all kinds of posed shots. Maris was irked; Mantle was bemused. "We've taken so many pictures together," he smiled, "that I'm beginning to feel like a Siamese twin."

There were all kinds of commercial capitalizations. An enterprising stripper went by the name of Mickey Maris. The sales of M&M candy skyrocketed—a tip of the cash register to the "M&M Boys," who had not endorsed the confection.

Newspapers printed endless stories and charts comparing Mantle and Maris, Maris and Ruth, Ruth and Mantle, and so forth, ad nauseum. Overreaching journalists invented stories that bickering and animosity existed between Mantle, who earned $75,000 that season, and Maris, who was paid $42,000. The stories were completely untrue. "Roger," Mantle insisted, "was one of my best friends."

The two shared a Queens apartment with Bob Cerv. The three young Yankee outfielders would ride in Maris's open convertible back and forth from Yankee Stadium. The closeness of the trio reflected the atmosphere on the team.

Tony Kubek, Clete Boyer, Bill Stafford, and others stayed at the Stadium Motor Lodge, a motel just an eight-block walk from the Stadium. After the game ended, the gathering place was the Dutchman, a steakhouse close by 161st Street. Two large Dobermans acted as doormen. The players ate and enjoyed replaying the day's game and hearing stories of the old Yankees from some of the veteran waiters. A favorite was about how the Babe used to like to have more than a few beers and then go practice his slide on the sawdust-covered floors.

Despite image-making efforts, such as the *Look* magazine photograph of the team in business suits and attaché cases, the 1961 Yankees were not a personification of corporate America. They were a collection of individuals with much pride in playing the game all-out with flair and professionalism. They were also a team helped immeasurably by a highly professional coaching staff at the ready with advice, insights, and direction.

The third-base coaching box was almost a second home for Frank Crosetti, who served as an infield tutor and a traffic cop for baserunners, making all those aggressively correct decisions. Pitching coach Johnny Sain preached less rest between appearances and made hurlers more effective. He was also a big believer in more spin on the ball for his pitchers. That philosophy turned Whitey Ford into a workhorse and Luis Arroyo into a winner. Wally Moses was the batting and first-base coach; Roger Maris and others credited him with top-notch tips. Former catcher Jim Hegan added class and experience.

On July 4, the weather, the Yankees, and Roger Maris were heating up. The Yanks were only a game behind first-place Detroit as they prepared to meet in a doubleheader at the Stadium. It was Whitey Ford versus Don Mossi in the first game. A six-run fifth highlighted by Howard's bases-loaded triple gave the Yankees the win. In the eighth inning of the nightcap Maris slammed a pitch by Frank Lary into the seats, his 31st roundtripper of the season. He was more than halfway to the 34-year-old record. But "Yankee killer" Lary dropped a nifty two-out, two-strike squeeze bunt in the 10th inning to give the Tigers a split of the doubleheader.

Casey Stengel was asked if he thought Maris had a shot at the Ruth record. "Why shouldn't he break it?" Casey responded. "My going after the record started off such a dream," Maris admitted. "I was living a fairy tale for a while. I never thought I'd ever get a chance to break such a record. Every day and every night people wanted to talk to me—and they all asked the same damn question: 'Do you think you can break Babe Ruth's record?'"

Maris, bombarded over and over again with the same question, had grown surly. "How the hell should I know?" was his standard reply to the standard question. "I was a disliked player," Maris said. "And there's a difference when you played as a liked player and a disliked player. I understand why it happened. A lot of people, especially older people, did not want me to break Ruth's record. They tried to make me fit the mold of Babe Ruth. I didn't want to fit anybody's mold."

The pattern being created by Maris and Mantle—booming home runs—was becoming one that other Yankees were following in their own way. There was no way Johnny Blanchard could crack the starting everyday lineup. But

Johnny Blanchard was the Yankees second catcher in 1961. Not to be outdone by the other bashers in the lineup, Blanchard tied a record by homering in four consecutive at-bats in July.

The graceful, balanced follow-through of the great Mickey Mantle.

he competently backed up Elston Howard and also served as pinch-hitter deluxe. And he had a tremendous impact on the 1961 Yankees—eight of his home runs that season tied games or were the go-ahead runs. In one amazing stretch from July 21 to 26, Blanchard homered in two pinch-hitting appearances. Then he homered twice in one game against Chicago. Hitting like that enabled him to crack 21 homers in just 243 at bats in 1961.

On July 25, in a twinight doubleheader at Yankee Stadium against the White Sox, Maris slammed two home runs in each game—37, 38, 39, 40! He was two-thirds of the way toward tying the Ruth record. Mantle homered in the first game of that doubleheader. The score in the home run race was Maris 40, Mantle 38.

But more important, the Yankees swept that doubleheader against Chicago. For most of July they had played musical chairs for first place in the standings with the Tigers. The double win over Chicago put the Yankees on top for good.

In first place, the Yankees kept the pressure on the rest of the league. For Maris, the pressure kept building day by day. Reporters lined up three and four deep by Maris's cubicle in all the ballparks. "I never had a minute to myself," he said. "People who knew nothing about sports were there in the clubhouse, and they kept asking the same question. I might have grown a bit impatient, but it was never as bad as they were writing."

Sitting at a huge oak table in the center of the clubhouse, sipping coffee and smoking Camels, Maris tried to escape the pressure by spending hours playing with a box trying to manipulate a steel ball through a 40-hole maze. When even this provided no respite, he would take to hiding in the training room. That provided some relief, but the race against the ghost of Babe Ruth was too big a story. Those who wanted to, needed to, found other places to ask questions of the Yankee slugger.

Some pointed out that the right-field fence in Yankee Stadium was just 296 feet away. Others said too many of Maris's home runs came with the bases empty. A few, such as Rogers Hornsby, snapped, "It would be a shame if a .270 hitter broke Ruth's record." Many pleaded openly for Mantle, not Maris.

"Yeah, they always said Mantle was the one to break the record," Maris explained. He was the favorite. I was never the fair-haired boy over there. When I'd get hurt, they'd think I could still play. When Mantle or someone else got hurt, they'd let them rest."

Fame's relentless bright light became a way of life for Maris. "They even ask for autographs at Mass," he snapped. Verbal abuse was just one of the prices he had to pay. There were bottles thrown at him from the stands—even at Yankee Stadium. A game at Detroit was held up as ushers cleared garbage that was tossed down at Maris. Vituperative hate letters and wild promotional schemes arrived daily in the mail.

Some teams attempted to pitch around the beleaguered Maris. In a game against the Los Angeles Angels, one the Yankees won, 2–1, in 12 innings, he was walked five times. "I felt I had to play every day or else I'd blow it," he said. "One little injury, and I'd blow it. The pressure from all sides was just tremendous."

On August 16, Maris homered twice off Chicago's Billy Pierce. That gave him home runs in seven straight games to tie an AL record. At the end of the day Maris had 48 home runs, three more than Mantle.

On August 22, Maris pounded number 50, becoming the first player ever to have that many home runs by August. "I never wanted all the hoopla," the beleaguered Maris explained after hitting number 50. "All I wanted was to be a good ballplayer, hit 25 or 30 home runs, drive in around 100 runs, and help my club win the pennant. I just wanted to be one of the guys, an average player having a good season." But what he wanted was not what he had.

Against his former Kansas City team on August 26, in his 128th game of the 1961 season, Maris recorded home run number 51. It was just about that time that Commissioner Ford Frick, who had been a ghostwriter for Ruth, ruled that if the Babe's single-season home run record was broken, the feat would be inscribed in the record books with an asterisk.

The rationale was that Ruth had recorded 60 home runs in a 154-game season. Maris was playing out a 162-game schedule due to expansion. The Frick ruling infuriated Yankee fans, who paraded about with placards that announced, "Frick—up your asterisk!"

The man pursuing the Ruth record was mellower, but plainly miffed: "Commissioner Frick makes the rules," Maris said. "If all I am entitled to will be an asterisk, it will be all right with me. However, I never make up any schedules. Do you know any other record that's been broken since they started playing 162 games that's got an asterisk? I don't. Commissioner Frick should have said that all records made during the new schedule should have an asterisk. But he decided on the asterisk when I had about 50 home runs and it looked like I'd break the record."

Despite the asterisk, the pressure of fans and the press, and the efforts of some Yankee executives, who attempted to encourage rookie manager Ralph Houk to change the lineup to diminish the chances of Ruth's record being broken, Maris kept on.

And so did the Yankees, who played at a 22–9 clip in August. But the Tigers were still hanging around. On September 1, the two teams met in a crucial series. The Yankees swept all three games and went off on a 13-game winning streak. The sweep broke the back of the deflated Tigers, who lost eight straight.

By September 10, the Yankee lead over Detroit was 11½ games. Mantle had 53 home runs. Maris had 56. Maris was driven. Mantle was debilitated. There were times that season that he was in so much discomfort from leg problems that Maris had to assist him in getting out of taxicabs. The nagging mass of aches and pains—a pulled arm muscle, a bad head cold, an abscess in his side from a flu shot—all brought the Mick down.

The Mick managed but one home run from September 10 on—number 54 would be his career high. With Mantle a shell of himself and no longer a factor in the home run race, with the Yankees having clinched their 26th pennant, the pressure was now totally on Roger Maris.

On September 18, the Yankees arrived in Baltimore for a four-game series. Controversy and media hype came along. Maris had 58 home runs. His chance to "officially" break Ruth's record was restricted by the Ford

If all I am entitled to will be an asterisk, it will be all right with me.
—Roger Maris

Manager Ralph Houk (center) poses with the M&M Boys, Mickey Mantle (left) and Roger Maris (right). The 1961 Yankees were one of the most explosive teams in baseball history.

Frick edict to the first three games. They fell within the 154-game schedule. Accomplishments after that date, the ruling read, would be designated by an asterisk.

In a twinight doubleheader, games 152 and 153, Maris was shut out. On September 20, in a night game, Maris faced Milt Pappas of the Orioles. It was a media circus with reporters from all over the country converged on the scene. But there were only 21,000 or so in the stands.

The man they called "Rajah" lined solidly to right field his first time up. In the third inning, Maris caught a Pappas pitch and blasted it almost 400 feet into the bleachers in right field— home run number 59! He had passed Jimmie Foxx and Hank Greenberg. Maris had three more chances that night to tie the Babe Ruth record. But he struck out, flied out, and grounded out.

"I really gave it all I had," Maris said. "It just wasn't enough." Lost in all the attention to Maris was the fact that the Yankees clinched the pennant with that win over Pappas and the Orioles.

Five days later, on September 26, in game number 159 for the Yankees, in the third inning Jack Fisher of Baltimore threw a high curveball. "The minute I threw the ball," Fisher moaned, "I said to myself, that does it. That's number 60."

The record-tying home run pounded onto the concrete steps of the sixth row in the third deck in Yankee Stadium. The ball bounced back onto the

field and was picked up by Earl Robinson, the Oriole right fielder, who tossed the ball to umpire Ed Hurley, who gave it to Yankee first-base coach Wally Moses, who rolled it into the Yankee dugout. The ball and Maris, running out the 60th home run, arrived in the dugout of the Bronx Bombers at about the same time.

Maris picked up the ball and barely looked at it; cheering fans kept calling for him to come out and take a bow. Finally, Maris emerged. Standing sheepishly on the top step of the dugout, he waved his cap. An especially interested onlooker was Mrs. Claire Ruth, widow of the Babe.

With three games left in the 1961 season, Roger Maris was questing after baseball's most fabled record, straining for home run number 61, the unreachable number that had stood for 34 seasons. The Red Sox were the competition.

Don Schwall of Boston stopped Maris in the first game of the series. Bill Monbouquette of the Sox stopped Maris in the second game of the series. Maris was frozen on 60.

"Maybe I'm not a great man," the Yankee slugger had said. "But I damn well want to break the record." On October 1, 1961, Mickey Mantle watched from his Manhattan hospital bed as the Yankees played their final game of

Roger Maris and Sal Durante, the fan who caught Maris' record-breaking 61st home run. Durante was paid a $5,000 reward by a California man for retrieving the ball and returning it to Maris.

Nicknamed "Chairman of the Board," Whitey Ford went 25–4 in 1961. The crafty left-hander also led the American League in winning percentage (.862) and innings pitched (283) as he copped the Cy Young award.

the season. Roger Maris, worn, frustrated, straining, was up against Tracy Stallard, a 24-year-old Boston right-hander, a rookie.

In the Yankee bullpen in right field, the pitchers and the catchers watched as the action played out. A $5,000 reward had been promised to the one who caught the ball.

"I told them," Maris said, "that if they got the ball not to give it to me. Take the $5,000 reward."

Stallard retired Maris in his first at bat. The 23,154 roaring fans at Yankee Stadium were quieted. In the fourth inning, Maris came to bat again.

"They're standing, waiting to see if Maris is gonna hit number 61." The voice of Phil Rizzuto, broadcasting the moment, was filled with more emotion than the usually hyper Scooter put forth.

"We've only got a handful of people sitting out in left field," Rizzuto continued, "but in right field, man, it's hogged out there. And they're standing up. Here's the windup, the pitch to Roger. Way outside, ball one . . . and the fans are starting to boo. Low, ball two. That one was in the dirt. And the boos get louder . . . two balls, no strikes on Roger Maris. Here's the windup. Fastball, hit deep to right! This could be it! Way back there! Holy Cow, he did it! Sixty-one for Maris!"

The ball went over outfielder Lu Clinton's head and slammed into box 163D of section 33 in the right-field seats. And a melee broke out as fans scuffled and scrambled, fighting for the ball and the $5,000 reward. The stands were chaos. But Maris, who had made the point that "you can't eat glamour," was eating up the moment as he trotted out the home run into the record books.

A youngster jumped out onto the field. He grabbed Maris's hand as the slugger passed first base. Maris shook hands. He also shook hands with third-base coach Frank Crosetti as he rounded third, heading home.

But he was confronted by a human wall of teammates who would not allow him to enter the dugout. Four times he tried to force his way in; each time he was pushed out onto the playing field. Finally, Maris gave in and waved his cap to the frenzied crowd.

The human wall dissolved; Maris was finally allowed to enter the relative sanctuary of the dugout.

"Maybe I wouldn't do it all over again if I had the chance," he said. "Sometimes I feel it wasn't worth the aggravation. But if I never hit another home run, this is the one they can never take away from me."

The home run and the achievement was never taken away, but it was designated for years by an asterisk, until that was finally taken away.

"People just remember the 61 home runs," said Bill Skowron. "They forget that Roger was an excellent base stealer and a superb right fielder. He was the best defensive right fielder in the majors. He was an all-around ballplayer, a humble guy, a real team player. History never gave him his due."

Overshadowed by the epic accomplishments of Roger Maris, who won his second straight MVP, were the record 240 home runs hit by the Yankees, who won 109 games, just one shy of the total of the 1927 Murderer's Row. The '61 Yankees were first in the league in fielding, made the fewest errors, turned the most double plays.

And also lost in all the hoopla were the 54 homers hit by Mantle, most ever by a switch-hitter in a season, the 30 road home runs—also a record for a switch-hitter in a season. Coupled with the 40 homers he hit in 1960, Mantle's two-season total of 94 was the most ever for a switch-hitter. Mantle and Maris combined for 115 home runs—a new record. And in back-to-back seasons Maris hit a total of 100 home runs—only Babe Ruth ever did as much.

The platoon switch of Berra and Lopez to left field made that position a little porous defensively and led to one of Yogi's great lines: "It gets late early out there this time of year." It was a reference to the September setting sun at the Stadium. But the move provided even more offensive punch for the Yankee lineup, as Yogi cracked 22 home runs in just 395 at bats.

Other Yankee big bats included Howard and Blanchard. Between them the catchers hammered 42 home runs and drove in 131 runs. In spring training, the man the Yankees called "Elly" suffered through the indignity of not being able to stay with the rest of the team at their hotel in segregated St. Petersburg. He had to be put up by a family in the African American section of town. But throughout that 1961 season he was a key member of the Yankee family. American League pitchers winced at Howard's quick bat, which, out of Howard's closed stance, sent so many line drives back through the mound. He wound up having a career year, batting .348 and stroking 21 homers.

Pitcher Ralph Terry posted a sparkling 16-3 record for the '61 Yankees. He would go on to star in the 1962 World Series vs. the Giants and, later, he became a professional golfer.

One of the biggest prizes in the early days of free agency, Jim "Catfish" Hunter fires toward the plate. 1977 was not one of Hunter's best seasons. After being struck on the foot by a line drive on opening day, Hunter could do no better than a 9-9 record.

Bill Skowron had a knack of using one hand to slam opposite-field homers when it seemed to all onlookers that he was fooled by outside curveballs. The "Moose" slugged 28 home runs and had 89 RBIs.

"Chairman of the Board" Whitey Ford posted a 25–4 record and claimed "nobody noticed because of the home run race." His .862 winning percentage was an American League best. His 283 innings pitched topped all AL hurlers. The Cy Young award winner, Ford was in the prime of a 16-year career that would see him post a 236–106 record and .690 winning percentage—best for any pitcher since 1900.

Ralph Terry was 16–3. Sophomore Bill Stafford was 14–9. Jim Coates and Rollie Sheldon had identical 11–5 records. And Little Louie "Yo-Yo" Arroyo, possessor of a multispeed screwball, accounted for a league-leading 29 saves, with 15 wins, and an ERA of 2.19. He even batted .280. It was a career year for the potbellied hurler whose record before 1961 was 23–23 with but 8 saves.

In the World Series against Cincinnati, Mantle, afflicted with an abscess, appeared in only the second and third games. A drained and exhausted Maris batted just .105. But the Yankees had a lot of other weapons. Johnny Blanchard batted .400. Bobby Richardson hit .391 and Bill Skowron .353. The Yanks easily beat the Reds in five games.

A highlight of the Fall Classic was Whitey Ford extending his string of World Series scoreless innings to 32, breaking Babe Ruth's 43-year-old record of 29 2/3 shutout innings.

"Maybe I'll get together with batting coach Wally Moses next spring and go after some of the Babe's batting records, too." Whitey Ford joked. "It wasn't such a good year for the Babe."

But it was a very good year for the New York Yankees. Ralph Houk became only the third rookie manager to win a World Series. And that 1961 pennant would be the second in a string of five straight for the Yankees. It was good times in the Bronx.

1977: THE BRONX ZOO

In sharp contrast to the years that preceded them, the middle 1970s were a time of excitement, controversy, confrontation, and accomplishment for the New York Yankees. One of the marker dates of that era for the team was New Year's Eve 1974.

Free-agent pitcher Jim "Catfish" Hunter signed on with the Yankees for five years at $3.75 million. It was the most lucrative contract for a baseball player to that time. Hunter had four straight 20-win seasons, leading Oakland to three World Championships. He knew how to win and gave the Yankees an image of a winner. The huge amount of money paid to the superstar hurler and the others who followed would trigger much criticism of Yankee owner George Steinbrenner. The Yankees would be referred to as "the best team money could buy."

Another marker date for the Yankees in the '70s was August 1, 1975. Bill Virdon was out as manager of the third-place New York Yankees. Alfred Manuel Martin was in.

By July of 1976, the brash Martin, who claimed he always dreamed of doing what Casey Stengel had done, was doing it, driving the Yankees to victory after victory. When Martin was hired by Steinbrenner, general manager Gabe Paul warned, "Your temperaments aren't compatible. There are going to be problems."

There were problems, but winning took care of that. The team played exciting, aggressive, gambling baseball. The writers called it "Billy Ball." Drawing over two million fans into the refurbished Stadium, the Yankees finished 10½ games ahead of the Baltimore Orioles in the American League East in 1976.

Then they came up against Kansas City in the League Championship Series. The teams split the first four games. On October 14 in game five George Brett hit an eighth-inning three-run home run to tie the game at 6–6. Chris Chambliss led off the bottom of the ninth against Mark Littell. He got all of the Kansas City relief pitcher's fastball, hammering it into the right-field seats. Bedlam broke out at Yankee Stadium. The Yankees had their 30th pennant, their first since 1964.

"By the time Chris got to third base," Munson recalled, "all hope of reaching the plate was gone. He never did make it." Hours later, in an empty ballpark under the protective eyes of two security guards, Chambliss touched home plate. That made it official.

"The Chambliss home run," Willie Randolph recalled, "was the highlight of our season. We celebrated that night and flew all the way to Cincinnati for a game the next day."

But the Yankees were swept in the World Series by the Big Red Machine. "We didn't show the country how good we really were," Randolph said. "We were totally embarrassed."

George Steinbrenner was not only embarrassed, he was bitterly disappointed. His reaction was to shake things up even more. Cincinnati's Don Gullett, who had helped defeat the Yankees in the World Series, was signed as a free agent for $2.09 million. But the most prized free agent of all was Reggie Jackson, and George Steinbrenner went after him with a passion.

There was a dinner with the muscular outfielder at the '21' Club in Manhattan, a Thanksgiving breakfast in Chicago, and many phone calls back and forth. Reggie signed for a reported $3.5 million over five years.

"Steinbrenner took it upon himself to hunt me down," Jackson explained. "Several clubs offered several hundred thousand dollars more, but the reason I'm a Yankee is that George Steinbrenner outhustled everybody else." And then he added that playing in New York he was sure they would name a candy bar after him.

The acquisition of the controversial Jackson added another element to the soap opera atmosphere on the Yankees. In spring training of 1977, the self-promoting Reginald Martinez Jackson, who was fond of talking about the "magnitude of me," announced: "I didn't come to New York to be a star. I brought my star with me."

He also claimed: "I'm the straw that stirs the drink. Munson thinks he is. But he isn't and can only stir it bad." It was his way of undercutting others on the team, especially Thurman Munson. Jackson may have in truth been the straw, the last straw, but it was Thurman Munson who was the heart of

Sparky Lyle was outstanding in 1977, named the league's Cy Young Award winner. Lyle won 13 regular-season games, two ALCS games and game one of the World Series.

Roy White, was a steady performer and a stabilizing presence in an otherwise unstable Yankee locker room.

those Yankee teams.

The solid catcher had been told he would be the highest-paid Yankee. But now Jackson was. Munson was miffed throughout spring training, as were Graig Nettles, who left camp, and Mickey Rivers, who pouted, and Sparky Lyle, who snapped, "Pay me [more] or trade me."

When Rivers heard Jackson bragging that he had a 160 IQ, Mickey snapped, "Out of what? A thousand?"

Even the mild-mannered Catfish Hunter found a way to get into the act. "Reggie would give you the shirt off his back. Of course, he'd call a press conference to announce it."

Jackson did not make many friends in spring training. But he wasn't a contented camper either. Billy Martin, who was never consulted about the acquisition of Jackson, announced that he was going to have Reggie DH exclusively and bat sixth in the order. That didn't sit too well with him. Neither did the fact that Martin had him play every day in spring training.

Spring training was no fun for Jackson and for most of the Yankees; the start of the season was just a continuation of the general down mood. Graig Nettles boycotted the Welcome Home Dinner. "If they want someone to play third base and hit home runs," he snapped, "they've got me. If they want someone to attend banquets, they can get George Jessel."

The 1977 Yankees Yearbook had a special insert celebrating the 50th anniversary of the 1927 team—Murderer's Row. But in the early going there

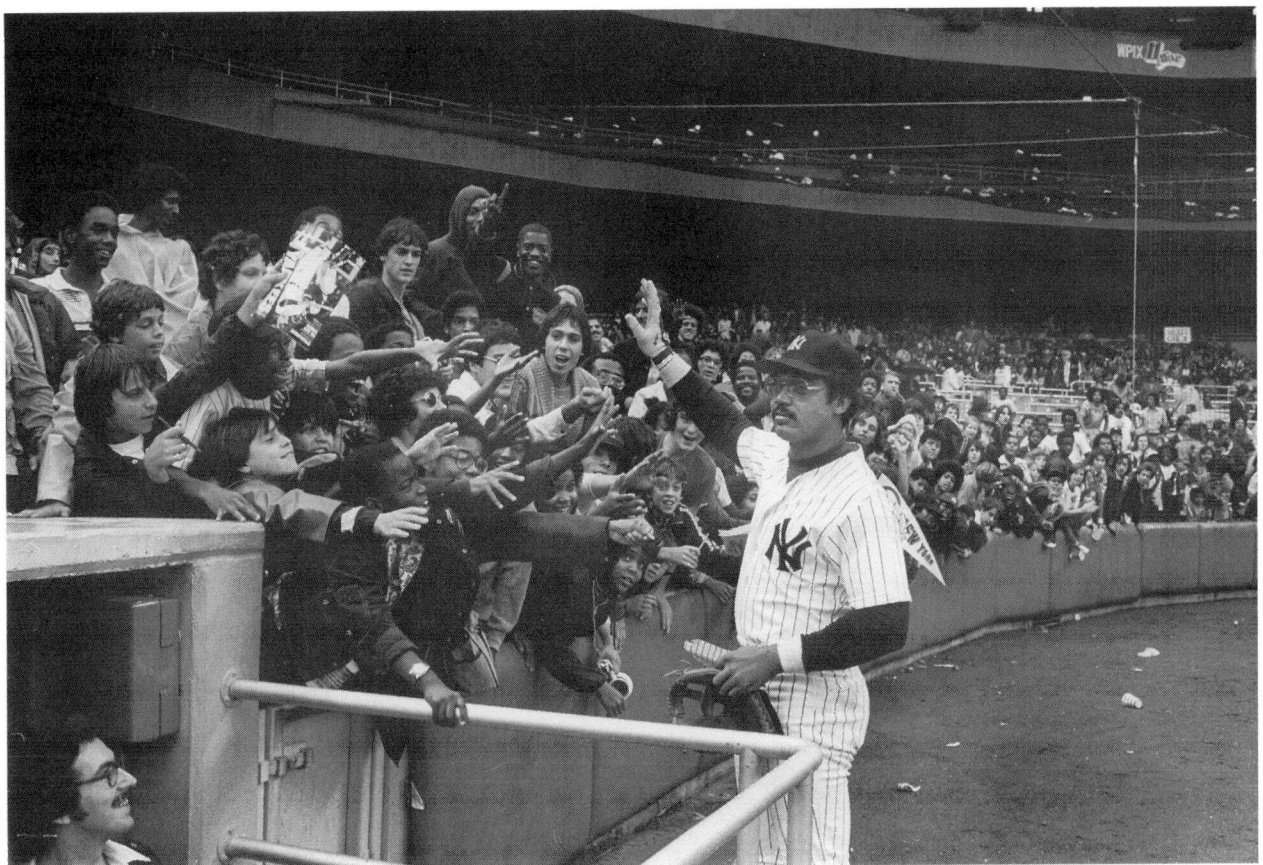

was not much celebrating for the Yankees, who dropped 8 of their first 10 games and were 5½ games out by April 19.

With less than a month elapsed in the season, Steinbrenner and Gabe Paul made more moves—moves that irritated the easily exacerbated Martin even more, as players who were his personal favorites were traded away. Oscar Gamble was one of them. The outfielder departed for Chicago along with pitcher LaMarr Hoyt and $200,000 for shortstop Bucky Dent, who replaced another Martin favorite, Fred Stanley.

"I was tickled about being traded to New York," Dent recalled, "because they had been in the World Series the year before and had the tools to get back."

Gabe Paul, who was annoyed with the earring and the attitude sported by Dock Ellis, and maybe at the fact that he was one of Martin's pets, peddled the pitcher to the A's for pitcher Mike Torrez. Cliff Johnson also came over from Houston in a trade.

With all this baggage on board, Martin seemed to take out his wrath on the 31-year-old Jackson, whom he batted fifth in the order and sometimes relegated to the bench against certain pitchers. The Jackson–Martin relationship could only be characterized as tense and hostile. At that, it was better than Reggie's relationship with teammates, whom he refused to shake hands with after hitting home runs.

The festering boil that was the 1977 Yankees finally burst June 17–19 in a three-game series against Don Zimmer's Red Sox before a series total of

"Mr. October," Reggie Jackson arrived in New York in 1977 and immediately brought emotions to a feverish level. Love him or hate him, no one could deny his ability to perform in the clutch.

91

Yankee players and coaches separate manager Billy Martin from Reggie Jackson. Martin had pulled Jackson from a game after accusing him of loafing after a fly ball. The two exchanged heated words but no blows were thrown.

103,910 fans at a windswept Fenway Park. In the first game of the series Catfish Hunter was pounded for first-inning home runs by Rick Burleson, Fred Lynn, Carlton Fisk, and George Scott. That was humiliating enough for the Yankees. But the most bizarre moment was to come in the nationally televised middle game of the series.

Boston was leading 7–4. Jim Rice checked his swing, and the ball landed in front of Reggie Jackson. "He jogged for the ball," Billy Martin exploded. "He fielded it on about the 50th hop, took his time throwing it in, and made a weak throw in the general direction of the pitcher's mound. I told my players if they ever embarrassed me on the field, I was going to embarrass them."

Out came Jackson. In came Paul Blair as a replacement. Entering the Yankee dugout Jackson yelled at Martin, "You showed me up on television!" Then he charged at his manager. Only the intervention of Elston Howard and Yogi Berra prevented punches from being landed.

"The writers were never late that year," recalled Phil Rizzuto, "because something was always going on. A lot of egos were vying for the headlines."

The next day the headline in the *Boston Herald American* read: "Yanks Go Down Fighting Themselves." The Sox scorched the Yankees 11–1 to complete the three-game sweep, in which they hammered 16 home runs to none for the New Yorkers. George Steinbrenner was furious about what the Boston faithful called "the Yankee massacre," furious about the way his team

had been humbled, and especially furious about the behavior of Billy
Martin, whom he thought had overstepped his bounds. Incredibly, as
the story goes, Martin was not fired, in large part due to the intervention
of Jackson. All kinds of meetings and discussions pushed the episode aside.
But it was not forgotten. Tumult and shouting would continue throughout
the season. Being on that Yankee team was like being part of a family feud.
And traveling to stadiums all over the American League as a Yankee was
like going into enemy territory. Invective and insults were always part of
the environment.

Despite the boos and the catcalls they experienced, the negative press,
and the mangled interpersonal relationships, the 1977 Yankees, a blend of
great balance and specialized roles, took it all in their stride. They were a
team of character, talent, depth, and All-Stars, including Reggie Jackson,
Sparky Lyle, Thurman Munson, Graig Nettles, and Willie Randolph.

The infield of first baseman Chris Chambliss, second baseman Willie
Randolph, shortstop Bucky Dent, and Gold Glove third baseman Graig
Nettles blended intelligence, defense, power, and experience.

The outfield of Roy White, Reggie Jackson, and Mickey Rivers made the
big plays, hit for average and power, and, with Rivers atop the lineup, had a
real base-stealing threat.

Thurman Munson was one of the best catchers in all of baseball—a
threat at the plate, a super defensive presence, and an expert handler of
pitchers. There were also the all-purpose players, such as Lou Piniella and

Mickey Rivers added much-
needed speed and pop to top
of the Yankee lineup. In 1977,
Rivers batted .326, hit 12 homers
and stole 22 bases.

Steady Chris Chambliss cranks a two-run home run off Dodger pitcher Burt Hooton in the deciding game six of the 1977 World Series.

Cliff Johnson.

The Yankees also had plenty of pitching to fuse with the ample supply of bats. Catfish Hunter, Ed Figueroa, Don Gullett, Mike Torrez, and slim south-paw Ron Guidry, who in spring training made the last roster spot, were starters. Dick Tidrow and Sparky Lyle were at the ready as relievers.

Six days after the Jackson–Martin confrontation, the Yankees and Red Sox were at it again. Boston had won seven straight, 13 of its last 24 games. The Yankees had fallen five games back. Catfish Hunter started the game and served up three home runs. The Sox led 5–3 with Bill Campbell on the mound in the bottom of the ninth, looking to nail down his 16th save. He got the first two outs with no difficulty. Willie Randolph stepped into the batter's box.

"Campbell had a pretty good screwball," Randolph recalled. "And I was just looking to hit it hard somewhere."

Randolph hit it hard somewhere. The ball skipped past Carl Yastrzemski in left field for a three-base hit. Then Roy White homered into the right-field stands to tie the game. In the bottom of the 11th inning Reggie Jackson singled, driving in Nettles, and the Yankees had a hard-fought 6–5 victory. The game proved to be a morale booster.

On June 30, there was another morale booster for the Yanks—a game that showcased what Yogi Berra would have called "deep depth." Cliff Johnson hammered three consecutive home runs, two of them in the eighth inning, as the Yankees trampled Toronto, 11–5.

Morale-boosting moments for the Yankees notwithstanding, nothing could mask that despite all the talent on hand and some dramatic game-winning moments, they were middling along at about the .500 level. They would win a few, lose a few. The parts were all there, but they didn't seem to be able to mesh.

Then, on August 7, Mike Torrez won his third straight game, snapping a three-game Yankee losing streak. Three days later Reggie Jackson was installed as the regular cleanup hitter. Then it all seemed to mesh. From that point on the Yankees won 40 of their final 53 games as Jackson hit 13 home runs and drove in 49 runs.

Reggie was a big part of the 1977 Yankee story on and off the field. But the team could not have accomplished what it did without what Jackson referred to as his supporting cast.

A case in point took place on August 16. Ron Guidry was on the mound against the White Sox. The Yankees had a comfortable lead going into the ninth inning, but Chicago scored six times to go ahead 10–9. In the bottom of the ninth Munson walked. Piniella sacrificed him to second. Chambliss slugged a two-run homer. Final score: Yankees 11, Chicago 10. Advantage supporting cast.

On August 21, a homer and double by Nettles locked up a 2–1 Yankee victory over Texas. Advantage supporting cast. The Red Sox lead was one-half game. Two days later Mickey Rivers put together a 5–5 day, and Torrez reeled off his seventh straight complete game. The Yankees defeated Chicago, 8–3, and took over first place by a half-game. Advantage supporting cast.

The season moved to mid-September, and baseball's greatest rivalry, Yankees versus Red Sox, was red-hot at Yankee Stadium. For Boston, it was a do-or-die three-game series. The middle game was played on September 13. It matched Ed Figueroa against Reggie Cleveland, who had won seven straight games against the Yankees. The game moved to the bottom of the ninth, scoreless.

Munson singled. Jackson faked a bunt on the first pitch and took it for a ball. He worked the count to 3–2. And then he worked his magic: home run deep into the right-field bleachers.

"I hit the ball on the screws," Jackson said, "and I knew it was gone."

For all intents and purposes, so were the Red Sox. The 2–0 Yankee victory pushed Boston $3\frac{1}{2}$ games back. They finished along with Baltimore tied for second place, $2\frac{1}{2}$ games out. And the Yankees, despite the rages and rancor, the imagined and real personality clashes, recorded another American League East pennant, winning 100 of the 162 games they played.

Mickey Rivers, the greyhound on a team of thumpers, hit .326. Piniella batted .330 and had 12 homers. Jackson had 32 home runs and 110 RBIs. Jackson, Chambliss, Nettles, and Munson all had 90 or more RBIs. The 107 RBIs and 37 home runs recorded by Nettles were both the most ever for a Yankee third baseman.

Cy Young award winner Sparky Lyle saved 26 games and had a 13–5 record. Ron Guidry, who said, "I made my emergence that year, which was a plus the club didn't expect," was true to his nickname, "Louisiana Lightning." He mixed his nasty slider and moving fastball to post a 16–7

"Louisiana Lightning" struck often for the Yankees during the 1977 season. Fan favorite Ron Guidry posted 16 regular-season wins and a complete game victory in game four of the World Series.

Some people call October a time of pressure. I call it a time of character.
—Reggie Jackson

record and a 2.82 ERA. Ed Figueroa was 16–11; Don Gullett was 14–4 and would have won more had his season not been cut short by injuries. Mike Torrez won 14 and lost 12, but his victories came when the Yankees needed them most. Dick Tidrow's 11–4 record was a bright spot, but a bad shoulder limited Catfish Hunter to a 9–9 mark.

Kansas City, in the middle year of three straight Western Division Championships, once again was the competition in the League Championship Series. And once again the Yanks eliminated the Whitey Herzog-led Royals in the ninth inning of the fifth game, this time on a Mickey Rivers game-winning hit—final score, 5–3. Working four of the five games, winning two of them, the mustached Sparky Lyle posted a gaudy 0.96 ERA.

"After losing four straight to Cincinnati," Piniella recalled, "we were determined in '77 to first win the division, to second win the pennant, and then get another crack at becoming World Champions. It wasn't as easy as it was in '76. We were a better club, but we were challenged all the way."

The Yankee route to the World Series was a rocky one. The Dodgers had an easy time of it. New York and Los Angeles prepared to square off in the Fall Classic, and Reggie Jackson said: "The only reason I don't like playing in the World Series is I can't watch myself play . . . October—that's when they pay off for playing ball."

The first two games were played at Yankee Stadium. The Yankees were 4–3 victors in game one in 12 innings. Jackson's defensive replacement, Paul Blair, singled home the game's winning run. The Dodgers came back to win game two, 6–1, behind right-hander Burt Hooton. Martin had played a hunch and started an ailing Catfish Hunter, but the gamble did not pay off. Reggie Smith and Ron Cey took him deep and out of the game.

The Yankees won the next two games, played in Los Angeles. A three-run first inning iced game three. Mike Torrez yielded a three-run homer to Dusty Baker but lasted the distance to pick up the 5–3 triumph. The Yankees won game four, 4–2. Reggie pounded a homer and a double. Ron Guidry went the distance and hurled a four-hitter.

Game five was a 10–4 Dodger romp behind Don Sutton. Steve Yeager hit a three-run homer and Reggie Smith also smacked a roundtripper. Little note was taken of the fact that Reggie Jackson was zeroing in on history—he homered in his final at bat that game.

The Series shifted back to New York City. It was knuckleballing Burt Hooton versus Torrez in game six. A Steve Garvey triple gave the Dodgers a 2–0 lead after one inning. A Chambliss two-run homer in the second inning tied the game. The score seesawed back in LA's favor as Reggie Smith homered in the third.

In his first at bat of the game, Reggie Jackson was walked on four pitches by Hooton. In the fourth inning Jackson disdained taking a pitch. Instead he rocked Hooton's first serve for a two-run homer into the lower bleacher seats in right field. As Jackson rounded the bases running out the "hook shot" he mouthed "Hi, Mom" two times to the television cameras.

In the fifth inning, Jackson came up against Elias Sosa. Again he slugged the first pitch into right-center field—another two-run home run. The roundtripper gave the Yankees a 7–3 lead. As the game moved to the late innings there was little doubt that the Yankees had the Series clinched. The only drama that remained was Reggie Jackson—Mr. October. What would he be able to do in his final at bat?

"All I had to do was show up at the plate," Jackson recalls. "They were going to cheer me even if I struck out." There were 60,000 or more stomping their feet and chanting "REGGIE! REGGIE! REGGIE!"

In the eighth inning, Jackson faced Charlie Hough. First pitch—home run deep into the blackness of the tarp in centerfield, 450 feet from home plate. Those who saw it at the Stadium or on television will never forget the image—Mr. October dropping the bat and watching the ball fly into the blackness of the fall night in the Bronx.

"I must admit," Steve Garvey said, "when Reggie hit his third home run and I was sure nobody was looking, I applauded in my glove."

"I felt like Superman," Jackson said. "If they had tied it up and we played eight more extra innings, I'd have hit three more home runs on the first pitch that night." Then warming up to the topic, Jackson added, "Nothing can top this. Who in hell's ever going to hit three home runs in a deciding World Series game? I won't. Babe Ruth, Hank Aaron, Joe DiMaggio—at least I was with them for one night."

The epic feat—three home runs on the first pitch off three different hurlers—helped the Yankees become World Champions for the 21st time, and for the first time in 15 years. Actually, going back to game five, Jackson had hammered four consecutive home runs in four straight official at bats. In all, Jackson wound up with five homers, eight RBIs, and a .450 average. He scored 10 runs and had 25 total bases. His Most Valuable Player award was well deserved.

The 8–4 Yankee win gave the franchise its first World Championship since 1962. Jackson was happy. Steinbrenner was happy. And Billy Martin, who called that time "my biggest thrill in baseball," was happy and had the last word:

> I was happy for George because George wanted it so bad. I said to myself, "Now he can really have fun at the '21' Club. He'll go around and give rings to his friends, and he'll be able to go around and talk about this one as long as he lives."

Wade Boggs taking batting practice prior to the start of the 1996 season. Ten years after the Red Sox crushing loss to the Mets in the 1986 World Series, Wade Boggs would finally taste sweet victory when the Yanks took the Braves in six games to become champions.

1996: NICE GUYS FINISH FIRST

In the Steinbrenner years, tumultuous change and much controversy have always characterized the New York Yankees. But as the 1996 season got under way the Boss seemed to be outdoing even himself.

The Yankees had a new general manager and a new manager. To say that they were damned with faint praise by fans and the media would be an exaggeration.

Yankee legend Don Mattingly was out of baseball. In his place was former Seattle first baseman Tino Martinez, who, along with Jeff Nelson, came over from the Mariners for Sterling Hitchcock and Russ Davis.

A 22-year-old rookie was set to take over at shortstop. Derek Jeter grew up as a Yankee fan and remembered the winning years. "It's a dream come

Andy Pettitte, the Yankees' newest pitching phenom, posted 21 wins during the 1996 season. Here he celebrates his 1-0 victory over the Braves in game five of the World Series.

true to play here but it would be an even bigger dream to play in the play-offs and World Series."

Pitcher Jack McDowell was gone, and in his place was Kenny Rogers. David Cone, a big-game pitcher but one with a lot of mileage, was back with the Yankees after a spirited off-season bidding war between New York and Baltimore. Jimmy Key, 35, was on the mend from off-season surgery for a torn rotator cuff. The Yankees' top pitcher was Andy Pettitte, a second-year player.

Catcher Mike Stanley now played for the Red Sox; Joe Girardi was his replacement. Randy Velarde was unceremoniously let go; Mariano Duncan, a career utility man, was his replacement.

"It was to the point where I was saying, 'Oh my God, they dismantled the whole team and we'll be lucky to finish fifth,'" Wade Boggs said. "Then, boom, everything started to fall into place. It's nice to see because there were a lot of unanswered questions in December."

The 1996 roster mixed and matched 49 different players—some old, some new, some borrowed, some not ready for prime time and others just coming into their own.

From July 29 to August 30, the revolving door that was the Yankee roster saw 23 different changes in personnel.

There were the career professionals like Tim Raines, Wade Boggs, and Paul O'Neill; youngsters like Mariano Rivera, Ruben Rivera, and Bernie Williams; and serviceable types like David Weathers, Charlie Hayes, and Graeme Lloyd.

Recycled and reunited after a five-year separation, former New York Mets Darryl Strawberry and Doc Gooden, former Wunderkinds, were major parts of the 1996 Yankee story. Strawberry would come to the Bronx via the Northern League St. Paul Saints. Gooden had an even tougher climb, out of drug and alcohol rehabilitation treatment.

Joe Girardi was paid $2.325 million a year, Tino Martinez was paid $2 million a year, Kenny Rogers was paid $5 million a year, and David Cone was paid $4 million a year. The club payroll totaled $66.6 million, the highest in baseball. It was truly the best team that money could buy.

The season began with the Yankees sweeping two games from the American League champion Cleveland Indians in Cleveland. Then Opening Day at Yankee Stadium, April 9, 1996, fans started lining up at the press gates at 7:30 A.M. The game-time temperature was 40 degrees. Snow fell throughout the game. Andy Pettitte, who had said, "I don't care if it's Ping-Pong, I'll kill you to win it," pitched six-plus innings and notched his second sub-40-degree triumph of the season. And Derek Jeter homered. The two would play key roles for the 1996 Yankees.

On April 30 and May 1, the Yanks won two games from the Orioles and took over first place. Through the bumps and the grinds of the ride through the long season, they held fast. Their record was 26–11 on May 8. Playing together, staying together, the Yankees took care of business on the field. Off the field there were the bonding scenes of players bumping fists, smiling at each other, sitting around in pairs and quietly talking about baseball and family. Even Yankee haters had to admit this batch of players was not arrogant, not smug, even likable.

There were a whole bunch of significant stats, marker moments, lasting images:

■ A manager who was not afraid to cry, not afraid to show his feelings; the image of Torre and bench coach Don Zimmer whispering to each other, always conferring.

■ An 11–6 victory in 15 innings on May 1 that showcased Jim Mecir, a career minor leaguer, who struck out Brady Anderson with the bases loaded, after having fallen behind by a 3–0 count, to keep the score tied into the 11th.

■ Darryl Strawberry hitting back-to-back two-run home runs against Baltimore, slugging three home runs in a game against Chicago, playing all-out, day in and day out.

■ Dwight Gooden put into the rotation, replacing David Cone, who had surgery to remove an aneurysm, no-hitting Seattle on May 14, winning 11 of 18 decisions to keep the Yankees going.

■ Mariano Rivera, signed as a 20-year-old free agent out of Panama, unimpressive in the early going, viewed by Torre as a wild card. The high-90s fastball, the streak of 26 scoreless innings pitched from April 19 to May 21.

■ "6–2–1!" Six innings from a starter, two innings from Rivera, and one inning to close the deal from John Wetteland. It was 10 o'clock lightning—Rivera and Wetteland. The Yankees won 29 of 31 regular-season games when that duo did their thing.

■ A pitching staff that yielded the fewest home runs in the American League.

■ Jimmy Key, off the DL, hurling a six-inning, one-run victory against the A's on the third day of June.

■ David Cone, back from aneurysm surgery, pitching a Labor Day beauty—seven innings of no-hit ball.

■ A 19–2 romp over Milwaukee on September 25, clinching the Eastern Division title for the Yankees, who finished the 1996 regular season with a 92–70 record.

During the 1996 season, Mariano Rivera became the premiere set-up man in baseball. The one-two punch of Rivera and Wetteland in the New York bullpen meant that teams had to be leading the Yanks by the end of the sixth inning or the game was over.

Texas won the opening game of the division series, but buoyed by their bullpen, which allowed just one earned run in 19²/₃ innings, the Yankees ended the Rangers' season. Tied with the Orioles after two games in the American League Championship Series, the Yankees left them in the lurch on their way to a date with Atlanta in the World Series.

Ted Turner's charges had beaten St. Louis in the National League Championship Series, pounding Cardinal pitching 32–1 in games five through seven. That gave some Yankee fans pause.

Torrential rain postponed the opening of the Series, but the Yankees had waited since 1981—another day was no problem. But the Braves were.

Charlie Hayes catches a foul pop off the bat of the Braves' Mark Lemke to record the final out of the 1996 World Series. It was the first Yankees World Series triumph since 1978, the longest dry spell in the team's history.

Game one was an Atlanta cakewalk, 12–1. John Smoltz was virtually unhittable while Andy Pettitte was ripped hard. It was the worst defeat in Yankee World Series history.

The Braves won game two, 4–0. Greg Maddux pitched an eight-inning, 82-pitch masterpiece. Joe Torre said, "We've seen pitchers who could really hump it up and throw a great game, but they're not all on one team." But it seemed they were.

The Series moved to Atlanta–Fulton County Stadium. One Atlanta writer noted: "Theirs is a higher standard." A couple of others went into much detail documenting how the Yankees were overmatched. But the New Yorkers knew it took four wins to be declared World Champions.

Torre tabbed David Cone to turn things around for the Yankees in game three. "It's as big a game as I've ever pitched," he said. Coney was up to it. The gritty veteran gutted it out, holding the Braves to one run and four hits in six innings. Mariano Rivera, Graeme Lloyd, and John Wetteland took over and the Yankees won 5–2.

The Yankees overcame a 6–0 Atlanta lead to win game four in 10 innings, 8–6. The big blow for the Yankees was a three-run homer by Jim Leyritz. They won the next game, 1–0. Andy Pettitte and John Wetteland were just a little better than John Smoltz and Mark Wohlers. The victory gave the Yankees a perfect 8–0 October road record. And incredibly, the written-off Yanks were now one game away from writing World Series history and winning the World Championship.

Cecil Fielder, another handy addition to the fully used Yankee roster, bellowed, "We're going home, man! The Bronx Zoo is going to be a zoo."

It was. The date was October 26, 1996. Game six. Yankee Stadium was rocking and rolling. The pitching matchup was Jimmy Key versus Greg Maddux. The Joe Torre "6–2–1" formula was in place. Key held the Braves at bay. Then, Hello, Mariano Rivera! Hello, John Wetteland!

The Yankees scored three runs off Maddux in the third, the big blow a Joe Girardi triple over the head of the center fielder. The score was 3–1 Yankees when Mariano Rivera came in. It was still 3–1 when he left after pitching the seventh and eighth innings. Enter John Wetteland, homed in on his fourth straight save. The Yankee closer's performance was not a thing of beauty. He gave up three singles and allowed the Braves to score another run and edge even more painfully close. But then Mark Lemke popped to Charlie Hayes at third base and it was over.

Atlanta might have been the team of the '90s, but the Yanks were the team of 1996. The Yankees became the first team in history to lose the first two games at home in a World Series and then win four straight and the World Championship, their 23rd.

All hell broke loose. It seemed the ground at the Stadium was shaking. Torre led the players in a victory lap around the ballpark. Strawberry did the Bronx boogie. Boggs rode a police horse around the running track and pumped his fist in the air. Don Zimmer was just overcome with the moment.

Then thousands of voices, most of them off-key and very loud, joined in with the Frank Sinatra recording of "New York, New York." It was a great time to be in the Big Apple. And everyone had something to say.

Even Greg Maddux, gentlemanly in defeat, appreciated the time: "Obviously it hurts losing, but the atmosphere here is matched nowhere. It's exciting to be out there on the mound in front of people going freaky. It's wild. Even though we lost, in a while we're going to appreciate being in this place."

"Joe Torre had one brother die and another waiting for a heart transplant and every day he came out with a positive attitude," noted Charlie Hayes. "Our team fed off that."

"This is a team," George Steinbrenner said, "that New York can be proud of."

"I look back at this World Series and the last month," Joe Torre said. "I think it was all supposed to happen. Once we got here it seemed like nothing could stop us. A team like this is a rarity. This team wasn't concerned about numbers, only winning. We used all the ingredients. That's what glued us together. The whole thing was like some out-of-body experience, it really is dreamlike."

There have been greater Yankee teams with more fabled stars. But the 1996 New York Yankees, their sum greater than their parts, were unique.

Yankee outfielder Bernie Williams is congratulated by third-base coach Willie Randolph after hitting a game-winning home run in the 11th inning of game one of the American League Championship Series.

Yankee catcher Joe Girardi and third base coach Willie Randolph celebrate Girardi's triple in game six of the 1996 World Series.

The Parade

It was a scene reminiscent of the old days in New York City when the Brooklyn Dodgers, New York Giants, and New York Yankees lorded it over the other teams and strutted their stuff in October.

This time it was Yankees, 1996 style, a celebration of their first World Championship since 1978, the 23rd in franchise history. The day was brisk, windy, beautiful, autumn in New York.

Ten buses loaded with Yankee players, wives, families and friends, team officials, and significant others departed from Yankee Stadium at 9:00 A.M. The caravan rolled into Battery Park 45 minutes later.

Then the scene turned into a sea of blue-and-white floats with Yankees on them. Up lower Broadway, the Canyon of Heroes that Charles Lindbergh and Douglas MacArthur and the Apollo astronauts and Ron Guidry and Reggie Jackson and Thurman Munson had been on.

It was labeled a Ticker Tape Parade. But ticker tape belonged to another time. So people made do, throwing shredded paper, confetti, toilet paper—

Wade Boggs take a ride around Yankee Stadium in celebration of the Yankees World Series victory.

even boxes of public and confidential unshredded records came hurtling out of windows of government agencies across from City Hall.

Tens of thousands of fans lined the streets, shouting, "Let's Go, Yankees, Let's Go Yankees, Let's Go Yankees!!!!" Some climbed traffic light poles or hung out of the windows of skyscrapers or stood atop cars. Others in the cheering throng had hungered so to be part of the moment that they showed up the night before and slept in tents and cars to be able to guarantee themselves unobstructed views.

"For a city the size of New York to take on that small-town feel, it was like Main Street, U.S.A.," said Joe Torre. "You see it all the time, but not in New York City. To have this kind of acclaim and support is mind-boggling."

Derek Jeter blushed at the wail of teenage girls. Kenny Rogers waved a huge Yankee flag. David Cone stared at the sea of celebration. Jim Leyritz blew kisses. Joe Torre smiled and waved. Darryl Strawberry signed autographs with pleasure and said, "This is definitely one of those days that I never expected to be a part of."

It was a day to play hooky, to take a long lunch, to take it all in—and millions did.

THREE

THE Yankee Immortals

Yogi Berra played on 10 World Championship Yankee teams.

YOGI BERRA

*H*e didn't look like a Yankee, walk like a Yankee, or talk like a Yankee, but Lawrence Peter Berra was pure Yankee in all other ways. Yet, at the start, it didn't seem that way to Yankee owner Larry MacPhail.

The Giants had offered $50,000 for the young Berra. The Yankees rebuffed them. MacPhail recalled the time: "So I waited for my first look at the prize package which was worth $50,000. The instant I saw him my heart sank and I wondered why I had been so foolish as to refuse to sell him. In busted a stocky little guy in a sailor suit. He had no neck and his muscles were virtually busting the buttons off his uniform. He was one of the most unprepossessing fellows I ever set eyes on in my life. And the sailor suit accentuated every defect."

But there were not too many baseball defects. In just 277 at bats at Newark in 1946, Berra smacked 15 home runs, drove in 59 runs, and batted .315. With the Yankees in 1947, Lawrence Peter Berra became a pet project for manager Bucky Harris, who brought him along slowly, playing him in 51 games as a catcher in 1947 and 24 games in the outfield.

Yogi would lash out at any pitch; Harris preached restraint. In one particular at bat, Berra took a pitch right down the center of the plate for a strike. The next pitch came over. Again Berra did not swing. Strike two. The third pitch was a called strike three.

Returning to the Yankee bench, Berra told an irritated Harris, "It's all your fault. How do you expect a guy to hit and think, to think and hit at the same time."

That could have been the start of what the world would call "Yogiisms." Or maybe it was when he was given a night that season in his hometown, St. Louis, and said in all sincerity, "I want to thank all of the people for making this night necessary."

And the lines kept coming: Yankee catching great Bill Dickey functioned as Berra's personal tutor. That relationship led to the line, "Bill is learning me all his experience."

Some of his teammates made negative comments about the way Yogi's face was put together. "You don't hit with your face," was his rejoinder. "A face has nothing to do with winning."

If there was anything Berra was, it was a winner. He was the heart and soul of the great Yankee teams from 1949 to 1955. In his prime of primes the team won five straight pennants and World Championships. Berra won three MVP awards and led the Yankees in RBIs each of those seasons. And even though he was a notorious bad-ball hitter, he rarely struck out. In 1950, he fanned just 12 times in 597 at bats.

Number 8 could beat the opposition with his bat, his glove, his arm, his head. "To me he is a great man," was Casey Stengel's comment on Yogi, whom he called "Mr. Berra, my assistant manager. I am lucky to have him and so are my pitchers."

A superb handler of the varied moods and different skills of Yankee pitchers, Berra was behind the plate for the Larsen Perfect Game and the

(Preceding page)
Joltin' Joe DiMaggio, voted baseball's "greatest living player."

two no-hitters pitched by Allie Reynolds. Berra underwhelmed and over-whelmed opposition hitters, either talking them into distraction or directing his pitchers on how to capitalize on batters' weaknesses.

As a fielder, he was in a class by himself. "He springs on a bunt," Stengel said, "like it was a dollar." Berra's lifetime fielding mark was a gaudy .988. He had a string of 148 consecutive games played without an error. From July 28, 1957, to May 10, 1959, he handled 950 chances flawlessly. He was also one of only four catchers to field 1.000 in a season. Six times he led the league in double plays. He also turned 175 lifetime double plays, second on the all-time list. Eight times he led the American League in games caught, chances accepted. In 1949, Berra played part of the season with a broken finger, innovating the practice of keeping one finger outside the catcher's mitt.

If Reggie Jackson was Mr. October, than Yogi was Mr. World Series. He played in 14 of them. In 75 games he had 259 at bats, 71 hits, and 10 dou-bles—all World Series records. He also threw out 36 runners attempting to steal in the Fall Classic, another all-time record. Perhaps his most notable record is the 10 World Championship Yankee teams he played on, a record that will probably never be topped.

Fourth all-time in games played and at bats in Yankee history, fifth in RBIs and home runs, sixth in runs scored, ninth in doubles, Berra's nine

Berra is shown here standing with teammates Gene Woodling (to his left), Allie Reynolds, and Joe Collins. Reynolds (holding up two fingers) had just completed his second no-hitter of the 1951 season.

Bill Dickey takes a break during spring training in St. Petersburg, Florida. He still holds the highest single season batting average (.362) by a catcher in baseball history.

career pinch-hit home runs is the best in team history. For 15 straight years he was an All-Star, and it surprised no one when he was elected to the Baseball Hall of Fame in 1971.

The legacy of Lawrence Peter Berra, who grew up on the Hill in St. Louis eating banana sandwiches with mustard, having his cake and eating it too, is not only outstanding accomplishments on the baseball field, but a repository of quips and one-liners that gave him a well-earned reputation as one of the national pastime's premier funnymen.

BILL DICKEY

With all due respect to Yogi Berra, Johnny Bench, Mickey Cochrane, and others, William Malcolm Dickey was, quite simply, the greatest catcher in baseball history.

Born in Bastrop, Louisiana, in 1907, the young Dickey was trying to make an impression on Yankee manager Miller Huggins in spring training in 1929. "Stop unbuttoning your shirt on every pitch," Hug snapped. "We pay one player for hitting home runs, and that's Babe Ruth. So choke the bat and drill the ball."

Dickey did as he was told. He batted .324 in 1929, the first of 11 seasons in which he batted .300 or better. He was the first in a long line of great Yankee catchers.

"Dickey isn't just a catcher," Dan Daniel wrote. "He's a ball club. He isn't just a player. He's an influence." The glue of those great Yankee teams of the 1930s, the backstop with the southern drawl never showed up an umpire, was a superb handler of pitchers, always helped out a teammate and, like his roommate Lou Gehrig, was quiet until aroused.

On July 4, 1932, Dickey was more than aroused. There was a bang-bang play at home plate. Dickey collided with Carl Reynolds of Washington. There were words exchanged, briefly, and then with one punch, Dickey broke Reynolds's jaw. Fined a thousand dollars and suspended for 30 days, a rested and restless Dickey returned on August 4 to the Yankees lineup. It was as if he wanted everyone to know he was back. He lashed a bases-loaded home run and three singles.

As with so many other Yankee immortals, the World Series was Dickey's time. In 1932, he batted .438. In 1938, he had a 4–4 game. In 1939, he averaged better than an RBI a game. In 1943, his two-run sixth-inning home run polished off St. Louis.

His stats are remarkable for any player, let alone a catcher who caught 100 games or more in 13 consecutive seasons. Eleven times Dickey was an American League All-Star, three times he led all catchers in fielding percentage. In 1936, he batted .362—a mark that no 20th-century catcher has exceeded. His lifetime batting average is .313. He struck out just 289 times in 6,300 at bats. His power years were 1936–39, when he hit 102 of his career 202 home runs. Previously, Dickey had never hit more than 15 in a season.

His rank among all those who ever played for the Yankees clearly shows just how talented Dickey was: batting average, 5th; games, doubles, and RBIs, 6th; hits, 7th; at bats, 9th; triples and home runs, 10th.

Dickey's uniform Number 8, worn by him and Yogi Berra, is fittingly retired in honor of both Yankee backstops. The kid from Bastrop, Louisiana, who had a very long Yankee playing career, a brief managing stint in 1946, a successful coaching tenure under Casey Stengel from 1949 to 1957, and then some time as a scout, was admitted to the Baseball Hall of Fame in 1954.

JOE DIMAGGIO

Even though Boston's Ted Williams hit .406 in 1941, DiMaggio was awarded the American League MVP.

When Joe DiMaggio played baseball on the streets of San Francisco in his growing-up years, the bases were concrete chunks and home plate was a flattened-out oil can. The only glove belonged to the catcher, and black friction tape was used over and over again on an old ball. The kids called him "Long Legs" in Italian. He was always tall for his age.

On October 1, 1932, the day Babe Ruth hit what became known as his "Called Shot," DiMaggio was a skinny 17-year-old shortstop playing his first game for the San Francisco Seals of the Pacific Coast League. He managed one hit. On July 26, 1933, DiMag, not quite 19 years old, had his 61-game hitting streak stopped. He had gone 104 for 257 for a .405 average.

On a bright sunny May day at Yankee Stadium in 1936, Babe Ruth, although annoyed at Yankee management, strolled into the clubhouse and greeted the rookie DiMaggio with a "Hello, Joe" and shook hands. Lefty Gomez was impressed. "With the Babe veterans are 'Doc' and rookies 'Kid,'" he told DiMaggio. "You're the first guy I ever heard him call by name."

It was truly the passing of the torch. The Babe must have known that Joseph Paul DiMaggio was going to be something special. And right off the bat the rookie showed he was. Although he missed 15 games, the stat line for that 1936 season read: .323 batting average, 29 home runs, 125 RBIs, 206 hits. He tied for the league lead in triples and collected 44 doubles. There were also the two home runs he hit in the same inning, making him the first Yankee to accomplish that feat.

He didn't have too bad a sophomore season either. Playing in his first All-Star Game, he also appeared in his first movie—*Manhattan Merry-Go Round*. In 1937, DiMaggio batted in 167 runs and hammered 46 home runs, both career highs for him. His 46 home runs led the American League, and that was unusual for a right-handed hitter in the old Yankee Stadium, where the power alley was in left field.

DiMaggio figured that all those accomplishments should have earned him a pay raise, a big one. And he held out before the 1938 season to get one. Fans, deeming him greedy, turned against him. He would turn them in his favor. But it would take a couple of years.

The public image of Number 5 was of a skinny, reserved kid from Fisherman's Wharf in San Francisco who rarely smiled, kept his feelings inside. His exterior was placid, some said it was sullen and unfeeling. "He wasn't the friendliest guy in the world," said Arthur Richman, "but DiMaggio was the Yankees."

The ultimate professional and perfectionist, DiMaggio was always well groomed and elegantly dressed. In 1936, he was voted one of the ten best-dressed men in the United States.

Joe DiMaggio practiced and played the game of baseball with passion on a daily basis. When asked why he still worked so hard after becoming a star in the big leagues, he replied: "There is always some kid who may be seeing me for the first or last time. I owe him my best."

(Opposite)
DiMaggio cashed in on his hitting streak with this 1941 advertisement for a breakfast cereal.

_110_

What feelings he had, he kept to himself. He was never thrown out of a game.

In the clubhouse he would partake of more than 12 half-cups of coffee and a pack of cigarettes. It was all a kind of buildup of caffeine and nicotine for the war outside. DiMaggio took it very personally when the Yankees lost.

"Joe had an elegance, an aura about him," longtime New York City sportswriter Red Foley noted. "They always said he didn't sweat—he perspired. He never made a really sensational catch. He was always right there."

"They'd hit the ball to center field," Joe McCarthy said, "and Joe would stretch out those long legs of his and run the ball down. He never made a mistake on the bases. He was the best baserunner I ever saw. He could have stolen 50, 60 bases a year if I had let him. He wasn't the fastest man alive. He just knew how to run bases better than anybody. I don't think in all the years he played for me he was ever thrown out stretching."

In 1939, the man they were calling "Yankee Clipper" hit .381. He won the batting title. In 1940, he hit .352 and there was another batting title. DiMaggio hit with power but was a rarity among power hitters in that he seldom struck out. He hit 361 home runs in his career and struck out just 369 times.

It seemed that Joe DiMaggio could do just about everything on a baseball field. Joe McCarthy was asked if DiMag could bunt. "I don't know," the Yankee manager said, "nor do I have any intention of finding out."

How to enjoy breakfast!

It's a *"Breakfast of Champions"* for champion hitter Joe Di Maggio

NICE GOING, JOE! *Baseball's outstanding individual performance this 1941 season was the record 56 game hitting streak of "the Yankee Clipper."* Joe DiMaggio, star center-fielder for the New York Yankees, *began his consecutive game hitting rampage back in May, and kept on hitting at least once in every game until he left all major league records far, far behind.*

As the photograph here shows, Champion Joe likes his Wheaties. He says, "I have been eating Wheaties since 1936, when I first joined the Yankees. I liked the flavor when I first tried them and I think they taste even better now." And Joe goes on to say, "I eat Wheaties four or five times a week the year around."

"Wheaties" and "Breakfast of Champions" are registered trade marks of General Mills, Inc. Copyright 1941, General Mills, Inc.

Tough day tomorrow? Then give yourself this double advantage. Eat a "Breakfast of Champions"—for real enjoyment *and* for valuable nourishment to help you get the day's work done.

Sit down to a bowlful of Wheaties, lots of those toasted whole wheat flakes, with plenty of milk or cream and some fruit—say a juicy peach.

There's flavor for you! A big helping of that famous Wheaties flavor which Joe DiMaggio thinks is "even better now." Flavor so good it has made Wheaties far and away America's favorite whole wheat flakes. (And you can enjoy Wheaties anywhere in the U.S.A.—in restaurants, hotels, dining cars, boats, planes.)

How about nourishment? Well, just try to beat this breakfast combination of three basic, protective foods—milk, fruit, and choice *whole wheat.* Yes,

Wheaties are whole wheat, guaranteed by General Mills to give you *all* the valuable varied nourishment that nature packs into our basic cereal grain. Including vitamin B_1 (Thiamin), vitamin G (Riboflavin), phosphorus and iron. For this reason Wheaties are accepted as a *preferred* wheat cereal by the Council on Foods of the American Medical Association. A *preferred* wheat cereal. That's what you want for your family.

Special Offer! Yours for only a 3c stamp! Family sample package of Wheaties (3 full servings). Also the new Betty Crocker booklet on food selection, vitamins and meal planning, "Thru Highway to Good Nutrition." Offer good only until November 26, 1941. Send premised today with name and address. Department 810, Mi (CONTINUED)

"WITH GO! VITAMIN B_1"

Printed in U.S.A.

When I was in San Francisco, Lefty O'Doul told me: "Joe, don't let the big city scare you. New York is the friendliest town in the world." This day proves it. I want to thank my fans, my friends, my manager Casey Stengel, my teammates, the gamest, fightingest bunch of guys that ever lived. And I want to thank the good Lord for making me a Yankee.
—Joe DiMaggio on his day in 1949

On February 17, 1943, DiMaggio gave up his $43,500 Yankees salary and prepared to receive the $50 a month given to enlisted men in the United States Army. He never even gave the Yankees advance notice of his plans. From 1943 to 1945 DiMaggio was in the service. When he returned to the Yankees, he never quite reached the same high levels of baseball accomplishments. But he was still one of the best. There was a third Most Valuable Player award in 1947; the following year he was the American League home run and RBI leader.

Bone spurs forced DiMaggio to miss the first two months of the season in 1949. When he returned in mid-June, the Yankees played a crucial series against the Red Sox. DiMag homered four times in that series. Mel Allen got so excited that he shouted, "How about that," originating that famous turn of phrase that came to be part of sports and Yankee lingo.

"The old boy can't be that bad," DiMaggio said after managing just a .263 average in 116 games and only 12 home runs for the 1951 season. The Yankees prepared to match up against Brooklyn in the World Series. The Dodger scouting report read, "He can't throw real hard. You can take an extra base on him if he's in motion away from the line of the throw. He won't throw on questionable plays. He can't run and can't pull the ball at all."

That 1951 World Series was the last hurrah for Joe DiMaggio. The Yankees attempted to get him to play one more season, but he knew it was time to go. "When baseball is no longer fun," he said, "it's no longer a game."

The only Yankee to win two batting titles, seventh all-time in games played in Yankee history, fourth in career batting average, home runs, runs, hits, and doubles, third in triples and RBIs, the Yankee Clipper left behind the memory of a man who moved about in the vast pastureland of Yankee Stadium with an almost poetical grace. He played when he was fatigued, when he was hurt, when it mattered a great deal, when it mattered little. He played with a style that has never been duplicated.

"We haven't seen that type since," Red Foley said. "We may never see it again."

"There was nothing they could teach Joe D.," former sports columnist Jimmy Cannon wrote. "When he came to the big leagues, it was all there. Other guys hit for higher averages, struck more home runs. But this is the whole ballplayer, complete and great. There are no defects to discuss."

"I'd like to thank the good Lord," Joe DiMaggio said, "for making me a Yankee."

So would millions of Yankee fans.

WHITEY FORD

Lefty Gomez gave him the nickname "Whitey." Casey Stengel called him "Slick." Elston Howard dubbed him "Chairman of the Board." But the label most fitting for Edward Charles Ford is, quite simply, the greatest pitcher in Yankee history.

Born on East 66th Street in Manhattan, raised in the Astoria section of Queens, Ford spent a lot of his growing-up years tossing a Spalding ball against the wall of a trolley garage. Then he became a baseball star on the sandlots of New York and just continued his natural progression with the Yankees. And what a progression it was.

In the spring of 1950, Casey Stengel received a phone call. "If you want to win the pennant," the caller said, "just bring up that kid Ford from the minors." To the very end Stengel insisted that the one who made the phone call was Whitey Ford.

The chunky southpaw was called up in late June and piled up nine straight wins. Then the rookie sensation was tabbed by Stengel to pitch in the fourth and deciding game of the 1950 World Series against the Phillies. There were 68,000 in attendance at Yankee Stadium. But the 21-year-old Ford said he felt no nervousness. "Why should I?" he quipped. "Half my relatives are here anyway."

Ford won the game and afterward ran into Dizzy Dean, then a broadcaster. "No wonder you won 30 games," he told the old Cardinal. "You were pitching in that crummy National League. I could win 40 in that league myself."

No one ever said that Whitey Ford was shy. But he backed up his bragging banter with a classy manner and businesslike approach that resulted in accomplishment after accomplishment on the pitcher's mound. He featured change-ups, sharp breaking curves, pitches thrown with pinpoint control at different speeds to different locations, and just enough pop on the fastball. "I think I could tell you just about every pitch I threw in 3,170 innings I pitched. I was really into every game."

A gifted all-around athlete, Ford was an excellent fielder and could swing the bat. He compiled 177 major league hits. His pickoff move was one of the best in history. Poised in pressure situations, never beating himself, Whitey Ford was the "money" pitcher on a team filled with "money" players. He posted a 236–106 lifetime record—the best winning percentage (.690) for a pitcher appearing in 200 games since 1900. His lifetime ERA (2.75) is among the lowest for southpaws. In 11 of his 16 seasons his ERA was below 3.00. Three times Ford led the American League in wins and winning percentage, twice in games started, innings pitched, shutouts, and ERA. Eight times he was picked for the All-Star team. Only twice did he win 20 games in a season, but from 1953 to 1960 he averaged almost 16 wins against only 7 defeats. And there were all those special times, the streaks of magnificence on the mound that awed teammates and opposition: back-to-back one-hitters in September of 1955, 14 straight victories in 1961, a career of pitching dominance over the Baltimore Orioles, with a lifetime mark of 30–16 against them, best of any pitcher ever. There were the 45 career shutouts, eight of them 1–0 wins.

Ford's prime years were 1961 to 1963, a time he started more games than ever and added a tough slider to his bag of tricks. In 1961 Ford posted a 25–4 mark, paced the league in wins, innings pitched, and won–lost percentage, and won the Cy Young award and the Babe Ruth award as the outstanding player in the World Series. He was 17–8 in 1962 and 24–7 in 1963.

Whitey Ford boasted an accurate arm and a highly competitive attitude. Ford is shown here pitching the opening game of the 1957 World Series. He defeated Milwaukee Braves ace Warren Spahn to earn one of his major league record 10 World Series victories.

Winning 11 Yankee pennants during his 16-year career gave Ford plenty to smile about.

"You kind of took it for granted around the Yankees," Ford said, "that there was always going to be baseball in October." One of the prime reasons for that was the pitching of the Chairman of the Board. In 11 of Ford's 16 seasons with the team, the Yankees won the pennant. The gifted southpaw's World Series pitching records include most games started (22), most games won (10), most games pitched (22), most innings pitched (146), and most strikeouts (94).

In the last few years of his career, the impish-looking Ford really lived up to his "Slick" nickname, sporting trick pitches like a mudball, a spitter, and a scuffball. On occasion, he used a specially designed rasp ring that worked wonders and made the baseball dance. He employed a spitter to strike out Willie Mays in the All-Star Game. "Look," he joked, "they don't call me 'Slick' for nothing."

On October 3, 1965, at Fenway Park in Boston, Whitey Ford won his 232nd game and became the top winner in franchise history. In his 16 seasons, the longest tenure of any pitcher in Yankee history, Ford was on the mound as the starter for a dozen Stadium openers. A study in reliability and steadiness, Ford ranks first on the all-time Yankee list in wins, strikeouts, innings pitched, and shutouts.

He retired on May 30, 1967. "I came here in 1950," Ford said, "and I was wearing $50 suits. And I'm leaving wearing $200 suits. And I'm gettin' 'em for $80. So I guess I'm doing all right."

In 1970, playing in an Old-Timers' Game, Ford was accused of scuffing up the ball. Always the competitor, he snapped, "Why not, I'm tired of losing these games." In 1974, the kid from New York City who led the Yankees to 11 pennants and a half-dozen World Championships was inducted into the Baseball Hall of Fame. That 1974 season his uniform Number 16 was retired by the Yankees.

Casey Stengel, always happy that he listened to the advice of the telephone caller back in 1950, said of Ford, "If you had one game to win and your life depended on it, you'd want him to pitch it."

LOU GEHRIG

Gehrig was a perfect gentleman off the field, and never allowed fame to affect his personality.

Born in 1903, Henry Louis Gehrig grew up on New York's Upper East Side, the son of poor German immigrants. His father was an ironworker. The youth attended school on the coldest of days clad only in a khaki shirt and pants, never even wearing a hat or an overcoat. His early baseball experience was as an awkward left-handed-throwing catcher whom the other kids teased with the term "chicken."

Athletic stardom at Commerce High School was followed by even more success in football and baseball at Columbia University, where his mother worked as a cook at a fraternity house. In 1921, Gehrig was declared ineligible for collegiate athletic competition when it was discovered that John J. McGraw had persuaded him to play professional baseball under an assumed name. But Gehrig's coach, Andy Coakley, a former major leaguer, was able to get him reinstated.

Gehrig went on to set Columbia season records for highest batting average, slugging percentage, and home runs. He was also a talented pitcher, striking out 17 in one game. Yankee scout Paul Krichell allegedly "discovered" the six-foot, 200-pound, broad-shouldered youngster when Gehrig slammed a home run that landed 400 feet from home plate on the steps of the Columbia library. As the story goes, sure he had seen "the next Babe Ruth," Krichell signed Gehrig to a $1,500 bonus after he graduated from Columbia. A sidebar to the story is that the Yankees allegedly paid Coakley $500 to influence Gehrig to sign with them.

Gehrig played two seasons at Hartford in the Eastern League, including 13 games for the 1923 Yankees and 10 games for the 1924 Yankees. And then on June 1, 1925, Gehrig's defining moment arrived. During batting practice veteran first baseman Wally Pipp was hit on the side of the head and was taking aspirin for a headache when Miller Huggins said, "Take a couple of days off. I'm going to start young Gehrig in your place."

Up to that moment Gehrig had played in just 23 games and batted just 38 times. But Huggins told him that if he did well there was a good chance that he would become the regular Yankee first baseman.

The misconception is that when Gehrig replaced Pipp the fabled consecutive-games-played streak of 2,130 games began. But it really started the day before. Gehrig pinch-hit for Pee Wee Wanninger, who ironically

Wally Pipp, Gehrig's predecessor at first base.

replaced shortstop Everett Scott, who had the record for consecutive games played at 1,307.

From that game on June 1, 1925, to April 30, 1939, a period of 14 years, Gehrig was never out of the Yankee lineup. But he was not an instant success. Three times in June, Huggins pinch-hit for him. On July 5, Gehrig didn't start a game but came in later. At season's end, the young first baseman had compiled a .295 average, 20 home runs, and 68 RBIs in 126 games. Almost half of his hits were for extra bases. With Lou Gehrig now a fixture on the Yankees, Wally Pipp was traded off to the Reds.

Much of the punch Gehrig generated came from his powerful leg muscles, honed each winter in a strenuous speed-skating program. He stood with his feet wide apart and took a short stride into the ball. "Babe set his entire body behind his blow," Gehrig explained. "I'm an arm hitter. It's the strength you have in your grip, in your forearm more than anything else."

By 1927, hitting behind Babe Ruth, finishing third in batting at .373, slugging at a .765 pace, drawing 109 walks, leading the American League in doubles, total bases, and RBIs, Gehrig had come into his own as a major league superstar.

They called him "Iron Horse," "Larrupin' Lou," "Pride of the Yankees," "Columbia Lou," and "Biscuit Pants." But the nickname that perhaps fit him best was concocted by Ruth. The Babe called him "Buster." And Lou Gehrig was "Buster" in one sense—a closemouthed, pipe-smoking, bridge-playing, bow-tie-wearing "mama's boy."

With a bat in his hand, he also was a "Buster" in another sense—busting a lot of pitchers' hearts.

In 1931, Gehrig's 184 RBIs set an American League record. He could have also led the league in home runs that season, but a baserunning error cost him a home run. Gehrig wound up tied with the Babe for the home run title at 46.

On June 23, 1932, Gehrig played in his 1,103rd straight game in a New York uniform, tying Cleveland Joe Sewell's mark of consecutive games played. By June, 14, 1933, the streak stood at 1,249. That day Gehrig and Joe McCarthy were tossed out of a game. The Yankee manager was suspended for three games but the Iron Horse was allowed to play on.

"The ballplayer who loses his head," Gehrig had remarked, "who can't keep his cool, is worse than no ballplayer at all." On that day and on July 26, 1933, the Iron Horse didn't follow his own feelings. He was tossed out of the second game of a doubleheader against Boston. Had it been the first game of the twin bill, the streak would have ended right there. But another streak was stopped that day—that of Joe DiMaggio of the San Francisco Seals at 61 consecutive games with a hit.

On August 17, 1933, Gehrig played in his 1,308th straight game, breaking the record of Everett Scott. The streak kept going. On July 13, 1934, pain in his back from what was diagnosed as lumbago was so severe that Gehrig had to be helped off the field in the first inning in a game against the Detroit Tigers. The streak stood at 1,426, but there were doubts about his chances of playing the next day. He did play, after a fashion. Listed first in the batting order and tabbed to play shortstop, the pain-ravaged Gehrig could barely stand up. But he managed to single. Then Red Rolfe pinch-ran for him and came in to play shortstop. That 1934 season Gehrig hit a career high 49 homers to lead the majors and became the first Yankee to win the Triple Crown.

Ruth was no longer on the Yankee scene in 1935. No longer in the Babe's shadow, Lou Gehrig was now the Pride of the Yankees. On June 8, 1935, the streak was again in jeopardy. Gehrig banged into Carl Reynolds of the Red Sox in a play at first base and had to leave the game. He complained of pain in his arm and shoulder. But a rainout and an open date gave Gehrig some recuperating time. Another attack of lumbago took him out of a game on August 5, 1935, but he was again back in action to keep on playing the next day. That 1935 season was the first of three straight years that Gehrig led the American League in walks—just another indication of the respect pitchers had for him.

On June 5, 1936, the Yankees defeated Cleveland, 4–3. It was Gehrig's 1,700th straight game. It was said that "nothing short of a locomotive will stop Lou Gehrig. He will go on forever." On August 1, 1937, Gehrig hit for the cycle for the second and final time in his career. Two days later, as the Iron Horse played before a Tuesday crowd of 66,767 at the Stadium, the streak was at 1,900.

On May 31, 1938, the streak was at 2,000. But in the final third of that season, Gehrig started to falter even though he managed to rap a first-inning grand-slam home run on August 20—the 23rd and final bases-loaded homer of his career. As the 1938 season ended, no one knew what was really wrong with him, but it was plain to all that his great strength was waning. His hand would tremble as he held a cup of coffee. He pushed himself more and more on the field, trying to fight off the lethargy. On September 9, 1938, Gehrig rapped out four hits, bringing his average to .300. The streak of consecutive games played was now at 2,100.

In spring training in 1939, Gehrig grew weaker. His Yankee teammates and his wife, Eleanor, told him to rest. They argued that his record would never be broken. But he would not let up. As the 1939 season began, Gehrig once again was positioned at first base for the New York Yankees. He took that famous big swing, but little fly balls replaced the booming, gargantuan home runs. Still he played on. Once, at Yankee Stadium, he bent over to tie his shoelaces and fell down. He would trip over his own feet. Manager Joe McCarthy looked away and continued to fill Gehrig's name in on the lineup card day after day. McCarthy could not break the heart of the man who had been so much to the Yankees.

Gehrig would come home to his wife, shaken. "Stop playing, Lou," she pleaded. "Take some time off and get yourself checked out and find out what is wrong with you."

"I have to play on," Gehrig said. "I will be able to work it out. This is the only way for me to go."

On April 30, 1939, a thin and weak Lou Gehrig decided there was another way to go. He told Joe McCarthy, "You'd better take me out, Joe, I guess that's all."

On May 2, 1939, Wally Pipp, whose place Gehrig had taken those 2,130 games before, came down from his home in Grand Rapids, Michigan, for the Yankees–Tigers game. He expected to see Gehrig perform. Instead, he saw

This Iron Man stuff is just baloney. I think he's making one of the worst mistakes a ballplayer can make. The guy ought to learn to sit on the bench and rest.
—Babe Ruth

From 1926 to 1937, Lou Gehrig never batted under .300, never hit fewer than 27 home runs, and drove in at least 107 runs in each season. His consecutive games streak was miraculous, but his consistency went way beyond being in the lineup every day.

the Iron Horse standing alone at home plate delivering the lineup card. At age 36, the highest-paid player in baseball, Gehrig was finished. His 1939 batting average was .143.

Lefty Gomez attempted to soften the moment. "Hey, Lou," he cracked. "It took 15 years to get you out of the game. Sometimes I'm out of there in 15 minutes."

Joe McCarthy said, "Lou just told me he felt it would be best for the club if I took him out of the lineup. I asked him if he really felt that way. He told me he was serious. He feels blue. He is dejected. He's been a great ballplayer. Fellows like him come along once in a hundred years. More than that, he's been a vital part of the Yankee club since he started. We'll miss him. You can't escape that fact. But I think he's doing the proper thing."

There was an announcement made to the fans about Gehrig's taking himself out of the starting lineup. Then, as he walked back to the dugout, he was given a huge ovation from the fans in Tiger Stadium. Gehrig took off his cap, doffed it to the fans, then settled into a corner of the Yankee bench. Alone. One can only wonder what thoughts he had.

Babe Dahlgren, Gehrig's replacement, who had waited three years for his chance, homered in the third inning. And the first person out of the Yankee dugout offering congratulations was Lou Gehrig. And when the game ended—a 22–2 Yankee thrashing of the Tigers—and the consecutive game streak was stopped at 2,130—the Iron Horse answered all the questions from reporters and went into a lengthy commentary about what had been and what was.

"I decided last Sunday on this move," Gehrig explained. "I haven't been a bit of good to the team since the season started. It would not be fair to the boys, to Joe, or to the baseball public. In fact, it wouldn't be fair to myself, and I'm the last consideration. It's tough to see your mates on base, have a chance to win a ballgame, and not be able to do anything about it. McCarthy has been swell about it all the time. He'd let me go until the cows came home. He is that considerate of my feelings, but I knew in Sunday's game that I should get out of there. I went up there four times with men on base. Once there were two there. A hit would have won the ballgame for the Yankees, but I missed, leaving five grounded as the Yankees lost. Maybe a rest will do me some good. Maybe it won't. Who knows? Who can tell? I'm just hoping.

On June 19, 1939, on his 36th birthday, Lou Gehrig left the Mayo Clinic with a sealed envelope. The results of his examination and diagnosis were in it: "Mr. Gehrig is suffering from amyotrophic lateral sclerosis. This type of illness involves the motor pathways and cells of the central nervous system and in lay terms is known as a form of infantile paralysis. The nature of this trouble makes it such that Mr. Gehrig will be unable to continue his active participation as a baseball player."

Gehrig returned to the Yankees on June 21. Retired, but still the captain, still the Pride of the Yankees, he took the lineup card out to the umpires before each game and looked out at the action on the playing field from his seat in the corner in the dugout.

July 4, 1939, was Lou Gehrig Appreciation Day at Yankee Stadium. The critically ill man stirred his 1927 Yankee teammates plus the 61,808 in attendance with his farewell address:

> *Fans, for the past two weeks you have been reading about the bad break I got. Yet today I consider myself the luckiest man on the face of the earth. I have been in ballparks for 17 years and have never received anything but kindness and encouragement from you fans. Look at these grand men. Which of you wouldn't consider it the highlight of your career to associate with them for even one day? Sure, I'm lucky. Who wouldn't have considered it an honor to have known Jacob Ruppert? Also the builder of baseball's greatest empire, Ed Barrow? To have spent six years with that wonderful little fellow, Miller Huggins? Then to have spent the next nine years with that outstanding leader, that smart student of psychology, the best manager in baseball today, Joe McCarthy? Sure I'm lucky. When the New York Giants, a team you would give your right arm to beat, and vice versa, sends you a gift—that's something. When everybody*

Gehrig considered playing the game of baseball every day a blessing rather than a job. Here he lets out a laugh as he swings and misses a pitch in batting practice during spring training.

Gehrig wipes his eyes as he delivers his farewell speech on July 4, 1939.

down to the groundskeepers and those boys in white coats remember you with trophies—that's something. When you have a wonderful mother-in-law who takes sides with you in squabbles with her own daughter—that's something. When you have a father and a mother who work all their lives so you can have an education and build your body—it's a blessing. When you have a wife who has been a tower of strength and shown more courage than you dreamed existed—that's the finest I know. So I close in saying that I may have had a tough break, but I have an awful lot to live for.

With the speech ended, Babe Ruth came over to Gehrig. "I put my arms around him and though I tried to smile and cheer him up, I wound up crying like a baby."

Gehrig's Number 4 was retired. Of all the retired Yankee uniform numbers, it is the only one worn by just one player. Throughout the 1939 season, the Iron Horse remained with the Yankees as captain. It gave him joy to see his team win the American League pennant by 17 games and sweep the

---

(Opposite)
Gehrig (far right) pictured with his family.

120

Cincinnati Reds in the World Series and become the first team to rack up four straight World Championships.

In December 1939, Gehrig was inducted into the Baseball Hall of Fame at Cooperstown. The mandatory five-year waiting period was waived because of his illness. In 1940, Gehrig was confined to a wheelchair, his powerful body now a shell of what it once was. On June 2, 1941, exactly 16 years to the day since he had replaced Wally Pipp as the New York Yankees first baseman, Gehrig died. He was 17 days shy of his 38th birthday. A ceremony in center field at Yankee Stadium honored his memory.

On July 4, 1941, a monument to his memory was placed in center field at Yankee Stadium:

> *HENRY LOUIS GEHRIG*
>
> *JUNE 19, 1903–JUNE 2, 1941. A MAN, A GENTLEMAN, AND A GREAT BALLPLAYER WHOSE AMAZING RECORD OF 2,130 CONSECUTIVE GAMES SHOULD STAND FOR ALL TIME. THIS MEMORIAL IS A TRIBUTE FROM THE YANKEE PLAYERS TO THEIR BELOVED CAPTAIN AND TEAMMATE.*

Lou Gehrig recorded 493 home runs, third best in Yankee history. His .340 lifetime batting average is second only to Ruth in franchise history. Thirteen straight seasons he drove in 100 or more runs; eight seasons he notched 200 or more hits; seven seasons he had 150 or more RBIs. Twice he was named the American League Most Valuable Player. Five times he led the league in RBIs, four times he led in runs scored, three times he tied or led the AL in home runs, twice he was the slugging percentage leader. His slugging percentage of .632 is the third best in history—only Babe Ruth and Ted Williams did better. His 1,990 lifetime RBIs place him third on the all-time list. In the World Series, Gehrig was at the top of his form. He hit 10 home runs, had 35 RBIs in 34 games, and batted .361.

His longtime roommate Bill Dickey said of Gehrig: "He just went out and did his job every day." That he did. He ranks first in Yankee history in hits, triples, doubles, and RBIs; second in games played, at bats, and runs scored. And although his consecutive-game record was broken by Cal Ripken, Gehrig's accomplishments go far beyond his remarkable endurance mark. He was truly the Pride of the Yankees.

LEFTY GOMEZ

Out of Rodeo, California, Vernon Louis Gomez was the product of a Spanish mother and an Irish dairyman father. As a 20-year-old in 1928, he posted a 12–14 record for Salt Lake City. The next season he was 18–11 with the San Francisco Seals. The Yankees paid $50,000 for his contract.

In 1930, the skinny hurler got into his first game for the Yankees. "I was making the long walk," Gomez recalled. "Thoughts kept running through my mind. Will I spike myself?" He finished out the season with St. Paul. By 1931, Gomez was back with the Yankees, firing his blazer of a fastball off a high leg kick, befuddling American League batters, posting a 21–9 record.

"I talk 'em out of hits," was his explanation for his success. That wasn't exactly true, but he was a man of constant banter, one-liners, and self-deprecating humor.

Ed Barrow told the 6-2, 150-pound Gomez that if he put on 20 pounds he'd make everyone forget 41-game winner Jack Chesbro. "I put on 20 pounds and almost made them forget Gomez," the fun-loving southpaw cracked. He just could not function with too much weight on his lanky frame.

There was a game in which the opposition loaded the bases on him. Joe McCarthy came out to the mound. "I know they're loaded up," Gomez cracked. "Do you think I thought they gave me another infield?"

Another time Bill Dickey came out to the mound. "What do you want to throw to Jimmie Foxx?" the Yankee catcher asked. "I don't want to throw him nothin'," Gomez responded. "Maybe he'll get tired of waitin' and leave."

Gomez loved to brag: "I roomed with Joe DiMaggio and made him famous. They didn't know he could go back on a ball until he played behind me."

In 1935, the Yankee pitcher had a subpar season. Ruppert was going to cut his salary from $20,000 to $7,500. "You keep the salary," Gomez quipped. "I'll take the cut."

It was lines like these and his pausing while pitching to watch an airplane fly over Yankee Stadium in the middle of a World Series game that earned Gomez a slew of colorful nicknames: the "Gay Castillian," "Goofy," "El Goofy," "The Happy Hidalgo," and the "Singular Señor."

The classic line of his career came in a game when all the outs were recorded by the fielders behind him: "I'd rather be lucky than good."

Lefty Gomez was lucky. On August 1, 1941, he was a 9–0 victor over the St. Louis Browns despite walking 11, the most walks ever in a shutout. But he was also very good. Throughout the 1930s, he teamed with Red Ruffing to give the Yankees the most potent lefty-righty pitching duo in the majors. His career year was 1934. He led the league in wins (26–5), strikeouts, and ERA. In All-Star and World Series competition Gomez was at the top of his form, posting a record 3–1 mark in All-Star games and a 6–0 record in the World Series—the most wins without a defeat in the Fall Classic. Overall, he won 189 games and three times led the American League in strikeouts.

Various arm problems afflicted Gomez throughout his career, and the velocity on his fastball kept deteriorating. He joked about it: "I'm throwing as hard as I ever did but the ball is just not getting there as fast."

In 1941, a season Gomez was 15–5, Phil Rizzuto was a nervous Yankee rookie shortstop. Gomez called him in from his infield position. "Is your mom in the stands?" he asked. Rizzuto nodded that she was.

"I'll make her proud of you."

"How's that?"

"Just stand here with me a minute and she'll be telling people that her little boy is giving advice to the great Gomez."

Great, he was. The man they called "Yankee Doodle Zany" is second in complete games, third in regular-season wins, fourth in shutouts and strikeouts, and seventh in winning percentage in franchise history. In 1972, he was inducted into the Baseball Hall of Fame. He wasn't so "Goofy" after all.

Lefty Gomez exhibits the form that made him the Yankees ace pitcher during the late 1930s.

Tommy Henrich gets a handshake from a security guard after hit the game-winning home run in the bottom of the ninth inning of game one of the 1949 World Series. Henrich's blast was the only run of the day as New York defeated Brooklyn, 1-0.

TOMMY HENRICH

He played in the same outfield in the shadow of Joe DiMaggio and Charlie Keller. His name is not to be found among the all-time Yankee leaders in statistical achievements. Others could run faster, throw more accurately, hit for a higher average or with more power. But when a clutch performance was needed, Tommy Henrich was always there.

The man they called "Old Reliable" came to the Yankees in April 1937 out of the Cleveland Indians farm system after Judge Landis had declared him a free agent. Eight teams sought to sign him, but the Masillon, Ohio, native had been a Yankee fan as a kid. He took the $25,000 bonus and reported to the Yankees of Joe DiMaggio, Lefty Gomez, Tony Lazzeri, Bill Dickey, and Red Ruffing. "I was in awe," Henrich recalled. "The atmosphere was one of nine guys getting ready to go out and play ball."

They played ball, and so did five-time All-Star Tommy Henrich, who spent his entire 11-year career with the Yankees. He especially stood out when it really mattered—at World Series time. His ninth-inning home run in the opener of the 1949 Fall Classic beat Brooklyn's Don Newcombe and gave Allie Reynolds a 1–0 win. In 1947, he drove in the winning run in the Yankee's seventh game, a 5–2 triumph over Brooklyn.

And in 1941, a season in which he hit 31 home runs, he came to bat in the ninth inning of game four of the World Series with the Yankees trailing the Dodgers, 4–3. There were two outs, nobody on base. A Brooklyn victory seemed wrapped up. Hugh Casey got two strikes on Henrich, who swung and missed for an apparent strike three. But catcher Mickey Owen mishandled the ball.

"Even as I was trying to hold up," Henrich recalled, "I was thinking that the ball had broken so fast that Owen might have trouble with it, too. When I saw that little white jackrabbit bouncing, I said, 'Let's go!'"

Henrich went—all the way down to first—and that was the play that turned the game and the Series around. Charlie Keller doubled in two runs to torque a four-run Yankee rally that gave them a 7–4 come-from-behind emotional win. The next day there was another Yankee win and their ninth World Championship. And it all started because of Henrich's heads-up play and hustle.

Heads-up play and hustle was the way Henrich lived his baseball life. "Catching a fly ball is a pleasure," Henrich said. "But knowing what to do with it after you catch it is a business." One of the great defensive outfielders in Yankee history, Henrich always knew what he was doing on the field. In 1946, he committed just two errors playing a tough right field.

His career year was 1948. Topping all American League batters in triples for the second straight season, Henrich was the league leader in runs scored (138). He batted .308, had 25 home runs, and 100 RBIs. But 1949 was the season that really underscored the aptness of his "Old Reliable" nickname. The Yankees were decimated by injuries, including those sustained by Henrich, who played in just 115 games. But day after day he made the most of his playing time, delivering clutch hits. He virtually carried the Yankees to the pennant with his 24 home runs and timely RBIs.

"Tommy," Casey Stengel said to him, "I don't want you to sit in a draft. Don't slip and fall in the shower. And under no circumstances are you to eat fish, because them bones could be murder. Drive carefully, and stay in the slow lane, and sit quietly in the clubhouse until the game begins. I can't let anything happen to you."

Casey wasn't taking any chances. He knew what he had—one of the classiest and most professional performers in the history of the New York Yankees.

ELSTON HOWARD

Although he was an All-Star for nine straight years and is in the top 20 Yankee all-time list for games played, at bats, hits, doubles, RBIs, and home runs, Elston Howard remains one of the most underrated performers in franchise history. Perhaps it was because he was steady and stoical, not flashy or noisy. But he was a talented and dedicated team player who just did whatever needed to be done to help the Yankees win.

Born in St. Louis in 1929, Elston Gene Howard came to the Yankees in 1955 from the Kansas City Monarchs of the Negro Leagues. He was the Yankees' first African American player. And he had to suffer through the indignity those first few spring trainings of being barred from staying in the Yankee hotel in St. Petersburg and having to live in a segregated part of town with an African American family.

In his first five Yankee seasons, with Yogi Berra on the scene, Howard was moved from his natural catcher's position to the outfield. "You can substitute," Stengel said, "but it's tough to replace. With Howard I have a replacement, not a substitute."

It was not until 1960 that Howard became the "replacement," the regular backstop, and Berra played the field. Howard was a master behind the plate, highly skilled in handling pitchers, incredibly adept at catching foul pops. He innovated the hinged catcher's mitt, the forerunner of the one-handed catching technique. His .993 career fielding mark is one of the best ever for catchers.

When he first came to the majors, Howard batted out of an exaggerated spread stance that became less and less pronounced as the years went on. Three times he batted over .300. In 1963, Howard became the American League's first African American Most Valuable Player. Statistically (.287, 28 home runs—his third straight year of 20 plus homers—85 RBIs), that was not his top season. But Mantle and Maris missed many games due to injuries, and "Ellie" was the constant on the Yankees, the leader.

Traded to the Red Sox in 1967, Howard returned to the Yankees two years later, becoming the American League's first African American coach. He coached for the Yankees for 11 years, until his death by heart failure on December 14, 1980.

WAITE HOYT

Born in Brooklyn, New York, in 1899, Waite Charles "Schoolboy" Hoyt was the son of a minstrel man. They called him the "Brooklyn Schoolboy," a nick-

Elston Howard as a rookie in 1955. Howard was a steady player for the Yankees both at and behind the plate.

name that came from his place of birth and the fact that he had been a star pitcher at Erasmus Hall High School.

He began his baseball career with Mt. Carmel in the Pennsylvania League in 1916 and ended it with Brooklyn in the National League in 1938. But his glory years were as a pitcher for the Yankees in the Roaring Twenties.

At age 15 Hoyt was signed by John McGraw to a New York Giants contract. He pitched in one game for the Giants in 1918, then joined the Red Sox, who traded him in December of 1920 to the Yankees, along with Wally Schang, Mike McNally, and Harry Harper, for Del Pratt, Muddy Ruel, Sammy Vick, and Hank Thormahlen.

Hoyt won 19 games in 1921 in his first Yankee season, pacing the Bronx Bombers to the pennant. That season set the stage for the stocky right-hander as workhorse and main man of the pitching staff for the first half-dozen Yankee pennant winners.

The fun-loving Waite enjoyed every single moment of those seasons. A sophisticated man, a writer, painter, and singer—he even had a few gigs at the Palace Theater in Manhattan—Hoyt was very close to Babe Ruth, who for some strange reason called him "Walter."

There were those who said that Hoyt's vocabulary was as developed as his pitching skills. In any event he knew more words than most of his contemporaries. Once he had an altercation with an umpire and fired off this one-liner: "You should be a traffic cop so you could stand in the middle of the street with a badge on your chest and insult people with impunity."

In the rough-and-tumble baseball world of his time, the broad right-handed hurler gave as good as he got. Pitching in the Polo Grounds in the 1921 World Series against the Giants, Hoyt had to dodge a bar of soap thrown at him by John McGraw. He picked up the soap and fired it, just missing the ear of the Giant manager. Then Hoyt took care of business, defeating the Giants, 3–0, on a two-hitter. In that World Series he hurled three complete games, allowing no earned runs.

"In the daytime you sat in the dugout and talked about women," cracked Hoyt. "In the nighttime you went out with women and talked about baseball. Small wonder—it's great to be young and a Yankee."

Despite Hoyt's winning ways, Jake Ruppert was not satisfied: "What's the matter with you?" the Yankee owner asked. "Other pitchers win their games 9–3, 10–2. You win yours 2–1, 1–0. Why don't you win your games like the others?"

In 1927, Hoyt had a career year, winning 22 of 29 decisions, posting a 2.63 ERA, topping all American League pitchers in wins, winning percentage, and ERA.

Hoyt had said, "A Yankee pitcher should never hold out because then he might be traded and would have to pitch against them." After his banner season in 1927, Hoyt disregarded his own advice and held out in the spring of 1928. But it didn't do him much good.

In fact, it may have done him some harm, for in May of 1930, Ruppert went along with the trade of Hoyt and Mark Koenig to Detroit for three players who never really helped the Yankees. Out of pinstripes and moving from team to team, Hoyt remained a Yankee at heart. In 1933, as a member of the Pittsburgh Pirates, he was being ragged by the opposition. His response was,

Waite Hoyt had only one losing season on the mound during his 9½ seasons with the Yankees.

(Opposite)
Elston Howard's .993 lifetime fielding percentage ranks him second all-time among catchers.

Reggie Jackson is all business in the Yankee dugout after hitting his second home run in the fifth inning of game six of the 1977 World Series. Jackson wasn't finished, however, as he hit his third of the game on the first pitch of the his next at-bat.

"Shut up you guys or I'll put my Yankee uniform on and scare the shit out of you."

In 1969, Waite Hoyt, who ranks 7th in complete games, 8th in wins, 9th in games pitched, 13th in winning percentage, 15th in strikeouts, and 17th in shutouts on the Yankee all-time list, was inducted into the Baseball Hall of Fame.

REGGIE JACKSON

The first player to have a candy bar named after him, Reginald Martinez Jackson helped three teams win 10 division titles, six pennants, and five World Series from 1971 to 1982. He is the only player to be an MVP in two World Series. His .755 slugging percentage is a World Series record. Jackson played for 21 tumultuous seasons, just five of those years with the Yankees. But when he was admitted to the Baseball Hall of Fame in 1993, he went in as a Yankee.

Reggie Jackson, like Babe Ruth, was born to be a Yankee. And like Babe Ruth, he was a circus, a parade, and a sideshow all rolled into one. Some of his one-liners were even greater attention-getters than those uttered by the Babe:

(Opposite)
Reggie Jackson's classic power swing.

128

"Fans don't boo nobodies."

"Hitting is better than sex."

"After Jackie Robinson, the most important black in baseball history is Reggie Jackson. I really mean that."

Dubbed "Mr. October" for his home run-hitting heroics in the World Series and "Mr. Obnoxious" for his unabashed arrogance, Jackson led the Yankees to four Eastern Division championships (1977, 1978, 1980, and 1981), two American League pennants, and back-to-back World Championships in 1977 and 1978. Throughout his Yankee years there were many on and off the field confrontations, controversies, and squabbles with Billy Martin, George Steinbrenner, and a cast of assorted players, coaches, and opponents.

At first it seemed that New York City and the self-promoting outfielder were a perfect marriage. But it didn't take long for the divorce proceedings to get under way.

"It's a fickle town," Jackson said, "a tough town. They getcha, boy. They don't let you escape with minor scratches and bruises. They put scars on you here."

The Yankees lost the 1981 World Series to the Dodgers. George Steinbrenner, frustrated and enraged, apologized at a news conference to Yankee fans for his team's poor play.

The supersensitive Jackson took umbrage at Steinbrenner's remarks. "I don't have to apologize to anyone," he snapped. "I played my best." Reggie missed the first three games of the Series with an injury but did give it his best. On January 22, 1982, the man who for five frenetic seasons had been the Yankee star of stars decided to give his best for California. He signed a five-year contract with the Angels.

When Jackson was a rookie with the Athletics in 1967, Joe DiMaggio was the batting coach. He tried to convince the youngster to cut down on his swing. But Jackson wouldn't listen to DiMag. He said he'd do it his way. The sixth leading home run hitter of all time (563) and also the all-time strikeout leader (2,597)—once every four at bats—for Jackson it was all or nothing.

MICKEY MANTLE

In spring training in 1962, former Yankee infielder Phil Linz recalled, "I was at shortstop taking ground balls. Mickey Mantle had come down to Florida a couple of days late and he walks out of the dugout in a sweatsuit. He had a couple of bats in his hand and walked over to the cage. Whoever was hitting walked out. Everything stopped—it was like the whole field was frozen. He was not even swinging hard. He was just warming up. But he hit the first nine pitches out."

Then there was the time in Detroit that Mantle told Linz and Joe Pepitone to get dressed in their finest clothing and meet him and Whitey Ford for dinner at a place called the Flame. "Ask for my table," Mantle said.

Pepitone and Linz took great pains to dress for the occasion, a night out with the stars. They hopped into a cab and after riding for more than a half hour arrived at the Flame. It was in a rundown part of town, a grimy hole-in-the-wall dump. Ford never showed. Neither did Mantle. There wasn't even a reserved table.

There was the Mickey Mantle, the "Oklahoma Kid," the blonde Adonis with the ingratiating smile who may have been the best all-around baseball player ever. And there was the Mickey Mantle, wise guy, cursing out reporters, pushing kids aside as they begged for autographs, demeaning teammates, playing practical jokes with no thought for the hurt they caused.

Mickey Charles Mantle was born on October 20, 1931, in Spavinaw, Oklahoma, population 300. He was named for Mickey Cochrane, his father's favorite player. When Mantle was just an infant, his father, Elven, a former semipro player, ordered a baseball cap for his son. At four Mickey moved with his family to Commerce, Oklahoma, population, 2,500. When he was six, his father dressed him up in a complete baseball uniform.

A worker in the lead mines of Commerce, Oklahoma, Mantle's father told everyone: "Mickey will be the best switch-hitter that ever lived if I have my way." He threw to his son right-handed so that Mickey would bat left-handed. Then the solidly built man whom they called "Mutt" threw left-handed so that Mickey would bat right-handed. The young Mantle balked at the regimen, but Mutt was unrelenting. Before long Mickey was hitting home runs left-handed and right-handed on the Alkali, a flat section of Oklahoma plain close by abandoned lead mine shafts. He was also playing a pretty fair shortstop.

When Mickey was 14 years old, Mutt bought him a "Marty Marion" glove. It cost $22, which was then a third of Mutt's weekly wages. Mickey was still using the glove a couple of years later as a member of the Baxter Springs (Kansas) Whiz Kids, the top team in the Ban Johnson League. In one memorable game he hit three homers, including one that traveled about 500 feet.

In a scene out of Hollywood casting, famed Yankee scout Tom Greenwade, in the front seat of his 1947 Oldsmobile with the Mantles, ather and son, in the back seat, negotiated a baseball contract. Greenwade offered $140 a month. "He can make that much playing Sunday ball and working in the mines during the week," Mutt Mantle said. They settled on a $1,150 bonus.

At 18, Mantle played for Independence, Missouri. A year later he was with Joplin in Class-C ball. In 137 games he hit .383 with 30 doubles, 26 homers, and 136 RBIs and led his team to the Western Association title. Just under six feet tall, the 200-pound, 19-year-old whom they called the "Commerce Comet" earned a trip to the Yankee spring-training camp in 1951.

"He was a real country boy," Whitey Ford recalled, "all shy and embarrassed. He arrived with a straw suitcase and two pairs of slacks and one blue sports jacket that probably cost about eight dollars."

Since Phil Rizzuto was a fixture at shortstop, and since Mantle made more than 50 errors playing that position at Joplin, Tommy Henrich and Joe DiMaggio were assigned the task of teaching the youngster some outfielding skills. It seemed there wasn't too much anyone could teach him about hit-

Though he doesn't quite get to this one, Mantle's great speed allowed him to run down a lot of balls in the Yankee outfield.

ting. Mantle batted .402 in spring training, slammed long home runs, was clocked at 3.1 seconds batting left-handed going from home to first base.

"He should lead the league in everything," Casey Stengel said of Mantle. "With his combination of speed and power he should win the triple batting crown every year. In fact, he should do anything he wants to do."

"I don't think I will ever experience a day like Opening Day 1951," Mantle said. "It was the worst day of my life. I don't think I slept a wink the night before, and I was trembling all over from the moment I reached Yankee Stadium. I was so scared."

The first major league home run for the 19-year-old switch-hitter was on May 1 off Chicago's Randy Gumpert. Fifteen days later, batting from the right side against Dick Rozek of Cleveland, Mantle recorded the first of 266 Yankee Stadium home runs—most for a player in major league history.

The power was there, the talent was there, but so was the immaturity. Lonely, striking out too much, pouting, exploding into temper tantrums, Mantle was not ready—yet. He was sent down in July to Kansas City in Triple-A, where in just 166 at bats he hit .361 with 11 home runs and 50 RBIs.

In August, Mickey Mantle came back to the Bronx to stay. Pete Sheehy changed his uniform from Number 6 to Number 7. It would become one of the most famous numbers in Yankee history.

"At five or six," former Yankee manager Buck Showalter said, "I remember standing in front of the TV set and trying to imitate his batting stance. Every kid in Little League wanted Number 7. When I got to the Yankees and played in the minor leagues, Number 7 didn't seem to be available, and rightfully so."

Batting .267 with 13 home runs and 65 RBIs, Mantle had a creditable if not sensational 1951 rookie season. In the World Series against the Giants he was the starting right fielder. For the moment Joe DiMaggio was still the Yankee center fielder. In game two at Yankee Stadium, Mantle, under orders from Stengel to go after anything hit to the outfield because of DiMag's bad heel, was chasing a ball hit by Willie Mays. DiMaggio called him off. Mantle's spikes caught in the drainpipe covering. He tore up his knee and was taken out of the game. He would not play another game for the rest of his career without some kind of pain.

Helping the Mick into a cab that would take them to Lenox Hill Hospital, Mutt Mantle hurt his back and collapsed. Both father and son watched the rest of the World Series on TV from hospital beds. It was determined that Mutt Mantle was fatally ill; the following summer Mutt died of Hodgkin's disease. One can only ponder the effect on the young Mantle of his father's death and that of his grandfather and two uncles. They all passed away when they were around 40 years old.

With DiMaggio retired, the Yankees became Mickey Mantle's team. His blond hair, blue eyes, crew cut, big muscles, and middle American background combined with his alliterative, almost lyrical, name to make him a symbol of the 1950s. He was an icon even if he didn't know what the word meant.

From 1952 to 1959, the Mick averaged 33 home runs and 97 RBIs each season. On April 17, 1953, in Griffith Stadium in Washington, D.C., Mantle hit what went down in baseball lore as the first "tape measure" home run.

The Mel Allen broadcast call brings back the moment:

> *Yogi Berra on first. Mickey Mantle at bat with the count of one ball, no strikes. Left-handed pitcher Chuck Stobbs on the mound. Mantle, a switch-hitter batting right-handed, digs in at the plate. Here's the pitch . . . Mantle swings . . . there's a tremendous drive going into deep left field! It's going, going, it's over the bleachers and over the sign atop the bleachers into the yards of houses across the street! It's got to be one of the longest home runs I've ever seen hit. How about that! . . . We have just learned that Yankee publicity director Red Patterson has gotten hold of a tape measure and he's going to go out there to see how far that ball actually did go."*

It was measured at an estimated 565 feet.

"Mickey had so much power," recalled former pitcher Pedro Ramos, who was touched up on more than one occasion by the Mick, "that if you made just a little mistake, even if he hit the ball bad he would hit it further than Maris, further than anyone.

Mickey Mantle takes batting practice during the 1960 World Series. Mantle's performances in the post season were legendary.

Mantle connects for his 18th and last World Series home run against Bob Gibson in the seventh game of the 1964 classic.

"When I came into the league in '55 with the Senators," Ramos continued, "the Yankees had Yogi Berra and Moose Skowron, Gil McDougald, Andy Carey. A little bit of Rizzuto. The outfield was Mickey Mantle, Hank Bauer, and all those guys. It was a tough lineup.

"The guy that I talked to the most was Mickey. He was number one. He was my hero. I was a pretty fast runner and was trying to race him all those years. Finally when I was playing for Cleveland he said he'd race for a thousand dollars.

"'Mickey, I think I can beat you,' I said, 'but I don't know. I only know I can't afford to lose a thousand dollars. I don't make so much money as you.' The Indian general manager, Gabe Paul, said he would put $2,000 down. But Mickey said, 'I don't need that kind of money, and there is a chance you might beat me and then I'd lose my reputation.'"

The reputation, however, was secure right from the start. If there was a flaw to that jewel of a ballplayer, Red Foley points out, it was a minor one.

"Mantle had a great arm," Foley said, "but it wasn't a disciplined arm and he'd make a mistake and lose sight of the ball or get a bad jump on a ball. But because of that raw speed he outran his mistakes."

And because of his raw power he turned on pitch after pitch throughout his career. He hammered 54 home runs in 1961, the most ever for a switch-hitter. Coupled with the 40 he hit in 1960, the total of 94 gave him another line in the record book for most home runs in consecutive seasons by a switch-hitter.

Five times he hit the façade at Yankee Stadium. One of those "façade shots" was on May 22, 1963, off Bill Fischer of Kansas City. The ball was still rising as it hit the façade in right field.

On May 13, 1967, Mantle hit his 500th career home run. Circling the bases, he was limping in pain as his knee gave in. There was probably not a day throughout those 18 Yankee seasons that Mantle did not have some kind of pain, some kind of physical problem. He was a man racked by the ravages of osteomyelitis in his left leg, sustained when he was kicked in a high-school football game. There were the assorted and cumulative injuries to leg muscles and knees and other parts of his body, such as the 1957 World Series play at second base when Red Schoendienst fell on Mantle's right shoulder. The Mick's throwing ability and left-handed batting effectiveness were thrown out of kilter. Season after season muscles and tendons were banged up, torn up. There were abscesses that sapped his energy and oozed blood.

Mantle missed a good part of the 1963 season when he slammed into a chain-link fence in center field and broke his left foot and suffered ligament damage to his left knee. Physical problems kept him out of at least 25 games in each of four other seasons.

The final decade of his career Mantle played with elastic bandages wrapped around his right leg from midcalf to upper thigh. His left leg was given the same treatment in his final few years. In his last two seasons he played first base, attempting to save his banged-up legs.

Dissipation, injuries, and natural causes destroyed that once-great machine of a ballplayer. It was said that he never lifted a weight in his life. Because of the condition of his knees, he would never push himself to be in condition, or maybe he didn't care. He never exercised his banged-up legs during the off-season, as he had been advised to.

But he always wanted to play. He would show up with hangovers and flaunt a kind of macho pride, ready for baseball. Oh, was he ready. He led the American League six times in runs scored, four times in homers, and once in homers, RBIs, and batting average. Ten times he homered from both sides of the plate in one game.

On September 20, 1968, Mantle homered in the third inning at Yankee Stadium, his last home run. It gave him a grand total of 536, most home runs for any switch-hitter in history.

Just before the 1969 season, the Mick called it a career. He really should have left sooner, but the $100,000 paychecks and the good times were too much of a lure. "I had three or four bad years in a row," Mantle explained. In those four years he hit only 82 total homers and his average kept dropping: .255, .288, .245, .237.

"I received the biggest disappointment of my career by falling under .300 as a lifetime average," Mantle said. "I was actually dreading playing another season. I was stupid. I thought it was never going to end. I was 36 years old when I had to quit, which is practically the prime of life."

After retirement, Mantle was once asked if he'd ever gone up to the plate trying to hit a home run and succeeded. He replied: "I tried to hit a home run every time I went up to the plate."

Mickey Mantle played in 2,401 games, the most ever for a Yankee. The retirement of his famed Number 7 took place on June 8, 1969. "Playing 18 years for you folks," he told the throng at Yankee Stadium, "has to be the best thing that ever happened to a ballplayer. I've always wondered how a man who was dying could stand here and say he was the luckiest man in the world. Now I know how Lou Gehrig felt. To have my number retired with Numbers 3, 4, and 5 tops everything I've ever done."

Yogi Berra made the point that Mantle "ran as fast as any man I ever saw. He could run, throw, and hit. There's no telling how good he'd have been on two good legs."

He was more than good enough. A three-time Most Valuable Player (1956, 1957, 1962), a 16-time All-Star, the Mick hit .300 or more 10 times. He is eighth in career home runs. Playing in a dozen World Series, he set records for runs scored (42), home runs (18), runs batted in (40), and total bases (123).

"I'm sorry Dad really never saw me make it big," Mantle said, referring to his father, whose dream of making his son the best switch-hitter who ever lived did come true.

In 1974 Mickey Mantle was inducted into the Baseball Hall of Fame. Year after year there was the sight of him at Old-Timers' Games at Yankee Stadium. Then there was the report of his illness and the poignant statements he issued: "When I retired, I was probably an alcoholic but didn't know it. I would like to say to the kids out there . . . this is a role model— don't be like me. God gave me a body and the ability to play baseball and I just wasted it."

The death of Mickey Mantle on August 13, 1995, at age 63 from complications from liver cancer gave a certain pathos to what he had once said only half in jest:

"If I'da known I was going to live this long I'da taken better care of myself."

"Mickey," Mel Allen said, "was a country boy who came to the big city and became one of the greatest and most powerful switch-hitters who ever lived. He was the most exciting player since Ruth and DiMag. As Casey Stengel said, he hit balls over buildings."

"Mickey Mantle," George Steinbrenner said, "is more than just a former Yankee ballplayer. He transcends any game and any team."

"When I first joined the Yankees as the organist," Eddie Layton recalled, "I got to know Mickey Mantle very well. He would ask me to play 'Over the Rainbow.' It's my favorite song, but I told him but I can't play it at Yankee Stadium—it's a ballad and I don't play ballads here. I never did play it until the day after he passed away. That was my opening number. It brought tears to everyone that day."

That day Bob Sheppard announced: "Today is a sad moment. We have lost one of our own, one of the greatest baseball players of all time, Mickey Mantle." Then Sheppard, whose first game as Yankee public address announcer was Mantle's first game, asked for a moment of silence.

Yankee players wearing black armbands, some with Number 7 on their caps, watched along with the throng at the Stadium as Diamond Vision moved time along from black and white to color and brought back the Mick

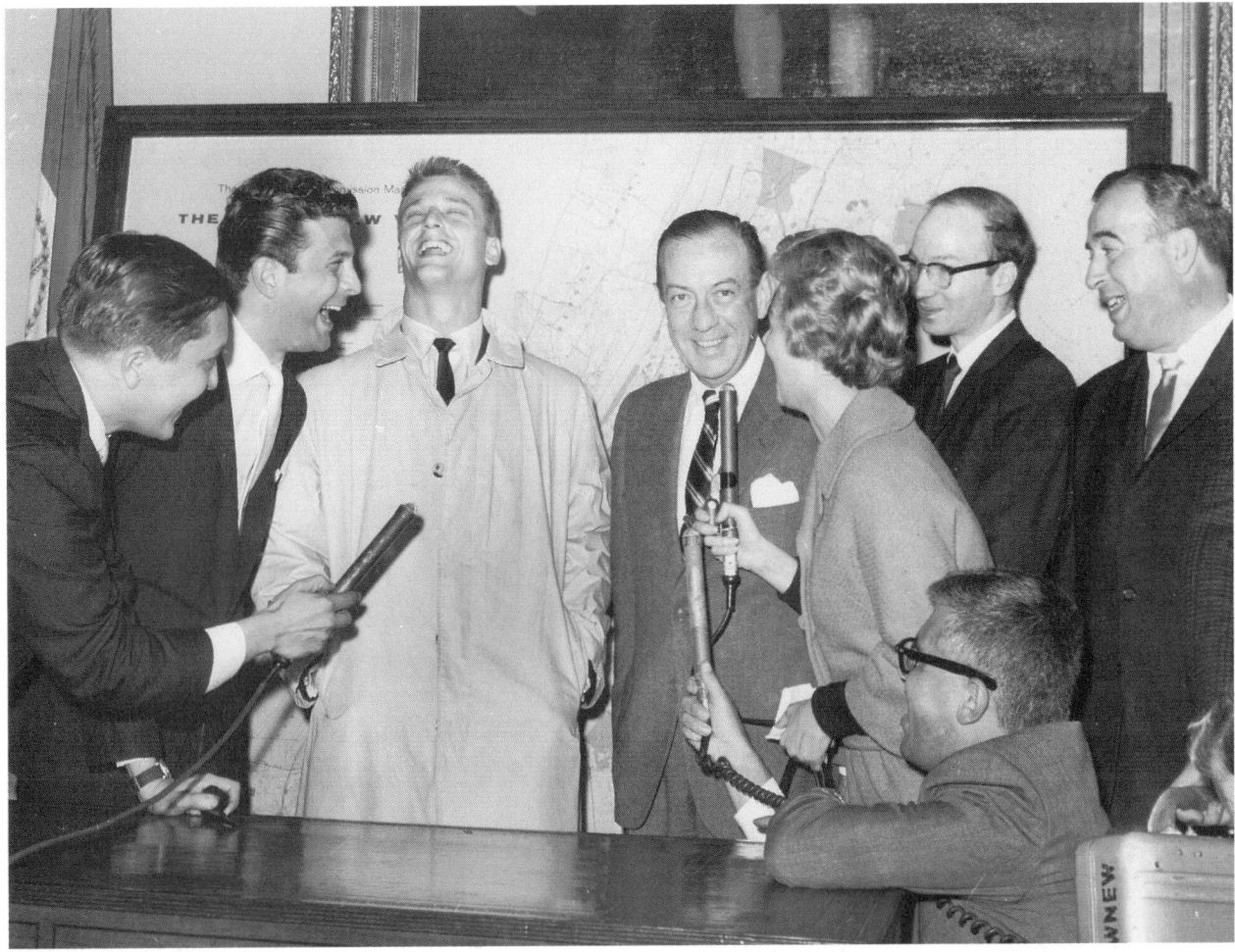

in all his youthful vigor wearing Number 6, then 7, hitting home runs left-handed and right-handed.

Casey Stengel once said of Mantle, "He was fairly amazin' in several respects."

That he was.

Maris genuinely disliked the constant media attention during the 1961 season, but enjoys a laugh here with New York Mayor Robert Wagner after the record was broken.

ROGER MARIS

"Roger Maris was just a quiet down-to-earth guy who didn't like fanfare and was wonderful with his teammates," Phil Linz recalled. "We all respected him as a player. He was a person who wanted to win above all else, above his individual statistics. He treated us like he had known us all his life. The public perception was that he was cold, but he didn't have an enemy on the team."

In his seven seasons as a Yankee, Roger Maris had a roller-coaster ride of success and frustration, of accomplishment and anger. Much maligned and misunderstood, the antihero Maris nevertheless has a special place in the history of the franchise.

In his very first game after coming to the Yankees from Kansas City in December 1959 in a multiple-player trade, Maris went 4–4: 2 home runs, a

Roger Maris watches his record-breaking 61st home run of the 1961 season. Maris hit it off of Tracy Stallard and the Yanks won the game, 1-0.

double, and a single. He wound up the season with 39 home runs—just one fewer than Mickey Mantle, who led the league. Maris topped all American League batters in slugging percentage and won the MVP award.

But the best and worst of times for the 26-year-old North Dakota-born Maris came in 1961, the year he hammered 61 home runs to break Babe Ruth's single-season record. The media circus and the controversy over the asterisk appended to the 61 home runs because they came in a season of 162 games turned the reticent superstar into a sometimes surly figure.

But lost in all the hype, hoopla, and histrionics in 1961 was the fact that Maris was a fine all-around baseball player. In addition to the record 61 home runs, he drove in 142 runs and scored 132 runs—leading the American League in those departments. One of the best defensive right fielders in Yankee history, Maris had an excellent arm and a hustling style. Both were showcased over and over again as he snared drives headed for the right-field seats that would have been home runs. That 1961 season Maris won a second straight Most Valuable Player award for his all-around value to the Yankees.

World Series time underscored all the things Roger Maris could do on a baseball field to help his team win. In 1960, in game one he homered in his first World Series at bat. In 1961, he homered in the ninth inning of game three to give the Yankees a win over the Reds. In game seven in 1962, on a rain-soaked field, his hustling play on a Willie Mays double and a strong throw kept Matty Alou on third base and ensured a Yankee 1–0 win over the Giants.

Some fans did not have much respect for him. But in 1962, in a 12-inning game he drew four intentional walks—it was just one of the ways other teams showed their respect for what he could do. For the third straight year Maris had 30-plus homers and 100 RBIs. By any standard it was another highly productive season. But it wasn't viewed that way by those who never forgave him for breaking the Babe's home run record. One wire service called Maris "the Flop of the Year," noting he had only hit 33 home runs.

He was the "Flop of the Year" again in 1963. But there were extenuating circumstances. A hand injury reduced his playing time to 90 games. Maris hit but 23 home runs. More of the cheers turned to boos. In 1964 he rebounded a bit, boosting his homer total to 26. But 1965 was a total loss. Racked by injuries, he played in just 46 games. In 1966 both Maris and the Yankees hit rock bottom. The Bronx Bombers crashed to last place. Maris played in 119 games, hit just 13 home runs, and batted a puny .233.

A fallen idol, Maris spent those last years with the Yankees being booed by fans, criticized by the media. "Every day I went to Yankee Stadium," he recalled, "as well as on the road people were on my back. The last six years in the American League were mental hell for me. I was drained of all my desire to play baseball."

In December 1966, Maris was traded to St. Louis in the other league. The feeling was that he was washed up. The feeling was wrong. He helped power the Cardinals to pennants in 1967 and 1968.

In retirement, Roger Maris returned to Yankee Stadium in 1978 for an Old-Timers' Game. He was surprised to be greeted with much warmth by the fans. "It's like obituaries," the snake-bitten Maris remarked. "When you die, they give you good reviews."

Death from lymph cancer came to Maris on December 14, 1985. A few months before, he had reflected on his life and career: "I always came across as being bitter," mused the man who ranks ninth in home runs on the Yankees all-time list. "People were reluctant to give me any credit. I thought hitting 61 home runs was something. But everyone shied off. Why, I don't know. Maybe I wasn't the chosen one, but I was the one who got the record. It would have been a helluva lot more fun if I never hit those home runs. All it brought me was headaches."

DON MATTINGLY

After 13 years and 1,785 regular-season games, 34-year-old Don Mattingly, perhaps the best of the Yankees never to appear in postseason play, finally made it in 1995. It ended a long drought for "Donnie Baseball" and also for the Yankees. Since 1981 they had been absent from postseason play.

"It's a great feeling," Mattingly said. "It's been 13 years for me and that's a long time. I said over the years that I was going to get there and I never gave up hope."

The Yankees were defeated by Seattle in a spirited postseason clash. A few weeks later Mattingly retired.

More than just one of the top stars of his time, Mattingly was a throwback to the Yankees of the past. The image of him is stamped on the franchise— the trademark lampblack always under the eyes, his cap settled low on his

Mattingly finally made the post-season in 1995, his last with the Yanks. Unfortunately, chronic back problems forced him out of baseball in 1996, the year New York captured their first World Series title in 18 years.

head with the bill pulled down, the full mustache, the professionalism in his play and demeanor. Blending power, situational hitting, and superb fielding, Mattingly had a steadiness and a sturdiness that set him apart from some of the gaudier types that came and went in his time with the Bronx Bombers.

Donald Arthur Mattingly, a skinny-necked 19-year-old from Evansville, Indiana, was a Yankee 19th-round selection in the June 1979 free-agent draft. He was an unprepossessing fellow. "Honestly," Mattingly said, "at one time I thought Babe Ruth was a cartoon character. I really did. I wasn't born until 1961 and I grew up in Indiana."

Shuttling from Columbus to New York in 1982 and 1983, playing a fringe role on the Yankees, a sometime first baseman, a sometime outfielder, Mattingly got his big break in 1984 when new manager Yogi Berra decided to play him full time at first base.

Day after day throughout that 1984 season Mattingly and Dave Winfield battled for the American League batting title. It was reminiscent of Roger Maris and Mickey Mantle competing for the home run title in 1961. On September 30, the final day of the season, Mattingly went 4–5 and wound up with a .343 average and the batting crown. The first Yankee to win the title since Mantle in 1956, Mattingly was also the first left-handed-hitting Yankee to bat over .340 since Lou Gehrig in 1937. His league-leading 207 hits were the most by a Yankee in 22 years.

From 1984 to 1989, Mattingly was perhaps the best player in all of baseball. Every one of those years he batted .300 or more, collected 186 hits or more, and except for 1988, drove in 100 or more runs. There were also five straight Gold Gloves.

Hitting third in the Yankee batting order in 1985, Mattingly hammered out 35 home runs and 145 RBIs. Not since Joe DiMaggio in 1948 had a Yankee driven in as many in a season. Mattingly won the American League Most Valuable Player award.

The Yankees finished in second place in 1986 when some key players had subpar seasons. For Mattingly, however, it was a career year. His .352 average was second best in the AL. He led all batters with a .573 slugging percentage and 388 total bases. His 238 hits were the most ever for a Yankee. The classy first baseman hit 31 home runs and led the majors with 53 doubles, eclipsing Gehrig on the all-time Yankee list. In the MVP voting, Mattingly finished second to Roger Clemens.

For his accomplishments in July of 1987, Mattingly could have been called "Mr. July." Homering in eight straight games from July 8 to July 18, Mattingly tied the record set in 1956 by Dale Long. Then on July 20, he made 22 putouts to tie the record for first baseman in a nine-inning game. For good measure, Mattingly also slammed a record six grand-slam home runs.

Back problems reduced the quiet star's productivity in the 1990s, but day in and day out, he was a constant in the Yankee lineup. And day in and day out the awards and records kept piling up. On February 28, 1991, Mattingly was named the tenth captain in franchise history. In 1994, he won his ninth Gold Glove award and established a league record by leading all first basemen in fielding for the seventh time. From 1990 to 1994, he ranked third in the American league as the toughest player to strike out.

When he was out there in Yankee pinstripes, there were some who took Mattingly for granted. But a look at the record shows that at the very least, "Donnie Baseball" was the most skilled of all the Yankees who had never played in a World Series.

"There is a silent torch that we all carried for Donnie," Buck Showalter said.

There are many who share that sentiment.

Yankee catcher Thurman Munson bears down on Milwaukee Brewer George Scott in 1976. Munson was the first Yankee player to be named captain since the legendary Lou Gehrig.

THURMAN MUNSON

Scouted at Kent State University, where he was an All-American, by former Yankee Gene Woodling, a major leaguer after just 99 minor league games, Thurman Munson batted .302 and won the American League Rookie of the Year award in 1970. He was another in the Yankee line of great catchers—Bill Dickey, Yogi Berra, Elston Howard. And like them, the rugged Munson led by doing.

To the media and the public Munson projected a gruff exterior. "He may have been gruff to outsiders," recalled Larry Hisle, who played on high-school All-Star teams together with Munson and against him in the

American League, "but those of us who knew him well knew that he was a caring, friendly, and loyal person."

Munson's Yankee teammates knew him as a driven professional whose hustling and aggressive style made everyone around him better. Possessing one of the quickest releases of any catcher in history, Munson was a great handler of pitchers, quick as a cat on bunts, solid as a wall in blocking the plate.

He took great pride in his role a Yankee catcher. "Look, I like hitting fourth," Munson said, "and I like the good batting average. But what I do every day behind the plate is a lot more important because it touches so many people and so many more aspects of the game."

Munson played in 1,423 games as a Yankee, collected 1,558 hits, and won three Gold Glove awards. His peak seasons were 1975 to 1977. In that span of time, Munson drove in over 100 runs and batted over .300 each year.

On April 17, 1976, Munson became the fifth captain in Yankee history, the first one since Lou Gehrig. That 1976 season was the best of his career. He won the Most Valuable Player award, batting .302, driving in 105 runs. In the 1976 World Series, he batted .529, and his six straight hits tied a record. Munson hit for a .320 average in the 1977 and 1978 World Series, making his Fall Classic lifetime average .373—third best in history. His overall post-season batting average is a glittering .357.

An avid flying enthusiast, on August 2, 1979, Munson was practicing take-offs and landings flying a new twin-engine Cessna jet near his home in Canton, Ohio, when his plane hit a tree and crashed. The Yankee catcher could not escape the burning plane.

On September 20, 1980, a bronze plaque honoring Thurman Munson was dedicated at Yankee Stadium. His uniform Number 15 was retired and a bronze plaque was placed in Yankee Stadium Memorial Park. His locker in the Yankees clubhouse remains permanently empty.

The description that was his epitaph reads: "I'm a little too belligerent. I cuss and swear at people. I yell at umpires and maybe I'm a little too tough at home sometimes. I don't sign as many autographs as I should and I haven't always been very good with the writers."

Like everyone else, Thurman Munson had his flaws, but on the baseball diamond he was a glittering presence who died much too soon.

ALLIE REYNOLDS

His one-quarter Creek Indian ancestry was one reason Allie Reynolds was called "Superchief." Another was the role he played as a Yankee powerhouse pitcher. Reynolds was acquired by the Yankees from Cleveland for Joe Gordon in 1946. In eight Yankee seasons the hard-throwing right-hander compiled a 131–60 record and 41 saves and was a five-time All-Star.

In 1951, he hurled two no-hitters, becoming the first American League pitcher to accomplish that feat. The first no-hitter was a taut 1–0 triumph over his old Cleveland team and former roommate Bob Feller on July 12. For five innings neither team was able to get a hit. A Gene Woodling home run in the seventh was the only run Reynolds needed. Facing only 29 batters, Reynolds

won his 10th game, hurled his 5th shutout of the year, and notched his 4th straight victory against the Tribe.

The second no-hitter was an 8–0 win against Boston on September 28 at Yankee Stadium before 40,000. But there was a moment of drama and uncertainty in the ninth inning that involved Ted Williams, who was winding up his 10th straight .300 season.

"I was very much aware of the no-hitter and the ninth inning," Reynolds recalled, "and all I had to get out was Ted Williams. Most times I tried to walk the damn guy. In my opinion it was just stupid to let an outstanding hitter like him beat you."

On that day Reynolds made up his mind to pitch to Williams. The first pitch was a fastball—strike one. The second pitch was again a fastball. Williams uncoiled. The ball was fouled into the air behind home plate. Berra was poised under it, but at the last moment the ball darted off his glove. He collided with Reynolds, who helped Yogi to his feet, saying, "Don't worry Yogi, we'll get him next time."

An annoyed Williams snapped at Berra: "You blew it. You son of a bitches put me in a hell of a spot. Now I've got to bear down even harder even though the game is decided and your man has a no-hitter going."

Allie Reynolds fired two no-hit games in 1951, and compiled a 131-50 record in his eight-year stint with the Yankees.

Phil Rizzuto's favorite offensive weapon was the bunt down the third base line. Here he drops one down during the 1950 World Series against the Philadelphia Phillies.

Yogi called for the same pitch. Reynolds reloaded. Williams swung. The ball was fouled off near the Yankee dugout. Yogi got that one. And the Yankees clinched their third straight pennant.

For his two no-hitters and route-going performances in 16 of his 17 wins, Reynolds was awarded the Hickock Belt as Professional Athlete of the Year in 1951. As an encore in 1952, the Superchief posted a 20–8 mark, notched six saves, and was the ERA and shutout leader. He wound up second in the Most Valuable Player award voting.

A money pitcher, best under pressure, Reynolds thrived in World Series competition, where he won seven of nine decisions and had four saves. One of his wins was a 1–0, two-hit performance against the Dodgers and Don Newcombe in 1949. Another was a 2–1, 10-inning triumph over Robin Roberts and the Phillies in 1950. The Yankee winning run was a Joe DiMaggio homer. "God bless DiMag," Reynolds told reporters. "If he hadn't hit it, I'd still be pitching."

If he hadn't been injured, Reynolds would have had a longer career. Nevertheless, the man from Bethany, Oklahoma, ranks 4th in winning percentage, 5th in shutouts, 8th in strikeouts, 9th in wins, 15th in complete games, and 20th in ERA among all those who ever pitched for the Bronx Bombers. Allie Pierce Reynolds was one of the great pitchers in Yankee history.

PHIL RIZZUTO

Philip Francis Rizzuto was born on September 25, 1917, in Brooklyn, the son of a streetcar conductor. In his growing-up years he rooted for the Dodgers. "But even though I was a Dodger fan," Rizzuto pointed out, "my uncle Mike always took me to Yankee Stadium. Babe Ruth was my idol."

As the story goes, Rizzuto tried out with the Dodgers and was dismissed by manager Casey Stengel: "Kid, you're too small. You ought to go out and shine shoes." Undaunted, the 5-6 Rizzuto showed up at a Yankee tryout in 1937. He was given a ham sandwich, a glass of milk, and a chance to show his stuff.

General Manager Ed Barrow was impressed with the little guy and signed him to a minor league contract at Bassett, Virginia, at $75 a month. "My dad pinned a $20 bill to my undershirt," Rizzuto said. "He read there were thieves on the train. He said he'd let me try it and if I didn't make it right away I would have to go out and work."

Coming off a .347 average at Kansas City and a Minor League Player of the Year award, Rizzuto reported to the Yankees in 1941. Frank Crosetti was an institution at shortstop and a very popular Yankee. Rizzuto had to endure a lot of snubs and unkind words.

"I was coming to take Crosetti's job," the Scooter said. "I was having trouble getting into the batter's cage." But Joe DiMaggio interceded, telling the other Yankees to give the kid a break and let him handle the bat.

Bat handling was just one of the specialties of Phil Rizzuto. From 1949 to 1952 he led the majors in sacrifice hits—no one ever did better. On September 17, 1951, a suicide squeeze in the ninth inning that scored Joe DiMaggio and beat Cleveland, 2–1, put the Yankees in first place to stay for the season and epitomized Rizzuto's bunting ability. No less an authority than Ty Cobb called Rizzuto "one of the best bunters of all time." His lifetime average was .273. But what would it have been had Rizzuto played for himself and not the team—using his at bats to move runners along.

As a fielder he was something to behold. Three times Rizzuto led the American League in double plays and total chances per game. Twice he was the league leader in fielding and putouts, once in assists. "My best pitch," former Yankee star hurler Vic Raschi used to say, "is anything the batter grounds, lines, or pops in the direction of Rizzuto."

"What about that shortstop, Rizzuto?" asked the same Stengel who had said the Scooter was too small when he tried out for the Dodgers. "He's got nothing but daughters but throws out the left-handed hitters in the double play. He's the greatest shortstop I have ever seen. Honus Wagner was a better hitter, but I've seen this kid make plays Wagner never did."

Rizzuto's best seasons were 1949 and 1950. Previously, he had batted down in the order. In 1949, Number 10 became the leadoff batter. He scored 110 runs, walked 72 times, batted .275, and was second to Ted Williams in the Most Valuable Player award balloting. In 1950, Rizzuto put together a career year: a .324 average (sixth), 125 runs (second), 36 doubles (third), and almost a hundred walks. Those numbers earned him the MVP award.

Loyalty, longevity, love for the game—all of these were part of the Phil Rizzuto package, as were a host of superstitions, such as fear of insects, never stepping on the baseline, and always stepping out of bed on the same side. He was the star shortstop on 10 Yankee pennant winners and 8 World Champions from 1941 to 1956, with three years out for military service. He is in the Yankee top-20 list for doubles, triples, stolen bases, games, at bats, and runs scored.

And through the years, despite always being snubbed for admission to the Baseball Hall of Fame, Rizzuto kept being honored by the Yankees. "I think I led the league in days," he quipped. "I don't know how many I've had, but Billy Martin kept track. He always told me, 'If Steinbrenner knew how many days you had . . . . But when they retired my number at my day in 1985, Tom Seaver upstaged me by winning his 300th game and then the cow they gave me stepped on my foot."

On February 25, 1994, Phil Rizzuto, after 28 years of eligibility, was finally elected to the Baseball Hall of Fame. Scooter cherished the moment: "I said 'Holy Cow' and almost fell to the floor. I never gave up about the Hall of Fame as long as I was eligible and still breathing."

Casey Stengel, who called Phil Rizzuto "my little fella," would have been proud.

RED RUFFING

Red Ruffing was the first pitching coach of the New York Mets in 1962, but his real claim to fame is as one of the great pitchers in Yankee history. In his prime in the 1930s, he ranked right there with Dizzy Dean as the best right-handed pitcher in baseball.

At age 15 Ruffing played for the Nokomis, Illinois, mining company team managed by his father. At 19, he joined the Red Sox, where he posted

Red Ruffing enters the locker-room after pitching the Yankees to their third straight World Series championship in 1938.

a 39–96 record with some sorry teams. In 1930, Ruffing, who had batted .300-plus in 1928 and 1929, was traded to the Yankees. It was a kind of a mirror image of Babe Ruth coming over from the Sox—another good-hitting pitcher. But the Yankees got the big right-hander for his arm even though they made use of his bat.

In his last year with Boston, Ruffing was a 22-game loser. In his first year with the Yankees, the powerfully built hurler posted a 15–5 mark and was the top pitcher on the team. Through the 1930s, Ruffing had just one losing season for the Yankees. He led the league in strikeouts in 1932, and in shutouts in 1938 and 1939. His four straight 20-win seasons were contemporaneous with four Yankee championships. Usually tabbed to open the World Series for the Yankees, Ruffing posted a 7–2 record in Fall Classic competition.

Bill Dickey, who was behind the plate handling Ruffing all those years, said of him, "If I were asked to choose the best pitcher I've ever caught, I would have to say Ruffing."

A true Yankee pitching immortal, Ruffing is first in complete games (261), second in innings pitched and wins (231) behind Whitey Ford, third in strikeouts and shutouts, and ninth in winning percentage.

One of the great-hitting pitchers, Ruffing had a career average of .269. His 520 hits rank him third best in history for a pitcher. Eight times he batted over .300, including a .364 mark in 1930 (40–110), the second-best single-season average for a pitcher.

Charles Herbert "Red" Ruffing accomplished all of this despite almost constant pain from the loss in a mining accident of four toes on his left foot. In 1967, the determined and durable right-hander was admitted to the Baseball Hall of Fame in his 15th and final year of eligibility.

BABE RUTH

They called him the "Bambino," "Sultan of Swat," "Wizard of Whack," "Goliath of Grand Slams," "Behemoth of Biff," "Prince of Pounders." They called him "Caliph of Clout," "Maharajah of Mash," "Wazir of Wham," "Rajah of Rap," "Infant Swatagy." The opposition called him "Baboon," "Monkey," "Big Monk." His teammates called him the "Big Fellow," "Big Guy," and "Jidge."

By any name Babe Ruth was simply the most compelling and exciting presence baseball had ever seen. Millions of fans, in his phrase, "came out in groves" to see him perform and read with joy the newspaper stories that began with the headline: "BAM HITS ONE."

George Herman Ruth was born in Baltimore in 1895. When he was seven years old, he was placed in St. Mary's Industrial School for Boys, an institution that treated "incorrigible behavior." It was there that Ruth learned how to play baseball. He left St. Mary's at 16 and joined the Baltimore Orioles owned by Jack Dunn. Players on the team called him "Dunn's Babe."

In 1914, the Red Sox purchased "the Babe." The following year he won 18 games, then 23 games in 1916. Ruth posted 24 victories in 1917 with Boston and also batted .325 in 123 at bats. By 1918, he was mainly an outfielder. Batting 317 times, he led the league with 11 home runs; Ruth also pitched in 20 games, posting a 13–7 record. In 1919, Ruth batted .322 and set a new major league record for home runs in a season—29. It was a mark many thought might last forever.

Babe Ruth had accomplished a great deal as a member of the Boston Red Sox. But no one could have predicted what he would achieve with the New York Yankees. Hype, hoopla, and histrionics ushered in his time with his new team. A godsend to the Yankee owners, Ruth was a bonanza of constant copy and headlines for the New York press. More writers than ever before were assigned to cover the team in spring training in 1920. Newspaper headlines blared: "YANKEES TRAINING ON SCOTCH."

The biggest consumer among the rollicking Yankees was the Babe. There were many mornings when he would quaff a pint of scotch or bourbon and ginger ale, a big steak, french-fried potatoes, four fried eggs, many slices of toast, and a pot of coffee. And that was just breakfast.

On May 1, 1920, the Babe hit his first home run as a Yankee. The ball went clear out of the Polo Grounds. Three times in his career he accomplished that powerful feat. Day after day through that 1920 season the 6-2, 215-pound Ruth swung his 44-ounce bat, a bat bigger than anyone else's, and when he swung for the home run, the swing itself was pure drama.

Most players of his time had a level, parallel swing. Ruth seemed to uppercut the ball, swinging in an upward arc of controlled aggression. The

A young, slim Babe Ruth takes his stance early on in his career. Though Ruth will always be remembered for his incredible power at the plate, he was also one of the best left-handed pitchers in the game. Because he was so dangerous with a bat in his hands, his pitching career was cut short.

swing was like that of Shoeless Joe Jackson, but with more heft and power behind it. When the ball was pitched, the Babe would inhale deeply on his backswing, hold his breath and then exhale only after swinging at the ball or letting it go by.

On July 15, the barrel-chested Babe tied his 1919 record of 29 home runs. He was doing a lot of swinging on the field and a lot of swinging off it, too. One of his favorite sports was tooting about town with the top down on his $6,700, maroon twin-six Packard roadster with the GHR monogram embossed on the driver's-side door. His teammates dubbed it "the ghost of Riverside Drive."

"On Sunday," Waite Hoyt recalled, "often after all night out, the Babe would haul a few of us protesting Protestants to Mass with him. When the collection came, he'd plunk down 50 bucks and figure he'd paid up for his sins for the week."

"I don't room with Babe Ruth," Ping Bodie, his official roommate, said, "I room with his suitcase." Ruth's wife, Helen, could have uttered the same comment. For even though the pair had an official New York City residence at the Ansonia Hotel on Broadway those first few years in New York, George Herman Ruth was out, it seemed, more times than he was in.

But on the baseball field it was the reverse. To opposing pitchers it seemed the Bambino was rarely out. "He liked the night life," recalled teammate Roger Peckinpaugh, "but he was always at the park early in time for batting practice and in good shape to play."

On September 29, 1920, Ruth hit his 54th home run, exceeding all team totals except that of the Phillies. He batted .376, third in the league, and was number one in RBIs (137) and runs scored (158). Of his 172 hits, 99 were for extra bases. He led the league with 148 walks, an average of more than one a game. He was on base 379 times in 1920 and piled up 457 total bases, an all-time record. His slugging percentage was an astonishing .847, still an unbroken record. No other player ever cracked the .800 slugging barrier. The Babe did it twice, slugging at an .846 pace in 1921, and he whacked away in 1927 at a .772 mark, third highest in history.

With Ruth, the 1920 Yankees finished only three games out of first place and became the first team to draw one million fans at home, double the attendance of any other major league team, more than 360,000 better than their Polo Grounds landlord, the New York Giants. The actual record attendance figure of 1,289,422 stood until 1946.

Ruppert and Huston were elated. They had one insurance policy on the whole team, and another $150,000 policy just for Ruth, one they hoped they never needed to collect.

In 1921, the Ruths adopted an infant named Dorothy. It was felt the new addition would benefit the marriage. Mother and daughter spent a lot of time together in the Ruth home close by Boston. The Babe resided where his spirit and spirits moved him. The toast of New York City in his second season as a Yankee, Babe Ruth became the first player to homer into the center-field bleachers at the Polo Grounds. He also set a major league home run record for the third straight year, slashing 59. He drove in 171 runs, rapped out 44 doubles, and set major league records that 1921 season for most total bases (457) and runs scored (177). His slugging percentage was a blistering .846. One would have thought that after a season like that Ruth would have had his fill of baseball. But his appetite for the sport and many other things was insatiable.

With the season over, desirous of picking up some extra cash, Ruth went on a barnstorming tour against the orders of Baseball Commissioner Landis, who suspended him, Bob Meusel, and Bill Piercy for "mutinous behavior." The suspension lasted 39 days into the 1922 season. Hopping mad when he finally got his chance to play on May 20, Ruth couldn't or wouldn't hide his feelings. Nonstop cursing was the least of his bad-boy behavior that season. He threw dirt in an umpire's face, went after a fan in the stands who was heckling him, climbed atop the dugout roof challenging one and all to a fight. In total, he was suspended five times during the 1922 season. He was also publicly dumped on.

American League president Ban Johnson snapped: "A man of your stamp bodes no good in the profession. The time has arrived when you should allow some intelligence to creep into a mind that has plainly been warped."

The Sporting News labeled Ruth the "Exploded Phenomenon" and commented: "The baseball public is on to his real worth as a batsmen and in future, let us hope, he will attract just ordinary attention." In all, 1922 was not the best of years for the Babe, who had the briefest tenure in history as Yankee captain that season—six days. But he still managed to hit .315 and rap out 35 home runs in just 110 games.

Ruth's Yankee salary was $20,000 in 1920, $30,000 in 1921. He signed a five-year deal in 1922 for $52,000 a season. It was supposed to be a round $50,000 a year, but the Babe told Ruppert: "It would be nice to make a grand a week."

About that time Ruth started to make much more than a grand a week with Christy Walsh on the scene as his agent, adviser, and confidant. All manner of endorsements, exhibitions, and events were staged. The Babe became a walking billboard of Christmas cards, books, magazine covers, vaudeville appearances, and ghosted articles and columns. He more than doubled his annual salary with all the goodies garnered by Walsh, who even set up a forced saving annuity fund so the Babe would have something for a rainy day. It was all a very far cry from the Boston days and the "Babe Ruth Cigar" that sold for five cents and had his image on each wrapper.

Walsh had one kind of influence on Ruth. Jimmy Walker, then a New York State senator, had another. He convinced the out-of-control superstar to give up some of his rebellious and rollicking ways and become a true role model for the youth of America. The Babe heeded Walker's advice, spent most of the off-season after the 1922 campaign chopping wood and staying with his wife and child at his Sudbury, Massachusetts, 190-acre farm, which he called Home Plate.

By Opening Day of 1923 he was 20 pounds lighter, more muscular, ready for baseball in the brand-new Yankee Stadium. But American League pitchers were not ready for him. Ruth recorded the highest season average of his career (.393), stroked 205 hits, slugged 41 home runs, drove in 131 runs, and for good measure stole 17 bases. He led the league in RBIs, slugging percentage, total bases, runs scored, and of course, home runs.

Born, hell, Babe Ruth wasn't born. He fell from a tree.
—Joe Dugan

"All I tell 'em is I pick a good one and sock it," he said. "I get back to the dugout and they ask me what it was I hit and I tell 'em I don't know except it looked good."

He was so intimidating at the plate that he drew an all-time record 170 walks. Three times that year Ruth batted right-handed to dissuade pitchers from walking him. Twice he was walked. A third time he took a pitch and then went back to hitting left-handed and smashed a home run. His efforts in 1923 powered the Yankees to their third straight pennant—16 games ahead of the runner-up Tigers. He truly earned the Most Valuable Player award. There has always been much debate over what season was the Babe's best. His personal choice was 1923, a season he topped off by batting .368 in the World Series and slugging three home runs.

But 1924 was just as good in many ways. The sacks of mail that came to Yankee Stadium addressed to the Babe showed just how good it was. Ruth hardly had time for the blizzard of messages of all kinds. "Open these for me, will ya, kid," was a familiar refrain of his as he walked around the clubhouse with a stack of mail in his hands. "Keep the ones with checks and the ones from the broads—throw out the others."

That 1924 season was Ruth's second straight season of 200 or more hits. He led all batters in walks, runs scored, slugging percentage, and total bases. He was the league leader in home runs (46). He batted .378 and became the first Yankee to win a batting title. It was also a season he came the closest in his career to winning the Triple Crown. But his 121 RBIs placed him second in that category.

Going into spring training in 1925, the Babe was a 30-year-old, moonfaced, potbellied, spindly legged veteran. But he still had that wonder bat and paced all Yankee batters in the spring with a .449 average. And then something turned on him as the Yankees headed north. He spent seven weeks in St. Vincent's Hospital in Manhattan. They called it "the bellyache heard round the world." Speculation about what was wrong ranged from too many hot dogs to the strong suspicion that he had contracted some kind of venereal disease.

Finally donning his Yankee uniform on June 1, 1925, Ruth played six innings until exhaustion forced him out of the game. June 1 was also game one of Lou Gehrig's 2,130-game streak.

By the start of August, Ruth was barely hitting his weight. But that was the least of his troubles. Violating curfews, carousing, showing up late for meetings when he showed up at all—the Babe had a serious attitude problem.

Finally, all the accumulated Ruthian excesses and excuses got to Huggins. On August 29, he suspended the Babe for showing up late and fined him $5,000. An enraged Ruth roared that he would not play another game for the Yankees as long as Huggins was manager. But Ruppert, who said "Ruth has the mentality of a boy of fifteen," supported Huggins and prevailed on the Babe to publicly apologize for his actions. It wasn't until September 7 that the chastened Ruth finally returned to the Yankees. The season was a disaster for him and the team. It underscored the slogan "As Ruth goes, so do the Yankees."

The Yankees finished in seventh place, almost 30 games off the pace. Playing in fewer than 100 games, the Babe hit 25 home runs and batted

.290. Those were good enough statistics for a mere mortal but not for George Herman Ruth. Speculation was rampant that he was washed up.

Anyone seeing Babe Ruth around Christmas of 1925 would have agreed with the speculation. He was 254 pounds of dissipated flab. Then he threw himself into a two-month training regimen at Artie McGovern's gym at 42nd Street and Madison Avenue. McGovern said: "He was as near to being a total loss as anyone I ever had under my care." The word "near" was the key word. For when spring training of 1926 arrived, McGovern had transformed the blubbery Babe into a robust and trim 212-pound athlete.

Flexing his new muscle tone, the Sultan of Swat pounded away at American League pitching throughout the '26 season. He blasted 47 home runs—more than five percent of the major league total that season. He drove in 145 runs. He scored 139 runs. In all, he led the league in 7 of 12 offensive categories. And he even took time out to become the first player to catch a ball dropped from an airplane.

There were those who claimed Ruth engaged in that stunt because there were many photographers present. They were probably correct. A camera was a prod for him to do anything—pet a snake, cuddle a chimp,

Having Gehrig follow Ruth in the line-up seemed almost unfair to opposing pitchers.

151

Ruth set numerous records on the field, but he also opened a lot of eyes off the field as well. Ruth had a large appetite for the high life and was a legend in his own way out on the town.

sit on a cow, do pullups, do pushups, put on any kind of hat, don any kind of uniform.

Politicians, well aware of how often Babe Ruth's image or news of him found its way into newspapers and magazines, never passed on the chance to get close to him. Some paid the price. One of them was President Calvin Coolidge. He was introduced to Ruth on a very warm day in Washington. "Hot as hell, ain't it, prez?" was the Babe's very unpolitic greeting.

The one who was really hot was George Herman Ruth. Along with his big cigar and high-top stockings, his name and face became known to more people in the United States than those of any other player in baseball. He was the most famous, most ballyhooed personality of his time. Even famed playwright George Bernard Shaw was curious. "Who is this Baby Ruth?" he asked on a visit to the United States. "And what does she do?"

People stood in the rain for hours waiting to see the moonfaced mountain of a man arrive by train in the little towns. Still others jumped on his taxi, ogled him through a window as he ate in a restaurant, trailed after him on his way to and from ballparks all over America. Many of them were kids. He was like a Pied Piper for children.

As the story goes, he paid a hospital visit to an 11-year-old boy who had an incurable disease. The Babe allegedly promised: "I'll knock a homer for you in Wednesday's game." True to his vow, Ruth hit the homer. The boy, Johnny Sylvester, improved and lived to the age of 74.

The Roaring Twenties was Babe Ruth's time; he loved every single moment of it, playing to the roar of the crowd, the nobodies and the notables alike. Two celebrities who had a special fondness for the Bambino were dancer Bill "Bojangles" Robinson and movie star Tom Mix. Both had choice seats behind the Yankee dugout where they had up close and personal viewing perches of the dramatics of Babe Ruth. Mix had a lot of fun waving his big cowboy hat and acting as chief cheerleader for the Sultan of Swat. Robinson showed his appreciation for a Ruth home run by tap-dancing atop the Yankee dugout as the Babe circled the bases.

Very few players ever had back-to-back years comparable to what Ruth accomplished in 1927–28. As the chief assassin of Murderer's Row, the Babe blasted 60 homers in 1927, setting a new record for the fourth time in nine years. The Yankees as a team tallied 158 home runs. Philadelphia, the second top home run-hitting team, had 56—four fewer than Ruth. His bat over those two seasons stung pitchers for 306 RBIs and 114 home runs. It was no wonder he felt like a colossus astride baseball.

His personal life was a far different matter. His marriage for all intents and purposes had been finished for a few years, but for what he claimed were religious reasons he had not sought a divorce. Then on January 11, 1929, his wife Helen died in a fire in her Massachusetts home.

That cleared the way for Ruth to marry Claire Hodgson, a woman he had been with since 1923. The marriage ceremony took place at 6:00 A.M. on April 17 to avoid the crush of reporters and fans. The very next day Ruth homered into the left-field seats at Yankee Stadium off Red Ruffing, paused at second base and tipped his cap to the new bride. He always had that special flair for the dramatic.

In March of 1930 Ruth was told that his salary was higher than that of President Herbert Hoover. "Why not," the Babe smiled, "I had a better year." With new manager Bob Shawkey running things and leaving Ruth on his own, the Babe had another typical Ruthian year: a .359 average, a league-leading 49 home runs, 153 RBIs. He even pitched the final game of the 1930 season, going the distance and winning, 9–3.

"It's hell to get older," the 37-year-old Ruth moaned in 1931. "All ballplayers should quit when it starts to feel as if all the baselines run uphill." Yet, despite the economic woes of the Depression, which prompted his first pay cut, all the years of abusing his body catching up to him, a dramatic drop in playing time, George Herman Ruth, like Old Man River, was still rolling along. In 1931 he batted .373, his best average in eight seasons, and tied Lou Gehrig for the league lead in home runs with 46. It was Ruth's 12th and last home run title and was an exclamation point to his last hurrah as a great hitter.

Beset by more and more aches and pains, diminished athletic skills, and less playing time, Ruth's stats dropped off in 1932 in virtually every major offensive category from the season before. In 1933, Ruth's decline was echoed

Ruth revolutionized offensive baseball by turning on the ball and lifting it in the air for power. Great hitters of his time, such as Ty Cobb, merely slapped at the ball to hit singles and doubles. When Ruth swung the bat, he swung with all his might.

Ruth is shown here visiting New York's Hospital for Joint Diseases during Christmas of 1944. Spending most of his childhood away from his father, Ruth always had a soft spot for youngsters.

by his shrinking salary. He was paid $52,000—quite a cut from the $75,000 he had earned the year before. "Times are changing," Ruppert told him. Still, the Bambino was the highest-paid performer in the major leagues. That season he batted .301, and on October 1, he pitched the last game of the season as an attendance gimmick. His home run was the Yankee margin of victory in the 6–5 game. "I had such a sore arm after pitching nine innings that I had to eat with my right hand for a week."

In 1934, Babe Ruth began his 21st season in baseball, a figure out of time and often out of place. All his former Yankee cronies were gone. Only Earle Combs, Tony Lazzeri, and Lou Gehrig remained from the glory days. He didn't speak to Gehrig. Lazzeri rarely had anything to say. And Combs admitted, "I had only one real serious conversation with him in all the years."

The Babe's 1934 salary was cut to $35,000, but it was still the major league high. A highlight of that season was Ruth's 700th career home run. It was a mighty shot over the right-field wall at Navin Field that rolled down the street for a couple of hundred feet. His last game in pinstripes was September 30, 1934. Only a couple of thousand showed up at Yankee Stadium on that chilly day to see him. He finished with a .288 average and 22 home runs, his lowest totals as a Yankee. And then the force that led the Yankees to seven pennants, the man who changed the game of baseball forever, was gone over to Boston in the National League. And then it was all over.

Like a Niagara, Ruth's epic feats flood the record books: the 16 seasons of more than 20 home runs, the 13 seasons when he had more than 30, the 12 times he won the home run title, the 11 times he recorded 40 or more home runs in a season, the 4 times he slashed 50 or more home runs in a season, the all-time record 114 home runs in 1927–28, the all-time record 72 times he hit two or more home runs in a game, the two seasons he out-homered all the other American League teams, the 714 career home runs—most by a left-handed batter.

From 1926 to 1931 he averaged more than 50 homers a season. Babe Ruth recorded the most consecutive seasons with a .600 plus, .700 plus, .800 plus slugging percentage. His .690 lifetime slugging percentage is the highest in history. In all, he led the majors in slugging percentage 13 times—7 in a row. He ranks first in career walks with 2,056—about once every four at bats. Who knows how much more he would have accomplished as a hitter if opposing pitchers hadn't taken the bat out his hands rather than face him.

His lifetime batting average was .342. "I could have had a lifetime .600 average," Ruth said, "but I would have had to hit them singles. The people were paying to see me hit home runs." Oh, did he hit home runs—more often, further, more dramatically than any other player in baseball history.

As a pitcher he was special, too. In all, he posted a 5–0 record for the Yankees, bringing his lifetime won–lost record to 94–46 with a 2.28 ERA. He was 3–0 in the World Series, with an 0.87 ERA.

In 1936, the Babe became one of the five charter members of the Baseball Hall of Fame in Cooperstown. His speech was surprisingly self-effacing. "You know, for me this is just like an anniversary myself, because 25 years ago yesterday I pitched my first baseball game in Boston for the Boston Red Sox. So it seems like an anniversary for me, too, and I'm surely glad and it's a pleasure to come up here and be picked also in the Hall of Fame."

There was Babe Ruth Day at Yankee Stadium and every major league ballpark and in Japan on April 27, 1947, and the retirement of his uniform Number 3. A seriously ill, drawn shell of himself, Ruth told the 58,339: "Thank you very much, ladies and gentlemen. You know how bad my voice sounds. Well, it feels just as bad . . . .There's been so many lovely things said about me. I'm glad I had the opportunity to thank everybody. Thank you."

On August 16, 1948, Babe Ruth passed away, a cancer victim. He was 53 years old. For the next two days his body lay in state in the main entrance to Yankee Stadium. More than 100,000 came to say their final farewell. Three days later there were almost 7,000 at the funeral at St. Patrick's Cathedral. The pallbearers were Whitey Witt, Connie Mack, sportswriter Fred Lieb, Joe Dugan, and Waite Hoyt, who called Ruth "a sainted sinner."

Struggling under the weight of the casket on that warm August day, Dugan said: "I'd give a hundred bucks for an ice-cold beer."

"So would the Babe," said Hoyt.

On Opening Day 1949 the monument to his memory was unveiled at Yankee Stadium:

Thank you very much, ladies and gentlemen. You know how bad my voice sounds. Well it feels just as bad. You know, this baseball game of ours comes up from the youth. That means the boys. And after you're a boy and grow up to play ball, then you come to the boys you see representing clubs today in your national pastime. The only real game in the world, I think, is baseball. As a rule, people think that if you give boys a football or a baseball or somthing like that, they naturally become athletes right away. But you can't do that in baseball. You've got to start from way down, at the bottom, when the boys are six or seven years of age. You can't wait until they're 15 or 16. You've got to let it grow up with you, if you're the boy. And if you try hard enough, you're bound to come out on top, just as these boys here have come to the top now. There have been so many lovely things said about me today, that I'm glad to have had the opportunity to thank everybody. Thank you.
—Babe Ruth at Babe Ruth Day,
April 27, 1947

GEORGE HERMAN "BABE" RUTH
1895-1948
A GREAT BALL PLAYER
A GREAT MAN
A GREAT AMERICAN
ERECTED BY THE YANKEES
AND THE NEW YORK BASEBALL WRITERS
April 19, 1949

Perhaps the most apt words ever said about the Babe are these uttered by Lefty Gomez: "You just can't imagine the kind of guy he was without seeing him play. He was a circus, a play, a movie, all rolled into one. Kids adored him. Men idolized him. Women loved him. There was something about him, something with men like that who come along once in a while, that made him great."

"To Hell with Babe Ruth"

Anyone seeing the old-time World War II movies probably recalls excited Japanese troops in the Pacific screaming loudly at GIs, "To hell with Babe Ruth!" That taunting cry had its origin back in 1934, when the Babe toured Japan, even playing first base in Tokyo in the rain, a colorful orange parasol held over his shoulder. So popular was the Sultan of Swat that the Japanese took the "Do Not Disturb" sign off his hotel-room door and woke him up early asking for autographs. He never lost his temper; he always obliged his newfound fans. That was just one of the reasons the Japanese called him "Beibu Rusu."

So it was no wonder that years later, with the memory of the impact and persona of the Babe still strong, Japanese soldiers resorted to the cry, "To hell with Babe Ruth," a phrase they deemed the unkindest cut of all.

DAVE WINFIELD

Branch Rickey said that to be truly great a player had to be able to hit, hit with power, run, and throw. The man they called the "Mahatma" was probably thinking of a player along the lines of Dave Winfield.

Born in St. Paul, Minnesota, on October 3, 1951, the day Bobby Thomson hit "the shot heard 'round the world," Winfield, it was said, exhibited all-around athletic skills almost from the time he was able to walk. He was a pitching star and an outstanding basketball player at the University of Minnesota. Pro scouts outdid each other serving up superlatives describing his potential. Winfield was drafted by four teams in three sports: the American Basketball Association, National Basketball Association, National Football League, and Major League Baseball. Baseball won. Winfield signed on as a first-round draft pick with the San Diego Padres. He never played a day in the minors.

In 1980, Winfield was a free agent. A bidding war began for his services. The two chief bidders were the Braves and the Yankees. George Steinbrenner had his way. Ten days before Christmas 1980, Dave Winfield

Dave Winfield launches a grand slam home run off Texas Ranger Dickie Noles in 1984. It was one of 205 homers that Winfield hit in a Yankee uniform.

signed a 10-year contract with the Yankees, making him the highest-paid player in baseball. The contract was worth at least $13 million with a cost-of-living clause pushing its value to $20 million.

On the Padres, Winfield was king of the hill. With the Yankees, he was one of many stars, but he had his own unique luster. His first home run at Yankee Stadium in 1981 won a game. That set the dramatic tone for the Winfield Yankee years.

The player they called "Daddy Longlegs" batted .294 in his first Yankee season and led the team in games played, at bats, slugging percentage, RBIs, doubles, and hits. His performance helped the Yankees move past Milwaukee and Oakland in postseason competition. But the Yankees lost to the Dodgers in the World Series in what was perhaps the low point of Winfield's career. He went 1–22 for an anemic .045 average. And it was probably about that time that George Steinbrenner came up with the sarcastic nickname "Mr. May" for him. It was the flipside to Reggie Jackson's "Mr. October" label for his World Series heroics.

The 1981 World Series was an aberration for Winfield, who drove in 100 runs in six of his first nine Yankee seasons. From 1982 to 1986, he drove

157

in 100 or more runs a year, becoming the first Yankee to do so since Joe DiMaggio. Winfield slammed 24 or more home runs in each of seven full seasons with New York, but not in 1984. That year he cut down on his swing and battled Don Mattingly for the batting title to the last day of the season. "Winny" wound up with a .340 average—runner-up to the Yankee first baseman.

The sight of Dave Winfield in a Yankee uniform was always high drama. At 6-6 and with those long arms and legs, he was one of the top defensive outfielders of his era. There were all those times he used his old basketball skills, digging his cleats into the padding, scampering up the outfield walls, and robbing players of home runs. That was just one of the reasons he won five Gold Gloves as a Yankee. His powerful arm was another.

But there were times when there was more publicity generated about Winfield because of his wars with Steinbrenner than for his baseball accomplishments, such as the 1988 season when at age 36 he batted .322 with 25 home runs and 107 RBIs.

The personable Winfield had a no-trade clause with the Yankees and always exercised it. In 1990, he finally agreed to a trade and was sent to the California Angels for Mike Witt.

A presence and a producer with the Yankees, in a little more than eight seasons Winfield hit 205 home runs to rank eighth all-time in franchise history. His 818 RBIs place him 12th in Yankee history. In addition to his great athletic skills and intelligent appreciation of all aspects of the game, Winfield had something within him that made him the success he was.

Perhaps his words best articulate what that something was: "Internally for a guy to be successful, you have to be like a clock spring—wound but loose at the same time."

MONUMENTS

Since 1932, monuments have existed at Yankee Stadium. The first one was in place on Memorial Day 1932 to honor Miller Huggins. Both Lou Gehrig in 1941 and Babe Ruth in 1949 were honored posthumously with monuments. The three red granite monuments were part of the playing field, 10 feet in front of the wall, dead center in front of the flagpole.

The monuments honored legendary Yankees past and looked more like gravestones than monuments. There were some who saw a macabre touch when a batted ball rolled between the monuments and outfielders had to grope about attempting to make a fielding play. A center-field gate led out to the warning track, providing access for fans to read the plaques or view the monuments.

Before the remodeling of Yankee Stadium, the monuments were removed because of fear of vandalism when the Yankees were on a road trip on September 23, 1973.

The first plaque was placed on the center-field wall in 1940 as a tribute to Jacob Ruppert. This was followed by others honoring Ed Barrow, Joe DiMaggio, and Mickey Mantle.

Plaques were put up to honor Casey Stengel and Joe McCarthy (1976), Thurman Munson (1980), Roger Maris and Elston Howard (1984), Phil Rizzuto (1985), Billy Martin (1986), Lefty Gomez and Whitey Ford (1987), Yogi Berra and Bill Dickey (1988), and Allie Reynolds (1989).

After the new Yankee Stadium opened, the monuments and plaques were moved to Monument Park, an area between the bullpens. Fans were no longer able to exit as they had in the past, so the viewing of Monument Park was from a distance.

In 1985, the Monument Park area was made accessible for viewing by fans. A special walk honoring Yankees whose numbers have been retired is now part of the expanded Monument Park.

Not only Yankee fans and players but all those who come to the Stadium—players, media representatives, and executives—are interested in Monument Park, one of the most unusual features of any ballpark.

FOUR

THE Greatest Games

LOU GEHRIG: FOUR HOME RUNS IN ONE GAME

*I*n the first inning at Shibe Park in Philadelphia on Friday, June 3, 1932, Lou Gehrig homered into the stands in left-center. Gehrig repeated the feat in the fourth inning, homering over the right-field wall. In the fifth inning, the Iron Horse homered into the stands in left-center. George Earnshaw, who had won more than 20 games for three straight seasons, was the victim of Gehrig's first three roundtrippers. Connie Mack mercifully put Roy Mahaffey in to replace Earnshaw.

"Connie Mack always liked Roy," Earnshaw recalled, "so he brought him in to cool Gehrig off. Boy, he sure did cool him off." Gehrig blasted a fourth homer off Mahaffey in the seventh inning that climbed over the right-field wall.

The 5,000 Philadelphia fans cheered for Gehrig to hit a home run as he came up in the eighth inning, but he grounded out. In the ninth inning, batting against Ed Rommel, the Yankee first baseman hit his hardest shot of the game. But Al Simmons made a one-handed leaping snare of the ball a few steps from the farthest point of the ballpark in deep center. Gehrig missed a fifth home run by inches.

The four home runs in one game was an epic slugging performance and tied Gehrig for the record with two 19th-century players—Bobby Lowe of Boston in 1894 and Ed Delahanty of Philadelphia in 1896. It was also a record fourth time he hit three or more home runs in a game.

The game itself was a wild affair. Even with all the home run hitting—Babe Ruth, Earle Combs, and Tony Lazzeri each homered—the Yankees twice lost the lead. They finally won the game, 20–13.

Despite his sensational slugging exhibition, Lou Gehrig's giant feat was dwarfed by extensive newspaper coverage of another New York City baseball legend, John J. McGraw, who retired that day after 31 years as manager of the New York Giants.

DON LARSEN: THE PERFECT GAME

Don Larsen, racked by the Brooklyn Dodgers for four runs in two innings in the second game of the 1956 World Series, had the ball again for the Yankees in the fifth game, played on October 8, 1956, before 64,519. But this was a different game and a different Larsen, one more like the pitcher who developed a no-windup delivery and won all four of his starts in September—all four-hitters.

The image of the Yankee right-hander almost casually tossing the ball from a no-stretch windup to Yogi Berra remains in the mind's eye for many. He struck out Junior Gilliam on a breaking ball to start the game. Then Larsen went to a 3–2 count on Pee Wee Reese. It was the only time in the game the 6-4, 240-pound hurler threw more than two balls to any batter. And then he struck out the Dodger captain.

And then it all blended together—the autumn shadows and the smoke and the haze at the Stadium, the World Series bunting adorning the railings

(Preceding page)
Don Larsen is mobbed by teammates after his Perfect Game in the 1956 World Series.

along the first- and third-base lines, the scoreboard and the zeroes for the Dodgers of Brooklyn mounting inning after inning.

Larsen threw no more than 15 pitches in any one inning against the Dodgers of Campanella, Reese, Hodges, Gilliam, Robinson, Snider, and Furillo. They adjusted their swings. They stepped out. They attempted to wait out Larsen.

Five times they threatened Larsen's perfection, and five times they were denied. A second-inning Jackie Robinson line drive off the glove of Andy Carey at third was picked up by Gil McDougald. Mantle got a great jump on a fifth-inning line drive by Gil Hodges and made a backhand grab of the ball. Hodges hit a hot shot down the third-base line in the eighth only to see it converted into an out by Carey. There were balls smacked into the right-field seats by Amoros and Snider—both were foul, but barely so.

That venerable baseball superstition of not talking about a no-hitter in progress was very much observed on the Yankee bench, observed by all except for Don Larsen. All he wanted to do was talk about it.

"I was down in the corner getting a drink of water," Mickey Mantle recalled, "and he came over to me. 'Hey, Mickey, wouldn't it be something if I pitched a no-hitter?'

"I said, 'Come on man, get out of here!' I didn't want to talk about it.'"

But the talk at the Stadium was all about the no-hitter, the Perfect Game. As the contest moved into the final three innings Larsen seemed to be gaining strength, to be more in rhythm, homed in.

Yankee pitcher Don Larsen made history when he pitched the only perfect game in World Series history, but he didn't do it alone. This sequence shows how close Jackie Robinson came to beating out a base hit in the second inning. After the ball glanced off third baseman Andy Carey's glove, shortstop Gil McDougald made the play deep in the hole to get Robinson by a hair.

163

Larsen takes his time to gain his composure before firing the final pitch of his Perfect Game. Larsen caught Dodger Dale Mitchell looking at a called third strike for the last out of the game.

The huge crowd at the Stadium cheered each out. The ballpark was like a huge boom box turned off as Larsen paused to pitch, then turned on after each pitch and increasing in decibel level as each out was recorded. The game moved to the bottom of the ninth inning.

Just two seasons before Larsen had had the worst record in the American League. He came to the Yankees in the fall of 1954 from Baltimore in a 18-player trade. It was said of him that the only thing he feared was sleep. In spring training of 1956 in St. Petersburg during the wee small hours of the morning he had wrapped his automobile around a telephone pole. "He went out to mail a letter," Casey Stengel joked.

Now Larsen was center stage at the World Series, the key figure in the Yankee–Dodger nail-biter. There were all kinds of concerns on the Yankee bench. "Everybody suddenly got scared we weren't playing the outfield right," Stengel said. "I never seen so many managers." The Yankee infield of first baseman Joe Collins, second baseman Billy Martin, shortstop Gil McDougald, and third baseman Andy Carey was ready for any kind of play.

"If it was 9–0, he would've been paying little attention," Berra remembered. "It was close and he had to be extremely disciplined. He was. At the start of the ninth I didn't say a thing about how well he was throwing. I went to the mound and reminded him that if he walked one guy and the next guy hit one out, the game was tied."

"The last three outs were the toughest," Larsen recalled. "I was so weak in the knees that I thought I was going to faint. I was so nervous I almost fell down. My legs were rubbery. My fingers didn't feel like they belonged to me. I said to myself, 'Please help me somebody.'"

The 64,519 in attendance were quiet, almost muted, as the ninth inning began to play out. Four pitches were fouled off by Furillo, and then he hit a fly ball out to Bauer in right field. Campanella grounded out weakly to Billy Martin at second base. Don Larsen needed just one more out to achieve perfection.

Left-handed batter Dale Mitchell stepped to the plate as a pinch hitter for Dodger pitcher Sal Maglie. It would be the final major league at bat for the 35-year-old lifetime .312 hitter. Here is how announcer Bob Wolff called it:

"Count is one and one. And this crowd just straining forward on every pitch. Here it comes . . . a swing and a miss! Two strikes, ball one to Dale Mitchell. Listen to this crowd! I'll guarantee that nobody—but nobody—has left this ballpark. And if somebody did manage to leave early, man, he's missing the greatest! Two strikes and a ball. Mitchell waiting, stands deep, feet close together. Larsen is ready, gets the sign. Two strikes, ball one, here comes the pitch. Strike three! A no-hitter! A perfect game for Don Larsen!"

That final pitch—Larsen's 97th of a game that took just 2 hours and 6 minutes—was the only one that elicited controversy.

"The third strike on Mitchell was absolutely, positively a strike on the outside corner," Berra maintains to this day. "No question about it. People say it was a ball and that I rushed the mound to hug Larsen to make the umpire think it was a strike. Nonsense. It was a perfect strike."

With the drama ended, a sea of fans swept out of the stands and onto the playing field. Security personnel were powerless to hold them back. Larsen was pounded and grasped at. Someone stole his cap. It was a struggle, but he finally made it into the relative safety of the Yankee dugout.

Lost in all the excitement of the first perfect game since 1922 was the performance of Sal Maglie, who allowed just five hits. The place that destiny put him in was not one the combative "Barber" was pleased about. "I don't want to talk about it," he snapped. "I don't want to think about it. I just want to forget it."

Arthur Richman, now a Yankee executive, then a *New York Daily Mirror* sportswriter and a good friend of Don Larsen's, will never forget the time. "After the fourth game the Series was tied 2–2, and everywhere I read that Larsen didn't know he was starting the fifth game of the series," Richman said.

"That's wrong, of course you know you're starting. We went out the night before as we always did, and I told him: 'I want you to get to bed at a decent hour tonight because if you blow it tomorrow there is no way the Yankees will keep you around.'

"So we had a few toddies downtown at Bill Taylor's gin mill on 57th Street. And we came back to the Bronx where he lived at the Concourse Plaza. And Don said, 'Let's have a pizza before going to sleep.' We did. Then he gave me $20 and said, 'Give this to your mother to give to church.'

"I said, 'My mother doesn't go to church. She goes to synagogue.'

"'Well, tell her to do whatever she can with it—say a little prayer for me.'

"I gave the money to my mother, and she gave it to the synagogue the next morning. And lightning struck!

"The next day, I wrote the story up for the *Daily Mirror*. The next night we went to all the spots that we had hit during the season. 'Let's go to the Copa and see Joey Lewis,' Don said.

"I called and asked for a reservation. 'Are you kidding?' they said. 'Not for two months.'

"I said, 'I got Don Larsen with me.'

"'If you've got Don Larsen with you, we'll put you up right on the floor in front of the show.'

"Joey Lewis joined us at the table. We ordered a bottle of vodka, Scotch, Canadian Club. Lots of food. They hit me with a tab for 400 bucks. We didn't have 40 dollars among us. And Joey Lewis said, 'Give me that check. I'll take care of it.' And he did."

Don Larsen—the man who was truly lit by lightning on October 8, 1956, the pitcher whom destiny favored, the player the *New York Daily News* called "Zero Hero"—went on to complete a 14-year major league career. He won 81 games and lost 91 and posted a 3.78 ERA.

But never again was Don James Larsen able to come close to the singular state that he reached on that October day—pitching the only perfect game in the history of the World Series.

THE CHRIS CHAMBLISS HOME RUN

The 1971 Rookie of the Year, first baseman Chris Chambliss came to the Yankees from Cleveland on April 27, 1974, in a seven-player trade. He bat-

Chris Chambliss leaps for joy as he watches his ninth inning home run clear the right field wall. Yankee catcher Thurman Munson (left) and teammate Sandy Alomar (right) join the celebration.

ted .304 in 1975, made the 1976 All-Star team, was the quiet, steady man on a team of talkers.

In game three of the 1976 League Championship Series against Kansas City, Chambliss's two-run homer and three RBIs paced a 5–3 Yankee win. But neither he nor the fans of the Bronx Bombers could anticipate what thunder he still had remaining in his bat.

The Royals and Yankees squared off on the misty night of October 14, 1976, at Yankee Stadium in the fifth and deciding game of the seesaw series. Going into the eighth inning, the Yankees had a 6–3 lead. New York fans were starting to count the outs remaining for Kansas City. But the counting stopped as the huge crowd was silenced by George Brett's three-run homer.

The game moved to the bottom of the ninth, tied 6–6. Relatively well behaved to that point, the fans turned ugly, throwing firecrackers, rolls of toilet paper, eggs, and other debris onto the playing field. The umpires called time, and the game was delayed as the field was cleared by groundskeepers.

Chris Chambliss waited at the bat rack, antsy. "I was a little anxious," he said. "It was cold, too. That was a trying time there."

Finally, the left-handed-hitting Chambliss stepped in against right-handed relief pitcher Mark Littell, who had saved 16 games and won 8 more that season.

"I knew Littell was going to throw a fastball," Chamblisss said.

It was a fastball, high and inside. The time was 11:13 P.M. when

Chambliss whipped his bat in his classic swing. The ball climbed over the right-field wall. All Royal outfielder Hal McRae could do was wave his glove as the ball disappeared into the night.

Yankee Stadium exploded with noise. It seemed that a good chunk of the 56,821 fans surged out onto the field. Many were screaming, "We're number one!" Second base was scooped up by a fan. Players' caps were clawed at. Gloves were taken. The field was a combat zone.

Pumping his fists in the air and running out the home run, Chambliss tried to make his way around the bases. "I was worried about getting trampled," he said. "I wasn't even worried about touching bases anymore."

"I was one of the fools running around trying to make room for him to get to home plate," Willie Randolph said. "I was pushing people and they were pushing me. That was total pandemonium."

"By the time Chris got to third base," Thurman Munson recalled, "all hope of reaching the plate was gone. He never did make it."

In the Yankees locker room New York City mayor Abe Beame, actor Cary Grant, George Steinbrenner, many members of the media, and especially the Yankees, hugged, kissed, rejoiced. A dozen years of waiting had ended. The Yankees had finally won another pennant, their 30th.

In that LCS, Chris Chambliss batted .524, tied or broke five series records for hits and RBIs. He would play in 911 games for the Yankees in his six years with the team. But the home run he hit that October day was the one that

Chambliss probably never imagined that hitting the home run would be the easy part. New York fans swarmed the field after his pennant-clinching blast, making it impossible for Chambliss to circle the bases. After the field finally cleared, Chambliss had to come back out of the clubhouse with a security guard to touch the area where home plate had been.

went down in New York City baseball history alongside those hit by Bobby Thomson, Bucky Dent, and Reggie Jackson.

Hours later, in an empty ballpark under the protective eyes of two security guards, Chambliss touched home plate. That made it official.

RON GUIDRY: 18 STRIKEOUTS IN ONE GAME

The date was June 17, 1978. Warming up to start against the California Angels, Ron Guidry told Sparky Lyle, "I've got nothing tonight." Those were not the words one would have expected to hear from a pitcher who had won 10 games and lost none. But Guidry was like that.

The game began with a Bobby Grich double. Then Guidry reached back and struck out two to get out of the first inning. But the word on the California bench was that Guidry could be hit that night.

The word was wishful thinking. The slim southpaw was virtually untouchable. "I wasn't trying to strike out guys," Guidry said. "I was throwing fastballs right down the middle, but they couldn't hit it. And then the crowd started getting into it."

Guidry had 9 strikeouts through four innings, 11 strikeouts after five innings, 14 after six innings. He picked up another strikeout in the seventh to make it 15 Angels down on strikes.

"I was not thinking about it," Guidry recalled, "and that helped me, but about the sixth or seventh, I knew they wouldn't score on me. It was just a matter of how many strikeouts."

There was another strikeout in the eighth. If Guidry fanned the side in the ninth he would tie the all-time single-game record. The first two batters went down on strikes. Guidry was almost there. The next batter was Don Baylor. "I wasn't going to be the 19th," he said. He singled, stopping Guidry's streak of 14 straight batters retired. The game ended when Ron Jackson forced Baylor at second.

Guidry's 18 strikeouts set an American League record for a left-handed pitcher. Each Angel fanned at least once in the game. Three times Guidry struck out the side. And in the middle innings of the game, a dozen of the 13 outs came via the strikeout route. The man they called "Louisiana Lightning" lit up the Angels that June night. It was truly a career performance.

BUCKY DENT'S PLAYOFF HOME RUN

The New York Yankees and the Boston Red Sox finished up the 1978 season with identical 99–63 records, setting the stage for the second one-game play-off in the history of the American League. All the years, all the frustrating moments of coming in second behind the Yankees were close to the surface, as the city of Boston and Red Sox rooters girded themselves for October 2, 1978.

In the season series the Yankees had won 9 of 16 games, but the Sox had won 59 of their 82 games played at Fenway. Boston was the "hot" team

with the home-field edge. But the Yankees had Ron Guidry (24–3) and Goose Gossage (26 saves). Guidry's opponent was Mike Torrez, who just the year before had worn pinstripes and was now aching to defeat his former teammates.

There were nearly 33,000 jammed into the Fens. National media were all over the place. Some were literally sitting on the roof. Millions more watched on television or heard it on local radio.

"That one game surpasses any other one I've been connected with," recalled former Yankee broadcaster Frank Messer. "Those two teams and the whole season boiling down to just one game at Fenway, It was quite a moment."

Boston got off to a 1–0 lead on Carl Yastrzemski's second inning home run down the right-field line. "Guidry wasn't the same guy we saw earlier," said Sox outfielder Fred Lynn. "I thought that when the old man (Yastrzemski) hit the home run that was going to do it. Torrez was throwing the ball real well and he wanted that win," said former Boston announcer Hawk Harrelson.

The Sox picked up another run in the sixth, and as the Yankees came to bat in the seventh, Torrez had given up but two hits. Then Chris Chambliss singled. Roy White singled. Pinch-hitter Jim Spencer flied out. The light-

Yankee shortstop Bucky Dent shocked the baseball world when he blasted this seventh inning three-run homer off Boston's Mike Torrez. Dent lifted New York to a 3–2 lead and left his mark in baseball history.

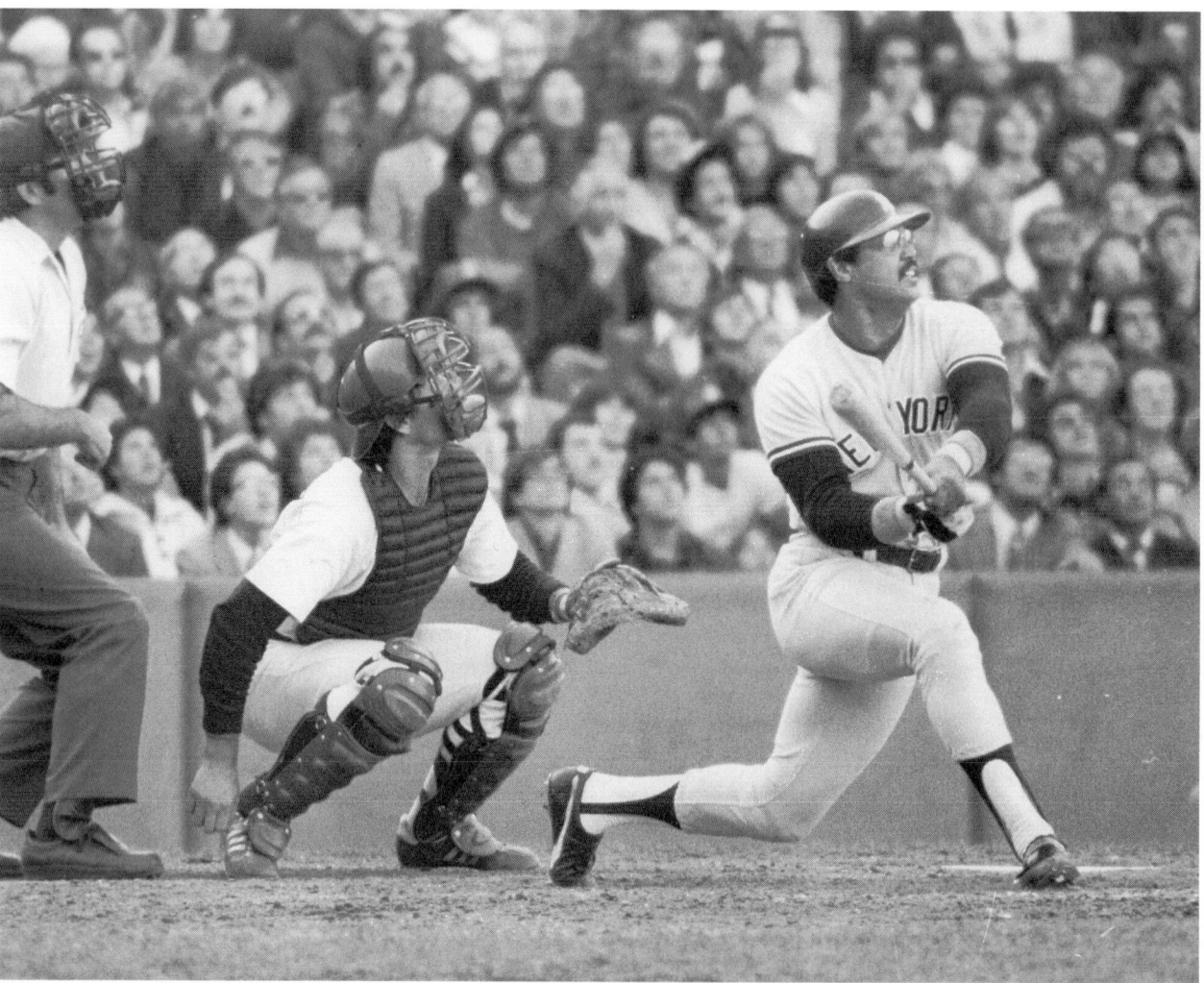

Reggie Jackson belted an eighth inning solo homer that gave the Yankees a 5-2 lead.

hitting Bucky Dent was due up next, and Sox fans relaxed a bit.

Dent had managed just four home runs in the 1978 season and batted only .140 in the last 20 games. The Yankee shortstop choked up on the bat. He was just out there trying to make contact. Torrez pitched. Dent fouled the ball off his foot. He moved about attempting to shake off the sting.

The on-deck batter, Mickey Rivers, noticed a crack in Dent's bat and told Bucky about it. He switched to a Mickey Rivers bat and stepped in. His Yankee teammates in the dugout screamed out encouragement; Red Sox fans screamed to Torrez, exhorting him to get Dent.

"Hit the tin, Bucky," Reggie Jackson's voice could be heard above the din. He was beseeching Dent to smack the ball off the left-field wall, to drive in the two Yankee runners.

The 6-5 Torrez came out of the windup and the pitch came in to the 5-9 Dent, who swung and got good wood on the ball. "The fact that it was at Fenway Park," said Messer, "as soon as it left the bat I thought it had a chance. Any time you hit a fly ball in Fenway there's a chance."

Clearing the infield, the ball climbed in its flight toward the left-field wall—the Green Monster. Yaz, on instinct, backed up, backed up. He had been in that position many times. But he had no chance. The ball went over the tin. Dent, racing around first base, knew he had put the ball into the left-field net.

White and Chambliss waited for Dent at home plate. The entire Yankee dugout emptied out. It was Bucky Dent's moment. With one swing he had given the Yankees a 3–2 lead, silenced the Fenway faithful, stunned Mike Torrez.

The Boston pitcher walked Rivers and was taken out of the game. Bob Stanley took over on the mound for the Sox. Rivers stole second. Doubling to deep center field, Thurman Munson gave the Yankees a 4–2 lead.

Gossage relieved Guidry in the seventh. Boston did not score. "I can still vividly remember standing out in right field in the latter part of the game wanting the game to get over," Lou Piniella said. "We had the Goose in there to short-circuit them. But we also knew that Boston was at home, and that Boston was going to come back at us."

Reggie Jackson smacked a Bob Stanley fastball into the center-field bleachers in the eighth inning. "I just thought it was an extra run," Jackson said. In the bottom of the eighth bedlam erupted in the stands as Sox fans tried to rally their team.

Jerry Remy doubled. There was more bedlam. Yaz singled Remy in. The score was 5–3. Fenway was rocking. Then Carlton Fisk singled. Fred Lynn singled Yaz home. The score was 5–4. Gossage got Butch Hobson on a lazy fly ball.

George Scott came to bat and the fans at Fenway, on their feet, stamping, screaming, urged the powerfully built batter to hit it out. Yankee manager Bob Lemon seemed to be the only one who was calm. He stayed with Gossage, who came into the game with a string of 30 appearances in which he had given up no home runs and notched 15 saves and 6 victories. Gossage versus Scott was truly power versus power. The Yankee pitcher's power prevailed. He fanned Scott.

The game and the season moved to the bottom of the ninth, 5–4 Yankees. Jackson's home run, which had seemed superfluous at the time, was all that separated the two teams.

There was one out. Then Rick Burleson coaxed a walk. Remy slashed a sinking liner to right. Piniella lost the ball for an instant in the sun. It dropped in front of him.

Jim Rice had hit 28 home runs in 1978 at Fenway. He came up looking for number 29. But all he got was a fly ball to deep right field. Burleson tagged at second and moved to third.

As if out of a movie script, Carl Yastrzemski came to the plate. An 18-year veteran, the favorite of Boston fans, dependable, durable, Yaz was the one batter all of Boston wanted up there at that moment.

Burleson led off third. Remy led off first base. Munson flashed the signs to Gossage. "I wasn't going to mess around with breaking junk," Gossage said later. "I wasn't going to get beaten by anything but my best. Yastrzemski's the greatest player I've ever played against. I just wound up and threw it as hard as I could. I couldn't tell you where."

All Yaz could manage was a gently arcing pop fly toward third base. Graig Nettles squeezed it in his glove. The Sox legend marched back to his dugout,

Yankee players bow their heads in a moment of silence in memory of their captain and teammate Thurman Munson.

disgusted. The Yankees charged out of their dugout, exultant.

And what happened that October day in Boston would always be remembered for the Bucky Dent home run.

WINNING ONE FOR THURMAN MUNSON

It was Yankees versus Orioles, the night of August 6, 1979. That afternoon Thurman Munson was buried in his hometown of Canton, Ohio. The entire Yankee team had been there to say a final farewell to their "Captain," who had died in a plane crash just four days earlier.

The game was played in a subdued and poignant atmosphere. Behind Dennis Martinez, the Orioles had an early 4–0 lead. Bobby Murcer, in his second go round with the Yankees after being reacquired from the Cubs on June 26, had delivered a stirring eulogy to Munson earlier that day. Murcer's three-run homer, his first Stadium home run since 1973, made the game close.

The game moved to the bottom of the ninth with Baltimore clinging to the one-run lead. Bucky Dent led off with a walk. Willie Randolph's bunt was mishandled by Tippy Martinez. Murcer came up with Yankees on second and third.

The count was 0–2. Then Murcer punched a hit to left field. Dent and Randolph came around to score, and the Yankees won the game, 5–4. The emotional win seemed to catapult all the Yankees out of the dugout, and they came racing to the first-base line, mobbing Murcer. It was a big win, an emotionally satisfying victory.

"Everybody was so tired," Murcer recalled. "I think we were playing in the spirit of Thurman. I think that's what carried us through the game."

THE PINE TAR INCIDENT

Going into late July 1983, the Yankee season had been an erratic one. Their record was 19–18, then 31–30. Then they won eight of nine games and were positioned to take over first place. Then they came up against the Kansas City Royals on July 24.

As the ninth inning began, the Yankees clung to a 4–3 lead. There were two outs, one Royal baserunner. Goose Gossage faced George Brett. The left-handed-batting Brett homered into the right-field stands, giving Kansas City a 5–4 lead.

Rounding the bases, circling third and coming home, Brett saw that Billy Martin had picked up his bat and that umpire Tim McClelland had called time. "I was confused," Brett said, "but not concerned. I figured they were checking the bat to see if it was corked."

But the checking determined that pine tar covered more than 18 inches from the knob of the bat. According to the rules, that was illegal. McClelland looked into the Kansas City dugout, stuck his thumb up in the air, and declared Brett out. Under his rules interpretation, the Yankees won the game.

But another game began—one of hot potato with the bat. Brett's sticky lumber was passed by him to KC pitcher Gaylord Perry, who started to walk off with it and then gave the bat to pitcher Steve Renko, who ran with it and then tossed it to Hal McRae. With police at their side, the umpires entered the Royals' locker room and retrieved the bat. The Yankees went off to Texas, where they won three straight and took over first place for the first time that season.

But the "Pine Tar Incident" was too sticky to go away. Overruling the umpires, American League president Lee MacPhail allowed the home run to stand and declared that the game would have to be continued from where it left off.

"Why a .356 hitter like George Brett," *Time* magazine noted, "would lumber along with a Marvelous Marv Throneberry model (lifetime .237) is the sort of paradox that, scientists say, has trees talking to themselves." The "Pine Tar Incident" had players and fans talking to themselves and each other as the controversy was debated and discussed ad nauseam.

"Mentally," Billy Martin said, "it really hurt us. We felt we had a game taken away from us because of a play that was illegal. It was hard for our guys to accept." The ruling sent the Yankees into a tailspin. They lost six of seven games and toppled to fourth place.

Murcer doffs his cap after his dramatic hit.

George Brett plants a kiss on his Louisville Slugger. Never has a baseball bat caused more controversy in a game than when Brett caked his with pine tar in July 1983.

173

Dwight Gooden sits atop his teammates' shoulders after completing his first career no-hitter.

In a circuslike atmosphere on August 18, the game resumed at Yankee Stadium. All fans were admitted free of charge. A livid Billy Martin made a travesty of the moment. His players appealed each base, charging that the Kansas City baserunners had not touched them all. Don Mattingly played second base, and pitcher Ron Guidry was in center field. George Frazier took the mound and struck out Hal McRae for the final out in the top of the ninth. But Kansas City relief ace Dan Quisenberry stifled the Yankees in the bottom of the ninth, securing the win for the Royals.

And George Brett had the final word: "In the end it counted, so while I may have been angry, I can't be known as a cheater because the league made it count."

DWIGHT GOODEN'S NO-HITTER

Just 19 years old, Dwight Gooden came up to the New York Mets in 1984. When he stepped onto a major league mound for the first time, he had pitched no higher than class-A ball. Featuring a fastball clocked in the high 90s and a roundhouse curveball that he dubbed "Lord Charles," Gooden used both of them to become one of the most dominating pitchers of the mid-1980s.

The youngest player ever to appear in an All-Star Game, Gooden won 17 games his first season and set a record of 11.39 strikeouts per nine innings. That earned him the nickname "Doctor K." Gooden was also the youngest player to win the Rookie of the Year and Cy Young awards. Only two pitchers in the 20th century reached the 100 victory mark faster than Gooden— Bob Feller and Frank "Noodles" Hahn.

Dwight Gooden was sitting atop the baseball world, and then it all began to come apart. From 1992 to 1994, he posted losing records. Then Gooden was suspended for part of the 1994 season and all of 1995 for continually violating the rules of his drug and alcohol aftercare program.

So it was no wonder that all kinds of controversy swirled around the Yankees' signing him to a one-year contract on October 16, 1995. In the view of many, Gooden was damaged goods, yesterday's hero.

George Steinbrenner defended his action. "I just think it's too early at age 31 to tell a young man—your life is over, you can't pitch anymore."

And Gooden explained: "This is the city where I started my career and the place where I wanted to finish it. I've always loved playing in New York. This is my home. I belong here. I grew up here."

Gooden showed up in spring training determined to make it all the way back. "I looked death in the eye many times," he said. He threw the ball 90-plus miles an hour in workouts. That was the upside.

The downside was his performance in spring-training game situations. Losing all three of his decisions, he posted a dismal 8.88 ERA. The 15 wins Steinbrenner had predicted Gooden could achieve in the 1996 season seemed mere public-relations banter.

Things only got worse for Gooden as the season got under way. He was racked up hard twice by Texas. Then the Twins got their licks in on April 19, scoring six runs in three innings off him.

Joe Torre had no alternative but to banish the fallen idol, his 0–3 record, and his 11.48 ERA to the bullpen. "I've just got to keep working on my mechanics," Gooden said. "It's complete frustration more than anything else. I never ever doubted myself. I wanted to do well so badly. But once they put me in the bullpen, I didn't know what was going on."

When David Cone developed an aneurysm in his right shoulder and the Yankee pitching staff was depleted, Joe Torre took a gamble and put Gooden back into the rotation on April 27. Gooden would joke later: "I guess I have Coney to thank for everything, if he didn't get hurt . . . "

Going up against the Twins, who had ravaged him less than a week before, sporting a more compact delivery that pitching coach Mel Stottlemyre had developed with him, Gooden managed six strong innings, struck out seven, yielded just one run.

In his next start he shut out the White Sox for six innings. Then he went up against Detroit. The final 20 Tigers he faced went down in a row. It was Gooden's first victory since June 19, 1994.

That set the stage for Tuesday night, May 14, 1996: New York Yankees versus Seattle Mariners. It was the first meeting of the two teams since the final game of the 1995 division series. A big-game atmosphere pervaded the Stadium. That was one subplot.

Another was the poignancy of Gooden's father in the hospital in Tampa, scheduled for double bypass surgery the next day. "You go home to your father if you have to," Joe Torre told him. "You have the option. You don't have to do this for me."

Doing it for his father, the 31-year-old Gooden took the mound. Both Mel Stottlemyre, who warmed him up in the bullpen, and Joe Girardi, who took the Doc's warm-up tosses from the mound, noticed the extra pop on the fastball, the quick bite on the slider.

And so did the Mariners as inning after inning played out. The hard-hitting Mariners were hitless through three innings, hitless through six innings. They could do nothing against Gooden's no-frills windup, the overpowering fastball, the deep, biting slider. Gooden took deep breaths, tried to keep control, worked on staying homed in.

The deafening din created by the more than 31,000 fans at the Stadium grew louder each inning. Gooden would say later that he wasn't aware of the possibility of the no-hitter until he came out for the seventh inning, that he started hoping for it then. The Mariners went down in order in the seventh. They went down in order in the eighth.

As the ninth inning began the Yankees had a 2–0 lead. The no-hitter was three outs away. But having thrown well over 100 pitches, Gooden was now pitching on sheer adrenaline.

Alex Rodriguez walked. The tension built. Ken Griffey, Jr., hit a grounder to Martinez at first. Gooden seemed frozen in place. The Yankee first baseman had to dive with an outstretched glove to the bag for the putout on the speedy runner. Then Edgar Martinez walked.

With Mariners on first and second, the game as well as the no-hitter now seemed in jeopardy. But for Joe Torre, "It was Dwight's game, all the way." The Yankee manager had no intention of taking Gooden out of the game.

With one swing of his bat, Jim Leyritz turned the 1996 World Series around.

The dangerous Jay Buhner stepped in. The noise level at the Stadium was turned up a notch. Perhaps that's what triggered the wild pitch that seemed to just get away from Gooden. Now there were runners on second and third for the Mariners. There was just one out.

Mel Stottlemyre jogged out to the mound to settle Gooden down. The count on Buhner was 2–2. Gooden reached back and fired the fastball. Strike three!

Paul Sorrento was all that stood in the way of the no-hitter. He swung at a swerving curveball and lifted the ball high to short. Derek Jeter squeezed it for the final out.

Yankee Stadium exploded. Gooden leaped into the arms of catcher Joe Girardi, was swarmed over by his teammates and carried off the field on their shoulders. "This is the greatest feeling of my life," he said. "I never, ever thought I could do this, not in my wildest dreams. A year and a half ago, at times, I thought I had played my last game. So being able not only to make it back but to throw a no-hitter, that's been an unbelievable blessing for me."

Ken Griffey, Jr., who had struck out twice on fastballs, said, "The things he went through, you have to take your hat off to him."

The morning after the no-hitter, Gooden, who hardly was able to get any sleep, flew to Tampa, Florida, to be with his 64-year-old father, who had successfully undergone surgery to repair his damaged heart. And Gooden, who mused about the times when his father would "get off work and we'd go into the field and he'd throw me balls, let me pitch to him, everything," presented his dad with the no-hitter game ball.

It was a marvelous moment in May for Dwight Gooden, one that foreshadowed the storybook season 1996 would be for the New York Yankees.

1996 WORLD SERIES GAME FOUR: THE LEYRITZ HOME RUN

Atlanta hurler Denny Neagle was coasting, and his team was ahead 6–0. It seemed the Braves were well on their way to winning game four of the 1996 World Series. But for teams who went up against the 1996 New York Yankees, as the Baltimore Orioles had learned, nothing was the way it seemed.

There was some concern in the Atlanta dugout when their lead was halved. The game played on to the top of the eighth inning. Atlanta 6, New York 3. The Yankees had two runners on. It was Jim Leyritz versus fastballer Mark Wohlers. The backup catcher fouled back a 98-mile-per-hour fastball. He fouled off another one. The count was 2–2. The 51,881 in attendance and the millions watching the game on national television were thinking fastball. Jim Leyritz was thinking right along with them, but he was also ready for anything.

Anything was a slider out over the plate—Wohlers's second-best pitch. The Yankee catcher drove the ball over the left-field wall. Game tied.

It was nail-biting time for fans of both teams as the game moved to the tenth inning. The Yankees and the Braves were tied, 6–6. Steve Avery was one out away from getting out of the inning. Then he walked Tim Raines on four pitches. The Atlanta southpaw got two strikes on Derek Jeter, but couldn't close him out. The Yankee shortstop singled to left field.

A beleaguered Bobby Cox, who would say after the game, "a lot of things went wrong for us," had Bernie Williams walked intentionally. Bases loaded. Andy Fox, who had entered the game as a pinch-runner for Cecil Fielder the inning before, was the next scheduled batter. Torre inserted Wade Boggs to pinch-hit for Fox.

It was the southpaw Avery versus the left-handed hitting Boggs. Avery had the count his way, 1–2. He tried to nibble away with a breaking pitch on the outside corner. Boggs, a five-time American League batting champion with the reputation of having an eagle eye, took the pitch. Umpire Steve Rippley called it a ball. It was a questionable call that made Avery grimace. He sent another pitch to the plate. Boggs took it. Full count. Avery's next pitch was not even close—a fastball, too high and too close to Boggs. The bases-loaded walk gave the Yankees a 7–6 lead.

Avery was out. Brad Clontz was in the game and so was Ryan Klesko to play first base and be ready to lead off for the Braves in the bottom of the tenth inning. Clontz pitched to Charlie Hayes, who popped the ball up to Klesko at first base. Unbelievably, Klesko muffed what looked like an easy catch. Did he lose the ball in the lights? Another Yankee run crossed the plate—the frosting on the cake, the insurance run.

John Wetteland closed out the Braves in the bottom of the tenth, and the Yankees had another of their patented come-from-behind victories.

It was a game that took 4 hours and 19 minutes to play, the longest in postseason history. It was a game that involved 41 players, 13 pitchers, 5 first basemen. It was a game that underscored the entire Yankee season, a game that will be long remembered.

FIVE

THE
Rivals

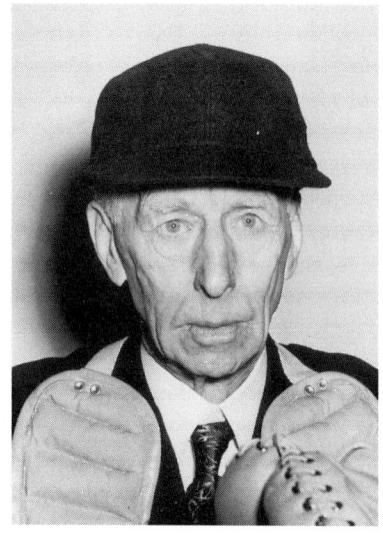

During the late 1920s and early 1930s, there was no bigger rivalry in baseball than the one between the Philadelphia Athletics and the New York Yankees. Philadelphia manager Connie Mack helped build the 1929 A's into one of the greatest teams in baseball history.

(Preceding page)
Ted Williams of the Boston Red Sox, one of the Yankees' fiercest rivals.

THE PHILADELPHIA ATHLETICS

*P*erhaps it was because of the close proximity of the cities, perhaps it was because Connie Mack, manager and owner, was on the scene for so long—whatever the reason the rivalry between the Yankees of New York and the Athletics of Philadelphia is one of the most storied in baseball history.

Perhaps the most telling commentary on the Yankee–Athletic competion was provided by Hall of Famer Al Simmons of Philadelphia. "We had a great team," he said, "a really great team. But when you compare us with the really great Yankee World Champions we simply weren't in their class. I'm not trying to kid myself or anyone else. I fought those Yankee teams as hard as anyone in the American League, but when they got us into a tough series they just batted our brains out."

The tough series took place almost every time the two rivals met during the late '20s and early '30s. Head-to-head battles from 1927 to 1932 saw the Yankees winning 73 games to Philadelphia's 59. There was one tie game in 1927. Both teams won three pennants in that six-year period. The rivalry was characterized by heavy hitting—35 times games were double-digit affairs. There were also many close, taut battles: 31 times in that six-year period the outcome of a game was decided by one run, 23 times by two runs.

The 1927 Yankees were probably the greatest team of all time. They won the pennant by 19 games. But even though they finished a distant second, the patiently built Athletics gave notice they would not be that far behind in the seasons to come. The '27 A's struck out just 326 times—an American League record. They featured Simmons, who batted .392, and Lefty Grove, who won 20 games and had even greater years ahead of him.

In 1928, the Bronx Bombers had a 12-game lead on the Fourth of July. Winning 25 of 33 July games, the Athletics cut the lead. Through August and into the first week in September, the two teams fought for first place. On September 9, they met at Yankee Stadium before a doubleheader crowd of 85,000. Sweeping both games and the next one, the Yankees finished 2½ games ahead of Philadelphia and notched their third straight pennant. But the A's, with seven of the players from that roster now in the Hall of Fame, with Ty Cobb and Tris Speaker in their final seasons, had served notice that they had the power and the pitching to more than contend with the Yankees.

"With those two monsters in the league," Cleveland manager Roger Peckinpaugh said in 1929, "you started the season fighting for second place." The Athletics started that 1929 season lusting for first place and they got it, winning the pennant by 18 games over the Yankees, their first pennant since 1914.

On May 30, 1930, in a show of offensive might, the Yankees ravaged the Athletics 20–13 in the second game of a doubleheader. Gehrig had three home runs. Ruth, who hit three homers the day before, and one in the first game of the doubleheader, hit two more in the nightcap.

But the Athletics of 1930 batted .294 as a team, and had Al Simmons, who batted .381, two points higher than Gehrig, and Lefty Grove, who posted a 28–5 record and the league's lowest ERA, 2.54. Connie Mack had said,

"A team cannot be considered great unless it repeats." The Athletics repeated, winning their second straight pennant.

Babe Ruth led the American League in home runs in 1929, 1930, and 1931. Yet the Yankees were behind Philadelphia in the standings all three seasons. The 1931 A's had a combined 72 wins from Lefty Grove, George Earnshaw, and Rube Walberg. Al Simmons took his second straight batting title and had 22 home runs and 165 RBIs; Jimmie Foxx, dubbed the "right-handed Babe Ruth," and "The Beast," batted .291, hammered 30 home runs, and drove in 120. It was all too much for the 1931 Yankees, who finished 13½ games behind the powerful A's, who won 107 games, becoming the first American League club to win 100 or more games a year for three straight seasons.

In 1932, a Jimmie Foxx homer landed in the third deck of Yankee Stadium, and Lefty Gomez cracked: "It took 45 minutes to walk up there." "Double X" cracked 58 home runs that '32 season, challenging Ruth's record. His Philadelphia team also challenged the Yankees for a time but wound up in second place—13 games off the pace. Connie Mack would manage 18 more seasons, but never again would one of his teams finish that high again.

Jimmie Foxx crosses home plate after blasting a home run during the 1932 season. Foxx was the main power source in the A's line-up and was tabbed as the "right-handed Babe Ruth."

Phil Rizzuto and Yogi Berra greet Joe DiMaggio after a 1949 home run in Boston.

On June 7, 1933, Jimmie Foxx homered in his last at bat. The next day he slashed three home runs against the Yankees in his first three at bats. Philadelphia won the game, 14–10. Then on June 9, Foxx uncorked his fifth homer in three games, but the Yankees outlasted the Athletics, 7–6. It was a game that symbolized the rivalry—the Yankees outlasting the men of Cornelius McGillicuddy.

As 1933 came to an end, Connie Mack, a half-million dollars in debt, started selling off his great stars. Simmons, Dykes, Haas, Grove, Bishop, Waldberg, Foxx—all were sent away. Mack had built the dynasty; now he destroyed it to survive. In 1934, the Athletics finished in the second division. For the next 13 years, a time of triumph for the Yankees, the Athletics would be consigned to the second division. The great rivalry was over.

THE BOSTON RED SOX

At a chilly morning news conference on January 5, 1920, the New York Yankees began the new decade on the right foot: "Gentlemen," Col. Jacob Ruppert announced, "we have just bought Babe Ruth from Harry Frazee of the Boston Red Sox. I can't give exact figures, but it was a pretty check—six figures. No players are involved. It was strictly a cash deal."

The price was $125,000 and a guaranteed loan of $300,000 on Fenway Park. Whatever the price, it was the steal of the century. "Ruth's 29 home runs in 1912 were more spectacular than useful," Frazee snapped. "They didn't help the Red Sox get out of sixth place." To intimates, Frazee was more candid: "I couldn't help it," he said. "I needed money desperately."

The owner of a theater on 42nd Street in Manhattan, close by the Yankees offices, Frazee was a show-business wheeler-dealer, always hustling for a buck. But this time he went too far. The sale of Babe Ruth totally changed the balance of power in the American League. In 19 seasons the Red Sox had won a half-dozen pennants and five World Championships. The Yankees had won nothing. With Babe Ruth and others (many coming over from Boston) the Yankees would win 14 pennants before the Red Sox won another one.

Some claim the Red Sox–Yankee rivalry and the "curse of the Bambino" began then. Others maintain the rivalry is rooted in the geographical proximity and placement of the two teams in the same league. Whatever, Boston versus New York, Yankees versus Red Sox has always been baseball's greatest rivalry.

On October 29, 1920, Edward Grant Barrow, who had managed Boston from 1918 to 1920, took over as Yankee general manager. A fixture on the Yankee scene for a quarter-century, Barrow presided as the stationmaster of the Boston–New York player shuttles, triggering the question, who did Frazee sell to the Yankees today?

Some of the major players leaving and diluting the Boston franchise were Waite Hoyt, Harry Harper, Wally Schang, Mike McNally, "Bullet Joe" Bush, "Sad Sam" Jones, "Jumping Joe" Dugan, Herb Pennock, and Red Ruffing. The starting rotation for the first Yankee World Championship in 1923 included four former Red Sox pitchers: Jones, Pennock, Bush, and Hoyt.

There is no greater rivalry anywhere in the world of sport than the Yankees and the Red Sox.
—George Steinbrenner

When Harry Frazee in 1933 sold the Red Sox to Tom Yawkey, the pipeline of Boston players coming to the Yankees dried up. Although the Sox could no longer be ravaged for players, the rivalry continued. And when the Sox swept the Yankees in a five-game series in 1933, an infuriated Jacob Ruppert demanded immediate payment on the Frazee mortgage given in the Babe Ruth deal that was never called in. That did not sit too well with Sox fans. Neither did the four frustrating second-place Boston finishes behind the Yankees in 1938, 1939, 1941, and 1942.

Always, there have been annoying, heartbreaking, agonizing moments for fans in New England, such as the Yankee win over Boston giving them the pennant and the Sox another runner-up finish on the final day of the 1949 season; the Bucky Dent three-run homer on October 2, 1978, that helped defeat Boston; the eight runs the Yankees scored in the ninth inning with two outs on September 8, 1937, to defeat Boston 9–6; and the five pitchers used by Boston in one inning and the squandering of a nine-run lead that led to a 15–10 loss to the Yankees on April 18, 1950.

There have also been the times the Red Sox have had the upper hand—when Mantle fanned five times and Williams scored from second on a sacrifice bunt on May 30, 1951; when Boston shut out the Yankees in both games of a key doubleheader at Shea Stadium on July 27, 1975; and when the Sox

Harry Frazee's sale of Babe Ruth was probably the most monumental blunder by a team's owner in baseball history. Boston has failed to win a world championship since Ruth was purchased by the Yankees. Harry Frazee and Frank Chance, owner and manger, respectively, of the Red Sox at Yankee Stadium in 1923.

A dejected Mike Torrez hangs his head in the Boston dugout after he giving up a three-run homer to Bucky Dent in 1978. The Yanks won the one-game playoff, 5–4, to capture the American League Eastern Division title.

scored seven runs in the eighth inning on September 19, 1981, defeating the Yankees, 8–5.

Marker moments in the rivalry include Babe Ruth's first major league home run as a member of the Red Sox, hit in 1915 against the Yankees at the Polo Grounds; Lou Gehrig's first home run, which was hit at Fenway Park; the first major league hit of Ted Williams's career in a game against the Yankees; the record-setting 61st home run in 1961 by Roger Maris, hit against Boston; Carl Yastrzemski's 3,000th career hit, recorded in a game against the Yankees.

The rivalry has featured many physical battles: Billy Martin versus Jimmy Piersall, Jake Powell versus Joe Cronin, Bill Lee's arm being injured in a fracas at Yankee Stadium. One of the wilder moments took place on August 1, 1973, at Fenway. Thurman Munson rammed into Carlton Fisk at home plate. The collision triggered a battle between the two catchers and a pushing, shoving, cursing melee among Red Sox and Yankee players and coaches.

The rivalry is Joe DiMaggio winning the MVP in 1941 over Ted Williams, to the consternation of Sox fans; the rumored trade in 1947 of DiMag for Williams; Mantle edging out Ted Williams in 1956 for the batting title; the Mick winning the MVP in 1957, angering Sox fans, who thought Ted Williams deserved it; the "Red Sox Suck" and the "Yankee Go Home" T-shirts.

"When I first came to the Yankees, the guys said you won't believe this series," Goose Gossage recalled. "You won't believe the way the two teams go at each other. In late June of 1978 I made my first appearance against the Red Sox. I wanted to go out there and kick hell out of them."

"I didn't even know there was a big rivalry until I came to the Red Sox," said Don Zimmer. "But I found out soon enough. I was coaching at third base at Yankee Stadium and the fans were throwing so much crap on the field that I had to put on a helmet for protection. The players don't really hate each other. It's a rivalry of fans."

"Every time we came into Fenway," Bobby Murcer said, "it was a war. Every time they came into Yankee Stadium it was a war."

Curse of the Bambino

The Boston Red Sox were World Champions in 1903, 1912, 1915, 1916, and 1918, making them winners of five of the first 15 World Series played. Then Sox owner Harry Frazee sold Babe Ruth to the Yankees for $125,000 and a guaranteed loan of $300,000 on Fenway Park to finance his Broadway play *No, No Nanette*.

With the sale of the Bambino to the Yankees, Boston hit rock bottom. Nine times they finished in last place. The team's fortunes improved somewhat when Tom Yawkey purchased the team in 1933. But the Red Sox have never won a World Series since that fateful day when Ruth was sold to the Yankees.

For that reason and for all the heartbreaking finishes behind the Yankees through the decades, the results of the movement of Ruth from Boston to New York has rightfully been called "the curse of the Bambino."

THE DODGERS—BROOKLYN AND LOS ANGELES

Back in 1889 *The New York Times* noted, "The competition between Brooklyn and New York as regards baseball is unparalleled in the history of the national game."

The competition may have been unparalleled. But it was also unequal. Through most of their history the Dodgers of Brooklyn were a sad-sack team of whom it was said, "Overconfidence may cost them sixth place." The Yankees were the royalty of baseball.

It wasn't until 1941 that the competition and rivalry reached fever pitch as the Dodgers and Yankees prepared to meet as equals for the first time in the World Series. With a team they could really brag about, one million rabid fans assembled as the Dodgers celebrated their pennant with a victory march down Flatbush Avenue. Yankee fans took as a matter of course the Bronx Bombers' 101-victory season and their finish 17 games ahead of the runner-up Red Sox.

The most memorable moment of the World Series took place in game four. Trailing two games to one, the Dodgers had a 4–3 lead. The Yankees came up for their final at bat. With two outs and the bases empty and two strikes on Tommy Henrich, the game seemed to belong to Brooklyn. But fickle fate had other plans. The left-handed-hitting Henrich swung at a Hugh Casey pitch and missed. That should have been strike three. But the ball got by Dodger catcher Mickey Owen. Henrich made it to first base; that opened the barn door. The Yankees won the game 7–4. They won again the next day, 3–1. And they had their eighth straight World Series triumph, dating all the way back to 1927. Brooklyn was held to a .182 team batting average, but the fans of "Dem Bums" took solace in the headline in the *Brooklyn Eagle*: "Wait 'Til Next Year."

But next year never came. Despite the hype and hoopla, the outlandish signs and banners through the '40s and '50s, such as "Moider the Yanks," "Reese for Mayor," "God Help Da Yanks," "Tear Out Their Hearts," and "Brooklyn Has Those Atomic Bums," next year was always the same old sad scenario—the Dodgers losing to the Yankees in the World Series in 1941, 1947, 1949, 1952, and 1953.

The 1955 World Series was once again Dodgers versus Yankees. Brooklyn had lost all seven Series it played—five of them to the Bronx Bombers. Casey Stengel's team took the first two games, 6–5 and 4–2. Since no team had ever won a seven-game Series after losing the first two games, Yankee fans were getting ready to celebrate; Brooklyn fans were starting to think of next year.

Then the Series shifted to Ebbets Field. Behind southpaw Johnny Podres, pitching on his 23rd birthday, the Bums won the third game, 8–3. Then they won the next two. The Yankees came back with a sixth-game win.

The starting pitchers for the seventh and deciding game were Johnny Podres of Brooklyn against 35-year-old Tommy Byrne for the Yankees. Dodger first baseman Gil Hodges drove in a run in the fourth. He drove in another in the sixth. As the Yankees came to bat in the bottom of the sixth inning, the huge Stadium crowd was antsy.

Brooklyn Dodger pitcher Johnny Podres celebrates after throwing a complete game 2–0 shutout over the Yankees to give Brooklyn their first world championship in 1955. Congratulating Podres are catcher Roy Campanella and third-baseman Don Hoak.

New York manager Casey Stengel shouts words of encouragement to his players during the 1955 World Series. An injured Mickey Mantle looks on from the bench (far right).

For defensive purposes, Dodger manager Walt Alston switched Jim Gilliam from left field to replace Don Zimmer at second base. Speedy Sandy Amoros took over for Gilliam in left. Billy Martin worked Podres for a walk leading off the sixth. Gil McDougald bunted for a single. The din was deafening.

Yogi Berra came up to the plate. He sliced a high fly ball. "When Yogi hit the ball," Podres recalled, "I thought it would be an easy out to left. But when I looked up the ball was slicing toward the foul line. Amoros was on his horse. He had been playing Yogi to pull."

It looked at first as if the ball was headed for home run territory in the left-field corner. But Amoros raced over. He lunged with his gloved right hand. He snared the ball by the railing about a dozen inches inside fair territory. Bouncing off the railing, setting himself, the Dodger outfielder threw the ball to relay man Pee Wee Reese, who threw to Hodges—double play.

"I didn't think Amoros would catch the ball," McDougald said. "I thought he would shy away from the fence. I had passed first and had no chance to return to first in time."

"If Amoros had been right-handed," Mel Allen notes, "the ball he caught would have probably dropped in for a double and the whole nature of that game would have been changed."

The game moved to the bottom of the ninth inning. Dodgers 2, Yankees 0. Bill Skowron grounded to the mound. Bob Cerv flied to left. Johnny Podres looked in to Roy Campanella to get his signs to pitch to the dangerous Elston Howard. "I'd thrown Howard all fastballs because I'd wanted to finish him off with a strikeout and Campy wanted another fastball," Podres said. "But then I thought Pee Wee has been waiting so long for this, I'll throw him a changeup. He'll get out in front of it and bounce it to Pee Wee to end the game. That's what happened."

The precise moment was 3:43 P.M. on October 4, 1955—pandemonium in Brooklyn. The Dodgers were World Champions. Walt Alston had done what no Dodger manager had ever done, what Brooklyn owner Walter O'Malley had hired him to do—beaten the Yankees in the World Series.

Brooklyn streets were clogged with celebrating fans. Honking car horns, clanging pots and pans, and shredded newspaper all punctuated that one singular moment. There was joy in Flatbush—the hated Yankees had been beaten.

Sandy Koufax delivers the first pitch of game four of the 1963 World Series to Tony Kubek. Despite giving up a seventh inning home run to Mickey Mantle, Koufax defeated the Yanks, 2–1, for his second win of the series, leading Los Angeles to a four-game sweep.

Willie Randolph scores the game-winning run in the twelfth inning of game one of the 1977 World Series. Randolph doubled and then scored on a base hit by Paul Blair.

But 1956 was another season, another story. The old Yankee hex was on parade in that World Series, one in which Yogi Berra blasted two home runs in the seventh game. That was more than enough of a cushion for Yankee right-hander Johnny Kucks, who allowed just three hits and sailed to a 9–0 win. It was the last World Series played between the Brooklyn Dodgers and the Yankees.

With the Dodgers playing on the West Coast, the rivalry with the Yankees became a sometime thing, mainly at World Series time. But memories of what had been between the two ancient rivals were always close to the surface. There was also a new equation. Former Brooklyn Dodger fans, who never forgave "Dem Bums" for moving to Los Angeles, now became another and highly partisan part of the Yankee–Dodger rivalry. The love they had for the old Brooklyn Dodgers was now transformed into hate for the Los Angeles Dodgers.

But they and Yankee fans had little to cheer about in 1963. Southpaw Sandy Koufax set a new World Series record, striking out 15 in game one of the World Series. "I can see why Koufax won 25 games," quipped Yogi Berra, "but I wonder how he ever managed to lose five." The Dodgers, using just four pitchers, swept Ralph Houk's team in four, holding the Yankees to a .171 team batting average.

In 1977, the Yankees and Dodgers met in the Fall Classic for the ninth time. That Series was the Reggie Jackson show. His five World Series homers gave not only Yankee fans but old-time Brooklyn fans a lot of satisfaction.

The two teams did it again in 1978. Maybe it was too much Dodger Blue, too much Hollywood glitz, too many beautiful people. Maybe it was because, as Gary Park, San Francisco broadcaster, said, "Only in Los Angeles do the guys in the radio booth wear makeup." Whatever. There was something in the air. There was more foul language than ever, more debris on the playing field at the Stadium.

It prompted Reggie Smith to snap out his anger at Yankee fans: "We're spending all our money to solve the problems in the Middle East. We ought to be spending it to educate these idiots here." The Yankees took the championship in six games.

In 1981, another transcoastal World Series was played. The Yankees got off to a two-game lead, and it seemed they were on their way to another title. But some key Yankee errors in the next two games allowed the Dodgers to even and then take the Series.

The Yankee–Dodger rivalry can never be what it was—the two teams in the same city with all those partisan fans getting into it all the time. But it has had its moments since the Dodgers moved from the Borough of Churches to the City of Angels. And the next time the two teams meet in games that matter, the old bad blood will surely rise again.

New York Giant manager John McGraw despised the neighboring Yankee team and even went as far as heckling Yankee players like Babe Ruh.

THE GIANTS—NEW YORK AND SAN FRANCISCO

There was a time that New York Giant manager John J. McGraw was all sweetness and light when it came to the Yankees. In fact, it was the Little Napoleon who acted as the go-between for the purchase of the Yankees by Ruppert and Huston. It was also McGraw who sanctioned the Yankees' playing at the Polo Grounds when the Giants were on the road.

But as the 1920s began with his Giants lagging behind the Yankees in attendance and newspaper headlines, McGraw felt only rage and hostility toward the boarders who played in his Polo Grounds. The new kid on the block was taking over the block. It seemed the only place for McGraw and his Giants to take out their anger, to humble the Yankees, was on the playing field.

McGraw had his chance in 1921. New York City braced for the first one-city World Series since 1906. It was the first New York versus New York Series, the first in which all games were to be played in the same park—the Polo Grounds. Although it irked McGraw that his team had to wear road gray uniforms for half the games in their own home ballpark, he was delighted that his Giants took the Series, winning five of eight games. The only discordant note was the .313 average put up by Babe Ruth to lead all Yankee batters. Stopping the Yankee slugger in the future became a priority for McGraw.

It was New York versus New York again in the 1922 World Series. Throughout that season American League hurlers pitched around Ruth. When reporters asked McGraw if he would have his hurlers pitch to Ruth, he snapped, "Why shouldn't we pitch to Babe Ruth? We pitch to better hitters in the National League."

"Lay it over for him!" the Giant manager screamed at his opening game pitcher, Art Nehf. "He can't hit it even if you tell him what's coming." Privately, the Giant pilot had told his pitchers: "Don't throw that big baboon anything but slow curves." Nehf followed orders, spinning out a succession of slow curves. Ruth swung from his heels and came up with air. With each swinging strike throughout the Series, McGraw taunted Ruth more and more. The jibes and the slow curves achieved the desired result for McGraw. The Babe wound up with a puny .118 average. The Giants beat the Yankees.

In 1923, fans all over New York City clamored for a rematch of the Yankees and Giants in the World Series. And one more time, it was indeed New York versus New York in the World Series. Only this time games were played at both the Polo Grounds and brand-new Yankee Stadium. The mighty Babe had smashed 41 home runs, driven in 131 and batted .393 in the regular season. And even though the 1923 Giants had won their third straight pennant and featured eight future Hall of Famers in their lineup, it was the Yankees who were now top dog in the Big Apple. McGraw's only bragging rights were that his team had beaten the hated American Leaguers in two straight Series.

The two teams split the first two games. In game three aging outfielder Casey Stengel's home run gave the Giants a 1–0 victory. Slow strutting out the homer and thumbing his nose, Casey got the attention of the Yankee bench. Perhaps he got too much attention. The Yankees went on to win the Series in six. The Giants just could not contain Babe Ruth, who slammed three home runs and hit for a .368 average.

The Giant–Yankee rivalry would continue, but the era of McGraw's domination of New York City baseball was over. With that first championship won, the Yankees established their claim to greatness. They had the biggest star in the game, the grandest stadium, and they played in the world's greatest city.

The Giants met the Yankees in the "Battle of Broadway" in the 1936 and 1937 World Series. McGraw was no longer on the scene, and the Giants were no longer a match for the heavily favored and powerful Yankees. The Bronx Bombers easily won both Series.

Although some years would pass before the Giants and Yankees met again in postseason play, with the teams playing in such proximity to each other, with the heritage of ill feeling always close to the surface, there were always things to stoke the rivalry—comparisons of managers, players, announcers, ballparks. But the rivalry was never as red-hot as when the teams met in the World Series.

In 1951, it was time for another meeting. The Giants, on the strength of the "Shot Heard 'Round the World," Bobby Thomson's home run that was the blow that defeated the Dodgers in the 1951 playoff, prepared to battle the Yankees in the World Series.

Fully expecting Brooklyn to be in the World Series, Dodger scout Andy High had followed the Yankees around for the final month of the 1951 season. Now he had no use for his copious scouting reports, so he turned them over to Giants manager Leo Durocher.

The Giants defeated the Yankees 5–1 in the first game of the Series, the first opening-game loss in a World Series for the Yankees since 1936. "The High reports are great," Durocher smiled. "I never saw anything like it."

But the Yankees bounced back and shredded the Giants in six. One of their wins was a 13–1 mauling. Losing to the Yankees was not pleasant for the Giants. But the euphoria of what they had done that 1951 season to their more hated rival, the Dodgers, softened the pain.

(Opposite)
The 1921 World Series was played exclusively at the Polo Grounds.

Yogi Berra and Phil Rizzuto show their appreciation for teammate Hank Bauer after Bauer hit a bases loaded triple to lead the Yankees to the World Championship over the Giants in 1951.

In 1962, it was like 1951 all over again. During the season the Giants had trailed, caught, then beaten the Dodgers in the playoff. Now they prepared to face off against the Yankees for the seventh time in the World Series, the first coast-to-coast encounter in baseball history. Horace Stoneham still owned the Giants, but this was a different group of players, with names like Cepeda, McCovey, and Alou. Only Willie Mays remained from the team that had played at the Polo Grounds.

The teams split the first two games in San Francisco. The next three were played at the Stadium, where, unlike the treatment given to the Los Angeles Dodgers, the Giants were treated almost respectfully by fans.

The Series moved to the pivotal game seven at Candlestick Park. The score was 1–0 Yankees as the Giants came to bat in the bottom of the ninth inning against Ralph Terry, winner of the fifth game of the Series.

Matty Alou beat out a bunt to second. Then Terry struck out Felipe Alou and Chuck Hiller. Willie Mays doubled to right. Muscular Willie McCovey was next. Ralph Houk came out of the Yankee dugout. "First base is open," the Major said. "Do you want to walk him and pitch to Cepeda?"

"I want to pitch to McCovey," Terry said. "I can get him out."

McCovey stepped in. The 40,000 plus begged for just a single to give the Giants of San Francisco their first World Championship. What they got was a line shot that second baseman Bobby Richardson speared.

"They had just moved him over to that spot," says McCovey, still wincing, "and like magic I hit it right at him." It was Yankee magic—the ball stuck in his glove. The Yanks won the game and the World Championship.

The ghost of Bill Terry may have been there, but it was Ralph Terry's time. He was voted the Series MVP.

Ralph Terry flips his glove in the air after the final out of game seven of the 1962 World Series. Willie McCovey lined out to second baseman Bobby Richardson with runners on second and third, securing Terry's 1–0 gem.

THE BALTIMORE ORIOLES

On the eve of the 1996 American League Championship Series, Baltimore manager Davey Johnson said, "I think it was fated. I think this was meant to be. There's always been a great rivalry between the Yankees and Orioles."

That was true. The rivalry between the Yankees of New York and the Orioles of Baltimore had once been red-hot. Through the decades the two teams, located in fairly close geographical proximity, had gone head to head many times. There were sometimes bruised egos, malicious words. Always there was a battle of major stars.

But in recent years the rivalry had declined, partly because both franchises took a backseat to other, more successful American League teams.

193

Now the Yankees were at the doorstep of their first pennant since 1981. Baltimore was in the LCS for the first time since 1983.

A sidebar to the renewed rivalry was the ego clash of owners—George Steinbrenner versus Baltimore owner Peter Angelos, who had almost as much mouth as and probably deeper pockets than the Yankee boss. Both owners spent money freely and competed aggressively for free agents. They had a tug of war over David Cone. Baltimore scored with its acquisitions of Roberto Alomar, B. J. Surhoff, and Eddie Murray. Angelos had a gleaming new stadium, Camden Yards. Steinbrenner had his old castle in the Bronx, which he kept talking about moving out of.

The '96 editions of both teams were true reversals of the past. The Yankees were built on pitching, spare parts, runners being moved along, a very strong bullpen, a blend of veterans and newcomers—something along the lines of the Baltimore teams that they had once battled. The Orioles hit more home runs than any other team in major league history. Seven Orioles hit 20 or more home runs. But as a team they were essentially one-dimensional, a group of individuals who did more than their share of whining, a team dubbed the "Tin Men" by the Baltimore media.

The first two games played between the Yankees and Orioles at Camden Yards set the tone for the 1996 season. The Yankees trailed 9–4 in a 4-hour-21-minute marathon—the longest nine-inning game in major league history. New York finally prevailed, 13–10. The next night, rainy and bitter, the teams played 15 innings. The Yankees won that game too, 11–6. The games showcased the resilience of the New York roster. Andy Pettitte, who lasted only to the second inning in the first game, was the winner in the second game, hurling three scoreless innings.

The victory gave the Yankees possession of first place by a half-game, and in first place they remained for the rest of the season. The Orioles, seemingly stunned, played below .500 baseball from mid-April to mid-July. A four-game Yankee sweep at Camden Yards following the All-Star break appeared to put the Orioles away. The Yankees opened a 12-game lead on July 29. But the Orioles went on a charge that saw them go 31–15 in a six-week period. That put the O's back in the hunt.

The Yankee lead was cut to three games when the two teams met on September 18. It was an encounter the O's had looked forward to all summer. The Yankees took two out of three—Baltimore was pushed back four games and that was that. In 13 regular-season games between the rivals, the Orioles managed to win only three. The Yankees won all six games played at Camden Yards.

But Baltimore would not go away. The Orioles became the first wild-card team to advance in the playoffs when they knocked off Cleveland. And it was New York versus Baltimore in the American League Championship Series. It was the first time that two teams from the same division had battled for the pennant.

"Whatever happened is in the past," said the Orioles' Roberto Alomar. "Now everybody is at the same level."

Always tactful Joe Torre said, "The way Baltimore played the second half of the year, I sort of expected this to happen."

The opening game of the LCS was delayed a day by rain. The pivotal moment of game one came in the eighth inning, with the Yankees trailing 4–3 and the Orioles' fastballing Armando Benitez pitching to Derek Jeter. The swing—the ball lofted out to right field and headed to the porch. Tony Tarasco back, back, seemingly poised to make the catch. Then, like magic, 12-year-old Jeffrey Maier from Old Tappan, New Jersey, gloved hand outstretched, deflects the ball away.

Pandemonium! Tarasco jumps, screams, and, along with his teammates, is all over umpire Rich Garcia, who rules that Jeter has hit a home run. The Orioles protest, rage, curse. Davey Johnson is ejected for over-zealous protesting. Game tied 4–4.

Four innings later, with Randy Myers on the mound, Bernie Williams swings—home run, the king-sized kind. Yankees win!

"It was a routine fly ball for me," Tarasco tells reporters later. "It was an out. The ball was very catchable."

Jeffrey Maier also found the ball to be very catchable. The next day he had an even better seat behind the Yankee dugout in the *New York Daily News* box. Maier became the toast of the town. He was on national television. His picture was in every newspaper. He made the rounds of the talk shows.

"It's pretty unbelievable," he said. "I didn't think it would happen to me. I feel like something amazing has happened."

The Orioles came back the next day to win 5–3. That set up three games at Camden Yards, the Yankees' home away from home. But Steinbrenner moaned, "We're going to go up there and get swept. They've got Eddie Murray. We've got Cecil Fielder and Charlie Hayes." Was he just shaking things up? Was the Boss taking another jab at General Manager Bob Watson? Or was he telling it the way he felt?

It didn't matter. The Yankees won game three, 5–2. They won game four, 8–4. They won game five, 6–4. The Orioles were done.

"We couldn't make the pitches when it counted, and that's been kind of the story all year," Orioles manager Davey Johnson said. "The Yankees have consistently done the job and have gotten the key hits with men on base."

Johnson's commentary said a lot but was not the whole story of the Yankee triumph. His team scored 19 runs against the Yankees in the playoff: All but six of the runs came across via the home run route. No Oriole stole a base, very few runners were moved along. The frequent sight of Baltimore players on second and third base, stranded in late innings, accentuated the kind of team they had.

But Peter Angelos was not done: "New York won a battle in a war that is ongoing," he said. "As far as the Orioles are concerned, we will continue in our efforts again and again until our pursuit is successful. And it will be. Baltimore will have a winner."

Jeffrey Maier holds up the morning newspaper the day after his infamous "catch" from the stands. Maier gained national attention from the incident.

SIX

SOME
Yankee Eccentrics

YOGI BERRA

When Lawrence Peter Berra was at Newark in 1946 dreaming of the time he would become a Yankee, he roomed with Bobby Brown, who was at work studying to be a doctor. Brown pored over medical texts before he went to sleep. Yogi read comic books. One night as they were getting ready to put out the lights, Berra asked, "How did your book come out, Bobby?"

Yogi Berra's book came out just fine. He made the great leap from being a ninth-grade dropout whose favorite subject was "recess" to becoming one of the great players in Yankee history. And beyond that he remains one of the most quoted, lovable, and legendary figures who ever donned pinstripes.

In 1947, Berra's first full year with the Yankees, veteran players poured sand in his shoes and put hot stuff in his jock. Berra had short, stubby fingers and a body to match, prompting Larry MacPhail to remark, "He looks like the bottom man on an unemployed tag team."

Berra earned the "Yogi" nickname in his growing-up years in St. Louis. He and his friends had seen a Hindu fakir in a movie sitting still with arms and legs folded. The image of the fakir reminded the kids of Berra as he sat on the bench between innings of their games.

In many ways Berra was the ugly duckling who turned into the prince—a charming one at that. Lively, eccentric, lovable, he even inspired the "Yogi Bear" cartoon character.

Asked if he wanted to see a "dirty" movie, Berra's response was, "Who's in it?" As another story goes, he got a new piano and called up one of his Yankee teammates. "Come on over here and show me how to work this thing." And as another story goes he saw an old Steve McQueen movie and told a few friends, "He must have made that before he died."

Although Berra claimed, "I really didn't say everything I said," and some attempted to depict him as a dim-witted, uncouth character, Yogi was smart enough to play in 14 World Series in 17 years, smart enough to play in more games in Yankee history than anyone except Mantle and Gehrig, smart enough to add up a gin rummy score with lightning speed, smart enough to have a memory like an elephant's.

Casey Stengel always called him "Mr. Berra" and "my assistant manager" and said Yogi "was second only to Joe DiMaggio in all-around ability among the players I managed."

About the only real mistake Yogi Berra ever made in his baseball career was in 1965 at age 40. He made it into four games with the New York Mets as player-coach. All that succeeded in doing was delaying his admission into the Baseball Hall of Fame.

Yogiisms

(Preceding page)
Yogi Berra, one of baseball's true characters.

"A nickel ain't worth a dime anymore."

"I've been with the Yankees 17 years watching games and learning. You can see a lot by observing."

After striking out on three way-out-of-strike-zone pitches: "How can a pitcher that wild stay in the league?"

"You know the trouble with the sun at Yankee Stadium in autumn: It gets late early out there."

When they asked him in spring training about his cap size: "I don't know. I'm not in shape yet."

He spoke about a restaurant this way: "Nobody goes there anymore. It's too crowded."

His advice to one player about another: "If you can't imitate him, don't copy him."

"Baseball is 90 percent mental. The other half is physical."

"Ninety percent of the game is half mental."

"If the people don't want to come out to the ballpark, nobody's going to stop them."

"It's déjà vu all over again."

"You've got to be careful if you don't know where you're going, because you might not get there."

"He's a big clog in their machine."

"I usually take a two-hour nap, from one o'clock to four."

"The game isn't over till it's over."

Asked what time it was: "You mean now?"

"I'd rather be the Yankees catcher than the president, and that makes me pretty lucky, I guess, because I could never be the president."

After Johnny Bench broke his all-time home run record for catchers, the following telegram was sent: "Congratulations on breaking my record. I always thought it would stand until it was broken."

Told he looked nice and cool by Mary Lindsay, the wife of then New York City mayor John V. Lindsay, Berra replied: "You don't look so hot yourself."

Handed a check that said "pay to the bearer," Berra complained: "That ain't the way to spell my name."

Berra was introduced by Toots Shor at his restaurant to a bearded, stocky man. "This is Ernie Hemingway, Yogi, he's a writer. You've read him, haven't you?" "I don't think so," Yogi said with a half-frown. "What paper are you with, bud?"

Then there was the time Berra attended a White House dinner and said, "It was hard to have a conversation with anyone, there was so many people talking."

JIM BOUTON

One of the more intellectual, witty, and exciting characters to hit the '60s baseball scene, fastballer Jim Bouton pitched with verve and emotion, sometimes too much of both. Most of the time when he came out of his windup to deliver the pitch, his cap flew off. But that was the least of the hyperactive characteristics of the player they called "Bulldog."

Jim Bouton is shown earning an 8–3 decision over the St. Louis Cardinals during the 1964 World Series. Bouton later authored the best-selling *Ball Four,* which uncovered many well-kept secrets about the life of a ballplayer off the field.

Some of Bouton's spare time was devoted to his "Crazy Guggenheim" routine. The shtick delighted many of his Yankee teammates but irritated management, who considered him undignified and things worse.

As a rookie in 1962, Bouton posted a 7–7 record. Making the 1963 American League All-Star team in 1963, he hit his stride, posting a 21–7 mark with a 2.53 ERA. In game three of the 1963 World Series Bouton had the misfortune to come up against Don Drysdale, who, in Walt Alston's phrase, pitched "one of the greatest games I ever saw." Bouton lost 1–0. It was a heartbreaking defeat; the lone Dodger run came across on a first-inning walk to Jim Gilliam, a wild pitch, and a Tommy Davis single.

In 1964, Bouton was 18–13 and seemed headed for stardom It was not to be. In 1965, both Bouton and the Yankees crashed. He blew out his arm, wound up losing 15 of 19 decisions. A year later the Yankees finished in last place. They were at rock bottom and so was Bouton. He was 3–8.

Over seven frenetic Yankee seasons the lively hurler compiled a 55–51 record. In October of 1968 Bouton was traded to the Seattle Pilots. He is best remembered for *Ball Four,* a kiss-and-tell look at the seamier side of baseball—its drinking, pill culture, womanizing.

Despite the zaniness and the craziness, the fact that he ranks right up there among the all-time Yankee kooks, Jim Bouton was a player with a lot of talent.

RYNE DUREN

Casey Stengel said of Ryne Duren: "He takes a drink or 10, comes in with them Coke bottles [eyeglasses], throws one on the screen, and scares the shit out of them. And when he starts pitching, people stop eating their popcorn."

Acquired in a trade from Kansas City, the 28-year-old Duren was 13–2 for the Yankees' Denver farm team in 1957. He was a Yankee for just three years, but he sure left his mark.

They called him "Blind Ryne," and for good reason. Duren's uncorrected vision was 20/70 and 20/200. Goggle-styled glasses seemed to occupy most of his face. He stared, squinted, struggled to see batters. His signature was his first warmup pitch—it usually hit high off the screen behind home plate. In the minors one of Duren's errant fastballs once hit a batter in the on-deck circle. There were many times that the Wisconsin native's warmup pitches went astray, winding up all over the place. Some said the wildness was all part of an act, but no one wanted to test the 6-2, 194-pound hurler and his 95-mile-per-hour fastball.

In the 1958 season Duren led all relief pitcher in saves with 20 in 44 games. Against Milwaukee in the World Series he saved a game, won a game, and notched a 1.93 ERA. In 1959, he was unscored-on in 36 innings over 18 games. Both those seasons, during which he recorded 183 strikeouts in 151 innings, he was an American League All-Star.

Hitters were reluctant to dig in the batter's box when Ryne Duren was on the mound. Duren possessed a blazing 95 mile per hour fastball, but also had perhaps the worst vision in baseball history.

LEO DUROCHER

Leo Ernest Durocher was born on July 27, 1905, in West Springfield, Massachusetts. Throughout his growing-up years his spare time was spent perfecting his pool-shooting and rock-throwing skills. School was nothing but trouble. When he finally and surprisingly reached the ninth grade he was tossed out school for thrashing his ninth-grade teacher. He went to work for an electric company, played on its semipro team, and started his move up the baseball ladder.

Scout Paul Krichell was impressed with the play of the young infielder at Hartford, noting that Durocher had "double-play hands." The Yankees paid $7,000 to acquire him in 1925, and he appeared in two games for the Bronx Bombers. After minor league stops at Atlanta, where he hit .238, and St. Paul, where he batted .253, Durocher resurfaced with the Yankees in 1928. He batted .270 as a utility player; in 1929 he was the starting shortstop and hit .246.

Yankee manager Miller Huggins loved him. "Little guys like us can win games," Hug told Durocher. "We can beat 'em up here," the little skipper continued, pointing to his head. Most of the Yankees did not share Huggins's opinion. They were irritated by the newcomer's high-fashion clothing, frequent fraternizing with gamblers, and nonstop talking.

At first Babe Ruth befriended him. But Durocher's foul mouth opened up once too often, and his attempts to cut into the Sultan of Swat's batting practice time turned the Bambino against him. Ruth dubbed Durocher the

Leo Durocher, then managing the Brooklyn Dodgers, is shown here being interviewed by Red Barber. The interview took place just prior to the first telecast of a major league baseball game in 1939.

"All American Out" because of his lack of hitting ability. Ruth also called him a thief, claiming that the "Lip" had stolen his watch.

Pugnacious, conceited, driven, and reckless, Durocher backed down from no one, not even superstars. Ty Cobb, 41, was in his final major league season and was running toward third base trying for a triple. Durocher stuck his hip in the way of the Georgia Peach. Cobb lost his balance, fell, and Durocher tagged him out.

"If you ever pull that stunt again," Cobb screamed, "I'll cut off your legs."

"You ain't gonna cut off anybody's legs," Durocher barked. "You've gotten away with murder all these years but you are through. You'll get a hip any time you come down my way, and if you try and cut me, you'll get a ball rammed down your throat. Go home, Grandpa, you're gonna get hurt playing at your age."

The two were ready to go at each other, but players from both teams jumped in and stopped what would have been a good fight.

In September 1929, Miller Huggins died. Durocher had called him "the only friend I ever had on the team." Embarrassed by Leo's unseemly behavior and crude language, that winter Ed Barrow used Durocher's asking for a salary raise as an excuse to unload him to Cincinnati. Had Huggins lived, Durocher would probably have gotten the raise and remained with the Yankees.

En route to spring training in 1930, Leo passed through New York City and decided to call on Barrow. All duded up in a velvet-adorned overcoat, spats, and a spiffy derby hat of the latest style, the 24-year-old was asked by Barrow, "What time does your train depart for Florida?"

"Oh," said the Lip, "I'm not going by train. Look out your window and you'll see my transportation."

Barrow looked and saw a big red convertible. Taken aback, the Yankee executive finally responded, "Well, Leo, one thing everyone can say is that you always go first class."

That he did. Leo Ernest Durocher's tempestuous major league career began with one at bat for the 1925 Yankees. It ended a half-century later with the Houston Astros. All that time he lived first class and by the creed, "I come to play! I come to beat you! I come to kill you! That's the way Miller Huggins, my first manager, brought me up, and that's the way it has always been for me."

WHITEY FORD

He had twinkly blue eyes and a cherubic face. But underneath that choirboy countenance was an impish, cocky, blithe spirit, a night prowler. That was Whitey Ford, one of the great characters in Yankee history.

"Off the mound," his teammate Tony Kubek said, "Ford was shockingly humble." He might have been, but he was also the master of audacious one-liners like "the only way to make coaches think you're in shape in the spring is to get a tan."

A day before the 1961 All-Star Game in San Francisco, Horace Stoneham, owner of the Giants, gave Ford and Mickey Mantle access to his local country club. The two Yankees enjoyed themselves and ran up a $400 bill.

"We'll forget it, if you can strike out Willie Mays in the game tomorrow," Stoneham told Whitey.

In the first inning Ford got two strikes on Mays. Then he threw a pitch that started above the Giant center fielder's shoulder and dropped to his belt. It was strike three and it paralyzed Mays. Mantle was so excited that he raced in from center field and pounded Whitey on the back. There were those who swore the pitch Ford threw was one of his creations—the mudball, one part dirt from the mound and one part saliva.

When it came to competing, the man they called "Chairman of the Board" was cold and calculating, strictly business. He was much more kind to teammates.

In one game he called John Blanchard out to the mound.

"What's wrong?" the catcher asked.

"Nothing."

"Then why call me out?"

"I just figured you could use a break."

On and off the mound Ford never took a break. "Hell, if I didn't drink or smoke I'd win 20 games every year. It's easy if you don't drink or smoke or horse around." But horsing around was part of his game.

Whitey Ford did whatever it took to win ballgames for the Yankees. A crafty southpaw with great control, Ford would often dirty the ball to distort a hitter's vision at the plate.

PHIL LINZ

Although best remembered for the infamous "harmonica incident," Phil Linz was a talented minor leaguer who never could quite find his niche in the Yankee scheme of things. But that was not too due to any lack of talent, effort, or spirit.

"I spent $4\frac{1}{2}$ years in the Yankee minor league chain," Linz noted. "In 1960, I led the Carolina League in hitting. In 1961, at Amarillo, I led the Texas League in hitting with a .349 average. I was also Most Valuable Player both years."

In 1962, Linz came to the Yankees. The shortstop position was open because Tony Kubek would be away on military duty until August. The opening at shortstop became a battle between Tom Tresh and Linz. "The reporters," Linz said, "asked me about my chances. 'Tommy Tresh has more power, has a stronger arm, runs faster. I think Tommy has a better shot at being the shortstop.'"

The honest answer shocked many and made some think of Linz as a bit off-center. "But," Linz said, "I didn't view myself as an eccentric. Whatever came into my mind I said."

That was one of the reasons Linz was given the nickname "Mr. Laffs." He also earned the nickname "Supersub" because of his versatility. "I probably would have started for any other major league team," Linz said, "but with the Yankees I couldn't. I made myself valuable by learning how to play second, third, and taking fly balls in the outfield."

Phil Linz, shown here making a diving stop during a game in 1965, was the ultimate utility man for the Yanks. But when he told Yankee front office, "Play me or trade me," they sent him to the Philadelphia Phillies.

Ultimately, Linz tired of his "Supersub" status. That led to his line, since used by a legion of players, "Play me or trade me." The Yankees took his line to heart. He was traded to the Phillies after the 1965 season.

The Harmonica Incident

Heading on the team bus to O'Hare Airport on August 20, 1964, the Yankees were just happy to get out of town. They had lost four straight to the White Sox, lost 10 of their last 15 games. The team had won four straight pennants, but it seemed a fifth one was slipping away. Manager Yogi Berra was in a foul mood.

"I sat in the back of the bus," Phil Linz recalled. "Tony Kubek, Tommy Tresh, and I had been in Neiman Marcus in Chicago and they bought harmonicas. Tony played 'Streets of Laredo' right there in the department store. It sounded great so I bought one. I never owned a harmonica in my life prior to that."

It was a hot and sticky day. The traffic did not move. "I was bored," Linz said. "I had the Learner's Sheet for 'Mary Had a Little Lamb,' so I started fiddling. You blow in and blow out notes. Then Yogi came from the front of the bus and yelled, 'Cut that out and shove that harmonica up your watchchacallitt.' And Mickey [Mantle] yelled: 'Play it louder.'

"I told Yogi that I didn't lose the game and tried to continue playing the harmonica," Linz said. "There was a lot of shouting back and forth." One version has it that Yogi slapped the harmonica out of Linz's hands. Another is that Linz flipped the instrument to his infuriated manager. Even the man who was there doesn't quite recall exactly what happened. But Linz did scream, "What are you getting on me for? I give a hundred percent Why don't you get on some of the guys who don't hustle?

"The next day all the newspapers had these giant headlines that the Yankees had a big fight," the player they called Supersub recalled. "That night I went to Yogi's office and apologized. "I didn't know what came over me," I told him. "I shouldn't have been doing that." We shook hands. Yogi said, 'I have to fine you 250 bucks because of the writers.'

"The next day the Hohner Company called, and I got a contract for $5,000 to endorse their harmonica," Linz said. "The whole thing became a big joke."

The harmonica incident seemed to awaken the sleepwalking Yankees. They won 22 of 28 September games and the American League pennant, but lost to the St. Louis Cardinals in seven games in the World Series. There were those who said that owner Del Webb and GM Ralph Houk viewed the harmonica incident as symbolic of the way Yogi Berra had lost control of the team and that postseason accomplishments notwithstanding, he was gone. They were right. Berra was fired after the World Series.

SPARKY LYLE

In another of the worst trades the Boston Red Sox ever made, Sparky Lyle came to the Yankees in March 1972 for first-baseman Danny Cater. Manager Ralph Houk said that Lyle would be the stopper coming out of the bullpen. And stopper he was. In his first Yankee season the left-handed hurler was 9–5, with a 1.91 ERA and a league-leading 35 saves.

With his bushy mustache and long sideburns, Lyle was a totally 1970s type. Rubber-armed, eccentric, boasting a sensational slider and a gift for gab, Albert Walter Lyle would do anything for a laugh. Exiting from a coffin, sitting around in his birthday suit, sitting on cakes, showing up at spring training with his limbs in casts, all were part of his bag of tricks.

The man they called "the Count" would come into a game at the Stadium riding in a pinstriped Toyota to the strains of "Pomp and Circumstance" to the delight of fans. But that lasted only for a time. Lyle decided to make his entrances a bit more sedate, explaining, "A guy at the game for the first time might think I'm king or what if I came in and got my butt kicked."

In seven seasons as a Yankee it was Lyle who was doing the butt kicking. Six of those years he pitched in more games than any other Yankee. Five times he had the most saves. Four seasons he was the team ERA leader. Lyle was a major factor as the Yankees won their first championship in 15 years in 1977. He was 13–5 with 26 saves and became the first relief pitcher to win the Cy Young award.

Always the suspicious type, Lyle took his World Championship ring and "cut the glass on my coffee table with it. I wanted to find out if the diamond was for real. Then I found out that the coffee table was worth more than my ring."

Sparky Lyle's long sideburns and "handlebar" mustache epitomized the ballplayer of the 1970s. In 1977 he became the first relief pitcher to win the Cy Young award, but the Yankees traded him to Texas after the 1978 season.

Reggie Jackson signs his new book for a young Yankee fan in 1978. Jackson, who could never be accused of not taking his due credit, proclaimed that he wrote every caption in the book himself.

In 1978, it seemed that newly signed free agent Goose Gossage was worth more to the Yankees than Lyle, who, in Graig Nettles's phrase, went from Cy Young to sayonara. He also went to Texas when the season ended.

Sparky Lyle, one of the best relief pitchers in Yankee history, ranks third in all-time saves in franchise history behind Goose Gossage and Dave Righetti.

REGGIE JACKSON

He talked the talk and hit the home runs. Great copy for sportswriters, who he said were the only ones he could relate to, a pain for managers, a distraction for teammates, and a serious threat at all times to the competition. Reggie Jackson was a piece of work.

"Your first name's white," Mickey Rivers told him. "Your second is Hispanic, and your third belongs to a black. No wonder you don't know who you are."

But Reginald Martinez Jackson did know who he was, and he wasn't bashful about articulating it. "The only difference," he said, "between me and the other great Yankees is my skin color."

Hitting and talking, talking and hitting, Reggie lit up New York in his time as a Yankee with one-liners, quips, asides, monologues. He also lit up

206

the baseball world with his flair for the dramatic. "I put the asses in the seats," he said. Sometimes they did not stay there, as there were always people jumping up to watch him do his stuff on the baseball field.

"God," he said, "do I love to hit that round sumbitch out of the park and make 'em say 'wow.'"

The fans might have said "Wow" and "Reggee! Reggee!" but others had less kind commentary. "I go back to 1964 with Reggie," Rick Monday said, "but I don't go far back enough to remember when he was shy."

"There isn't enough mustard in the whole world to cover that hot dog," pitcher Darold Knowles noted.

On a key play in the 1978 World Series, Jackson deflected a thrown ball with his hip. "Something odd always happens around him," was the reaction of manager Bob Lemon.

Eccentric, egotistical, enigmatic, exciting, Reggie Jackson, in his phrase, did "represent both the underdog and the overdog in society."

Graig Nettles leaps into the air to snare a line drive off the bat of Davey Lopes in the 1978 World Series. Nettles's extraordinary fielding skills found the spotlight during the '78 Series.

GRAIG NETTLES

A Yankee from 1973 to 1983, Graig Nettles was the best all-around third baseman of the 1970s, possibly the best-fielding third baseman of all time. Only Reggie Jackson and Carl Yastrzemski collected more RBIs in the '70s.

Born in San Diego in 1944, Nettles was a hard-nosed, no-nonsense competitor. His fielding ability was something to behold. He got to balls in the hole, saw the ball into his glove, used his strong arm to gun out frustrated runners. His career year was 1977, when he hit 37 home runs, scored 99, and drove in 107.

His whole fielding package was on display in the 1978 World Series against the Dodgers, who won the first two games of the Series. In game three, Nettles made four tremendous stops. His fielding fired up the Yankees. They won that game and the next three to take the World Championship.

The talent was there for Nettles, but so was the moodiness and the mouth. And that earned him the reputation of being slightly off-center. More than a bit disconcerted about some of the antics of the Yankees on and off the field, Nettles snapped, "When I was a kid, I wanted to play baseball and join the circus. With the Yankees, I've been able to do both." He is also remembered for the line, "What the Yankees need is a second-base coach."

On January 29, 1982, Graig Nettles became the sixth captain in Yankee history. He seemed an odd choice considering his negative comments about teammates and the organization. But Nettles's tenure as captain was brief.

His nickname was "Puff," a reference, some claimed, to his fielding ability and sharp tongue. Joe Garagiola had another view. "They call him 'Puff' because he's always provoking fights and then when they start, *puff,* he's gone."

In 1984, Nettles, who averaged 26 home runs and 88 RBIs a year from 1973 to 1979, was gone from the Yankees—traded to San Diego.

Brooklyn-born Joe Pepitone never lived up to his enormous potential.

JOE PEPITONE

With his long hair, mod clothing, and a hair blower that he brought into the locker room, Joe Pepitone was not your typical Yankee. He had squandered his $20,000 signing bonus on a sports car and a motor boat. Out of Brooklyn, New York, left-handed all the way, "Pepi" came to the Yankees in 1962. He had marvelous minor league stats and a reputation as a flake, and he lived up to both.

For a time he was a backup to Bill Skowron at first base. This did not please some of Pepitone's tough friends. They offered to break the Moose's legs to give "Pepi" more playing time. But he declined the favor.

By 1963, with Skowron traded off to the Dodgers, the first-base job belonged to Pepitone. And he made the most of it. He hit 25 or more home runs in each of four seasons and three times won the Gold Glove award. The potential was always there for Pepitone to be a great one, but so was the outrageous behavior—fights on the field, weird one-liners, and even more absurd monologues.

"I roomed with Pepitone for a time," said Pedro Ramos, "but he was so crazy that I changed and roomed alone."

But with all this, Pepitone was a fixture in the Yankee lineup, a crowd favorite, generous with his time to fans. "I seldom refused autograph seekers," he said, "unless they were old enough to look like collection agents."

The never-at-a-loss-for-words Pepitone was shifted to center field in 1967–68, trading places with Mickey Mantle, who moved to first base to save his legs. The end for Pepitone as a Yankee came in December 1969, when he was traded to Houston. "The Astrodome," he quipped, "is the biggest hairdryer in the world."

From the Astros, Pepitone moved on to play for the Cubs and then the Braves and then in Japan. "I heard he wasn't happy there, either," Leo Durocher said. "The Japanese people were very inconsiderate. They insisted upon speaking Japanese."

In one way or another Joe Pepitone insisted on wasting his talent. If he had not, he would have been one of the better players in Yankee history.

MICKEY RIVERS

"Ain't no sense in worrying about things you got control over, 'cause if you got control over them, ain't no sense worrying. And there ain't no sense worrying about things you got no control over, 'cause if you got no control over them, ain't no sense worrying."

That was the motto of John Milton Rivers, better known as Mickey Rivers or "Mick the Quick." He came over to the Yankees from the California Angels along with Ed Figueroa for Bobby Bonds in December 1975. Installed as the leadoff hitter in a power-laden batting order, Rivers helped push the team to three straight pennants from 1976 to 1978.

One of the fastest players the Yankees ever had, Rivers stole 43 bases in 1976—most for the franchise since 1944. And the way he covered ground in center field evoked memories of Earle Combs, Joe DiMaggio, and Mickey Mantle, but not exactly.

The only time it seemed that he rushed was on the baseball field and on his way to the racetrack, a place where he spent a lot of time. Most of the time Rivers walked slowly and with a slouch. That earned him the nickname "The Almighty Tired Man." He was also fond of using his own language, words he claimed he had picked up in the ghetto. "Gozzlehead" and "Marplehead" were two of his favorites, and he employed them as adjectives, verbs, expletives, and salutations. It was said in all truth that Mickey Rivers had a gift for gab, and that gift was on display many times at kangaroo courts when he held forth as the sometimes wise presiding officer.

In four Yankee seasons, Mick the Quick batted .299 and stole 93 bases. He was traded to Texas in 1979. "We had to get him out of the New York environment," George Steinbrenner said. "He's just a sweet, sweet kid."

The Yankees acquired Mickey Rivers for his speed to complement their power-hitting lineup. Rivers helped New York win three straight American League pennants, but at times it seemed as if his mouth moved even more quickly than his feet.

PHIL RIZZUTO

"I started my career being naive," Phil Rizzuto recalled, "and finished my career the same way. In my rookie year in one game we were tied and it was getting very late. Games then started at 3:00 P.M. I guess I got lucky and hit a home run. The fans went wild. As I rounded third, one of them jumped out

A steady shortstop throughout his playing days, Phil Rizzuto's colorful personality gleamed when he began broadcasting for the Yankees.

of the stands and grabbed my hat and ran back into the stands. I thought that was great, that it was the customary thing to do. The next day I was called into Ed Barrow's office. I figured I'd get a raise or a pat on the back for winning the game, but he started yelling at me for losing my hat and told my that I'd have to pay for it. Can you imagine that?"

One can imagine anything when it comes to Phil Rizzuto. He was dismissed as being too small to make it in the majors. But despite the raps, the Scooter became the heart and soul of nine pennant winners, one of the best big league shortstops, most entertaining announcers, and most unusual personalities in the game.

Hyper, superstitious, loquacious, Phil Rizzuto always had a lot in common with his fellow New Yorkers—and that was one just of the reasons they loved him so much. The first American Leaguer to wear a batting helmet, the slight Rizzuto was also one of the first to bring his glove into the dugout between innings. But that caused all kinds of problems. Players were aware that he was fearful of all things that crawled. And a lot of those things made their way into his glove.

When he was in the minor leagues, Rizzuto was twice knocked to the ground by lightning. So he was afraid of lightning and thunder and flying in an airplane. His superstitions included closing his eyes when passing a cemetery. That was to insure his getting a hit that day. He also kept a large glop of gum on the top of his cap during a Yankee 19-game winning streak to keep it going. The smell became so noxious that no one would go near him.

Ed Barrow said of Rizzuto, "His signing cost me 15 cents, 10 cents for postage and five cents for a cup of coffee we gave him the day he worked out at the Stadium." Philip Francis Rizzuto, who during his playing days could have been mistaken for a batboy, said, "I'll take any way to get into the Hall of Fame. If they want a batboy, I'll go in as a batboy." But Rizzuto didn't go in as a batboy. He went in as one of the great shortstops and most unusual characters in Yankee history.

BABE RUTH

"The first game I ever saw was in 1934 at Yankee Stadium," said Red Foley, who went on to be a sportswriter for the *New York Daily News* for 37 years and official scorer for almost three decades. "My uncle took me to that game," Foley continued. "It was Babe Ruth's last year and the Yankees played the White Sox a day in August. When you're five years old and see a guy as big as him—he looked like a balloon in the Macy's Day Parade. I was fascinated seeing him running out to right field with that peculiar-like waddle. He didn't get a home run that day but just seeing him run was enough."

Seeing him run, hit, field, listening to him talk, just being around the Babe was enough. The character of all characters in baseball history, George Herman Ruth assaulted the senses. Crude, vulgar, he spoke in a big booming baritone voice. And he mangled language with the best of them. "As the duke of Wellington once said, the Battle of Waterloo was won on the playing fields of Elkton," the Babe explained.

When it was explained to him that the correct reference was the playing fields of Eton, Ruth retorted, "Well, I married my first wife in Elkton, Maryland, and I always hated the goddamn place and it must have stuck."

The Babe loved to listen to the radio. His favorite program was *The Lone Ranger* and his favorite song was "Deep Purple." Just barely literate, he claimed he gave up reading because it wasn't good for a ballplayer. "If my eyes went bad even a little bit," he said, "I couldn't hit home runs."

While reading was not his thing, penmanship was. There were the hundreds of thousands of times he signed "Babe Ruth" neatly and with a flourish. Idiosyncratic, he ate scallions to get out of a batting slump, had an air rifle at the ready when playing golf to fend off squirrels, never remembered a name. Those who were young the Babe greeted with a "Hiya, Kid." To those who were not so young he said, "Hiya, Doc."

One spring in the twilight of Ruth's career an old Baltimore friend asked him what he thought of the potential of the new Yankee second-base hopeful, a kid called Don Heffner.

"Who?"

"Don Heffner."

"Who the hell is that?"

Heffner had been playing for nearly a month in front of the Babe, but Ruth didn't even know his name.

Babe Ruth took the baseball world by storm in the 1920s, and from there on after there was seldom a dull moment.

SEVEN

Yankee Skippers

RALPH HOUK

*A*s the 1961 season got under way, legendary Casey Stengel was out and virtually unknown Ralph Houk was in as manager of the New York Yankees. The 41-year-old Houk had played in 91 games in parts of eight seasons for the Yankees. Where Stengel was his own man, Ralph Houk was the organization man. Where Stengel was eccentric and excitable, Ralph Houk was calm and collected. Stengel's path to the Bronx Bombers had been haphazard and circuitous. Houk seemed to have been born and bred to be a Yankee manager.

The solidly built Houk grew up on a farm in Stull, Kansas, and played briefly as a Yankee farmhand at Binghamton. In 1942, he enlisted in the army. The headlines of his military career read like the script for a Hollywood movie. He advanced from private to major in the Rangers, was at Omaha Beach on D-Day, was awarded the Silver Star, Purple Heart, and Bronze Star.

From 1947 on Houk shuttled back and forth from the Yankees to the minors. Yogi Berra was on the scene, and the native Kansan was locked into being a perennial backup and bullpen catcher, and a sometime coach. In 1955, Houk became manager of Denver in the American Association. Two years later he led Denver to the Little World Series championship. At Denver, he groomed players like Tony Kubek, Ryne Duren, Ralph Terry, Johnny Blanchard, and Bobby Richardson. Yankee owner Dan Topping was grooming Houk for his time as Yankee manager.

In 1958, Topping installed Houk as a Yankee coach, replacing Bill Dickey. A favorite of the players he had managed at Denver, the upbeat Houk was a sharp contrast to other Yankee coaches like Frank Crosetti and 65-year-old pitching coach Jim Turner, who went by the old school ways. Houk, a kind of gentle version of Patton in pinstripes, came to the ballpark early, did his job, and bided his time. In 1961, when his time came, he was ready.

Houk's way involved the hiring of his own coaches: Jim Hegan, who had handled the top Cleveland pitching staff a decade before, as bullpen coach; Wally Moses, a 17-year American League veteran, as batting instructor; and former star hurler Johnny Sain as pitching coach. Houk and Sain had spent a lot of time together in the bullpen when they were both players on the Yankees.

Houk informed Mickey Mantle that it was his time to take over as leader of the Yankees. He made it clear to infielders Bobby Richardson and Clete Boyer, who had been platooned under Casey, that they were going to be everyday players. Whitey Ford was "saved" by Casey. Houk gave the classy southpaw the ball every fourth day like clockwork.

Although Houk admitted he learned all he knew from Stengel, he was his own man and he had his own style. Unlike Casey, Houk did not like to or want to take chances playing hunches or juggling lineups. He played percentages and believed in continuity. Stengel's platooning became a thing of the past, as did rotating the positions of players. Houk's hallmark was the set

(Preceding page)
Casey Stengel (center) with two of his coaches, Bill Dickey (left) and Jim Turner (right) in 1953.

New Yankee manager Ralph Houk (left) stands with coaches Johnny Sain, Frank Crosetti, and Wally Moses. This photo was taken during spring training in St. Petersburg, Florida, in 1961.

lineup, a specific role for each player on the team. He was also a morale booster and generally had something positive to say about each player. The Major did not make waves and was opposed to curfews and elaborate rules of behavior for his team. He let the Yankees play ball.

"I'm on the player's side," Houk said. "They must do things that are good for the club as a whole. If ballplayers know a manager is on their side but won't put up with any foolishness they will play ball for you."

The Yankees posted a 9–19 record in spring training in 1961. But things got much better for everyone concerned once the season started. Day after day Ralph Houk penciled in the set Yankee lineup: Bobby Richardson, Tony Kubek, Roger Maris, Mickey Mantle, Elston Howard, Yogi Berra, Bill Skowron, Clete Boyer, and the pitcher. Day after day Houk, who never hit a major league home run, held sway over his Yankee wrecking crew, which pounded a record 240 home runs and crushed their American League competition.

That 1961 season he became the first former Yankee to pilot the Bronx Bombers to a pennant. The Bronx Bombers racked the Reds in five games

Manager Ralph Houk puffs on a celebratory cigar after the Yankees won their third consecutive American League pennant in 1963. They eventually lost the World Series to the Los Angeles Dodgers and Houk was moved upstairs to become vice-president and general manager of the organization.

in the World Series. For the rookie manager, a part of the Yankee organization from the time he was 19 years old, that season was the culmination of all his boyhood dreams.

In 1962, Mantle missed about a quarter of the season and hit just 30 home runs. Maris hit 33. Kubek was away in military service. But the slack was taken up by rookie Tom Tresh, who recorded 20 home runs and drove in 93 runs, and Ralph Terry, who won 23 games. Houk notched his second straight pennant.

The San Francisco Giants were the World Series competition. It came down to the bottom of the ninth inning in the seventh game. Ralph Terry and the Yankee clung to a 1–0 lead. With two outs the Giants had runners at second and third. Houk had to make a decision—pitch to power-hitting, left-handed batter Willie McCovey or walk him intentionally and have Terry face right-handed power-hitter Orlando Cepeda.

Houk chose McCovey. And the big Giant whacked a Terry pitch right at second-baseman Bobby Richardson. World Championship, Yankees! But had the ball been hit a few inches to the left or right of Richardson it could have been 1960 and Bill Mazeroski—whose homer in the bottom of the ninth of game seven gave the Pirates the win over the Yankees—all over again.

In 1963, Mickey Mantle missed almost 100 games because of injuries. Maris played in just 90 games. But the Yankees had other weapons to take up the slack. They were pitching-rich, with Whitey Ford (24–7), Jim Bouton (21–7), rookie Al Downing (13–5), and 17-game winner Ralph Terry. That season was Elston Howard's time, as he finally took over as the regular catcher, hitting 28 home runs and winning the MVP award. Elston was very underrated, notes Phil Linz. "He was a better catcher than Thurman Munson, a better hitter."

Houk assented to the trading of Bill Skowron to the Dodgers to create an opening in the lineup for fun-loving first baseman Joe Pepitone, and he made the most of it, smashing 27 home runs.

But the 1963 World Series against LA was a disappointment. The Dodgers swept the Yanks behind the pitching of Sandy Koufax, Don Drysdale, and Johnny Podres, who held Houk's team to a puny .171 batting average. Nevertheless, it was an unbelievable run for the Major —309 victories in his first three seasons, three straight pennants, two World Championships.

On October 22, 1963, Ralph Houk moved upstairs, becoming vice-president and general manager of the Yankees. Installed as manager was Yogi Berra, the man who always stood in the way of Houk's getting a regular catching job with the Yankees.

"It was a real switch," Phil Linz recalls. "Houk had the image of disciplinarian and had a rough demeanor. But he was easygoing. We respected him from his reputation. He treated the players like men and let us be on our own. He was very good at keeping the fringe players, the substitutes like myself, happy. But we all liked Yogi, who was different from Houk and was unfairly knocked, but he knew the game. He knew pitching better than anybody."

With Berra at the helm the Yankees, with a 22–6 September surge, won their 29th pennant, their fifth in a row. But they were beaten in seven in the 1964 World Series by St. Louis. In a move reminiscent of Casey Stengel's firing a few years back, Yogi was out and Johnny Keane, manager of the World Champion St. Louis Cardinals, was in.

Under Keane the Yankees finished sixth in 1965. Then, on a Friday night in California in 1966 with the Yankees at 4–16, Houk fired Keane and took over for his second tour of duty as manager.

But even the Major's magic could not revive a decimated Yankee team. Maris, Mantle, Ford, and Howard were all shadows of what they had once been. The team's top pitchers were Fritz Peterson and Mel Stottlemyre. Each won a dozen games in 1966. But Peterson lost 11 games and Stottlemyre lost 20.

Managing just 70 wins, the Yanks finished 28½ games out in 10th place for the only time in their history, in a season in which the rival Mets wound up in ninth place for the first time in their history.

Over the next seven seasons, Ralph Houk had his hands full attempting to bring back some semblance of respectability to the once-mighty Yankee franchise. There was a ninth-place finish, two fifth-place finishes, three fourth-place finishes.

There was the one shining season of 1970. Houk piloted the Yankees to 93 wins and a second-place finish behind the powerful Baltimore Orioles. For that accomplishment he was voted the Manager of the Year award. That patchwork Yankee team had Danny Cater playing first base, Horace Clarke installed at second base, Gene Michael playing shortstop, and Jerry Kenney at third base. The catcher was Thurman Munson in his first full season. The outfielders were Bobby Murcer, Curt Blefary, and Roy White. The pitching staff had such performers as Mel Stottlemyre, Fritz Peterson, Stan Bahnsen, and Lindy McDaniel. Some of those athletes would be part of Houk's legacy; others would be mediocre footnotes to Yankee history.

On September 30, 1973, on the final day of the 50th anniversary season of Yankee Stadium, after eight years as manager, unhappy with the CBS ownership, Ralph Houk resigned. In his tenure as the field boss of the Yankees he won 944 games and lost 805 for a percentage of .539.

And even though Mickey Mantle had his greatest years under Casey Stengel he called Ralph Houk "the best manager I ever played for."

MILLER HUGGINS

"Huggins is Ready to Mold Yankees" was the headline in the February 2, 1918, issue of *The New York Times*. The ninth manager in 16 seasons of the New York American League franchise, Huggins was not even interested at first in the job. He viewed the American League and the Yankees as a step down from his five years piloting the Cardinals in the National League, where he had earned praise for his tenacity, his analytical mind, and his ability to handle a pitching staff.

Huggins did not want the Yankees. And Jake Ruppert at first did not want Huggins. When the two men first met, the beer baron looked at what

Miller Huggins (left) managed the Yankees to their first three World Championships.

he called "the worker's clothes, the cap perched oddly on Huggins's head, the smallness of the man—it seemed to all add up to a drabness of personality not at all fitting for a manager of the New York Yankees."

In truth, Miller Huggins was the unlikeliest of candidates to become what he became. He suffered from real and imagined medical problems, was fretful, aloof, superstitious. He had a law degree from the University of Cincinnati, where one of his professors had been William Howard Taft. But Huggins never practiced law.

At 5-4, 146 pounds, the Cincinnati native presented such a frail presence that a contemporary noted, "That fellow does not seem able to find a uniform small enough to fit him." Dwarfed by Babe Ruth and other Yankees in reputation and size, Huggins said, "New York is a hell of a town. Everywhere I go in St. Louis or Cincinnati, it's always 'Hiya, Hug.' But here in New York I can walk the length of 42nd Street and not a soul knows me."

The puny pilot was also dwarfed at the start by his Giant counterpart, John J. McGraw. "We could both enter a crowded room at the same time and be introduced," Huggins noted, "and in two minutes the crowd would be all around McGraw and nobody would even know I was there."

And when he was noticed, sometimes that caused problems. There were a couple of instances when he was barred from banquets. "How can a little twerp like you be Babe Ruth's manager?"

Those who rooted for the opposition called him "the Mouse," a kind of acknowledgment of his fidgety movements on the bench and his squeaky, high-pitched voice that constantly piped out directions to his pitchers: "Coive him! Coive the busher!"

A bachelor all his life, Huggins lived with his sister Myrtle in a Manhattan apartment. And there were many moments in those early years that he came home to her disgusted and deflated. "Ah, it's just too frustrating. Life is too short for this kind of rotten stuff and rowdy players I have to put up with. I think I'll chuck the whole thing."

It was lucky for the Yankees that he never did, for with the "Mighty Mite" on the scene the team moved into its first era of greatness. The 1921 Yankees won 98 games and their first American League pennant. They had to beat out a Cleveland team that had seven regulars who batted .320 or more. The World Series competition was the Giants. Despite the 27 scoreless innings hurled by Waite Hoyt, the Giants won, limiting Yankee bats to a .207 average.

There was another pennant in 1922. But again there was no World Championship. "Huggins is through," announced Til Huston, who had always intensely disliked the little manager. "We want a World Champion." But it was Huston who left: Ruppert bought him out.

With his prime adversary gone, Huggins now fully asserted himself as Yankee manager. There was another pennant in 1923 and a World Series victory over the New York Giants. Triumphant over McGraw, no longer saddled with the sniping interference of Huston, tiny Miller Huggins was now a giant managerial force.

But Hug, throughout his time as head man of the Yankees, had to contend with another giant force—Babe Ruth. The dynamo that stoked the Yankees machine, the Babe was also a blubbery, boisterous headache for Huggins. Throughout the 1925 season Ruth was more a discipline problem than ever—showing up late for games, breaking curfews, carousing to all hours. Huggins even had to resort to hiring a private detective to keep an eye on his great star.

With the Yankees in seventh place on August 29, 1925, the Huggins–Ruth soap opera came to a head. The Babe arrived for a game at Sportsman's Park in St. Louis. He was more than a half-hour late.

Huggins told Ruth that he was through. "You're off the ball club," the little man said, "and furthermore, you're fined $5,000."

An enraged Ruth snarled, "You can't make a mug out of me. If you weren't such a little twerp, I'd slam the stuffing out of you."

Huggins did not back down. "I can't make a mug out of you. God made you what you are. But I'm not afraid of you. If I weighed just 40 pounds more, I'd lick you in a good fight. Right now—get out. You're suspended."

Ruth complained to Jake Ruppert and general manager Ed Barrow to no avail. They closed ranks behind Huggins. The Babe paid the $5,000 fine and apologized to Huggins. The whole episode was a calculated risk taken by Huggins, but it worked. With Ruth in line the Yankees were reshaped for the 1926 season.

But there were horrendous losses in spring training, a lot of fan hostility, and bad press clippings. Journalist Westbrook Pegler wrote that "Huggins wouldn't know what to do with capable players even if the Yankees had them."

Always the master psychologist, Huggins called a clubhouse meeting. He began by telling his players that he and Yankee scouts had assembled the best team in baseball. "But maybe we were wrong," Huggins said. "Maybe we'll have to start all over again and reassemble the team. Pegler and the others didn't write those stories. You fellows did, the way you play. Show all the critics they are wrong. Show them you are the best team in baseball, and they'll only have good things to say about you."

The pep talk worked—it especially did wonders for a rookie second baseman. "You could tell the kind of man," Tony Lazzeri said, "Miller Huggins was watching him bring along a kid player hopeless for anyone but him."

The Yankees won 16 straight games in May, wound up with 91 victories, and Huggins had another pennant winner. There was another in 1927, and a World Championship, as Huggins presided over Murderer's Row.

When he had managed the Cardinals, his philosophy of managing was the inside game—bunting, running. With the Yankees it was the power game. "A manager has his cards dealt to him," the sad-faced pilot explained, "and he must play them. New York is a home run town."

In 1928, Miller Huggins piloted the Yankees to their third straight pennant, their sixth in eight seasons. A four-game sweep over St. Louis gave the Yanks a string of eight straight World Series game victories. That '28 Yankee team had a utility player who was befriended by the little Yankee manager who said, "Hug was the best pal I ever had. I learned a lot about managing being around him." The utility player's name was Leo Durocher.

The two sweeps in the World Series and the half-dozen pennants in just eight years were unprecedented for the Yankees. The "Mite Manager" was the mighty manager. He was also self-effacing, claiming, "Great players make great managers."

And he was also a man of no illusions. "Two things happen to players on a championship team," Huggins said of the 1929 Yankees. "First, they think they're better than they are. Then when they begin to lose they don't know what to do. That's when the manager has to step in and hold the wires. That's when the players depend on the manager more than the manager depends on the players."

Always ritualistic, always superstitious, Huggins had a habit of changing his seat on the bench to change the luck of the Yankees. Day in and day out throughout the 1929 season he was like a jack-in-the-box moving about in the dugout searching for the "lucky" seat. Nothing worked.

Then he engaged in more and more frequent team meetings, sessions on strategy, pep talks. All of these had worked in his previous eleven seasons with the Yankees, but they did not work in 1929. The powerful Philadelphia Athletics kept winning, widening their lead over the Yankees. With each setback, the health of Huggins declined. He lost his appetite, suffered from insomnia, sulked about in a near depression. By the middle of August the Yankees were 25 games over the .500 mark, but the Athletics were 45 games over.

In early September there was a red spot under the beleaguered manager's eye. He refused all offers of medical attention. "Me, who took the spikes of Frank Chance and Fred Clarke, see a doctor just because of a little blotch on my face?"

On September 20, Huggins left Yankee Stadium and made the short walk he had made so many times to his apartment. Only this time he barely had the strength to put one foot in front of the other. His sister took his temperature when he finally reached their apartment. It was 105 degrees.

He was diagnosed at St. Vincent's Hospital as having severe blood poisoning caused by a carbuncle. On September 25, 1929, Miller James Huggins passed away. He was just 50 years old. His sister said her brother had often remarked that managing the Yankees had taken five years off his life, but that "Miller had always said it was worth it."

Lou Gehrig said, "He was more like a father to me than anything else. He never became impatient when I made a mistake. He would take me aside and tell me he had confidence in me. There was never a more patient or pleasant man to work for. I call him the squarest shooter in all of baseball."

For a couple of days Babe Ruth would not talk to anyone. Then he made this statement: "You know what I owe to him. You know what I thought of him. I cannot realize yet that we won't have him with us again on the bench."

On May 30, 1932, the first monument at Yankee Stadium was dedicated to "the odd little man," in Waite Hoyt's phrase, "the greatest manager who ever lived," who moved the franchise from mediocrity to greatness. The field the Yankee practiced on in St. Petersburg was named Huggins Field. In 1964, Miller Huggins was admitted to the Baseball Hall of Fame.

It was Joe McCarthy who said of him: "This is the man who cut the Yankee pennant pattern."

BILLY MARTIN

The tempestuous life and times of Alfred Manuel Martin began in Berkeley, California, on May 16, 1928. When he was old enough to listen, he heard his mother's command: "Don't take nothing from nobody. If you can't hit 'em, bite 'em."

It was reported that young Billy did a lot of hitting and biting in his growing-up years on the streets of Berkeley. "When I was a kid," he recalled, "I had to fight three of my friends for when I joined the YMCA they thought I was getting too ritzy for them." He also did a lot of baseball playing, and he was almost as good at that as he was with his fists.

After he graduated from high school it was on to playing baseball at Idaho Falls and then with Oakland in the Pacific Coast League. It was there that he became Casey's boy. "If liking a kid who will never let you down in the clutch is favoritism," Stengel said, "then I plead guilty."

The Ole Perfesser became manager of the Yankees in 1949 and Billy was reunited with his mentor the following year. "We gave him Number 1 when he first joined the club," former equipment manager Pete Sheehy explained, "because he was so thin that was the only number that would fit on his back."

Playing in his first game on April 18, 1950, Billy Martin established a major league record for the most hits in an inning in the first game for a player in the majors. Batting twice in the eighth inning, Martin managed a hit each time.

Feisty, undersized, pugnacious, Martin did not fit the typical Yankee image, and his ability was obscured by the surplus of talent around. Nevertheless, he was a valuable member of those great Yankee teams of the 1950s, playing on half a dozen pennant winners, batting .333 lifetime in the World Series, making the 1956 All-Star team.

But it was Martin's toughness that Casey most admired: "A lot of times when we'd lose a few games," Mantle recalled, "Casey would say, 'We're gettin' in a rut. Martin, get out there and start a fight today.' Just as soon as Billy would get on the field, he'd start a fight. Casey loved him for that."

Casey also loved him for his savvy. "There ain't nothing he don't think he can do," said Stengel. "He thinks he knows more about baseball than anybody else, and it won't surprise me if he was right."

But the mutual admiration society that was Billy Martin and Casey Stengel came to a dramatic and abrupt end in 1957. Mickey Mantle, Yogi Berra, Hank Bauer, Whitey Ford, and Johnny Kucks were celebrating Martin's 29th birthday at the Copacabana. Mantle recalled what happened: "Two bowling teams came in to celebrate their victories. Sammy Davis, Jr., was the entertainer. They kept calling him Little Black Sambo and stuff like that. Billy and Hank kept telling them a couple of times to sit down. They kept standing up. The next thing I knew was that the cloakroom was filled with people swinging. I was so drunk I didn't know who threw the first punch."

Billy Martin was first named Yankee manager in 1975, after being fired by the Texas Rangers two weeks earlier.

Billy Martin is tagged out by Dodger Roy Campanella after attempting to steal home during the 1955 World Series. Martin, a fiery competitor, later refuted the call; it would not be the last time he would tangle with an umpire.

That incident at the Copa was the end of Martin's time as a player with the Yankees. He was traded off to Kansas City on June 15, 1957. Said Mantle: "Billy thought that Casey got rid of him. I never thought that. It was the farthest thing from the truth. Casey loved Billy."

In exile from the Yankees, Martin did not love Stengel. "I needed him this one time in my life," Martin groused, "and Casey let me down." In exile from the Yankees, Martin became a baseball vagabond, playing for Kansas City, then Detroit, then Cleveland, then Cincinnati, then Milwaukee, then Minnesota, where he ended his playing career in 1961. Eight years later he began his major league managing career with the Twins.

Martin piloted the 1969 Twins to the American League West title but was fired at the end of the season. His confrontational and controversial behavior was cited as the reason. One glaring episode was his barring of Vice-President Hubert Humphrey from the dressing room after Minnesota suffered a tough loss. Resurfacing with Detroit in 1971, Martin won the division title the next year. But on September 1, 1973, Billy the Kid was again out of a job. Confrontational behavior was again the reason.

In 1974, Martin was again running a major league team—this time it was the Texas Rangers. He coaxed and pushed them to a second-place finish. But by July 20, 1975, he was fired again. Personality clashes were the official reason.

At that moment in time Martin could have trotted out the old Casey Stengel quip: "I was fired more times than a cap pistol." Instead he was able to make better use of a 1975 character reference: "He's a good manager," Casey said. "He might be a little selfish about some of the things he does, and he may think he knows more about baseball than anybody else, but it wouldn't surprise me if he was right."

On Old-Timers' Day 1975, after 18 years, one month, and 16 days of wandering about the baseball landscape, Billy Martin returned to his first love, put on the uniform with Number 1 and took over as manager of the New York Yankees. The team finished in third place. There was a pennant in 1976, another pennant in 1977, and a World Series win over the Dodgers. It was love-in time for the fans of the Bronx Bombers.

The Yankees had the talent, but they also had a manager armed from years of managing in all kinds of locales in all kinds of situations with an arsenal of ploys, tricks, insights, and knowledge. And these Martin used to give him and the Yankees an edge over the competition. The writers called it "Billy Ball."

Part of it was the ability to make do with the weapons he had at his disposal. He could orchestrate the power game, the inside baseball game, the big-inning game. Part of it was the constant motion of the peripatetic manager in the dugout, the talking to players, the swapping of insights, the gauging of moods, the offering of suggestions. Part of it was the constant surveillance of all actions on the field. He scrutinized the umpires as they called plays to detect if they were correctly positioned. It was a tactic designed to give him an arguing edge for any decisions that went against the Yankees.

Like a hawk, Martin also surveyed his prey—the opposition. He studied the catcher's position to ascertain the pitch that had been called, and when he picked up a hint of what pitch was coming, he signaled his batter. He also studied how the opposition infielders positioned themselves to determine a pitching pattern. He especially studied the opposition pitchers, their arm movements, the location of pitches.

"If they get tired, pitchers reach back for a little extra," Martin said. "They will get the ball up high. You can then alert your batters. If it's your own pitcher it's probably time to take him out."

Unorthodox moves were normal moves for Martin as a manager. "Billy Ball" was a fusion of speed, daring, and unpredictability. The squeeze was used in situations in which other managers would have their players swing away. "A lot of managers are afraid to make those unorthodox moves," Bobby Murcer noted. "They are afraid of the heat of the second-guessers. Billy was not."

Billy was not afraid of anything, but he should have been afraid of himself. In 1978, he was drinking more and more and was a mass of mood swings that changed daily, some would say hourly, as he attempted to balance the myriad problems of bruised egos, battered infielders, and dissatisfied players. At the All-Star break the Yankees were in third place, $11\frac{1}{2}$ games behind the first-place Red Sox.

By July 18, the Boston lead was up to 14 games. "Even Affirmed couldn't catch the Red Sox," quipped Reggie Jackson, a reference to the 1978 Triple Crown winning horse.

Dissension, sniping at each other, and a general feeling of one-upmanship characterized the Yankee environment. It was like a scene out of *The*

Martin played hard on the field, and partied even harder off of it. Here Martin (far left) is shown with Yankee teammates Yogi Berra, Whitey Ford, Mickey Mantle, and Darrell Johnson. Martin's nightlife antics with Ford and Mantle were legendary.

Caine Mutiny, with Martin playing Captain Queeg. He fined Sparky Lyle for removing himself from a game. He suspended Reggie Jackson for five days for ignoring a bunt sign in the 10th inning of a game against Kansas City.

Allegedly ordered by Steinbrenner to reinstate Jackson in the lineup, irritated by reports that the principal owner was considering trading him to Chicago for manager Bob Lemon, a frazzled Martin burned the ears of reporters with a lengthy monologue on the situation. The choicest lines: "The two of them deserve each other. One is a confirmed liar [Jackson] and the other is a convicted felon [Steinbrenner]."

It was just a matter of time. That time came on July 25, 1978. Billy Martin, who had remarked, "The only real way to know you've been fired is when you arrive at the ballpark and find your name has been scratched from the parking list," was fired as Yankee manager. Then four days later at Old-Timers' Day at the Stadium, the news was put out that Martin would return as Yankee manager in 1980.

But the return of "Billy the Kid" came quicker than anyone expected. On July 19, 1979, with the Yankee record at 34–30, Billy Martin returned, replacing Bob Lemon, who had replaced him as manager. The fans at Yankee Stadium gave Martin a standing ovation. "When you're a professional," the hyper manager was fond of saying, "you come back no matter what happened the day before."

In his second stint in control of the Yankees, Martin piloted the Yankees to a fourth-place finish in the American League East. Some key injuries to Goose Gossage and Ed Figueroa and the ineffectiveness of pitcher Catfish Hunter were major reasons for the team's mediocre showing. But Martin pointed to the death of Thurman Munson in a plane crash in August as making "the bottom fall out for the whole team. It was difficult from then on. Wins didn't matter quite so much and losses became tougher. Thurman's death took everything out of the club."

Nevertheless, the 1979 season concluded on a positive note for the Yanks as they won their last eight games. Prospects seemed bright. The Yankees seemed to have a lot of winning potential. Billy Martin's erratic behavior seemed to have stabilized.

Then in October 1979 the old self-destructiveness came back. Martin was involved in a fight with a marshmallow salesman in a Minnesota hotel. "I stood there looking down at him," Martin said, "and it was an old story. I was saying to myself. 'How in the hell did I get into this?'" An exasperated Steinbrenner fired Martin for the second time.

The 1981 baseball season was the time of the players' strike. A much-criticized split-season format saw the winner of the first half of the season compete against the winner of the second half of the season. The Yankees also had a split season with managers. Gene Michael recorded a 48–34 record; he was replaced by Bob Lemon, who went 11–14. The Yankees edged the Milwaukee Brewers 3–2 in the AL East playoff and headed into the American League Championship Series. The competition was Oakland, managed by Billy Martin, who had taken control of the moribund franchise in 1980 and driven it to a second-place finish and won the Manager of the Year award for his efforts.

They called it "Bobby Ball" (Bob Lemon) versus "Billy Ball" as Martin stared across at the Yankees, determined to use all of his tactics to pull a victory rabbit out of his hat. But the Yankees just had too much talent; they swept Oakland in three games, recording their 33rd pennant. Martin got a nice consolation prize—Manager of the Year for the third time. And there were those who swore there were moments during that Oakland–New York series that they saw a gleam in the eye of George Steinbrenner.

Both the Yankees and Oakland, managed by Martin, followed different scenarios in 1982 with the same final results. The 1982 Yankees added speed, acquiring outfielders Ken Griffey and Dave Collins. Versatility came with the addition of shortstop Roy Smalley and catcher Butch Wynegar. And chaos came with a crazy-quilt shuttle system of players, pitching coaches, batting instructors, and managers. Bob Lemon yielded to Gene Michael, who gave way to Clyde King. Nothing helped. At season's end the Yankees finished in fifth place, a game out of last place.

"Martin's a great manager," former pilot Whitey Herzog said. "The first year or two with a team, he gets players to respond to his system, his way." The implication was that after that it all fell apart. It did in 1982 for Oakland. Martin and his players seemed to just lose interest. The A's finished in fifth place, and there were many who said the fiery manager had lost his fire.

225

Martin gives instructions from the dugout during a game against Kansas City in 1985. He was hired and fired for the fifth and final time in 1988, ending a tumultuous 13-year soap opera between him and owner George Steinbrenner.

In December 1982 the Yankees signed free-agent power-hitter Don Baylor to a five-year, $5-million contract. But on January 11, 1983, a far more significant signing was announced. "Billy Ball" was replaced by "Billy's back!" It was the third incarnation in eight years of Billy Martin as manager of the New York Yankees.

"Billy's back," one writer noted: "May the Lord have mercy on the big guys wherever they are."

George Steinbrenner went to great pains to explain why he had brought Martin back. "A sailing ship with no wind goes nowhere," said the Yankee principal owner. "Sometimes you have to have a little turmoil. You've got to go with a winner to have a winner. There are only two or three managers in baseball who have a winning record since they started and Alfred Martin is one of them. We never had so many calls about any one thing before. Everyone wanted us to bring Billy back."

Martin also had a lot to say. He was especially fond of telling the story of his mother. "She was happy when I came home to Oakland," he said. "But she never stopped being a Yankee fan. She still had her same CB handle on her radio she had had for years. "It's 'Yankee One.' That's the way she thinks of herself, of me and of the New York Yankees. The Yankee pinstripes, they stay with you wherever you go. To me, being a Yankee always meant playing with pride, desire, self-confidence, the will to win. That's what I want to teach these guys. That's what I want to bring to this team."

The 1983 Yankees lost 11 of 20 games they played in April. That was for starters. On May 16, they were in sixth place. Billy Martin "puts behinds in seats," George Steinbrenner had said. But Yankee attendance was down. And Martin was out of control. He was suspended for three days in midsummer for kicking dirt on one umpire and then was suspended for a couple of games for calling another umpire "a stone liar."

Overmanaging, undermanaging, juggling, ignoring, insulting—all were part of Martin's managerial profile. The lineup would sometimes not be posted until just a few minutes before game time. Martin would close himself off in the manager's office away from his players, the press, his coaches. He was drinking more and more. His nastiness increased. It was a mess. The 1983 Yankees finished in third place with a 91-71 record, 7 games behind the Baltimore Orioles, who would go on to win the World Series.

"When I get through managing," Martin had remarked, "I'm going to open up a kindergarten. Out of 25 guys there should be five who would run through a wall for you, two or three who don't like you at all, five who are indifferent, and maybe three undecided. My job is to keep the last two groups from going the wrong way."

But he didn't. Coach Don Zimmer made it clear that he would not return to the Yankees. Players like Steve Kemp, Ken Griffey, and Goose Gossage, who at the start of the season had said, "Billy knows how to win, no doubt about it. He lets his players know when they're not doing the job, but he gives you a pat on the back when you're getting the job done. I'm excited to have him around again," also made it clear that if Billy was back in 1984, they wanted out.

On December 16, 1983, it was, "HELLO, YOGI. GOOD BYE, BILLY!" Yogi Berra took over as Yankee manager from Billy Martin. Taking great pains to explain that he had not really fired his embattled manager, Steinbrenner said, "I'm shifting people around. Nobody is leaving. I'm doing what's best for everybody's best interests, not just mine and Billy's but the team's too."

The fifty-five-year-old Martin remained as an official member of the Yankee family—"kicked upstairs," as some called it. And when the principal Yankee owner was asked about the chance of Martin coming back one day as Yankee manager, his answer was, "Nothing is sure but death and taxes."

The 1985 Yankees had added speedster Ricky Henderson to a lineup that included Don Mattingly, Dave Winfield, and Don Baylor. Henderson became the table-setter leading the league in runs scored and stolen bases two years in a row. But the Yanks got off to a disappointing 6–10 start.

On April 25, 1985, the headlines announced: "YOGI'S OUT, BILLY'S BACK." If Yogi had been in a better mood he would have probably trotted out his famous line, "It's déjà vu all over again."

Billy Martin was Yankee manager for the fourth time. Despite the MVP season of Don Mattingly, the 20-win season of Ron Guidry, the 20-plus home run totals for Winfield, Henderson, and Baylor, it was another close-but-no-cigar season. The Yankees fell two games shy of Toronto in the American League East.

On October 27, 1985, the Yankee managerial chair revolved again. Billy Martin was canned for the fourth time. Lou Piniella, who had been the hitting instructor for the team, took over.

It was becoming a New York ritual. On October 19, 1987, Billy Martin returned as manager for the fifth time. Martin tried to start the new year off right when he issued this statement on January 4, 1988: "George and I are agreed that we are friends and we won't let the media get in between us. I've got to try and not get mad and yell back. He [George Steinbrenner] has my heart, and I have his bank."

On June 23, 1988, the Yankees were in fourth place and had just returned from a 2–7 road trip. Billy Martin was out as manager. "I'm a 10-year manager if the front office interferes with my running of the club," Martin once said. "If it leaves me alone, I'm a 20-year manager."

He was a 16-year manager. With five different franchises, Billy Martin managed 2,267 games, winning 1,253, losing 1,013. But the team he really belonged to was the New York Yankees, where he was Number 1.

Five times in the 1970s and 1980s, Billy Martin managed the New York Yankees. His comings and goings were a familiar and almost anticipated part of the New York scene. The obsessive–compulsive, love–hate relationship between him and George Steinbrenner was front-page news. The duo even had a beer commercial on television poking fun at the hirings and firings. The gritty and abrasive manager was like New York City itself—battered, bruised, but somehow always coming back. "All I know is I pass people on the street these days," Martin said, "and they don't know whether to say hello or good-bye."

On Christmas Day 1989 it was time to say good-bye. Billy Martin, 61, was killed in an automobile accident. His record as Yankee manager was 556 wins, 385 losses, a winning percentage of .591, two American League titles, and one World Championship.

Joe McCarthy and Babe Ruth at spring training in 1933.

JOE MCCARTHY

The Yankees finished the 1930 season in third place, behind Philadelphia and Washington. Bob Shawkey, who had succeeded Miller Huggins as manager, had not done the job for Ruppert and Huston. And Joe McCarthy was hired as the 12th manager in the history of the franchise. He would hold the job for a longer period than any other Yankee pilot.

Born April 21, 1877, in Philadelphia, Joe McCarthy spent many days of his growing-up years hanging around the ballpark after games just to get a look at the way Connie Mack handled the Athletics. Years later Mack would dub McCarthy "the greatest manager of all."

But at the start in 1931 with the Yankees, the square-jawed McCarthy had his problems, especially with Babe Ruth. The Babe had hungered for the Yankee managing job after Shawkey was fired. He was furious that this "weak-hitting busher," whom he had pitched against in the International League, was in charge of the team's destiny. It was a matter of record that McCarthy had toiled away as a minor league infielder for 15 seasons but never played in the major leagues. Ruth and other Yankees harbored hostility against him for that and for his National League roots. They also made much of the fact that in four seasons he pushed the Cubs from last place to the World Series, but could never win the big one.

The low-keyed McCarthy heard the criticism and then went about his business. He knew that coexistence with Ruth was paramount. But the two strong-willed men hardly ever spoke to each other. McCarthy put in one set of rules for the team and another for the Babe. "He was an institution in himself," McCarthy said of Ruth, "and I tried to treat him accordingly. It would have been silly to curb him in any way."

The same philosophy did not apply to McCarthy's treatment of others. Silliness or sloppiness in his players were things McCarthy would not tolerate. He was focused on winning, and that was what he wanted his players to be obsessed with, even in spring training.

Winning exhibition games was important. So was effort and so was dedication to the job at hand. "Guys who rush in and out of the clubhouse," the gum-chewing manager said, "rush in and out of the big leagues."

All players were required to be dressed in jackets and ties on the road and be in the dining room for breakfast by 8:30. Peering out from behind his morning newspaper, the Yankee manager would check the condition of each player. Bed checks weren't needed—morning face checks sufficed.

Shaving was banned in the clubhouse, as were card games. "This is a clubhouse," McCarthy said, "and not a club room." He had the card table smashed. "I want players here to think of baseball and nothing else."

During his first season as Yankee manager, when McCarthy came home to his wife he was down, depressed. "We still have each other," said his wife, who had instructions to always pray at early Mass for the Yankees.

"Yes, dear," he responded with a half-smile, "I know. But in the ninth inning today I would've traded you in for a sacrifice fly."

A man who played no favorites and treated players with respect, McCarthy was solicitous about the older ones. The younger ones he encouraged. He abhorred "get-over" types, expected players to be ready to play day in and day out even with minor hurts.

"So I eat, drink, and sleep baseball 24 hours a day," he said. "What's wrong with that? The idea of this game is to win and keep winning." Baseball was his thing—the only thing. During the season the only reading he ever did was baseball related.

But part of his baseball reading involved coming across the phrase "Second-place Joe" over and over again. That was the negative label stuck on him by sportswriters, who pointed out not too kindly that in his first five seasons at the Yankee helm, there was one World Championship and four second-place finishes.

Being second-best infuriated McCarthy. Perfection was his goal. Perhaps it was the memory of the hard days as a youth working in a textile mill, the fact that he was only three years old when his father died, the long years of wandering around in the minor leagues and eating in broken-down hotels and going from city to city on dilapidated buses. To the outside world McCarthy's long-sleeved uniforms and short fat cigars were his trademarks. But those were external trappings. A fire inside was what made him go.

The studious pilot functioned without notes, without charts. "You store up little impressions," he said, "and then one day a bell rings and you have

An unfamiliar sight, McCarthy gives instructions to his players on the field while Lou Gehrig sits on the bench in 1939. Gehrig requested that McCarthy take him out of the lineup because he was too ill to play.

an edge." He remembered everything. General manager Ed Barrow claimed that McCarthy had a baseball memory that was "astonishing." And McCarthy used that memory, a lot of patience, and a knack for recognizing ability and knowing what to do with it to mold the Yankees. He was enamored of the name "Bronx Bombers" and encouraged its use for what it conveyed. He saw to it that Yankee caps were cut larger and squarer to enhance the power look. He had uniforms tailored larger so that his players looked bigger and stronger.

In 1936, with Babe Ruth no longer a Yankee, McCarthy began a string of excellence with what he called "his good citizens." All adhered to his Ten Commandments of Baseball:

1. Nobody ever became a ballplayer by walking after a ball.

2. You will never become a .300 hitter unless you take that bat off your shoulder.

3. An outfielder who throws back of the runner is locking the barn door after the horse is stolen.

4. Keep your head up, and you may not have to keep it down.

5. When you start to slide, S-L-I-D-E. He who changes his mind may have to change a good leg for a bad one.

6. Do not alibi on bad hops. Anybody can field a good one.

7. Always run them out. You can never tell.

8. Do not quit.

9. Do not find too much fault with the umpires. You cannot expect them to be as perfect as you are.

10. A pitcher who hasn't control hasn't anything.

From 1936 to 1939 there were four straight World Championships, two over the Giants, then the Cubs and the Reds. The Yankee pennant-winning margins were $19\frac{1}{2}$, 13, $9\frac{1}{2}$, and 17. Even more astounding was that those McCarthy teams lost just three games total in the four World Series.

Calm, concentrated, he watched the good times play out. "I never roamed the dugout," he said. "I was there seated in the middle, the command post." He was rarely thrown out of a game for arguing.

"I never challenged an umpire except on rules," the Yankee pilot said. "I wanted to be around to manage. I'm no good to the team if I'm not there. Only second-division clubs argue with umpires."

There didn't seem much for McCarthy to argue about. The Yankee victories season after season seemed to come with ruthless efficiency, with apparent ease. "Second-place Joe" belonged to the past. Now they were calling Joe McCarthy the "push-button manager."

He bristled at the nickname: "I spend all my summers in Atlantic City," he snapped, "and only come back for the World Series."

A master psychologist, McCarthy knew his way around all kinds of players. A Yankee infielder made a couple of errors that cost the team a victory. "I was just terrible," the player said over and over again. "I shouldn't even be a New York Yankee."

"If you think you were lousy," McCarthy smiled, "you should have seen me when I was a player. Don't worry about it. Things will get better."

A deft touch with all kinds of pitchers was another of McCarthy's strengths. In the late '30s, he employed Johnny Murphy as a reliever. Over and over again the "Fireman" would come in and get the job done. A variety of starting pitchers was used—all as the need arose. He worked the young ones hard and husbanded the strength of the older hurlers. Red Ruffing in his twilight years with the Yankees became virtually a Sunday pitcher, working on six day's rest, and it paid dividends for him and the Yanks.

"He said hello to me the first day of training camp," Ruffing recalled, "and said good-bye to me the last day of the season. In between, McCarthy just put the ball in my hand. That was all I wanted."

Former New York City sports columnist Dick Young recalled one of his earliest experiences with the McCarthy Yankees. "We were in the Copley Plaza Hotel in Boston, an old-fashioned place with marble stairways. Some of the Yankees were sitting on the marble stairs. McCarthy came in. He had his straw hat on as usual. He walked over to the players. 'Are these the World Championship Yankees,' he asked, 'sitting on the steps?'

"They got up right away and moved onto chairs. I was very young and very impressed at the time and I said to myself, 'God, if he could get them to jump over a trivial thing like that imagine how he can control them on the field.'"

Control was one of McCarthy's outstanding characteristics. Tolerance was not. In 1937, the Yankees lost two straight to Detroit. He was very upset and let his players know it. "What does McCarthy want?" asked Yankee outfielder Roy Johnson. "Does he expect us to win every day?" Feeling that Johnson was not sufficiently committed to winning, McCarthy unloaded him. The replacement was minor league outfielder Tommy Henrich, who was committed to winning.

Winning was on display for the McCarthy Yankees of 1941, 1942, and 1943. The 1941 World Series was a matchup of the Dodgers, who had celebrated their pennant with a victory march down Flatbush Avenue before a crowd of about one million rabid fans, and the vaunted Yankees, who won 101 games and finished 17 lengths ahead of the runnerup Red Sox.

The most memorable moment of the World Series took place in game four. Behind two games to one, the Dodgers were leading, 4–3. The Yankees came up for their final at bat. With two outs and the bases empty and two strikes on Tommy Henrich, the game seemed to belong to Brooklyn. But fickle fate had other plans. The left-handed-hitting Henrich swung at a Hugh Casey pitch and missed. That should have been out number three. But Dodger catcher Mickey Owen let the ball get by him. Henrich made it to first base; that opened the barn door. The Yankees won the game, 7–4. They won again the next day, 3–1. And they had their eighth straight World Series triumph, dating back to 1927. In that stretch they lost only four of 36 Series games.

There was another Yankee pennant in 1942, and another in 1943, plus a World Championship—their seventh under Joe McCarthy. Charlie Keller's 31 homers supplied the power for the '43 Yankees. Right-hander Spurgeon Ferdinand Chandler, better known as Spud, anchored the Yankee pitching staff. He posted a 20–4 record, and his 1.64 ERA was the lowest in the American League in 24 seasons.

In 1944, however, diminished by the loss of key players to the World War II effort, the Yanks slipped to third place. It was the time of a new Yankee—Joe Page. Dubbed the "Gay Reliever," Page loved the night life. Joe McCarthy did not love the night life and did not love Page's passion for it. The two had many confrontations.

"I hated his guts," Page said. "But there was never a better manager. A day never went by when you didn't learn something from McCarthy."

Despite the problems the stone-willed manager had with Page, there were never public confrontations. "That was one of his big strengths," recalled Phil Rizzuto, who as a Yankee rookie first played for McCarthy in 1941. "He never told a player off in public—all problems were settled behind closed doors."

McCarthy had his own problem behind closed doors. It never really came out when things were going well that the Yankee manager was a drinker, one who consumed his alcohol out of the spotlight. It never became a problem. But in 1944 and 1945, with the Yankees winning less and McCarthy drinking more, it became a problem.

The Yankees finished in fourth place in 1945. McCarthy had once remarked: "Sometimes I think I'm in the greatest business in the world. Then you lose four straight and want to change places with the farmer."

On May 24, 1946, McCarthy did trade places with the farmer. The man who used to tell reporters, "Let me do the worrying," had grown tired of worrying. He called it quits. "He was drinking too much," Joe DiMaggio said, "and he wasn't eating right, and he was worried about the team because it was playing so lousy."

That was part of the reason McCarthy retired. His past gallbladder woes also resurfaced. The new Yankee owners—Dan Topping, Del Webb, and especially Larry MacPhail—were not his kind of people. But the main reason was that after 21 years as a major league manager, he felt that it was time to go.

Bill Dickey took over as manager of the Yankees. And Joe McCarthy retired to his 61-acre farm in Tonawanda, New York. He took with him a record of eight pennants, seven World Championships, 1,460 wins—most ever for a manager in the history of the franchise—and a winning percentage of .627, also a Yankee franchise best.

McCarthy returned to baseball in 1948 as manager of the Boston Red Sox, and there were many battles with the Yankees—the team he had had his greatest glory with. In 1957, he was admitted to the Baseball Hall of Fame. In 1976, he was memorialized on a plaque in Yankee Stadium. A year later Joseph Vincent McCarthy, the man Lefty Gomez had called "Einstein in flannels," passed away at age 90.

CASEY STENGEL

Bucky Harris began his 22nd year as a major league manager, his second with the Yankees, in 1948. Larry MacPhail was gone and George Weiss was in place as general manager. The easygoing, carefree Harris and the sour-dispositioned and businesslike Weiss were like fire and ice, grating on each other's nerves. Weiss called Harris a "four-hour manager," a sniping reference to the structured time the jovial pilot spent at the ballpark and his unavailability after games.

The Yankees, with an injured Joe DiMaggio and weaknesses at a couple of positions, finished in third place in 1948. A scapegoat was needed. Harris was available. He was fired.

Just six days later, on October 12, 1948, rubber-faced, gravel-voiced Casey Stengel was introduced at a news conference as the manager of the New York Yankees. He went by many names, including "the Ole Perfesser," an appellation affixed to him in 1914, when he had a spring-training baseball-coaching stint at the University of Mississippi. The 58-year-old Stengel's résumé included many years of wandering through baseball's wilderness. He had played for 14 seasons. He had managed such mediocrities as the Boston Braves and the Brooklyn Dodgers for nine years and never brought a team

Casey Stengel during his playing years as an outfielder for the New York Giants in 1921.

in higher than fifth place. His checkered history made him seem a dubious choice to take command of the destiny of the Bronx Bombers.

"I didn't get the job through friendship," Casey said at his initial press conference in 1949. "The Yankees represent an investment of millions of dollars. They don't hand out jobs like this just because they like your company. I got the job because the people here think I can produce for them. I know I can make people laugh. And some of you think I'm a damn fool."

"It was a shock," former Yankee pitcher Eddie Lopat recalled. "We thought we got us a clown. When spring training started in 1949, we just sat back and watched his reaction. He never said too much to anyone about anything. It was a treat for him to be with us after all the donkey clubs he had been with. He was something."

At the start, anyone seeing Charles Dillon Stengel would never have imagined he would reach the major leagues—let alone become the manager of the most fabled franchise in baseball history.

Born on July 30, 1890, in Kansas City, Missouri, the young Stengel plugged away at cab driving and then dentistry before he settled into a baseball life. "I'm just glad I had baseball knuckles," he used to joke, "and couldn't become a dentist." In 1910, Stengel began his baseball career with the Kankakee, Illinois, team of the Northern League. The league disbanded.

Always resourceful, Stengel linked up with Maysville, Kentucky, in the Bluegrass League. An insane asylum was behind center field in the Maysville ballpark, and whenever Casey came in from his outfield position, he made a big deal of practicing his sliding skills at third base. The residents of the asylum acknowledged each slide with a roar of approval. Stengel's manager was not as impressed. Tapping his forehead and pointing to the asylum, the pilot warned Casey: "For you to wind up there—it's only a matter of time."

By 1912, Casey had progressed to the major leagues as a member of the Brooklyn Dodgers. Rookies were not allowed to take part in batting practice. So Stengel had little business cards printed up, which he handed out with a flourish to his bemused teammates: "Hi, I'm Dutch Stengel. I'm a new player on this team. I'd like to take batting practice."

It is unclear just how effective the business cards were, but according to Casey, "I broke in with four hits and the writers promptly decided they had seen the new Ty Cobb. It took me a few days to correct that impression. . . I had many years that I had no success as a ballplayer as it is a game of skill."

On April 9, 1913, Casey's Brooklyn team played its first game in brand-new Ebbets Field. The opposition was the Philadelphia Phillies. "A cold, raw wind kept the attendance down to about 12,000 but did not affect the players, who put up a remarkable battle," an account of the game read. "Both Tom Seaton (Philadelphia) and Nap Rucker (Brooklyn) pitched brilliant ball, the former just shading the noted southpaw in a 1 to 0 shutout. The opening ceremonies were impressive, the two teams parading across the field headed by a band . . . Casey Stengel made a sensational catch."

By 1918, Stengel was a member of the Pittsburgh Pirates. When he first showed up at his old stomping grounds, Ebbets Field, and came to bat, Casey was greeted by a long chorus of boos from the Brooklyn fans. They remembered him. He called time. He took off his cap, and a little sparrow flew out. The crowd went "Ohhhhh!"

There were more uggghs than ohhhhs for Casey from 1934 to 1936, when he toiled away as manager of some sorry Brooklyn teams. He was fond of telling stories about those years. "Whenever I decided to release a guy," he winked, "I used to have his room searched first. You couldn't take a chance with some of those birds."

During that era Casey used to instruct his barber: "Don't cut my throat, friend, I'm saving that for myself." And he got out the word: "Anyone comes looking for me, tell 'em I'm being embalmed."

The big-eared Casey took over as manager of the hapless Braves in 1938. It was his 13th job switch in 28 years and prompted the line: "I was fired more times than a cap pistol." He lasted with Boston until 1943.

In 1946, Casey resurfaced as a manager, this time with the Yankee Oakland farm team in the Pacific Coast League. Playing a hunch, George Weiss, who knew Stengel from their minor league days together, gave him the job. Casey won the pennant with the Oaks in 1948. "I had a couple of cases of beer delivered to the dressing room after each game," was how Stengel explained the success of the Oakland team. "The more the players drank, the more they won."

With Casey on the scene, the Yankees did a lot of winning. In 1949, they defeated the Red Sox in the last two games of the season to win the flag—the first in a string of five straight pennants and World Championships. In the clubhouse celebration Stengel announced: "I want to thank all these players for giving me the greatest thrill of my life. And to think they pay me for managing so great a bunch of boys." Casey was voted the 1949 Manager of the Year.

That winter Casey ran into Pittsburgh's Billy Meyer, who had been the 1948 Manager of the Year. "Ain't it funny, Bill," Casey cracked, "now all of a sudden I got so smart and you got so dumb."

But Casey was smart, very smart. "He didn't need any notes," recalled Eddie Lopat. "He knew what every hitter and pinch-hitter could do against certain pitchers. He could make the moves, all the moves."

In part, Stengel could make the moves because of the incredible depth of the Bronx Bombers. "That's a lot of bunk about them five-year building plans," Casey said. "Look at us. We build and win at the same time." The team's extensive farm system, highlighted by the three top Triple-A clubs at Newark, Kansas City, and Oakland, underscored Casey's desire to have "three Yankees for every position."

"We had guys on the bench," Lopat said, "who could play as good as the starters, who hated to get on the bench because they knew they might not get out there for three or four weeks."

Platooning players became a Stengel managing trademark. The power on the bench was as good as if not better than the starting lineups of other teams. "None of these guys board here," said Casey. "They all work. That's why they give us 25 players, to let the manager play games with them."

During the Casey Stengel era at one time or another first base was played by Tommy Henrich, Johnny Mize, Bill Skowron, and Joe Collins. The second basemen included Jerry Coleman, Billy Martin, Gil McDougald, and Bobby Richardson. Taking a turn at third base were Gil McDougald, Billy Johnson, Bobby Brown, Hector Lopez, and Andy Carey. Shortstop was mainly the province of Phil Rizzuto, but there were also Billy Hunter and Tony Kubek and McDougald. The Yankee roster was like a human jigsaw puzzle that Stengel enjoyed toying and tinkering with. Versatility and flexibility were cornerstones of his approach to managing.

Batting orders were quite varied and sometimes very odd. Gil McDougald at one time or another hit in every spot in the order except ninth. Hank Bauer saw his name penciled in from leadoff batter all the way through seventh in the order. Starters like Allie Reynolds and Johnny Sain became relievers. Pinch-hitters were inserted on a hunch.

"Casey remembered," former American League shortstop and president Joe Cronin said, "what an opposing manager did to counter a certain move years back on a May 12 with the wind blowing in on a cloudy day and a Democratic administration in office. Maybe you'd think there was no sense to some of the lineup shifts he'd constantly be making. But you'd be wrong. He was a great manager. Patient, imaginative, and he had that great memory."

Players were given new positions—Yogi Berra played everywhere but center field, shortstop, and second base. A shortstop in the minors, Mickey Mantle was converted to a center fielder. Skowron was transformed into a full-time first baseman when he reached the Yankees. Platooning of players was a common practice—to make the parts add up to more than the whole. Left-handed-hitting Gene Woodling and right-handed-hitting Hank Bauer shared outfield duties.

"Gene and I didn't like it when it was going on," Bauer admitted, "but later on we relaxed a bit. You'd come into the dugout and look at the lineup and find out if you were playing. He did just that. We didn't like it, but you couldn't complain. We respected authority in them days. We all respected Casey. Besides, you couldn't complain too much—we walked into the bank every October."

"If it weren't for Casey," Bill Skowron noted, "I would not be where I am now in the record books. 'Sign with the Yankees,' he said, 'and I'll have you up in the majors in three years.' . . . And he did in 1954. He got players to come up early from the minors. He felt it was good for us to play together as a unit. He always wanted us to play together with no jealousy no matter what our roles were.

"Once I got taken out in one game for a pinch-hitter and I was batting cleanup. I came back to the bench and Eddie Robinson came in to pinch-hit. Eddie got a bases-loaded double and we won, 3–0. I was angry as heck because I had never been pinch-hit for before. I complained to some people."

The following day Skowron was summoned into Stengel's office. "He started off with, 'Don't ever show me up again,' the man they called Moose recalled. 'I don't care how you feel. I'm out here to win ball games.'

"And I said, 'Sir, it will never happen again.' It never did."

Skowron had very little to complain about as a member of Stengel's Yankees. He played in seven World Series in nine years.

The depth of the Yankees was mind-boggling, especially to their competition. The Ole Perfesser pulled out all the syntax stops, waxing poetical over his Yankee empire in this spring-training 1955 monologue:

"And now we come to Collins which may be an outfielder. He played center field at Newark and also played right field for me in the World Series. You can look it up, but he had Novikoff on one side of him and someone else whose name I have forgotten on the other but you can look it up. That should prove he's a great outfielder in order to do it with them guys on either side of him.

"There's a kid infielder named Richardson who was in our rookie camp which he doesn't look like he can play because he's as stiff as a stick—but whoosh—and the ball's there and he does it so fast it would take some of them Sunshine Park handicappers with the field glasses on to see him do it so fast does he do it. He never misses. As soon as he misses a ball, we'll send him back home.

"We started out to get us a shortstop and now we got eight of them. We don't fool, we don't. I ain't yet found a way to play more than one man in each position although we can shift them around and make them maybe outfielders outa them or put 'em all at ketch like we done with Howard.

"You ask me what kind of ballclub I want, one with power or one with speed, well a lot of power but not too much, and a lot of speed but not too much. The best club is the versatile club, the one that has a homer hitter here and a bunter there, a fastball pitcher here and a change-of-pace pitcher there. That way, the other team never knows what's going to hit it next."

The other team never really did know what was going to hit it next. The Yankees of Casey Stengel became so very successful that the line "Rooting for the Yankees is like rooting for General Motors" became popular. Methodical, precisionlike, the Yankees rolled on. The opposition hated the Yankees, but newspapermen loved Old Casey, who claimed, "The Yankees don't pay me to win every day—just two out of three."

Throughout his Yankee years Stengel and his wife, Edna, lived the high life at the posh Essex House in Manhattan. He was a big spender and a big tipper. "I got so much money," he said, "I don't know what to do with it."

The couple owned a beautiful home in Glendale, California, a place where nieces and nephews of Edna's and Yankee players and their families would gather. Casey and Edna never had children of their own, but there were sometimes 50 to 75 children frolicking about. The huge house was stocked with antiques. There was a Chinese room and a Japanese room and varied collectibles brought back from trips around the world.

Edna had been a glamorous silent-screen star, a fact that Casey was very proud of. "C'mon," Casey would nudge her. "Edna, you tell 'em all about the times you played with Hoot Gibson." And Edna would oblige.

"It was real Yankee family back then," Yogi Berra mused. "Casey and Edna were like father and mother to us."

The Yankee environment with Casey at the helm was laid back, easygoing most of the time. "Spring training was a time," Skowron noted, "when Casey would leave us on our own to get in shape. But when those last 10 days of spring training came around you knew you had better be ready to play."

There were those who pointed out that Casey slept on the bench, was forgetful, at times seemed uninterested, complained about all kinds of aches and pains. That was the shell. He was nobody's fool and could rise to any occasion when he needed to. "Sure he wasn't that young," Skowron recalled.

Stengel's 63 World Series games and 37 victories are records for a manager.

"But he knew and we knew what we had to do. He'd leave us alone when we were winning. He'd holler 'Butcher boy' and 'Don't swing too hard at ground balls' and 'Don't beat yourselves.' But when he saw us making mistakes, he'd get excited and do some yelling. A lot of people thought Casey talked doubletalk, but when he was angry , he talked real good English and we understood everything he said."

Stengel's disciplining of players was kept to a minimum. "The hotel bar is mine," he said. "Let the players go somewhere else where I won't see them." If their off-the-field behavior didn't affect how they played he didn't care. But Casey wasn't afraid to let his players know that they couldn't fool him. "I pulled every stunt that wuz ever thought up," he was fond of saying, "and I did them 50 years before you ever got here."

Casey knew all the words—and those he didn't know he made up. He had an opinion about everything. A master of the one-liner, the cutting jest, the sarcastic jab, the droll story, and the insightful pun, he delighted in mastering and mangling the English language with lines like these:

> These old-timers' games, they're like airplane landings. If you can walk away from them, they're successful.
>
> About the autograph business—once somebody sent up a picture to me and I write: 'Do good in school.' I look up to see who was gettin' the picture. This guy is 78 years old.
>
> If you're in a pennant race, you can put up with any kind of character except a man who is lazy. A lazy man is a terrible thing. He stinks up a ballclub. And he may be a man that never breaks a rule. He says, 'I go to bed at 11:00 every night,' but he's not awake when he's on the ballfield.
>
> I don't like them, fellas who drive in two runs and let in three.
>
> Good pitching, you know, will always stop good hitting and vice versa.

The Ole Perfesser even had his own code words: Lowballs were "worm killers," sportswriters were "my writers," good fielders were "plumbers," naiveté was "Ned in the third reader," a bum was a "road apple," and a rookie was a "green pea."

"Green pea" Tony Kubek, 20, joined the Yankees in 1957 along with Bobby Richardson, and was just astonished at the atmosphere on the team, created in large part by Stengel.

"Jerry Coleman and Gil McDougald went out of their way to help us, and we were to ultimately take their jobs," Kubek said. "It was typical of the pinstripe loyalty."

Despite the fact that Kubek never knew from day to day where he would be playing or batting in the lineup—Stengel had him play shortstop, second base, third base, and the outfield—Kubek batted .297 and won the American League Rookie of the Year award.

"There was the Casey of the public-relations image," Kubek recalled. "There was the Casey who could talk for hours at a stretch on the 36 hours of train trips to Kansas City; there was the Casey who was highly sensitive . . . there was the Casey Stengel of the Yankee pride."

"Make 'em pay you a thousand dollars," was Casey's advice on personal appearances for his players. "Don't go help those people with their shows for coffee-and-cake money. You're the Yankees—the best."

The best of the Yankees for Casey Stengel was Mickey Mantle. The Old Man groomed the Mick to be the successor to Joe DiMaggio. Stengel admired the pure raw talent he saw in the power-hitting switch-hitter who he said "had more power than Staleen" (Joseph Stalin).

Casey recalled a time he was explaining to Mantle how to play the right-field wall at Ebbets Field as the Yankees prepared to battle the Dodgers in the World Series. "I told him how I used to do it," Stengel said. "He looked at me like I wuz crazy and asked me if I ever played. 'What the hell do you think,' I said, 'that I was born on this bench as an old manager?'"

Mantle and Stengel had many moments of revelry. Perhaps the most publicized one was on July 19, 1958, in Washington when the duo appeared at the congressional hearings on baseball's reserve clause. "They asked Casey one question," Mickey recalled, "and he answered for an hour and a half. He began with in Kankakee, Illinois, or someplace like that, I tore my suit sitting in the stands . . . now they've got good seats." He then went on to talk about how good the railroads were getting and how fast the planes of today are. He was really fast-talking and going on."

Senator Langer asked: "I want to know whether you intend to keep on monopolizing the World's Championship in New York City?"

"Well, I will tell you," Casey began his reply. "I got a little concern yesterday in the first three innings when I saw the three players I had gotten rid of, and I said when I lost nine what am I going to do and when I had a couple of my players I thought so great of that did not do so good up to the sixth inning I was more confused but I finally had to go and call on a young man in Baltimore that we don't own and the Yankees don't own him, and he is doing pretty good, and I would actually have to tell you that we are more the Greta Garbo type now from success.

"We are being hated, I mean from the ownership and all, we are being hated. Every sport that gets too great or one individual—but if we made 27 cents and it pays to have a winner at home, why would you have a good winner in your own park if you were an owner?

"That is the result of baseball. An owner get most of the money at home and it up to him and his staff to do better or they ought to be discharged."

The one who was discharged was Casey Stengel. "They couldn't get him out of there fast enough," Mantle recalled. "Then they called me up. I said, 'I agree completely with everything Casey said.'"

Phil Linz was another one who earlier that year got the scrambled-syntax treatment. Given a trip to the Yankees spring-training camp in 1958 as part of his signing bonus, the 17-year-old met the 68-year-old Stengel. "I was rounding third base in one of our drills and my scout, Johnny Neun, brought Casey over and introduced me. Casey talked to me for five minutes. I was so awestruck I didn't understand a word he said, me and a lot of other people."

Like a living quotation dictionary, Casey Stengel let the good times roll and the words come out in torrents. Sometimes he was incoherent, but he made sense when he talked about the art and science of managing:

Casey Stengel speaks to a Senate subcommittee in 1958 in support of the sport of baseball. Stengel testified on a bill to exempt baseball and other major sports from the antitrust laws.

Manager of the New York Mets in 1963, Stengel receives the Mayor's Trophy. The trophy was awarded to Stengel and the Mets for defeating the Yankees in an exhibition game played in June.

You got to get 27 outs to win.

What I learned from McGraw [whom he played for in the 1920s] I used with all of them. They are still using a round ball, a round bat and nine guys on a side.

What the hell is it but telling the umpire who's gonna play and then watching them play?

The best thing to do is to have players who can hit right-handed and left-handed and hit farther one way and farther sometimes the other way and run like the wind.

With players like these on the roster the Yankees took the 1958 pennant by 10 games. Eight players hit 11 or more home runs. Mantle had 42. Bob Turley won 21 games and the Cy Young award. And the Yankees rallied from a 3–1 deficit to defeat the Braves in the World Series.

The 1959 Yankees finished in third place—their low point in Stengel's time as manager. There were some who thought it was the beginning of the end for him, that all the long years were catching up on him. Nearing 70, impatient, sometimes peevish with young players, he was making moves in games that seemed highly unorthodox even for him.

But in 1960, in a tough pennant race, the Ole Perfesser rallied the Yankees to another flag. The Fall Classic, between the Yankees and Pirates, came down to the seventh game. The Yankees, losing 4–1 in the top of the sixth, scored four times. As the game progressed they stretched the lead to 7–4. But the Pirates came back and took a 9–7 lead. Then the Yankees scored two runs in the top of the ninth, knotting the score at 9–9. That set the stage for Pirate Bill Mazeroski's home run over the left-field wall. World Championship—Pittsburgh.

Casey Stengel had always lived by the creed that "the secret of success is to keep the guys who hate you away from the guys who are undecided." For a dozen years he had done that—and then he could do it no more. All the termites came out of the woodwork.

They criticized him for underusing Whitey Ford in the Series. They criticized him for having Ralph Terry warm up four times before he came in to serve up the home run pitch to Mazeroski. The rap on Casey was that he no longer had his "best stuff" and that he should have been aware Terry left his "best stuff" in the bullpen.

Shortly after the World Series ended—a dozen years and six days after Casey was introduced to the New York City media as the manager of the Yankees—the official announcement was made that the highest-paid manager in baseball was retiring.

But blunt to a fault, Casey, who always said "baseball is my very life, my one consuming interest," made it clear that leaving the Yankees was not his choice. Speaking before dozens of reporters, Casey told them that he was fired.

"I commenced winning pennants when I got here," Stengel rasped, "but I didn't commence getting any younger. They told me my services were no longer desired because they wanted to put in a youth program as an advance way of keeping the club going. When a club gets to discharging a man on account of age, they can if they want to. The trick is growing up without grow-

Stengel, celebrating his 76th birthday; is embraced by his wife, Edna, on July 30, 1966. Stengel had been elected to the Baseball Hall of Fame five days earlier.

ing old. Most guys are dead at my age anyway. You could look it up. I'll never make the mistake of being 70 years old again."

When Casey first came on the scene as manager, the 1949 Yankees had 37 different players on the roster at one time or another. By 1960, only Yogi Berra remained. In a dozen years as manager Casey led the Yankees to 1,149 wins, a pennant each year except for 1954 and 1959. There were five straight pennants and World Championships from 1949 to 1953, four more pennants from 1955 to 1958, another in 1960. In all, there were seven World Championships.

There was never anyone who managed the Yankees quite like the Ole Perfesser, and no one else ever piled up the record of success he did. In his time Casey Stengel presided over a Who's Who of baseball talent: Mickey Mantle, Tommy Henrich, Bill Skowron, Eddie Lopat, Hank Bauer, Whitey Ford, Jerry Coleman, Gil McDougald, Yogi Berra, Joe DiMaggio, Vic Raschi, Elston Howard, Allie Reynolds, Johnny Mize, Phil Rizzuto, Enos Slaughter, Tony Kubek, Billy Martin. But it was the irrepressible Charles Dillon Stengel who always held center stage.

In 1966, he was enshrined in the Baseball Hall of Fame. Three years later he was given the title of Baseball's Greatest Manager during the centennial observation of the national pastime.

He passed away on September 29, 1975. His epitaph at Forest Lawn Memorial Park, in Glendale, California, reads: "There comes a time in every man's life and I've had a few." That he did.

Stengelese

Casey Stengel didn't always talk his doubletalk. He used it only when he wanted to avoid answering questions, to stifle conversation, to befuddle or irritate, to put people on. He could make sense when he wanted to, but his scrambled syntax was much more fun than the words he served up straight. What follows is a sampler of Casey's always winning, sometimes wacky Stengelese:

As great as the other men were on the ball club, there comes a time when you get a weakness and it might be physical.

[Yogi Berra] would fall in a sewer and come up with a gold watch.

I can make a living telling the truth.

Satchel Paige threw the ball as far from the bat and as close to the plate as possible.

I never woulda done it without my players.

Tommy [Henrich], I don't want you to sit in a draft. Don't slip and fall in the shower. And under no circumstances are you to eat fish, because them bones can be murder. Drive carefully, and stay in the slow lane, and sit quietly in the clubhouse until the game begins. I can't let anything happen to you.

When I played in Brooklyn, I could go to the ballpark for a nickel carfare. But now I live in Pasadena, and it costs me $15 or $16 to take a cab to Glendale. If I was a young man, I'd study to become a cab driver.

They say some of my stars drink whiskey, but I have found that the ones who drink milkshakes don't win many games.

Right now we playin' bad every place. Not hittin', not pitchin', and not fieldin' too good. And judging by what I read in the newspapers, the Yankee writers are in a slump, too.

Left-handers have more enthusiasm for life. They sleep on the wrong side of the bed and their heads get more stagnant on that side.

I came in here and a fella asked me to have a drink. I said I don't drink. Then another fella said I hear you and Joe DiMaggio aren't speaking and I said I'll take that drink.

If we had batting helmets when I was playing, John McGraw would have insisted that we go up to the plate and get hit on the head.

JOE TORRE

His family has been his life. His father was a New York City policeman. He grew up in Brooklyn, the youngest by almost nine years of three brothers and two sisters, one of whom became a nun. He thought of becoming a doctor or a priest. But baseball always had the strongest pull for Joe Torre.

A standout major league player with the Braves and Cardinals, Torre finished his playing career with the Mets. The man they called "The Godfather" was a Gold Glove catcher, a nine-time All-Star with the St. Louis Cardinals. In 1971, Torre put together a career year, leading the National League in batting average, RBIs, total bases, and hits. He was a popular choice for the MVP award.

But Joe Torre was not a popular choice when it was it announced that he would manage the New York Yankees in 1996. Buck Showalter had departed under cloudy conditions. The last Yankee manger had been an organization man, a fan favorite, popular with the media, steeped in Yankee tradition. Sixteen years older than Showalter, the 55-year-old Torre was an outsider.

His upside was managing stints with the Mets, Braves, and Cardinals, a successful run as a broadcaster for the California Angels. He was intelligent, cultured, a skilled communicator. There were those who said those experiences gave him a broad overview of the game.

The downside was that Torre had been fired three times and had a career winning percentage of .471 as a major league manager. He was recycled, old news, a National League manager with too much mileage. All he accomplished in five years with the New York Mets were three straight last-place finishes. Fourth place was his high-water mark with the team. Sure, he had won a division title his first year as manager of the Braves. But that was yesterday. And he had worn out his welcome with the Braves, as he had with the Cardinals, where his best season win total was 87 games.

Upside and downside notwithstanding, Joe Torre was the manager of the New York Yankees as the 1996 season got under way. He was being paid $500,000—he had earned more than that as a broadcaster. He didn't need the money, didn't even need the job. And perhaps that was part of his strength. He could always walk away.

But he was there, in his phrase, because in 18 years as a player and 14 years as a manager he had never gotten a World Series ring. Now he thought he had "a perfect chance to get to the World Series with the Yankees, maybe my last chance." Torre said he had never managed so much talent. "I'm impressed," he said.

There were others who begged to differ. They touted the Boston Red Sox and the Baltimore Orioles as the season began and thought that the Yankees would bring up the rear behind those teams.

Joe Torre's family became a subtheme to the 1996 Yankee season. He had been married since 1987 to his third wife, Alice, who, he said, "wouldn't let me stop chasing my dreams." They had an infant daughter. "We're on the same schedule," he quipped. "We're both up three times every night."

His brother Rocco died in June watching a Yankee game on television. And Torre took the lineup card from the last game his brother ever saw and placed it and a Yankee cap in his brother's coffin at the wake.

The other brother, Frank, was a member of the 1957 and 1958 Milwaukee Braves World Series teams. A ring from the 1958 World Series that Frank had given Joe was stolen in 1972 from Torre's Manhattan hotel room.

The Yankee manger kept reminding people all season long how he ached to get a World Series ring which he would give to Frank's son. As for

Joe Torre is shown taking some practice cuts during spring training in 1971. Torre went on to win the National League Most Valuable Player award that season.

Torre is joined by his brother Frank after receiving *The Sporting News* "Sportsman of the Year" award on December 10, 1996.

Frank, he was a shell of his former self, a very sick man who waited and waited throughout the summer and fall of 1996 for a heart transplant at Columbia Presbyterian Medical Center.

Winning baseball for his Yankees throughout the 1996 season was paramount for Joe Torre. But he also knew there were other things that were more important. And perhaps it was this perspective that enabled him to cope with the garish media spotlight that never went away, to roll with the ebb and flow of the long season.

"He is one of the steadiest men I've ever known," noted John Wetteland. "Sometimes I couldn't believe how calm he was. I thought, is this a mask? To this day, I don't know if it was a mask."

There was a game in September when the Yankees' 12-game lead over Baltimore was almost gone. Torre came out to the mound to a gathering that included Tino Martinez, Wade Boggs, and Derek Jeter.

"Everyone was so serious," Martinez recalled. "We were waiting for Joe to say something and he goes, 'This is some game, isn't it?' Everybody cracked up. He wasn't going to let anything bother him. He never panicked."

On the surface Torre was warm, affable, a great storyteller, a manager who was able to get along with his players. But there was also the manager who wanted things done his way. Ruben Sierra didn't get it, and was traded away. Tino Martinez got it and followed Torre's message to relax and became a better player for it. John Wetteland took to heart Torre's words that it was unacceptable to scoot about on inline skates with a strained groin. Darryl Strawberry learned patience. Wade Boggs believed it when Torre said, "I don't play names."

There was also the Torre temper, most of the time out of sight, but it came out from time to time. "Everybody's got his envelope," Torre explained. "I've got no patience for mental mistakes or nonpreparation."

Led by Joe Torre, the 1996 Yankees made few mental mistakes and they were a team prepared for any situation. "We heard different bad news every day, but everyone was focused once they got to the ballpark," Paul O'Neill said. "That's a credit to Joe."

When the Yankees defeated Baltimore to move into the World Series, there was Torre poised on the top step of the Yankee dugout. The many years of waiting, all those whom he had played for and against, all those he had managed and managed against—it all came together. "So many people wanted this for me," he said.

And when he led the Yankees to triumph in the World Series, their first since 1978, Joseph Paul Torre out of Marine Park, out of St. Francis Prep, became the first native New Yorker to bring a World Championship to the Bronx. After 4,272 games as player and manager, he would finally have his World Series ring.

The deep, dark eyes lightened, the sadness about him lessened, the rumples on his face diminished. He took the Yankee team fashioned in his image on a victory lap around the Stadium. "I've never been so happy. I never thought this would happen to me."

"His impact is all over this team and it's all over every player," Darryl Strawberry said. "The reason we won the World Series is because of our manager."

"He kept saying, 'We will win this thing,'" Wetteland said. "Joe was the constant. No matter what happened, he never got too high or too low. He remained a rock for this team."

For his steadiness, his grace under pressure, his ability to shape the 1996 Yankees, Joe Torre was selected as Manager of the Year, along with Johnny Oates of Texas.

At long last, Joe Torre takes a victory lap around Yankee Stadium after the Yankees 3–2 game six victory over the Atlanta Braves. The win gave Torre his first World Series title after 4,272 games as a player and manager.

EIGHT

THE
Owners

Col. Tillinghast L'Hommedieu Huston co-owned the Yankees until Jacob Ruppert bought him out in 1922 for $1.5 million.

JACOB RUPPERT AND TILLINGHAST L'HOMMEDIEU HUSTON

Shrewd and calculating—some would say cold—Jacob Ruppert was the heir to his father's Manhattan brewery, which he headed for 42 years. His personal wealth was immense. A millionaire many times over, he enhanced his fortune with shrewd real-estate investments. Even during Prohibition he did all right, producing what was called near beer—the nonalcoholic kind.

The man they called the "Prince of Beer" was a lifelong bachelor who lived in a 15-room townhouse at 1120 Fifth Avenue and a castle on the Hudson opposite West Point. He called everybody by a last name or a corruption of it. Thus, Babe Ruth was "Root," Ed Barrow, "Barrows," and so on.

The Colonel never wanted for company. In constant attendance at his residences were a butler, maid, valet, cook, and laundress. He was driven about in a gleaming Pierce-Arrow automobile that some said was as big as a Pullman car. He had an extensive and expensive wardrobe that he changed a few times a day. He was an impeccably dressed dandy. A yachtsmen, a hunter, he bred Saint Bernards and trotters, owned a racing stable, financed expeditions, and collected animals—there were 20 monkeys in his collection. He also collected jade, first editions, porcelains, and Indian relics.

Ruppert's Prussian roots were evident in his Teutonic mustache, the cold and piercing look he gave when displeased, his ease in giving orders. "Colonel" was an honorary title bestowed on him when he was 22 years old. His only military background was membership in the politically and socially correct New York National Guard's 7th Regiment, Company B. From 1896 on, he served four terms in Congress.

The Ruppert brewery offices were located on the Upper East Side of Manhattan. They were a place of hustle and bustle, but also of a carefully thought-out organization. The floors were covered with expensive rugs and the white marble walls showed off hunting trophies.

"I found out a long time ago," he said in response to a league plan to share profits during the Depression, "that there is no charity in baseball, and that every club owner must make his own fight for existence. I went into baseball purely for the fun of it. I had no idea I would spend so much money. The only return I ever sought was to make ends meet." He did much more than make ends meet as the owner of the most fabled franchise in sports history.

In many ways Captain Tillinghast L'Hommedieu Huston was as strong-willed as Ruppert. But that is where the comparisons ended. Huston wore the same rumpled clothes over and over again. He was called "the man in the iron hat," because of the derby he always squashed onto his head. A self-made man whom players and sportswriters called "Cap" and felt at ease with, the large-bodied Huston hailed from a small town in Ohio. His first real employment was as a civil engineer in Cincinnati. He went from that to a captaincy during the Spanish-American War, in which he served as an engineer.

(Preceding page)
"The Boss," George Steinbrenner.

(Opposite)
Ruppert's beer as advertised in a World Series program.

Jacob Ruppert is all smiles when he signs Babe Ruth in 1932 to play for $75,000 a year.

He enjoyed the company of friends and hangers-on at his 30,000-acre hunting lodge in Georgia. One of his favorite pastimes was to slow sip corn whiskey, perfectly aged, of course, before a crackling fire. Building and designing things were his passions. Using the Petit Trianon at Versailles as a model, he built an estate in the middle of the Altamaha River in Georgia.

When World War I began, Huston served in France and rose to the rank of colonel. In his absence, Ruppert took control of the Yankees. Some said he was always in control, listed as he was as club president while Huston held the title of vice-president.

The two Yankee owners never got along that well. The one thing they had in common was a singleminded pursuit of excellence for their team and a willingness to spend as much money as was needed to accomplish their goal. They outspent all other owners as they transformed the Yankees from a mediocre team to a great franchise.

Miller Huggins was the biggest source of contention between the two millionaires. Ruppert was for the tiny manager; Huston could not abide Huggins. When the Yankees lost the 1922 World Series, Huston announced: "Miller Huggins has managed the Yankees for the last time."

But it was Huston who owned the Yankees for the last time. On May 21, 1923, the formal transfer of T. L. Huston's interest in the Yankees was completed and Jake Ruppert became sole owner. For his half-interest in the team, Huston received $1.5 million—a tidy profit of almost 650 percent over seven years. There were rumors that Huston was going to buy the Boston Red Sox. But that never came to be. It would have been interesting had it happened. But Huston's selling of his Yankee ownership ended his relationship with baseball.

Perhaps to show that he was really cleaning house, in an unprecedented move for baseball back then, Ruppert purchased two more sets of uniforms, stating that he did it so that his players could wear a clean outfit each day. The Ruppert Yankees were not only baseball's greatest franchise, they were also the most smartly dressed team.

As sole owner of the Yankees, Ruppert presided over some of the marker moments in the team's history. And he loved every moment of it. In his 24-year ownership tenure, the Yankees recorded 10 pennants and seven World Championships.

Ruppert passed away at age 71 on January 13, 1939. Four days later Ed Barrow was elected president of the Yankees. On April 23, 1940, a plaque honoring Ruppert was placed in Yankee Stadium.

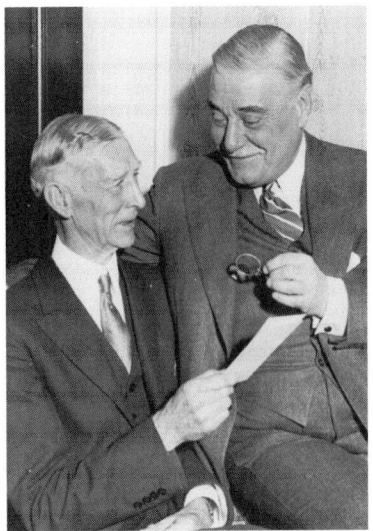

Ruppert and Philadelphia manager Connie Mack talk things over during an American League officials meeting during the off-season in 1932.

LARRY MACPHAIL, DAN TOPPING, AND DEL WEBB

On January 25, 1945, Larry MacPhail along with Dan Topping and Del Webb purchased the Yankees for $2.8 million from the heirs of Col. Jacob Ruppert—a woman and two nieces. The purchase price included the Yankees, the Stadium, the entire farm system including Newark and Kansas City, and the ballparks.

Dan Topping was in the Marines but was described in press releases as a "millionaire sportsman, heir to fortune, a café society headline maker." Del Webb was just out of the military. His fortune had been made in contracting work in Phoenix, much of the Southwest, and especially in Las Vegas. The most interesting of the trio was Leland "Larry" Stanford MacPhail.

"There was no doubt in my mind that MacPhail was a genius," Leo Durocher observed. "But there is that thin line between genius and insanity, and in Larry's case it was sometimes so thin that you could see him drifting back and forth."

A native of Michigan, a large, red-haired man, MacPhail left a successful position as general manager of the Reds to take over in the same role with the Dodgers in 1938. His challenge with Brooklyn was to give the team a new image, to go against the Yankees and the Giants for the affection of New York City baseball fans, to reverse the losing ways and madcap habits of "Dem Bums." He succeeded.

Challenge and change for MacPhail was a passion. Just as he had done with the Dodgers, MacPhail got busy with the Yankees, who became the first team to travel by airplane on a regular basis in 1946, a season in which MacPhail replaced the flagpoles on the Stadium roof with electric light structures and staged the first night game at Yankee Stadium. MacPhail also wheeled and dealed to arrange the first major league TV contract at a time when there were but 500 television sets in all of New York City. The Yankee

Dan Topping (left) and Del Webb (right) celebrate with manager Casey Stengel after winning the 1950 World Series.

offices were moved from their historic 42nd Street address to a classier and posher location on Fifth Avenue. A Stadium club was created with a bar for Yankee season-ticket holders. All kinds of promotions were put in place—an archery skills competition, foot races, free nylon stockings for women attending games.

MacPhail's way was not the traditional Yankee way, but it paid huge dividends at the box office. Attendance in 1946 was 2.2. million, doubling the previous high, making the Yankees the first team to break the two-million mark.

Surprisingly, MacPhail was on the Yankee scene for less than three tumultuous years. All kinds of controversies and confrontations characterized his tenure. In 1946, Joe McCarthy, Bill Dickey, and Johnny Neun all quit rather than manage for him. After the 1947 World Series ended, the tempestuous MacPhail let it all hang out in the postgame Yankee victory party. He attempted to punch out both Topping and Webb, cursed out a few bystanders, and threw a punch at a writer. All of this was capped off with the announcement that MacPhail was selling his one-third share of the Yankees for $2 million.

With MacPhail out of the picture, the former "silent partners," Topping and Webb, now presided over the Yankee empire. Ed Barrow, 79, retired,

George Weiss (middle, sitting down) became general manager after Ed Barrow retired. Weiss was largely responsible for hiring Casey Stengel.

and George Weiss took over as general manager. "There is no such thing as second place," the arrogant Weiss was fond of saying. "Either you're first or you're nothing." It was Weiss who engineered the hiring of Casey Stengel as manager with the encouragement of Webb, who had a special liking for the Ole Perfesser from his playing days.

Webb was into owning the Yankees more for the fun of it than the money. But he and Topping made plenty of money as Yankee owners. They also let the baseball people like Weiss run the show and take the heat. Weiss seemed immune from heat. "To hell with newspapermen," he said. "You can buy them with a steak."

In 1960, Topping had to take the heat when he fired Casey Stengel. "Twelve years ago we were ridiculed when we hired him," Topping snapped. "Today when Casey is leaving we are ridiculed again."

Without Casey, the Yankees kept on winning. There were five straight first place finishes in the early 1960s. On the surface it seemed to all that the franchise was set to be solidly perched atop the baseball world for years to come. Apparently Topping and Webb felt and knew otherwise. They were

Mike Burke took over as President and Chairman of the Board of the New York Yankees organization in 1966. Burke was a good businessman, and had a background in sports, but failed miserably with the Yanks.

not spending money to maintain the franchise. The vaunted farm system was eroding. In 1963, the four top Yankee minor league teams all finished in last place. On November 2, 1964, after 20 seasons, 15 pennants, and 10 World Championships, Topping and Webb sold 80 percent of the Yankees to CBS (which later bought the remaining 20 percent). The total price for the Yankees came to about $14.4 million.

CBS

The old line that "Rooting for the Yankees was like rooting for General Motors" was now changed to "Rooting for the Yankees is like rooting for CBS." It was the first time a corporation had owned a major league franchise. One of the ironies of the CBS ownership time was that former Yankee farm director Lee MacPhail, son of Larry, was general manager.

On September 20, 1966, Mike Burke succeeded Dan Topping as Yankee president. A 50-year-old CBS executive, the upbeat, politically well-connected, modish Burke added a lively touch. He had played football at the University of Pennsylvania and had a sports background. But nothing prepared Burke for the challenge of the failed franchise he was now charged with resurrecting.

In 1965, the Yankees experienced their first losing season in 40 years and plummeted to sixth place. It got worse. The 1966 Yankees wound up in last place—the lowest finish for the team since 1908.

"CBS did not affect us," Phil Linz recalled. "We felt we still had a good team, but they were not replenishing the farm system. That was pretty obvious. Mantle's leg was starting to bother him and he no longer was the great impact player that he had been and there really was no one around to take his place."

The Stadium was painted blue and white in the winter of 1966–67. There were added promotion days for the team. But these things were window dressing. The CBS ownership decade was a time of corporate unwillingness to put the money that was needed into the franchise, mediocre teams, fan frustration, and political infighting and unhappiness at the network. The CBS era also coincided with the rise of the New York Mets, who were playing at Shea Stadium, a new ballpark in Queens. The National Leaguers outdrew their Bronx cousins by a better than 2–1 margin for several seasons. In 1969, the "Miracle Mets" took the baseball world by storm, winning the World Series in just their eighth season of existence.

The purchase of the Yankees had been thought of as a tactic to give added luster and prestige to CBS. It wound up having the reverse effect. The network lost $11 million on the deal.

By 1972, with Yankee attendance dropping to 966,328, with radio and television revenues falling to $200,000 for 1973, CBS chairman William Paley told Mike Burke that he could purchase the team or sell it to another party.

GEORGE STEINBRENNER

Born on the Fourth of July, 1930, George Steinbrenner is the most famous owner of the most famous franchise in sports history. Earthy yet erudite, crude yet compassionate, arrogant yet altruistic, the Yankee owner is a complex piece of work.

On January 3, 1973, he headed the investment group that purchased the New York Yankees from CBS. The price was a bargain—just $10 million, approximately $4.4 million less than the media conglomerate had paid to buy the franchise from Dan Topping and Del Webb. With Steinbrenner around things have not been the same throughout baseball or with the Yankees. For just as he transformed his ailing family business and the American Ship Building Company, tripling its volume, Steinbrenner took the Yankees out of the CBS ash heap and revitalized the franchise.

Mike Burke was part of the Steinbrenner limited partnership group and then he was not. He resigned as club president on April 29, 1973. Never at a loss for words, Graig Nettles quipped: "Was his hair too long?" Also out was MacPhail. He moved up to become president of the American League in 1974. Gabe Paul, who as general manager of Cleveland had introduced Burke to Steinbrenner, became Yankee president and general manager.

"I won't be active in the day-to-day operations of the club at all," George Steinbrenner told the press early on. "I can't spread myself so thin. I've got enough headaches with my shipbuilding company. We plan on absentee ownership. I'll stick to building ships."

For a time Steinbrenner kept his word, busy as he was with a charge that he illegally contributed $100,000 to President Nixon's 1972 campaign. In August 1974, Steinbrenner pleaded guilty and was fined $15,000. Baseball Commissioner Bowie Kuhn suspended the principal owner from involvement with the Yankees for two years. Steinbrenner returned in March 1976.

Free at last to focus his energies on the Yankees, Steinbrenner went to work. They called him the "Boss" and earthier things and for good reason. Talkative, driven, Steinbrenner was concerned and consumed by every aspect of the Yankees. And he took charge. "Nothing is more limited," limited partner John McMullen noted, "than being a limited partner of George's."

Right off the bat Steinbrenner took umbrage at some of the shaggy-haired Yankees, giving a list of them to manager Ralph Houk. Among those with orders to report promptly to the barber shop were Thurman Munson, Bobby Murcer, and Sparky Lyle. That began some of the resentment against Steinbrenner, even though many welcomed the fact that there was a real human being whose hand was on every aspect of the fortunes of the team and not a faceless corporation like CBS. But the hand proved heavy.

In his first 17 seasons as owner, Steinbrenner's managerial revolving door saw 17 pilots come and go. "They know what the bottom line is," the

Since shipbuilder George Steinbrenner purchased the Yankees from CBS in 1973, the term "Manager of the Year" has had its own definition at Yankee Stadium.

Yankee owner snapped. Billy Martin racked up a record five times as Yankee manager. Gene Michael managed twice, as did Lou Piniella. In and out, and in and out as Yankee manager, Bob Lemon cracked, "I don't own the boat, I only row it." Dallas Green, who managed the Philadelphia Phillies to a world championship in 1980, lasted less than a season on the job as Yankee manager in 1989. Sick of Steinbrenner's interference, Green dubbed the owner "Manager George," which led to his firing after 121 games.

Not only managers have come and gone. There has also been a constant parade in Steinbrenner's time of general managers, pitching coaches, and players. "Every year is like being traded," snapped third-baseman Graig Nettles, "a new manager and a whole new team."

Dramatic changes in managerial, coaching, and player personnel have echoed Steinbrenner's fondness for free agents. At first he declared that he was "dead set against free agency. It can ruin baseball." Then Steinbrenner went out and signed Catfish Hunter for almost three million dollars for five years—a record in 1974. Reggie Jackson, Tommy John, Phil Niekro, Dave Winfield, Don Baylor, Jimmy Key, Wade Boggs, David Cone, and others who were not as successful have worn pinstripes not so proudly through the years.

Part of the Steinbrenner ownership profile has been his tendency to shoot from the hip, throw his mouth and his weight around. It is not the kind of behavior one would expect of a Williams College graduate, one who was an English major, fond of Shakespeare, who wrote his senior thesis on

256

the heroines in Thomas Hardy's novels. But nothing about George Steinbrenner has ever been predictable.

In 1981, the player's strike created a postseason format pitting the winner of the first half of the season against the winner of the second half. In the American League East playoff against Milwaukee after game four, there was a well-publicized shouting match in the Yankees locker room between the Boss and catcher Rick Cerone. That was just a warmup for Steinbrenner. In an elevator in a hotel in Los Angeles following game five of the World Series against the Dodgers, Steinbrenner was taunted by a couple of LA fanatics. There was a fight. "I clocked them," the former military academy athlete proudly proclaimed. "There are two guys in this town looking for their teeth."

The Yankees won the first two games of the Series, but the Dodgers came roaring back and beat the Bombers in six. "I'm like Archie Bunker," Steinbrenner had said. "I get mad as hell when my teams blows one." The Boss was "mad as hell," and he took it out on his players.

Early in 1985, Berra was fired as Yankee skipper. Steinbrenner had said that Yogi would be his manager all year. There was a lot of criticism of that firing and also a lot of noise coming from unhappy players. "I keep hearing about this guy and that guy being unhappy," the Boss responded. "Well, if they're not happy let them get jobs as cabdivers, firemen, or policemen in New York City. Then they'll see what it's like to work for a living."

The constant cascade of sharp-edged Steinbrenner words and the precipitous and sometimes unkind actions annoyed players and opponents alike: "He should stick to horses," said Reggie Jackson in 1982, then wearing a California Angels uniform. "At least he can shoot them if they spit the bit."

"How do you know when George Steinbrenner is lying?" asked Chicago White Sox owner Jerry Reinsdorf in 1983. "When his lips are moving."

Graig Nettles was particularly soured on the Steinbrenner way. "When I was a kid, I wanted to join the circus and play baseball," he said. "With the Yankees, I got to do both." Another zinger from the third baseman was: "The more we lose, the more he'll [Steinbrenner] fly in. And the more he flies in, the better chance that there'll be a plane crash. Some teams are under the gun; we're under the thumb. The sweetest words to George are 'Yes, Boss.'"

In 1988, the Yankees signed a Madison Square Garden cable TV and WABC radio contract assuring the franchise of a half-billion dollars in income over its next 15 seasons. The value of the Yankees was estimated to be more than 20 times what it had been when it was purchased from CBS. In the 1980s, the Yankees led all teams in victories. That was all the upside for Steinbrenner. The downside of the '80s was just one World Series appearance and a lot of chaos. The chaos continued in the 1990s.

On July 30, 1990, Commissioner Fay Vincent forced Steinbrenner to give up control of the Yankees because of reported payments to a New York City gambler for damaging information about Dave Winfield. *Newsweek* magazine's cover characterized him as "The most hated man in baseball." The chant at Yankee Stadium that day was "No More George."

It was No More George until March 1993, when the Boss was given back full control of the Yankees. George M. Steinbrenner had said at the start that he would not be active in the day-to-day operations of the club at all.

Buck Showalter lasted longer (four years) than any other manager had under Steinbrenner. But after the Yanks made the postseason for the first time since 1981, Showalter resigned due to differences with "The Boss".

Apparently, those words were just for press purposes. But others have become part of the Steinbrenner creed: "Owning the Yankees is like owning the Mona Lisa; it's something that you'd never sell." The stitching on a pillow in his Yankee Stadium office reads, "Give me a bastard with talent." Omnipresent, vocal, always hovering about—love him or hate him, George M. Steinbrenner is the ultimate hands-on owner.

In exile, as the first owner in the history of the American League to be removed by disciplinary action, "the Big Guy in the Sky" watched his Yankees finish out the 1990 season in seventh place, 21 games off the pace. Their winning percentage was the lowest since 1913.

In 1992, Buck Showalter became manager. The Yankees stumbled through their fourth straight losing season—10 games under .500. Not since 1912–15 had the Yankees posted such a string of losing seasons.

The 1994 Yankees, with the best hitter in Paul O'Neill and the best pitcher in Jimmy Key, had the best record in the American League. Then the baseball strike aborted everything. "It's a very terrible day," Steinbrenner said. "We were doing so well and it looked like we were going to win our division."

They didn't win their division in 1995 either, but as a wild-card team the Yankees made the postseason for the first time since 1981, the longest drought in franchise history. Guiding the fortunes of the highest-payrolled team in baseball was Buck Showalter, in his fourth straight year as Yankee skipper, the longest consecutive tenure of any pilot in Steinbrenner's regime. There were two Yankee wins over Seattle at the Stadium. Then the teams traveled west. With a stunning extra-inning come-from-behind victory in game five, the Mariners swept the Yankees in Seattle. Throughout the playoffs, Steinbrenner was omnipresent, neatly attired, impeccably groomed, hovering about.

As the Yankees prepared for 1996 there was a new general manager, Bob Watson, the team's 15th in 23 seasons. There was also a new manager, Joe Torre, making a total of 20 in Steinbrenner's time, factoring in the multiple terms of four managers. Buck Showalter became the second manager in the 23-year tenure of Steinbrenner as principal owner who voluntarily exited. The other was Ralph Houk.

Strangely, like a man mellowing with age, Steinbrenner kept a low profile throughout the 1996 season. A low profile for him. There were jabs at general manager Bob Watson and some of the players, but Joe Torre survived unscathed. And George M. Steinbrenner got what he hungered for—a World Championship.

YANKEE MANAGERS IN THE STEINBRENNER ERA

1973	Ralph Houk
1974–75	Bill Virdon
1975–78	Billy Martin
1978–79	Bob Lemon
1979	Billy Martin
1980	Dick Howser
1981	Gene Michael

1981-82	Bob Lemon
1982	Gene Michael
1982	Clyde King
1983	Billy Martin
1984–85	Yogi Berra
1985	Billy Martin
1986–87	Lou Piniella
1988	Billy Martin
1988	Lou Piniella
1989	Dallas Green
1989–90	Bucky Dent
1990–91	Stump Merrill
1992–95	Buck Showalter
1996–	Joe Torre

Voices OF THE *Yankees*

*I*t was 1921 when Yankee baseball was heard for the first time on the radio.

World Series games between the Yanks and New York Giants were transmitted by an experimental station that became part of NBC. Graham McNamee, previously a concert baritone, handled the mike. His was a voice that was at once theatrical, authoritative, and some said unforgettable.

The next year it was Yanks–Giants again in the World Series. Grantland Rice, sports editor of the *New York Herald Tribune* and the best-known sportswriter in the United States, did the play by play.

In 1923, McNamee, partnered with Phillips Carlin, again did the Fall Classic play by play. Headlines were made as McNamee sat through one of the games in an open box in drenching rain and gave the game account. The McNamee–Carlin duo did it again in 1926, 1927, and 1928.

It was a lucky thing for fans that the Yankees were so successful. For the only time they could hear play by play about their favorite team on the radio was at World Series time. The Yankees, Dodgers, and Giants had agreed not to put regular-season games on radio for fear of cutting into attendance at the ballparks.

That changed in 1939, when Dodger general manager Larry MacPhail decided that Brooklyn would broadcast its games on radio to a local audience. MacPhail served as the prod that convinced the Yankees and Giants to transmit regular-season games on the radio.

Arch McDonald, previously the voice of the Washington Senators, was brought in as Yankee announcer at the urging of sponsor General Mills. Dubbed the "Old Pine Tree" and the "Rembrandt of Re-Creations," McDonald was partnered with an unknown and very young law-school graduate of the University of Alabama. His name, Mel Allen.

That first Yankee regular-season home-game (it was only home games then) broadcast took place on April 20, 1939. Wheaties was the sponsor. The Red Sox were the competition. Rookie Ted Williams recorded his first major league hit. When the Yankees were on the road, McDonald and Allen switched over and broadcast Giant home games.

McDonald returned to broadcasting games in Washington in 1940. Part of his legacy was the "Yankee Clipper" nickname he gave to Joe DiMaggio and the tips he passed on to Mel Allen, who would be the Voice of the Yankees for the next quarter-century.

There were musical chairs in the Yankee broadcast boooth from 1943 to 1946, a time Mel Allen was away on military service. At first Don Dunphy teamed with Al Schacht. In 1945, he was replaced by Bill Slater. Dunphy became the broadcaster of Newark Bears games and then moved on to become the most famous boxing announcer of the postwar era.

Allen returned to the booth in 1946 and was paired with Russ Hodges, who had been the number-two announcer in Washington behind McDonald. It was Hodges who gave Tommy Henrich the nickname "Old Reliable." In 1949, Hodges took his signature home run call of "Bye, bye baby" and left to broadcast for the Giants. Curt Gowdy replaced him for two years and then moved on to Boston as the lead announcer. Allen's new partner in 1951 for local broadcasts was Art Gleason.

(Preceding page)
Mel Allen, the "voice of the Yankees" for over 25 years.

In 1950, the Yankees created the "Home of Champions Network," transmitting games to 15 cities. Allen, along with Dizzy Dean, the man who warbled the "Wabash Cannon Ball," Bill Crowley, and Geoff Davis were all part of the network, which by 1955 had expanded to 33 stations.

In 1954, Red Barber joined Mel Allen and Jim Woods as a broadcaster for the Yankees. The man Barber replaced was comedian Joe E. Brown, who had his own way of delivering "color commentary" throughout the 1953 season.

Phil Rizzuto was hired on December 18, 1956, to join Allen and Barber. The next decade both would be gone, but the Scooter would remain on the scene, a fixture as a Yankee broadcaster.

Other broadcast voices have included Joe Garagiola, who replaced Mel Allen in 1965 in the radio booth. The former Cardinal catcher mixed humor and storytelling, but his stay with the Yankees was brief. Frank Messer was added in 1968, when Garagiola left for NBC. Messer's greeting, "Good evening, ladies and gentlemen, wherever you may be listening to Yankee baseball," was both a welcome and an acknowledgment of the far-flung listening audience. Bill White was hired in 1971 and stayed on the scene until 1988, when he replaced Bart Giamatti as National League president. John Sterling and Michael Kay, in their fifth season together, teamed up to broadcast the Yankees' exciting run to the 1996 World Championship.

Some others who have formed the long pinstriped broadcast line for the Yankees are Jerry Coleman, noted for marvelous malapropisms, Tony Kubek, who made a living out of on-target baseball analysis, Fran Healy, who was the perfect foil for Phil Rizzuto, Jay Johnstone, Billy Martin, Bobby Murcer, Bob Gamere, Spencer Ross, Hank Greenwald, Tommy Hutton, DeWayne Staats, Dave Cohen, Jim Kaat, Al Trautwig, and Paul Olden. Yankee baseball in Spanish has come across through the voices of Eloy "Buck" Canel, the man who broadcast and was the "voice" of Franklin D. Roosevelt's World War II speeches in Spanish, and Juan Vene.

Yankee postgame broadcasters have included Joe DiMaggio, Dizzy Dean, and the comedian Joe E. Brown.

The shuffle of announcers has been echoed by a shuffling of stations: WCBS, WMCA, WINS, and then, in 1981, WABC, where the Yankees have remained. Yankee baseball on local television (WPIX–TV) began its 46th straight year in 1996. In 1996 Madison Square Garden Network transmitted Yankee games for the eighth season as the team's cable TV outlet.

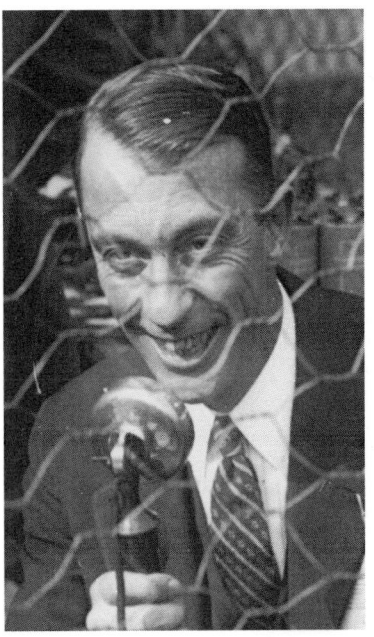

Graham McNamee calls the action for WEAF at the Polo Grounds in 1924.

MEL ALLEN

Born on February 14, 1913, in Birmingham, Alabama, Melvin Allen Israel lettered in football, basketball, and baseball during his high-school years. A graduate of the University of Alabama, Allen recalled: "I was supposed to practice law. I went to law school and got my degree. I never intended to be in broadcasting. But I was in the right place at the right time."

Allen broadcast sports programs for CBS and covered the 1938 World Series between the Chicago Cubs and the Yankees. It was the first of thousands of times he would witness baseball games from a broadcasting booth.

Allen (left) is pictured here with Eddie Mathews at the Baseball Hall of Fame in 1978. Allen received the Ford C. Frick award and Mathews was inducted into the Hall of Fame.

Before Allen, game accounts were fairly straightforward, reportorial. He changed the entire face of baseball broadcasting and brought the drama and excitement of Yankee baseball to millions, with insight and flair.

A witness to and messenger of history, Mel Allen was on the scene for Joe DiMaggio's 56-game hitting streak, the two no-hitters in the same season hurled by Allie Reynolds, the 61 home runs hit by Roger Maris, Don Larsen's Perfect Game, and hundreds of other marker moments in the history of baseball's greatest franchise.

"We always had something exciting going on," Allen said, "and it made it easier to broadcast."

His style and way with words made Yankee games easy to listen to. From his signature opening, "Hello there, everybody," to pet expressions like, "Foul by the length of a White Owl," Mel Allen was always "on." There were the home run calls in deference to sponsors: "Ballantine Blasts" and "White Owl Wallops."

"Going, going, gone" was his familiar home run call. "How about that!" was the way he marveled at something special accomplished by a Yankee. At his peak the man who lived and breathed the game of baseball, especially Yankee baseball, received 1,000 letters a week. But there were those who accused Allen of rooting too hard for the Yankees.

"How could he have been otherwise," former Yankee pitcher Eddie Lopat said. "One year we won 39 games in the seventh, eighth, and ninth innings. He had to get riled up."

A man with a gift for language, Allen gave nicknames to many Yankees, including "Steady Eddie" (Eddie Lopat), "Springfield Rifle" (Vic Raschi), "Superchief" (Allie Reynolds), "Plowboy" (Tom Morgan).

When the 1964 season ended, Mel Allen, the man who broadcast more World Series games than any announcer in history, was fired. It came as a shock to the baseball world and to Yankee fans in particular. He returned in the 1980s as a member of their cable TV broadcast crew. Mel Allen was a major part of the team's rich heritage. He passed away on June 16, 1996.

RED BARBER

Walter Lanier Barber was perhaps the most literate and well read of all baseball announcers. And his graciousness and eloquence enriched a baseball broadcast. In 1954, in another of the crazy crossovers in New York City baseball history, Red Barber, the "Voice of the Dodgers" since 1939, became a Yankee announcer. For Brooklyn fans it was as if he had been traded. There were some Dodgers fanatics who could not accept the fact that Barber was with the "enemy."

It was a golden era of broadcasters, Hall of Famer Monte Irvin noted. "Red Barber and Mel Allen . . . it was impossible to choose between them as to who was number one."

Walter Lanier "Red" Barber was born in Columbus, Mississippi, and he retained his soft southern speech. Like Allen, Barber delivered the narrative of baseball through those years and peppered it with signature lines and phrases like "hold the phone" (when the manager went to the mound); "the gate is shut on him" (for when a baserunner was tagged out); "Oh, Doctor!" (when something sensational took place on the playing field); "the rhubarb patch" (when something controversial transpired); "tearing up the pea patch" (when there was some commotion on the playing field); "the fat's in the fire" (when things were coming to a head).

One of Barber's props was a three-minute egg timer that he positioned near the microphone. When the grains of sand ran out, Barber gave the game score and turned the glass over, setting up the ritual again.

Barber was in his 13th season in 1966 as a Yankee announcer when, on September 22, 1966, there were only 413 fans in attendance for a makeup game on a weekday and Barber suggested that cameras pan the empty seats at the Stadium to show just how far the mighty franchise had fallen. But it was the talented Barber who was panned. He became the fall guy and was fired by CBS.

More than just a little bitter, Barber said: "I worked day and night to learn my business. I respected it to the end. When I left it was almost the end of professional broadcasting and then the jocks took over. I thank the almighty for the timing of my years." In his exit press conference, the "Old Redhead" blew a farewell kiss—to Brooklyn.

He also sent a card out to all who wished him well: "My removal from Mike Burke's peerage is a blessing."

Longtime announcer Red Barber calling a game in 1945. Barber joined Mel Allen in 1978 as a recipient of the Hall of Fame's Ford C. Frick Award.

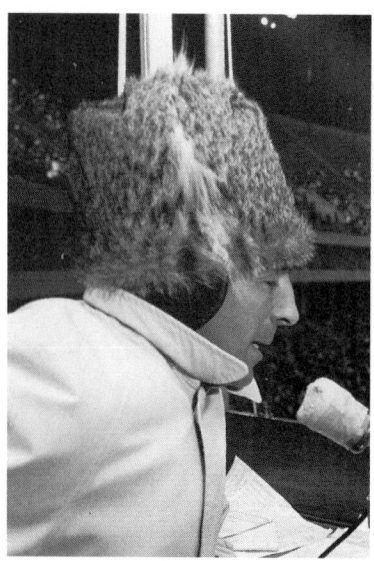

Phil Rizzuto keeps warm with a fur hat and ear muffs during a cold April night in Baltimore.

In 1978, Barber and Mel Allen were the first to be honored with the Ford C. Frick award for broadcasting and were inducted into the broadcaster section of the Baseball Hall of Fame.

PHIL RIZZUTO

He was told by Howard Cosell that he'd never make it as a broadcaster because he talked like Groucho Marx and looked like George Burns. As an announcer, besides his trade mark "holy cow" call, he invented the scoring symbol *WW* for "wasn't watching." Rizzuto shot from the lip such lines as, "They should take that stat for the game-winning RBI and shove it!" And sometimes his extemporaneously hyper quality almost got him into difficulty, like the Mother's Day he began a broadcast with, "Good afternoon and greetings to all you mothers out there." Rizzuto is also famous for his birthday salutes and on-the-air discussion of anything from his favorite foods to his fear of lightning.

But all things considered, malapropisms aside, slips of the tongue disregarded, the man they call the Scooter has been doing it behind the microphone for more than half a century for the New York Yankees—almost as well as he did it on the playing field. In addition to his election to the Baseball Hall of Fame, Rizzuto is also a member of of the American Sportscaster's Hall of Fame.

SOME MARKER MOMENTS AT THE MIKE

October 1, 1932

Tom Manning: The umpire again warns the Cubs! Charlie Root get his signal. And Babe Ruth steps out of the batter's box again! He's holding up his two and two. Oh, oh, and now Babe Ruth is pointing out to center field and he's yelling at the Cubs that the next pitch over is going into center field! . . . Someone just tossed a lemon down there. Babe Ruth has picked up the lemon and now he tosses it over to the Cubs bench. He didn't throw anything, he sort of kicked over there. After he turns, he points again to center field. And here's the pitch. . . It's going! Babe Ruth connects and here it goes! The ball is going, going, going—high into the center-field stands, into the scoreboard! And it's a home run. It's gone! Whoopee! Listen to that crowd!

July 17, 1941

Mel Allen: Sixty-seven thousand fans here at Municipal Stadium in Cleveland to see if Joe DiMaggio can keep his 56-game hitting streak alive. Jim Bagby on the mound works the count to one and one. A runner on first base. Here's the pitch. Joe DiMaggio swings. There's a ground ball out to short to Lou Boudreau. He flips the ball to Grannie Mack for one out. The relay to Grimes at first. . . It's in time for a double play! Joe DiMaggio's 56-game hitting streak is stopped.

May 14, 1967

Joe Garagiola: Three balls, two strikes. Mantle waits. Stu Miller is ready. Here's the payoff pitch by Miller to Mantle. Swung on! There she goes! . . . Mickey Mantle has hit the 500th home run [of his career], and the score at the end of seven complete innings: New York 6, Baltimore 4.

October 17, 1978

Bill White: Popped up behind the plate! Coming back. Munson! Throws the mask away! He's there. It's all over! It's all over—the Yankees charge out on the field. They mob Goose Gossage. The Yankees have won their second straight World Championship.

THE MAN WHO SINGS THE NATIONAL ANTHEM: ROBERT MERRILL

"I became a Yankee fan when I was about eight years old and saw Babe Ruth play," explains Robert Merrill. "But living in Brooklyn I also rooted for

One of the baseball broadcasting's best teams was the trio composed of Bill White, Bobby Murcer, and Phil Rizzuto. Murcer is pictured here announcing his first game in 1983, one day after he retired as a player.

267

the Dodgers. But when they moved I disowned them and gave my total allegiance to the Yankees. Baseball is big business, but it's still a game that kids play.

"Whenever I walk out there in front of all those people at Yankee Stadium and sing the national anthem I still have a lot of little boy in me. When I leave the Stadium, there are people of all colors and ethnic groups waiting for the ballplayers. And as I walk out they recognize me. They call out: 'There's the Oh, Can You See, Kid!' They all start to sing the national anthem with me outside the gates of Yankee Stadium.

"Where else could it happen but in New York with the Yankees. . . an opera singer standing there along with the players and signing autographs for the fans?"

EDDIE LAYTON

Playing organ background music for three daytime soap operas on CBS TV, Eddie Layton was happily set in a way of life. Then in 1967 Mike Burke, former CBS executive and president of the Yankees, asked Layton if he would play the organ between innings at Yankee Stadium.

"I thought," Layton recalled, "heck, why not. But I knew nothing about baseball. I thought a sacrifice fly was when they took a fly and sacrificed its life." In the first inning of Layton's first game at Yankee Stadium, Mickey Mantle homered and started to run around the bases. At that time the organ was in the press area opposite first base. "I screamed out, 'He's running around the bases the wrong way.' That comment made the back pages of all the newspapers," Layton smiled. "But I've learned a lot about the game since then."

The trim Layton arrives early for every Yankee home game and leisurely settles into his little booth in the press box overlooking home plate. His organ repertoire includes about 60 different gimmicks and 25 or more set songs. A few of his staples are: "I'm a Yankee Doodle Dandy," "Anything Goes," and "Hava Nagila."

"I play everything upbeat," Layton explained. I use "New York, New York" as my opening number before the game begins. I've played it in every game since that song come out. I like 'Yankee Doodle Dandy' at the start of the game. It gets the crowd into a mood."

In some ways Layton is like the 10th man out there for the Yankees. "But," he made the point, "I never do anything to embarrass the other team. When they're up at bat, I am quiet—I can even leave my booth."

Everyone pays attention when Layton plays those spine-tingling organ chords when the count is 3–2 on a Yankee batter. "Maybe it shakes up a young pitcher," Layton smiled, "and he walks a guy." Rallies are keyed musically by Layton when he strikes a few chords on the organ, leading fans in a cry of "Charge!"

Eddie Layton has one of the best seats in the house at Yankee Stadium and provides a lot of musical backdrop for the goings-on. The only discordant note he sounded was that "organ playing is a dying art—especially at ballparks." But not at Yankee Stadium.

Mr. Public Address Announcer: Bob Sheppard

Back in the 1920s, Jack Lenz moved about Yankee Stadium with a cheerleader's megaphone and a strong voice and announced the lineups and the goings-on on the field. He was the first Yankee public-address announcer. His sound was a far cry from the articulate and cultivated tones of Bob Sheppard.

"Good evening, ladies and gentlemen, and welcome to Yankee Stadium. Here are the starting lineups" is a phrase in a voice familiar to all Yankee fans. "No one has been doing this job as long as I have with one ball club," Sheppard says. And no on has been doing it as well. The St. John's speech professor began behind the microphone for the Yankees in April 1951.

"We were playing the Boston Red Sox," he said. "The Yankee team was made up of Johnny Mize at first base. Jerry Coleman was at second. Phil Rizzuto was the shortstop. Billy Johnson played third base. Jackie Jensen was in left. DiMaggio was in center and a rookie named Mickey Mantle was in right field. The catcher was Yogi Berra. The pitcher was Vic Raschi. That was some team. Five of them are in the Hall of Fame and if Whitey Ford had been pitching that day that would have been six out of nine."

More than 45 years later, Bob Sheppard is still on the scene, still bringing to the fans at the Stadium the lineups, the headlines, high moments, and the sad times.

"They ask me to do the eulogy," he said, "if you can call it a eulogy. I try to tailor my remarks to the person I am eulogizing. Thurman Munson, Dick Howser, and Billy Martin—all those who have died I've done it. Mickey's seemed to strike a chord in the hearts of the people perhaps because his death happened the night before."

Favorite Yankee moments stand out for Sheppard in his time above the Stadium looking down on the action on the field from his soundproofed small glass both: "One was Larsen's Perfect Game," he said. "Maris hitting the 61, Reggie Jackson's three home runs against the Dodgers, and Mantle hitting one almost over the roof."

> Every kid growing up has dreamed of lining up at Yankee Stadium in October and having Bob Sheppard announce his name.
> —Buck Showalter

CHAN...
DREWS. K.
GUMPERT. R.   R
JOHNSON. D.   R   X 6 7
NEWSOM. L.   R   7
RASCHI. V.   R
REYNOLDS. A   R
SHEA. F.
WENSLOFF. C.   R
STARR. R.   R

PAGE. J.   L   7

MCQUINN B   IF
BROWN. R.   IF   X 1 X X X 7
CROSETTI. F.   IF   7
FREY. L.   IF
JOHNSON. W.   IF
RIZZUTO. P.   IF
STIRNWEISS. G.   IF
PHILLIPS. J.   IF

CLARK. A.   OF
DiMAGGIO. J.   OF
HENRICH. T.   OF
KELLER. C.   OF
LINDELL. J.   OF

TEN

THE Farm System

$\mathcal{A}$s the 1930s got under way Yankee owner Jacob Ruppert decided in earnest to develop his own baseball talent. With new ownership in Boston, the quick-fix talent that had come from the Red Sox was no longer available, and Ruppert had noticed the success of Branch Rickey and the Cardinal farm system.

Purchasing the Newark Bears franchise of the International League, Ruppert shopped during the winter meetings before the 1931 season for a general manager for the Bears, a man to run the new Yankee farm system.

George Weiss was that man. A Yalie of German descent, the short, rotund Weiss was hired away from the Baltimore Orioles. It was a move that not only changed the balance of power in the International League but also assured decades of success for the Yankees.

Weiss not only copied the farm system created by Rickey, the taciturn but brilliant executive wheeled and dealed and eventually outdid the Mahatma even in frugality. Passionate about the Yankees, Weiss was just as passionate about not spending a dollar when he didn't have to.

Many scouts were hired to fan out over the country looking for prospects.

Paul Krichell was already on the scene in 1920, functioning as superscout. It was Krichell who scouted Lou Gehrig, Tony Lazzeri, Mark Koenig, Phil Rizzuto, Whitey Ford, and many others. Tom Greenwade, 40 years with the Yankees, was another legendary scout. He discovered Mickey Mantle, Hank Bauer, Bobby Murcer, Tom Sturdivant, Ralph Terry, and others. Bill Essick worked the West Coast through the '30s and '40s. On his recommendation Weiss spent the money to purchase Joe DiMaggio from the San Francisco Seals. In 1960, Bill Yancey became the Yankees' first African American scout. He signed Al Downing and others. Latin American scouting was headed by José Seda from the 1950s through the 1970s. His efforts brought Horace Clarke, among others, to the Yankees. Other Yankee scouts through the years were Whitey Ford, Luis Arroyo, Mickey Vernon, Dick Williams, Del Rice, Bill Monbouquette, Roy Hamey, Bob Lemon, Clyde King, Birdie Tebbetts, Mike Gazella, Jack Butterfield, Bill Bergesch, and many more.

Yankee farm teams were ultimately located all over the United States: Kansas City; Butler, Pennsylvania; Norfolk, Virginia; Springfield, Massachusetts; Augusta, Georgia; Akron, Ohio; Bassett, Virginia; Beaumont, Texas; Oakland; Portland; Richmond; Binghamton, New York; Denver; Columbus, Ohio—cities and towns east and west, north and south.

The glittering centerpiece of the farm system was the Newark Bears. From 1932 to 1938, the Bears finished first five times. The 1937 team posted a 109–43 record and wound up $25\frac{1}{2}$ games ahead of the competition. Six-teen of the players on that roster became major leaguers, including Minor League Player of the Year Charlie Keller, who batted .353, first baseman George McQuinn (.330), second baseman Joe Gordon, and third baseman Babe Dahlgren (.340).

The Bears swept through two rounds of playoffs, 4–0, 4–0. In the Little World Series they came up against the powerful Columbus Redbirds, led by Enos Slaughter. Columbus won the first three games, played in Newark. The Bears rallied to win four straight in Columbus. That Newark team was so strong that there were many who wagered it could beat most major league

(Preceding page)
George Weiss (left), the architect of the Yankee farm system in their glory years, with Yankee Manager Bucky Harris.

teams. From 1932 to 1942, the Bears won seven pennants and three playoffs and never finished lower than fourth.

The talent in the farm system was spread so thick that the Yankees could deal a batch of players for a star. There were always players who wanted to sign with the Yankees. The World Series share seemed always there. In the time before free agency a paycheck could be increased as much as one-third with that Series check.

Yankee players knew the score. "There was always some kid at Newark or elsewhere," George Selkirk recalled. "I'd read the papers every day to see how players were doing. Believe me it made me try harder. It made us all try harder."

The 1942 Bears sent Hank Borowy, Marius Russo, Johnny Lindell, and Spud Chandler to the Yankees. But there was still plenty of talent with Newark, including third baseman Hank Majeski, who won the batting title and the RBI title and became the Bears' fourth and final winner of the International League MVP award.

By 1949, the Bears had gone out of business as a result of Dodger, Giant, and Yankee TV transmission of games that reached into New Jersey. Fans just stopped coming to Ruppert Stadium. But just as the Yankees always were able to replace one superstar with another, Triple-A teams in Kansas City, then Denver, and then Richmond became near clones of the Newark operation.

The 1953 Kansas City Blues might have had the best minor league line-up ever—certainly the best in the 1950s. The team had players like Bill Skowron, Elston Howard, Bob Cerv, Vic Power, and Bill Virdon. Only a lack of pitching destined the team to a second-place finish.

The 1956 Denver team, managed by Ralph Houk, was another Yankee minor league powerhouse. Bobby Richardson and Tony Kubek formed the keystone combination. Third baseman Woody Held recorded 35 homers and 125 RBIs. First baseman Marv Throneberry batted .315 with 42 home runs and 145 RBIs. Johnny Blanchard was a superb catcher, and Ralph Terry was the star of the pitching staff.

George Weiss told prospects, "It might be four years before the Yankees will need you. However, you'll have good food, a good bed to sleep in, and when you come up you'll be coming up to the Yankees."

When they came up there was an amazing scenario at work. Tony Kubek recalled what it was like when he and Bobby Richardson joined the Yankees as rookies. "Bobby and I were astonished that Jerry Coleman and Gil McDougald went out of their way to help us, for we were to ultimately take their jobs. It was typical of the Yankee pinstripe loyalty. There was such an atmosphere of helping on the club—the Mantles, the McDougalds, the Careys, the Colemans were eager to help out. They had been through it and they were there to show us the way."

The farm system lost its way in the 1960s under CBS ownership, via penny-pinching and poor management. But it was resurrected in the 1970s by George Steinbrenner. He was the first baseball owner to assign a pitching and batting coach to each minor league team. Much emphasis was placed on instruction, using Yankees of the past as coaches, managers, and scouts. In 1980, six of the seven Yankee farm teams finished in first place.

"The tradition with the Yankees carries all the way down to the minor leagues," said J. T. Snow, who came up through the system. "From the first moment I signed back in A-ball to Triple-A I felt the Yankee way. We were always treated first class. Then when I got drafted and was part of the organization I got a taste of the tradition. My first big league camp was in 1992. Whitey Ford was there. Anybody that was a past Yankee could show up—it was like a big family."

The chart on the next page shows just how far-flung the Yankees farm system has been.

The Yankee Farm System Today

Columbus Clippers (International League—AAA), Cooper Stadium (15,000)

Norwich Navigators (Eastern League—AA), Senator Thomas Dodd Stadium (6,000), P.O. Box 6003, Norwich, CT

Tampa Yankees (Florida State League), Legends Field (10,373), 3802 Dr. Martin Luther King, Jr. Blvd., Tampa, FL

Greensboro Bats (South Atlantic League—A), War Memorial Stadium (7,500), 510 Yanceyville Street, Greensboro, NC

Oneonta Yankees (New York–Penn League SS—A), 95 River Street, Oneonta, NY

Gulf Coast Yankees (Gulf Coast League—A), 3102 N. Himes Avenue, Tampa, FL

Yankee Triple-A Minor League Clubs Past and Present

Newark, 1932–49

Kansas City, 1938–54

Denver, 1955–58

Richmond, 1956–64

Toledo, 1965–66

Syracuse, 1967–68

Tacoma, 1978

Columbus, 1979–

Minor League Notes

Columbus alumni include Don Mattingly, Derek Jeter, Dave Righetti, Doug Drabek, and Roberto Kelly. The right-field fence at Cooper Stadium in Columbus is 20 feet closer to home plate than the left-field fence. This gives the park a configuration similar to that of Yankee Stadium. Steve Balboni loved to play there. His 92 home runs from 1981 to 1983 is still an all-time Clippers record.

The Norwich Navigators team is named for the seafarers who wended their way to Norwich over the Quinebaug River. Alums include Bernie Williams, Pat Kelly, and Jimmy Leyritz.

Greenboro Bats (previously Hornets) alumni include Don Mattingly, Otis Nixon, Andy Pettitte, and Mike Pagliarulo. The team has been a Yankee affiliate since 1980.

The Tampa Yankees are owned by George Steinbrenner and moved to their present location in 1993 after completing 30 years in Ft. Lauderdale. The franchise previously sent to the Yankees Don Mattingly, Scott Kamieniecki, and Steve Balboni, who hit 16 homers for the team in 1979.

Year	# of Farm Teams	Year	# of Farm Teams	Year	# of Farm Teams
1936	11	1957	10	1977	4
1937	15	1958	10	1978	4
1938	15	1959	8	1979	5
1939	15	1960	8	1980	7
1940	14	1961	7	1981	7
1941	12	1962	7	1982	7
1942	9	1963	6	1983	5
1943	5	1964	5	1984	6
1944	5	1965	7	1985	5
1946	15	1966	7	1986	5
1947	22	1967	7	1987	6
1948	24	1968	6	1988	6
1949	22	1969	6	1989	6
1950	15	1970	6	1990	7
1951	14	1971	6	1991	7
1952	11	1972	5	1992	7
1953	11	1973	5	1993	6
1954	9	1974	5	1994	6
1955	10	1975	4	1995	6
1956	11	1976	4	1996	6

LEGENDS FIELD

Legends Field is the state-of-the-art spring-training home of the New York Yankees, the largest in the major leagues. Combining baseball management, training, and event operation, the complex has three fields, a 10,000-seat stadium, a community-use field, and a major league practice field.

Legends Field in Tampa, Florida, is also the home of the Tampa Yankees Class-A program. Yankee tradition is everywhere—from a replica of the monuments at Yankee Stadium, located outside the park, to the signs identifying rows and seats to the six vomitories entering Legends Field.

The name Legends Field, said Yankee general partner Joseph Molloy, "is designed to reflect and recognize not only the numerous Yankee players from past years but also the current legends who play here during spring training and the future legends developing from the Tampa Yankees."

Legends Field, "the house that George built," has dimensions identical to those of Yankee Stadium. Reggie Jackson and Gene Michael appeared at the Opening Day festivities in 1994. "It's nice to be able to get an idea of what it will be like to play in Yankee Stadium," Reggie Jackson said. "You'll be able to look at what a kid is doing in Tampa, and you'll be able to tell what he'd do in Yankee stadium. I think it's great that the kids will get the chance to play in the same ballpark as the one they'll eventually play in."

Total seating, 10,382

Luxury suites, 13,168 seats

Reserved seats, 10,082

First game, March 1, 1996, versus Cleveland

Stadium dimensions, identical to Yankee Stadium

Left-field foul line, 318 feet

Center-field, 408 feet

Right-field foul line, 314 feet

ELEVEN

THE Ballparks

The short porch down the lines at the Polo Grounds was very inviting to pull hitters.

POLO GROUNDS

*W*ith Broadway stars sitting in the sun in the stands at the Polo Grounds, with his players among the elite in all of baseball, John J. McGraw, manager of the New York Giants, was the toast of the town in 1913.

The lackluster New York Yankees, their Hilltop Park just about ready to be torn down, took up residence that season at the Polo Grounds, at 155th Street and Eighth Avenue in Manhattan, as boarders of the Giants. The Yankees posed no threat to the haughty Giants. In fact, they were there to provide the Giants with some extra cash.

But in their time at the Polo Grounds—April 11, 1913, to October 8, 1922—the Yankees went from struggling boarder to fat cat. It was that damned Babe Ruth. That's how John McGraw would have put it. With Babe Ruth acting like a Pied Piper for fans, the 1920 Yankees doubled their previous season's home attendance, drawing 1,289,422—more than 350,000 more than the talented Giants. The Yankees also became the first team in baseball history to break the one-million-season attendance mark.

In 1921 and 1922, the Polo Grounds was the setting for the first two Subway Series—Giants versus Yankees. McGraw's team won both times. But

(Preceding page)
Yankee Stadium in 1948 with the flags at half-mast following Babe Ruth's death.

278

he and Giant ownership were tired of the tug of war for fans and newspaper space with the upstart Yankees. The American League team was told its lease at the Polo Grounds would not be renewed. And John McGraw snapped: "The Yankees will have to build a park in Queens or some out-of-the-way place. Let them go away and wither on the vine."

Jake Ruppert did not pick some out-of-the-way place. He picked a spot just across the Harlem River from the Polo Grounds, a location that would be in full view of those watching Giant games. It was at the mouth of a stream called Crowell's Creek, city plot 2106, lot 100, former farm of John Lion Gardiner, granted to him by the British before the Revolutionary War. It was a location where baseball originated in the Bronx. The Unions of Morrisania, "Champions of the World" in 1866, played at the site where the old Melrose station of the Harlem Railroad was situated.

THE HOUSE THAT RUTH BUILT

The Osborn Engineering Company of Cleveland was hired to design the new stadium. White Construction Company broke ground on May 5, 1922, on the 10 acres in the West Bronx that cost $675,00 and were just 16 minutes by subway from Times Square. Seventeen days later construction began.

A press release indicated that the new stadium was going to be shaped like the Yale Bowl. Towering battlements, the release explained, would enclose the entire park. Those without tickets would not even get to glimpse the action.

In less than nine months, on 240,000 square feet of land, once part of the estate of millionaire William Waldorf Astor, over the completely filled-in bed of Crowell's Creek, construction crews labored to create a ballpark out of steel and reinforced concrete. Over 950,000 board feet of Pacific Coast fir were shipped through the Panama Canal for the construction of the bleachers. Some 2,200 tons of structural steel helped to create the imposing first triple decked structure in baseball history. A copper frieze was constructed 16 feet deep from the roof's top. It was this façade that gave a nobility, a sense of grandeur, to the whole park.

Built at a cost of $2.5 million, originally named "The Yankee Stadium," the massive ballpark stretched from 157th Street to 161st Street, from River Avenue to Doughty Avenue in the Bronx. Seating 20,000 more than any other park of its day, Yankee Stadium was both the "House That Ruth Built" and the House Built for Ruth. Its dimensions caused much controversy, tailored as they were for the Babe's left-handed power.

The right-field fence was just 296 feet away along the foul line extension, and 367 to dead right field. Just 43 inches high, the fence was the lowest in the majors. One of the park's most distinctive features was "Death Valley," 461 feet to center field—death to straightaway hitters. The park was also a short 301 feet down the left-field line.

One of the Stadium's oddities was a brick-lined vault with electronic equipment under second base, making it possible to have a boxing ring and press area on the infield.

The original designs called for a fully enclosed park. But these were changed so that the triple decks came to an end near the foul poles and one deck of wooden bleachers extended the length of the outfield. The original seating capacity was called 80,000. But this attendance depended on the number and size of those fans who sat on the wooden planks that served as bleacher seats.

Yankee Stadium was a gigantic horseshoe shaped by the triple-decked grandstands. The huge wooden bleachers circled the park. The 10,712 upper-grandstand seats and 14,543 lower-grandstand seats were fixed in place by 135,000 individual steel castings on which 400,000 pieces of maple lumber were fastened by more than a million screws.

April 18, 1923, was Opening Day at brand-new Yankee Stadium—the first ball park to be called a stadium, the last privately financed major league park. The Opening Day program showcased the Colonels—Ruppert and Huston. A massive throng showed up for the proudest moment in the history of the South Bronx. Thousands trudged up the ramps of the triple-tiered park. Many in the huge assemblage wore heavy sweaters, coats, hats. Some sported dinner jackets. The announced attendance was 74,217, later changed to 60,000. More than 25,000 were turned away. They would linger outside in the cold listening to the sounds of music and the roar of the crowd inside the Stadium.

The temperature at game time was a nippy 49 degrees. Wind whipped the Yankee pennants and blew dust from the dirt road that led to the Stadium. The dominant sound of the day was the march beat played by the Seventh Regiment Band, directed by John Philip Sousa. Seated in the celebrity box were Commissioner Kenesaw Mountain Landis, New York State governor Al Smith, and Colonel Jacob Ruppert, who said, "Yankee Stadium was a mistake, not mine, but the Giants'."

At 3:25 P.M. Babe Ruth was presented with an oversized bat handsomely laid out in a glass case. At 3:30 Governor Smith threw out the first ball to Yankee catcher Wally Schang. At 3:35 home-plate umpire Tommy Connolly, who had officiated the first Highlander game in 1903, bellowed, "Play ball."

Babe Ruth had hit 54 home runs and 59 home runs in the Polo Grounds in 1920 and 1921. "I cried when they took me out of the Polo Grounds," Babe Ruth said. "Boy, how I used to sock 'em in there. I'd give a year of my life if I can hit a home run in the first game in this new park."

Ruth's wish and that of the tens of thousands in attendance came true. In the third inning the Babe came to bat. There were two Yankee base-runners. Howard Ehmke tried to fool Ruth with a slow pitch. The Sultan of Swat jumped on the ball, hammered it on a line into the right-field bleachers. The first home run in Yankee Stadium history! The huge crowd was on its feet roaring as Ruth crossed the plate, removed his cap, extended it at arm's length in front of him, and waved to the ecstatic assemblage, who realized they were witnesses to baseball history. "Sailor Bob" Shawkey, sporting a red sweatshirt under his jersey, pitched the Yankees to a 4–1 victory over the Red Sox.

With the Yankees now officially in residence in their new ballpark, property values escalated in the surrounding neighborhood. Parking lots, bars, a small theater, and little restaurants opened for business. Lunch counters sprouted up in drug stores. The nearby Concourse Plaza Hotel became the favorite lodging for visiting ballplayers.

President Warren Harding was in attendance on April 24 at Yankee Stadium as the Babe's homer powered a Yankee 4–0 victory. But it wasn't only Ruth's homers that delighted fans during the Stadium's inaugural season. They were also excited by the 20 inside-the-park home runs that were hit. Outfielders had difficulty accustoming themselves to the dimensions of the dull-green oval edifice; the late-afternoon sun shaped strange mosaic designs on the center-field grass and hampered their vision.

The Yankees met the Giants in the World Series of 1923. Still miffed, John McGraw refused to allow his team to use the visitors' clubhouse. He issued orders to the Giants to dress in their own clubhouse at the Polo Grounds. Then, in full uniform, his players took the short taxi ride over the Harlem River across the Central Bridge to Yankee Stadium.

Jacob Ruppert looked down on McGraw's behavior. But his eyes looked up to bigger goals, such as making his Yankees and the Stadium they played in more and more successful. Constant change and improvement was a way of life for the Yankee owner.

In 1927, he cut the price of Yankee Stadium's 22,000 bleacher seats from 75 cents to 50 cents. He had the most bleacher seats in the big leagues and was determined to keep them filled. He did.

In the rafters and beams of the park, pigeons took up residence. Fat from the peanuts and popcorn that spilled out into the aisles, they bolted into flight every time the big crowds jumped to their feet, excited over a dramatic moment on the playing field.

Through the years more structural changes were effected. In 1927–28, a second and third deck were added in left and center field. A decade later a deck was added in right field. In 1928, the triple-decked grandstand was extended past the foul pole in left field.

The 1937 season opened with the right-field stands enlarged—the triple decking went past the right-field foul pole. Upper-deck homers were possible now in left and right field. "Ruthville, "the original old wooden bleachers that Ruth pounded most of his home runs into, was replaced in 1937–38 by an enlarged grandstand.

Yankee Stadium was rented out during the 1930s and 1940s to the Black Yankees when the Yanks were on the road. The Black Yankees were the flip side to the Yankees, almost always last-place finishers in the Negro League.

A great many of the Yankees' patrons came from the more affluent communities in the Bronx, Westchester, Queens, New Jersey, and Connecticut. They were more sedate than Dodgers and Giants fans and though they cheered the home team on at Yankee Stadium, it was a quieter, more controlled kind of cheering that fit in with the atmosphere of the "House That Ruth Built."

"Prior to World War II," Red Foley recalls, "box seats were regular wooden chairs that went back about two or three rows from third base to first base. They cost about $2.50. You had the low fences in left and right field only about three feet high. Players could lean into them to make a catch. There were a lot of pillars and people sat behind them and couldn't see very well. They called it an obstructed view.

"In 1946, when Larry MacPhail came in," Foley added, "he moved the Yankees to the first-base dugout. Both clubs had to go through third base to get to the clubhouse." It was MacPhail who was responsible for the installation of lights for night baseball. The first night game at the Stadium was played on May 28, 1946. MacPhail also created the Stadium Club and season box seats. Corporate patronage increased with the individualized dining and seating arrangements. In 1959, the first message scoreboard was in place. In the winter of 1966–67, Foley said, "the Stadium was painted blue and white. That was a light blue—much bluer than the color used today."

But aside from a paint job, a more modern scoreboard, and some structural changes, Yankee Stadium was caught in a time warp as the 1970s began. Nineteen inches wide, the old wooden seats were still in use.

The "House That Ruth Built" cried out for a makeover. And it got one.

SHEA STADIUM (1974–75)

On April 6, 1974, the Yankees played at Shea Stadium, on 126th Street and Roosevelt Avenue in Flushing, New York. It was their first home game outside Yankee Stadium since 1922. They played at Shea until September 28, 1975, while the $160-million (it was originally supposed to cost $23 million), two-year remodeling of Yankee Stadium took place.

A total of 1,273,075 came out to see them play at Shea—their best home attendance since 1964. But it was an otherworldly type of experience for all concerned. The Mets' 1973 National League pennant flapped in the breeze on the flagpole. The field was unkempt, especially with two teams using it. And then there were the Met fans who came to the games mainly to boo the hated Yankees.

"It was like we were guests there," Doc Medich said, "and every game was an away game."

THE REFURBISHED YANKEE STADIUM (1976)

On April 15, 1976, the remodeled "new" Yankee Stadium opened. There were 52,613 jammed in—the biggest Opening Day attendance since 1946. Present for the historic occasion were Joe DiMaggio and Mickey Mantle, Mrs. Babe Ruth and Mrs. Lou Gehrig, Yogi Berra, and other Yankee legends The pregame prayer was delivered by Bobby Richardson. George Steinbrenner was present for his first home Opening Day since 1973—nine months had been taken off his suspension from baseball by Commissioner Bowie Kuhn. It was a day that honored the 1923 Yankees team. Bob Shawkey, 85, who won the 1923 opener for the Yanks, threw out the first ball.

"They changed a lot of it," Fred Stanley said. "There were some things about it that were the same, but it wasn't the old Yankee Stadium."

The magnificent copper art deco frieze façade that had encircled the roof was taken down. A portion was saved and placed on top of the bleachers in center field. The seating capacity was now about 54,200—approximately 11,600 fewer seats. But all of them had unobstructed views, because the iron pillars in the park were gone.

"Death Valley" was reduced from 457 to 417 feet. By 1988, it would be down to 399 feet. Right field increased from 296 feet to 310. Left field increased from 301 to 312.

It became more difficult to hit a fair ball out with the upper deck becoming higher and deeper. The historic monuments and plaques that had been part of the playing field were moved into Monument Park, between the Yankee and visiting bullpens. Fans no longer exited the great ballpark via the outfield.

"The new ballpark," Red Foley said, "had sort of a plastic look. When they took the frieze down, they found out that it was made of galvanized steel. The dugouts before were different, a little bigger." Overall, the refurbished Stadium was more comfortable, but the changes took away some of the character.

But Yankee Stadium was still a ballpark with much character, still the most famous ballpark in history. "It is the most magic baseball park ever built," Phil Linz said. "Playing there as a Yankee was like being in the Marines, the feeling that you were in a special ballpark, special town, special uniform, special history."

"When I was a kid I used to listen in Cuba on the radio to the World Series and hear names like Yogi Berra and Joe DiMaggio," Pedro Ramos remembered. "I got them in my head. I knew that Yankee Stadium was history and like somebody wants to see the Grand Canyon or one of the wonders of the world, to me Yankee Stadium was and is the wonder of the baseball world."

The late 1980s were tough times for the Yankees and their fans as only 126 people showed up for the start of the first game of a September double-header between the Yanks and the Milwaukee Brewers in 1989.

283

I LOVE MICKEY

Words and Music by
TERESA BREWER · RUTH ROBERTS · BILL KATZ

Price 50c

Appendix

PLAYS

As William Shakespeare said, "The play's the thing." In other words, even if the play focuses on the Yankees there is no guarantee of its success. In fact, the only Yankee-oriented play that ever really made it big was *Damn Yankees*.

The 1955 musical based on the novel *The Year the Yankees Lost the Pennant* by Douglass Wallop featured wonderfully catchy music and lyrics by Richard Adler and Jerry Ross. It opened on May 5, 1955, and ran for 1,019 performances. The superb direction of George Abbott and the skills of Gwen Verdon as Lola and Ray Walston as Applegate, the Devil, made the play a piece of Americana and gave Yankee haters a chance to laugh and applaud. Some other plays with a Yankee reference were:

All She Cares About is the Yankees (1984) was a one-act play by John Ford Noonan.

The Amazin' Casey Stengel or Can't Anybody Here Speak This Game? (1981), by Michael Zettler and Shelly Altman, had two acts and lasted 13 performances.

The Babe (1984), a three-scene play with one character, dramatized Ruth's life.

Lou Gehrig Did Not Die of Cancer (1970), a one-act play by Jason Miller lasted three performances at Lincoln Center.

Mickey Mantle Ruined My Life (1984), a one-act comedy by Roy London, lasted a few weeks.

Yankee Wives (1982), a one-act play by David Rimmer, ran for five performances and looked at baseball through the eyes of the wives of Yankee players.

SONGS

"New York, New York" has been adopted as a New York Yankees theme song, but the John Kander and Fred Ebb piece was not written as a baseball song. In fact, it celebrates the city, not the team.

But there are dozens of other songs that were written with the Yankees in mind.

Almost 20 songs celebrate Babe Ruth:

"Batterin' Babe" (1919).

"Oh! You Babe Ruth" (1920) boasts: "Babe Ruth's a treasure beyond earthy measure."

"The Babe Ruth Song" (1921) contains the line: "When Babe Ruth grabs his hickory and ambles to the base, the pitcher hitches up his belt, and pulls a cheerless face."

"Babe Ruth at the Bat" (1922).

"Babe Ruth, He Is a Home Run Guy" (1923).

"Babe Ruth! Babe Ruth! We Know What He Can Do" (1928).

"Along Came Ruth" was written by Irving Berlin. ("We were looking for a home run hero, when along came Ruth.") In 1928, the song became one of special tribute to the Babe.

When Ruth was stricken with cancer several songs were composed:

"Come On Babe" (1947).

"Safe at Home" (1948) proclaimed, "He was called out, here below, but he's safe up there I know."

"Our Bambino" (1948).

The first big hit recording of a song as tribute to a baseball star was the Les Brown orchestra's "Joltin' Joe DiMaggio" (1941), which celebrated the 56-game hitting streak. Words and music for the song came from Alan Courtney and Ben Homer. The hit musical *Damn Yankees* (1955) contained "Six Months Out of Every Year," "The Game," and "Heart."

Other Yankee related-records are:

"I Love Mickey," by Teresa Brewer and Mickey Mantle. (1956)

"Here Come the Yankees" (1967), by the Sid Bass Orchestra and Chorus.

"Babe Ruth, the Winner of Them All" (1975), Cathy Lynn's pop tribute to the Sultan of Swat.

"Catfish" (1975), written by Bob Dylan and Jacques Levy, a folk ballad tribute to Catfish Hunter.

"The Catfish Kid" (1976).

"Be a Believer in Yankee Fever" (1979).

"Playing Catch With the Babe" (1979), a tribute to Thurman Munson.

"The Bambino, the Clipper, and the Mick" (1982), Terry Cashman's tribute to Ruth, DiMaggio, and Mantle.

"I Wanna Be a Yankee" (1982), by Carmen Cassanova.

"Reggie For Christmas" (1982), a humorous tip of the hat to Reggie Jackson.

"Seasons in the Sun" (1985), a Terry Cashman tribute to Mickey Mantle.

Some of the more miscellaneous Yankee songs are:

"I Can't Get to First Base Without You" (1935), written by Mrs. Lou Gehrig and Fred Fisher, dedicated to "Lou Gehrig, famous first baseman."

"Here Come the Yanks" (1938) served for a time as a fight song for the team.

"Big Charley! (The Yankee Pitcher Man)" (1942), dedicated to Charley "Red" Ruffing.

"Yankees! My Boys" (1949), a tribute to Casey Stengel and the Yankees.

"The Ballad of Don Larsen" (1956), commemorated the Yankee hurler's World Series Perfect Game.

THE MOVIES

Film critic Jeffrey Lyons made the point that the New York Yankees are "the number one team, playing in the number one city, playing the number one game." And that's perhaps the reason for the Yankees' topping the field in most cinematic references of all time. A quantatative but not necessarily qualitative list of some of the more famous ones follows:

The Scout (1995), a story about a Yankee scout filmed at Yankee Stadium with cameo roles played by Bobby Murcer and George Steinbrenner.

The Babe (1991), with John Goodman as Babe Ruth.

Safe at Home (1962), made to capitalize on the breaking of Ruth's home-run record. Mickey Mantle, Roger Maris, Ralph Houk, and Whitey Ford all got work playing themselves.

That Touch of Mink (1962), with Cary Grant and Doris Day, and also Roger Maris, Mickey Mantle, and Yogi Berra in cameos.

Damn Yankees (1958), with Gwen Verdon as Lola, who made it all happen.

Angels in the Outfield (1951), with Joe DiMaggio in a cameo role.

The Babe Ruth Story (1948), William Bendix as Babe; a movie filled with distortions.

Pride of the Yankees (1942), Gary Cooper earned an Academy Award nomination as a convincing Lou Gehrig—best Yankee movie ever. Ruth, Koenig, Dickey, and Meusel played themselves in the film.

Rawhide (1938), starred Lou Gehrig, about a baseball player who settles on a ranch after the season ends.

Slide, Kelly, Slide (1927), gave bit roles to Bob Meusel and Tony Lazzeri, featured a catcher named Munson and a boy named Mickey Martin.

The Babe Comes Home (1927), a comedy that starred Babe Ruth.

Speedy (1927), a comedy with Babe Ruth and comedian Harold Lloyd.

Heading Home (1920), Babe played a small-town All-American boy.

Other films with Yankee references include *Bang the Drum Slowly, Casey at the Bat, Field of Dreams, Mr. Baseball, The Natural, The Dream Team, City Slickers, Manhattan Merry-Go Round, Woman of the Year,* and *The Sandlot.*

FREE-AGENT SIGNINGS

Catfish Hunter	December 31, 1974	John Candelaria	January 15, 1988
Don Gullett	November 18, 1976	Jose Cruz	February 25, 1988
Reggie Jackson	November 29, 1976	Steve Sax	November 23, 1988
Rich Gossage	November 23, 1977	Dave LaPoint	December 3, 1988
Rawly Eastwick	December 12, 1977	Andy Hawkins	December 8, 1988
Luis Tiant	November 13, 1978	Jamie Quirk	December 20, 1988
Tommy John	November 22, 1978	Ron Guidry	February 3, 1989
Rudy May	November 8, 1979	Tommy John	February 13, 1989
Bob Watson	November 8, 1979	Pascual Perez	November 21, 1989
Dave Winfield	December 15, 1980	Mel Hall	November 30, 1989
Bill Castro	February 17, 1981	Rick Cerone	December 22, 1989
Ron Guidry	December 15, 1981	Damaso Garcia	December 22, 1989
Dave Collins	December 23, 1981	Tim Leary	November 19, 1990
Don Baylor	December 1, 1982	Steve Farr	November 26, 1990
Steve Kemp	December 9, 1982	Danny Tartabull	January 6, 1992
Bob Shirley	December 15, 1982	Mike Gallego	January 7, 1992
Dale Murray	November 21, 1983	Spike Owen	December 4, 1992
Phil Niekro	January 6, 1984	Steve Howe	December 8, 1992
Ed Whitson	December 27, 1984	Jimmy Key	December 10, 1992
Joe Niekro	January 8, 1986	Wade Boggs	December 15, 1992
Butch Wynegar	January 8, 1986	Luis Polonia	December 20, 1993
Al Holland	February 6, 1986	Donn Pall	January 18, 1994
Tommy John	May 2, 1986	Scott Bankhead	November 1, 1994
Rod Scurry	December 5, 1986	Tony Fernandez	December 15, 1994
Claudell Washington	December 11, 1986	Dwight Gooden	October 16, 1996
Lenn Sakata	December 16, 1986	Wade Boggs	December 5, 1995
Gary Ward	December 24, 1986	Mariano Duncan	December 11, 1995
Tommy John	January 8, 1987	David Cone	December 21, 1995
Wayne Tolleson	January 8, 1987	Pat Kelly	December 27, 1995
Willie Randolph	January 8, 1987	Kenny Rogers	January 4, 1996
Bob Shirley	January 28, 1987	Jim Leyritz	January 18, 1996
Rick Cerone	February 13, 1987	Mike Stanton	December 11, 1996
Ron Guidry	May 1, 1987	David Wells	December 18, 1996
Dave Righetti	December 23, 1987	Mark Whiten	January 9, 1997
Jack Clark	January 6, 1988		

YANKEES IN THE HALL OF FAME

Babe Ruth	1936		Clark C. Griffith	1945
Lou Gehrig	1939		Frank Chance	1946
Willie Keeler	1939		Jack Chesbro	1946
Herb Pennock	1948		George M. Weiss	1970
Paul Waner	1952		Yogi Berra	1971
Edward G. Barrow	1953		Lefty Gomez	1972
Bill Dickey	1954		Mickey Mantle	1974
Frank (Home Run) Baker	1955		Whitey Ford	1974
Joe DiMaggio	1955		Bucky Harris	1975
Dazzy Vance	1955		Joe Sewell	1977
Joe McCarthy	1957		Larry MacPhail	1978
Bill McKechnie	1962		Johnny Mize	1981
Burleigh Grimes	1964		Enos Slaughter	1985
Miller Huggins	1964		Catfish Hunter	1987
Casey Stengel	1966		Gaylord Perry	1991
Branch Rickey	1967		Tony Lazzeri	1991
Red Ruffing	1967		Reggie Jackson	1993
Stan Covelski	1969		Phil Rizzuto	1994
Waite Hoyt	1969		Phil Niekro	1997
Earle Combs	1970			

THE NUMBERS GAME

The famous Number 3 worn by Babe Ruth was actually a bit shopworn by the time the Yankees permanently retired it in 1948, a brief time before the Babe passed away. Other Yankees who had worn the fabled "3" include George Selkirk, Allie Clark, Bud Metheny, and Cliff Mapes. Even Joe Medwick sported the "3" during spring training.

As rookies Joe DiMaggio (9), Yogi Berra (35), and Mickey Mantle (6) all wore numbers that they subsequently gave up. Mantle wore Number 6 for a few months of the 1951 season. Number 7 was being worn by Cliff Mapes. On July 31, 1951, Mapes was traded to the St. Louis Browns. Mantle returned from Kansas City in the minors and put on Number 7, making it one of the famous numbers in New York Yankees history.

RETIRED NUMBERS

1	Billy Martin	1986		32	Elston Howard	1984
3	Babe Ruth	1948		37	Casey Stengel	1970
4	Lou Gehrig	1939		44	Reggie Jackson	1993
5	Joe DiMaggio	1952				
7	Mickey Mantle	1969				
8	Bill Dickey and Yogi Berra	1972				
9	Roger Maris	1984				
10	Phil Rizzuto	1985				
15	Thurman Munson	1979				
16	Whitey Ford	1974				
23	Don Mattingly	1997				

AWARDS

Cy Young

Bob Turley	1958
Whitey Ford	1961
Sparky Lyle	1977
Ron Guidry	1978

Most Valuable Player

Babe Ruth	1923
Lou Gehrig	1927, 1936
Joe DiMaggio	1939, 1941, 1947
Joe Gordon	1942
Spud Chandler	1943
Phil Rizzuto	1950
Yogi Berra	1951, 1954, 1955
Mickey Mantle	1956, 1957, 1962
Roger Maris	1960, 1961
Elston Howard	1963
Thurman Munson	1976
Don Mattingly	1985

American League Rookie of the Year

Gil McDougald 3b	1951
Bob Grim p	1954
Tony Kubek if-of	1957
Tom Tresh ss-of	1962
Stan Bahnsen p	1968
Thurman Munson c	1970
Dave Righetti p	1981
Derek Jeter ss	1996

No-Hitters

Throughout their history, Yankee pitchers have hurled 11 no-hitters. Opponents have managed to no-hit the Yankees seven times. The no-hitters have been spaced out throughout the years—each one has its own story.

The first no-hitter pitched by a Yankee took place on August 30, 1910. Tom Hughes was on the mound in the second game of a doubleheader against Cleveland. Using "inshoots" and "outshoots," Hughes had things well under control. By the end of the ninth only 28 batters had faced him. But in the 11th inning, an arm-weary Hughes yielded five runs and lost the game, 5–0. (Under current rules, this game is not considered a no-hitter.)

April 24, 1917: Southpaw George Mogridge nipped Boston, 2–1. The Red Sox run came on two walks, an error and a sacrifice fly.

September 4, 1923: In the year the Yankees won their first World Championship, "Sad Sam" Jones no-hit the Athletics, 2–0.

August 27, 1938: Right-hander Monte Pearson no-hit Cleveland in the second game of a doubleheader. The final score was 13–0. It was the first no-hitter pitched in Yankee Stadium.

July 12, 1951: Allie Reynolds no-hit Cleveland in a 1–0 night-game win.

September 28, 1951: Allie Reynolds pitched his second no-hitter of the season in the first game of a doubleheader, giving the Yankees an 8–0 win over the Red Sox.

October 8, 1956: In game five of the World Series against the Brooklyn Dodgers, Don Larsen pitched the only perfect game in the history of the Fall Classic.

July 4, 1983: Southpaw Dave Righetti struck out nine and pitched a no-hitter against the Red Sox at Yankee Stadium.

July 1, 1990: In a game played in Chicago, Andy Hawkins's no-hitter was for naught as the Yankees lost 4–0. Three Yankee errors allowed the runs to score.

September 4, 1993: Jim Abbott no-hit Cleveland, 4–0.

May 14, 1996: Dwight Gooden hurled a no-hitter against the Seattle Mariners in a night game at the Stadium. The Yankees won the game, 2–0.

Seven no-hitters have been pitched against the Yankees. The first was hurled by Cy Young and the last by Melido Perez. Here is the complete list.

June 30, 1908: Cy Young of Boston, 8–0 at New York.

June 21, 1916: George Foster of Boston, 2–0 at Boston.

September 10, 1919: First game of doubleheader, Ray Caldwell of Cleveland, 3–0 at New York.

April 30, 1946: Bob Feller of Cleveland, 1–0 at New York.

August 25, 1952: Virgil Trucks of Detroit, 1–0 at New York.

September 20, 1958: Hoyt Wilhelm of Baltimore, 1–0 at Baltimore.

July 12, 1990: Melido Perez of Chicago, 8–0 at New York (6 1/2-inning game).

YANKEES AND THE ALL-STAR GAME

"I was the starting second baseman in the 1977 All-Star Game at Yankee Stadium," Willie Randoph recalled. "I was a young kid in front of my home-town fans, my family. I played the whole game. I was there playing with guys I had grown up idolizing—Rod Carew, Reggie Jackson."

From Willie Randoph to all the Yankees through the decades who have played in the midsummer classic, the All-Star Game has brought special memories and much pride.

Yankee All-Star roots stretch back to the first game in 1933, played in Comiskey Park, Chicago. Lefty Gomez was on the mound for the first of three straight starts, five overall. Not only was "El Goofo" the winning pitcher, he also became the first player to drive in an All-Star run. And he did all of that on one day's rest. But it was Babe Ruth, age 38, fat and flabby, who grabbed the big headlines. Hammering a two-run homer, pulling off a sensational running catch, the Babe almost singlehandedly made possible the American League 4–2 victory. Other Yankees on the 1933 squad included Ben Chapman, Bill Dickey, and Tony Lazzeri.

Lou Gehrig played in the first six All-Star games. In 1936, the Iron Horse homered off Curt Davis. In 1937, with President Roosevelt looking on at the game played in Washington, Gehrig homered and doubled to drive in half the American League's eight runs in an easy American League win. Lefty Gomez started his fourth All-Star Game in five years, winning his third.

Bill Dickey was behind the plate for eight All-Star Games. His most dramatic moment was in 1934, when his single snapped Carl Hubbell's string of five straight strikeouts of immortals Babe Ruth, Lou Gehrig, Jimmie Foxx, Al Simmons, and Joe Cronin.

Joe DiMaggio, a rookie in 1936, started the All-Star Game and played the entire contest in right field. No other rookie had ever started an All-Star Game. But DiMag was not your average rookie. He was batting .358 and playing like a seasoned veteran. Unfortunately, it was not one of the best days the Yankee Clipper had on a baseball field. He muffed a shoestring catch, then committed an error, setting up the National League winning run. He also came to bat five times and couldn't manage a hit.

Joe McCarthy was an All-Star Game fixture. In 1943, in the first game played at night, Marse Joe, serving for the sixth time as American League manager, saw to it that no Yankees played. It was the only time in All-Star history that no Yankee participated even though six had been selected. McCarthy wanted to make the point that he could beat the National League without using any of his own players—and he did. The American League won the game, 5–3.

The next year Marse Joe made up for his omissions. At Forbes Field in Pittsburgh, with all his stars in wartime service, McCarthy still started an all-Yankee battery—pitcher Hank Borowy and catcher Rollie Hemsley. Borowy pitched three scoreless innings.

Other Yankee All-Star Game highlights include Ryne Duren's three innings in 1959, in which he allowed one hit and struck out four; Yogi Berra's two-run homer in 1959; Vic Raschi's three shutout innings for the Americans in the 1949 and 1950; the 1949 game won by the AL, 11–7, in which Joe Dee collected two hits and three RBIs to pace the American League offense.

Yankee Stadium has played host to the All-Star Game on three different occasions. The first time was on July 11, 1939. Six Yankees started the game. Pinstripes were all over the place—Frank Crosetti, Bill Dickey, Joe DiMaggio, Lefty Gomez, Joe Gordon, Johnny Murphy, Red Rolfe, Red Ruffing, and George Selkirk. The AL won the game. DiMag hit the only home run, and most of the 62,892 went home happy.

On July 13, 1960, Yankee Stadium was again the scene of the Summer Classic. There were 38,362 on hand and seven Yankees on the AL team: Whitey Ford, Roger Maris, Mickey Mantle, Bill Skowron, Elston Howard, Jim

Coates, and Yogi Berra. But Willie Mays spoiled the day for the American League and Whitey Ford. He singled in the first off "Slick" and then homered off Whitey in the third inning. That gave Mays a 6–6 performance off Ford in All-Star competition. The AL went down to a 6–0 defeat. Whitey Ford was the losing pitcher.

July 19, 1977, was the third All-Star Game played at Yankee Stadium. That was the one Willie Randoph played in that included Reggie, Sparky Lyle, Thurman Munson, and Graig Nettles. Lyle took his lumps, giving up three hits and two runs in two innings. The only bright spot for Yankee fans among the 56,683 in attendance was an RBI single by Randolph.

Yankee milestones and oddities of All-Star play include Lefty Gomez starting his third All-Star Game in 1935, pitching a record six innings, and picking up his second All-Star win; Whitey Ford's three starts; and the two starts each by Red Ruffing and Vic Raschi.

Mantle and Gehrig were the only Yankees to hit two home runs in All-Star competion. Mantle homered in 1955 and 1956 as Gehrig had done in 1936 and 1937. Gil McDougald was one of the most versatile of Yankee participants. A five-time All-Star, he started at shortstop, second base, and third base. All-time Yankee leaders in All-Star games played are Mickey Mantle (16), Berra (15), and DiMag (11).

WORLD SERIES MVP AWARD

1949	Joe Page
1950	Jerry Coleman
1951	Phil Rizzuto
1952	Johnny Mize
1953	Billy Martin
1956	Don Larsen
1958	Elston Howard (BBWA)
1958	Bob Turley (*Sport Magazine*)
1960	Bobby Richardson
1961	Whitey Ford
1962	Ralph Terry
1977	Reggie Jackson
1978	Bucky Dent
1996	Cecil Fielder (BBWA)
1996	John Wetteland (*Sport Magazine*)

YANKEE CAPTAINS

Hal Chase	?–12
Roger Peckinpaugh	1914–21
Babe Ruth (six games)	1922
Everett Scott	1922–25
Lou Gehrig	1935 until he died 6/2/41
Thurman Munson	1976 until he died 8/2/79
Graig Nettles	1982 until traded 3/30/84
Ron Guidry	1986 until retirement 7/12/89
Willie Randolph	1986 until signing with the Dodgers 12/10/88
Don Mattingly	1991–95

SILVER BAT AWARD (1980—96)

Given by *The Sporting News* and Hillerich and Bradsby to the best offensive player at each position in the AL.

1980	Willie Randolph (2B)
	Reggie Jackson (DH)
1981	Dave Winfield (OF)
1982	Dave Winfield (OF)
1983	Dave Winfield (OF)
	Don Baylor (DH)
1984	Dave Winfield (OF)
1985	Don Mattingly (1B)
	Rickey Henderson (OF)
	Dave Winfield (OF)
	Don Baylor (DH)
1986	Don Mattingly (1B)
1987	Don Mattingly (1B)
1993	Mike Stanley (C)
	Wade Boggs (3B)
1995	Wade Boggs (3B)

TRIPLE CROWN WINNERS (1903–96)

1934	Lou Gehrig (.363, 49 HRs, 165 RBIs)
1956	Mickey Mantle (.353, 52 HRs, 130 RBIs)

Yankee League Leaders 1903–96

Offense

AT BATS

1923	Joe Dugan	644
1927	Earle Combs	648
1939	Frank Crosetti	656
1945	Snuffy Stirnweiss	632
1962	Bobby Richardson	692
1963	Bobby Richardson	630
1964	Bobby Richardson	679
1969	Horace Clarke	641
1970	Horace Clarke	686
1973	Roy White	639
1989	Steve Sax	651

RUNS

1920	Babe Ruth	158
1921	Babe Ruth	177
1923	Babe Ruth	151
1924	Babe Ruth	143
1926	Babe Ruth	139
1927	Babe Ruth	158
1928	Babe Ruth	163
1931	Lou Gehrig	163
1933	Lou Gehrig	138
1935	Lou Gehrig	125
1936	Lou Gehrig	167
1937	Joe DiMaggio	151
1939	Red Rolfe	139
1944	Snuffy Stirnweiss	125
1945	Snuffy Stirnweiss	107
1948	Tommy Henrich	138
1954	Mickey Mantle	129
1956	Mickey Mantle	132
1957	Mickey Mantle	121
1958	Mickey Mantle	127
1960	Mickey Mantle	119
1961	Mickey Mantle	132
	Roger Maris	132
1972	Bobby Murcer	102
1976	Roy White	104
1986	Rickey Henderson	130

HITS

1927	Earle Combs	231
1931	Lou Gehrig	211
1939	Red Rolfe	213
1944	Snuffy Stirnweiss	205
1945	Snuffy Strinweiss	195
1962	Bobby Richardson	209
1984	Don Mattingly	207
1986	Don Mattingly	238

DOUBLES

1927	Lou Gehrig	52
1928	Lou Gehrig	47
1939	Red Rolfe	46
1984	Don Mattingly	44
1985	Don Mattingly	48
1986	Don Mattingly	53

TRIPLES

1924	Wally Pipp	19
1926	Lou Gehrig	20
1927	Earle Combs	23
1928	Earle Combs	21
1930	Earle Combs	22
1934	Ben Chapman	13
1936	Joe DiMaggio	15
	Red Rolfe	15
1943	Johnny Lindell	12
1944	Johnny Lindell	16
	Snuffy Stirnweiss	16
1945	Snuffy Stirnweiss	22
1947	Tommy Henrich	13
1948	Tommy Henrich	14
1955	Andy Carey	11
	Mickey Mantle	11
1957	Hank Bauer	9
	Gil McDougald	9

HOME RUNS

1917	Wally Pipp	9
1920	Babe Ruth	54
1921	Babe Ruth	59
1923	Babe Ruth	41
1924	Babe Ruth	46

1925	Bob Meusel	33
1926	Babe Ruth	47
1927	Babe Ruth	60
1928	Babe Ruth	54
1929	Babe Ruth	46
1930	Babe Ruth	49
1931	Babe Ruth	46
	Lou Gehrig	46
1934	Lou Gehrig	49
1936	Lou Gehrig	49
1937	Joe DiMaggio	46
1944	Nick Etten	22
1948	Joe DiMaggio	39
1955	Mickey Mantle	37
1956	Mickey Mantle	52
1958	Mickey Mantle	42
1960	Mickey Mantle	40
1961	Roger Maris	61
1976	Graig Nettles	32
1980	Reggie Jackson	41

RBIS

1920	Babe Ruth	137
1921	Babe Ruth	171
1923	Babe Ruth	131
1925	Bob Meusel	138
1926	Babe Ruth	145
1927	Lou Gehrig	175
1928	Lou Gehrig	142
	Babe Ruth	142
1930	Lou Gehrig	174
1931	Lou Gehrig	184
1934	Lou Gehrig	165
1941	Joe DiMaggio	125
1945	Nick Etten	111
1948	Joe DiMaggio	155
1956	Mickey Mantle	130
1960	Roger Maris	112
1985	Don Mattingly	145

STOLEN BASES

| 1914 | Fritz Maisel | 74 |
| 1931 | Ben Chapman | 61 |

1932	Ben Chapman	38
1933	Ben Chapman	27
1938	Frank Crosetti	27
1944	Snuffy Stirnweiss	55
1945	Snuffy Stirnweiss	33
1985	Rickey Henderson	80
1986	Rickey Henderson	87
1988	Rickey Henderson	93

BASES ON BALLS

1920	Babe Ruth	148
1921	Babe Ruth	144
1922	Whitey Witt	89
1923	Babe Ruth	170
1924	Babe Ruth	142
1926	Babe Ruth	144
1927	Babe Ruth	138
1928	Babe Ruth	135
1930	Babe Ruth	136
1931	Babe Ruth	128
1932	Babe Ruth	130
1933	Babe Ruth	114
1935	Lou Gehrig	132
1936	Loue Gehrig	130
1937	Lou Gehrig	127
1940	Charlie Keller	106
1943	Charlie Keller	106
1944	Nick Etten	97
1955	Mickey Mantle	113
1957	Mickey Mantle	146
1958	Mickey Mantle	129
1961	Mickey Mantle	126
1962	Mickey Mantle	122
1972	Roy White	99
1980	Willie Randolph	119

BATTING AVERAGE

1924	Babe Ruth	.378
1934	Lou Gehrig	.363
1939	Joe DiMaggio	.381
1940	Joe DiMaggio	.352
1945	Snuffy Stirnweiss	.309
1956	Mickey Mantle	.353

1984	Don Mattingley	.343
1994	Paul O'Neill	.359

SLUGGING AVERAGE

1920	Babe Ruth	.847
1921	Babe Ruth	.846
1922	Babe Ruth	.672
1923	Babe Ruth	.764
1924	Babe Ruth	.739
1926	Babe Ruth	.737
1927	Babe Ruth	.772
1928	Babe Ruth	.709
1929	Babe Ruth	.697
1930	Babe Ruth	.732
1931	Babe Ruth	.700
1934	Lous Gehrig	.706
1936	Lou Gehrig	.696
1937	Joe DiMaggio	.673
1945	Snuffy Stirnweiss	.476
1950	Joe DiMaggio	.585
1955	Mickey Mantle	.611
1956	Mickey Mantle	.705
1960	Roger Maris	.581
1961	Mickey Mantle	.687
1962	Mickey Mantle	.605
1986	Don Mattingly	.573

Pitching (1903–96)

WINS

1904	Jack Chesbro	41
1906	Al Orth	27
1921	Carl Mays	27
1927	Waite Hoyt	22
1928	George Pipgras	24
1934	Lefty Gomez	26
1937	Lefty Gomez	21
1938	Red Ruffing	21
1943	Spud Chandler	20
1955	Whitey Ford	18
1958	Bob Turley	21
1961	Whitey Ford	25

1962	Ralph Terry	23
1963	Whitey Ford	24
1975	Catfish Hunter	23
1978	Ron Guidry	25
1985	Ron Guidry	22
1994	Jimmy Key	17
1996	Andy Pettitte	21

WIN PERCENTAGE

1904	Jack Chesbro	.774 (41–12)
1921	Carl Mays	.750 (27–9)
1922	Bullet Joe Bush	.788 (26–7)
1923	Herb Pennock	.760 (19–6)
1927	Waite Hoyt	.759 (22–7)
1932	Johnny Allen	.810 (17–4)
1934	Lefty Gomez	.839 (26–5)
1936	Monte Pearson	.731 (19–7)
1938	Red Ruffing	.750 (21–7)
1941	Lefty Gomez	.750 (15–5)
1942	Ernie Bonham	.808 (21–5)
1943	Spud Chandler	.833 (20–4)
1947	Allie Reynolds	.704 (19–8)
1950	Vic Raschi	.724 (21–8)
1953	Ed Lopat	.800 (16–4)
1955	Tommy Byrne	.762 (16–5)
1956	Whitey Ford	.760 (19–6)
1957	Tom Sturdivant	.727 (16–6)
1958	Bob Turley	.750 (21–7)
1961	Whitey Ford	.862 (25–4)
1963	Whitey Ford	.774 (24–7)
1978	Ron Guidry	.893 (25–3)
1985	Ron Guidry	.786 (22–6)
1993	Jimmy Key	.750 (18–6)

GAMES PITCHED

1904	Jack Chesbro	55
1906	Jack Chesbro	49
1918	George Mogridge	45
1921	Carl Mays	49
1948	Joe Page	55
1949	Joe Page	60
1961	Luis Arroyo	65
1977	Sparky Lyle	72

1986	Dave Righetti	74		1960	Whitey Ford	4
1994	Bob Wickman	53		1978	Ron Guidry	9
				1980	Tommy John	6

GAMES STARTED

SAVES

1904	Jack Chesbro	51
1906	Jack Chesbro	42
1928	George Pipgras	38
1949	Vic Raschi	37
1951	Vic Raschi	34
1961	Whitey Ford	39
1962	Ralph Terry	39
1963	Whitey Ford	37
	Ralph Terry	37

SAVES

1916	Bob Shawkey	8
1918	George Mogridge	7
1921	Carl Mays	7
1922	Sad Sam Jones	8
1927	Wilcy Moore	13
1928	Waite Hoyt	8
1936	Pat Malone	9
1938	Johnny Murphy	11
1939	Johnny Murphy	19
1941	Johnny Murphy	15
1943	Johnny Murphy	11
1945	Jim Turner	10
1947	Joe Page	17
1949	Joe Page	27
1954	Johnny Sain	22
1957	Bob Grim	19
1958	Ryne Duren	20
1961	Luis Arroyo	29
1972	Sparky Lyle	35
1976	Sparky Lyle	23
1978	Rich Gossage	27
1980	Rich Gossage	33
1986	Dave Righetti	46
1996	John Wetteland	43

COMPLETE GAMES

1904	Jack Chesbro	48
1906	Al Orth	36
1934	Lefty Gomez	25
1942	Ernie Bonham	22
1943	Spud Chandler	20
1955	Whitey Ford	18
1958	Bob Turley	19
1963	Ralph Terry	18
1965	Mel Stottlemyre	18
1969	Mel Stottlemyre	24
1975	Catfish Hunter	30
1983	Ron Guidry	21
1995	Jack McDowell	8

SHUTOUTS

1920	Carl Mays	6
1928	Herb Pennock	5
1930	George Pipgras	3
1934	Lefty Gomez	6
1937	Lefty Gomez	6
1938	Lefty Gomez	3
	Red Ruffing	3
1939	Red Ruffing	5
1942	Ernie Bonham	6
1943	Spud Chandler	5
1951	Allie Reynolds	7
1952	Allie Reynolds	6
1958	Whitey Ford	7

ERA

1920	Bob Shawkey	2.45
1927	Wilcy Moore	2.28
1934	Lefty Gomez	2.33
1937	Lefty Gomez	2.33
1943	Spud Chandler	1.64
1947	Spud Chandler	2.46
1952	Allie Reynolds	2.06
1953	Ed Lopat	2.42
1956	Whitey Ford	2.47
1957	Bobby Shantz	2.45
1958	Whitey Ford	2.01
1978	Ron Guidry	1.74

| 1979 | Ron Guidry | 2.78 |
| 1980 | Rudy May | 2.47 |

STRIKEOUTS

1932	Red Ruffing	190
1933	Lefty Gomez	163
1934	Lefty Gomez	158
1937	Lefty Gomez	194
1951	Vic Raschi	164
1962	Ralph Terry	299
1952	Allie Reynolds	160
1964	Al Downing	217

INNINGS PITCHED

1904	Jack Chesbro	455
1906	Al Orth	339
1921	Carl Mays	337
1925	Herb Pennock	277
1928	George Pipgras	301
1934	Lefty Gomez	282
1961	Whitey Ford	283
1963	Whitey Ford	269
1965	Mel Stottlemyre	291
1975	Catfish Hunter	328

ALL-TIME YANKEE RECORDS
Yankee Career Leaders 1903–96

GAMES PLAYED

1.	Mickey Mantle	2,401
2.	Lou Gehrig	2,164
3.	Yogi Berra	2,116
4.	Babe Ruth	2,084
5.	Roy White	1,881
6.	Bill Dickey	1,789
7.	Don Mattingly	1,785
8.	Joe DiMaggio	1,736
9.	Willie Randolph	1,694
10.	Frank Crosetti	1,682

AT-BATS

| 1. | Mickey Mantle | 8,102 |
| 2. | Lou Gehrig | 8,001 |

3.	Yogi Berra	7,546
4.	Babe Ruth	7,217
5.	Don Mattingly	7,003
6.	Joe DiMaggio	6,821
7.	Roy White	6,650
8.	Willie Randolph	6,303
9.	Bill Dickey	6,300
10.	Frank Crosetti	6,277

RUNS SCORED

1.	Babe Ruth	1,959
2.	Lou Gehrig	1,888
3.	Mickey Mantle	1,677
4.	Joe DiMaggio	1,390
5.	Earle Combs	1,186
6.	Yogi Berra	1,174
7.	Willie Randolph	1,027
8.	Don Mattingly	1,007
9.	Frank Crosetti	1,006
10.	Roy White	964

HITS

1.	Lou Gehrig	2,721
2.	Babe Ruth	2,518
3.	Mickey Mantle	2,415
4.	Joe DiMaggio	2,214
5.	Don Mattingly	2,153
6.	Yogi Berra	2,148
7.	Bill Dickey	1,969
8.	Earle Combs	1,866
9.	Roy White	1,803
10.	Tony Lazzeri	1,784

DOUBLES

1.	Lou Gehrig	535
2.	Don Mattingly	442
3.	Babe Ruth	424
4.	Joe DiMaggio	389
5.	Mickey Mantle	344
6.	Bill Dickey	343
7.	Bob Meusel	338
8.	Tony Lazzeri	327
9.	Yogi Berra	321
10.	Earle Combs	309

TRIPLES

1.	Lou Gehrig	162
2.	Earle Combs	154
3.	Joe DiMaggio	131
4.	Wally Pipp	121
5.	Tony Lazzeri	115
6.	Babe Ruth	106
7.	Bob Meusel	87
8.	Tommy Henrich	73
9.	Bill Dickey	72
10.	Mickey Mantle	72

HOME RUNS

1.	Babe Ruth	659
2.	Mickey Mantle	536
3.	Lou Gehrig	493
4.	Joe DiMaggio	361
5.	Yogi Berra	358
6.	Graig Nettles	250
7.	Don Mattingly	222
8.	Dave Winfield	205
9.	Roger Maris	203
10.	Bill Dickey	202

RUNS BATTED IN

1.	Lou Gehrig	1,991
2.	Babe Ruth	1,970
3.	Joe DiMaggio	1,537
4.	Mickey Mantle	1,509
5.	Yogi Berra	1,430
6.	Bill Dickey	1,209
7.	Tony Lazzeri	1,154
8.	Don Mattingly	1,099
9.	Bob Meusel	1,005
10.	Graig Nettles	834

BASES ON BALLS

1.	Babe Ruth	1,847
2.	Mickey Mantle	1,733
3.	Lou Gehrig	1,508
4.	Willie Randolph	1,005
5.	Roy White	934
6.	Tony Lazzeri	831

7.	Frank Crosetti	792
8.	Joe DiMaggio	790
9.	Charlie Keller	760
10.	Tommy Henrich	712

STOLEN BASES

1.	Rickey Henderson	326
2.	Willie Randolph	251
3.	Hal Chase	248
4.	Roy White	233
5.	Ben Chapman	184
	Wid Conroy	184
7.	Fritz Maisel	183
8.	Mickey Mantle	153
9.	Horace Clarke	151
	Roberto Kelly	151

BATTING AVERAGE
(At least 500 games played.)

1.	Babe Ruth	.349
2.	Lou Gehrig	.340
3.	Earle Combs	.325
	Joe DiMaggio	.325
5.	Paul O'Neill	.315
6.	Bill Dickey	.313
7.	Bob Meusel	.311
8.	Don Mattingly	.307
9.	Ben Chapman	.305
10.	Mickey Mantle	.298

YANKEE CAREER LEADERS BY POSITION 1903–96

(At least 75 percent of the games played by the player must be at the position shown.)

CATCHERS

Games	Yogi Berra	2,116
At-Bats	Yogi Berra	7,546
Runs	Yogi Berra	1,174
Hits	Yogi Berra	2,148
Doubles	Bill Dickey	343
Triples	Bill Dickey	72
Home Runs	Yogi Berra	358

Runs Batted In	Yogi Berra	1,430
Bases on Balls	Yogi Berra	704
Batting Average		
(1,500 at-bats)	Bill Dickey	.313

FIRST BASEMEN

Games	Lou Gehrig	2,164
At-Bats	Lou Gehrig	8,001
Runs	Lou Gehrig	1,888
Hits	Lou Gehrig	2,721
Doubles	Lou Gehrig	535
Triples	Lou Gehrig	162
Home Runs	Lou Gehrig	493
Runs Batted In	Lou Gehrig	1,991
Bases on Balls	Lou Gehrig	1,508
Stolen Bases	Hal Chase	248
Batting Average		
(1,500 at-bats)	Lou Gehrig	.340

SECOND BASEMEN

Games	Willie Randolph	1,694
At-Bats	Willie Randolph	6,303
Runs	Willie Randolph	1,027
Hits	Tony Lazzeri	1,784
Doubles	Tony Lazzeri	327
Triples	Tony Lazzeri	115
Home Runs	Tony Lazzeri	169
Runs Batted In	Tony Lazzeri	1,154
Bases on Balls	Willie Randolph	1,005
Stolen Bases	Willie Randolph	251
Batting Average		
(1,500 at-bats)	Tony Lazzeri	.293

THIRD BASEMEN

Games	Graig Netles	1,535
At-Bats	Graig Nettles	5,519
Runs	Red Rolfe	942
Hits	Graig Nettles	1,396
Doubles	Red Rolfe	257
Triples	Red Rolfe	67
Home Runs	Graig Nettles	250
Runs Batted In	Graig Nettles	834

Bases on Balls	Graig Nettles	627
Stolen Bases	Fritz Maisel	183
Batting Average		
(1,500 at-bats)	Wade Boggs	.317

SHORTSTOPS

Games	Frank Crosetti	1,682
At-Bats	Frank Crosetti	6,277
Runs	Frank Crosetti	1,006
Hits	Rhil Rizzuto	1,588
Doubles	Frank Crosetti	260
Triples	Frank Crosetti	65
Home Runs	Frank Crosetti	98
Runs Batted In	Frank Crosetti	649
Bases on Balls	Frank Crosetti	792
Stolen Bases	Phil Rizzuto	149
Batting Average		
(1,500 at-bats)	Mark Koenig	.285

OUTFIELDERS

Games	Mickey Mantle	2,401
At-Bats	Mickey Mantle	8,102
Runs	Babe Ruth	1,959
Hits	Babe Ruth	2,518
Doubles	Babe Ruth	424
Triples	Earle Combs	154
Home Runs	Babe Ruth	659
Runs Batted In	Babe Ruth	1,970
Bases on Balls	Babe Ruth	1,847
Stolen Bases	Rickey Henderson	326
Batting Average		
(1,500 at-bats)	Babe Ruth	.349

CLUB SINGLE-SEASON LEADERS 1903–96

(By category.)

AT-BATS

1.	Bobby Richardson	692	(1962)
2.	Horace Clarke	686	(1970)
3.	Bobby Richardson	679	(1964)
4.	Don Mattingly	677	(1986)
5.	Bobby Richardson	664	(1965)

RUNS SCORED

1.	Babe Ruth	177	(1921)**
2.	Lou Gehrig	167	(1936)
3.	Babe Ruth	163	(1928)
	Lou Gehrig	163	(1931)
5.	Babe Ruth	158	(1920)
	Babe Ruth	158	(1927)

HITS

1.	Don Mattingly	238	(1986)
2.	Earle Combs	231	(1927)
3.	Lou Gehrig	220	(1930)
4.	Lou Gehrig	218	(1927)
5.	Joe DiMaggio	215	(1937)

DOUBLES

1.	Don Mattingly	53	(1986)
2.	Lou Gehrig	52	(1927)
3.	Don Mattingly	48	(1985)
4.	Lou Gehrig	47	(1926)
	Bob Meusel	47	(1927)
	Lou Gehrig	47	(1928)

TRIPLES

1.	Earle Combs	23	(1927)
2.	Birdie Cree	22	(1911)
	Earle Combs	22	(1930)
	Snuffy Stirnweiss	22	(1945)
5.	Earle Combs	21	(1928)

HOME RUNS

1.	Roger Maris	61	(1961)**
2.	Babe Ruth	60	(1927)
3.	Babe Ruth	59	(1921)
4.	Babe Ruth	54	(1920)
	Babe Ruth	54	(1928)
	Mickey Mantle	54	(1961)

RUNS BATTED IN

1.	Lou Gehrig	184	(1931)*
2.	Lou Gehrig	175	(1927)
3.	Lou Gehrig	174	(1930)
4.	Babe Ruth	171	(1921)
5.	Joe DiMaggio	167	(1937)

BASES ON BALLS

1.	Babe Ruth	170	(1923)**
2.	Babe Ruth	148	(1920)

3.	Mickey Mantle	146	(1957)
4.	Babe Ruth	144	(1921)
	Babe Ruth	144	(1926)

STOLEN BASES

1.	Rickey Henderson	93	(1988)
2.	Rickey Henderson	87	(1986)
3.	Rickey Henderson	80	(1985)
4.	Fritz Maisel	74	(1914)
5.	Ben Chapman	61	(1931)

BATTING AVERAGE

(At least 350 at-bats.)

1.	Babe Ruth	.393	(1923)
2.	Joe DiMaggio	.381	(1939)
3.	Lou Gehrig	.379	(1930)
4.	Babe Ruth	.378	(1921)
	Babe Ruth	.378	(1924)

TOTAL BASES

1.	Babe Ruth	457	(1921)
2.	Lou Gehrig	447	(1927)
3.	Lou Gehrig	419	(1930)
4.	Joe DiMaggio	418	(1937)
5.	Babe Ruth	417	(1927)

*A.L. Record

**M.L. Record

PITCHING LEADERS
YANKEE RECORDS

Most Years on Club: 16 Whitey Ford—1950, 1953–67

Most Games Pitched, Right-hander, Season: 73 Jeff Nelson, 1996

Most Games Pitched, Left-Hander, Season: 74 Dave Righetti, 1985, 1986

Most Games Pitched, Right-Hander, With Club: 426 Red Ruffing, 1930–42, 1945–46

Most Games Pitched, Left-Hander, With Club: 498 Whitey Ford, 1950, 1953–67

Most Games Started, Right-Hander, Season: 5 Jack Chesbro, 1904

Most Games Started, Left-Hander, Season: 3 Whitey Ford, 1961

Most Games Started, Left-Hander, With Club: 438 Whitey Ford, 1950, 1953–67

Most Games Started, Right-Hander, With Club: 391 Red Ruffing, 1930–42, 1945–46

Most Complete Games, Right-Hander, Season: 48 Jack Chesbro, 1904

Most Complete Games, Left-Hander, Season: 25 Herb Pennock, 1924; Lefty Gomez, 1934, 1937

Most Complete Games, Right-Hander, With Club: 261 Red Ruffing, 1930–42, 1945–46

Most Complete Games, Left-Hander, With Club: 173 Lefty Gomez, 1930–42

Most Innings Pitched, Right-Hander, Season: 454 Jack Chesbro, 1904

Most Innings Pitched, Left-Hander, Season: 286 Herb Pennock, 1924

Most Innings Pitched, Left-Hander, With Club: 3, 171 Whitey Ford, 1950, 1953–67

Most Innings Pitched, Right-Hander, With Club: 3, 169 Red Ruffing, 1930–42, 1945–46

Most Games Won, Right-Hander, Season: 41 Jack Chesbro, 1904

Most Games Won, Left-Hander, Season: 26 Lefty Gomez, 1934

Most Games Won, Left-Hander, With Club: 236 Whitey Ford, 1950, 1953–67

Most Games Won, Right-Hander, With Club: 231 Red Ruffing, 1930–42, 1945–46

Most Years Winning 20 or More Games: 4 Bob Shawkey, 1916, 1919, 1920, 1922; Lefty Gomez, 1931, 1932, 1934, 1937; Red Ruffing, 1936, 1937, 1938, 1939

Highest Percentage Games Won, Season: .893 Ron Guidry, 1978 (won 25, lost 3)

Most Consecutive Games Won, Season: 14 Jack Chesbro, 1904; Whitey Ford, 1961

Most Consecutive Games Won, Start of Season: 13 Ron Guidry, 1978

Most Games Lost, Right-Hander, Season: 22 Joe Lake, 1908

Most Games Lost, Left-Hander, Season: 17 Herb Pennock, 1925

Most Games Lost, Right-Hander, With Club: 139 Mel Stottlemyre, 1964–74

Most Games Lost, Left-Hander, With Club: 106 Whitey Ford, 1950, 1953–67

Most Consecutive Games Lost, Season: 9 Bill Hogg, 1908;Thad Tillotson, 1967

Most Saves, Left-Hander, Season: 46 Dave Righetti, 1986

Most Saves, Right-Hander, Season: 43, John Wetteland, 1996

Most Saves, Left-Hander, With Club: 224, Dave Righetti, 1979, 1981–90

Most Saves, Right-Hander, With Club: 151, Rich Gossage, 1978–83

Most Strikeouts, Left-Hander, Season: 248, Ron Guidry, 1978

Most Strikeouts, Right-Hander Season: 239, Jack Chesbro, 1904

Most Strikeouts, Left-Hander, With Club: 1,956, Whitey Ford, 1950, 1953–67

Most Strikeouts, Right-Hander With Club: 1,526, Red Ruffing, 1930–42, 1945–46

Most Strikeouts, Nine-Inning Game: 18, Ron Guidry, June 17, 1978

Most Bases on Balls, Left-Hander, Season: 179, Tommy Byrne, 1949

Most Bases on Balls, Right-Hander, Season: 177, Bob Turley, 1955

Most Bases on Balls, Left-Hander, With Club: 1,090, LeftyGomez, 1930–42

Most Bases on Balls, Right-Hander, With Club: 1,066, Red Ruffing, 1930–42, 1945–46

Most Shutouts, Left-Hander, Season: 9, Ron Guidry, 1978

Most Shutouts, Right-Hander, Season: 8, Russ Ford, 1910

Most Shutouts, Left-Hander, With Club: 45, Whitey Ford, 1950, 1953–67

Most Shutouts, Right-Hander, With Club: 40, Mel Stottlemyre, 1964–74

Most 1–0 Shutouts Won, With Club: 7, Bob Shawkey, 1915–27

Most Shutouts Lost, Season: 7, Bill Zuber, 1945

Most 1–0 Shutouts Lost, Season: 5, Jack Warhop, 1914

Lowest ERA, Right-Hander, Season: 1.64, Spud Chandler, 1943 (253 innings pitched)

Lowest ERA, Left-Hander, Season: 1.74, Ron Guidry, 1978 (274 innings pitched)

Lowest ERA, Right-Hander, With Club: 2.54, Russ Ford, 1909–13

Lowest ERA, Left-Hander, With Club: 2.75, Whitey Ford, 1950, 1953–67

Most Earned Runs Allowed, Season: 127, Sam Jones, 1925

Most Runs Allowed, Season: 165, Russ Ford, 1912

Most Batsmen Faced, Season: 1,406, Carl Mays, 1921

Most Hits Given Up, Season: 338, Jack Chesbro, 1904

Most Home Runs Given Up, Season: 40, Ralph Terry, 1962

Most Hit Batsmen, Season: 26, Jack Warhop, 1909

Most Wild Pitches, Season: 23, Tim Leary, 1990

YANKEE CAREER LEADERS 1903–96

(By pitching category.)

WINS

1.	Whitey Ford	236
2.	Red Ruffing	231
3.	Lefty Gomez	189
4.	Ron Guidry	170
5.	Bob Shawkey	168
6.	Mel Stottlemyre	164
7.	Herb Pennock	162
8.	Waite Hoyt	157
9.	Allie Reynolds	131
10.	Jack Chesbro	126

WINNING PERCENTAGE

(At least 100 decisions.)

1.	Spud Chandler	.717	(109–43)
2.	Vic Raschi	.706	(110–50)
3.	Whitey Ford	.690	(236–106)
4.	Allie Reynolds	.686	(131–60)
5.	Carl Mays	.669	(80–39)
6.	Ed Lopat	.657	(113–59)
7.	Lefty Gomez	.652	(189–101)
8.	Ron Guidry	.651	(170–91)
	Red Ruffing	.651	(231–124)
10.	Herb Pennock	.643	(162–90)
	Tommy Byrne	.643	(72–40)

SAVES

1.	Dave Righetti	224
2.	Rich Gossage	150
3.	Sparky Lyle	141
4.	Johnny Murphy	104
5.	Steve Farr	78
6.	Joe Page	76
7.	John Wetteland	74
8.	Lindy McDaniel	58
9.	Luis Arroyo	43
	Ryne Duren	43

GAMES PITCHED

1.	Dave Righetti	522
2.	Whitey Ford	498
3.	Red Ruffing	426
4.	Sparky Lyle	420
5.	Bob Shawkey	415
6.	Johnny Murphy	383
7.	Ron Guidry	368
8.	Lefty Gomez	367
9.	Waite Hoyt	365
10.	Mel Stottlemyre	360

GAMES STARTED

1.	Whitey Ford	438
2.	Red Ruffing	391
3.	Mel Stottlemyre	356
4.	Ron Guidry	323
5.	Lefty Gomez	319
6.	Waite Hoyt	275
7.	Bob Shawkey	274
8.	Herb Pennock	268
9.	Fritz Peterson	265
10.	Jack Chesbro	227

SHUTOUTS

1.	Whitey Ford	45
2.	Mel Stottlemyre	40
3.	Red Ruffing	37
4.	Allie Reynolds	27
5	Spud Chandler	26

6.	Lefty Gomez	26
	Ron Guidry	26
	Bob Shawkey	26
9.	Vic Raschi	24
10.	Bob Turley	21

EARNED RUN AVERAGE

(At least 800 innings pitched.)

1.	Russ Ford	2.54
2.	Jack Chesbro	2.58
3.	Al Orth	2.72
4.	Ernie Bonham	2.73
5.	Whitey Ford	2.75
6.	Spud Chandler	2.84
7.	Ray Fisher	2.91
8.	Mel Stottlemyre	2.97
9.	Ray Caldwell	2.99
10.	Jack Warhop	3.09

COMPLETE GAMES

1.	Red Ruffing	261
2.	Lefty Gomez	173
3.	Jack Chesbro	169
4.	Herb Pennock	165
5.	Bob Shawkey	161
6.	Whitey Ford	156
	Waite Hoyt	156
8.	Mel Stottlemyre	152
9.	Ray Caldwell	151
10.	Spud Chandler	109

INNINGS PITCHED

1.	Whitey Ford	3,170
2.	Red Ruffing	3,169
3.	Mel Stottlemyre	2,662
4.	Lefty Gomez	2,498
5.	Bob Shawkey	2,489
6.	Ron Guidry	2,392
7.	Waite Hoty	2,273
8.	Herb Pennock	2,190
9.	Jack Chesbro	1,953
10.	Fritz Peterson	1,857

STRIKEOUTS

1.	Whitey Ford	1,956
2.	Ron Guidry	1,778
3.	Red Ruffing	1,526
4.	Lefty Gomez	1,468
5.	Mel Stottlemyre	1,257
6.	Bob Shawkey	1,163
7.	Al Downing	1,028
8.	Allie Reynolds	967
9.	Dave Righetti	940
10.	Jack Chesbro	913

CLUB SINGLE-SEASON LEADERS 1903–96

(By pitching category.)

WINS

1.	Jack Chesbro	41	(1904)**
2.	Al Orth	27	(1906)
	Carl Mays	27	(1921)
4.	Russ Ford	26	(1910)
	Carl Mays	26	(1920)
	Bullet Joe Bush	26	(1922)
	Lefty Gomez	26	(1934)

SAVES

1.	Dave Righetti	46	(1986)
2.	John Wetteland	43	(1996)
3.	Dave Righetti	36	(1990)
4.	Sparky Lyle	35	(1972)
5.	Rich Gossage	33	(1980)

GAMES PITCHED

1.	Dave Righetti	74	(1985)
	Dave Righetti	74	(1986)
3.	Jeff Nelson	73	(1996)
4.	Sparky Lyle	72	(1977)
5.	Lee Guetterman	70	(1989)

GAMES STARTED

1.	Jack Chesbro	51	(1904)**
2.	Jack Powell	45	(1904)
3.	Jack Chesbro	42	(1906)
4.	Al Orth	39	(1906)
	Whitey Ford	39	(1961)
	Ralph Terry	39	(1962)

Mel Stottlemyre	39	(1969)
Pat Dobson	39	(1974
Catfish Hunter	39	(1975)

COMPLETE GAMES

1.	Jack Chesbro	48	(1904)**
2.	Jack Powell	38	(1904)
3.	Al Orth	36	(1906)
4.	Jack Chesbro	33	(1903)
5.	Russ Ford	30	(1912)

INNINGS PITCHED

1.	Jack Chesbro	455	(1904)
2.	Jack Powell	390	(1904)
3.	Al Orth	339	(1906)
4.	Carl Mays	337	(1921)
5.	Catfish Hunter	328	(1975)

STRIKEOUTS

1.	Ron Guidry	248	(1978)
2.	Jack Chesbro	239	(1904)
3.	Melido Perez	218	(1992)
4.	Al Downing	217	(1964)
5.	Bob Turley	210	(1955)

SHUTOUTS

1.	Ron Guidry	9	(1978)
2.	Russ Ford	8	(1910)
	Whitey Ford	8	(1964)
4.	Allie Reynolds	7	(1951)
	Whitey Ford	7	(1958)
	Mel Stottlemyre	7	(1971)
	Mel Stottlemyre	7	(1972)
	Catfish Hunter	7	(1975)

EARNED RUN AVERAGE (STARTING PITCHERS)

1.	Spud Chandler	1.64	(1943)
2.	Russ Ford	1.65	(1910)
3.	Ron Guidry	1.74	(1978)
4.	Jack Chesbro	1.82	(1904)
5.	Hippo Vaughn	1.83	(1910)

*A.L. Record

**M.L. Record

PERFORMANCE AS A TEAM

Yankee Team Records

Most Players Used in a Season: 49, 1989

Fewest Players Used in a Season: 25, 1923, 1927

Most Games Played: 164, 1964, 1968

Fewest Games Played: 107, 1981

Most At-Bats: 5,705, 1964

Most Runs: 1,067, 1931

Fewest Runs: 459, 1908

Most Runs by Opponents: 898, 1930

Most Hits: 1,683, 1930

Fewest Hits: 1,137, 1968

Most Singles: 1,237, 1988

Most Doubles: 315, 1936

Most Triples: 110, 1930

Most Home Runs: 240, 1961

Most Home Runs by Pinch-Hitters: 10, 1961

Most Grand Slam Home Runs: 10, 1987

Most Extra-Base Hits: 580, 1936

Most Total Bases: 2,703, 1936

Most Sacrifices (hits and flies): 218, 1922, 1926

Most Sacrifice Hits: 178, 1906

Most Sacrifice Flies: 72, 1974

Most Stolen Bases: 289, 1910

Most Caught Stealing: 82, 1920

Most Bases on Balls: 766, 1932

Most Strikeouts: 1,043, 1967

Fewest Strikeouts: 420, 1924

Most Batters Hit by a Pitched Ball: 53, 1990

Fewest Batters Hit by a Pitched Ball: 14, 1969

Most Runs Batted In: 995, 1936

Highest Batting Average: .309, 1930

Lowest Batting Average: .214, 1968

Highest Slugging Average: .489, 1927

Lowest Slugging Average: .287, 1914

Most Double Plays Grounded Into: 153, 1996

Fewest Double Plays Grounded Into: 91, 1963

Most Left on Bases: 1,258, 1996

Fewest Left on Bases: 1,010, 1920

Most .300 Hitters: 9, 1930

Most Putouts: 4,520, 1964

Fewest Putouts: 3,993, 1935

Most Assists: 2,086, 1904

Fewest Assists: 1,493, 1948

Most Chances Accepted: 6,383, 1980

Fewest Chances Accepted: 5,551, 1935

Most Errors: 386, 1912

Fewest Errors: 91, 1996

Most Double Plays Made: 214, 1956

Fewest Double Plays Made: 81, 1912

Most Consecutive Games, One or More Double Plays Made: 19, 1992

Most Passed Balls: 32, 1913

Fewest Passed Balls: 0, 1931

Highest Fielding Average: .985, 1996

Lowest Fielding Average: .939, 1912

Most Games Won: 110, 1927

Most Games Lost: 103, 1908

Highest Percentage Games Won: .714, 1927 (won 110, lost 44)

Lowest Percentage Games Won: .329, 1912 (won 50, lost 102)

Most Shutouts Won: 24, 1951

Most Shutouts Lost: 27, 1914

Most 1–0 Games Won: 6, 1908, 1968

Most 1–0 Games Lost: 9, 1914

Most Consecutive Games Won: 19, 1947

Most Consecutive Games Lost: 13, 1913

Most Saves: 58, 1986

Most Complete Games Pitched: 123, 1904

Most Innings Pitched: 1,507, 1964

Most Strikeouts Recorded by Pitchers: 1,139, 1996

Lowest Earned Run Average: 2.57, 1904

Most Runs Scored, Game: 25, 5/24/36 Yankees, 25; Philadelphia A's, 2

Most Runs Scored, Shutout Game: 21, 08/13/39 Yankees, 21; Philadelphia A's, 0 (8 innings)

Most Runs Scored, Inning: 14, 7/06/20 5th inning vs. Washington

Most Runs Scored, Game, by Opponent: 24, 7/29/28 (Cleveland Indians, 24; Yankees, 6)

Most Runs Scored, Shutout Game, by Opponent: 15 (twice). (7/15/07, Chicago White Sox, 15; Yankees, 0; 5/04/50, Chicago White Sox, 15; Yankees, 0)

Most Hits, Game: 30, 9/28/23 vs. Boston

Most Home Runs, Game: 8, 6/28/39 vs. Philadelphia

Most Consecutive Games, One or More Home Runs: 25, 1941 (40 HRs in all)

Most Home Runs in Consecutive Games in Which Home Runs Were Hit: 40, 1941 (25 games)

Most Total Bases, Game: 53, 6/28/39 vs. Philadelphia

Longest and Shortest Games in Yankee History

Longest Extra-Inning Game, by Time: 7 hours, 0 minutes. At Detroit, June 24, 1962 (Yankees, 9; Detroit Tigers, 7)

Longest Extra-Inning Game, by Innings: 22 innings At Detroit, June 24, 1962 (Yankees, 9; Detroit Tigers, 7)

Longest Extra-Inning Game EVER Played at the Polo Grounds: 19 innings, May 24, 1918 (Cleveland Indians, 3; Yankees, 2)

Longest Extra-Inning Game Played at Yankee Stadium: 20 innings, August 29, 1967 (Yankees, 4; Boston Red Sox, 3)

Shortest Nine-Inning Game, by Time: 55 minutes At St. Louis, September 26, 1926 (St. Louis Browns, 6; Yankees, 2—second game)

Shortest 18-Inning Doubleheader, by Time: 2 hours, 7 minutes. At St. Louis, September 26, 1926

PLAYER, PITCHER, AND MANAGER

Register

AND YEAR-BY-YEAR

Record

Player Register

The Player Register is an alphabetical listing of every man who has played in the major leagues and played for the New York Yankees from 1903 through today, except for those players who were primarily pitchers. However, players who pinch-hit and played in other positions for a total of 25 games or more are listed in this Player Register. Included are facts about the players and their year-by-year batting records for the Yankees.

Year	Gms.	BA	SA	AB	H	2B	3B	HR	RBI	SB	G. by Pos

Mickey Mantle

MICKEY CHARLES MANTLE
B. Oct. 20, 1931, Spavinaw, Okla.
D. Aug. 13, 1995, Dallas, Tex.
Hall of Fame 1974

BB TR
5' 11½" 195 lbs.

Year	Gms.	BA	SA	AB	H	2B	3B	HR	RBI	SB	G. by Pos
1951	96	.267	.443	341	91	11	5	13	65	8	OF-86
1952	142	.311	.530	549	171	37	7	23	87	4	OF-141, 3B-1
1953	127	.295	.497	461	136	24	3	21	92	8	OF-121, SS-1
1954	146	.300	.525	543	163	17	12	27	102	5	OF-144, SS-4, 2B-1
1955	147	.306	.611	517	158	25	11	37	99	8	OF-145, SS-2
1956	150	.353	.705	533	188	22	5	52	130	10	OF-144
1957	144	.365	.665	474	173	28	6	34	94	16	OF-139
1958	150	.304	.592	519	158	21	1	42	97	18	OF-150
1959	144	.285	.514	541	154	23	4	31	75	21	OF-143
1960	153	.275	.558	527	145	17	6	40	94	14	OF-150
1961	153	.317	.687	514	163	16	6	54	128	12	OF-150
1962	123	.321	.605	377	121	15	1	30	89	9	OF-117
1963	65	.314	.622	172	54	8	0	15	35	2	OF-52
1964	143	.303	.591	465	141	25	2	35	111	6	OF-132
1965	122	.255	.452	361	92	12	1	19	46	4	OF-108
1966	108	.288	.538	333	96	12	1	23	56	1	OF-97
1967	144	.245	.434	440	108	17	0	22	55	1	1B-131
1968	144	.237	.398	435	103	14	1	18	54	6	1B-131
18 yrs.	2401	.298	.557	8102	2415	344	72	536	1509	153	OF-2019, 1B-262, SS-7, 2B-1, 3B-1

World Series

Year	Gms.	BA	SA	AB	H	2B	3B	HR	RBI	SB	G. by Pos
1951	2	.200	.200	5	1	0	0	0	0	0	OF-2
1952	7	.345	.655	29	10	1	1	2	3	0	OF-7
1953	6	.208	.458	24	5	0	0	2	7	0	OF-6
1955	3	.200	.500	10	2	0	0	1	1	0	OF-2
1956	7	.250	.667	24	6	1	0	3	4	1	OF-7
1957	6	.263	.421	19	5	0	0	1	2	0	OF-5
1958	7	.250	.583	24	6	0	1	2	3	0	OF-7
1960	7	.400	.800	25	10	1	0	3	11	0	OF-7
1961	2	.167	.167	6	1	0	0	0	0	0	OF-2
1962	7	.120	.160	25	3	1	0	0	0	2	OF-7
1963	4	.133	.333	15	2	0	0	1	1	0	OF-4
1964	7	.333	.792	24	8	2	0	3	8	0	OF-7
12 yrs.	65	.257	.535	230	59	6	2	18	40	3	OF-63

Key

Year	Year Played
Gms.	Games Played
BA	Batting Average
SA	Slugging Average
AB	At-Bats
H	Hits
2B	Doubles
3B	Triples
HR	Home Runs
RBI	Runs Batted In
SB	Stolen Bases
G. by Pos	Games by Position
BB	Bats Both
BL	Bats Left
BR	Bats Right
TL	Throws Left
TR	Throws Right

(Preceding page)
Third baseman Andy Carey,
a Yankee from 1952 to 1960.

Spencer Adams

SPENCER DEWEY ADAMS BL TR
B. Jul. 21, 1898, Layton, Utah 5' 9" 158 lbs.
D. Nov. 24, 1970, Salt Lake City, Utah

Year	Gms.	BA	SA	AB	H	2B	3B	HR	RBI	SB	G. by Pos
1926	28	.120	.160	25	3	1	0	0	1	1	2B-4, 3B-1
World Series											
1926	2	—	—	0	0	0	0	0	0	0	

Luis Aguayo

LUIS AGUAYO BR TR
B. Mar. 13, 1959, Vega Baja, Puerto Rico 5' 9" 173 lbs.

Year	Gms.	BA	SA	AB	H	2B	3B	HR	RBI	SB	G. by Pos
1988	50	.250	.343	140	35	4	0	3	8	0	3B-33, 2B-13, SS-6

Mike Aldrete

MICHAEL PETER ALDRETE BL TL
B. Jan. 29, 1961, Carmel, Calif. 5' 11" 180 lbs.

Year	Gms.	BA	SA	AB	H	2B	3B	HR	RBI	SB	G. by Pos
1996	32	.250	.456	68	17	5	0	3	12	0	OF-9, DH-9, 1B-8, P-1
League Championship Series											
1996	1	—	—	0	0	0	0	0	0	0	
World Series											
1996	2	.000	.000	1	0	0	0	0	0	0	OF-1

Walt Alexander

WALTER ERNEST ALEXANDER BR TR
B. Mar. 5, 1891, Atlanta, Ga. 5' 10½" 165 lbs.
D. Dec. 29, 1978, Ft. Worth, Tex.

Year	Gms.	BA	SA	AB	H	2B	3B	HR	RBI	SB	G. by Pos
1915	25	.250	.353	68	17	4	0	1	5	2	C-24
1916	36	.256	.359	78	20	6	1	0	3	0	C-27
1917	20	.137	.216	51	7	2	1	0	4	1	C-20
3 yrs.	81	.223	.320	197	44	12	2	1	12	3	C-71

Bernie Allen

BERNARD KEITH ALLEN BL TR
B. Apr. 16, 1939, East Liverpool, Ohio 6' 175 lbs.

Year	Gms.	BA	SA	AB	H	2B	3B	HR	RBI	SB	G. by Pos
1972	84	.227	.391	220	50	9	0	9	21	0	3B-44, 2B-20
1973	16	.180	.320	50	9	1	0	2	9	0	2B-9, 3B-8, DH-2
2 yrs.	100	.219	.378	270	59	10	0	11	30	0	3B-52, 2B-29, DH-2

Sandy Alomar

SANTOS ALOMAR., SR. BB TR
B. Oct. 19, 1943, Salinas, Puerto Rico 5' 9" 140 lbs.

Year	Gms.	BA	SA	AB	H	2B	3B	HR	RBI	SB	G. by Pos
1974	76	.269	.308	279	75	8	0	1	27	6	2B-76, DH-1
1975	151	.239	.305	489	117	18	4	2	39	28	2B-150, SS-1
1976	67	.239	.282	163	39	4	0	1	10	12	2B-38, DH-9, SS-6, 3B-3, 1B-1, OF-1
3 yrs.	294	.248	.302	931	231	30	4	4	76	46	2B-264, DH-10, SS-7, 3B-3, 1B-1, OF-1
League Championship Series											
1976	2	.000	.000	1	0	0	0	0	0	0	DH-1

Felipe Alou

FELIPE ALOU BR TR
May 12, 1935, Haina, Dominican Republic 6' 195 lbs.

Year	Gms.	BA	SA	AB	H	2B	3B	HR	RBI	SB	G. by Pos
1971	131	.289	.410	461	133	20	6	8	69	5	OF-80, 1B-42
1972	120	.278	.395	324	90	18	1	6	37	1	1B-95, OF-15
1973	93	.236	.321	280	66	12	0	4	27	0	1B-67, OF-22
3 yrs.	344	.271	.382	1065	289	50	7	18	133	6	1B-204, OF-117

Matty Alou

MATEO ALOU BL TL
Dec. 22, 1938, Haina, Dominican Republic 5' 9" 160 lbs.

Year	Gms.	BA	SA	AB	H	2B	3B	HR	RBI	SB	G. by Pos
1973	123	.296	.356	497	147	22	1	2	28	5	OF-85, 1B-40, DH-1

Dell Alston

WENDELL ALSTON BL TR
B. Sep. 22, 1952, Valhalla, N.Y. 6' 180 lbs.

Year	Gms.	BA	SA	AB	H	2B	3B	HR	RBI	SB	G. by Pos
1977	22	.325	.500	40	13	4	0	1	4	3	DH-10, OF-2
1978	3	.000	.000	3	0	0	0	0	0	0	
2 yrs.	25	.302	.465	43	13	4	0	1	4	3	DH-10, OF-2

Ruben Amaro

RUBEN AMARO, SR. BR TR
B. Jan. 6, 1936, Veracruz, Mexico 5' 11" 170 lbs.

Year	Gms.	BA	SA	AB	H	2B	3B	HR	RBI	SB	G. by Pos
1966	14	.217	.217	23	5	0	0	0	3	0	SS-14
1967	130	.223	.259	417	93	12	0	1	17	3	SS-123, 3B-3, 1B-2
1968	47	.122	.146	41	5	1	0	0	0	0	SS-23, 1B-22
3 yrs.	191	.214	.247	481	103	13	0	1	20	3	SS-160, 1B-24, 3B-3

John Anderson

JOHN JOSEPH ANDERSON BB TR
B. Dec. 14, 1873, Sarpsborg, Norway 6' 2" 180 lbs.
D. Jul 23, 1949, Worcester, Mass.

Year	Gms.	BA	SA	AB	H	2B	3B	HR	RBI	SB	G. by Pos
1904	143	.278	.385	558	155	27	12	3	82	20	OF-111, 1B-33
1905	32	.232	.283	99	23	3	1	0	14	9	OF-22, 1B-3
2 yrs.	175	.271	.370	657	178	30	13	3	96	29	OF-133, 1B-36

Angel Aragon

ANGEL ARAGON BR TR
B. Aug. 2, 1890, Havana, Cuba 5' 5" 150 lbs.
D. Jan. 24, 1952, New York, N.Y.

Year	Gms.	BA	SA	AB	H	2B	3B	HR	RBI	SB	G. by Pos
1914	6	.143	.143	7	1	0	0	0	0	0	OF-1
1916	13	.185	.185	27	5	0	0	0	3	2	3B-8, OF-3
1917	14	.067	.089	45	3	1	0	0	2	0	OF-6, 3B-4, SS-2
3 yrs.	33	.114	.127	79	9	1	0	0	5	2	3B-12, OF-10, SS-2

Tucker Ashford

THOMAS STEVEN ASHFORD BR TR
B. Dec. 4, 1954, Memphis, Tenn. 6' 1" 195 lbs.

Year	Gms.	BA	SA	AB	H	2B	3B	HR	RBI	SB	G. by Pos
1981	3	—	—	0	0	0	0	0	0	0	2B-2

Jimmy Austin

JAMES PHILIP AUSTIN BB TR
B. Dec. 8, 1879, Swansea, Wales 5' 7½" 155 lbs.
D. Mar. 6, 1965, Laguna Beach, Calif.

Year	Gms.	BA	SA	AB	H	2B	3B	HR	RBI	SB	G. by Pos
1909	136	.231	.286	437	101	11	5	1	39	30	3B-111, SS-23, 2B-1
1910	133	.218	.275	432	94	11	4	2	36	22	3B-133
2 yrs.	269	.224	.281	869	195	22	9	3	75	52	3B-244, SS-23, 2B-1

Martin Autry

MARTIN GORDON AUTRY BR TR
B. Mar. 5, 1903, Martindale, Tex. 6' 180 lbs.
D. Jan. 26, 1950, Savannah, Ga.

Year	Gms.	BA	SA	AB	H	2B	3B	HR	RBI	SB	G. by Pos
1924	2	—	—	0	0	0	0	0	0	0	C-2

Oscar Azocar

OSCAR GREGORIO AZOCAR BL TL
B. Feb. 21, 1965, Soro, Venezuela 6' 1" 170 lbs.

Year	Gms.	BA	SA	AB	H	2B	3B	HR	RBI	SB	G. by Pos
1990	65	.248	.355	214	53	8	0	5	19	7	OF-57, DH-1

Loren Babe

LOREN ROLLAND BABE BL TR
B. Jan. 11, 1928, Pisgah, Iowa 5' 10" 180 lbs.
D. Feb. 14, 1984, Omaha, Neb.

Year	Gms.	BA	SA	AB	H	2B	3B	HR	RBI	SB	G. by Pos
1952	12	.095	.143	21	2	1	0	0	0	1	3B-9
1953	5	.333	.722	18	6	1	0	2	6	0	3B-5
2 yrs.	17	.205	.410	39	8	2	0	2	6	1	3B-14

Bill Bailey

HARRY LEWIS BAILEY BL TR
B. Nov. 19, 1881, Shawnee, Ohio 5' 10½" 170 lbs.
D. Oct. 27, 1967, Seattle, Wash.

Year	Gms.	BA	SA	AB	H	2B	3B	HR	RBI	SB	G. by Pos
1911	5	.111	.111	9	1	0	0	0	0	0	OF-2, 3B-1

Frank Baker

JOHN FRANKLIN BAKER BL TR
B. Mar. 13, 1886, Trappe, Md. 5' 11" 173 lbs.
D. Jun. 28, 1963, Trappe, Md.
Hall of Fame 1955

Year	Gms.	BA	SA	AB	H	2B	3B	HR	RBI	SB	G. by Pos
1916	100	.269	.428	360	97	23	2	10	52	15	3B-96
1917	146	.282	.365	553	156	24	2	6	71	18	3B-146
1918	126	.306	.409	504	154	24	5	6	68	8	3B-126
1919	141	.293	.388	567	166	22	1	10	83	13	3B-141
1921	94	.294	.436	330	97	16	2	9	71	8	3B-83

Year	Gms.	BA	SA	AB	H	2B	3B	HR	RBI	SB	G. by Pos

Frank Baker *continued*

Year	Gms.	BA	SA	AB	H	2B	3B	HR	RBI	SB	G. by Pos
1922	69	.278	.444	234	65	12	3	7	36	1	3B-60
6 yrs.	676	.288	.404	2548	735	121	15	48	381	63	3B-652
World Series											
1921	4	.250	.250	8	2	0	0	0	0	0	3B-2
1922	1	.000	.000	1	0	0	0	0	0	0	
2 yrs.	5	.222	.222	9	2	0	0	0	0	0	3B-2

Frank Baker

FRANK WATTS BAKER BL TR
B. Oct. 29, 1946, Meridian, Miss. 6' 2" 178 lbs.

Year	Gms.	BA	SA	AB	H	2B	3B	HR	RBI	SB	G. by Pos
1970	35	.231	.282	117	27	4	1	0	11	1	SS-35
1971	43	.139	.165	79	11	2	0	0	2	3	SS-38
2 yrs.	78	.194	.235	196	38	6	1	0	13	4	SS-73

Steve Balboni

STEPHEN CHARLES BALBONI BR TR
B. Jan. 16, 1957, Brockton, Mass. 6' 3" 225 lbs.

Year	Gms.	BA	SA	AB	H	2B	3B	HR	RBI	SB	G. by Pos
1981	4	.286	.714	7	2	1	1	0	2	0	1B-3, DH-1
1982	33	.187	.280	107	20	2	1	2	4	0	1B-26, DH-5
1983	32	.233	.430	86	20	2	0	5	17	0	1B-23, DH-4
1989	110	.237	.460	300	71	12	2	17	59	0	DH-82, 1B-20
1990	116	.192	.406	266	51	6	0	17	34	0	DH-72, 1B-28
5 yrs.	295	.214	.415	766	164	23	4	41	116	0	DH-164, 1B-100

Neal Ball

CORNELIUS BALL BR TR
B. Apr. 22, 1881, Grand Haven, Mich. 5' 7" 145 lbs.
D. Oct. 15, 1957, Bridgeport, Conn.

Year	Gms.	BA	SA	AB	H	2B	3B	HR	RBI	SB	G. by Pos
1907	15	.205	.273	44	9	1	1	0	4	1	SS-11, 2B-5
1908	132	.247	.291	446	110	16	2	0	38	32	SS-130, 2B-1
1909	8	.207	.310	29	6	1	1	0	3	2	2B-8
3 yrs.	155	.241	.291	519	125	18	4	0	45	35	SS-141, 2B-14

Jesse Barfield

JESSE LEE BARFIELD BR TR
B. Oct. 29, 1959, Joliet, Ill. 6' 1" 200 lbs.

Year	Gms.	BA	SA	AB	H	2B	3B	HR	RBI	SB	G. by Pos
1989	129	.240	.410	441	106	19	1	18	56	5	OF-129
1990	153	.246	.456	476	117	21	2	25	78	4	OF-151
1991	84	.225	.447	284	64	12	0	17	48	1	OF-81
1992	30	.137	.221	95	13	2	0	2	7	1	OF-30
4 yrs.	396	.231	.421	1296	300	54	3	62	189	11	OF-391

Ray Barker

RAYMOND HERRELL BARKER BL TR
B. Mar. 12, 1936, Martinsburg, W. Va. 6' 192 lbs.

Year	Gms.	BA	SA	AB	H	2B	3B	HR	RBI	SB	G. by Pos
1965	98	.254	.410	205	52	11	0	7	31	1	1B-61, 3B-3
1966	61	.187	.373	75	14	5	0	3	13	0	1B-47
1967	17	.077	.077	26	2	0	0	0	0	0	1B-13
3 yrs.	176	.222	.373	306	68	16	0	10	44	1	1B-121, 3B-3

Honey Barnes

JOHN FRANCIS BARNES BL TR
B. Jan. 29, 1900, Fulton, N. Y. 5' 10" 175 lbs.
D. Jun. 18, 1981, Lockport, N. Y.

Year	Gms.	BA	SA	AB	H	2B	3B	HR	RBI	SB	G. by Pos
1926	1	—	—	0	0	0	0	0	0	0	C-1

Ed Barney

EDMUND J. BARNEY BL TR
B. Jan. 23, 1890, Amery, Wis. 5' 10½" 178 lbs.
D. Oct. 4, 1967, Rice Lake, Wis.

Year	Gms.	BA	SA	AB	H	2B	3B	HR	RBI	SB	G. by Pos
1915	11	.194	.194	36	7	0	0	0	8	2	OF-10

George Batten

GEORGE BURNETT BATTEN BR TR
B. Oct. 7, 1891, Haddonfield, N. J. 5' 11" 165 lbs.
D. Aug. 4, 1972, New Port Ritchey, Fla.

Year	Gms.	BA	SA	AB	H	2B	3B	HR	RBI	SB	G. by Pos
1912	1	.000	.000	3	0	0	0	0	0	0	2B-1

Hank Bauer

HENRY ALBERT BAUER BR TR
B. Jul. 31, 1922, East St. Louis, Ill. 6' 192 lbs.

Year	Gms.	BA	SA	AB	H	2B	3B	HR	RBI	SB	G. by Pos
1948	19	.180	.300	50	9	1	1	1	9	1	OF-14

Hank Bauer *continued*

Year	Gms.	BA	SA	AB	H	2B	3B	HR	RBI	SB	G. by Pos
1949	103	.272	.432	301	82	6	6	10	45	2	OF-95
1950	113	.320	.463	415	133	16	2	13	70	2	OF-110
1951	118	.296	.454	348	103	19	3	10	54	5	OF-107
1952	141	.293	.463	553	162	31	6	17	74	6	OF-139
1953	133	.304	.446	437	133	20	6	10	57	2	OF-126
1954	114	.294	.459	377	111	16	5	12	54	4	OF-108
1955	139	.278	.461	492	137	20	5	20	53	8	OF-133, C-1
1956	147	.241	.445	539	130	18	7	26	84	4	OF-146
1957	137	.259	.455	479	124	22	9	18	65	7	OF-135
1958	128	.268	.423	452	121	22	6	12	50	3	OF-123
1959	114	.238	.375	341	81	20	0	9	39	4	OF-111
12 yrs.	1406	.277	.444	4784	1326	211	56	158	654	48	OF-1347, C-1
World Series											
1949	3	.167	.167	6	1	0	0	0	0	0	OF-3
1950	4	.133	.133	15	2	0	0	0	1	0	OF-4
1951	6	.167	.278	18	3	0	1	0	3	0	OF-6
1952	7	.056	.056	18	1	0	0	0	1	0	OF-7
1953	6	.261	.348	23	6	0	1	0	1	0	OF-6
1955	6	.429	.429	14	6	0	0	0	1	0	OF-5
1956	7	.281	.375	32	9	0	0	1	3	1	OF-7
1957	7	.258	.581	31	8	2	1	2	6	0	OF-7
1958	7	.323	.710	31	10	0	0	4	8	0	OF-7
9 yrs.	53	.245	.399	188	46	2	3	7	24	1	OF-52

Paddy Baumann

CHARLES JOHN BAUMANN BR TR
B. Dec. 20, 1885, Indianapolis, Ind. 5' 9" 160 lbs.
D. Nov. 20, 1969, Indianapolis, Ind.

Year	Gms.	BA	SA	AB	H	2B	3B	HR	RBI	SB	G. by Pos
1915	76	.292	.388	219	64	13	1	2	28	9	2B-43, 3B-19
1916	79	.287	.346	237	68	5	3	1	25	10	OF-28, 3B-26, 2B-9
1917	49	.218	.255	110	24	2	1	0	8	2	2B-18, OF-7, 3B-1
3 yrs.	204	.276	.345	566	156	20	5	3	61	21	2B-70, 3B-46, OF-35

Don Baylor

DON EDWARD BAYLOR BR TR
B. Jun 28, 1949, Austin, Tex. 6' 1" 190 lbs.

Year	Gms.	BA	SA	AB	H	2B	3B	HR	RBI	SB	G. by Pos
1983	144	.303	.494	534	162	33	3	21	85	17	DH-136, OF-5, 1B-1
1984	134	.262	.489	493	129	29	1	27	89	1	DH-127, 1B-5
1985	142	.231	.430	477	110	24	1	23	91	0	DH-140
3 yrs.	420	.267	.472	1504	401	86	5	71	265	18	DH-403, 1B-6, OF-5

Zinn Beck

ZINN BERTRAM BECK BR TR
B. Sep. 30, 1885, Steubenville, Ohio 5' 10½" 160 lbs.
D. Mar. 19, 1981, West Palm Beach, Fla.

Year	Gms.	BA	SA	AB	H	2B	3B	HR	RBI	SB	G. by Pos
1918	11	.000	.000	8	0	0	0	0	1	0	1B-5

John Bell

JOHN BELL BR TR
B. Jan. 1, 1881, Wausau, Wis. 5' 8½" 158 lbs.
D. Jul. 28, 1955, Albuquerque, N. M.

Year	Gms.	BA	SA	AB	H	2B	3B	HR	RBI	SB	G. by Pos
1907	17	.212	.288	52	11	2	1	0	3	4	OF-17

Zeke Bella

JOHN BELLA BR TL
B. Aug. 23, 1930, Greenwich, Conn. 5' 11" 185 lbs.

Year	Gms.	BA	SA	AB	H	2B	3B	HR	RBI	SB	G. by Pos
1957	5	.100	.100	10	1	0	0	0	0	0	OF-4

Benny Bengough

BERNARD OLIVER BENGOUGH BR TR
B. Jul. 27, 1898, Niagara Falls, N. Y. 5' 7½" 168 lbs.
D. Dec. 22, 1968, Philadelphia, Pa.

Year	Gms.	BA	SA	AB	H	2B	3B	HR	RBI	SB	G. by Pos
1923	19	.132	.170	53	7	2	0	0	3	0	C-19
1924	11	.313	.500	16	5	1	1	0	3	0	C-11
1925	95	.258	.322	283	73	14	2	0	23	0	C-94
1926	36	.381	.452	84	32	6	0	0	14	1	C-35
1927	31	.247	.353	85	21	3	3	0	10	0	C-30
1928	58	.267	.298	161	43	3	1	0	9	0	C-58
1929	23	.194	.258	62	12	2	1	0	7	0	C-23
1930	44	.235	.314	102	24	4	2	0	12	0	C-44
8 yrs.	317	.257	.322	846	217	35	10	0	81	2	C-314

Year	Gms.	BA	SA	AB	H	2B	3B	HR	RBI	SB	G. by Pos

Benny Bengough continued

World Series

Year	Gms.	BA	SA	AB	H	2B	3B	HR	RBI	SB	G. by Pos
1927	2	.000	.000	4	0	0	0	0	0	0	C-2
1928	4	.231	.231	13	3	0	0	0	1	0	C-4
2 yrs.	6	.176	.176	17	3	0	0	0	1	0	C-6

Juan Beniquez

JUAN JOSE BENIQUEZ BR TR
B. May 13, 1950, San Sebastian, 5' 11" 150 lbs.
Puerto Rico

Year	Gms.	BA	SA	AB	H	2B	3B	HR	RBI	SB	G. by Pos
1979	62	.254	.394	142	36	6	1	4	17	3	OF-60, 3B-3

Lou Berberet

LOUIS JOSEPH BERBERET BL TR
B. Nov. 20, 1929, Long Beach, Calif. 5' 11" 200 lbs.

Year	Gms.	BA	SA	AB	H	2B	3B	HR	RBI	SB	G. by Pos
1954	5	.400	.400	5	2	0	0	0	3	0	C-3
1955	2	.400	.400	5	2	0	0	0	2	0	C-1
2 yrs.	7	.400	.400	10	4	0	0	0	5	0	C-4

Dave Bergman

DAVID BRUCE BERGMAN BL TL
B. Jun. 6, 1953, Evanston, Ill. 6' 1½" 185 lbs.

Year	Gms.	BA	SA	AB	H	2B	3B	HR	RBI	SB	G. by Pos
1975	7	.000	.000	17	0	0	0	0	0	0	OF-6
1977	5	.250	.250	4	1	0	0	0	1	0	OF-3, 1B-2
2 yrs.	12	.048	.048	21	1	0	0	0	1	0	OF-9, 1B-2

Juan Bernhardt

JUAN RAMON BERNHARDT BR TR
B. Aug. 31, 1953, San Pedro 5' 11" 160 lbs.
de Macoris, Dominican Republic

Year	Gms.	BA	SA	AB	H	2B	3B	HR	RBI	SB	G. by Pos
1976	10	.190	.238	21	4	1	0	0	1	0	OF-4, DH-2, 3B-1

Dale Berra

DALE ANTHONY BERRA BR TR
B. Dec. 13, 1956, Ridgewood, N. J. 6' 180 lbs.

Year	Gms.	BA	SA	AB	H	2B	3B	HR	RBI	SB	G. by Pos
1985	48	.229	.321	109	25	5	1	1	8	1	3B-41, SS-6
1986	42	.231	.352	108	25	7	0	2	13	0	SS-19, 3B-18, DH-4
2 yrs.	90	.230	.336	217	50	12	1	3	21	1	3B-59, SS-25, DH-4

Yogi Berra

LAWRENCE PETER BERRA BL TR
B. May 12, 1925, St. Louis, Mo. 5' 7½" 185 lbs.
Hall of Fame 1972

Year	Gms.	BA	SA	AB	H	2B	3B	HR	RBI	SB	G. by Pos
1946	7	.364	.682	22	8	1	0	2	4	0	C-6
1947	83	.280	.464	293	82	15	3	11	54	0	C-51, OF-24
1948	125	.305	.488	469	143	24	10	14	98	3	C-71, OF-50
1949	116	.277	.480	415	115	20	2	20	91	2	C-109
1950	151	.322	.533	597	192	30	6	28	124	4	C-148
1951	141	.294	.492	547	161	19	4	27	88	5	C-141
1952	142	.273	.478	534	146	17	1	30	98	2	C-140
1953	137	.296	.523	503	149	23	5	27	108	0	C-133
1954	151	.307	.488	584	179	28	6	22	125	0	C-149, 3B-1
1955	147	.272	.470	541	147	20	3	27	108	1	C-145
1956	140	.298	.534	521	155	29	2	30	105	3	C-135, OF-1
1957	134	.251	.438	482	121	14	2	24	82	1	C-121, OF-6
1958	122	.266	.471	433	115	17	3	22	90	3	C-85, OF-21, 1B-2
1959	131	.284	.462	472	134	25	1	19	69	1	C-116, OF-7
1960	120	.276	.446	359	99	14	1	15	62	2	C-63, OF-36
1961	119	.271	.466	395	107	11	0	22	61	2	OF-87, C-15
1962	86	.224	.388	232	52	8	0	10	35	0	C-31, OF-28
1963	64	.293	.497	147	43	6	0	8	28	1	C-35
18 yrs.	2116	.285	.483	7546	2148	321	49	358	1430	30	C-1694, OF-260, 1B-2, 3B-1

World Series

Year	Gms.	BA	SA	AB	H	2B	3B	HR	RBI	SB	G. by Pos
1947	6	.158	.316	19	3	0	0	1	2	0	C-4, OF-2
1949	4	.063	.063	16	1	0	0	0	1	0	C-4
1950	4	.200	.400	15	3	0	0	1	2	0	C-4
1951	6	.261	.304	23	6	1	0	0	0	0	C-6
1952	7	.214	.464	28	6	1	0	2	3	0	C-7
1953	6	.429	.619	21	9	1	0	1	4	0	C-6
1955	7	.417	.583	24	10	1	0	1	2	0	C-7
1956	7	.360	.800	25	9	2	0	3	10	0	C-7

Yogi Berra continued

Year	Gms.	BA	SA	AB	H	2B	3B	HR	RBI	SB	G. by Pos
1957	7	.320	.480	25	8	1	0	1	2	0	C-7
1958	7	.222	.333	27	6	3	0	0	2	0	C-7
1960	7	.318	.455	22	7	0	0	1	8	0	OF-4, C-3
1961	4	.273	.545	11	3	0	0	1	3	0	OF-4
1962	2	.000	.000	2	0	0	0	0	0	0	C-1
1963	1	.000	.000	1	0	0	0	0	0	0	
14 yrs.	75	.274	.452	259	71	10	0	12	39	0	C-63, OF-10

Monte Beville

HENRY MONTE BEVILLE BL TR
B. Feb. 24, 1875, Dublin, Ind. 5' 11" 180 lbs.
D. Jan. 24, 1955, Grand Rapids, Mich.

Year	Gms.	BA	SA	AB	H	2B	3B	HR	RBI	SB	G. by Pos
1903	82	.194	.256	258	50	14	1	0	29	4	C-75, 1B-3
1904	9	.273	.364	22	6	2	0	0	2	0	1B-4, C-3
2 yrs.	91	.200	.264	280	56	16	1	0	31	4	C-78, 1B-7

Rick Bladt

RICHARD ALAN BLADT BR TR
B. Dec. 9, 1946, Santa Cruz, Calif. 6' 1" 160 lbs.

Year	Gms.	BA	SA	AB	H	2B	3B	HR	RBI	SB	G. by Pos
1975	52	.222	.291	117	26	3	1	1	11	6	OF-51

Paul Blair

PAUL L. BLAIR BR TR
B. Feb. 1, 1944, Cushing, Okla. 6' 168 lbs.

Year	Gms.	BA	SA	AB	H	2B	3B	HR	RBI	SB	G. by Pos
1977	83	.262	.396	164	43	4	3	4	25	3	OF-79, DH-1
1978	75	.176	.264	125	22	5	0	2	13	1	OF-64, 2B-5, SS-4, 3B-3
1979	2	.200	.200	5	1	0	0	0	0	0	OF-2
1980	12	.000	.000	2	0	0	0	0	0	0	OF-12
4 yrs.	172	.223	.334	296	66	9	3	6	38	4	OF-157, 2B-5, SS-4, 3B-3, DH-1

League Championship Series

Year	Gms.	BA	SA	AB	H	2B	3B	HR	RBI	SB	G. by Pos
1977	3	.400	.400	5	2	0	0	0	0	0	OF-3
1978	4	.000	.000	6	0	0	0	0	0	0	OF-3, 2B-1
2 yrs.	7	.182	.182	11	2	0	0	0	0	0	OF-6, 2B-1

World Series

Year	Gms.	BA	SA	AB	H	2B	3B	HR	RBI	SB	G. by Pos
1977	4	.250	.250	4	1	0	0	0	1	0	OF-3
1978	6	.375	.500	8	3	1	0	0	0	0	OF-6
2 yrs.	10	.333	.417	12	4	1	0	0	1	0	OF-9

Walter Blair

WALTER ALLEN BLAIR BR TR
B. Oct. 13, 1883, Landrus, Pa. 6' 185 lbs.
D. Aug. 20, 1948, Lewisburg, Pa.

Year	Gms.	BA	SA	AB	H	2B	3B	HR	RBI	SB	G. by Pos
1907	7	.182	.182	22	4	0	0	0	1	0	C-7
1908	76	.190	.237	211	40	5	1	1	13	4	C-60, OF-9, 1B-3
1909	42	.209	.264	110	23	2	2	0	11	2	C-42
1910	6	.227	.318	22	5	0	1	0	2	0	C-6
1911	85	.194	.252	222	43	9	2	0	26	2	C-84, 1B-1
5 yrs.	216	.196	.249	587	115	16	6	1	53	8	C-199, OF-9, 1B-4

Johnny Blanchard

JOHN EDWIN BLANCHARD BL TR
B. Feb. 26, 1933, Minneapolis, Minn. 6' 1" 193 lbs.

Year	Gms.	BA	SA	AB	H	2B	3B	HR	RBI	SB	G. by Pos
1955	1	.000	.000	3	0	0	0	0	0	0	C-1
1959	49	.169	.288	59	10	1	0	2	4	0	C-12, OF-8, 1B-1
1960	53	.242	.414	99	24	3	0	4	14	0	C-28
1961	93	.305	.613	243	74	10	1	21	54	1	C-48, OF-15
1962	93	.232	.419	246	57	7	0	13	39	0	OF-47, C-15, 1B-2
1963	76	.225	.463	218	49	4	0	16	45	0	OF-64
1964	77	.255	.435	161	41	8	0	7	28	1	C-25, OF-14, 1B-3
1965	12	.147	.265	34	5	1	0	1	3	0	C-12
8 yrs.	454	.245	.461	1063	260	34	2	64	187	2	OF-148, C-141, 1B-6

World Series

Year	Gms.	BA	SA	AB	H	2B	3B	HR	RBI	SB	G. by Pos
1960	5	.455	.636	11	5	2	0	0	2	0	C-2
1961	4	.400	1.100	10	4	1	0	2	3	0	OF-2
1962	1	.000	.000	1	0	0	0	0	0	0	
1963	1	.000	.000	3	0	0	0	0	0	0	OF-1
1964	4	.250	.500	4	1	1	0	0	0	0	
5 yrs.	15	.345	.690	29	10	4	0	2	5	0	OF-3, C-2

Curt Blefary

CURTIS LEROY BLEFARY
B. Jul. 5, 1943, Brooklyn, N. Y.
BL TR   6' 2" 195 lbs.

Year	Gms.	BA	SA	AB	H	2B	3B	HR	RBI	SB	G. by Pos
1970	99	.212	.335	269	57	6	0	9	37	1	OF-79, 1B-6
1971	21	.194	.306	36	7	1	0	1	2	0	OF-6, 1B-4
2 yrs.	120	.210	.331	305	64	7	0	10	39	1	OF-85, 1B-10

Elmer Bliss

ELMER WARD BLISS
B. Mar. 9, 1875, Penfield, Pa.
D. Mar. 18, 1962, Bradford, Pa.
BL TR   6' 180 lbs.

Year	Gms.	BA	SA	AB	H	2B	3B	HR	RBI	SB	G. by Pos
1903	1	.000	.000	3	0	0	0	0	0	0	P-1
1904	1	.000	.000	1	0	0	0	0	0	0	OF-1
2 yrs.	2	.000	.000	4	0	0	0	0	0	0	P-1, OF-1

Ron Blomberg

RONALD MARK BLOMBERG
B. Aug. 23, 1948, Atlanta, Ga.
BL TR   6' 1½" 195 lbs.

Year	Gms.	BA	SA	AB	H	2B	3B	HR	RBI	SB	G. by Pos
1969	4	.500	.500	6	3	0	0	0	0	0	OF-2
1971	64	.322	.477	199	64	6	2	7	31	2	OF-57
1972	107	.268	.488	299	80	22	1	14	49	0	1B-95
1973	100	.329	.498	301	99	13	1	12	57	2	DH-55, 1B-41
1974	90	.311	.481	264	82	11	2	10	48	2	DH-58, OF-19
1975	34	.255	.481	106	27	8	2	4	17	0	DH-27, OF-1
1976	1	.000	.000	2	0	0	0	0	0	0	DH-1
7 yrs.	400	.302	.486	1177	355	60	8	47	202	6	DH-141, 1B-136, OF-79

Mike Blowers

MICHAEL ROY BLOWERS
B. Apr. 24, 1965, Wurzburg, Germany
BR TR   6' 2" 190 lbs.

Year	Gms.	BA	SA	AB	H	2B	3B	HR	RBI	SB	G. by Pos
1989	13	.263	.263	38	10	0	0	0	3	0	3B-13
1990	48	.188	.319	144	27	4	0	5	21	1	3B-45, DH-2
1991	15	.200	.286	35	7	0	0	1	1	0	3B-14
3 yrs.	76	.203	.304	217	44	4	0	6	25	1	3B-72, DH-2

Eddie Bockman

JOSEPH EDWARD BOCKMAN
B. Jul. 26, 1920, Santa Ana, Calif.
BR TR   5' 9" 175 lbs.

Year	Gms.	BA	SA	AB	H	2B	3B	HR	RBI	SB	G. by Pos
1946	4	.083	.167	12	1	1	0	0	0	0	3B-4

Ping Bodie

FRANK STEPHAN BODIE
B. Oct. 8, 1887, San Francisco, Calif.
D. Dec. 17, 1961, San Francisco, Calif.
BR TR   5' 8" 195 lbs.

Year	Gms.	BA	SA	AB	H	2B	3B	HR	RBI	SB	G. by Pos
1918	91	.256	.358	324	83	12	6	3	46	6	OF-90
1919	134	.278	.406	475	132	27	8	6	59	15	OF-134
1920	129	.295	.446	471	139	26	12	7	79	6	OF-129
1921	31	.172	.241	87	15	2	2	0	12	0	OF-25
4 yrs.	385	.272	.398	1357	369	67	28	16	196	27	OF-378

Len Boehmer

LEONARD JOSEPH STEPHEN BOEHMER
B. Jun. 28, 1941, Flinthill, Mo.
BR TR   6' 1" 192 lbs.

Year	Gms.	BA	SA	AB	H	2B	3B	HR	RBI	SB	G. by Pos
1969	45	.176	.213	108	19	4	0	0	7	0	1B-21, 3B-8, 2B-1, SS-1
1971	3	.000	.000	5	0	0	0	0	0	0	3B-1
2 yrs.	48	.168	.204	113	19	4	0	0	7	0	1B-21, 3B-9, 2B-1, SS-1

Wade Boggs

WADE ANTHONY BOGGS
B. Jun. 15, 1958, Omaha, Neb.
BL TR   6' 2" 190 lbs.

Year	Gms.	BA	SA	AB	H	2B	3B	HR	RBI	SB	G. by Pos
1993	143	.302	.362	560	169	26	1	2	59	0	3B-134, DH-8
1994	97	.342	.489	366	125	19	1	11	55	2	3B-93, 1B-4
1995	126	.324	.422	460	149	22	4	5	63	1	3B-117, 1B-9
1996	132	.311	.389	501	156	29	2	2	41	1	3B-123, DH-4
4 yrs.	498	.317	.409	1887	599	96	8	20	218	4	3B-467, 1B-13, DH-12

Divisional Playoffs

Year	Gms.	BA	SA	AB	H	2B	3B	HR	RBI	SB	G. by Pos
1995	4	.263	.526	19	5	2	0	1	3	0	3B-4
1996	3	.083	.167	12	1	1	0	0	0	0	3B-3
2 yrs.	7	.194	.387	31	6	3	0	1	3	0	3B-7

Wade Boggs *continued*

League Championship Series

Year	Gms.	BA	SA	AB	H	2B	3B	HR	RBI	SB	G. by Pos
1996	3	.133	.133	15	2	0	0	0	0	0	3B-3

World Series

Year	Gms.	BA	SA	AB	H	2B	3B	HR	RBI	SB	G. by Pos
1996	4	.273	.364	11	3	1	0	0	2	0	3B-4

Don Bollweg

DONALD RAYMOND BOLLWEG
B. Feb. 12, 1921, Wheaton, Ill.
D. May 26, 1996, Wheaton, Ill.
BL TL   6' 1" 190 lbs.

Year	Gms.	BA	SA	AB	H	2B	3B	HR	RBI	SB	G. by Pos
1953	70	.297	.503	155	46	6	4	6	24	1	1B-43

World Series

Year	Gms.	BA	SA	AB	H	2B	3B	HR	RBI	SB	G. by Pos
1953	3	.000	.000	2	0	0	0	0	0	0	1B-1

Bobby Bonds

BOBBY LEE BONDS
B. Mar. 15, 1946, Riverside, Calif.
BR TR   6' 1" 190 lbs.

Year	Gms.	BA	SA	AB	H	2B	3B	HR	RBI	SB	G. by Pos
1975	145	.270	.512	529	143	26	3	32	85	30	OF-129, DH-12

Juan Bonilla

JUAN GUILLERMO BONILLA
B. Jan. 12, 1956, Santurce, Puerto Rico
BR TR   5' 9" 170 lbs.

Year	Gms.	BA	SA	AB	H	2B	3B	HR	RBI	SB	G. by Pos
1985	8	.125	.188	16	2	1	0	0	2	0	2B-7
1987	23	.255	.364	55	14	3	0	1	3	0	2B-22, 3B-1
2 yrs.	31	.225	.324	71	16	4	0	1	5	0	2B-29, 3B-1

Luke Boone

LUTE JOSEPH BOONE
B. May. 6, 1890, Pittsburgh, Pa.
D. Jul. 29, 1982, Pittsburgh, Pa.
BR TR   5' 9" 160 lbs.

Year	Gms.	BA	SA	AB	H	2B	3B	HR	RBI	SB	G. by Pos
1913	5	.333	.333	12	4	0	0	0	1	0	SS-4
1914	106	.222	.254	370	82	8	2	0	21	10	2B-90, 3B-9
1915	130	.204	.276	431	88	12	2	5	43	14	2B-115, SS-12, 3B-3
1916	46	.185	.242	124	23	4	0	1	8	7	3B-25, SS-12, 2B-7
4 yrs.	287	.210	.264	937	197	24	4	6	73	31	2B-212, 3B-37, SS-28

Frenchy Bordagaray

STANLEY GEORGE BORDAGARAY
B. Jan. 3, 1910, Coalinga, Calif.
BR TR   5' 7½" 175 lbs.

Year	Gms.	BA	SA	AB	H	2B	3B	HR	RBI	SB	G. by Pos
1941	36	.260	.274	73	19	1	0	0	4	1	OF-19

World Series

Year	Gms.	BA	SA	AB	H	2B	3B	HR	RBI	SB	G. by Pos
1941	1	—	—	0	0	0	0	0	0	0	

Babe Borton

WILLIAM BAKER BORTON
B. Aug. 14, 1888, Marion, Ill.
D. Jul. 29, 1954, Berkeley, Calif.
BL TL   6' 178 lbs.

Year	Gms.	BA	SA	AB	H	2B	3B	HR	RBI	SB	G. by Pos
1913	33	.130	.167	108	14	1	0	1	11	1	1B-33

Daryl Boston

DARYL LAMONT BOSTON
B. Jan. 4, 1963, Cincinnati, Ohio
BL TL   6' 3" 185 lbs.

Year	Gms.	BA	SA	AB	H	2B	3B	HR	RBI	SB	G. by Pos
1994	52	.182	.364	77	14	2	0	4	14	0	OF-16, DH-8

Clete Boyer

CLETIS LEROY BOYER
B. Feb. 8, 1937, Cassville, Mo.
BR TR   6' 165 lbs.

Year	Gms.	BA	SA	AB	H	2B	3B	HR	RBI	SB	G. by Pos
1959	47	.175	.193	114	20	2	0	0	3	1	SS-26, 3B-16
1960	124	.242	.405	393	95	20	1	14	46	2	3B-99, SS-33
1961	148	.224	.347	504	113	19	5	11	55	1	3B-141, SS-12, OF-1
1962	158	.272	.413	566	154	24	1	18	68	3	3B-157
1963	152	.251	.363	557	140	20	3	12	54	4	3B-141, SS-9, 2B-1
1964	147	.218	.304	510	111	10	5	8	52	4	3B-123, SS-21
1965	148	.251	.424	514	129	23	6	18	58	4	3B-147, SS-2
1966	144	.240	.384	500	120	22	4	14	57	6	3B-85, SS-59
8 yrs.	1068	.241	.371	3658	882	140	25	95	393	27	3B-909, SS-162, 2B-1, OF-1

World Series

Year	Gms.	BA	SA	AB	H	2B	3B	HR	RBI	SB	G. by Pos
1960	4	.250	.583	12	3	2	1	0	1	0	3B-4, SS-1

Clete Boyer *continued*

Year	Gms.	BA	SA	AB	H	2B	3B	HR	RBI	SB	G. by Pos
1961	5	.267	.400	15	4	2	0	0	3	0	3B-5
1962	7	.318	.500	22	7	1	0	1	4	0	3B-7
1963	4	.077	.077	13	1	0	0	0	0	0	3B-4
1964	7	.208	.375	24	5	1	0	1	3	1	3B-7
5 yrs.	27	.233	.395	86	20	6	1	2	11	1	3B-27, SS-1

Scott Bradley

SCOTT WILLIAM BRADLEY   BL TR
B. Mar. 22, 1960, Glen Ridge, N.J.   5' 11" 175 lbs.

Year	Gms.	BA	SA	AB	H	2B	3B	HR	RBI	SB	G. by Pos
1984	9	.286	.333	21	6	1	0	0	2	0	OF-5, C-3
1985	19	.163	.245	49	8	2	1	0	1	0	DH-9, C-3
2 yrs.	28	.200	.271	70	14	3	1	0	3	0	DH-9, C-6, OF-5

Marshall Brant

MARSHALL LEE BRANT   BR TR
B. Sep. 17, 1955, Garberville, Calif.   6' 5" 185 lbs.

Year	Gms.	BA	SA	AB	H	2B	3B	HR	RBI	SB	G. by Pos
1980	3	.000	.000	6	0	0	0	0	0	0	1B-2, DH-1

Fritzie Brickell

FRITZ DARRELL BRICKELL   BR TR
B. Mar. 19, 1935, Wichita, Kans.   5' 5½" 157 lbs.
D. Oct. 15, 1965, Wichita, Kans.

Year	Gms.	BA	SA	AB	H	2B	3B	HR	RBI	SB	G. by Pos
1958	2	—	—	0	0	0	0	0	0	0	2B-2
1959	18	.256	.359	39	10	1	0	1	4	0	SS-15, 2B-3
2 yrs.	20	.256	.359	39	10	1	0	1	4	0	SS-15, 2B-5

Jim Brideweser

JAMES EHRENFELD BRIDEWESER   BR TR
B. Feb. 13, 1927, Lancaster, Ohio   6' 165 lbs.
D. Aug. 25, 1989, El Toro, Calif.

Year	Gms.	BA	SA	AB	H	2B	3B	HR	RBI	SB	G. by Pos
1951	2	.375	.375	8	3	0	0	0	0	0	SS-2
1952	42	.263	.263	38	10	0	0	0	2	0	SS-22, 2B-4, 3B-1
1953	7	1.000	1.667	3	3	0	1	0	3	0	SS-3
3 yrs.	51	.327	.367	49	16	0	1	0	5	0	SS-27, 2B-4, 3B-1

Harry Bright

HARRY JAMES BRIGHT   BR TR
B. Sep. 22, 1929, Kansas City, Mo.   6' 190 lbs.

Year	Gms.	BA	SA	AB	H	2B	3B	HR	RBI	SB	G. by Pos
1963	60	.236	.414	157	37	7	0	7	23	0	1B-35, 3B-12
1964	4	.200	.200	5	1	0	0	0	0	0	1B-2
2 yrs.	64	.235	.407	162	38	7	0	7	23	0	1B-37, 3B-12
World Series											
1963	2	.000	.000	2	0	0	0	0	0	0	

Ed Brinkman

EDWIN ALBERT BRINKMAN   BR TR
B. Dec. 8, 1941, Cincinnati, Ohio   6' 170 lbs.

Year	Gms.	BA	SA	AB	H	2B	3B	HR	RBI	SB	G. by Pos
1975	44	.175	.270	63	11	4	1	0	2	0	SS-39, 2B-3, 3B-3

Tom Brookens

THOMAS DALE BROOKENS   BR TR
B. Aug. 10, 1953, Chambersburg, Pa.   5' 10" 165 lbs.

Year	Gms.	BA	SA	AB	H	2B	3B	HR	RBI	SB	G. by Pos
1989	66	.226	.333	168	38	6	0	4	14	1	3B-51, SS-7, 2B-5, OF-3, DH-3

Bob Brower

ROBERT RICHARD BROWER   BR TR
B. Jan. 10, 1960, Jamaica, N.Y.   5' 11" 185 lbs.

Year	Gms.	BA	SA	AB	H	2B	3B	HR	RBI	SB	G. by Pos
1989	26	.232	.362	69	16	3	0	2	3	3	OF-25, DH-1

Bobby Brown

ROBERT WILLIAM BROWN   BL TR
B. Oct. 25, 1924, Seattle, Wash.   6' 1" 180 lbs.

Year	Gms.	BA	SA	AB	H	2B	3B	HR	RBI	SB	G. by Pos
1946	7	.333	.375	24	8	1	0	0	1	0	SS-5, 3B-2
1947	69	.300	.373	150	45	6	1	1	18	0	3B-27, SS-11, OF-3
1948	113	.300	.405	363	109	19	5	3	48	0	3B-41, SS-26, 2B-17, OF-4
1949	104	.283	.399	343	97	14	4	6	61	4	3B-86, OF-3
1950	95	.267	.339	277	74	4	2	4	37	0	3B-82
1951	103	.268	.387	313	84	15	2	6	51	1	3B-90
1952	29	.247	.303	89	22	2	0	1	14	1	3B-24

Bobby Brown *continued*

Year	Gms.	BA	SA	AB	H	2B	3B	HR	RBI	SB	G. by Pos
1954	28	.217	.283	60	13	1	0	1	7	0	3B-17
8 yrs.	548	.279	.376	1619	452	62	14	22	237	9	3B-369, SS-42, 2B-17, OF-10
World Series											
1947	4	1.000	1.667	3	3	2	0	0	3	0	
1949	4	.500	.917	12	6	1	2	0	5	0	3B-3
1950	4	.333	.583	12	4	1	1	0	1	0	3B-4
1951	5	.357	.429	14	5	1	0	0	0	0	3B-4
4 yrs.	17	.439	.707	41	18	5	3	0	9	0	3B-11

Bobby Brown

ROGERS LEE BROWN   BB TR
B. May 25, 1954, Norfolk, Va.   6' 2" 190 lbs.

Year	Gms.	BA	SA	AB	H	2B	3B	HR	RBI	SB	G. by Pos
1979	30	.250	.324	68	17	3	1	0	3	2	OF-27, DH-1
1980	137	.260	.415	412	107	12	5	14	47	27	OF-131, DH-1
1981	31	.226	.242	62	14	1	0	0	6	4	OF-29, DH-2
3 yrs.	198	.255	.384	542	138	16	6	14	56	33	OF-187, DH-4
Divisional Playoffs											
1981	1	—	—	0	0	0	0	0	0	0	
League Championship Series											
1980	3	.000	.000	10	0	0	0	0	0	0	OF-3
1981	3	1.000	1.000	1	1	0	0	0	0	0	OF-2
2 yrs.	6	.091	.091	11	1	0	0	0	0	0	OF-5
World Series											
1981	4	.000	.000	1	0	0	0	0	0	0	OF-2

Billy Bryan

WILLIAM RONALD BRYAN   BL TR
B. Dec. 4, 1938, Morgan, Ga.   6' 4" 200 lbs.

Year	Gms.	BA	SA	AB	H	2B	3B	HR	RBI	SB	G. by Pos
1966	27	.217	.420	69	15	2	0	4	5	0	C-14, 1B-3
1967	16	.167	.417	12	2	0	0	1	2	0	C-1
2 yrs.	43	.210	.420	81	17	2	0	5	7	0	C-15, 1B-3

Jay Buhner

JAY CAMPBELL BUHNER   BR TR
B. Aug. 13, 1964, Louisville, Ky.   6' 3" 205 lbs.

Year	Gms.	BA	SA	AB	H	2B	3B	HR	RBI	SB	G. by Pos
1987	7	.227	.318	22	5	2	0	0	1	0	OF-7
1988	25	.188	.319	69	13	0	0	3	13	0	OF-22
2 yrs.	32	.198	.319	91	18	2	0	3	14	0	OF-29

George Burns

GEORGE HENRY BURNS   BR TR
B. Jan. 31, 1893, Niles, Ohio   6' 1½" 180 lbs.
D. Jan. 7, 1978, Kirkland, Wash.

Year	Gms.	BA	SA	AB	H	2B	3B	HR	RBI	SB	G. by Pos
1928	4	.500	.500	4	2	0	0	0	0	0	1B-2
1929	9	.000	.000	9	0	0	0	0	0	0	
2 yrs.	13	.154	.154	13	2	0	0	0	0	0	1B-2

Alex Burr

ALEXANDER THOMSON BURR   BR TR
B. Nov. 1, 1893, Chicago, Ill.   6' 3½" 190 lbs.
D. Oct. 12, 1918, Cazaux, France

Year	Gms.	BA	SA	AB	H	2B	3B	HR	RBI	SB	G. by Pos
1914	1	—	—	0	0	0	0	0	0	0	OF-1

Joe Buzas

JOSEPH JOHN BUZAS   BR TR
B. Oct. 2, 1919, Alpha, N.J.   6' 1" 180 lbs.

Year	Gms.	BA	SA	AB	H	2B	3B	HR	RBI	SB	G. by Pos
1945	30	.262	.323	65	17	2	1	0	6	2	SS-12

Sammy Byrd

SAMUEL DEWEY BYRD   BR TR
B. Oct. 15, 1907, Bremen, Ga.   5' 10½" 175 lbs.
D. May 11, 1981, Mesa, Ariz.

Year	Gms.	BA	SA	AB	H	2B	3B	HR	RBI	SB	G. by Pos
1929	62	.312	.471	170	53	12	0	5	28	1	OF-54
1930	92	.284	.440	218	62	12	2	6	31	5	OF-85
1931	115	.270	.395	248	67	18	2	3	32	5	OF-88
1932	104	.297	.478	209	62	12	1	8	30	1	OF-90
1933	85	.280	.411	107	30	6	1	2	11	0	OF-71
1934	106	.246	.335	191	47	8	0	3	23	1	OF-104
6 yrs.	564	.281	.422	1143	321	68	6	27	155	13	OF-492
World Series											
1932	1	—	—	0	0	0	0	0	0	0	OF-1

Tommy Byrne

THOMAS JOSEPH BYRNE   BL TL
B. Dec. 31, 1919, Baltimore, Md.   6' 1" 182 lbs.

Year	Gms.	BA	SA	AB	H	2B	3B	HR	RBI	SB	G. by Pos
1943	13	.091	.091	11	1	0	0	0	0	0	P-11
1946	14	.222	.222	9	2	0	0	0	0	0	P-4
1947	4	—	—	0	0	0	0	0	0	0	P-4
1948	31	.326	.500	46	15	3	1	1	7	0	P-31
1949	35	.193	.289	83	16	4	2	0	13	0	P-32
1950	34	.272	.407	81	22	3	1	2	16	1	P-31
1951	9	.222	.556	9	2	0	0	1	3	0	P-9
1954	7	.368	.684	19	7	4	1	0	6	0	P-5
1955	45	.205	.282	78	16	1	1	1	6	0	P-27
1956	44	.269	.500	52	14	1	1	3	10	0	P-37
1957	35	.189	.486	37	7	2	0	3	8	0	P-30
11 yrs.	271	.240	.393	425	102	18	7	11	69	1	P-221
World Series											
1949	1	1.000	1.000	1	1	0	0	0	0	0	P-1
1955	3	.167	.167	6	1	0	0	0	2	0	P-2
1956	2	.000	.000	1	0	0	0	0	0	0	P-1
1957	2	.500	.500	2	1	0	0	0	0	0	P-2
4 yrs.	8	.300	.300	10	3	0	0	0	2	0	P-6

Ray Caldwell

RAYMOND BENJAMIN CALDWELL   BL TR
B. Apr. 26, 1888, Croydon, Pa.   6' 2" 190 lbs.
D. Aug. 17, 1967, Salamanca, N. Y.

Year	Gms.	BA	SA	AB	H	2B	3B	HR	RBI	SB	G. by Pos
1910	6	.000	.000	6	0	0	0	0	0	0	P-6
1911	58	.272	.313	147	40	4	1	0	17	5	P-41, OF-11
1912	41	.237	.303	76	18	1	2	0	6	4	P-30
1913	55	.289	.361	97	28	3	2	0	11	3	P-27, OF-3
1914	59	.195	.230	113	22	4	0	0	10	2	P-31, 1B-6
1915	72	.243	.368	144	35	4	1	4	20	4	P-36
1916	45	.204	.226	93	19	2	0	0	4	1	P-21, OF-3
1917	63	.258	.371	124	32	6	1	2	12	2	P-32, OF-8
1918	65	.291	.377	151	44	10	0	1	18	2	P-24, OF-19
9 yrs.	464	.250	.323	951	238	34	7	7	98	23	P-248, OF-44, 1B-6

Johnny Callison

JOHN WESLEY CALLISON   BL TR
B. Mar. 12, 1939, Qualls, Okla.   5' 10" 175 lbs.

Year	Gms.	BA	SA	AB	H	2B	3B	HR	RBI	SB	G. by Pos
1972	92	.258	.393	275	71	10	0	9	34	3	OF-74
1973	45	.176	.228	136	24	4	0	1	10	1	OF-32, DH-10
2 yrs.	137	.231	.338	411	95	14	0	10	44	4	OF-106, DH-10

Howie Camp

HOWARD LEE CAMP   BL TR
B. Jul. 1, 1893, Munford, Ala.   5' 9" 169 lbs.
D. May. 8, 1960, Eastaboga, Ala.

Year	Gms.	BA	SA	AB	H	2B	3B	HR	RBI	SB	G. by Pos
1917	5	.286	.333	21	6	1	0	0	0	0	OF-5

Bert Campaneris

DAGOBERTO CAMPANERIS   BR TR
B. Mar. 9, 1942, Pueblo Nuevo, Cuba   5' 10" 160 lbs.

Year	Gms.	BA	SA	AB	H	2B	3B	HR	RBI	SB	G. by Pos
1983	60	.322	.357	143	46	5	0	0	11	6	2B-32, 3B-24

Andy Carey

ANDREW ARTHUR CAREY   BR TR
B. Oct. 18, 1931, Oakland, Calif.   6' 1½" 190 lbs.

Year	Gms.	BA	SA	AB	H	2B	3B	HR	RBI	SB	G. by Pos
1952	16	.150	.150	40	6	0	0	0	1	0	3B-14, SS-1
1953	51	.321	.531	81	26	5	0	4	8	2	3B-40, SS-2, 2B-1
1954	122	.302	.423	411	124	14	6	8	65	5	3B-120
1955	135	.257	.378	510	131	19	11	7	47	3	3B-135
1956	132	.237	.339	422	100	18	2	7	50	7	3B-131
1957	85	.255	.393	247	63	6	5	6	33	2	3B-81
1958	102	.286	.486	315	90	19	4	12	45	1	3B-99
1959	41	.257	.356	101	26	1	0	3	9	1	3B-34
1960	4	.333	.333	3	1	0	0	0	1	0	3B-2, OF-1
9 yrs.	688	.266	.397	2130	567	82	28	47	259	23	3B-656, SS-3, 2B-1, OF-1
World Series											
1955	2	.500	1.500	2	1	0	1	0	1	0	
1956	7	.158	.158	19	3	0	0	0	0	0	3B-7
1957	2	.286	.429	7	2	1	0	0	1	0	3B-2

Andy Carey *continued*

Year	Gms.	BA	SA	AB	H	2B	3B	HR	RBI	SB	G. by Pos
1958	5	.083	.083	12	1	0	0	0	0	0	3B-5
4 yrs.	16	.175	.250	40	7	1	1	0	2	0	3B-14

Roy Carlyle

ROY EDWARD CARLYLE   BL TR
B. Dec. 10, 1900, Buford, Ga.   6' 2½" 195 lbs.
D. Nov. 22, 1956, Norcross, Ga.

Year	Gms.	BA	SA	AB	H	2B	3B	HR	RBI	SB	G. by Pos
1926	35	.377	.509	53	20	5	1	0	11	0	OF-16

Duke Carmel

LEON JAMES CARMEL   BL TL
B. Apr 23, 1937, New York, N. Y.   6' 3" 202 lbs.

Year	Gms.	BA	SA	AB	H	2B	3B	HR	RBI	SB	G. by Pos
1965	6	.000	.000	8	0	0	0	0	0	0	1B-2

Tommy Carroll

THOMAS EDWARD CARROLL   BR TR
B. Sep. 17, 1936, Jamaica, N. Y.   6' 3" 186 lbs.

Year	Gms.	BA	SA	AB	H	2B	3B	HR	RBI	SB	G. by Pos
1955	14	.333	.333	6	2	0	0	0	0	0	SS-4
1956	36	.353	.353	17	6	0	0	0	0	1	3B-11, SS-1
2 yrs.	50	.348	.348	23	8	0	0	0	0	1	3B-11, SS-5
World Series											
1955	2	—	—	0	0	0	0	0	0	0	

Danny Cater

DANNY ANDERSON CATER   BR TR
B. Feb. 25, 1940, Austin, Tex.   6' 170 lbs.

Year	Gms.	BA	SA	AB	H	2B	3B	HR	RBI	SB	G. by Pos
1970	155	.301	.393	582	175	26	5	6	76	4	1B-131, 3B-42, OF-7
1971	121	.276	.364	428	118	16	5	4	50	0	1B-78, 3B-52
2 yrs.	276	.290	.381	1010	293	42	10	10	126	4	1B-209, 3B-94, OF-7

Rick Cerone

RICHARD ALDO CERONE   BR TR
B. May 19, 1954, Newark, N. J.   5' 11" 192 lbs.

Year	Gms.	BA	SA	AB	H	2B	3B	HR	RBI	SB	G. by Pos
1980	147	.277	.432	519	144	30	4	14	85	1	C-147
1981	71	.244	.342	234	57	13	2	2	21	0	C-69
1982	89	.227	.310	300	68	10	0	5	28	0	C-89
1983	80	.220	.272	246	54	7	0	2	22	0	C-78, 3B-1
1984	38	.208	.283	120	25	3	0	2	13	1	C-38
1987	113	.243	.335	284	69	12	1	4	23	0	C-111, P-2, 1B-2
1990	49	.302	.388	139	42	6	0	2	11	0	C-35, DH-6, 2B-1
7 yrs.	587	.249	.351	1842	459	81	7	31	203	2	C-567, DH-6, P-2, 1B-2, 2B-1, 3B-1
Divisional Playoffs											
1981	5	.333	.611	18	6	2	0	1	5	0	C-5
League Championship Series											
1980	3	.333	.583	12	4	0	0	1	2	0	C-3
1981	3	.100	.100	10	1	0	0	0	0	0	C-3
2 yrs.	6	.227	.364	22	5	0	0	1	2	0	C-6
World Series											
1981	6	.190	.381	21	4	1	0	1	3	0	C-6

Bob Cerv

ROBERT HENRY CERV   BR TR
B. May. 5, 1926, Weston, Neb.   6' 200 lbs.

Year	Gms.	BA	SA	AB	H	2B	3B	HR	RBI	SB	G. by Pos
1951	12	.214	.250	28	6	1	0	0	2	0	OF-9
1952	36	.241	.356	87	21	3	2	1	8	0	OF-27
1953	8	.000	.000	6	0	0	0	0	0	0	OF-3
1954	56	.260	.470	100	26	6	0	5	13	0	OF-24
1955	55	.341	.541	85	29	4	2	3	22	4	OF-20
1956	54	.304	.530	115	35	5	6	3	25	0	OF-44
1960	87	.250	.421	216	54	11	1	8	28	0	OF-51, 1B-3
1961	57	.271	.483	118	32	5	1	6	20	1	OF-30, 1B-3
1962	14	.118	.176	17	2	1	0	0	0	0	OF-3
9 yrs.	379	.266	.444	772	205	36	12	26	118	5	OF-208, 1B-6
World Series											
1955	5	.125	.313	16	2	0	0	1	1	0	OF-4
1956	1	1.000	1.000	1	1	0	0	0	0	0	
1960	4	.357	.357	14	5	0	0	1	1	0	OF-3
3 yrs.	10	.258	.355	31	8	0	0	1	1	0	OF-7

Year	Gms.	BA	SA	AB	H	2B	3B	HR	RBI	SB	G. by Pos

Chris Chambliss

CARROLL CHRISTOPHER CHAMBLISS BL TR
B. Dec. 26, 1948, Dayton, Ohio   6' 1" 195 lbs.

Year	Gms.	BA	SA	AB	H	2B	3B	HR	RBI	SB	G. by Pos
1974	110	.242	.343	400	97	16	3	6	43	0	1B-106
1975	150	.304	.434	562	171	38	4	9	72	0	1B-147
1976	156	.293	.441	641	188	32	6	17	96	1	1B-155, DH-1
1977	157	.287	.445	600	172	32	6	17	90	4	1B-157
1978	162	.274	.382	625	171	26	3	12	90	2	1B-155, DH-7
1979	149	.280	.437	554	155	27	3	18	63	3	1B-134, DH-16
1988	1	.000	.000	1	0	0	0	0	0	0	
7 yrs.	885	.282	.417	3383	954	171	25	79	454	10	1B-854, DH-24

League Championship Series

Year	Gms.	BA	SA	AB	H	2B	3B	HR	RBI	SB	G. by Pos
1976	5	.524	.952	21	11	1	1	2	8	2	1B-5
1977	5	.059	.059	17	1	0	0	0	0	0	1B-5
1978	4	.400	.400	15	6	0	0	0	2	0	1B-4
3 yrs.	14	.340	.509	53	18	1	1	2	10	2	1B-14

World Series

Year	Gms.	BA	SA	AB	H	2B	3B	HR	RBI	SB	G. by Pos
1976	4	.313	.375	16	5	1	0	0	1	0	1B-4
1977	6	.292	.500	24	7	2	0	1	4	0	1B-6
1978	3	.182	.182	11	2	0	0	0	5	0	1B-3
3 yrs.	13	.275	.392	51	14	3	0	1	5	0	1B-13

Frank Chance

FRANK LEROY CHANCE BR TR
B. Sep. 9, 1877, Fresno, Calif.   6' 190 lbs.
D. Sep. 15, 1924, Los Angeles, Calif.
Hall of Fame 1946

Year	Gms.	BA	SA	AB	H	2B	3B	HR	RBI	SB	G. by Pos
1913	11	.208	.208	24	5	0	0	0	6	1	1B-8
1914	1	—	—	0	0	0	0	0	0	0	1B-1
2 yrs.	12	.208	.208	24	5	0	0	0	6	1	1B-9

Les Channell

LESTER CLARK CHANNELL BL TL
B. Mar. 3, 1886, Crestline, Ohio   6' 180 lbs.
D. May. 7, 1954, Denver, Colo.

Year	Gms.	BA	SA	AB	H	2B	3B	HR	RBI	SB	G. by Pos
1910	6	.316	.316	19	6	0	0	0	3	2	OF-6
1914	1	1.000	2.000	1	1	1	0	0	0	0	
2 yrs.	7	.350	.400	20	7	1	0	0	3	2	OF-6

Ben Chapman

WILLIAM BENJAMIN CHAPMAN BR TR
B. Dec. 25, 1908, Nashville, Tenn.   6' 190 lbs.
D. Jul. 7, 1993, Hoover, Ala.

Year	Gms.	BA	SA	AB	H	2B	3B	HR	RBI	SB	G. by Pos
1930	138	.316	.474	513	162	31	10	10	81	14	3B-91, 2B-45
1931	149	.315	.483	600	189	28	11	17	122	61	OF-137, 2B-11
1932	150	.299	.473	581	174	41	15	10	107	38	OF-149
1933	147	.312	.437	565	176	36	4	9	98	27	OF-147
1934	149	.308	.413	588	181	21	13	5	86	26	OF-149
1935	140	.289	.430	553	160	38	8	8	74	17	OF-138
1936	36	.266	.432	139	37	14	3	1	21	1	OF-36
7 yrs.	909	.305	.451	3539	1079	209	64	60	589	184	OF-756, 3B-91, 2B-56

World Series

Year	Gms.	BA	SA	AB	H	2B	3B	HR	RBI	SB	G. by Pos
1932	4	.294	.353	17	5	1	0	0	6	0	OF-4

Mike Chartak

MICHAEL GEORGE CHARTAK BL TL
B. Apr. 28, 1916, Brooklyn, N. Y.   6' 2" 180 lbs.
D. Jul. 25, 1967, Cedar Rapids, Iowa

Year	Gms.	BA	SA	AB	H	2B	3B	HR	RBI	SB	G. by Pos
1940	11	.133	.200	15	2	1	0	0	3	0	OF-3
1942	5	.000	.000	5	0	0	0	0	0	0	
2 yrs.	16	.100	.150	20	2	1	0	0	3	0	OF-3

Hal Chase

HAROLD HOMER CHASE BR TL
B. Feb. 13, 1883, Los Gatos, Calif.   6' 175 lbs.
D. May 18, 1947, Colusa, Calif.

Year	Gms.	BA	SA	AB	H	2B	3B	HR	RBI	SB	G. by Pos
1905	126	.249	.329	465	116	16	6	3	49	22	1B-122, 2B-1, SS-1
1906	151	.323	.395	597	193	23	10	0	76	28	1B-150, 2B-1
1907	125	.287	.357	498	143	23	3	2	68	32	1B-121, OF-4
1908	106	.257	.306	405	104	11	3	1	36	27	1B-96, 2B-3, 3B-2, P-1

Hal Chase *continued*

Year	Gms.	BA	SA	AB	H	2B	3B	HR	RBI	SB	G. by Pos
1909	118	.283	.357	474	134	17	3	4	63	25	1B-118
1910	130	.290	.365	524	152	20	5	3	73	40	1B-130
1911	133	.315	.419	527	166	32	7	3	62	36	1B-124, OF-7, 2B-2, SS-1
1912	131	.274	.372	522	143	21	9	4	58	33	1B-121, 2B-8
1913	39	.212	.281	146	31	2	4	0	9	5	1B-29, 2B-5, OF-5
9 yrs.	1059	.284	.362	4158	1182	165	50	20	494	248	1B-1011, 2B-20, OF-16, 3B-2, SS-2, P-1

Allie Clark

ALFRED ALOYSIUS CLARK BR TR
B. Jun. 16, 1923, South Amboy, N. J.   6' 195 lbs.

Year	Gms.	BA	SA	AB	H	2B	3B	HR	RBI	SB	G. by Pos
1947	24	.373	.493	67	25	5	0	1	14	0	OF-16

World Series

Year	Gms.	BA	SA	AB	H	2B	3B	HR	RBI	SB	G. by Pos
1947	3	.500	.500	2	1	0	0	0	1	0	OF-1

Jack Clark

JACK ANTHONY CLARK BR TR
B. Nov. 10, 1955, New Brighton, Pa.   6' 2" 205 lbs.

Year	Gms.	BA	SA	AB	H	2B	3B	HR	RBI	SB	G. by Pos
1988	150	.242	.433	496	120	14	0	27	93	3	DH-112, OF-19, 1B-10

Horace Clarke

HORACE MEREDITH CLARKE BB TR
B. Jun. 2, 1940, Frederiksted, Virgin Islands   5' 9" 170 lbs.

Year	Gms.	BA	SA	AB	H	2B	3B	HR	RBI	SB	G. by Pos
1965	51	.259	.296	108	28	1	0	1	9	2	3B-17, 2B-7, SS-1
1966	96	.266	.381	312	83	10	4	6	28	5	SS-63, 2B-16, 3B-4
1967	143	.272	.316	588	160	17	0	3	29	21	2B-140
1968	148	.230	.254	579	133	6	1	2	26	20	2B-139
1969	156	.285	.367	641	183	26	7	4	48	33	2B-156
1970	158	.251	.309	686	172	24	4	4	46	23	2B-157
1971	159	.250	.318	625	156	23	7	2	41	17	2B-156
1972	147	.241	.302	547	132	20	2	3	37	18	2B-143
1973	148	.263	.308	590	155	21	0	2	35	11	2B-147
1974	24	.234	.255	47	11	1	0	0	1	1	2B-20, DH-1
10 yrs.	1230	.257	.315	4723	1213	149	23	27	300	151	2B-1081, SS-64, 3B-21, DH-1

Lu Clinton

LUCIEAN LOUIS CLINTON BR TR
B. Oct. 13, 1937, Ponca City, Okla.   6' 1" 185 lbs.

Year	Gms.	BA	SA	AB	H	2B	3B	HR	RBI	SB	G. by Pos
1966	80	.220	.403	159	35	10	2	5	21	0	OF-63
1967	6	.500	.750	4	2	1	0	0	2	0	OF-1
2 yrs.	86	.227	.411	163	37	11	2	5	23	0	OF-64

Jim Cockman

JAMES COCKMAN BR TR
B. Apr. 26, 1873, Guelph, Ont., Canada 5' 6" 145 lbs.
D. Sep. 28, 1947, Guelph, Ont., Canada

Year	Gms.	BA	SA	AB	H	2B	3B	HR	RBI	SB	G. by Pos
1905	13	.105	.105	38	4	0	0	0	2	2	3B-13

Rich Coggins

RICHARD ALLEN COGGINS BL TL
B. Dec. 7, 1950, Indianapolis, Ind.   5' 8" 170 lbs.

Year	Gms.	BA	SA	AB	H	2B	3B	HR	RBI	SB	G. by Pos
1975	51	.224	.262	107	24	1	0	1	6	3	OF-36, DH-9
1976	7	.250	.250	4	1	0	0	0	1	1	OF-2, DH-1
2 yrs.	58	.225	.261	111	25	1	0	1	7	4	OF-38, DH-10

Rocky Colavito

ROCCO DOMENICO COLAVITO BR TR
B. Aug. 10, 1933, New York, N. Y.   6' 3" 190 lbs.

Year	Gms.	BA	SA	AB	H	2B	3B	HR	RBI	SB	G. by Pos
1968	39	.220	.451	91	20	2	2	5	13	0	OF-28, P-1

Curt Coleman

CURTIS HANCOCK COLEMAN BL TR
B. Feb. 18, 1887, Salem, Ore.   5' 11" 180 lbs.
D. Jul. 1, 1980, Newport, Ore.

Year	Gms.	BA	SA	AB	H	2B	3B	HR	RBI	SB	G. by Pos
1912	12	.243	.351	37	9	4	0	0	4	0	3B-10

Jerry Coleman

GERALD FRANCIS COLEMAN BR TR
B. Sep. 14, 1924, San Jose, Calif. 6' 165 lbs.

Year	Gms.	BA	SA	AB	H	2B	3B	HR	RBI	SB	G. by Pos
1949	128	.275	.358	447	123	21	5	2	42	8	2B-122, SS-4
1950	153	.287	.381	522	150	19	6	6	69	3	2B-152, SS-6
1951	121	.249	.315	362	90	11	2	3	43	6	2B-102, SS-18
1952	11	.405	.500	42	17	2	1	0	4	0	2B-11
1953	8	.200	.200	10	2	0	0	0	0	0	2B-7, SS-1
1954	107	.217	.277	300	65	7	1	3	21	3	2B-79, SS-30, 3B-1
1955	43	.229	.281	96	22	5	0	0	8	0	SS-29, 2B-13, 3B-1
1956	80	.257	.295	183	47	5	1	0	18	1	2B-41, SS-24, 3B-18
1957	72	.268	.376	157	42	7	2	2	12	1	2B-45, 3B-21, SS-4
9 yrs.	723	.263	.339	2119	558	77	18	16	217	22	2B-572, SS-116, 3B-41
World Series											
1949	5	.250	.400	20	5	3	0	0	4	0	2B-5
1950	4	.286	.357	14	4	1	0	0	3	0	2B-4
1951	5	.250	.250	8	2	0	0	0	0	0	2B-5
1955	3	.000	.000	3	0	0	0	0	0	0	SS-3
1956	2	.000	.000	2	0	0	0	0	0	0	2B-2
1957	7	.364	.455	22	8	2	0	0	2	0	2B-7
6 yrs.	26	.275	.362	69	19	6	0	0	9	0	2B-23, SS-3

Bob Collins

ROBERT JOSEPH COLLINS BR TR
B. Sep. 18, 1909, Pittsburgh, Pa. 5' 11" 176 lbs.
D. Apr. 19, 1969, Pittsburgh, Pa.

Year	Gms.	BA	SA	AB	H	2B	3B	HR	RBI	SB	G. by Pos
1944	3	.333	.333	3	1	0	0	0	0	0	C-3

Dave Collins

DAVID SCOTT COLLINS BB TL
B. Oct. 20, 1952, Rapid City, S. D. 5' 10" 175 lbs.

Year	Gms.	BA	SA	AB	H	2B	3B	HR	RBI	SB	G. by Pos
1982	111	.253	.330	348	88	12	3	3	25	13	OF-60, 1B-52, DH-1

Joe Collins

JOSEPH EDWARD COLLINS BL TL
B. Dec. 3, 1922, Scranton, Pa. 6' 185 lbs.
D. Aug. 30, 1989, Union, N. J.

Year	Gms.	BA	SA	AB	H	2B	3B	HR	RBI	SB	G. by Pos
1948	5	.200	.400	5	1	1	0	0	2	0	
1949	7	.100	.100	10	1	0	0	0	4	0	1B-5
1950	108	.234	.420	205	48	8	3	8	28	5	1B-99, OF-2
1951	125	.286	.458	262	75	8	5	9	48	9	1B-114, OF-15
1952	122	.280	.481	428	120	16	8	18	59	4	1B-119
1953	127	.269	.439	387	104	11	2	17	44	2	1B-113, OF-4
1954	130	.271	.446	343	93	20	2	12	46	2	1B-117
1955	105	.234	.414	278	65	9	1	13	45	0	1B-73, OF-27
1956	100	.225	.347	262	59	5	3	7	43	3	OF-51, 1B-43
1957	79	.201	.248	149	30	1	0	2	10	2	1B-32, OF-15
10 yrs.	908	.256	.421	2329	596	79	24	86	329	27	1B-715, OF-114
World Series											
1950	1	—	—	0	0	0	0	0	0	0	1B-1
1951	6	.222	.389	18	4	0	0	1	3	0	1B-6, OF-1
1952	6	.000	.000	12	0	0	0	0	0	0	1B-6
1953	6	.167	.333	24	4	1	0	1	2	0	1B-6
1955	5	.167	.667	12	2	0	0	2	3	1	1B-5, OF-1
1956	6	.238	.333	21	5	2	0	0	2	0	1B-5
1957	6	.000	.000	5	0	0	0	0	0	0	1B-5
7 yrs.	36	.163	.326	92	15	3	0	4	10	1	1B-34, OF-2

Orth Collins

ORTH STEIN COLLINS BL TR
B. Apr. 27, 1880, Lafayette, Ind. 6' 150 lbs.
D. Dec. 13, 1949, Fort Lauderdale, Fla.

Year	Gms.	BA	SA	AB	H	2B	3B	HR	RBI	SB	G. by Pos
1904	5	.353	.529	17	6	1	1	0	1	0	OF-5

Pat Collins

THARON PATRICK COLLINS BR TR
B. Sep. 13, 1896, Sweet Springs, Mo. 5' 11½" 178 lbs.
D. May 20, 1960, Kansas City, Kans.

Year	Gms.	BA	SA	AB	H	2B	3B	HR	RBI	SB	G. by Pos
1926	102	.286	.417	290	83	11	3	7	35	3	C-100
1927	92	.275	.418	251	69	9	3	7	36	0	C-89
1928	70	.221	.390	136	30	5	0	6	14	0	C-70
3 yrs.	264	.269	.412	677	182	25	6	20	85	3	C-259

Pat Collins *continued*

Year	Gms.	BA	SA	AB	H	2B	3B	HR	RBI	SB	G. by Pos
World Series											
1926	3	.000	.000	2	0	0	0	0	0	0	C-3
1927	2	.600	.800	5	3	1	0	0	0	0	C-2
1928	1	1.000	2.000	1	1	1	0	0	0	0	C-1
3 yrs.	6	.500	.750	8	4	2	0	0	0	0	C-6

Frank Colman

FRANK LLOYD COLMAN BL TL
B. Mar. 2, 1918, London, Ont., Canada 5' 11" 186 lbs.
D. Feb. 19, 1983, London, Ont., Canada

Year	Gms.	BA	SA	AB	H	2B	3B	HR	RBI	SB	G. by Pos
1946	5	.267	.467	15	4	0	0	1	5	0	OF-5
1947	22	.107	.321	28	3	0	0	2	6	0	OF-6
2 yrs.	27	.163	.372	43	7	0	0	3	11	0	OF-11

Earle Combs

EARLE BRYAN COMBS BL TR
B. May 14, 1899, Pebworth, Ky. 6' 185 lbs.
D. Jul. 21, 1976, Richmond, Ky.
Hall of Fame 1970

Year	Gms.	BA	SA	AB	H	2B	3B	HR	RBI	SB	G. by Pos
1924	24	.400	.543	35	14	5	0	0	2	0	OF-11
1925	150	.342	.462	593	203	36	13	3	61	12	OF-150
1926	145	.299	.429	606	181	31	12	8	56	8	OF-145
1927	152	.356	.511	648	231	36	23	6	64	15	OF-152
1928	149	.310	.463	626	194	33	21	7	56	10	OF-149
1929	142	.345	.468	586	202	33	15	3	65	11	OF-141
1930	137	.344	.523	532	183	30	22	7	82	16	OF-135
1931	138	.318	.446	563	179	31	13	5	58	11	OF-129
1932	143	.321	.455	591	190	32	10	9	65	3	OF-138
1933	122	.298	.463	419	125	22	16	5	60	6	OF-104
1934	63	.319	.434	251	80	13	5	2	25	3	OF-62
1935	89	.282	.362	298	84	7	4	3	35	1	OF-70
12 yrs.	1454	.325	.462	5748	1866	309	154	58	629	96	OF-1386
World Series											
1926	7	.357	.429	28	10	2	0	0	2	0	OF-7
1927	4	.313	.313	16	5	0	0	0	2	0	OF-4
1928	1			0	0	0	0	0	1	0	
1932	4	.375	.625	16	6	1	0	1	4	0	OF-4
4 yrs.	16	.350	.450	60	21	3	0	1	9	0	OF-15

Tom Connelly

THOMAS MARTIN CONNELLY BL TR
B. Oct. 20, 1897, Chicago, Ill. 5' 11½" 165 lbs.
D. Feb. 18, 1941, Hines, Ill.

Year	Gms.	BA	SA	AB	H	2B	3B	HR	RBI	SB	G. by Pos
1920	1	.000	.000	1	0	0	0	0	0	0	
1921	4	.200	.200	5	1	0	0	0	0	0	OF-3
2 yrs.	5	.167	.167	6	1	0	0	0	0	0	OF-3

Joe Connor

JOSEPH FRANCIS CONNOR BR TR
B. Dec. 8, 1874, Waterbury, Conn. 6' 2" 185 lbs.
D. Nov. 8, 1957, Waterbury, Conn.

Year	Gms.	BA	SA	AB	H	2B	3B	HR	RBI	SB	G. by Pos
1905	8	.227	.273	22	5	1	0	0	2	1	C-6, 1B-2

Wid Conroy

WILLIAM EDWARD CONROY BR TR
B. Apr. 5, 1877, Camden, N. J. 5' 9" 158 lbs.
D. Dec. 6, 1959, Mt. Holly, N. J.

Year	Gms.	BA	SA	AB	H	2B	3B	HR	RBI	SB	G. by Pos
1903	126	.272	.372	503	137	23	12	1	45	33	3B-123, SS-4
1904	140	.243	.335	489	119	18	12	1	52	30	3B-110, SS-27, OF-3
1905	102	.273	.395	385	105	19	11	2	25	25	3B-48, OF-21, SS-18, 1B-9, 2B-3
1906	148	.245	.332	567	139	17	10	4	54	32	OF-97, SS-49, 3B-2
1907	140	.234	.315	530	124	12	11	3	51	41	OF-100, SS-38
1908	141	.237	.296	531	126	22	3	1	39	23	3B-119, 2B-12, OF-10
6 yrs.	797	.250	.338	3005	750	111	59	12	266	184	3B-402, OF-231, SS-136, 2B-15, 1B-9

Year	Gms.	BA	SA	AB	H	2B	3B	HR	RBI	SB	G. by Pos

Doc Cook

LUTHER ALMUS COOK BL TR
B. Jun. 24, 1886, Witt, Tex. 6' 170 lbs.
D. Jun. 30, 1973, Lawrenceburg, Tenn.

Year	Gms.	BA	SA	AB	H	2B	3B	HR	RBI	SB	G. by Pos
1913	20	.264	.319	72	19	2	1	0	1	1	OF-20
1914	131	.283	.326	470	133	11	3	1	40	26	OF-126
1915	132	.271	.338	476	129	16	5	2	33	29	OF-131
1916	3	.100	.100	10	1	0	0	0	1	0	OF-3
4 yrs.	286	.274	.329	1028	282	29	9	3	75	56	OF-280

Dusty Cooke

ALLEN LINDSEY COOKE BL TR
B. Jun. 23, 1907, Swepsonville, N. C. 6' 1" 205 lbs.
D. Nov. 21, 1987, Raleigh, N. C.

Year	Gms.	BA	SA	AB	H	2B	3B	HR	RBI	SB	G. by Pos
1930	92	.255	.421	216	55	12	3	6	29	4	OF-73
1931	27	.333	.436	39	13	1	0	1	6	4	OF-11
1932	3	—	—	0	0	0	0	0	0	0	
3 yrs.	122	.267	.424	255	68	13	3	7	35	8	OF-84

Johnny Cooney

JOHN WALTER COONEY BR TL
B. Mar. 18, 1901, Cranston, R. I. 5' 10" 165 lbs.
D. Jul. 8, 1986, Sarasota, Fla.

Year	Gms.	BA	SA	AB	H	2B	3B	HR	RBI	SB	G. by Pos
1944	10	.125	.125	8	1	0	0	0	1	0	OF-2

Phil Cooney

PHILIP CLARENCE COONEY BR TR
B. Sep. 14, 1882, New York, N. Y. 5' 8" 155 lbs.
D. Oct. 6, 1957, New York, N. Y.

Year	Gms.	BA	SA	AB	H	2B	3B	HR	RBI	SB	G. by Pos
1905	1	.000	.000	3	0	0	0	0	0	0	3B-1

Dan Costello

DANIEL FRANCIS COSTELLO BL TR
B. Sep. 9, 1891, Jessup, Pa. 6' ½" 185 lbs.
D. Mar. 26, 1936, Pittsburgh, Pa.

Year	Gms.	BA	SA	AB	H	2B	3B	HR	RBI	SB	G. by Pos
1913	2	.500	.500	2	1	0	0	0	0	0	

Henry Cotto

HENRY COTTO BR TR
B. Jan. 5, 1961, Bronx, N. Y. 6' 2" 180 lbs.

Year	Gms.	BA	SA	AB	H	2B	3B	HR	RBI	SB	G. by Pos
1985	34	.304	.375	56	17	1	0	1	6	1	OF-30
1986	35	.212	.287	80	17	3	0	1	6	3	OF-29, DH-1
1987	68	.235	.403	149	35	10	0	5	20	4	OF-57
3 yrs.	137	.242	.365	285	69	14	0	7	32	8	OF-116, DH-1

Clint Courtney

CLINTON DAWSON COURTNEY BL TR
B. Mar. 16, 1927, Hall Summit, La. 5' 8" 180 lbs.
D. Jun. 16, 1975, Rochester, N. Y.

Year	Gms.	BA	SA	AB	H	2B	3B	HR	RBI	SB	G. by Pos
1951	1	.000	.000	2	0	0	0	0	0	0	C-1

Ernie Courtney

EDWARD ERNEST COURTNEY BL TR
B. Jan. 20, 1875, Des Moines, Iowa 5' 10" lbs.
D. Feb. 29, 1920, Buffalo, N. Y.

Year	Gms.	BA	SA	AB	H	2B	3B	HR	RBI	SB	G. by Pos
1903	25	.266	.418	79	21	3	1	1	8	1	SS-19, 2B-4, 1B-1

Billy Cowan

BILLY ROLAND COWAN BR TR
B. Aug. 28, 1938, Calhoun City, Miss. 6' 170 lbs.

Year	Gms.	BA	SA	AB	H	2B	3B	HR	RBI	SB	G. by Pos
1969	32	.167	.229	48	8	0	0	1	3	0	OF-14, 1B-6

Bobby Cox

ROBERT JOE COX BR TR
B. May 21, 1941, Tulsa, Okla. 5' 11" 180 lbs.

Year	Gms.	BA	SA	AB	H	2B	3B	HR	RBI	SB	G. by Pos
1968	135	.229	.316	437	100	15	1	7	41	3	3B-132
1969	85	.215	.293	191	41	7	1	2	17	0	3B-56, 2B-6
2 yrs.	220	.225	.309	628	141	22	2	9	58	3	3B-188, 2B-6

Birdie Cree

WILLIAM FRANKLIN CREE BR TR
B. Oct. 22, 1882, Khedive, Pa. 5' 6" 150 lbs.
D. Nov. 8, 1942, Sunbury, Pa.

Year	Gms.	BA	SA	AB	H	2B	3B	HR	RBI	SB	G. by Pos
1908	21	.269	.321	78	21	0	2	0	4	1	OF-21
1909	104	.262	.315	343	90	6	3	2	27	10	OF-77, SS-6, 2B-4, 3B-1

Birdie Cree *continued*

Year	Gms.	BA	SA	AB	H	2B	3B	HR	RBI	SB	G. by Pos
1910	134	.287	.422	467	134	19	16	4	73	28	OF-134
1911	137	.348	.513	520	181	30	22	4	88	48	OF-137, SS-4, 2B-1
1912	50	.332	.453	190	63	11	6	0	22	12	OF-50
1913	145	.272	.346	534	145	25	6	1	63	22	OF-144
1914	77	.309	.411	275	85	18	5	0	40	4	OF-76
1915	74	.214	.276	196	42	8	2	0	15	7	OF-53
8 yrs.	742	.292	.398	2603	761	117	62	11	332	132	OF-692, SS-10, 2B-5, 3B-1

Lou Criger

LOUIS CRIGER BR TR
B. Feb. 3, 1872, Elkhart, Ind. 5' 10" 165 lbs.
D. May 14, 1934, Tucson, Ariz.

Year	Gms.	BA	SA	AB	H	2B	3B	HR	RBI	SB	G. by Pos
1910	27	.188	.217	69	13	2	0	0	4	0	C-27

Herb Crompton

HERBERT BRYAN CROMPTON BR TR
B. Nov. 7, 1911, Taylor Ridge, Ill. 6' 185 lbs.
D. Aug. 5, 1963, Moline, Ill.

Year	Gms.	BA	SA	AB	H	2B	3B	HR	RBI	SB	G. by Pos
1945	36	.192	.222	99	19	3	0	0	12	0	C-33

Frankie Crosetti

FRANK PETER JOSEPH CROSETTI BR TR
B. Oct. 4, 1910, San Francisco, Calif. 5' 10" 165 lbs.

Year	Gms.	BA	SA	AB	H	2B	3B	HR	RBI	SB	G. by Pos
1932	115	.241	.374	398	96	20	9	5	57	3	SS-83, 3B-33, 2B-1
1933	136	.253	.379	451	114	20	5	9	60	4	SS-133
1934	138	.265	.401	554	147	22	10	11	67	5	SS-119, 3B-23, 2B-1
1935	87	.256	.430	305	78	17	6	8	50	3	SS-87
1936	151	.288	.437	632	182	35	7	15	78	18	SS-151
1937	149	.234	.352	611	143	29	5	11	49	13	SS-147
1938	157	.263	.371	631	166	35	3	9	55	27	SS-157
1939	152	.233	.332	656	153	25	5	10	56	11	SS-152
1940	145	.194	.273	546	106	23	4	4	31	14	SS-145
1941	50	.223	.284	148	33	2	1	1	22	0	SS-32, 3B-13
1942	74	.242	.337	285	69	5	5	4	23	1	3B-62, SS-8, 2B-2
1943	95	.233	.279	348	81	8	1	2	20	4	SS-90
1944	55	.239	.355	197	47	4	2	5	30	3	SS-55
1945	130	.238	.293	441	105	12	0	4	48	7	SS-126
1946	28	.288	.339	59	17	3	0	0	3	0	SS-24
1947	3	.000	.000	1	0	0	0	0	0	0	2B-1, SS-1
1948	17	.286	.429	14	4	0	1	0	0	0	2B-6, SS-5
17 yrs.	1682	.245	.354	6277	1541	260	65	98	649	113	SS-1515, 3B-131, 2B-11

World Series

Year	Gms.	BA	SA	AB	H	2B	3B	HR	RBI	SB	G. by Pos
1932	4	.133	.200	15	2	1	0	0	0	0	SS-4
1936	6	.269	.346	26	7	2	0	0	3	0	SS-6
1937	5	.048	.048	21	1	0	0	0	0	0	SS-5
1938	4	.250	.688	16	4	1	1	1	6	0	SS-4
1939	4	.063	.063	16	1	0	0	0	1	0	SS-4
1942	1	.000	.000	3	0	0	0	0	0	0	3B-1
1943	5	.278	.278	18	5	0	0	0	1	1	SS-5
7 yrs.	29	.174	.261	115	20	5	1	1	11	1	SS-28, 3B-1

Jose Cruz

JOSE CRUZ BL TL
B. Aug. 8, 1947, Arroyo, Puerto Rico 6' 170 lbs.

Year	Gms.	BA	SA	AB	H	2B	3B	HR	RBI	SB	G. by Pos
1988	38	.200	.263	80	16	2	0	1	7	0	DH-12, OF-8

Roy Cullenbine

ROY JOSEPH CULLENBINE BB TR
B. Oct. 18, 1913, Nashville, Tenn. 6' 1" 195 lbs.
D. May 28, 1991, Mt. Clemens, Mich.

Year	Gms.	BA	SA	AB	H	2B	3B	HR	RBI	SB	G. by Pos
1942	21	.364	.532	77	28	7	0	2	17	0	OF-19, 1B-1

World Series

Year	Gms.	BA	SA	AB	H	2B	3B	HR	RBI	SB	G. by Pos
1942	5	.263	.316	19	5	1	0	0	2	1	OF-5

Nick Cullop

HENRY NICHOLAS CULLOP BR TR
B. Oct. 16, 1900, St. Louis, Mo. 6' 200 lbs.
D. Dec. 8, 1978, Gahanna, Ohio

Year	Gms.	BA	SA	AB	H	2B	3B	HR	RBI	SB	G. by Pos
1926	2	.500	.500	2	1	0	0	0	0	0	

Jim Curry

JAMES L. CURRY BR TR
B. Mar. 10, 1893, Camden, N.J. 5' 11" 160 lbs.
D. Sep. 2, 1938, Grenloch, N.J.

Year	Gms.	BA	SA	AB	H	2B	3B	HR	RBI	SB	G. by Pos
1911	4	.182	.182	11	2	0	0	0	0	0	2B-4

Fred Curtis

FREDERICK MARION CURTIS BR TR
B. Oct. 30, 1880, Beaver Lake, Mich. 6' 1" lbs.
D. Apr. 5, 1939, Minneapolis, Minn.

Year	Gms.	BA	SA	AB	H	2B	3B	HR	RBI	SB	G. by Pos
1905	2	.222	.333	9	2	1	0	0	2	1	1B-2

Babe Dahlgren

ELLSWORTH TENNEY DAHLGREN BR TR
B. Jun. 15, 1912, San Francisco, Calif. 6' 190 lbs.
D. Sep. 4, 1996, Arcadia, Calif.

Year	Gms.	BA	SA	AB	H	2B	3B	HR	RBI	SB	G. by Pos
1937	1	.000	.000	1	0	0	0	0	0	0	
1938	29	.186	.209	43	8	1	0	0	1	0	3B-8, 1B-6
1939	144	.235	.377	531	125	18	6	15	89	2	1B-144
1940	155	.264	.384	568	150	24	4	12	73	1	1B-155
4 yrs.	329	.248	.374	1143	283	43	10	27	163	3	1B-305, 3B-8

World Series

Year	Gms.	BA	SA	AB	H	2B	3B	HR	RBI	SB	G. by Pos
1939	4	.214	.571	14	3	2	0	1	2	0	1B-4

Tom Daley

THOMAS FRANCIS DALEY BL TR
B. Nov. 13, 1884, Du Bois, Pa. 5' 5" 168 lbs.
D. Dec. 2, 1934, Los Angeles, Calif.

Year	Gms.	BA	SA	AB	H	2B	3B	HR	RBI	SB	G. by Pos
1914	67	.251	.325	191	48	6	4	0	9	8	OF-57
1915	10	.250	.250	8	2	0	0	0	1	1	OF-2
2 yrs.	77	.251	.322	199	50	6	4	0	10	9	OF-59

Bert Daniels

BERNARD ELMER DANIELS BR TR
B. Oct. 31, 1882, Danville, Ill. 5' 9½" 180 lbs.
D. Jun. 6, 1958, Cedar Grove, N.J.

Year	Gms.	BA	SA	AB	H	2B	3B	HR	RBI	SB	G. by Pos
1910	95	.253	.343	356	90	13	8	1	17	41	OF-85, 3B-6, 1B-4
1911	131	.286	.372	462	132	16	9	2	31	40	OF-120
1912	133	.274	.381	496	136	25	11	2	41	37	OF-131
1913	93	.216	.287	320	69	13	5	0	22	27	OF-87
4 yrs.	452	.261	.352	1634	427	67	33	5	111	145	OF-423, 3B-6, 1B-4

Kiddo Davis

GEORGE WILLIS DAVIS BR TR
B. Feb. 12, 1902, Bridgeport, Conn. 5' 11" 178 lbs.
D. Mar. 4, 1983, Bridgeport, Conn.

Year	Gms.	BA	SA	AB	H	2B	3B	HR	RBI	SB	G. by Pos
1926	1	—	—	0	0	0	0	0	0	0	OF-1

Lefty Davis

ALFONZO DEFORD DAVIS BL TL
B. Feb. 4, 1875, Nashville, Tenn. 5' 10" 170 lbs.
D. Feb. 7, 1919, Collins, N.Y.

Year	Gms.	BA	SA	AB	H	2B	3B	HR	RBI	SB	G. by Pos
1903	104	.237	.263	372	88	10	0	0	25	11	OF-102, SS-1

Russ Davis

RUSSELL STUART DAVIS BR TR
B. Sep. 13, 1969, Birmingham, Ala. 6' 170 lbs.

Year	Gms.	BA	SA	AB	H	2B	3B	HR	RBI	SB	G. by Pos
1994	4	.143	.143	14	2	0	0	0	1	0	3B-4
1995	40	.276	.429	98	27	5	2	2	12	0	3B-34, DH-4, 1B-2
2 yrs.	44	.259	.393	112	29	5	2	2	13	0	3B-38, DH-4, 1B-2

Divisional Playoffs

Year	Gms.	BA	SA	AB	H	2B	3B	HR	RBI	SB	G. by Pos
1995	2	.200	.200	5	1	0	0	0	0	0	3B-2

Brian Dayett

BRIAN KELLY DAYETT BR TR
B. Jan. 22, 1957, New London, Conn. 5' 10" 180 lbs.

Year	Gms.	BA	SA	AB	H	2B	3B	HR	RBI	SB	G. by Pos
1983	11	.207	.276	29	6	0	1	0	5	0	OF-9
1984	64	.244	.409	127	31	9	0	4	23	0	OF-62, DH-1
2 yrs.	75	.237	.385	156	37	9	1	4	28	0	OF-71, DH-1

Joe De Maestri

JOSEPH PAUL DE MAESTRI BR TR
B. Dec. 9, 1928, San Francisco, Calif. 6' 170 lbs.

Year	Gms.	BA	SA	AB	H	2B	3B	HR	RBI	SB	G. by Pos
1960	49	.229	.257	35	8	1	0	0	2	0	2B-19, SS-17
1961	30	.146	.146	41	6	0	0	0	2	0	SS-18, 2B-5, 3B-4
2 yrs.	79	.184	.197	76	14	1	0	0	4	0	SS-35, 2B-24, 3B-4

Joe De Maestri *continued*

World Series

Year	Gms.	BA	SA	AB	H	2B	3B	HR	RBI	SB	G. by Pos
1960	4	.500	.500	2	1	0	0	0	0	0	SS-3

Ivan DeJesus

IVAN DEJESUS BR TR
Jan. 9, 1953, Santurce, Puerto Rico 5' 11" 175 lbs.

Year	Gms.	BA	SA	AB	H	2B	3B	HR	RBI	SB	G. by Pos
1986	7	.000	.000	4	0	0	0	0	0	0	SS-7

Al DeVormer

ALBERT E. DEVORMER BR TR
B. Aug. 19, 1891, Grand Rapids, Mich. 6' ½" 175 lbs.
D. Aug. 29, 1966, Grand Rapids, Mich.

Year	Gms.	BA	SA	AB	H	2B	3B	HR	RBI	SB	G. by Pos
1921	22	.347	.429	49	17	4	0	0	7	2	C-17
1922	24	.203	.305	59	12	4	1	0	11	0	C-17, 1B-1
2 yrs.	46	.269	.361	108	29	8	1	0	18	2	C-34, 1B-1

World Series

Year	Gms.	BA	SA	AB	H	2B	3B	HR	RBI	SB	G. by Pos
1921	2	.000	.000	1	0	0	0	0	0	0	C-1

Jim Deidel

JAMES LAWRENCE DEIDEL BR TR
B. Jun. 6, 1949, Denver, Colo. 6' 2" 195 lbs.

Year	Gms.	BA	SA	AB	H	2B	3B	HR	RBI	SB	G. by Pos
1974	2	.000	.000	2	0	0	0	0	0	0	C-2

Bobby Del Greco

ROBERT GEORGE DEL GRECO BR TR
B. Apr. 7, 1933, Pittsburgh, Pa. 5' 10½" 185 lbs.

Year	Gms.	BA	SA	AB	H	2B	3B	HR	RBI	SB	G. by Pos
1957	8	.429	.429	7	3	0	0	0	0	1	OF-6
1958	12	.200	.200	5	1	0	0	0	0	0	OF-12
2 yrs.	20	.333	.333	12	4	0	0	0	0	1	OF-18

Frank Delahanty

FRANK GEORGE DELAHANTY BR TR
B. Jan. 29, 1883, Cleveland, Ohio 5' 9" 160 lbs.
D. Jul. 22, 1966, Cleveland, Ohio

Year	Gms.	BA	SA	AB	H	2B	3B	HR	RBI	SB	G. by Pos
1905	9	.222	.259	27	6	1	0	0	2	0	1B-5, OF-3
1906	92	.238	.345	307	73	11	8	2	41	11	OF-92
1908	37	.256	.296	125	32	1	2	0	10	9	OF-36
3 yrs.	138	.242	.327	459	111	13	10	2	53	20	OF-131, 1B-5

Jim Delsing

JAMES HENRY DELSING BL TR
B. Nov. 13, 1925, Rudolph, Wis. 5' 10" 175 lbs.

Year	Gms.	BA	SA	AB	H	2B	3B	HR	RBI	SB	G. by Pos
1949	9	.350	.550	20	7	1	0	1	3	0	OF-5
1950	12	.400	.400	10	4	0	0	0	2	0	
2 yrs.	21	.367	.500	30	11	1	0	1	5	0	

Ray Demmitt

CHARLES RAYMOND DEMMITT BL TR
B. Feb. 2, 1884, Illiopolis, Ill. 5' 8½" 170 lbs.
D. Feb. 19, 1956, Glen Ellyn, Ill.

Year	Gms.	BA	SA	AB	H	2B	3B	HR	RBI	SB	G. by Pos
1909	123	.246	.358	427	105	12	12	4	30	16	OF-109

Rick Dempsey

JOHN RIKARD DEMPSEY BR TR
B. Sep. 13, 1949, Fayetteville, Tenn. 6' 180 lbs.

Year	Gms.	BA	SA	AB	H	2B	3B	HR	RBI	SB	G. by Pos
1973	6	.182	.182	11	2	0	0	0	0	0	C-5
1974	43	.239	.321	109	26	3	0	2	12	1	C-31, OF-2, DH-1
1975	71	.262	.338	145	38	8	0	1	11	0	C-19, DH-18, OF-8, 3B-1
1976	21	.119	.119	42	5	0	0	0	2	0	C-9, OF-4
4 yrs.	141	.231	.296	307	71	11	0	3	25	1	C-64, DH-19, OF-14, 3B-1

Bucky Dent

RUSSELL EARL DENT BR TR
B. Nov. 25, 1951, Savannah, Ga. 5' 9" 170 lbs.

Year	Gms.	BA	SA	AB	H	2B	3B	HR	RBI	SB	G. by Pos
1977	158	.247	.352	477	118	18	4	8	49	1	SS-157
1978	123	.243	.317	379	92	11	1	5	40	3	SS-123
1979	141	.230	.285	431	99	14	2	2	32	0	SS-141
1980	141	.262	.354	489	128	26	2	5	52	0	SS-141
1981	73	.238	.379	227	54	11	0	7	27	0	SS-73
1982	59	.169	.188	160	27	1	1	0	9	0	SS-58
6 yrs.	695	.239	.324	2163	518	81	10	27	209	4	SS-693

Year	Gms.	BA	SA	AB	H	2B	3B	HR	RBI	SB	G. by Pos

Bucky Dent *continued*

League Championship Series

Year	Gms.	BA	SA	AB	H	2B	3B	HR	RBI	SB	G. by Pos
1977	5	.214	.286	14	3	1	0	0	2	0	SS-5
1978	4	.200	.200	15	3	0	0	0	4	0	SS-4
1980	3	.182	.182	11	2	0	0	0	0	0	SS-3
3 yrs.	12	.200	.225	40	8	1	0	0	6	0	SS-12

World Series

Year	Gms.	BA	SA	AB	H	2B	3B	HR	RBI	SB	G. by Pos
1977	6	.263	.263	19	5	0	0	0	2	0	SS-6
1978	6	.417	.458	24	10	1	0	0	7	0	SS-6
2 yrs.	12	.349	.372	43	15	1	0	0	9	0	SS-12

Claud Derrick

CLAUD LESTER DERRICK BR TR
B. Jun. 11, 1886, Burton, Ga. 6' 175 lbs.
D. Jul. 15, 1974, Clayton, Ga.

Year	Gms.	BA	SA	AB	H	2B	3B	HR	RBI	SB	G. by Pos
1913	22	.292	.354	65	19	1	0	1	7	2	SS-13, 3B-4, 2B-2

Russ Derry

ALVA RUSSELL DERRY BL TR
B. Oct. 7, 1916, Princeton, Mo. 6' 1" 180 lbs.

Year	Gms.	BA	SA	AB	H	2B	3B	HR	RBI	SB	G. by Pos
1944	38	.254	.386	114	29	3	0	4	14	1	OF-28
1945	78	.225	.419	253	57	6	2	13	45	1	OF-68
2 yrs.	116	.234	.409	367	86	9	2	17	59	2	OF-96

Orestes Destrade

ORESTES DESTRADE BB TR
B. May. 8, 1962, Santiago de Cuba, 6' 4" 210 lbs.
Cuba

Year	Gms.	BA	SA	AB	H	2B	3B	HR	RBI	SB	G. by Pos
1987	9	.263	.263	19	5	0	0	0	1	0	1B-3, DH-2

Joe DiMaggio

JOSEPH PAUL DIMAGGIO BR TR
B. Nov. 25, 1914, Martinez, Calif. 6' 2" 193 lbs.
Hall of Fame 1955

Year	Gms.	BA	SA	AB	H	2B	3B	HR	RBI	SB	G. by Pos
1936	138	.323	.576	637	206	44	15	29	125	4	OF-138
1937	151	.346	.673	621	215	35	15	46	167	3	OF-150
1938	145	.324	.581	599	194	32	13	32	140	6	OF-145
1939	120	.381	.671	462	176	32	6	30	126	3	OF-117
1940	132	.352	.626	508	179	28	9	31	133	1	OF-130
1941	139	.357	.643	541	193	43	11	30	125	4	OF-139
1942	154	.305	.498	610	186	29	13	21	114	4	OF-154
1946	132	.290	.511	503	146	20	8	25	95	1	OF-131
1947	141	.315	.522	534	168	31	10	20	97	3	OF-139
1948	153	.320	.598	594	190	26	11	39	155	1	OF-152
1949	76	.346	.596	272	94	14	6	14	67	0	OF-76
1950	139	.301	.585	525	158	33	10	32	122	0	OF-137, 1B-1
1951	116	.263	.422	415	109	22	4	12	71	0	OF-113
13 yrs.	1736	.325	.579	6821	2214	389	131	361	1537	30	OF-1721, 1B-1

World Series

Year	Gms.	BA	SA	AB	H	2B	3B	HR	RBI	SB	G. by Pos
1936	6	.346	.462	26	9	3	0	0	3	0	OF-6
1937	5	.273	.409	22	6	0	0	1	4	0	OF-5
1938	4	.267	.467	15	4	0	0	1	2	0	OF-4
1939	4	.313	.500	16	5	0	0	1	3	0	OF-4
1941	5	.263	.263	19	5	0	0	0	1	0	OF-5
1942	5	.333	.333	21	7	0	0	0	3	0	OF-5
1947	7	.231	.462	26	6	0	0	2	5	0	OF-7
1949	5	.111	.278	18	2	0	0	1	2	0	OF-5
1950	4	.308	.615	13	4	1	0	1	2	0	OF-4
1951	6	.261	.478	23	6	2	0	1	5	0	OF-6
10 yrs.	51	.271	.422	199	54	6	0	8	30	0	OF-51

Bill Dickey

WILLIAM MALCOLM DICKEY BL TR
B. Jun. 6, 1907, Bastrop, La. 6' 1½" 185 lbs.
D. Nov. 12, 1993, Little Rock, Ark.
Hall of Fame 1954

Year	Gms.	BA	SA	AB	H	2B	3B	HR	RBI	SB	G. by Pos
1928	10	.200	.400	15	3	1	1	0	2	0	C-10
1929	130	.324	.485	447	145	30	6	10	65	4	C-127
1930	109	.339	.486	366	124	25	7	5	65	7	C-101
1931	130	.327	.442	477	156	17	10	6	78	2	C-125
1932	108	.310	.482	423	131	20	4	15	84	2	C-108
1933	130	.318	.490	478	152	24	8	14	97	3	C-127
1934	104	.322	.494	395	127	24	4	12	72	0	C-104

Bill Dickey *continued*

Year	Gms.	BA	SA	AB	H	2B	3B	HR	RBI	SB	G. by Pos
1935	120	.279	.458	448	125	26	6	14	81	1	C-118
1936	112	.362	.617	423	153	26	8	22	107	0	C-107
1937	140	.332	.570	530	176	35	2	29	133	3	C-137
1938	132	.313	.568	454	142	27	4	27	115	3	C-126
1939	128	.302	.512	480	145	23	3	24	105	5	C-126
1940	106	.247	.355	372	92	11	1	9	54	0	C-102
1941	109	.284	.417	348	99	15	5	7	71	2	C-104
1942	82	.295	.373	268	79	13	1	2	37	2	C-80
1943	85	.351	.492	242	85	18	2	4	33	2	C-71
1946	54	.261	.366	134	35	8	0	2	10	0	C-39
17 yrs.	1789	.313	.486	6300	1969	343	72	202	1209	36	C-1712

World Series

Year	Gms.	BA	SA	AB	H	2B	3B	HR	RBI	SB	G. by Pos
1932	4	.438	.438	16	7	0	0	0	4	0	C-4
1936	6	.120	.240	25	3	0	0	1	5	0	C-6
1937	5	.211	.316	19	4	0	1	0	3	0	C-5
1938	4	.400	.600	15	6	0	0	1	2	1	C-4
1939	4	.267	.667	15	4	0	0	2	5	0	C-4
1941	5	.167	.222	18	3	1	0	0	1	0	C-5
1942	5	.263	.263	19	5	0	0	0	0	0	C-5
1943	5	.278	.444	18	5	0	0	1	4	0	C-5
8 yrs.	38	.255	.379	145	37	1	1	5	24	1	C-38

Kerry Dineen

KERRY MICHAEL DINEEN BL TL
B. Jul. 1, 1952, Englewood, N. J. 5' 11" 165 lbs.

Year	Gms.	BA	SA	AB	H	2B	3B	HR	RBI	SB	G. by Pos
1975	7	.364	.409	22	8	1	0	0	1	0	OF-7
1976	4	.286	.286	7	2	0	0	0	1	1	OF-4
2 yrs.	11	.345	.379	29	10	1	0	0	2	1	OF-11

Cozy Dolan

ALBERT J. DOLAN BR TR
B. Dec. 23, 1889, Chicago, Ill. 5' 10" 160 lbs.
D. Dec. 10, 1958, Chicago, Ill.

Year	Gms.	BA	SA	AB	H	2B	3B	HR	RBI	SB	G. by Pos
1911	19	.304	.420	69	21	1	2	1	6	12	3B-19
1912	17	.200	.317	60	12	1	3	0	11	5	3B-17
2 yrs.	36	.256	.372	129	33	2	5	1	17	17	3B-36

Mike Donovan

MICHAEL BERCHMAN DONOVAN BR TR
B. Oct. 18, 1881, Brooklyn, N. Y. 5' 8" 155 lbs.
D. Feb. 3, 1938, New York, N. Y.

Year	Gms.	BA	SA	AB	H	2B	3B	HR	RBI	SB	G. by Pos
1908	5	.263	.316	19	5	1	0	0	2	0	3B-5

Brian Dorsett

BRIAN RICHARD DORSETT BR TR
B. Apr. 9, 1961, Terre Haute, Ind. 6' 3" 215 lbs.

Year	Gms.	BA	SA	AB	H	2B	3B	HR	RBI	SB	G. by Pos
1989	8	.364	.409	22	8	1	0	0	4	0	C-8
1990	14	.143	.200	35	5	2	0	0	0	0	C-9, DH-5
2 yrs.	22	.228	.281	57	13	3	0	0	4	0	C-17, DH-5

Patsy Dougherty

PATRICK HENRY DOUGHERTY BL TR
B. Oct. 27, 1876, Andover, N. Y. 6' 2" 190 lbs.
D. Apr. 30, 1940, Bolivar, N. Y.

Year	Gms.	BA	SA	AB	H	2B	3B	HR	RBI	SB	G. by Pos
1904	106	.283	.396	452	128	13	10	6	22	11	OF-106
1905	116	.263	.335	418	110	9	6	3	29	17	OF-108, 3B-1
1906	12	.192	.231	52	10	2	0	0	4	0	OF-12
3 yrs.	234	.269	.359	922	248	24	16	9	55	28	OF-226, 3B-1

John Dowd

JOHN LEO DOWD BR TR
B. Jan. 3, 1891, Weymouth, Mass. 5' 8" 170 lbs.
D. Jan. 31, 1981, Fort Lauderdale, Fla.

Year	Gms.	BA	SA	AB	H	2B	3B	HR	RBI	SB	G. by Pos
1912	10	.194	.226	31	6	1	0	0	0	0	SS-10

Brian Doyle

BRIAN REED DOYLE BL TR
B. Jan. 26, 1955, Glasgow, Ky. 5' 10" 160 lbs.

Year	Gms.	BA	SA	AB	H	2B	3B	HR	RBI	SB	G. by Pos
1978	39	.192	.192	52	10	0	0	0	0	0	2B-29, SS-7, 3B-5
1979	20	.125	.188	32	4	2	0	0	5	0	2B-13, 3B-6
1980	34	.173	.227	75	13	1	0	1	5	1	2B-20, SS-12, 3B-2
3 yrs.	93	.170	.208	159	27	3	0	1	10	1	2B-62, SS-19, 3B-13

Year	Gms.	BA	SA	AB	H	2B	3B	HR	RBI	SB	G. by Pos

Brian Doyle *continued*

League Championship Series
Year	Gms.	BA	SA	AB	H	2B	3B	HR	RBI	SB	G. by Pos
1978	3	.286	.286	7	2	0	0	0	1	0	2B-3

World Series
Year	Gms.	BA	SA	AB	H	2B	3B	HR	RBI	SB	G. by Pos
1978	6	.438	.500	16	7	1	0	0	2	0	2B-6

Jack Doyle

JOHN JOSEPH DOYLE   BR TR
B. Oct. 25, 1869, Killorglin, Ireland 5' 9" 155 lbs.
D. Dec. 31, 1958, Holyoke, Mass.

Year	Gms.	BA	SA	AB	H	2B	3B	HR	RBI	SB	G. by Pos
1905	1	.000	.000	3	0	0	0	0	0	0	1B-1

Bill Drescher

WILLIAM CLAYTON DRESCHER   BL TR
B. May 23, 1921, Congers, N. Y.   6' 2" 190 lbs.
D. May 15, 1968, Haverstraw, N. Y.

Year	Gms.	BA	SA	AB	H	2B	3B	HR	RBI	SB	G. by Pos
1944	4	.143	.143	7	1	0	0	0	0	0	C-1
1945	48	.270	.310	126	34	3	1	0	15	0	C-33
1946	5	.333	.500	6	2	1	0	0	1	0	C-3
3 yrs.	57	.266	.309	139	37	4	1	0	16	0	C-37

Joe Dugan

JOSEPH ANTHONY DUGAN   BR TR
B. May 12, 1897, Mahanoy City, Pa. 5' 11" 160 lbs.
D. Jul. 7, 1982, Norwood, Mass.

Year	Gms.	BA	SA	AB	H	2B	3B	HR	RBI	SB	G. by Pos
1922	60	.286	.365	252	72	9	1	3	25	1	3B-60
1923	146	.283	.384	644	182	30	7	7	67	4	3B-146
1924	148	.302	.390	610	184	31	7	3	56	1	3B-148, 2B-2
1925	102	.292	.359	404	118	19	4	0	31	2	3B-96
1926	123	.288	.362	434	125	19	5	1	64	2	3B-122
1927	112	.269	.362	387	104	24	3	2	43	1	3B-111
1928	94	.276	.381	312	86	15	0	6	34	1	3B-91
7 yrs.	785	.286	.374	3043	871	147	27	22	320	12	3B-774, 2B-2

World Series
Year	Gms.	BA	SA	AB	H	2B	3B	HR	RBI	SB	G. by Pos
1922	5	.250	.300	20	5	1	0	0	0	0	3B-5
1923	6	.280	.560	25	7	2	1	1	5	0	3B-6
1926	7	.333	.375	24	8	1	0	0	2	0	3B-7
1927	4	.200	.200	15	3	0	0	0	0	0	3B-4
1928	3	.167	.167	6	1	0	0	0	1	0	3B-3
5 yrs.	25	.267	.367	90	24	4	1	1	8	0	3B-25

Mariano Duncan

MARIANO DUNCAN   BR TR
B. Mar. 13, 1963, San Pedro de Macoris, 6' 165 lbs.
Dominican Republic

Year	Gms.	BA	SA	AB	H	2B	3B	HR	RBI	SB	G. by Pos
1996	109	.340	.500	400	136	34	3	8	56	4	2B-104, 3B-3, OF-3, DH-2

Divisional Playoffs
Year	Gms.	BA	SA	AB	H	2B	3B	HR	RBI	SB	G. by Pos
1996	4	.313	.313	16	5	0	0	0	3	0	2B-4

League Championship Series
Year	Gms.	BA	SA	AB	H	2B	3B	HR	RBI	SB	G. by Pos
1996	4	.200	.333	15	3	2	0	0	0	0	2B-4

World Series
Year	Gms.	BA	SA	AB	H	2B	3B	HR	RBI	SB	G. by Pos
1996	6	.053	.053	19	1	0	0	0	0	1	2B-6

Leo Durocher

LEO ERNEST DUROCHER   BR TR
B. Jul. 27, 1905, W. Springfield, Mass. 5' 10" 160 lbs.
D. Oct. 7, 1991, Palm Springs, Calif.
Hall of Fame 1994

Year	Gms.	BA	SA	AB	H	2B	3B	HR	RBI	SB	G. by Pos
1925	2	.000	.000	1	0	0	0	0	0	0	
1928	102	.270	.338	296	80	8	6	0	31	1	2B-66, SS-29
1929	106	.246	.287	341	84	4	5	0	32	3	SS-93, 2B-12
3 yrs.	210	.257	.310	638	164	12	11	0	63	4	SS-122, 2B-78

World Series
Year	Gms.	BA	SA	AB	H	2B	3B	HR	RBI	SB	G. by Pos
1928	4	.000	.000	2	0	0	0	0	0	0	2B-4

Cedric Durst

CEDRIC MONTGOMERY DURST   BL TL
B. Aug. 23, 1896, Austin, Tex.   5' 11" 160 lbs.
D. Feb. 16, 1971, San Diego, Calif.

Year	Gms.	BA	SA	AB	H	2B	3B	HR	RBI	SB	G. by Pos
1927	65	.248	.326	129	32	4	3	0	25	0	OF-36, 1B-2
1928	74	.252	.326	135	34	2	1	2	10	1	OF-33, 1B-3

Cedric Durst *continued*

Year	Gms.	BA	SA	AB	H	2B	3B	HR	RBI	SB	G. by Pos
1929	92	.257	.361	202	52	3	3	4	31	3	OF-72, 1B-1
1930	8	.158	.211	19	3	1	0	0	5	0	OF-8
4 yrs.	239	.249	.336	485	121	10	7	6	71	4	OF-149, 1B-6

World Series
Year	Gms.	BA	SA	AB	H	2B	3B	HR	RBI	SB	G. by Pos
1927	1	.000	.000	1	0	0	0	0	0	0	
1928	4	.375	.750	8	3	0	0	1	2	0	OF-4
2 yrs.	5	.333	.667	9	3	0	0	1	2	0	OF-4

Mike Easler

MICHAEL ANTHONY EASLER   BL TR
B. Nov. 29, 1950, Cleveland, Ohio   6' 190 lbs.

Year	Gms.	BA	SA	AB	H	2B	3B	HR	RBI	SB	G. by Pos
1986	146	.302	.449	490	148	26	2	14	78	3	DH-129, OF-11
1987	65	.281	.389	167	47	6	0	4	21	1	DH-32, OF-15
2 yrs.	211	.297	.434	657	195	32	2	18	99	4	DH-161, OF-26

Doc Edwards

HOWARD RODNEY EDWARDS   BR TR
B. Dec. 10, 1936, Red Jacket, W. Va.   6' 2" 215 lbs.

Year	Gms.	BA	SA	AB	H	2B	3B	HR	RBI	SB	G. by Pos
1965	45	.190	.250	100	19	3	0	1	9	1	C-43

Robert Eenhoorn

ROBERT EENHOORN   BR TR
Feb. 9, 1968, Rotterdam, Netherlands 6' 3" 170 lbs.

Year	Gms.	BA	SA	AB	H	2B	3B	HR	RBI	SB	G. by Pos
1994	3	.500	.750	4	2	1	0	0	0	0	SS-3
1995	5	.143	.214	14	2	1	0	0	2	0	2B-3, SS-2
1996	12	.071	.071	14	1	0	0	0	2	0	2B-10, 3B-2
3 yrs.	20	.156	.219	32	5	2	0	0	4	0	2B-13, SS-5, 3B-2

Kid Elberfeld

NORMAN ARTHUR ELBERFELD   BR TR
B. Apr. 13, 1875, Pomeroy, Ohio   5' 7" 158 lbs.
D. Jan. 13, 1944, Chattanooga, Tenn.

Year	Gms.	BA	SA	AB	H	2B	3B	HR	RBI	SB	G. by Pos
1903	90	.287	.367	349	100	18	5	0	45	16	SS-90
1904	122	.263	.328	445	117	13	5	2	46	18	SS-122
1905	111	.262	.318	390	102	18	2	0	53	18	SS-108
1906	99	.306	.384	346	106	11	5	2	31	19	SS-98
1907	120	.271	.336	447	121	17	6	0	51	22	SS-118
1908	19	.196	.250	56	11	3	0	0	5	1	SS-17
1909	106	.237	.288	379	90	9	5	0	26	23	SS-61, 3B-43
7 yrs.	667	.268	.333	2412	647	89	28	4	257	117	SS-614, 3B-43

Gene Elliott

EUGENE BIRMINGHOUSE ELLIOTT BL TR
B. Feb. 8, 1889, Fayette City, Pa.   5' 7" 150 lbs.
D. Jan. 5, 1976, Huntingdon, Pa.

Year	Gms.	BA	SA	AB	H	2B	3B	HR	RBI	SB	G. by Pos
1911	5	.077	.154	13	1	1	0	0	1	0	OF-2, 3B-1

John Ellis

JOHN CHARLES ELLIS   BR TR
B. Aug. 21, 1948, New London, Conn. 6' 2½" 225 lbs.

Year	Gms.	BA	SA	AB	H	2B	3B	HR	RBI	SB	G. by Pos
1969	22	.290	.403	62	18	4	0	1	8	0	C-15
1970	78	.248	.403	226	56	12	1	7	29	0	1B-53, 3B-5, C-2
1971	83	.244	.340	238	58	12	1	3	34	0	1B-65, C-2
1972	52	.294	.456	136	40	5	1	5	25	0	C-25, 1B-8
4 yrs.	235	.260	.391	662	172	33	3	16	96	0	1B-126, C-44, 3B-5

Kevin Elster

KEVIN DANIEL ELSTER   BR TR
B. Aug. 3, 1964, San Pedro, Calif.   6' 2" 180 lbs.

Year	Gms.	BA	SA	AB	H	2B	3B	HR	RBI	SB	G. by Pos
1994	7	.000	.000	20	0	0	0	0	0	0	SS-7
1995	10	.118	.176	17	2	1	0	0	0	0	SS-10, 2B-1
2 yrs.	17	.054	.081	37	2	1	0	0	0	0	SS-17, 2B-1

Clyde Engle

ARTHUR CLYDE ENGLE   BR TR
B. Mar. 19, 1884, Dayton, Ohio   5' 10" 190 lbs.
D. Dec. 26, 1939, Boston, Mass.

Year	Gms.	BA	SA	AB	H	2B	3B	HR	RBI	SB	G. by Pos
1909	135	.278	.358	492	137	20	5	3	71	18	OF-134
1910	5	.231	.231	13	3	0	0	0	0	1	OF-3
2 yrs.	140	.277	.354	505	140	20	5	3	71	19	OF-137

Year	Gms.	BA	SA	AB	H	2B	3B	HR	RBI	SB	G. by Pos

Juan Espino

JUAN ESPINO
B. Mar. 16, 1956, Bonao, Dominican Republic
BR TR 6' 1" 190 lbs.

Year	Gms.	BA	SA	AB	H	2B	3B	HR	RBI	SB	G. by Pos
1982	3	.000	.000	2	0	0	0	0	0	0	C-3
1983	10	.261	.391	23	6	0	0	1	3	0	C-10
1985	9	.364	.364	11	4	0	0	0	0	0	C-9
1986	27	.162	.216	37	6	2	0	0	5	0	C-27
4 yrs.	49	.219	.288	73	16	2	0	1	8	0	C-49

Alvaro Espinoza

ALVARO ALBERTO ESPINOZA
B. Feb. 19, 1962, Valencia, Venezuela
BR TR 6' 160 lbs.

Year	Gms.	BA	SA	AB	H	2B	3B	HR	RBI	SB	G. by Pos
1988	3	.000	.000	3	0	0	0	0	0	0	2B-2, SS-1
1989	146	.282	.332	503	142	23	1	0	41	3	SS-146
1990	150	.224	.274	438	98	12	2	2	20	1	SS-150
1991	148	.256	.344	480	123	23	2	5	33	4	SS-147, 3B-2, P-1
4 yrs.	447	.255	.317	1424	363	58	5	7	94	8	SS-444, 2B-2, 3B-2, P-1

Nick Etten

NICHOLAS RAYMOND THOMAS ETTEN
B. Sep. 19, 1913, Spring Grove, Ill.
D. Oct. 18, 1990, Hinsdale, Ill.
BL TL 6' 2" 198 lbs.

Year	Gms.	BA	SA	AB	H	2B	3B	HR	RBI	SB	G. by Pos
1943	154	.271	.420	583	158	35	5	14	107	3	1B-154
1944	154	.293	.466	573	168	25	4	22	91	4	1B-154
1945	152	.285	.437	565	161	24	4	18	111	2	1B-152
1946	108	.232	.365	323	75	14	1	9	49	0	1B-84
4 yrs.	568	.275	.429	2044	562	98	14	63	358	9	1B-544
World Series											
1943	5	.105	.105	19	2	0	0	0	2	0	1B-5

Barry Evans

BARRY STEVEN EVANS
B. Nov. 30, 1955, Atlanta, Ga.
BR TR 6' 1" 185 lbs.

Year	Gms.	BA	SA	AB	H	2B	3B	HR	RBI	SB	G. by Pos
1982	17	.258	.355	31	8	3	0	0	2	0	2B-8, 3B-6, SS-4

Charlie Fallon

CHARLES AUGUSTUS FALLON
B. Mar. 7, 1881, New York, N. Y.
D. Jun. 10, 1960, King's Park, N. Y.
BR TR 5' 6" lbs.

Year	Gms.	BA	SA	AB	H	2B	3B	HR	RBI	SB	G. by Pos
1905	1	—	—	0	0	0	0	0	0	0	

Doc Farrell

EDWARD STEPHEN FARRELL
B. Dec. 26, 1901, Johnson City, N. Y.
D. Dec. 20, 1966, Livingston, N. J.
BR TR 5' 8" 160 lbs.

Year	Gms.	BA	SA	AB	H	2B	3B	HR	RBI	SB	G. by Pos
1932	26	.175	.222	63	11	1	1	0	4	0	2B-16, SS-5, 1B-2, 3B-1
1933	44	.269	.269	93	25	0	0	0	6	0	SS-22, 2B-20
2 yrs.	70	.231	.250	156	36	1	1	0	10	0	2B-36, SS-27, 1B-2, 3B-1

Frank Fernandez

FRANK FERNANDEZ
B. Apr. 16, 1943, Staten Island, N. Y.
BR TR 6' 185 lbs.

Year	Gms.	BA	SA	AB	H	2B	3B	HR	RBI	SB	G. by Pos
1967	9	.214	.393	28	6	2	0	1	4	1	C-7, OF-2
1968	51	.170	.385	135	23	6	1	7	30	1	C-45, OF-4
1969	89	.223	.415	229	51	6	1	12	29	1	C-65, OF-14
3 yrs.	149	.204	.403	392	80	14	2	20	63	3	C-117, OF-20

Tony Fernandez

OCTAVIO ANTONIO FERNANDEZ
B. Jun. 30, 1962, San Pedro de Macoris, Dominican Republic
BB TR 6' 1" 160 lbs.

Year	Gms.	BA	SA	AB	H	2B	3B	HR	RBI	SB	G. by Pos
1995	108	.245	.346	384	94	20	2	5	45	6	SS-103, 2B-4
Divisional Playoffs											
1995	5	.238	.333	21	5	2	0	0	0	0	SS-5

Mike Ferraro

MICHAEL DENNIS FERRARO
B. Aug. 14, 1944, Kingston, N. Y.
BR TR 5' 11" 175 lbs.

Year	Gms.	BA	SA	AB	H	2B	3B	HR	RBI	SB	G. by Pos
1966	10	.179	.179	28	5	0	0	0	0	0	3B-10
1968	23	.161	.184	87	14	0	1	0	1	0	3B-22
2 yrs.	33	.165	.183	115	19	0	1	0	1	0	3B-32

Chick Fewster

WILSON LLOYD FEWSTER
B. Nov. 10, 1895, Baltimore, Md.
D. Apr. 16, 1945, Baltimore, Md.
BR TR 5' 11" 160 lbs.

Year	Gms.	BA	SA	AB	H	2B	3B	HR	RBI	SB	G. by Pos
1917	11	.222	.222	36	8	0	0	0	1	1	2B-11
1918	5	.500	.500	2	1	0	0	0	0	0	2B-2
1919	81	.283	.357	244	69	9	3	1	15	8	OF-41, SS-23, 2B-4, 3B-2
1920	21	.286	.333	21	6	1	0	0	1	0	SS-5, 2B-2
1921	66	.280	.386	207	58	19	0	1	19	4	OF-43, 2B-15
1922	44	.242	.311	132	32	4	1	1	9	2	OF-38, 2B-2
6 yrs.	228	.271	.349	642	174	33	4	3	45	15	OF-122, 2B-36, SS-28, 3B-2
World Series											
1921	4	.200	.500	10	2	0	0	1	2	0	OF-4

Cecil Fielder

CECIL GRANT FIELDER
B. Sep. 21, 1963, Los Angeles, Calif.
BR TR 6' 3" 230 lbs.

Year	Gms.	BA	SA	AB	H	2B	3B	HR	RBI	SB	G. by Pos
1996	53	.260	.495	200	52	8	0	13	37	0	DH-43, 1B-9
Divisional Playoffs											
1996	3	.364	.636	11	4	0	0	1	4	0	DH-3
League Championship Series											
1996	5	.167	.500	18	3	0	0	2	8	0	DH-5
World Series											
1996	6	.391	.478	23	9	2	0	0	2	0	1B-3, DH-3

Mike Fischlin

MICHAEL THOMAS FISCHLIN
B. Sep. 13, 1955, Sacramento, Calif.
BR TR 6' 1" 165 lbs.

Year	Gms.	BA	SA	AB	H	2B	3B	HR	RBI	SB	G. by Pos
1986	71	.206	.225	102	21	2	0	0	3	0	SS-42, 2B-27

Gus Fisher

AUGUST HARRIS FISHER
B. Oct. 21, 1885, Pottsborough, Tex.
D. Apr. 8, 1972, Portland, Ore.
BL TR 5' 10" 175 lbs.

Year	Gms.	BA	SA	AB	H	2B	3B	HR	RBI	SB	G. by Pos
1912	4	.100	.100	10	1	0	0	0	0	0	C-4

Mike Fitzgerald

JUSTIN HOWARD FITZGERALD
B. Jun. 22, 1890, San Mateo, Calif.
D. Jan. 17, 1945, San Mateo, Calif.
BL TR 5' 8" 160 lbs.

Year	Gms.	BA	SA	AB	H	2B	3B	HR	RBI	SB	G. by Pos
1911	16	.270	.297	37	10	1	0	0	6	4	OF-9

Tim Foli

TIMOTHY JOHN FOLI
B. Dec. 8, 1950, Culver City, Calif.
BR TR 6' 179 lbs.

Year	Gms.	BA	SA	AB	H	2B	3B	HR	RBI	SB	G. by Pos
1984	61	.252	.319	163	41	11	0	0	16	0	SS-28, 2B-21, 3B-10, 1B-2

Barry Foote

BARRY CLIFTON FOOTE
B. Feb. 16, 1952, Smithfield, N. C.
BR TR 6' 3" 205 lbs.

Year	Gms.	BA	SA	AB	H	2B	3B	HR	RBI	SB	G. by Pos
1981	40	.208	.384	125	26	4	0	6	10	0	C-34, DH-4, 1B-1
1982	17	.146	.250	48	7	5	0	0	2	0	C-17
2 yrs.	57	.191	.347	173	33	9	0	6	12	0	C-51, DH-4, 1B-1
Divisional Playoffs											
1981	1	—	—	0	0	0	0	0	0	0	
League Championship Series											
1981	2	1.000	1.000	1	1	0	0	0	0	0	C-1
World Series											
1981	1	.000	.000	1	0	0	0	0	0	0	

Eddie Foster

EDWARD CUNNINGHAM FOSTER
B. Feb. 13, 1887, Chicago, Ill.
D. Jan. 15, 1937, Washington, D. C.
BR TR 5' 6½" 145 lbs.

Year	Gms.	BA	SA	AB	H	2B	3B	HR	RBI	SB	G. by Pos
1910	30	.133	.157	83	11	2	0	0	1	2	SS-22

Jack Fournier

JOHN FRANK FOURNIER
B. Sep. 28, 1889, Au Sable, Mich.
D. Sep. 5, 1973, Tacoma, Wash.
BL TR 6' 195 lbs.

Year	Gms.	BA	SA	AB	H	2B	3B	HR	RBI	SB	G. by Pos
1918	27	.350	.430	100	35	6	1	0	12	7	1B-27

Ray French

RAYMOND EDWARD FRENCH
BR TR
B. Jan. 9, 1895, Alameda, Calif.
D. Apr. 3, 1978, Alameda, Calif.
5' 9½" 158 lbs.

Year	Gms.	BA	SA	AB	H	2B	3B	HR	RBI	SB	G. by Pos
1920	2	.000	.000	2	0	0	0	0	1	0	SS-1

Lonny Frey

LINUS REINHARD FREY
BL TR
B. Aug. 23, 1910, St. Louis, Mo.
5' 10" 160 lbs.

Year	Gms.	BA	SA	AB	H	2B	3B	HR	RBI	SB	G. by Pos
1947	24	.179	.250	28	5	2	0	0	2	3	2B-8
1948	1	—	—	0	0	0	0	0	0	0	
2 yrs.	25	.179	.250	28	5	2	0	0	2	3	2B-8
World Series											
1947	1	.000	.000	1	0	0	0	0	1	0	

Dave Fultz

DAVID LEWIS FULTZ
BR TR
B. May 29, 1875, Staunton, Va.
D. Oct. 29, 1959, Deland, Fla.
5' 11" 170 lbs.

Year	Gms.	BA	SA	AB	H	2B	3B	HR	RBI	SB	G. by Pos
1903	79	.224	.271	295	66	12	1	0	25	29	OF-77, 3B-2
1904	97	.274	.366	339	93	17	4	2	32	17	OF-90
1905	130	.232	.277	422	98	13	3	0	42	44	OF-122
3 yrs.	306	.243	.304	1056	257	42	8	2	99	90	OF-289, 3B-2

Liz Funk

ELIAS CALVIN FUNK
BL TL
B. Oct. 28, 1904, La Cygne, Kans.
D. Jan. 16, 1968, Norman, Okla.
5' 8½" 160 lbs.

Year	Gms.	BA	SA	AB	H	2B	3B	HR	RBI	SB	G. by Pos
1929	1	—	—	0	0	0	0	0	0	0	

Joe Gallagher

JOSEPH EMMETT GALLAGHER
BR TR
B. Mar. 7, 1914, Buffalo, N. Y.
6' 2" 210 lbs.

Year	Gms.	BA	SA	AB	H	2B	3B	HR	RBI	SB	G. by Pos
1939	14	.244	.439	41	10	1	0	2	9	1	OF-12

Mike Gallego

MICHAEL ANTHONY GALLEGO
BR TR
B. Oct. 31, 1960, Whittier, Calif.
5' 8" 160 lbs.

Year	Gms.	BA	SA	AB	H	2B	3B	HR	RBI	SB	G. by Pos
1992	53	.254	.358	173	44	7	1	3	14	0	2B-40, SS-14
1993	119	.283	.412	403	114	20	1	10	54	3	SS-55, 2B-52, 3B-27, DH-1
1994	89	.239	.359	306	73	17	1	6	41	0	SS-72, 2B-26
3 yrs.	261	.262	.383	882	231	44	3	19	109	3	SS-141, 2B-118, 3B-27, DH-1

Oscar Gamble

OSCAR CHARLES GAMBLE
BL TR
B. Dec. 20, 1949, Ramer, Ala.
5' 11" 160 lbs.

Year	Gms.	BA	SA	AB	H	2B	3B	HR	RBI	SB	G. by Pos
1976	110	.232	.426	340	79	13	1	17	57	5	OF-104, DH-1
1979	36	.389	.735	113	44	4	1	11	32	0	OF-27, DH-15
1980	78	.278	.567	194	54	10	2	14	50	2	OF-49, DH-20
1981	80	.238	.439	189	45	8	0	10	27	0	OF-43, DH-33
1982	108	.272	.522	316	86	21	2	18	57	6	DH-74, OF-29
1983	74	.261	.456	180	47	10	2	7	26	0	OF-32, DH-21
1984	54	.184	.440	125	23	2	0	10	27	1	DH-26, OF-12
7 yrs.	540	.259	.496	1457	378	68	8	87	276	14	OF-296, DH-190
Divisional Playoffs											
1981	4	.556	1.333	9	5	1	0	2	3	0	DH-4
League Championship Series											
1976	3	.250	.375	8	2	1	0	0	1	0	OF-3
1980	2	.200	.200	5	1	0	0	0	0	0	OF-1, DH-1
1981	3	.167	.167	6	1	0	0	0	1	0	DH-2, OF-1
3 yrs.	8	.211	.263	19	4	1	0	0	2	0	OF-5, DH-3
World Series											
1976	3	.125	.125	8	1	0	0	0	1	0	OF-2
1981	3	.333	.333	6	2	0	0	0	1	0	OF-2
2 yrs.	6	.214	.214	14	3	0	0	0	2	0	OF-4

John Ganzel

JOHN HENRY GANZEL
BR TR
B. Apr. 7, 1874, Kalamazoo, Mich.
D. Jan. 14, 1959, Orlando, Fla.
6' ½" 195 lbs.

Year	Gms.	BA	SA	AB	H	2B	3B	HR	RBI	SB	G. by Pos
1903	129	.277	.378	476	132	25	7	3	71	9	1B-129
1904	130	.260	.376	465	121	16	10	6	48	13	1B-118, 2B-9, SS-1
2 yrs.	259	.269	.377	941	253	41	17	9	119	22	1B-247, 2B-9, SS-1

Mike Garbark

MICHAEL NATHANIEL GARBARK
BR TR
B. Feb. 2, 1916, Houston, Tex.
D. Aug. 31, 1994, Charlotte, N. C.
6' 200 lbs.

Year	Gms.	BA	SA	AB	H	2B	3B	HR	RBI	SB	G. by Pos
1944	89	.261	.328	299	78	9	4	1	33	0	C-85
1945	60	.216	.295	176	38	5	3	1	26	0	C-59
2 yrs.	149	.244	.316	475	116	14	7	2	59	0	C-144

Damaso Garcia

DAMASO DOMINGO GARCIA
BR TR
B. Feb. 7, 1957, Moca,
Dominican Republic
6' 1" 165 lbs.

Year	Gms.	BA	SA	AB	H	2B	3B	HR	RBI	SB	G. by Pos
1978	18	.195	.195	41	8	0	0	0	1	1	2B-16, SS-3
1979	11	.263	.289	38	10	1	0	0	4	2	SS-10, 3B-1
2 yrs.	29	.228	.241	79	18	1	0	0	5	3	2B-16, SS-13, 3B-1

Billy Gardner

WILLIAM FREDERICK GARDNER
BR TR
B. Jul. 19, 1927, Waterford, Conn.
6' 170 lbs.

Year	Gms.	BA	SA	AB	H	2B	3B	HR	RBI	SB	G. by Pos
1961	41	.212	.293	99	21	5	0	1	2	0	3B-33, 2B-6
1962	4	.000	.000	1	0	0	0	0	0	0	2B-1, 3B-1
2 yrs.	45	.210	.290	100	21	5	0	1	2	0	3B-34, 2B-7
World Series											
1961	1	.000	.000	1	0	0	0	0	0	0	

Earl Gardner

EARLE McCLURKIN GARDNER
BR TR
B. Jan. 24, 1884, Sparta, Ill.
D. Mar. 2, 1943, Sparta, Ill.
5' 11" 160 lbs.

Year	Gms.	BA	SA	AB	H	2B	3B	HR	RBI	SB	G. by Pos
1908	20	.213	.240	75	16	2	0	0	4	0	2B-20
1909	22	.329	.376	85	28	4	0	0	15	4	2B-22
1910	86	.244	.284	271	66	4	2	1	24	9	2B-70
1911	102	.263	.311	357	94	13	2	0	39	14	2B-101
1912	43	.281	.313	160	45	3	1	0	26	11	2B-43
5 yrs.	273	.263	.304	948	249	26	5	1	108	38	2B-256

Mike Gazella

MICHAEL GAZELLA
BR TR
B. Oct. 13, 1896, Olyphant, Pa.
D. Sep. 11, 1978, Odessa, Tex.
5' 7½" 165 lbs.

Year	Gms.	BA	SA	AB	H	2B	3B	HR	RBI	SB	G. by Pos
1923	8	.077	.077	13	1	0	0	0	1	0	SS-4, 2B-2, 3B-2
1926	66	.232	.268	168	39	6	0	0	21	2	3B-45, SS-11
1927	54	.278	.417	115	32	8	4	0	9	4	3B-44, SS-6
1928	32	.232	.232	56	13	0	0	0	2	2	3B-14, 2B-4, SS-3
4 yrs.	160	.241	.304	352	85	14	4	0	33	8	3B-105, SS-24, 2B-6
World Series											
1926	1	—	—	0	0	0	0	0	0	0	3B-1

Joe Gedeon

ELMER JOSEPH GEDEON
BR TR
B. Dec. 5, 1893, Sacramento, Calif.
D. May 19, 1941, San Francisco, Calif.
6' 167 lbs.

Year	Gms.	BA	SA	AB	H	2B	3B	HR	RBI	SB	G. by Pos
1916	122	.211	.262	435	92	14	4	0	27	14	2B-122
1917	33	.239	.299	117	28	7	0	0	8	4	2B-31
2 yrs.	155	.217	.270	552	120	21	4	0	35	18	2B-153

Lou Gehrig

HENRY LOUIS GEHRIG
BL TL
B. Jun. 19, 1903, New York, N. Y.
D. Jun. 2, 1941, New York, N. Y.
Hall of Fame 1939
6' 200 lbs.

Year	Gms.	BA	SA	AB	H	2B	3B	HR	RBI	SB	G. by Pos
1923	13	.423	.769	26	11	4	1	1	9	0	1B-9
1924	10	.500	.583	12	6	1	0	0	5	0	1B-2, OF-1
1925	126	.295	.531	437	129	23	10	20	68	6	1B-114, OF-6
1926	155	.313	.549	572	179	47	20	16	107	6	1B-155
1927	155	.373	.765	584	218	52	18	47	175	10	1B-155
1928	154	.374	.648	562	210	47	13	27	142	4	1B-154
1929	154	.300	.582	553	166	33	9	35	126	4	1B-154
1930	154	.379	.721	581	220	42	17	41	174	12	1B-153, OF-1
1931	155	.341	.662	619	211	31	15	46	184	17	1B-154, OF-1
1932	156	.349	.621	596	208	42	9	34	151	4	1B-155
1933	152	.334	.605	593	198	41	12	32	139	9	1B-152
1934	154	.363	.706	579	210	40	6	49	165	9	1B-153, SS-1

Lou Gehrig *continued*

Year	Gms.	BA	SA	AB	H	2B	3B	HR	RBI	SB	G. by Pos
1935	149	.329	.583	535	176	26	10	30	119	8	1B-149
1936	155	.354	.696	579	205	37	7	49	152	3	1B-155
1937	157	.351	.643	569	200	37	9	37	159	4	1B-157
1938	157	.295	.523	576	170	32	6	29	114	6	1B-157
1939	8	.143	.143	28	4	0	0	0	1	0	1B-8
17 yrs.	2164	.340	.632	8001	2721	535	162	493	1990	102	1B-2136, OF-9, SS-1

World Series

Year	Gms.	BA	SA	AB	H	2B	3B	HR	RBI	SB	G. by Pos
1926	7	.348	.435	23	8	2	0	0	3	0	1B-7
1927	4	.308	.769	13	4	2	2	0	5	0	1B-4
1928	4	.545	1.727	11	6	1	0	4	9	0	1B-4
1932	4	.529	1.118	17	9	1	0	3	8	0	1B-4
1936	6	.292	.583	24	7	1	0	2	7	0	1B-6
1937	5	.294	.647	17	5	1	1	1	3	0	1B-5
1938	4	.286	.286	14	4	0	0	0	0	0	1B-4
7 yrs.	34	.361	.731	119	43	8	3	10	35	0	1B-34

Bob Geren

ROBERT PETER GEREN   BR TR
B. Sep. 22, 1961, San Diego, Calif.   6' 3" 205 lbs.

Year	Gms.	BA	SA	AB	H	2B	3B	HR	RBI	SB	G. by Pos
1988	10	.100	.100	10	1	0	0	0	0	0	C-10
1989	65	.288	.454	205	59	5	1	9	27	0	C-60, DH-2
1990	110	.213	.325	277	59	7	0	8	31	0	C-107, DH-1
1991	64	.219	.289	128	28	3	0	2	12	0	C-63
4 yrs.	249	.237	.356	620	147	15	1	19	70	0	C-240, DH-3

Jake Gibbs

JERRY DEAN GIBBS   BL TR
B. Nov. 7, 1938, Grenada, Miss.   6' 180 lbs.

Year	Gms.	BA	SA	AB	H	2B	3B	HR	RBI	SB	G. by Pos
1962	2	—	—	0	0	0	0	0	0	0	3B-1
1963	4	.250	.250	8	2	0	0	0	0	0	C-1
1964	3	.167	.167	6	1	0	0	0	0	0	C-2
1965	37	.221	.324	68	15	1	0	2	7	0	C-21
1966	62	.258	.341	182	47	6	0	3	20	5	C-54
1967	116	.233	.289	374	87	7	1	4	25	7	C-99
1968	124	.213	.277	423	90	12	3	3	29	9	C-121
1969	71	.224	.283	219	49	9	2	0	18	3	C-66
1970	49	.301	.542	153	46	9	2	8	26	2	C-44
1971	70	.218	.335	206	45	9	0	5	21	2	C-51
10 yrs.	538	.233	.321	1639	382	53	8	25	146	28	C-459, 3B-1

Frank Gilhooley

FRANK PATRICK GILHOOLEY   BL TR
B. Jun. 10, 1892, Toledo, Ohio.   5' 8" 155 lbs.
D. Jul. 11, 1959, Toledo, Ohio.

Year	Gms.	BA	SA	AB	H	2B	3B	HR	RBI	SB	G. by Pos
1913	24	.341	.388	85	29	2	1	0	14	6	OF-24
1914	1	.667	.667	3	2	0	0	0	0	0	OF-1
1915	1	.000	.000	4	0	0	0	0	0	0	OF-1
1916	58	.278	.341	223	62	5	3	1	10	16	OF-57
1917	54	.242	.291	165	40	6	1	0	8	6	OF-46
1918	112	.276	.337	427	118	13	5	1	23	7	OF-111
6 yrs.	250	.277	.334	907	251	26	10	2	55	35	OF-240

Joe Girardi

JOSEPH ELLIOTT GIRARDI   BR TR
B. Oct. 14, 1964, Peoria, Ill.   5' 11" 195 lbs.

Year	Gms.	BA	SA	AB	H	2B	3B	HR	RBI	SB	G. by Pos
1996	124	.294	.374	422	124	22	3	2	45	13	C-120, DH-2

Divisional Playoffs

Year	Gms.	BA	SA	AB	H	2B	3B	HR	RBI	SB	G. by Pos
1996	4	.222	.222	9	2	0	0	0	0	0	C-4

League Championship Series

Year	Gms.	BA	SA	AB	H	2B	3B	HR	RBI	SB	G. by Pos
1996	4	.250	.417	12	3	0	1	0	0	0	C-4

World Series

Year	Gms.	BA	SA	AB	H	2B	3B	HR	RBI	SB	G. by Pos
1996	4	.200	.400	10	2	0	1	0	1	0	C-4

Frank Gleich

FRANK ELMER GLEICH   BL TR
B. Mar. 7, 1894, Columbus, Ohio.   5' 11" 175 lbs.
D. Mar. 27, 1949, Columbus, Ohio.

Year	Gms.	BA	SA	AB	H	2B	3B	HR	RBI	SB	G. by Pos
1919	5	.250	.250	4	1	0	0	0	1	0	OF-4
1920	24	.122	.122	41	5	0	0	0	3	0	OF-15
2 yrs.	29	.133	.133	45	6	0	0	0	4	0	OF-19

Joe Glenn

JOSEPH CHARLES GLENN   BR TR
B. Nov. 19, 1908, Dickson City, Pa.   5' 11" 175 lbs.
D. May. 6, 1985, Tunkhannock, Pa.

Year	Gms.	BA	SA	AB	H	2B	3B	HR	RBI	SB	G. by Pos
1932	6	.125	.125	16	2	0	0	0	0	0	C-5
1933	5	.143	.143	21	3	0	0	0	1	0	C-5
1935	17	.233	.326	43	10	4	0	0	6	0	C-16
1936	44	.271	.349	129	35	7	0	1	20	1	C-44
1937	25	.283	.396	53	15	2	2	0	4	0	C-24
1938	41	.260	.350	123	32	7	2	0	25	1	C-40
6 yrs.	138	.252	.332	385	97	20	4	1	56	2	C-134

Jesse Gonder

JESSE LEMAR. GONDER   BL TR
B. Jan. 20, 1936, Monticello, Ark.   5' 10" 180 lbs.

Year	Gms.	BA	SA	AB	H	2B	3B	HR	RBI	SB	G. by Pos
1960	7	.286	.714	7	2	0	0	1	3	0	C-1
1961	15	.333	.417	12	4	1	0	0	3	0	
2 yrs.	22	.316	.526	19	6	1	0	1	6	0	C-1

Fernando Gonzalez

JOSE FERNANDO GONZALEZ   BR TR
B. Jun. 19, 1950, Arecibo, Puerto Rico   5' 10" 165 lbs.

Year	Gms.	BA	SA	AB	H	2B	3B	HR	RBI	SB	G. by Pos
1974	51	.215	.298	121	26	5	1	1	7	0	2B-42, 3B-7, SS-3, DH-1

Pedro Gonzalez

PEDRO GONZALEZ   BR TR
B. Dec. 12, 1937, San Pedro de Macoris, 6' 176 lbs.
Dominican Republic

Year	Gms.	BA	SA	AB	H	2B	3B	HR	RBI	SB	G. by Pos
1963	14	.192	.231	26	5	1	0	0	1	0	2B-7
1964	80	.277	.366	112	31	8	1	0	5	3	1B-31, OF-20, 3B-9, 2B-6
1965	7	.400	.600	5	2	1	0	0	0	0	
3 yrs.	101	.266	.350	143	38	10	1	0	6	3	1B-31, OF-20, 2B-13, 3B-9

World Series

Year	Gms.	BA	SA	AB	H	2B	3B	HR	RBI	SB	G. by Pos
1964	1	.000	.000	1	0	0	0	0	0	0	3B-1

Joe Gordon

JOSEPH LOWELL GORDON   BR TR
B. Feb. 18, 1915, Los Angeles, Calif. 5' 10" 180 lbs.
D. Apr. 14, 1978, Sacramento, Calif.

Year	Gms.	BA	SA	AB	H	2B	3B	HR	RBI	SB	G. by Pos
1938	127	.255	.502	458	117	24	7	25	97	11	2B-126
1939	151	.284	.506	567	161	32	5	28	111	11	2B-151
1940	155	.281	.511	616	173	32	10	30	103	18	2B-155
1941	156	.276	.466	588	162	26	7	24	87	10	2B-131, 1B-30
1942	147	.322	.491	538	173	29	4	18	103	12	2B-147
1943	152	.249	.413	543	135	28	5	17	69	4	2B-152
1946	112	.210	.338	376	79	15	0	11	47	2	2B-108
7 yrs.	1000	.271	.467	3686	1000	186	38	153	617	68	2B-970, 1B-30

World Series

Year	Gms.	BA	SA	AB	H	2B	3B	HR	RBI	SB	G. by Pos
1938	4	.400	.733	15	6	2	0	1	6	1	2B-4
1939	4	.143	.143	14	2	0	0	0	1	0	2B-4
1941	5	.500	.929	14	7	1	1	1	5	0	2B-5
1942	5	.095	.143	21	2	1	0	0	0	0	2B-5
1943	5	.235	.471	17	4	1	0	1	2	0	2B-5
5 yrs.	23	.259	.457	81	21	5	1	3	14	1	2B-23

Dick Gossett

JOHN STAR GOSSETT   BR TR
B. Aug. 21, 1891, Denison, Ohio.   5' 11" 185 lbs.
D. Oct. 6, 1962, Massillon, Ohio.

Year	Gms.	BA	SA	AB	H	2B	3B	HR	RBI	SB	G. by Pos
1913	39	.162	.181	105	17	2	0	0	9	1	C-38
1914	9	.143	.143	21	3	0	0	0	1	0	C-9
2 yrs.	48	.159	.175	126	20	2	0	0	10	1	C-47

Johnny Grabowski

JOHN PATRICK GRABOWSKI   BR TR
B. Jan. 7, 1900, Ware, Mass.   5' 10" 185 lbs.
D. May 23, 1946, Albany, N. Y.

Year	Gms.	BA	SA	AB	H	2B	3B	HR	RBI	SB	G. by Pos
1927	70	.277	.328	195	54	2	4	0	25	0	C-68
1928	75	.238	.297	202	48	7	1	1	21	0	C-75
1929	22	.203	.220	59	12	1	0	0	2	1	C-22
3 yrs.	167	.250	.300	456	114	10	5	1	48	1	C-165

Johnny Grabowski *continued*

Year	Gms.	BA	SA	AB	H	2B	3B	HR	RBI	SB	G. by Pos
World Series											
1927	1	.000	.000	2	0	0	0	0	0	0	C-1

Willie Greene

PATRICK JOSEPH GREENE   BR TR
B. Mar. 20, 1875, Providence, R. I.   5' 8" 150 lbs.
D. Oct. 20, 1934, Providence, R. I.

Year	Gms.	BA	SA	AB	H	2B	3B	HR	RBI	SB	G. by Pos
1903	4	.308	.385	13	4	1	0	0	0	0	3B-2, SS-1

Ken Griffey

GEORGE KENNETH GRIFFEY, SR.   BL TL
B. Apr. 10, 1950, Donora, Pa.   5' 11" 190 lbs.

Year	Gms.	BA	SA	AB	H	2B	3B	HR	RBI	SB	G. by Pos
1982	127	.277	.407	484	134	23	2	12	54	10	OF-125
1983	118	.306	.437	458	140	21	3	11	46	6	1B-101, OF-14, DH-2
1984	120	.273	.381	399	109	20	1	7	56	2	OF-82, 1B-27, DH-2
1985	127	.274	.425	438	120	28	4	10	69	7	OF-110, DH-7, 1B-1
1986	59	.303	.475	198	60	7	0	9	26	2	OF-51, DH-2
5 yrs.	551	.285	.419	1977	563	99	10	49	251	27	OF-382, 1B-129, DH-13

Oscar Grimes

OSCAR RAY GRIMES, JR.   BR TR
B. Apr. 13, 1915, Minerva, Ohio   5' 11" 178 lbs.
D. May 19, 1993, Westlake, Ohio

Year	Gms.	BA	SA	AB	H	2B	3B	HR	RBI	SB	G. by Pos
1943	9	.150	.150	20	3	0	0	0	1	0	SS-3, 1B-1
1944	116	.279	.403	387	108	17	8	5	46	6	3B-97, SS-20
1945	142	.265	.358	480	127	19	7	4	45	7	3B-141, 1B-1
1946	14	.205	.231	39	8	1	0	0	4	0	SS-7, 2B-5
4 yrs.	281	.266	.367	926	246	37	15	9	96	13	3B-238, SS-30, 2B-5, 1B-2

Brad Gulden

BRADLEY LEE GULDEN   BL TR
B. Jun. 10, 1956, New Ulm, Minn.   5' 10" 175 lbs.

Year	Gms.	BA	SA	AB	H	2B	3B	HR	RBI	SB	G. by Pos
1979	40	.163	.207	92	15	4	0	0	6	0	C-40
1980	2	.333	1.333	3	1	0	0	1	2	0	C-2
2 yrs.	42	.168	.242	95	16	4	0	1	8	0	C-42

Kent Hadley

KENT WILLIAM HADLEY   BL TL
B. Dec. 17, 1934, Pocatello, Ida.   6' 3" 190 lbs.

Year	Gms.	BA	SA	AB	H	2B	3B	HR	RBI	SB	G. by Pos
1960	55	.203	.422	64	13	2	0	4	11	0	1B-24

Ed Hahn

WILLIAM EDGAR HAHN   BL TR
B. Aug. 27, 1875, Nevada, Ohio   160 lbs.
D. Nov. 29, 1941, Des Moines, Iowa

Year	Gms.	BA	SA	AB	H	2B	3B	HR	RBI	SB	G. by Pos
1905	43	.319	.350	160	51	5	0	0	11	1	OF-43
1906	11	.091	.136	22	2	1	0	0	1	2	OF-7
2 yrs.	54	.291	.324	182	53	6	0	0	12	3	OF-50

Hinkey Haines

HENRY LUTHER HAINES   BR TR
B. Dec. 23, 1898, Red Lion, Pa.   5' 10" 170 lbs.
D. Jan. 9, 1979, Sharon Hill, Pa.

Year	Gms.	BA	SA	AB	H	2B	3B	HR	RBI	SB	G. by Pos
1923	28	.160	.240	25	4	2	0	0	3	3	OF-14
World Series											
1923	2	.000	.000	1	0	0	0	0	0	0	OF-2

George Halas

GEORGE STANLEY HALAS   BB TR
B. Feb. 2, 1895, Chicago, Ill.   6' 164 lbs.
D. Oct. 31, 1983, Chicago, Ill.

Year	Gms.	BA	SA	AB	H	2B	3B	HR	RBI	SB	G. by Pos
1919	12	.091	.091	22	2	0	0	0	0	0	OF-6

Bob Hale

ROBERT HOUSTON HALE   BL TL
B. Nov. 7, 1933, Sarasota, Fla.   5' 10" 195 lbs.

Year	Gms.	BA	SA	AB	H	2B	3B	HR	RBI	SB	G. by Pos
1961	11	.154	.385	13	2	0	0	1	1	0	1B-5

Jimmie Hall

JIMMIE RANDOLPH HALL   BL TR
B. Mar. 17, 1938, Mt. Holly, N. C.   6' 175 lbs.

Year	Gms.	BA	SA	AB	H	2B	3B	HR	RBI	SB	G. by Pos
1969	80	.236	.363	212	50	8	5	3	26	8	OF-50, 1B-7

Mel Hall

MELVIN HALL, JR.   BL TL
B. Sep. 16, 1960, Lyons, N. Y.   6' 185 lbs.

Year	Gms.	BA	SA	AB	H	2B	3B	HR	RBI	SB	G. by Pos
1989	113	.260	.427	361	94	9	0	17	58	0	OF-75, DH-34
1990	113	.258	.433	360	93	23	2	12	46	0	DH-54, OF-50
1991	141	.285	.455	492	140	23	2	19	80	0	OF-120, DH-10
1992	152	.280	.429	583	163	36	3	15	81	4	OF-136, DH-11
4 yrs.	519	.273	.437	1796	490	91	7	63	265	4	OF-381, DH-109

Mike Handiboe

ALOYSIUS JAMES HANDIBOE   BL TL
B. Jul. 21, 1887, Washington, D. C.   5' 10" 155 lbs.
D. Jan. 31, 1953, Savannah, Ga.

Year	Gms.	BA	SA	AB	H	2B	3B	HR	RBI	SB	G. by Pos
1911	5	.067	.067	15	1	0	0	0	0	0	OF-4

Truck Hannah

JAMES HARRISON HANNAH   BR TR
B. Jun. 5, 1889, Larimore, N. D.   6' 1" 190 lbs.
D. Apr. 27, 1982, Fountain Valley, Calif.

Year	Gms.	BA	SA	AB	H	2B	3B	HR	RBI	SB	G. by Pos
1918	90	.220	.268	250	55	6	0	2	21	5	C-88
1919	75	.238	.313	227	54	8	3	1	21	0	C-73, 1B-1
1920	79	.247	.320	259	64	11	1	2	25	2	C-78
3 yrs.	244	.235	.300	736	173	25	4	5	67	7	C-239, 1B-1

Ron Hansen

RONALD LAVERN HANSEN   BR TR
B. Apr. 5, 1938, Oxford, Neb.   6' 3" 190 lbs.

Year	Gms.	BA	SA	AB	H	2B	3B	HR	RBI	SB	G. by Pos
1970	59	.297	.473	91	27	4	0	4	14	0	SS-15, 3B-11, 2B-1
1971	61	.207	.269	145	30	3	0	2	20	0	3B-30, 2B-9, SS-3
2 yrs.	120	.242	.347	236	57	7	0	6	34	0	3B-41, SS-18, 2B-10

Joe Hanson

HARRY FRANCIS HANSON   BR TR
B. Jan. 17, 1896, Elgin, Ill.   5' 11" lbs.
D. Oct. 5, 1966, Savannah, Ga.

Year	Gms.	BA	SA	AB	H	2B	3B	HR	RBI	SB	G. by Pos
1913	1	.000	.000	2	0	0	0	0	0	0	C-1

Bubbles Hargrave

EUGENE FRANKLIN HARGRAVE   BR TR
B. Jul. 15, 1892, New Haven, Ind.   5' 10½" 174 lbs.
D. Feb. 23, 1969, Cincinnati, Ohio

Year	Gms.	BA	SA	AB	H	2B	3B	HR	RBI	SB	G. by Pos
1930	45	.278	.343	108	30	7	0	0	12	0	C-34

Toby Harrah

COLBERT DALE HARRAH   BR TR
B. Oct. 26, 1948, Sissonville, W. Va.   6' 175 lbs.

Year	Gms.	BA	SA	AB	H	2B	3B	HR	RBI	SB	G. by Pos
1984	88	.217	.296	253	55	9	4	1	27	3	3B-74, 2B-4, OF-1

Joe Harris

JOSEPH HARRIS   BR TR
B. May 20, 1891, Coulters, Pa.   5' 9" 170 lbs.
D. Dec. 10, 1959, Renton, Pa.

Year	Gms.	BA	SA	AB	H	2B	3B	HR	RBI	SB	G. by Pos
1914	2	.000	.000	1	0	0	0	0	0	0	1B-1, OF-1

Jim Ray Hart

JAMES RAY HART   BR TR
B. Oct. 30, 1941, Hookerton, N. C.   5' 11" 185 lbs.

Year	Gms.	BA	SA	AB	H	2B	3B	HR	RBI	SB	G. by Pos
1973	114	.254	.419	339	86	13	2	13	52	0	DH-106
1974	10	.053	.053	19	1	0	0	0	0	0	DH-4
2 yrs.	124	.243	.399	358	87	13	2	13	52	0	DH-110

Roy Hartzell

ROY ALLEN HARTZELL   BL TR
B. Jul. 6, 1881, Golden, Colo.   5' 8½" 155 lbs.
D. Nov. 6, 1961, Golden, Colo.

Year	Gms.	BA	SA	AB	H	2B	3B	HR	RBI	SB	G. by Pos
1911	144	.296	.387	527	156	17	11	3	91	22	3B-124, SS-12, OF-8

Year	Gms.	BA	SA	AB	H	2B	3B	HR	RBI	SB	G. by Pos

Roy Hartzell *continued*

Year	Gms.	BA	SA	AB	H	2B	3B	HR	RBI	SB	G. by Pos
1912	123	.272	.356	416	113	10	11	1	38	20	3B-56, OF-55, SS-10, 2B-2
1913	141	.259	.300	490	127	18	1	0	38	26	2B-81, OF-30, 3B-21, SS-4
1914	137	.233	.308	481	112	15	9	1	32	22	OF-128, 2B-5
1915	119	.251	.313	387	97	11	2	3	60	7	OF-107, 2B-5, 3B-2
1916	33	.188	.203	64	12	1	0	0	7	1	OF-28
6 yrs.	697	.261	.330	2365	617	72	34	8	266	98	OF-356, 3B-203, 2B-93, SS-26

Buddy Hassett

JOHN ALOYSIUS HASSETT BL TL
B. Sep. 5, 1911, New York, N. Y. 5' 11" 180 lbs.

Year	Gms.	BA	SA	AB	H	2B	3B	HR	RBI	SB	G. by Pos
1942	132	.284	.364	538	153	16	6	5	48	5	1B-132
World Series
1942	3	.333	.444	9	3	1	0	0	2	0	1B-3

Ron Hassey

RONALD WILLIAM HASSEY BL TR
B. Feb. 27, 1953, Tucson, Ariz. 6' 2" 200 lbs.

Year	Gms.	BA	SA	AB	H	2B	3B	HR	RBI	SB	G. by Pos
1985	92	.296	.509	267	79	16	1	13	42	0	C-69, 1B-2, DH-2
1986	64	.298	.466	191	57	14	0	6	29	1	C-51, DH-3
2 yrs.	156	.297	.491	458	136	30	1	19	71	1	C-120, DH-5, 1B-2

Chicken Hawks

NELSON LOUIS HAWKS BL TL
B. Feb. 3, 1896, San Francisco, Calif. 5' 11" 167 lbs.
D. May 26, 1973, San Rafael, Calif.

Year	Gms.	BA	SA	AB	H	2B	3B	HR	RBI	SB	G. by Pos
1921	41	.288	.479	73	21	2	3	2	15	0	OF-15

Charlie Hayes

CHARLES DEWAYNE HAYES BR TR
B. May 29, 1965, Hattiesburg, Miss. 6' 224 lbs.

Year	Gms.	BA	SA	AB	H	2B	3B	HR	RBI	SB	G. by Pos
1992	142	.257	.409	509	131	19	2	18	66	3	3B-139, 1B-4
1996	20	.284	.418	67	19	3	0	2	13	0	3B-19
2 yrs.	162	.260	.410	576	150	22	2	20	79	3	3B-158, 1B-4
Divisional Playoffs
1996	3	.200	.200	5	1	0	0	0	1	0	3B-2
League Championship Series
1996	4	.143	.143	7	1	0	0	0	0	0	3B-2, DH-1
World Series
1996	5	.188	.188	16	3	0	0	0	1	0	3B-4, 1B-1

Fran Healy

FRANCIS XAVIER HEALY BR TR
B. Sep. 6, 1946, Holyoke, Mass. 6' 5" 220 lbs.

Year	Gms.	BA	SA	AB	H	2B	3B	HR	RBI	SB	G. by Pos
1976	46	.267	.292	120	32	3	0	0	9	3	C-31
1977	27	.224	.299	67	15	5	0	0	7	1	C-26
1978	1	.000	.000	1	0	0	0	0	0	0	C-1
3 yrs.	74	.250	.293	188	47	8	0	0	16	4	C-58

Mike Heath

MICHAEL THOMAS HEATH BR TR
B. Feb. 5, 1955, Tampa, Fla. 5' 11" 180 lbs.

Year	Gms.	BA	SA	AB	H	2B	3B	HR	RBI	SB	G. by Pos
1978	33	.228	.283	92	21	3	1	0	8	0	C-33
World Series
1978	1	—	—	0	0	0	0	0	0	0	C-1

Don Heffner

DONALD HENRY HEFFNER BR TR
B. Feb. 8, 1911, Rouzerville, Pa. 5' 10" 155 lbs.
D. Aug. 1, 1989, Pasadena, Calif.

Year	Gms.	BA	SA	AB	H	2B	3B	HR	RBI	SB	G. by Pos
1934	72	.261	.320	241	63	8	3	0	25	1	2B-68
1935	10	.306	.444	36	11	3	1	0	8	0	2B-10
1936	19	.229	.313	48	11	2	1	0	6	0	3B-8, 2B-5, SS-3
1937	60	.249	.328	201	50	6	5	0	21	1	2B-38, SS-13, 3B-3, 1B-1, OF-1
4 yrs.	161	.257	.331	526	135	19	10	0	60	2	2B-121, SS-16, 3B-11, 1B-1, OF-1

Mike Hegan

JAMES MICHAEL HEGAN BL TL
B. Jul. 21, 1942, Cleveland, Ohio 6' 1" 188 lbs.

Year	Gms.	BA	SA	AB	H	2B	3B	HR	RBI	SB	G. by Pos
1964	5	.000	.000	5	0	0	0	0	0	0	1B-2
1966	13	.205	.256	39	8	0	1	0	2	1	1B-13
1967	68	.136	.212	118	16	4	1	1	3	7	1B-54, OF-10
1973	37	.275	.466	131	36	3	2	6	14	0	1B-37
1974	18	.226	.377	53	12	2	0	2	9	1	1B-17
5 yrs.	141	.208	.335	346	72	9	4	9	28	9	1B-123, OF-10
World Series
1964	3	.000	.000	1	0	0	0	0	0	0	

Woodie Held

WOODSON GEORGE HELD BR TR
B. Mar. 25, 1932, Sacramento, Calif. 5' 10½" 167 lbs.

Year	Gms.	BA	SA	AB	H	2B	3B	HR	RBI	SB	G. by Pos
1954	4	.000	.000	3	0	0	0	0	0	0	SS-4, 3B-1
1957	1	.000	.000	1	0	0	0	0	0	0	
2 yrs.	5	.000	.000	4	0	0	0	0	0	0	SS-4, 3B-1

Charlie Hemphill

CHARLES JUDSON HEMPHILL BL TL
B. Apr. 20, 1876, Greenville, Mich. 5' 9" 160 lbs.
D. Jun. 22, 1953, Detroit, Mich.

Year	Gms.	BA	SA	AB	H	2B	3B	HR	RBI	SB	G. by Pos
1908	142	.297	.356	505	150	12	9	0	44	42	OF-142
1909	73	.243	.282	181	44	5	1	0	10	10	OF-45
1910	102	.239	.288	351	84	9	4	0	21	19	OF-94
1911	69	.284	.338	201	57	4	2	1	15	9	OF-56
4 yrs.	386	.271	.323	1238	335	30	16	1	90	80	OF-337

Rollie Hemsley

RALSTON BURDETT HEMSLEY BR TR
B. Jun. 24, 1907, Syracuse, Ohio 5' 10" 170 lbs.
D. Jul. 31, 1972, Washington, D. C.

Year	Gms.	BA	SA	AB	H	2B	3B	HR	RBI	SB	G. by Pos
1942	31	.294	.353	85	25	3	1	0	15	1	C-29
1943	62	.239	.339	180	43	6	3	2	24	0	C-52
1944	81	.268	.366	284	76	12	5	2	26	0	C-76
3 yrs.	174	.262	.355	549	144	21	9	4	65	1	C-157

Rickey Henderson

RICKEY HENLEY HENDERSON BR TL
B. Dec. 25, 1957, Chicago, Ill. 5' 10" 180 lbs.

Year	Gms.	BA	SA	AB	H	2B	3B	HR	RBI	SB	G. by Pos
1985	143	.314	.516	547	172	28	5	24	72	80	OF-141, DH-1
1986	153	.263	.469	608	160	31	5	28	74	87	OF-146, DH-5
1987	95	.291	.497	358	104	17	3	17	37	41	OF-69, DH-24
1988	140	.305	.399	554	169	30	2	6	50	93	OF-136, DH-3
1989	65	.247	.349	235	58	13	1	3	22	25	OF-65
5 yrs.	596	.288	.455	2302	663	119	16	78	255	326	OF-557, DH-33

Harvey Hendrick

HARVEY HENDRICK BL TR
B. Nov. 9, 1897, Mason, Tenn. 6' 2" 190 lbs.
D. Oct. 29, 1941, Covington, Tenn.

Year	Gms.	BA	SA	AB	H	2B	3B	HR	RBI	SB	G. by Pos
1923	37	.273	.485	66	18	3	1	3	12	3	OF-12
1924	40	.263	.303	76	20	0	0	1	11	1	OF-17
2 yrs.	77	.268	.387	142	38	3	1	4	23	4	OF-29
World Series
1923	1	.000	.000	1	0	0	0	0	0	0	

Ellie Hendricks

ELROD JEROME HENDRICKS BL TR
B. Dec. 22, 1940, Charlotte Amalie, 6' 1" 175 lbs.
Virgin Islands

Year	Gms.	BA	SA	AB	H	2B	3B	HR	RBI	SB	G. by Pos
1976	26	.226	.415	53	12	1	0	3	5	0	C-18
1977	10	.273	.636	11	3	1	0	1	5	0	C-6
2 yrs.	36	.234	.453	64	15	2	0	4	10	0	C-24
League Championship Series
1976	1	1.000	1.000	1	1	0	0	0	0	0	
World Series
1976	2	.000	.000	2	0	0	0	0	0	0	

Tim Hendryx

TIMOTHY GREEN HENDRYX BR TR
B. Jan. 31, 1891, LeRoy, Ill. 5' 9" 170 lbs.
D. Aug. 14, 1957, Corpus Christi, Tex.

Year	Gms.	BA	SA	AB	H	2B	3B	HR	RBI	SB	G. by Pos
1915	13	.200	.250	40	8	2	0	0	1	0	OF-12

Year	Gms.	BA	SA	AB	H	2B	3B	HR	RBI	SB	G. by Pos

Tim Hendryx continued

Year	Gms.	BA	SA	AB	H	2B	3B	HR	RBI	SB	G. by Pos
1916	15	.290	.435	62	18	7	1	0	5	4	OF-15
1917	125	.249	.359	393	98	14	7	5	44	6	OF-107
3 yrs.	153	.251	.360	495	124	23	8	5	50	10	OF-134

Tommy Henrich

THOMAS DAVID HENRICH   BL TL
B. Feb. 20, 1913, Massillon, Ohio   6' 180 lbs.

Year	Gms.	BA	SA	AB	H	2B	3B	HR	RBI	SB	G. by Pos
1937	67	.320	.553	206	66	14	5	8	42	4	OF-59
1938	131	.270	.490	471	127	24	7	22	91	6	OF-130
1939	99	.277	.429	347	96	18	4	9	57	7	OF-88, 1B-1
1940	90	.307	.539	293	90	28	5	10	53	1	OF-76, 1B-2
1941	144	.277	.519	538	149	27	5	31	85	3	OF-139
1942	127	.267	.431	483	129	30	5	13	67	4	OF-119, 1B-7
1946	150	.251	.411	565	142	25	4	19	83	5	OF-111, 1B-41
1947	142	.287	.485	550	158	35	13	16	98	3	OF-132, 1B-6
1948	146	.308	.554	588	181	42	14	25	100	2	OF-102, 1B-46
1949	115	.287	.526	411	118	20	3	24	85	2	OF-61, 1B-52
1950	73	.272	.536	151	41	6	8	6	34	0	1B-34
11 yrs.	1284	.282	.491	4603	1297	269	73	183	795	37	OF-1017, 1B-189
World Series											
1938	4	.250	.500	16	4	1	0	1	1	0	OF-4
1941	5	.167	.389	18	3	1	0	1	1	0	OF-5
1947	7	.323	.484	31	10	2	0	1	5	0	OF-7
1949	5	.263	.421	19	5	0	0	1	1	0	1B-5
4 yrs.	21	.262	.452	84	22	4	0	4	8	0	OF-16, 1B-5

Leo Hernandez

LEONARDO JESUS HERNANDEZ   BR TR
B. Nov. 6, 1959, Santa Lucia,   5' 11" 170 lbs.
Venezuela

Year	Gms.	BA	SA	AB	H	2B	3B	HR	RBI	SB	G. by Pos
1986	7	.227	.455	22	5	2	0	1	4	0	3B-7, 2B-1, SS-1

Ed Herrmann

EDWARD MARTIN HERRMANN   BL TR
B. Aug. 27, 1946, San Diego, Calif.   6' 1" 195 lbs.

Year	Gms.	BA	SA	AB	H	2B	3B	HR	RBI	SB	G. by Pos
1975	80	.255	.410	200	51	9	2	6	30	0	DH-35, C-24

Hugh High

HUGH JENKIN HIGH   BL TL
B. Oct. 24, 1887, Pottstown, Pa.   5' 7½" 155 lbs.
D. Nov. 16, 1962, St. Louis, Mo.

Year	Gms.	BA	SA	AB	H	2B	3B	HR	RBI	SB	G. by Pos
1915	119	.258	.342	427	110	19	7	1	43	22	OF-117
1916	115	.263	.326	377	99	13	4	1	28	13	OF-109
1917	103	.236	.307	365	86	11	6	1	19	8	OF-100
1918	7	.000	.000	10	0	0	0	0	0	0	OF-4
4 yrs.	344	.250	.323	1179	295	43	17	3	90	43	OF-330

Jesse Hill

JESSE TERRILL HILL   BR TR
B. Jan. 20, 1907, Yates, Mo.   5' 9" 165 lbs.
D. Aug. 31, 1993, Pasadena, Ca.

Year	Gms.	BA	SA	AB	H	2B	3B	HR	RBI	SB	G. by Pos
1935	107	.293	.390	392	115	20	3	4	33	14	OF-94

Mack Hillis

MALCOLM DAVID HILLIS   BR TR
B. Jul. 23, 1901, Cambridge, Mass.   5' 10" 165 lbs.
D. Jun. 16, 1961, Cambridge, Mass.

Year	Gms.	BA	SA	AB	H	2B	3B	HR	RBI	SB	G. by Pos
1924	1	.000	.000	1	0	0	0	0	0	0	2B-1

Myril Hoag

MYRIL OLIVER HOAG   BR TR
B. Mar. 9, 1908, Davis, Calif.   5' 11" 180 lbs.
D. Jul. 28, 1971, High Springs, Fla.

Year	Gms.	BA	SA	AB	H	2B	3B	HR	RBI	SB	G. by Pos
1931	44	.143	.214	28	4	2	0	0	3	0	OF-23, 3B-1
1932	46	.370	.519	54	20	5	0	1	7	1	OF-35, 1B-1
1934	97	.267	.351	251	67	8	2	3	34	1	OF-86
1935	48	.255	.336	110	28	4	1	1	13	4	OF-37
1936	45	.301	.468	156	47	9	4	3	34	3	OF-39
1937	106	.301	.423	362	109	19	8	3	46	4	OF-99
1938	85	.277	.352	267	74	14	3	0	48	4	OF-70
7 yrs.	471	.284	.390	1228	349	61	18	11	185	17	OF-389, 1B-1, 3B-1

Myril Hoag continued

Year	Gms.	BA	SA	AB	H	2B	3B	HR	RBI	SB	G. by Pos
World Series											
1932	1	—	—	0	0	0	0	0	0	0	
1937	5	.300	.500	20	6	1	0	1	2	0	OF-5
1938	2	.400	.600	5	2	1	0	0	1	0	OF-1
3 yrs.	8	.320	.520	25	8	2	0	1	3	0	OF-6

Butch Hobson

CLELL LAVERN HOBSON, JR.   BR TR
B. Aug. 17, 1951, Tuscaloosa, Ala.   6' 1" 193 lbs.

Year	Gms.	BA	SA	AB	H	2B	3B	HR	RBI	SB	G. by Pos
1982	30	.172	.207	58	10	2	0	0	3	0	DH-15, 1B-11

Danny Hoffman

DANIEL JOHN HOFFMAN   BL TL
B. Mar. 12, 1880, Canton, Conn.   5' 9" 175 lbs.
D. Mar. 14, 1922, Manchester, Conn.

Year	Gms.	BA	SA	AB	H	2B	3B	HR	RBI	SB	G. by Pos
1906	100	.256	.325	320	82	10	6	0	23	32	OF-98
1907	136	.253	.308	517	131	10	3	4	46	30	OF-135
2 yrs.	236	.254	.314	837	213	20	9	4	69	62	OF-233

Solly Hofman

ARTHUR FREDERICK HOFMAN   BR TR
B. Oct. 29, 1882, St. Louis, Mo.   6' 160 lbs.
D. Mar. 10, 1956, St. Louis, Mo.

Year	Gms.	BA	SA	AB	H	2B	3B	HR	RBI	SB	G. by Pos
1916	6	.296	.407	27	8	1	0	0	2	1	OF-6

Fred Hofmann

FRED HOFMANN   BR TR
B. Jun. 10, 1894, St. Louis, Mo.   5' 11½" 175 lbs.
D. Nov. 19, 1964, St. Helena, Calif.

Year	Gms.	BA	SA	AB	H	2B	3B	HR	RBI	SB	G. by Pos
1919	1	.000	.000	1	0	0	0	0	0	0	C-1
1920	15	.292	.292	24	7	0	0	0	1	0	C-14
1921	23	.177	.274	62	11	1	1	1	5	0	C-18, 1B-1
1922	37	.297	.484	91	27	5	3	2	10	0	C-29
1923	72	.290	.403	238	69	10	4	3	26	2	C-70
1924	62	.175	.241	166	29	6	1	1	11	2	C-54
1925	3	.000	.000	2	0	0	0	0	0	0	C-1
7 yrs.	213	.245	.349	584	143	22	9	7	53	4	C-187, 1B-1
World Series											
1923	2	.000	.000	1	0	0	0	0	0	0	

Bill Holden

WILLIAM PAUL HOLDEN   BR TR
B. Sep. 7, 1889, Birmingham, Ala.   6' 170 lbs.
D. Sep. 14, 1971, Pensacola, Fla.

Year	Gms.	BA	SA	AB	H	2B	3B	HR	RBI	SB	G. by Pos
1913	18	.302	.396	53	16	3	1	0	8	0	OF-16
1914	50	.182	.224	165	30	3	2	0	12	2	OF-45
2 yrs.	68	.211	.266	218	46	6	3	0	20	2	OF-61

Fred Holmes

FREDERICK C. HOLMES   BR TR
B. Jul. 1, 1878, Chicago, Ill.   ' " lbs.
D. Feb. 13, 1956, Norwood Park, Ill.

Year	Gms.	BA	SA	AB	H	2B	3B	HR	RBI	SB	G. by Pos
1903	1	—	—	0	0	0	0	0	0	0	1B-1

Roger Holt

ROGER BOYD HOLT   BB TR
B. Apr. 8, 1956, Daytona Beach, Fla.   5' 11" 165 lbs.

Year	Gms.	BA	SA	AB	H	2B	3B	HR	RBI	SB	G. by Pos
1980	2	.167	.167	6	1	0	0	0	1	0	2B-2

Johnny Hopp

JOHN LEONARD HOPP   BL TL
B. Jul. 18, 1916, Hastings, Neb.   5' 10" 170 lbs.

Year	Gms.	BA	SA	AB	H	2B	3B	HR	RBI	SB	G. by Pos
1950	19	.333	.593	27	9	2	1	1	8	0	1B-12, OF-6
1951	46	.206	.317	63	13	1	0	2	4	2	1B-25
1952	15	.160	.160	25	4	0	0	0	2	2	1B-12
3 yrs.	80	.226	.348	115	26	3	1	3	14	4	1B-49, OF-6
World Series											
1950	3	.000	.000	2	0	0	0	0	0	0	1B-3
1951	1	—	—	0	0	0	0	0	0	0	
2 yrs.	4	.000	.000	2	0	0	0	0	0	0	1B-3

Shags Horan

JOSEPH PATRICK HORAN BR TR
B. Sep. 6, 1895, St. Louis, Mo. 5' 10" 170 lbs.
D. Feb. 13, 1969, Torrance, Calif.

Year	Gms.	BA	SA	AB	H	2B	3B	HR	RBI	SB	G. by Pos
1924	22	.290	.323	31	9	1	0	0	7	0	OF-13

Ralph Houk

RALPH GEORGE HOUK BR TR
B. Aug. 9, 1919, Lawrence, Kans. 5' 11" 193 lbs.

Year	Gms.	BA	SA	AB	H	2B	3B	HR	RBI	SB	G. by Pos
1947	41	.272	.326	92	25	3	1	0	12	0	C-41
1948	14	.276	.345	29	8	2	0	0	3	0	C-14
1949	5	.571	.571	7	4	0	0	0	1	0	C-5
1950	10	.111	.222	9	1	1	0	0	1	0	C-9
1951	3	.200	.200	5	1	0	0	0	2	0	C-3
1952	9	.333	.333	6	2	0	0	0	0	0	C-9
1953	8	.222	.222	9	2	0	0	0	1	0	C-8
1954	1	.000	.000	1	0	0	0	0	0	0	
8 yrs.	91	.272	.323	158	43	6	1	0	20	0	C-89
World Series											
1947	1	1.000	1.000	1	1	0	0	0	0	0	
1952	1	.000	.000	1	0	0	0	0	0	0	
2 yrs.	2	.500	.500	2	1	0	0	0	0	0	

Elston Howard

ELSTON GENE HOWARD BR TR
B. Feb. 23, 1929, St. Louis, Mo. 6' 2" 196 lbs.
D. Dec. 14, 1980, New York, N. Y.

Year	Gms.	BA	SA	AB	H	2B	3B	HR	RBI	SB	G. by Pos
1955	97	.290	.477	279	81	8	7	10	43	0	OF-75, C-9
1956	98	.262	.362	290	76	8	3	5	34	0	OF-65, C-26
1957	110	.253	.379	356	90	13	4	8	44	2	OF-71, C-32, 1B-2
1958	103	.314	.479	376	118	19	5	11	66	1	C-67, OF-24, 1B-5
1959	125	.273	.476	443	121	24	6	18	73	0	1B-50, C-43, OF-28
1960	107	.245	.353	323	79	11	3	6	39	3	C-91, OF-1
1961	129	.348	.549	446	155	17	5	21	77	0	C-111, 1B-9
1962	136	.279	.474	494	138	23	5	21	91	1	C-129
1963	135	.287	.528	487	140	21	6	28	85	0	C-132
1964	150	.313	.455	550	172	27	3	15	84	1	C-146
1965	110	.233	.345	391	91	15	1	9	45	0	C-95, 1B-5, OF-1
1966	126	.256	.356	410	105	19	2	6	35	0	C-100, 1B-13
1967	66	.196	.271	199	39	6	0	3	17	0	C-48, 1B-1
13 yrs.	1492	.279	.436	5044	1405	211	50	161	733	8	C-1029, OF-265, 1B-85
World Series											
1955	7	.192	.308	26	5	0	0	1	3	0	OF-7
1956	1	.400	1.200	5	2	1	0	1	1	0	OF-1
1957	6	.273	.545	11	3	0	0	1	3	0	1B-3
1958	6	.222	.222	18	4	0	0	0	2	1	OF-6
1960	5	.462	.923	13	6	1	1	1	4	0	C-4
1961	5	.250	.550	20	5	3	0	1	1	0	C-5
1962	6	.143	.190	21	3	1	0	0	1	0	C-6
1963	4	.333	.333	15	5	0	0	0	1	0	C-4
1964	7	.292	.333	24	7	1	0	0	2	0	C-7
9 yrs.	47	.261	.418	153	40	7	1	5	18	1	C-26, OF-14, 1B-3

Harry Howell

HENRY HARRY HOWELL BR TR
B. Nov. 14, 1876, New Jersey 5' 9"
D. May 22, 1956, Spokane, Wash.

Year	Gms.	BA	SA	AB	H	2B	3B	HR	RBI	SB	G. by Pos
1903	40	.217	.311	106	23	3	2	1	12	1	P-25, 3B-7, SS-5, 1B-1, 2B-1

Dick Howser

RICHARD DALTON HOWSER BR TR
B. May 14, 1936, Miami, Fla. 5' 8" 155 lbs.
D. Jun. 17, 1987, Kansas City, Mo.

Year	Gms.	BA	SA	AB	H	2B	3B	HR	RBI	SB	G. by Pos
1967	63	.268	.309	149	40	6	0	0	10	1	2B-22, 3B-12, SS-3
1968	85	.153	.180	150	23	2	1	0	3	0	2B-29, 3B-2, SS-1
2 yrs.	148	.211	.244	299	63	8	1	0	13	1	2B-51, 3B-14, SS-4

Rex Hudler

REX ALLEN HUDLER BR TR
B. Sep. 2, 1960, Tempe, Ariz. 6' 1" 180 lbs.

Year	Gms.	BA	SA	AB	H	2B	3B	HR	RBI	SB	G. by Pos
1984	9	.143	.286	7	1	1	0	0	0	0	2B-9
1985	20	.157	.196	51	8	0	1	0	1	0	2B-16, 1B-1, SS-1
2 yrs.	29	.155	.207	58	9	1	1	0	1	0	2B-25, 1B-1, SS-1

Keith Hughes

KEITH WILLS HUGHES BL TL
B. Sep. 12, 1963, Bryn Mawr, Pa. 6' 3" 210 lbs.

Year	Gms.	BA	SA	AB	H	2B	3B	HR	RBI	SB	G. by Pos
1987	4	.000	.000	4	0	0	0	0	0	0	

John Hummel

JOHN EDWIN HUMMEL BR TR
B. Apr. 4, 1883, Bloomsburg, Pa. 5' 11" 160 lbs.
D. May 18, 1959, Springfield, Mass.

Year	Gms.	BA	SA	AB	H	2B	3B	HR	RBI	SB	G. by Pos
1918	22	.295	.377	61	18	1	2	0	4	3	OF-15, 1B-3, 2B-1

Mike Humphreys

MICHAEL BUTLER HUMPHREYS BR TR
B. Apr. 10, 1967, Dallas, Tex. 6' 185 lbs.

Year	Gms.	BA	SA	AB	H	2B	3B	HR	RBI	SB	G. by Pos
1991	25	.200	.200	40	8	0	0	0	3	2	OF-9, DH-7, 3B-6
1992	4	.100	.100	10	1	0	0	0	0	0	OF-2, DH-1
1993	25	.171	.371	35	6	2	1	1	6	2	OF-21, DH-3
3 yrs.	54	.176	.259	85	15	2	1	1	9	4	OF-32, DH-11, 3B-6

Ken Hunt

KENNETH LAWRENCE HUNT BR TR
B. Jul. 13, 1934, Grand Forks, N. D. 6' 1" 205 lbs.

Year	Gms.	BA	SA	AB	H	2B	3B	HR	RBI	SB	G. by Pos
1959	6	.333	.417	12	4	1	0	0	1	0	OF-5
1960	25	.273	.364	22	6	2	0	0	1	0	OF-24
2 yrs.	31	.294	.382	34	10	3	0	0	2	0	OF-29

Billy Hunter

GORDON WILLIAM HUNTER BR TR
B. Jun. 4, 1928, Punxsutawney, Pa. 6' 180 lbs.

Year	Gms.	BA	SA	AB	H	2B	3B	HR	RBI	SB	G. by Pos
1955	98	.227	.298	255	58	7	1	3	20	9	SS-98
1956	39	.280	.427	75	21	3	4	0	11	0	SS-32, 3B-4
2 yrs.	137	.239	.327	330	79	10	5	3	31	9	SS-130, 3B-4

Ham Hyatt

ROBERT HAMILTON HYATT BL TR
B. Nov. 1, 1884, Buncombe County, N. C. 6' 1" 185 lbs.
D. Sep. 11, 1963, Liberty Lake, Wash.

Year	Gms.	BA	SA	AB	H	2B	3B	HR	RBI	SB	G. by Pos
1918	53	.229	.336	131	30	8	0	2	10	1	OF-25, 1B-5

Fred Jacklitsch

FREDERICK LAWRENCE JACKLITSCH BR TR
B. May 24, 1876, Brooklyn, N. Y. 5' 9" 180 lbs.
D. Jul. 18, 1937, Brooklyn, N. Y.

Year	Gms.	BA	SA	AB	H	2B	3B	HR	RBI	SB	G. by Pos
1905	1	.000	.000	3	0	0	0	0	1	0	C-1

Reggie Jackson

REGINALD MARTINEZ JACKSON BL TL
B. May 18, 1946, Wyncote, Pa. 6' 195 lbs.
Hall of Fame 1993

Year	Gms.	BA	SA	AB	H	2B	3B	HR	RBI	SB	G. by Pos
1977	146	.286	.550	525	150	39	2	32	110	17	OF-127, DH-18
1978	139	.274	.477	511	140	13	5	27	97	14	OF-104, DH-35
1979	131	.297	.544	465	138	24	2	29	89	9	OF-125, DH-11
1980	143	.300	.597	514	154	22	4	41	111	1	OF-94, DH-46
1981	94	.237	.428	334	79	17	1	15	54	0	OF-61, DH-33
5 yrs.	653	.281	.526	2349	661	115	14	144	461	41	OF-511, DH-143
Divisional Playoffs											
1981	5	.300	.600	20	6	0	0	2	4	0	OF-5
League Championship Series											
1977	5	.125	.125	16	2	0	0	0	1	1	OF-4, DH-1
1978	4	.462	1.000	13	6	1	0	2	6	0	DH-3, OF-1
1980	3	.273	.364	11	3	1	0	0	0	0	OF-3
1981	2	.000	.000	4	0	0	0	0	1	1	OF-2
4 yrs.	14	.250	.432	44	11	2	0	2	8	2	OF-10, DH-4
World Series											
1977	6	.450	1.250	20	9	1	0	5	8	0	OF-6
1978	6	.391	.696	23	9	1	0	2	8	0	DH-6
1981	3	.333	.667	12	4	1	0	1	1	0	OF-3
3 yrs.	15	.400	.891	55	22	3	0	8	17	0	OF-9, DH-6

Dion James

DION JAMES BL TL
B. Nov. 9, 1962, Philadelphia, Pa. 6' 1" 170 lbs.

Year	Gms.	BA	SA	AB	H	2B	3B	HR	RBI	SB	G. by Pos
1992	67	.262	.379	145	38	8	0	3	17	1	OF-46, DH-5
1993	115	.332	.466	343	114	21	2	7	36	0	OF-103, 1B-1, DH-1

Dion James *continued*

Year	Gms.	BA	SA	AB	H	2B	3B	HR	RBI	SB	G. by Pos
1995	85	.287	.354	209	60	6	1	2	26	4	OF-29, DH-27, 1B-6
1996	6	.167	.167	12	2	0	0	0	0	1	OF-4, DH-1
4 yrs.	273	.302	.410	709	214	35	3	12	79	6	OF-182, DH-34, 1B-7

Divisional Playoffs

Year	Gms.	BA	SA	AB	H	2B	3B	HR	RBI	SB	G. by Pos
1995	4	.083	.083	12	1	0	0	0	0	0	OF-4

Stan Javier

STANLEY JULIAN JAVIER BB TR
B. Jan. 9, 1964, San Francisco de Macoris, 6' 180 lbs.
Dominican Republic

Year	Gms.	BA	SA	AB	H	2B	3B	HR	RBI	SB	G. by Pos
1984	7	.143	.143	7	1	0	0	0	0	0	OF-5

Stan Jefferson

STANLEY JEFFERSON BB TR
B. Dec. 4, 1962, New York, N.Y. 5' 11" 175 lbs.

Year	Gms.	BA	SA	AB	H	2B	3B	HR	RBI	SB	G. by Pos
1989	10	.083	.083	12	1	0	0	1	1	1	OF-7, DH-1

Jackie Jensen

JACK EUGENE JENSEN BR TR
B. Mar. 9, 1927, San Francisco, Calif. 5' 11" 190 lbs.
D. Jul. 14, 1982, Charlottesville, Va.

Year	Gms.	BA	SA	AB	H	2B	3B	HR	RBI	SB	G. by Pos
1950	45	.171	.300	70	12	2	2	1	5	4	OF-23
1951	56	.298	.500	168	50	8	1	8	25	8	OF-48
1952	7	.105	.263	19	2	1	1	0	2	1	OF-5
3 yrs.	108	.249	.428	257	64	11	4	9	32	13	OF-76

World Series

Year	Gms.	BA	SA	AB	H	2B	3B	HR	RBI	SB	G. by Pos
1950	1	—	—	0	0	0	0	0	0	0	

Derek Jeter

DEREK SANDERSON JETER BR TR
B. Jun. 26, 1974, Pequannock, N.J. 6' 3" 175 lbs.

Year	Gms.	BA	SA	AB	H	2B	3B	HR	RBI	SB	G. by Pos
1995	15	.250	.375	48	12	4	1	0	7	0	SS-15
1996	157	.314	.430	582	183	25	6	10	78	14	SS-157
2 yrs.	172	.310	.425	630	195	29	7	10	85	14	SS-172

Divisional Playoffs

Year	Gms.	BA	SA	AB	H	2B	3B	HR	RBI	SB	G. by Pos
1996	4	.412	.471	17	7	1	0	0	1	0	SS-4

League Championship Series

Year	Gms.	BA	SA	AB	H	2B	3B	HR	RBI	SB	G. by Pos
1996	5	.417	.625	24	10	2	0	1	1	2	SS-5

World Series

Year	Gms.	BA	SA	AB	H	2B	3B	HR	RBI	SB	G. by Pos
1996	6	.250	.250	20	5	0	0	0	1	1	SS-6

Elvio Jimenez

FELIX ELVIO JIMENEZ BR TR
B. Jan. 6, 1940, San Pedro de Macoris, 5' 9" 170 lbs.
Dominican Republic

Year	Gms.	BA	SA	AB	H	2B	3B	HR	RBI	SB	G. by Pos
1964	1	.333	.333	6	2	0	0	0	0	0	OF-1

Alex Johnson

ALEXANDER JOHNSON BR TR
B. Dec. 7, 1942, Helena, Ark. 6' 205 lbs.

Year	Gms.	BA	SA	AB	H	2B	3B	HR	RBI	SB	G. by Pos
1974	10	.214	.357	28	6	1	0	1	2	0	DH-3, OF-1
1975	52	.261	.345	119	31	5	1	1	15	2	DH-28, OF-7
2 yrs.	62	.252	.347	147	37	6	1	2	17	2	DH-31, OF-8

Billy Johnson

WILLIAM RUSSELL JOHNSON BR TR
B. Aug. 30, 1918, Montclair, N.J. 5' 10" 180 lbs.

Year	Gms.	BA	SA	AB	H	2B	3B	HR	RBI	SB	G. by Pos
1943	155	.280	.367	592	166	24	6	5	94	3	3B-155
1946	85	.260	.382	296	77	14	5	4	35	1	3B-74
1947	132	.285	.417	494	141	19	8	10	95	1	3B-132
1948	127	.294	.446	446	131	20	6	12	64	0	3B-118
1949	113	.249	.374	329	82	11	3	8	56	1	3B-81, 1B-21, 2B-1
1950	108	.260	.376	327	85	16	2	6	40	1	3B-100, 1B-5
1951	15	.300	.375	40	12	3	0	0	4	0	3B-13
7 yrs.	735	.275	.395	2524	694	107	30	45	388	7	3B-673, 1B-26, 2B-1

World Series

Year	Gms.	BA	SA	AB	H	2B	3B	HR	RBI	SB	G. by Pos
1943	5	.300	.450	20	6	1	1	0	3	0	3B-5
1947	7	.269	.500	26	7	0	3	0	2	0	3B-7
1949	2	.143	.143	7	1	0	0	0	0	1	3B-2
1950	4	.000	.000	6	0	0	0	0	0	0	3B-4
4 yrs.	18	.237	.390	59	14	1	4	0	5	1	3B-18

Cliff Johnson

CLIFFORD JOHNSON, JR. BR TR
B. Jul. 22, 1947, San Antonio, Tex. 6' 4" 215 lbs.

Year	Gms.	BA	SA	AB	H	2B	3B	HR	RBI	SB	G. by Pos
1977	56	.296	.606	142	42	8	0	12	31	0	DH-25, C-15, 1B-11
1978	76	.184	.351	174	32	9	1	6	19	0	DH-39, C-22, 1B-1
1979	28	.266	.453	64	17	6	0	2	6	0	DH-18, C-4
3 yrs.	160	.239	.463	380	91	23	1	20	56	0	DH-82, C-41, 1B-12

League Championship Series

Year	Gms.	BA	SA	AB	H	2B	3B	HR	RBI	SB	G. by Pos
1977	5	.400	.733	15	6	2	0	1	2	0	DH-4
1978	1	.000	.000	1	0	0	0	0	0	0	
2 yrs.	6	.375	.688	16	6	2	0	1	2	0	DH-4

World Series

Year	Gms.	BA	SA	AB	H	2B	3B	HR	RBI	SB	G. by Pos
1977	2	.000	.000	1	0	0	0	0	0	0	C-1
1978	2	.000	.000	2	0	0	0	0	0	0	
2 yrs.	4	.000	.000	3	0	0	0	0	0	0	C-1

Darrell Johnson

DARRELL DEAN JOHNSON BR TR
B. Aug. 25, 1928, Horace, Neb. 6' 1" 180 lbs.

Year	Gms.	BA	SA	AB	H	2B	3B	HR	RBI	SB	G. by Pos
1957	21	.217	.304	46	10	1	0	1	8	0	C-20
1958	5	.250	.250	16	4	0	0	0	0	0	C-4
2 yrs.	26	.226	.290	62	14	1	0	1	8	0	C-24

Deron Johnson

DERON ROGER JOHNSON BR TR
B. Jul. 17, 1938, San Diego, Calif. 6' 2" 200 lbs.
D. Apr. 23, 1992, Poway, Calif.

Year	Gms.	BA	SA	AB	H	2B	3B	HR	RBI	SB	G. by Pos
1960	6	.500	.750	4	2	1	0	0	0	0	3B-5
1961	13	.105	.105	19	2	0	0	0	2	0	3B-8
2 yrs.	19	.174	.217	23	4	1	0	0	2	0	3B-13

Ernie Johnson

ERNEST RUDOLPH JOHNSON BL TR
B. Apr. 29, 1888, Chicago, Ill. 5' 9" 151 lbs.
D. May. 1, 1952, Monrovia, Calif.

Year	Gms.	BA	SA	AB	H	2B	3B	HR	RBI	SB	G. by Pos
1923	17	.354	.479	48	17	1	1	1	8	0	SS-12, 3B-1
1924	64	.353	.597	119	42	4	8	3	12	1	2B-27, SS-9, 3B-2
1925	76	.282	.412	170	48	5	1	5	17	6	2B-34, SS-28, 3B-2
3 yrs.	157	.318	.487	337	107	10	10	9	37	7	2B-61, SS-49, 3B-5

World Series

Year	Gms.	BA	SA	AB	H	2B	3B	HR	RBI	SB	G. by Pos
1923	2	—	—	0	0	0	0	0	0	0	SS-1

Otis Johnson

OTIS L. JOHNSON BB TR
B. Nov. 5, 1883, Fowler, Ind. 5' 9" 185 lbs.
D. Nov. 9, 1915, Johnson City, N.Y.

Year	Gms.	BA	SA	AB	H	2B	3B	HR	RBI	SB	G. by Pos
1911	71	.234	.378	209	49	9	6	3	36	12	SS-47, 2B-15, 3B-3

Roy Johnson

ROY CLEVELAND JOHNSON BL TR
B. Feb. 23, 1903, Pryor, Okla. 5' 9" 175 lbs.
D. Sep. 10, 1973, Tacoma, Wash.

Year	Gms.	BA	SA	AB	H	2B	3B	HR	RBI	SB	G. by Pos
1936	63	.265	.367	147	39	8	2	1	19	3	OF-33
1937	12	.294	.353	51	15	3	0	0	6	1	OF-12
2 yrs.	75	.273	.364	198	54	11	2	1	25	4	OF-45

World Series

Year	Gms.	BA	SA	AB	H	2B	3B	HR	RBI	SB	G. by Pos
1936	2	.000	.000	1	0	0	0	0	0	0	

Jay Johnstone

JOHN WILLIAM JOHNSTONE BL TR
B. Nov. 20, 1945, Manchester, Conn. 6' 1" 175 lbs.

Year	Gms.	BA	SA	AB	H	2B	3B	HR	RBI	SB	G. by Pos
1978	36	.262	.308	65	17	0	1	1	6	0	OF-22, DH-5
1979	23	.208	.292	48	10	1	0	1	7	1	OF-19, DH-3
2 yrs.	59	.239	.301	113	27	1	0	2	13	1	OF-41, DH-8

World Series

Year	Gms.	BA	SA	AB	H	2B	3B	HR	RBI	SB	G. by Pos
1978	2	—	—	0	0	0	0	0	0	0	OF-2

Darryl Jones

DARRYL LEE JONES BR TR
B. Jun. 5, 1951, Meadville, Pa. 5' 10" 175 lbs.

Year	Gms.	BA	SA	AB	H	2B	3B	HR	RBI	SB	G. by Pos
1979	18	.255	.404	47	12	5	1	0	6	0	DH-15, OF-2

Ruppert Jones

RUPPERT SANDERSON JONES BL TL
B. Mar. 12, 1955, Dallas, Tex. 5' 10" 170 lbs.

Year	Gms.	BA	SA	AB	H	2B	3B	HR	RBI	SB	G. by Pos
1980	83	.223	.357	328	73	11	3	9	42	18	OF-82

Year	Gms.	BA	SA	AB	H	2B	3B	HR	RBI	SB	G. by Pos

Tim Jordan

TIMOTHY JOSEPH JORDAN BL TL
B. Feb. 14, 1879, New York, N. Y. 6' 1" 170 lbs.
D. Sep. 13, 1949, Bronx, N. Y.

Year	Gms.	BA	SA	AB	H	2B	3B	HR	RBI	SB	G. by Pos
1903	2	.125	.125	8	1	0	0	0	0	0	1B-2

Arndt Jorgens

ARNDT LUDWIG JORGENS BR TR
B. May 18, 1905, Modum, Norway 5' 9" 160 lbs.
D. Mar. 1, 1980, Wilmette, Ill.

Year	Gms.	BA	SA	AB	H	2B	3B	HR	RBI	SB	G. by Pos
1929	18	.324	.412	34	11	3	0	0	4	0	C-15
1930	16	.367	.467	30	11	3	0	0	1	0	C-16
1931	46	.270	.320	100	27	1	2	0	14	0	C-40
1932	55	.219	.318	151	33	7	1	2	19	0	C-55
1933	21	.220	.400	50	11	3	0	2	13	1	C-19
1934	58	.208	.251	183	38	6	1	0	20	2	C-56
1935	36	.238	.262	84	20	2	0	0	8	0	C-33
1936	31	.273	.348	66	18	3	1	0	5	0	C-30
1937	13	.130	.174	23	3	1	0	0	3	0	C-11
1938	9	.235	.353	17	4	2	0	0	2	0	C-8
1939	3	—	—	0	0	0	0	0	0	0	C-2
11 yrs.	306	.238	.310	738	176	31	5	4	89	3	C-285

Frank Kane

FRANCIS THOMAS KANE BL TR
B. Mar. 9, 1895, Whitman, Mass. 5' 11½" 175 lbs.
D. Dec. 2, 1962, Brockton, Mass.

Year	Gms.	BA	SA	AB	H	2B	3B	HR	RBI	SB	G. by Pos
1919	1	.000	.000	1	0	0	0	0	0	0	

Bill Karlon

WILLIAM JOHN KARLON BR TR
B. Jan. 21, 1909, Palmer, Mass. 6' 1" 190 lbs.
D. Dec. 7, 1964, Ware, Mass.

Year	Gms.	BA	SA	AB	H	2B	3B	HR	RBI	SB	G. by Pos
1930	2	.000	.000	5	0	0	0	0	0	0	OF-1

Benny Kauff

BENJAMIN MICHAEL KAUFF BL TL
B. Jan. 5, 1890, Pomeroy, Ohio 5' 8" 157 lbs.
D. Nov. 17, 1961, Columbus, Ohio

Year	Gms.	BA	SA	AB	H	2B	3B	HR	RBI	SB	G. by Pos
1912	5	.273	.273	11	3	0	0	0	2	1	OF-4

Eddie Kearse

EDWARD PAUL KEARSE BR TR
B. Feb. 23, 1916, San Francisco, Calif. 6' 1" 195 lbs.
D. Jul. 15, 1968, Eureka, Calif.

Year	Gms.	BA	SA	AB	H	2B	3B	HR	RBI	SB	G. by Pos
1942	11	.192	.192	26	5	0	0	0	2	1	C-11

Willie Keeler

WILLIAM HENRY KEELER BL TL
B. Mar. 3, 1872, Brooklyn, N. Y. 5' 4½" 140 lbs.
D. Jan. 1, 1923, Brooklyn, N. Y.
Hall of Fame 1939

Year	Gms.	BA	SA	AB	H	2B	3B	HR	RBI	SB	G. by Pos
1903	132	.318	.373	515	164	14	7	0	32	24	OF-128, 3B-4
1904	143	.343	.409	543	186	14	8	2	40	21	OF-142
1905	149	.302	.362	560	169	14	4	4	38	19	OF-139, 2B-12, 3B-3
1906	152	.304	.338	592	180	8	3	2	33	23	OF-152
1907	107	.234	.255	423	99	5	2	0	17	7	OF-107
1908	91	.263	.288	323	85	3	1	1	14	14	OF-88
1909	99	.264	.319	360	95	7	5	1	32	10	OF-95
7 yrs.	873	.295	.342	3316	978	65	30	10	206	118	OF-851, 2B-12, 3B-7

Charlie Keller

CHARLES ERNEST KELLER BL TR
B. Sep. 12, 1916, Middletown, Md. 5' 10" 185 lbs.
D. May 23, 1990, Frederick, Md.

Year	Gms.	BA	SA	AB	H	2B	3B	HR	RBI	SB	G. by Pos
1939	111	.334	.500	398	133	21	6	11	83	6	OF-105
1940	138	.286	.508	500	143	18	15	21	93	8	OF-136
1941	140	.298	.580	507	151	24	10	33	122	6	OF-137
1942	152	.292	.513	544	159	24	9	26	108	14	OF-152
1943	141	.271	.525	512	139	15	11	31	86	7	OF-141
1945	44	.301	.577	163	49	7	4	10	34	0	OF-44
1946	150	.275	.533	538	148	29	10	30	101	1	OF-149
1947	45	.238	.550	151	36	6	1	13	36	0	OF-43
1948	83	.267	.417	247	66	15	2	6	44	1	OF-66

Charlie Keller *continued*

Year	Gms.	BA	SA	AB	H	2B	3B	HR	RBI	SB	G. by Pos
1949	60	.250	.379	116	29	4	1	3	16	2	OF-31
1952	2	.000	.000	1	0	0	0	0	0	0	OF-1
11 yrs.	1066	.286	.518	3677	1053	163	69	184	723	45	OF-1005
World Series
1939	4	.438	1.188	16	7	1	1	3	6	0	OF-4
1941	5	.389	.500	18	7	2	0	0	5	0	OF-5
1942	5	.200	.500	20	4	0	0	2	5	0	OF-5
1943	5	.222	.333	18	4	0	1	0	2	1	OF-5
4 yrs.	19	.306	.611	72	22	3	2	5	18	1	OF-19

Pat Kelly

PATRICK FRANKLIN KELLY BR TR
B. Oct. 14, 1967, Philadelphia, Pa. 6' 180 lbs.

Year	Gms.	BA	SA	AB	H	2B	3B	HR	RBI	SB	G. by Pos
1991	96	.242	.339	298	72	12	4	3	23	12	3B-80, 2B-19
1992	106	.226	.374	318	72	22	2	7	27	8	2B-101, DH-1
1993	127	.273	.389	406	111	24	1	7	51	14	2B-125
1994	93	.280	.399	286	80	21	2	3	41	6	2B-93
1995	89	.237	.333	270	64	12	1	4	29	8	2B-87, DH-1
1996	13	.143	.143	21	3	0	0	0	2	0	2B-10, DH-3
6 yrs.	524	.251	.366	1599	402	91	10	24	173	48	2B-435, 3B-80, DH-5
Divisional Playoffs
1995	5	.000	.000	3	0	0	0	0	1	0	2B-4

Roberto Kelly

ROBERTO CONRADO KELLY BR TR
Oct.. 1, 1964, Panama City, Panama 6' 2" 180 lbs.

Year	Gms.	BA	SA	AB	H	2B	3B	HR	RBI	SB	G. by Pos
1987	23	.269	.385	52	14	3	0	1	7	9	OF-17
1988	38	.247	.364	77	19	4	1	1	7	5	OF-30
1989	137	.302	.417	441	133	18	3	9	48	35	OF-137
1990	162	.285	.418	641	183	32	4	15	61	42	OF-160, DH-1
1991	126	.267	.444	486	130	22	2	20	69	32	OF-125
1992	152	.272	.384	580	158	31	2	10	66	28	OF-146
6 yrs.	638	.280	.412	2277	637	110	12	56	258	151	OF-615, DH-1

Steve Kemp

STEVEN F. KEMP BL TL
B. Aug. 7, 1954, San Angelo, Tex. 6' 195 lbs.

Year	Gms.	BA	SA	AB	H	2B	3B	HR	RBI	SB	G. by Pos
1983	109	.241	.399	373	90	17	3	12	49	1	OF-101, DH-2
1984	94	.291	.403	313	91	12	1	7	41	4	OF-75, DH-12
2 yrs.	203	.264	.401	686	181	29	4	19	90	5	OF-176, DH-14

John Kennedy

JOHN EDWARD KENNEDY BR TR
B. May 29, 1941, Chicago, Ill. 6' 185 lbs.

Year	Gms.	BA	SA	AB	H	2B	3B	HR	RBI	SB	G. by Pos
1967	78	.196	.235	179	35	4	0	1	17	2	SS-36, 3B-34, 2B-2

Jerry Kenney

GERALD TENNYSON KENNEY, JR. BL TR
B. Jun. 30, 1945, St. Louis, Mo. 6' 1" 170 lbs.

Year	Gms.	BA	SA	AB	H	2B	3B	HR	RBI	SB	G. by Pos
1967	20	.310	.397	58	18	2	0	1	5	2	SS-18
1969	130	.257	.311	447	115	14	2	2	34	25	3B-83, OF-31, SS-10
1970	140	.193	.282	404	78	10	7	4	35	20	3B-135, 2B-2
1971	120	.262	.311	325	85	10	3	0	20	9	3B-109, SS-5, 1B-1
1972	50	.210	.227	119	25	2	0	0	7	3	SS-45, 3B-1
5 yrs.	460	.237	.299	1353	321	38	12	7	101	59	3B-328, SS-78, OF-31, 2B-2, 1B-1

Steve Kiefer

STEVEN GEORGE KIEFER BR TR
B. Oct. 18, 1960, Chicago, Ill. 6' 1" 175 lbs.

Year	Gms.	BA	SA	AB	H	2B	3B	HR	RBI	SB	G. by Pos
1989	5	.125	.125	8	1	0	0	0	0	0	3B-5

Dave Kingman

DAVID ARTHUR KINGMAN BR TR
B. Dec. 21, 1948, Pendleton, Ore. 6' 6" 210 lbs.

Year	Gms.	BA	SA	AB	H	2B	3B	HR	RBI	SB	G. by Pos
1977	8	.250	.833	24	6	2	0	4	7	0	DH-6

Henry Kingman

HENRY LEES KINGMAN BL TL
B. Apr. 3, 1892, Tientsin, China 6' 1½" 165 lbs.
D. Dec. 27, 1982, Oakland, Calif.

Year	Gms.	BA	SA	AB	H	2B	3B	HR	RBI	SB	G. by Pos
1914	4	.000	.000	3	0	0	0	0	0	0	1B-1

329

Ron Kittle

RONALD DALE KITTLE   BR TR
B. Jan. 5, 1958, Gary, Ind.   6' 4" 200 lbs.

Year	Gms.	BA	SA	AB	H	2B	3B	HR	RBI	SB	G. by Pos
1986	30	.237	.412	80	19	2	0	4	12	2	DH-24, OF-1
1987	59	.277	.535	159	44	5	0	12	28	0	DH-49, OF-2
2 yrs.	89	.264	.494	239	63	7	0	16	40	2	DH-73, OF-3

Red Kleinow

JOHN PETER KLEINOW   BR TR
B. Jul. 20, 1879, Milwaukee, Wis.   5' 10" 165 lbs.
D. Oct. 9, 1929, New York, N. Y.

Year	Gms.	BA	SA	AB	H	2B	3B	HR	RBI	SB	G. by Pos
1904	68	.206	.282	209	43	8	4	0	16	4	C-62, 3B-2, OF-1
1905	88	.221	.281	253	56	6	3	1	24	7	C-83, 1B-3
1906	96	.220	.276	268	59	9	3	0	31	8	C-95, 1B-1
1907	90	.264	.316	269	71	6	4	0	26	5	C-86, 1B-1
1908	96	.168	.204	279	47	3	2	1	13	5	C-89, 2B-2
1909	78	.228	.320	206	47	11	4	0	15	7	C-77
1910	6	.417	.417	12	5	0	0	0	2	2	C-5
7 yrs.	522	.219	.279	1496	328	43	20	2	127	38	C-497, 1B-5, 2B-2, 3B-2, OF-1

Mickey Klutts

GENE ELLIS KLUTTS   BR TR
B. Sep. 20, 1954, Montebello, Calif.   5' 11" 170 lbs.

Year	Gms.	BA	SA	AB	H	2B	3B	HR	RBI	SB	G. by Pos
1976	2	.000	.000	3	0	0	0	0	0	0	SS-2
1977	5	.267	.533	15	4	1	0	1	4	0	3B-4, SS-1
1978	1	1.000	1.500	2	2	1	0	0	0	0	3B-1
3 yrs.	8	.300	.550	20	6	2	0	1	4	0	3B-5, SS-3

Bill Knickerbocker

WILLIAM HART KNICKERBOCKER   BR TR
B. Dec. 29, 1911, Los Angeles, Calif.   5' 11" 170 lbs.
D. Sep. 8, 1963, Sebastopol, Calif.

Year	Gms.	BA	SA	AB	H	2B	3B	HR	RBI	SB	G. by Pos
1938	46	.250	.383	128	32	8	3	1	21	0	2B-34, SS-3
1939	6	.154	.231	13	2	1	0	0	1	0	2B-2, SS-2
1940	45	.242	.347	124	30	8	1	1	10	1	SS-19, 3B-17
3 yrs.	97	.242	.358	265	64	17	4	2	32	1	2B-36, SS-24, 3B-17

John Knight

JOHN WESLEY KNIGHT   BR TR
B. Oct. 6, 1885, Philadelphia, Pa.   6' 2½" 180 lbs.
D. Dec. 19, 1965, Walnut Creek, Calif.

Year	Gms.	BA	SA	AB	H	2B	3B	HR	RBI	SB	G. by Pos
1909	116	.236	.286	360	85	8	5	0	40	15	SS-78, 1B-19, 2B-18
1910	117	.312	.413	414	129	25	4	3	45	23	SS-79, 1B-23, 2B-7, 3B-4, OF-1
1911	132	.268	.351	470	126	16	7	3	62	18	SS-82, 1B-27, 2B-21, 3B-1
1913	70	.236	.276	250	59	10	0	0	24	7	1B-50, 2B-21
4 yrs.	435	.267	.340	1494	399	59	16	6	171	63	SS-239, 1B-119, 2B-67, 3B-5, OF-1

Mark Koenig

MARK ANTHONY KOENIG   BB TR
B. Jul. 19, 1904, San Francisco, Calif.   6' 180 lbs.
D. Apr. 22, 1993, Willows, Calif.

Year	Gms.	BA	SA	AB	H	2B	3B	HR	RBI	SB	G. by Pos
1925	28	.209	.282	110	23	6	1	0	4	0	SS-28
1926	147	.271	.363	617	167	26	8	5	62	4	SS-141
1927	123	.285	.382	526	150	20	11	3	62	3	SS-122
1928	132	.319	.415	533	170	19	10	4	63	3	SS-125
1929	116	.292	.416	373	109	27	5	3	41	1	SS-61, 3B-37, 2B-1
1930	21	.230	.297	74	17	5	0	0	9	0	SS-19
6 yrs.	567	.285	.382	2233	636	103	35	15	241	11	SS-496, 3B-37, 2B-1

World Series

Year	Gms.	BA	SA	AB	H	2B	3B	HR	RBI	SB	G. by Pos
1926	7	.125	.156	32	4	1	0	0	2	0	SS-7
1927	4	.500	.611	18	9	2	0	0	2	0	SS-4
1928	4	.158	.158	19	3	0	0	0	0	0	SS-4
3 yrs.	15	.232	.275	69	16	3	0	0	4	0	SS-15

Andy Kosco

ANDREW JOHN KOSCO   BR TR
B. Oct. 5, 1941, Youngstown, Ohio   6' 3" 205 lbs.

Year	Gms.	BA	SA	AB	H	2B	3B	HR	RBI	SB	G. by Pos
1968	131	.240	.382	466	112	19	1	15	59	2	OF-95, 1B-28

Ernie Krueger

ERNEST GEORGE KRUEGER   BR TR
B. Dec. 27, 1890, Chicago, Ill.   5' 10½" 185 lbs.
D. Apr. 22, 1976, Waukegan, Ill.

Year	Gms.	BA	SA	AB	H	2B	3B	HR	RBI	SB	G. by Pos
1915	10	.172	.207	29	5	1	0	0	0	0	C-8

Dick Kryhoski

RICHARD DAVID KRYHOSKI   BL TL
B. Mar. 24, 1925, Leonia, N. J.   6' 2" 182 lbs.

Year	Gms.	BA	SA	AB	H	2B	3B	HR	RBI	SB	G. by Pos
1949	54	.294	.401	177	52	10	3	1	27	2	1B-51

Tony Kubek

ANTHONY CHRISTOPHER KUBEK   BL TR
B. Oct. 12, 1936, Milwaukee, Wis.   6' 3" 190 lbs.

Year	Gms.	BA	SA	AB	H	2B	3B	HR	RBI	SB	G. by Pos
1957	127	.297	.381	431	128	21	3	3	39	6	OF-50, SS-41, 3B-38, 2B-1
1958	138	.265	.317	559	148	21	1	2	48	5	SS-134, OF-3, 1B-1, 2B-1
1959	132	.279	.391	512	143	25	7	6	51	3	SS-67, OF-53, 3B-17, 2B-1
1960	147	.273	.401	568	155	25	3	14	62	3	SS-136, OF-29
1961	153	.276	.395	617	170	38	6	8	46	1	SS-145
1962	45	.314	.432	169	53	6	1	4	17	2	SS-35, OF-6
1963	135	.257	.343	557	143	21	3	7	44	4	SS-132, OF-1
1964	106	.229	.340	415	95	16	3	8	31	4	SS-99
1965	109	.218	.295	339	74	5	3	5	35	1	SS-93, OF-3, 1B-1
9 yrs.	1092	.266	.364	4167	1109	178	30	57	373	29	SS-882, OF-145, 3B-55, 2B-3, 1B-2

World Series

Year	Gms.	BA	SA	AB	H	2B	3B	HR	RBI	SB	G. by Pos
1957	7	.286	.500	28	8	0	0	2	4	0	OF-5, 3B-2
1958	7	.048	.048	21	1	0	0	0	1	0	SS-7
1960	7	.333	.367	30	10	1	0	0	3	0	SS-7, OF-2
1961	5	.227	.227	22	5	0	0	0	1	0	SS-5
1962	7	.276	.310	29	8	1	0	0	1	0	SS-7
1963	4	.188	.188	16	3	0	0	0	0	0	SS-4
6 yrs.	37	.240	.295	146	35	2	0	2	10	0	SS-30, OF-7, 3B-2

Frank LaPorte

FRANK BREYFOGLE LAPORTE   BR TR
B. Feb. 6, 1880, Uhrichsville, Ohio   5' 8" 175 lbs.
D. Sep. 25, 1939, Newcomerstown, Ohio

Year	Gms.	BA	SA	AB	H	2B	3B	HR	RBI	SB	G. by Pos
1905	11	.400	.500	40	16	1	0	1	12	1	2B-11
1906	123	.264	.368	454	120	23	9	2	54	10	3B-114, 2B-5, OF-1
1907	130	.270	.360	470	127	20	11	0	48	10	3B-64, OF-63, 1B-1
1908	39	.262	.352	145	38	3	5	0	15	3	2B-26, OF-11
1909	89	.298	.379	309	92	19	3	0	31	5	2B-83
1910	124	.264	.338	432	114	14	6	2	67	16	2B-79, OF-24, 3B-15
6 yrs.	516	.274	.362	1850	507	80	34	5	227	45	2B-204, 3B-193, OF-99, 1B-1

Bill Lamar

WILLIAM HARMONG LAMAR   BL TR
B. Mar. 21, 1897, Rockville, Md.   6' 1" 185 lbs.
D. May 24, 1970, Rockport, Mass.

Year	Gms.	BA	SA	AB	H	2B	3B	HR	RBI	SB	G. by Pos
1917	11	.244	.244	41	10	0	0	0	3	1	OF-11
1918	28	.227	.255	110	25	3	0	0	2	2	OF-27
1919	11	.188	.250	16	3	1	0	0	0	1	OF-3, 1B-1
3 yrs.	50	.228	.251	167	38	4	0	0	5	4	OF-41, 1B-1

Hal Lanier

HAROLD CLIFTON LANIER   BR TR
B. Jul. 4, 1942, Denton, N. C.   6' 2" 180 lbs.

Year	Gms.	BA	SA	AB	H	2B	3B	HR	RBI	SB	G. by Pos
1972	60	.214	.243	103	22	5	0	0	6	1	3B-47, SS-9, 2B-3
1973	35	.209	.244	86	18	3	0	0	5	0	SS-26, 2B-8, 3B-1
2 yrs.	95	.212	.243	189	40	6	0	0	11	1	3B-48, SS-35, 2B-11

Don Larsen

DON JAMES LARSEN   BR TR
B. Aug. 7, 1929, Michigan City, Ind.   6' 4" 215 lbs.

Year	Gms.	BA	SA	AB	H	2B	3B	HR	RBI	SB	G. by Pos
1955	21	.146	.317	41	6	1	0	2	7	0	P-19
1956	45	.241	.380	79	19	5	0	2	12	0	P-38
1957	31	.250	.339	56	14	5	0	0	5	0	P-27
1958	28	.306	.571	49	15	1	0	4	13	0	P-19

Don Larsen *continued*

Year	Gms.	BA	SA	AB	H	2B	3B	HR	RBI	SB	G. by Pos
1959	29	.255	.298	47	12	2	0	0	8	0	P-25
5 yrs.	154	.243	.382	272	66	14	0	8	45	0	P-128
World Series											
1955	1	.000	.000	2	0	0	0	0	0	0	P-1
1956	2	.333	.333	3	1	0	0	0	1	0	P-2
1957	2	.000	.000	2	0	0	0	0	0	0	P-2
1958	2	.000	.000	2	0	0	0	0	0	0	P-2
4 yrs.	7	.111	.111	9	1	0	0	0	1	0	P-7

Lyn Lary

LYNFORD HOBART LARY BR TR
B. Jan. 28, 1906, Armona, Calif. 6' 165 lbs.
D. Jan. 9, 1973, Downey, Calif.

Year	Gms.	BA	SA	AB	H	2B	3B	HR	RBI	SB	G. by Pos
1929	80	.309	.428	236	73	9	2	5	26	4	3B-55, SS-14, 2B-2
1930	117	.289	.386	464	134	20	8	3	52	14	SS-113
1931	155	.280	.416	610	171	35	9	10	107	13	SS-155
1932	91	.232	.343	280	65	14	4	3	39	9	SS-80, 1B-5, 2B-2, 3B-2, OF-1
1933	52	.220	.291	127	28	3	3	0	13	2	3B-28, SS-16, 1B-3, OF-1
1934	1	—	—	0	0	0	0	0	0	0	1B-1
6 yrs.	496	.274	.388	1717	471	81	26	21	237	42	SS-378, 3B-85, 1B-9, 2B-4, OF-2

Marcus Lawton

MARCUS DWAYNE LAWTON BB TR
B. Aug. 18, 1965, Gulfport, Miss. 6' 1" 160 lbs.

Year	Gms.	BA	SA	AB	H	2B	3B	HR	RBI	SB	G. by Pos
1989	10	.214	.214	14	3	0	0	0	0	1	OF-8, DH-1

Gene Layden

EUGENE FRANCIS LAYDEN BL TL
B. Mar. 14, 1894, Pittsburgh, Pa. 5' 10" 160 lbs.
D. Dec. 12, 1984, Pittsburgh, Pa.

Year	Gms.	BA	SA	AB	H	2B	3B	HR	RBI	SB	G. by Pos
1915	3	.286	.286	7	2	0	0	0	0	0	OF-2

Tony Lazzeri

ANTHONY MICHAEL LAZZERI BR TR
B. Dec. 6, 1903, San Francisco, Calif. 5' 11½" 170 lbs.
D. Aug. 6, 1946, San Francisco, Calif.
Hall of Fame 1991

Year	Gms.	BA	SA	AB	H	2B	3B	HR	RBI	SB	G. by Pos
1926	155	.275	.462	589	162	28	14	18	114	16	2B-149, SS-5, 3B-1
1927	153	.309	.482	570	176	29	8	18	102	22	2B-113, SS-38, 3B-9
1928	116	.332	.535	404	134	30	11	10	82	15	2B-116
1929	147	.354	.561	545	193	37	11	18	106	9	2B-147, SS-61
1930	143	.303	.462	571	173	34	15	9	121	4	2B-77, 3B-60, SS-8, 1B-1, OF-1
1931	135	.267	.401	484	129	27	7	8	83	18	2B-90, 3B-39
1932	141	.300	.506	510	153	28	16	15	113	11	2B-133, 3B-5
1933	139	.294	.486	523	154	22	12	18	104	15	2B-138
1934	123	.267	.445	438	117	24	6	14	67	11	2B-92, 3B-30
1935	130	.273	.417	477	130	18	6	13	83	11	2B-118, SS-9
1936	150	.287	.441	537	154	29	6	14	109	8	2B-148, SS-2
1937	126	.244	.399	446	109	21	3	14	70	7	2B-125
12 yrs.	1658	.293	.467	6094	1784	327	115	169	1154	147	2B-1446, 3B-144, SS-123, 1B-1, OF-1
World Series											
1926	7	.192	.231	26	5	1	0	0	3	0	2B-7
1927	4	.267	.333	15	4	1	0	0	2	0	2B-4
1928	4	.250	.333	12	3	1	0	0	0	2	2B-4
1932	4	.294	.647	17	5	0	0	2	5	0	2B-4
1936	6	.250	.400	20	5	0	0	1	7	0	2B-6
1937	5	.400	.733	15	6	0	1	1	2	0	2B-5
6 yrs.	30	.267	.429	105	28	3	1	4	19	2	2B-30

Joe Lefebvre

JOSEPH HENRY LEFEBVRE BL TR
B. Feb. 22, 1956, Concord, N. H. 5' 10" 170 lbs.

Year	Gms.	BA	SA	AB	H	2B	3B	HR	RBI	SB	G. by Pos
1980	74	.227	.407	150	34	1	1	8	21	0	OF-71
League Championship Series											
1980	1	—	—	0	0	0	0	0	0	0	OF-1

Frank Leja

FRANK JOHN LEJA BL TL
B. Feb. 7, 1936, Holyoke, Mass. 6' 4" 205 lbs.
D. May. 3, 1991, Boston, Mass.

Year	Gms.	BA	SA	AB	H	2B	3B	HR	RBI	SB	G. by Pos
1954	12	.200	.200	5	1	0	0	0	0	0	1B-6
1955	7	.000	.000	2	0	0	0	0	0	0	1B-2
2 yrs.	19	.143	.143	7	1	0	0	0	0	0	1B-8

Jack Lelivelt

JOHN FRANK LELIVELT BL TL
B. Nov. 14, 1885, Chicago, Ill. 5' 11" 175 lbs.
D. Jan. 20, 1941, Seattle, Wash.

Year	Gms.	BA	SA	AB	H	2B	3B	HR	RBI	SB	G. by Pos
1912	36	.362	.537	149	54	6	7	2	23	7	OF-36
1913	17	.214	.286	28	6	0	1	0	4	1	OF-5
2 yrs.	53	.339	.497	177	60	6	8	2	27	8	OF-41

Eddie Leon

EDUARDO ANTONIO LEON BR TR
B. Aug. 11, 1946, Tucson, Ariz. 6' 170 lbs.

Year	Gms.	BA	SA	AB	H	2B	3B	HR	RBI	SB	G. by Pos
1975	1	—	—	0	0	0	0	0	0	0	SS-1

Ed Levy

EDWARD CLARENCE LEVY BR TR
B. Oct. 28, 1916, Birmingham, Ala. 6' 5½" 190 lbs.

Year	Gms.	BA	SA	AB	H	2B	3B	HR	RBI	SB	G. by Pos
1942	13	.122	.122	41	5	0	0	0	3	1	1B-13
1944	40	.242	.418	153	37	11	2	4	29	1	OF-36
2 yrs.	53	.216	.356	194	42	11	2	4	32	2	OF-36, 1B-13

Duffy Lewis

GEORGE EDWARD LEWIS BR TR
B. Apr. 18, 1888, San Francisco, Calif. 5' 10½" 165 lbs.
D. Jun. 17, 1979, Salem, N. H.

Year	Gms.	BA	SA	AB	H	2B	3B	HR	RBI	SB	G. by Pos
1919	141	.272	.365	559	152	23	4	7	89	8	OF-141
1920	107	.271	.332	365	99	8	1	4	61	2	OF-99
2 yrs.	248	.272	.352	924	251	31	5	11	150	10	OF-240

Jim Leyritz

JAMES JOSEPH LEYRITZ BR TR
B. Dec. 27, 1963, Lakewood, Ohio 6' 190 lbs.

Year	Gms.	BA	SA	AB	H	2B	3B	HR	RBI	SB	G. by Pos
1990	92	.257	.356	303	78	13	1	5	25	2	3B-69, OF-14, C-11
1991	32	.182	.221	77	14	3	0	0	4	0	3B-18, C-5, 1B-3, DH-1
1992	63	.257	.444	144	37	6	0	7	26	0	DH-31, C-18, 1B-2, 3B-2, OF-2, 2B-1
1993	95	.309	.525	259	80	14	0	14	53	0	1B-29, OF-28, DH-21, C-12
1994	75	.265	.518	249	66	12	0	17	58	0	C-37, DH-25, 1B-10
1995	77	.269	.394	264	71	12	0	7	37	1	C-46, 1B-18, DH-15
1996	88	.264	.381	265	70	10	0	7	40	2	C-55, 3B-13, DH-13, 1B-5, OF-3, 2B-2
7 yrs.	522	.266	.422	1561	416	70	1	57	243	5	C-184, DH-106, 3B-102, 1B-67, OF-47, 2B-3
Divisional Playoffs											
1995	2	.143	.571	7	1	0	0	1	2	0	C-2
1996	2	.000	.000	3	0	0	0	0	1	0	C-1, DH-1
2 yrs.	4	.100	.400	10	1	0	0	1	3	0	C-3, DH-1
League Championship Series											
1996	3	.250	.625	8	2	0	0	1	2	0	C-2, OF-1
World Series											
1996	4	.375	.750	8	3	0	0	1	3	1	C-3

Johnny Lindell

JOHN HARLAN LINDELL BR TR
B. Aug. 30, 1916, Greeley, Colo. 6' 4½" 217 lbs.
D. Aug. 27, 1985, Newport Beach, Calif.

Year	Gms.	BA	SA	AB	H	2B	3B	HR	RBI	SB	G. by Pos
1941	1	.000	.000	1	0	0	0	0	0	0	
1942	27	.250	.292	24	6	1	0	0	4	0	P-23
1943	122	.245	.365	441	108	17	12	4	51	2	OF-122
1944	149	.300	.500	594	178	33	16	18	103	5	OF-149
1945	41	.283	.377	159	45	6	3	1	20	0	OF-41
1946	102	.259	.410	332	86	10	5	10	40	4	OF-74, 1B-14
1947	127	.275	.412	476	131	18	7	11	67	1	OF-118
1948	88	.317	.511	309	98	17	2	13	55	0	OF-79

Johnny Lindell *continued*

Year	Gms.	BA	SA	AB	H	2B	3B	HR	RBI	SB	G. by Pos
1949	78	.242	.374	211	51	10	0	6	27	3	OF-65
1950	7	.190	.190	21	4	0	0	0	2	0	OF-6
10 yrs.	742	.275	.428	2568	707	112	45	63	369	17	OF-654, P-23, 1B-14

World Series

Year	Gms.	BA	SA	AB	H	2B	3B	HR	RBI	SB	G. by Pos
1943	4	.111	.111	9	1	0	0	0	0	0	OF-4
1947	6	.500	.778	18	9	3	1	0	7	0	OF-6
1949	2	.143	.143	7	1	0	0	0	0	0	OF-2
3 yrs.	12	.324	.471	34	11	3	1	0	7	0	OF-12

Phil Linz

PHILIP FRANCIS LINZ
B. Jun. 4, 1939, Baltimore, Md.
BR TR 6' 1" 180 lbs.

Year	Gms.	BA	SA	AB	H	2B	3B	HR	RBI	SB	G. by Pos
1962	71	.287	.372	129	37	8	0	1	14	6	SS-21, 3B-8, 2B-5, OF-2
1963	72	.269	.349	186	50	9	0	2	12	1	SS-22, 3B-13, OF-12, 2B-6
1964	112	.250	.364	368	92	21	3	5	25	3	SS-55, 3B-41, 2B-5, OF-3
1965	99	.207	.277	285	59	12	1	2	16	2	SS-71, 3B-4, OF-4, 2B-1
4 yrs.	354	.246	.337	968	238	50	4	10	67	12	SS-169, 3B-66, OF-21, 2B-17

World Series

Year	Gms.	BA	SA	AB	H	2B	3B	HR	RBI	SB	G. by Pos
1963	3	.333	.333	3	1	0	0	0	0	0	
1964	7	.226	.452	31	7	1	0	2	2	0	SS-7
2 yrs.	10	.235	.441	34	8	1	0	2	2	0	SS-7

Bryan Little

RICHARD BRYAN LITTLE
B. Oct. 8, 1959, Houston, Tex.
BB TR 5' 11" 155 lbs.

Year	Gms.	BA	SA	AB	H	2B	3B	HR	RBI	SB	G. by Pos
1986	14	.195	.220	41	8	1	0	0	0	0	2B-14

Jack Little

WILLIAM ARTHUR LITTLE
B. Mar. 12, 1891, Mart, Tex.
D. Jul. 27, 1961, Dallas, Tex.
BR TR 5' 11" 175 lbs.

Year	Gms.	BA	SA	AB	H	2B	3B	HR	RBI	SB	G. by Pos
1912	3	.250	.250	12	3	0	0	0	0	2	OF-3

Gene Locklear

GENE LOCKLEAR
B. Jul. 19, 1949, Lumberton, N. C.
BL TR 5' 10" 165 lbs.

Year	Gms.	BA	SA	AB	H	2B	3B	HR	RBI	SB	G. by Pos
1976	13	.219	.250	32	7	1	0	0	1	0	DH-6, OF-3
1977	1	.600	.600	5	3	0	0	0	2	0	OF-1
2 yrs.	14	.270	.297	37	10	1	0	0	3	0	DH-6, OF-4

Sherm Lollar

JOHN SHERMAN LOLLAR
B. Aug. 23, 1924, Durham, Ark.
D. Sep. 24, 1977, Springfield, Mo.
BR TR 6' 1" 185 lbs.

Year	Gms.	BA	SA	AB	H	2B	3B	HR	RBI	SB	G. by Pos
1947	11	.219	.375	32	7	0	1	1	6	0	C-9
1948	22	.211	.211	38	8	0	0	0	4	0	C-10
2 yrs.	33	.214	.286	70	15	0	1	1	10	0	C-19

World Series

Year	Gms.	BA	SA	AB	H	2B	3B	HR	RBI	SB	G. by Pos
1947	2	.750	1.250	4	3	2	0	0	1	0	C-2

Phil Lombardi

PHILLIP ARDEN LOMBARDI
B. Feb. 20, 1963, Abilene, Tex.
BR TR 6' 2" 200 lbs.

Year	Gms.	BA	SA	AB	H	2B	3B	HR	RBI	SB	G. by Pos
1986	20	.278	.528	36	10	3	0	2	6	0	OF-8, C-3
1987	5	.125	.125	8	1	0	0	0	0	0	C-3
2 yrs.	25	.250	.455	44	11	3	0	2	6	0	OF-8, C-6

Dale Long

RICHARD DALE LONG
B. Feb. 6, 1926, Springfield, Mo.
D. Jan. 27, 1991, Palm Coast, Fla.
BL TL 6' 4" 205 lbs.

Year	Gms.	BA	SA	AB	H	2B	3B	HR	RBI	SB	G. by Pos
1960	26	.366	.707	41	15	3	1	3	10	0	1B-11
1962	41	.298	.468	94	28	4	0	4	17	1	1B-31
1963	14	.200	.200	15	3	0	0	0	0	0	1B-2
3 yrs.	81	.307	.507	150	46	7	1	7	27	1	1B-44

Dale Long *continued*

World Series

Year	Gms.	BA	SA	AB	H	2B	3B	HR	RBI	SB	G. by Pos
1960	3	.333	.333	3	1	0	0	0	0	0	
1962	2	.200	.200	5	1	0	0	0	1	0	1B-2
2 yrs.	5	.250	.250	8	2	0	0	0	1	0	1B-2

Herman Long

HERMAN C. LONG
B. Apr. 13, 1866, Chicago, Ill.
D. Sep. 17, 1909, Denver, Colo.
BL TR 5' 8½" 160 lbs.

Year	Gms.	BA	SA	AB	H	2B	3B	HR	RBI	SB	G. by Pos
1903	22	.188	.225	80	15	3	0	0	8	3	SS-22

Art Lopez

ARTURO LOPEZ
B. Jun. 8, 1937, Mayaguez, Puerto Rico
BL TL 5' 9" 170 lbs.

Year	Gms.	BA	SA	AB	H	2B	3B	HR	RBI	SB	G. by Pos
1965	38	.143	.143	49	7	0	0	0	0	0	OF-16

Hector Lopez

HECTOR HEADLEY LOPEZ
B. Jul. 9, 1929, Colon, Panama
BR TR 5' 11" 182 lbs.

Year	Gms.	BA	SA	AB	H	2B	3B	HR	RBI	SB	G. by Pos
1959	112	.283	.451	406	115	16	2	16	69	3	3B-76, OF-35
1960	131	.284	.414	408	116	14	6	9	42	1	OF-106, 2B-5, 3B-1
1961	93	.222	.305	243	54	7	2	3	22	1	OF-72
1962	106	.275	.391	335	92	19	1	6	48	0	OF-84, 2B-1, 3B-1
1963	130	.249	.395	433	108	13	4	14	52	1	OF-124, 2B-1
1964	127	.260	.418	285	74	9	3	10	34	1	OF-103, 3B-1
1965	111	.261	.392	283	74	12	2	7	39	0	OF-75, 1B-2
1966	54	.214	.368	117	25	4	1	4	16	0	OF-29
8 yrs.	864	.262	.399	2510	658	94	21	69	322	7	OF-628, 3B-79, 2B-7, 1B-2

World Series

Year	Gms.	BA	SA	AB	H	2B	3B	HR	RBI	SB	G. by Pos
1960	3	.429	.429	7	3	0	0	0	0	0	OF-1
1961	4	.333	.889	9	3	0	1	1	7	0	OF-3
1962	2	.000	.000	2	0	0	0	0	0	0	
1963	3	.250	.500	8	2	2	0	0	0	0	OF-2
1964	3	.000	.000	2	0	0	0	0	0	0	OF-1
5 yrs.	15	.286	.536	28	8	2	1	1	7	0	OF-7

Baldy Louden

WILLIAM P. LOUDEN
B. Aug. 27, 1885, Piedmont, W. Va.
D. Dec. 8, 1935, Piedmont, W. Va.
BR TR 5' 11" 175 lbs.

Year	Gms.	BA	SA	AB	H	2B	3B	HR	RBI	SB	G. by Pos
1907	5	.111	.111	9	1	0	0	0	0	1	3B-3

Torey Lovullo

SALVATORE ANTHONY LOVULLO
B. Jul. 25, 1965, Santa Monica, Calif.
BB TR 6' 185 lbs.

Year	Gms.	BA	SA	AB	H	2B	3B	HR	RBI	SB	G. by Pos
1991	22	.176	.216	51	9	2	0	0	2	0	3B-22

Johnny Lucadello

JOHN LUCADELLO
B. Feb. 22, 1919, Thurber, Tex.
BB TR 5' 11" 160 lbs.

Year	Gms.	BA	SA	AB	H	2B	3B	HR	RBI	SB	G. by Pos
1947	12	.083	.083	12	1	0	0	0	0	0	2B-5

Roy Luebbe

ROY JOHN LUEBBE
B. Sep. 17, 1900, Parkersburg, Iowa
D. Aug. 21, 1985, Papillon, Neb.
BB TR 6' 175 lbs.

Year	Gms.	BA	SA	AB	H	2B	3B	HR	RBI	SB	G. by Pos
1925	8	.000	.000	15	0	0	0	0	3	0	C-8

Jerry Lumpe

JERRY DEAN LUMPE
B. Jun. 2, 1933, Lincoln, Mo.
BL TR 6' 2" 185 lbs.

Year	Gms.	BA	SA	AB	H	2B	3B	HR	RBI	SB	G. by Pos
1956	20	.258	.306	62	16	3	0	0	4	1	SS-17, 3B-1
1957	40	.340	.437	103	35	6	2	0	11	2	3B-30, SS-6
1958	81	.254	.362	232	59	8	4	3	32	1	3B-65, SS-5
1959	18	.222	.222	45	10	0	0	0	2	0	3B-12, SS-4, 2B-1
4 yrs.	159	.271	.357	442	120	17	6	3	49	4	3B-108, SS-32, 2B-1

World Series

Year	Gms.	BA	SA	AB	H	2B	3B	HR	RBI	SB	G. by Pos
1957	6	.286	.286	14	4	0	0	0	2	0	3B-3

Jerry Lumpe *continued*

Year	Gms.	BA	SA	AB	H	2B	3B	HR	RBI	SB	G. by Pos
1958	6	.167	.167	12	2	0	0	0	0	0	3B-3, SS-2
2 yrs.	12	.231	.231	26	6	0	0	0	2	0	3B-6, SS-2

Scott Lusader

SCOTT EDWARD LUSADER BL TL
B. Sep. 30, 1964, Chicago, Ill. 5' 10" 165 lbs.

Year	Gms.	BA	SA	AB	H	2B	3B	HR	RBI	SB	G. by Pos
1991	11	.143	.143	7	1	0	0	0	1	0	OF-4, DH-1

Jim Lyttle

JAMES LAWRENCE LYTTLE BL TR
B. May 20, 1946, Hamilton, Ohio 6' 180 lbs.

Year	Gms.	BA	SA	AB	H	2B	3B	HR	RBI	SB	G. by Pos
1969	28	.181	.229	83	15	4	0	0	4	1	OF-28
1970	87	.310	.452	126	39	7	1	3	14	3	OF-70
1971	49	.198	.291	86	17	5	0	1	7	0	OF-29
3 yrs.	164	.241	.342	295	71	16	1	4	25	4	OF-127

Kevin Maas

KEVIN CHRISTIAN MAAS BL TL
B. Jan. 20, 1965, Castro Valley, Calif. 6' 3" 195 lbs.

Year	Gms.	BA	SA	AB	H	2B	3B	HR	RBI	SB	G. by Pos
1990	79	.252	.535	254	64	9	0	21	41	1	1B-57, DH-18
1991	148	.220	.390	500	110	14	1	23	63	5	DH-109, 1B-36
1992	98	.248	.406	286	71	12	0	11	35	3	DH-62, 1B-22
1993	59	.205	.411	151	31	4	0	9	25	1	DH-31, 1B-17
4 yrs.	384	.232	.427	1191	276	39	1	64	164	10	DH-220, 1B-132

Ray Mack

RAYMOND JAMES MACK BR TR
B. Aug. 31, 1916, Cleveland, Ohio 6' 200 lbs.
D. May. 7, 1969, Bucyrus, Ohio

Year	Gms.	BA	SA	AB	H	2B	3B	HR	RBI	SB	G. by Pos
1947	1	—	—	0	0	0	0	0	0	0	

Bunny Madden

THOMAS JOSEPH MADDEN BL TL
B. Jul. 31, 1883, Philadelphia, Pa. 5' 11" 160 lbs.
D. Jul. 26, 1930, Philadelphia, Pa.

Year	Gms.	BA	SA	AB	H	2B	3B	HR	RBI	SB	G. by Pos
1910	1	.000	.000	1	0	0	0	0	0	0	

Elliott Maddox

ELLIOTT MADDOX BR TR
B. Dec. 21, 1947, East Orange, N. J. 5' 11" 180 lbs.

Year	Gms.	BA	SA	AB	H	2B	3B	HR	RBI	SB	G. by Pos
1974	137	.303	.386	466	141	26	2	3	45	6	OF-135, 2B-2, 3B-1
1975	55	.307	.394	218	67	10	3	1	23	9	OF-55, 2B-1
1976	18	.217	.261	46	10	2	0	0	3	0	OF-13, DH-2
3 yrs.	210	.299	.381	730	218	38	5	4	71	15	OF-203, 2B-3, DH-2, 3B-1

League Championship Series

Year	Gms.	BA	SA	AB	H	2B	3B	HR	RBI	SB	G. by Pos
1976	3	.222	.333	9	2	1	0	0	1	0	OF-3

World Series

Year	Gms.	BA	SA	AB	H	2B	3B	HR	RBI	SB	G. by Pos
1976	2	.200	.600	5	1	0	1	0	0	0	OF-1, DH-1

Lee Magee

LEO CHRISTOPHER MAGEE BB TR
B. Jun. 4, 1889, Cincinnati, Ohio 5' 11" 165 lbs.
D. Mar. 14, 1966, Columbus, Ohio

Year	Gms.	BA	SA	AB	H	2B	3B	HR	RBI	SB	G. by Pos
1916	131	.257	.325	510	131	18	4	3	45	29	OF-128, 2B-2
1917	51	.220	.254	173	38	4	1	0	8	3	OF-50
2 yrs.	182	.247	.307	683	169	22	5	3	53	32	OF-178, 2B-2

Stubby Magner

EDMUND BURKE MAGNER BR TR
B. Feb. 20, 1888, Kalamazoo, Mich. 5' 3" 135 lbs.
D. Sep. 6, 1956, Chillicothe, Ohio

Year	Gms.	BA	SA	AB	H	2B	3B	HR	RBI	SB	G. by Pos
1911	13	.212	.212	33	7	0	0	0	4	1	SS-6, 2B-5

Fritz Maisel

FREDERICK CHARLES MAISEL BR TR
B. Dec. 23, 1889, Catonsville, Md. 5' 7½" 170 lbs.
D. Apr. 22, 1967, Baltimore, Md.

Year	Gms.	BA	SA	AB	H	2B	3B	HR	RBI	SB	G. by Pos
1913	51	.257	.310	187	48	4	3	0	12	25	3B-51
1914	149	.239	.325	548	131	23	9	2	47	74	3B-148

Fritz Maisel *continued*

Year	Gms.	BA	SA	AB	H	2B	3B	HR	RBI	SB	G. by Pos
1915	135	.281	.357	530	149	16	6	4	46	51	3B-134
1916	53	.228	.259	158	36	5	0	0	7	4	OF-26, 3B-11, 2B-4
1917	113	.198	.228	404	80	4	4	0	20	29	2B-100, 3B-7
5 yrs.	501	.243	.305	1827	444	52	22	6	132	183	3B-351, 2B-104, OF-26

Hank Majeski

HENRY MAJESKI BR TR
B. Dec. 13, 1916, Staten Island, N. Y. 5' 9" 174 lbs.
D. Aug. 9, 1991, Staten Island, N. Y.

Year	Gms.	BA	SA	AB	H	2B	3B	HR	RBI	SB	G. by Pos
1946	8	.083	.250	12	1	0	1	0	0	0	3B-2

Pat Maloney

PATRICK WILLIAM MALONEY BR TR
B. Jan. 19, 1888, Grosvenordale, Conn. 6' 150 lbs.
D. Jun. 27, 1979, Pawtucket, R. I.

Year	Gms.	BA	SA	AB	H	2B	3B	HR	RBI	SB	G. by Pos
1912	22	.215	.228	79	17	1	0	0	4	3	OF-20

Mickey Mantle

MICKEY CHARLES MANTLE BB TR
B. Oct. 20, 1931, Spavinaw, Okla. 5' 11½" 195 lbs.
D. Aug. 13, 1995, Dallas, Tex.
Hall of Fame 1974

Year	Gms.	BA	SA	AB	H	2B	3B	HR	RBI	SB	G. by Pos
1951	96	.267	.443	341	91	11	5	13	65	8	OF-86
1952	142	.311	.530	549	171	37	7	23	87	4	OF-141, 3B-1
1953	127	.295	.497	461	136	24	3	21	92	8	OF-121, SS-1
1954	146	.300	.525	543	163	17	12	27	102	5	OF-144, SS-4, 2B-1
1955	147	.306	.611	517	158	25	11	37	99	8	OF-145, SS-2
1956	150	.353	.705	533	188	22	5	52	130	10	OF-144
1957	144	.365	.665	474	173	28	6	34	94	16	OF-139
1958	150	.304	.592	519	158	21	1	42	97	18	OF-150
1959	144	.285	.514	541	154	23	4	31	75	21	OF-143
1960	153	.275	.558	527	145	17	6	40	94	14	OF-150
1961	153	.317	.687	514	163	16	6	54	128	12	OF-150
1962	123	.321	.605	377	121	15	1	30	89	9	OF-117
1963	65	.314	.622	172	54	8	0	15	35	2	OF-52
1964	143	.303	.591	465	141	25	2	35	111	6	OF-132
1965	122	.255	.452	361	92	12	1	19	46	4	OF-108
1966	108	.288	.538	333	96	12	1	23	56	1	OF-97
1967	144	.245	.434	440	108	17	0	22	55	1	1B-131
1968	144	.237	.398	435	103	14	1	18	54	6	1B-131
18 yrs.	2401	.298	.557	8102	2415	344	72	536	1509	153	OF-2019, 1B-262, SS-7, 2B-1, 3B-1

World Series

Year	Gms.	BA	SA	AB	H	2B	3B	HR	RBI	SB	G. by Pos
1951	2	.200	.200	5	1	0	0	0	0	0	OF-2
1952	7	.345	.655	29	10	1	1	2	3	0	OF-7
1953	6	.208	.458	24	5	0	0	2	7	0	OF-6
1955	3	.200	.500	10	2	0	0	1	1	0	OF-2
1956	7	.250	.667	24	6	1	0	3	4	1	OF-7
1957	6	.263	.421	19	5	0	0	1	2	0	OF-5
1958	7	.250	.583	24	6	0	1	2	3	0	OF-7
1960	7	.400	.800	25	10	1	0	3	11	0	OF-7
1961	2	.167	.167	6	1	0	0	0	0	0	OF-2
1962	7	.120	.160	25	3	1	0	0	0	0	OF-7
1963	4	.133	.333	15	2	0	0	1	1	0	OF-4
1964	7	.333	.792	24	8	2	0	3	8	0	OF-7
12 yrs.	65	.257	.535	230	59	6	2	18	40	3	OF-63

Cliff Mapes

CLIFFORD FRANKLIN MAPES BL TR
B. Mar. 13, 1922, Sutherland, Neb. 6' 3" 205 lbs.

Year	Gms.	BA	SA	AB	H	2B	3B	HR	RBI	SB	G. by Pos
1948	53	.250	.432	88	22	11	1	1	12	1	OF-21
1949	111	.247	.378	304	75	13	3	7	38	6	OF-108
1950	108	.247	.421	356	88	14	6	12	61	1	OF-102
1951	45	.216	.431	51	11	3	1	2	8	0	OF-34
4 yrs.	317	.245	.407	799	196	41	11	22	119	8	OF-265

World Series

Year	Gms.	BA	SA	AB	H	2B	3B	HR	RBI	SB	G. by Pos
1949	2	.100	.200	10	1	1	0	0	2	0	OF-4
1950	1	.000	.000	4	0	0	0	0	0	0	OF-1
2 yrs.	5	.071	.143	14	1	1	0	0	2	0	OF-5

Year	Gms.	BA	SA	AB	H	2B	3B	HR	RBI	SB	G. by Pos

Roger Maris

ROGER EUGENE MARIS BL TR
B. Sep. 10, 1934, Hibbing, Minn. 6' 197 lbs.
D. Dec. 14, 1985, Houston, Tex.

Year	Gms.	BA	SA	AB	H	2B	3B	HR	RBI	SB	G. by Pos
1960	136	.283	.581	499	141	18	7	39	112	2	OF-131
1961	161	.269	.620	590	159	16	4	61	141	0	OF-160
1962	157	.256	.485	590	151	34	1	33	100	1	OF-154
1963	90	.269	.542	312	84	14	1	23	53	1	OF-86
1964	141	.281	.464	513	144	12	2	26	71	3	OF-137
1965	46	.239	.439	155	37	7	0	8	27	0	OF-43
1966	119	.233	.382	348	81	9	2	13	43	0	OF-95
7 yrs.	850	.265	.515	3007	797	110	17	203	547	7	OF-806

World Series

Year	Gms.	BA	SA	AB	H	2B	3B	HR	RBI	SB	G. by Pos
1960	7	.267	.500	30	8	1	0	2	2	0	OF-7
1961	5	.105	.316	19	2	1	0	1	2	0	OF-5
1962	7	.174	.348	23	4	1	0	1	5	0	OF-7
1963	2	.000	.000	5	0	0	0	0	0	0	OF-2
1964	7	.200	.300	30	6	0	0	1	1	0	OF-7
5 yrs.	28	.187	.355	107	20	3	0	5	10	0	OF-28

Armando Marsans

ARMANDO MARSANS BR TR
B. Oct. 3, 1887, Matanzas, Cuba 5' 10" 157 lbs.
D. Sep. 3, 1960, Havana, Cuba

Year	Gms.	BA	SA	AB	H	2B	3B	HR	RBI	SB	G. by Pos
1917	25	.227	.273	88	20	4	0	0	15	6	OF-25
1918	37	.236	.293	123	29	5	1	0	9	3	OF-36
2 yrs.	62	.232	.284	211	49	9	1	0	24	9	OF-61

Billy Martin

ALFRED MANUEL MARTIN BR TR
B. May 16, 1928, Berkeley, Calif. 5' 11½" 165 lbs.
D. Dec. 25, 1989, Johnson City, N. Y.

Year	Gms.	BA	SA	AB	H	2B	3B	HR	RBI	SB	G. by Pos
1950	34	.250	.361	36	9	1	0	1	8	0	2B-22, 3B-1
1951	51	.259	.345	58	15	1	2	0	2	0	2B-23, SS-6, 3B-2, OF-1
1952	109	.267	.344	363	97	13	3	3	33	3	2B-107
1953	149	.257	.395	587	151	24	6	15	75	6	2B-146, SS-18
1955	20	.300	.371	70	21	2	0	1	9	1	2B-17, SS-3
1956	121	.264	.397	458	121	24	5	9	49	7	2B-105, 3B-16
1957	43	.241	.324	145	35	5	2	1	12	2	2B-27, 3B-13
7 yrs.	527	.262	.376	1717	449	70	18	30	188	19	2B-447, 3B-32, SS-27, OF-1

World Series

Year	Gms.	BA	SA	AB	H	2B	3B	HR	RBI	SB	G. by Pos
1951	1	—	—	0	0	0	0	0	0	0	
1952	7	.217	.348	23	5	0	0	1	4	0	2B-7
1953	6	.500	.958	24	12	1	2	2	8	1	2B-6
1955	7	.320	.440	25	8	1	1	0	4	0	2B-7
1956	7	.296	.519	27	8	0	0	2	3	0	2B-7, 3B-2
5 yrs.	28	.333	.566	99	33	2	3	5	19	1	2B-27, 3B-2

Hersh Martin

HERSHEL RAY MARTIN BB TR
B. Sep. 19, 1909, Birmingham, Ala. 6' 2" 190 lbs.
D. Nov. 17, 1980, Cuba, Mo.

Year	Gms.	BA	SA	AB	H	2B	3B	HR	RBI	SB	G. by Pos
1944	85	.302	.445	328	99	12	4	9	47	5	OF-80
1945	117	.267	.392	408	109	18	6	7	53	4	OF-102
2 yrs.	202	.283	.416	736	208	30	10	16	100	9	OF-182

Jack Martin

JOHN CHRISTOPHER MARTIN BR TR
B. Apr. 19, 1887, Plainfield, N. J. 5' 9" 159 lbs.
D. Jul. 4, 1980, Bronx, N. Y.

Year	Gms.	BA	SA	AB	H	2B	3B	HR	RBI	SB	G. by Pos
1912	69	.225	.260	231	52	6	1	0	17	14	SS-64, 3B-4, 2B-1

Tino Martinez

CONSTANTINO MARTINEZ BL TR
B. Dec. 7, 1967, Tampa, Fla. 6' 2" 205 lbs.

Year	Gms.	BA	SA	AB	H	2B	3B	HR	RBI	SB	G. by Pos
1996	155	.292	.466	595	174	28	0	25	117	2	1B-151, DH-3

Divisional Playoffs

Year	Gms.	BA	SA	AB	H	2B	3B	HR	RBI	SB	G. by Pos
1996	4	.267	.400	15	4	2	0	0	0	0	1B-4

League Championship Series

Year	Gms.	BA	SA	AB	H	2B	3B	HR	RBI	SB	G. by Pos
1996	5	.182	.227	22	4	1	0	0	0	0	1B-5

World Series

Year	Gms.	BA	SA	AB	H	2B	3B	HR	RBI	SB	G. by Pos
1996	6	.091	.091	11	1	0	0	0	0	0	1B-5

Jim Mason

JAMES PERCY MASON BL TR
B. Aug. 14, 1950, Mobile, Ala. 6' 2" 185 lbs.

Year	Gms.	BA	SA	AB	H	2B	3B	HR	RBI	SB	G. by Pos
1974	152	.250	.352	440	110	18	6	5	37	1	SS-152
1975	94	.152	.211	223	34	3	2	4	16	0	SS-93, 2B-1
1976	93	.180	.235	217	39	7	1	1	14	0	SS-93
3 yrs.	339	.208	.287	880	183	28	9	8	67	1	SS-338, 2B-1

League Championship Series

Year	Gms.	BA	SA	AB	H	2B	3B	HR	RBI	SB	G. by Pos
1976	2	—	—	0	0	0	0	0	0	0	SS-2

World Series

Year	Gms.	BA	SA	AB	H	2B	3B	HR	RBI	SB	G. by Pos
1976	3	1.000	4.000	1	1	0	0	1	1	0	SS-3

Vic Mata

VICTOR JOSE MATA BR TR
B. Jun. 17, 1961, Santiago, 6' 1" 165 lbs.
Dominican Republic

Year	Gms.	BA	SA	AB	H	2B	3B	HR	RBI	SB	G. by Pos
1984	30	.329	.443	70	23	5	0	1	6	1	OF-28
1985	6	.143	.143	7	1	0	0	0	0	0	OF-3
2 yrs.	36	.312	.416	77	24	5	0	1	6	1	OF-31

Don Mattingly

DONALD ARTHUR MATTINGLY BL TL
B. Apr. 20, 1961, Evansville, Ind. 6' 185 lbs.

Year	Gms.	BA	SA	AB	H	2B	3B	HR	RBI	SB	G. by Pos
1982	7	.167	.167	12	2	0	0	0	1	0	OF-6, 1B-1
1983	91	.283	.409	279	79	15	4	4	32	0	OF-48, 1B-42, 2B-1
1984	153	.343	.537	603	207	44	2	23	110	1	1B-133, OF-19
1985	159	.324	.567	652	211	48	3	35	145	2	1B-159
1986	162	.352	.573	677	238	53	2	31	113	0	1B-160, 3B-3, DH-1
1987	141	.327	.559	569	186	38	2	30	115	1	1B-140, DH-1
1988	144	.311	.462	599	186	37	0	18	88	1	1B-143, OF-1, DH-1
1989	158	.303	.477	631	191	37	2	23	113	3	1B-145, DH-17, OF-1
1990	102	.256	.335	394	101	16	0	5	42	1	1B-89, DH-13, OF-1
1991	152	.288	.394	587	169	35	0	9	68	2	1B-127, DH-22
1992	157	.287	.416	640	184	40	0	14	86	3	1B-143, DH-15
1993	134	.291	.445	530	154	27	2	17	86	0	1B-130, DH-5
1994	97	.304	.411	372	113	20	1	6	51	0	1B-97
1995	128	.288	.413	458	132	32	2	7	49	0	1B-125, DH-1
14 yrs.	1785	.307	.471	7003	2153	442	20	222	1099	14	1B-1634, OF-76, DH-76, 3B-3, 2B-1

Divisional Playoffs

Year	Gms.	BA	SA	AB	H	2B	3B	HR	RBI	SB	G. by Pos
1995	5	.417	.708	24	10	4	0	1	6	0	1B-5

Carlos May

CARLOS MAY BL TR
B. May 17, 1948, Birmingham, Ala. 5' 11" 200 lbs.

Year	Gms.	BA	SA	AB	H	2B	3B	HR	RBI	SB	G. by Pos
1976	87	.278	.361	288	80	11	2	3	40	1	DH-74, OF-7, 1B-1
1977	65	.227	.309	181	41	7	1	2	16	0	DH-52, OF-4
2 yrs.	152	.258	.341	469	121	18	3	5	56	1	DH-126, OF-11, 1B-1

League Championship Series

Year	Gms.	BA	SA	AB	H	2B	3B	HR	RBI	SB	G. by Pos
1976	3	.200	.300	10	2	1	0	0	0	0	DH-3

World Series

Year	Gms.	BA	SA	AB	H	2B	3B	HR	RBI	SB	G. by Pos
1976	4	.000	.000	9	0	0	0	0	0	0	DH-4

John Mayberry

JOHN CLAIBORN MAYBERRY BL TL
B. Feb. 18, 1949, Detroit, Mich. 6' 3" 215 lbs.

Year	Gms.	BA	SA	AB	H	2B	3B	HR	RBI	SB	G. by Pos
1982	69	.209	.353	215	45	7	0	8	27	0	1B-63, DH-4

Lee Mazzilli

LEE LOUIS MAZZILLI BB TR
B. Mar. 25, 1955, New York, N. Y. 6' 1" 180 lbs.

Year	Gms.	BA	SA	AB	H	2B	3B	HR	RBI	SB	G. by Pos
1982	37	.266	.422	128	34	2	0	6	17	2	1B-23, DH-9, OF-2

Joe McCarthy

JOSEPH N. McCARTHY BR TR
B. Dec. 25, 1881, Syracuse, N. Y.
D. Jan. 12, 1937, Syracuse, N. Y.

Year	Gms.	BA	SA	AB	H	2B	3B	HR	RBI	SB	G. by Pos
1905	1	.000	.000	2	0	0	0	0	0	0	C-1

Pat McCauley

PATRICK M. McCAULEY B TR
B. Jun. 10, 1870, Ware, Mass. 5' 10½" 156 lbs.
D. Jan. 23, 1917, Newark, N. J.

Year	Gms.	BA	SA	AB	H	2B	3B	HR	RBI	SB	G. by Pos
1903	6	.053	.053	19	1	0	0	0	1	0	C-6

Larry McClure

LAWRENCE LEDWITH MCCLURE BR TR
B. Oct. 3, 1885, Wayne, W. Va. 5' 6½" 130 lbs.
D. Aug. 31, 1949, Huntington, W. Va.

Year	Gms.	BA	SA	AB	H	2B	3B	HR	RBI	SB	G. by Pos
1910	1	.000	.000	1	0	0	0	0	0	0	OF-1

George McConnell

GEORGE NEELY MCCONNELL BR TR
B. Sep. 16, 1877, Shelbyville, Tenn. 6' 3" 190 lbs.
D. May 10, 1964, Chattanooga, Tenn.

Year	Gms.	BA	SA	AB	H	2B	3B	HR	RBI	SB	G. by Pos
1909	13	.209	.256	43	9	0	1	0	5	1	1B-11, P-2
1912	42	.297	.385	91	27	4	2	0	8	0	P-23, 1B-2
1913	39	.179	.209	67	12	2	0	0	2	0	P-35, 1B-1
3 yrs.	94	.239	.299	201	48	6	3	0	15	1	P-60, 1B-14

Mickey McDermott

MAURICE JOSEPH MCDERMOTT BL TL
B. Aug. 29, 1928, Poughkeepsie, N. Y. 6' 2" 170 lbs.

Year	Gms.	BA	SA	AB	H	2B	3B	HR	RBI	SB	G. by Pos
1956	46	.212	.269	52	11	0	0	1	4	0	P-23
World Series
1956	1	1.000	1.000	1	1	0	0	0	0	0	P-1

Dave McDonald

DAVID BRUCE MCDONALD BL TR
B. May 20, 1943, New Albany, Ind. 6' 3" 215 lbs.

Year	Gms.	BA	SA	AB	H	2B	3B	HR	RBI	SB	G. by Pos
1969	9	.217	.261	23	5	1	0	0	2	0	1B-7

Gil McDougald

GILBERT JAMES MCDOUGALD BR TR
B. May 19, 1928, San Francisco, Calif. 6' 175 lbs.

Year	Gms.	BA	SA	AB	H	2B	3B	HR	RBI	SB	G. by Pos
1951	131	.306	.488	402	123	23	4	14	63	14	3B-82, 2B-55
1952	152	.263	.369	555	146	16	5	11	78	6	3B-117, 2B-38
1953	141	.285	.416	541	154	27	7	10	83	3	3B-136, 2B-26
1954	126	.259	.416	394	102	22	2	12	48	3	2B-92, 3B-35
1955	141	.285	.407	533	152	10	8	13	53	6	2B-126, 3B-17
1956	120	.311	.443	438	136	13	3	13	56	3	SS-92, 2B-31, 3B-5
1957	141	.289	.442	539	156	25	9	13	62	2	SS-121, 2B-21, 3B-7
1958	138	.250	.376	503	126	19	1	14	65	6	2B-115, SS-19
1959	127	.251	.353	434	109	16	8	4	34	0	2B-53, SS-52, 3B-25
1960	119	.258	.401	337	87	16	4	8	34	2	3B-84, 2B-42
10 yrs.	1336	.276	.410	4676	1291	187	51	112	576	45	2B-599, 3B-508, SS-284
World Series
1951	6	.261	.435	23	6	1	0	1	7	0	3B-5, 2B-4
1952	7	.200	.320	25	5	0	0	1	3	1	3B-7
1953	6	.167	.500	24	4	0	1	2	4	0	3B-6
1955	7	.259	.370	27	7	0	0	1	1	0	3B-7
1956	7	.143	.143	21	3	0	0	0	1	0	SS-7
1957	7	.250	.250	24	6	0	0	0	2	1	SS-7
1958	7	.321	.607	28	9	2	0	2	4	0	2B-7
1960	6	.278	.333	18	5	1	0	0	2	0	3B-6
8 yrs.	53	.237	.379	190	45	4	1	7	24	2	3B-31, SS-14, 2B-11

Herm McFarland

HERMAS WALTER MCFARLAND BL TR
B. Mar. 11, 1870, Des Moines, Iowa 5' 6" 150 lbs.
D. Sep. 21, 1935, Richmond, Va.

Year	Gms.	BA	SA	AB	H	2B	3B	HR	RBI	SB	G. by Pos
1903	103	.243	.378	362	88	16	9	5	45	13	OF-103

Deacon McGuire

JAMES THOMAS MCGUIRE BR TR
B. Nov. 18, 1863, Youngstown, Ohio 6' 1" 185 lbs.
D. Oct. 31, 1936, Duck Lake, Mich.

Year	Gms.	BA	SA	AB	H	2B	3B	HR	RBI	SB	G. by Pos
1904	101	.208	.258	322	67	12	2	0	20	2	C-97, 1B-1
1905	72	.219	.268	228	50	7	2	0	33	3	C-71
1906	51	.299	.333	144	43	5	0	0	14	0	C-49, 1B-1
1907	1	.000	.000	1	0	0	0	0	0	0	C-1
4 yrs.	225	.230	.276	695	160	24	4	0	67	8	C-218, 1B-2

Irish McIlveen

HENRY COOKE MCILVEEN BL TL
B. Jul. 27, 1880, Belfast, Ireland 5' 11½" 180 lbs.
D. Oct. 18, 1960, Lorain, Ohio

Year	Gms.	BA	SA	AB	H	2B	3B	HR	RBI	SB	G. by Pos
1908	44	.213	.266	169	36	3	3	0	8	6	OF-44

Irish McIlveen *continued*

Year	Gms.	BA	SA	AB	H	2B	3B	HR	RBI	SB	G. by Pos
1909	4	.000	.000	3	0	0	0	0	0	0	
2 yrs.	48	.209	.262	172	36	3	3	0	8	6	OF-44

Tim McIntosh

TIMOTHY ALLEN MCINTOSH BR TR
B. Mar. 21, 1965, Minneapolis, Minn. 5' 11" 195 lbs.

Year	Gms.	BA	SA	AB	H	2B	3B	HR	RBI	SB	G. by Pos
1996	3	.000	.000	3	0	0	0	0	0	0	C-1, 1B-1, 3B-1

Bill McKechnie

WILLIAM BOYD MCKECHNIE BB TR
B. Aug. 7, 1886, Wilkinsburg, Pa. 5' 10" 160 lbs.
D. Oct. 29, 1965, Bradenton, Fla.
Hall of Fame 1962

Year	Gms.	BA	SA	AB	H	2B	3B	HR	RBI	SB	G. by Pos
1913	44	.134	.134	112	15	0	0	0	8	2	2B-27, SS-7, 3B-2

Rich McKinney

CHARLES RICHARD MCKINNEY BR TR
B. Nov. 22, 1946, Piqua, Ohio 5' 11" 185 lbs.

Year	Gms.	BA	SA	AB	H	2B	3B	HR	RBI	SB	G. by Pos
1972	37	.215	.256	121	26	2	0	1	7	1	3B-33

Frank McManus

FRANCIS E. MCMANUS B TR
B. Sep. 21, 1875, Lawrence, Mass. 5' 10" lbs.
D. Sep. 1, 1923, Syracuse, N. Y.

Year	Gms.	BA	SA	AB	H	2B	3B	HR	RBI	SB	G. by Pos
1904	4	.000	.000	7	0	0	0	0	0	0	C-4

Norm McMillan

NORMAN ALEXIS MCMILLAN BR TR
B. Oct. 5, 1895, Latta, S. C. 6' 175 lbs.
D. Sep. 28, 1969, Marion, S. C.

Year	Gms.	BA	SA	AB	H	2B	3B	HR	RBI	SB	G. by Pos
1922	33	.256	.321	78	20	1	2	0	11	4	OF-23, 3B-5
World Series
1922	1	.000	.000	2	0	0	0	0	0	0	OF-1

Tommy McMillan

THOMAS LAW MCMILLAN BR TR
B. Apr. 18, 1888, Pittston, Pa. 5' 5" 130 lbs.
D. Jul. 15, 1966, Orlando, Fla.

Year	Gms.	BA	SA	AB	H	2B	3B	HR	RBI	SB	G. by Pos
1912	41	.228	.242	149	34	2	0	0	12	18	SS-41

Mike McNally

MICHAEL JOSEPH MCNALLY BR TR
B. Sep. 9, 1892, Minooka, Pa. 5' 11" 150 lbs.
D. May 29, 1965, Bethlehem, Pa.

Year	Gms.	BA	SA	AB	H	2B	3B	HR	RBI	SB	G. by Pos
1921	71	.260	.312	215	56	4	2	1	24	5	3B-48, 2B-16
1922	52	.252	.294	143	36	2	2	0	18	2	3B-32, 2B-9, SS-4, 1B-1
1923	30	.211	.211	38	8	0	0	0	1	2	SS-13, 3B-7, 2B-5
1924	49	.246	.246	69	17	0	0	0	2	1	2B-25, 3B-13, SS-6
4 yrs.	202	.252	.288	465	117	6	4	1	45	10	3B-100, 2B-55, SS-23, 1B-1
World Series
1921	7	.200	.250	20	4	1	0	0	1	2	3B-7
1922	1	—	—	0	0	0	0	0	0	0	2B-1
2 yrs.	8	.200	.250	20	4	1	0	0	1	2	3B-7, 2B-1

George McQuinn

GEORGE HARTLEY MCQUINN BL TL
B. May 29, 1910, Arlington, Va. 5' 11" 165 lbs.
D. Dec. 24, 1978, Alexandria, Va.

Year	Gms.	BA	SA	AB	H	2B	3B	HR	RBI	SB	G. by Pos
1947	144	.304	.437	517	157	24	3	13	80	0	1B-142
1948	94	.248	.421	302	75	11	4	11	41	0	1B-90
2 yrs.	238	.283	.431	819	232	35	7	24	121	0	1B-232
World Series
1947	7	.130	.130	23	3	0	0	0	1	0	1B-7

Bobby Meacham

ROBERT ANDREW MEACHAM BB TR
B. Aug. 25, 1960, Los Angeles, Calif. 6' 1" 180 lbs.

Year	Gms.	BA	SA	AB	H	2B	3B	HR	RBI	SB	G. by Pos
1983	22	.235	.275	51	12	2	0	0	4	8	SS-18, 3B-4
1984	99	.253	.328	360	91	13	4	2	25	9	SS-96, 2B-2

Year	Gms.	BA	SA	AB	H	2B	3B	HR	RBI	SB	G. by Pos

Bobby Meacham *continued*

Year	Gms.	BA	SA	AB	H	2B	3B	HR	RBI	SB	G. by Pos
1985	156	.218	.266	481	105	16	2	1	47	25	SS-155
1986	56	.224	.280	161	36	7	1	0	10	3	SS-56
1987	77	.271	.409	203	55	11	1	5	21	6	SS-56, 2B-25
1988	47	.217	.296	115	25	9	0	0	7	7	SS-24, 2B-21, 3B-5
6 yrs.	457	.236	.308	1371	324	58	8	8	114	58	SS-405, 2B-48, 3B-9

Charlie Meara

CHARLES EDWARD MEARA   BL TR
B. Apr. 13, 1891, New York, N. Y.   5' 10" 160 lbs.
D. Feb. 8, 1962, Bronx, N. Y.

Year	Gms.	BA	SA	AB	H	2B	3B	HR	RBI	SB	G. by Pos
1914	4	.286	.286	7	2	0	0	0	1	0	OF-3

Bob Melvin

ROBERT PAUL MELVIN   BR TR
B. Oct. 28, 1961, Palo Alto, Calif.   6' 4" 205 lbs.

Year	Gms.	BA	SA	AB	H	2B	3B	HR	RBI	SB	G. by Pos
1994	9	.286	.500	14	4	0	0	1	3	0	C-4, 1B-4, DH-1

Fred Merkle

FREDERICK CHARLES MERKLE   BR TR
B. Dec. 20, 1888, Watertown, Wis.   6' 1" 190 lbs.
D. Mar. 2, 1956, Daytona Beach, Fla.

Year	Gms.	BA	SA	AB	H	2B	3B	HR	RBI	SB	G. by Pos
1925	7	.385	.462	13	5	1	0	0	1	1	1B-5
1926	1	.000	.000	2	0	0	0	0	0	0	1B-1
2 yrs.	8	.333	.400	15	5	1	0	0	1	1	1B-6

Bud Metheny

ARTHUR BEAUREGARD METHENY   BL TL
B. Jun. 1, 1915, St. Louis, Mo.   5' 11" 190 lbs.

Year	Gms.	BA	SA	AB	H	2B	3B	HR	RBI	SB	G. by Pos
1943	103	.261	.397	360	94	18	2	9	36	2	OF-91
1944	137	.239	.355	518	124	16	1	14	67	5	OF-132
1945	133	.248	.338	509	126	18	2	8	53	5	OF-128
1946	3	.000	.000	3	0	0	0	0	0	0	
4 yrs.	376	.247	.359	1390	344	52	5	31	156	12	OF-351
World Series											
1943	2	.125	.125	8	1	0	0	0	0	0	OF-2

Hensley Meulens

HENSLEY FILEMON ACASIO MEULENS   BR TR
B. Jun. 23, 1967, Willemstad, Curacao   6' 4" 200 lbs.

Year	Gms.	BA	SA	AB	H	2B	3B	HR	RBI	SB	G. by Pos
1989	8	.179	.179	28	5	0	0	0	1	0	3B-8
1990	23	.241	.434	83	20	7	0	3	10	1	OF-23
1991	96	.222	.319	288	64	8	1	6	29	3	OF-73, DH-13, 1B-7
1992	2	.600	1.200	5	3	0	0	1	1	0	3B-2
1993	30	.170	.340	53	9	1	1	2	5	0	OF-24, 1B-3, 3B-1
5 yrs.	159	.221	.344	457	101	16	2	12	46	4	OF-120, DH-13, 3B-11, 1B-10

Bob Meusel

ROBERT WILLIAM MEUSEL   BR TR
B. Jul. 19, 1896, San Jose, Calif.   6' 3" 190 lbs.
D. Nov. 28, 1977, Downey, Calif.

Year	Gms.	BA	SA	AB	H	2B	3B	HR	RBI	SB	G. by Pos
1920	119	.328	.517	460	151	40	7	11	83	4	OF-64, 3B-45, 1B-2
1921	149	.318	.559	598	190	40	16	24	135	17	OF-147
1922	121	.319	.522	473	151	26	11	16	84	13	OF-121
1923	132	.313	.478	460	144	29	10	9	91	13	OF-121
1924	143	.325	.494	579	188	40	11	12	120	26	OF-143, 3B-2
1925	156	.290	.542	624	181	34	12	33	138	10	OF-131, 3B-27
1926	108	.315	.470	413	130	22	3	12	81	16	OF-107
1927	135	.337	.510	516	174	47	9	8	103	24	OF-131
1928	131	.297	.467	518	154	45	5	11	113	6	OF-131
1929	100	.261	.391	391	102	15	3	10	57	2	OF-96
10 yrs.	1294	.311	.500	5032	1565	338	87	146	1005	131	OF-1192, 3B-74, 1B-2
World Series											
1921	8	.200	.267	30	6	2	0	0	3	1	OF-8
1922	5	.300	.350	20	6	1	0	0	2	1	OF-5
1923	6	.269	.462	26	7	1	2	0	8	0	OF-6
1926	7	.238	.381	21	5	1	1	0	0	0	OF-7
1927	4	.118	.118	17	2	0	0	0	1	1	OF-4
1928	4	.200	.467	15	3	1	0	1	3	2	OF-4
6 yrs.	34	.225	.341	129	29	6	3	1	17	5	OF-34

Gene Michael

EUGENE RICHARD MICHAEL   BB TR
B. Jun. 2, 1938, Kent, Ohio   6' 2" 183 lbs.

Year	Gms.	BA	SA	AB	H	2B	3B	HR	RBI	SB	G. by Pos
1968	61	.198	.250	116	23	3	0	1	8	3	SS-43, P-1
1969	119	.272	.364	412	112	24	4	2	31	7	SS-118
1970	134	.214	.255	435	93	10	1	2	38	3	SS-123, 3B-4, 2B-3
1971	139	.224	.276	456	102	15	0	3	35	3	SS-136
1972	126	.233	.279	391	91	7	4	1	32	4	SS-121
1973	129	.225	.278	418	94	11	1	3	47	1	SS-129
1974	81	.260	.311	177	46	9	0	0	13	0	2B-45, SS-39, 3B-2
7 yrs.	789	.233	.289	2405	561	79	10	12	204	21	SS-709, 2B-48, 3B-6, P-1

Ezra Midkiff

EZRA MILLINGTON MIDKIFF   BL TR
B. Nov. 13, 1882, Salt Rock, W. Va.   5' 10" 180 lbs.
D. Mar. 20, 1957, Huntington, W. Va.

Year	Gms.	BA	SA	AB	H	2B	3B	HR	RBI	SB	G. by Pos
1912	21	.244	.256	86	21	1	0	0	9	4	3B-21
1913	83	.197	.236	284	56	9	1	0	14	9	3B-76, SS-4, 2B-2
2 yrs.	104	.208	.241	370	77	10	1	0	23	13	3B-97, SS-4, 2B-2

Larry Milbourne

LAWRENCE WILLIAM MILBOURNE   BB TR
B. Feb. 14, 1951, Port Norris, N. J.   6' 161 lbs.

Year	Gms.	BA	SA	AB	H	2B	3B	HR	RBI	SB	G. by Pos
1981	61	.313	.399	163	51	7	2	1	12	2	SS-39, 2B-14, 3B-3
1982	14	.148	.185	27	4	1	0	0	0	0	SS-9, 2B-3, 3B-3
1983	31	.200	.257	70	14	4	0	0	2	1	2B-19, SS-6, 3B-4
3 yrs.	106	.265	.338	260	69	12	2	1	14	3	SS-54, 2B-36, 3B-10, DH-3
Divisional Playoffs											
1981	5	.316	.368	19	6	1	0	0	0	0	SS-5
League Championship Series											
1981	3	.462	.462	13	6	0	0	0	1	0	SS-3
World Series											
1981	6	.250	.350	20	5	2	0	0	3	0	SS-6

Elmer Miller

ELMER MILLER   BR TR
B. Jul. 28, 1890, Sandusky, Ohio   6' 175 lbs.
D. Nov. 28, 1944, Beloit, Wis.

Year	Gms.	BA	SA	AB	H	2B	3B	HR	RBI	SB	G. by Pos
1915	26	.145	.157	83	12	1	0	0	3	0	OF-26
1916	43	.224	.289	152	34	3	2	1	18	8	OF-42
1917	114	.251	.319	379	95	11	3	3	35	11	OF-112
1918	67	.243	.322	202	49	9	2	1	22	2	OF-62
1921	56	.298	.450	242	72	9	8	4	36	2	OF-56
1922	51	.267	.384	172	46	7	2	3	18	2	OF-51
6 yrs.	357	.250	.340	1230	308	40	17	12	132	25	OF-349
World Series											
1921	8	.161	.194	31	5	1	0	0	2	0	OF-8

John Miller

JOHN ALLEN MILLER   BR TR
B. Mar. 14, 1944, Alhambra, Calif.   5' 11" 195 lbs.

Year	Gms.	BA	SA	AB	H	2B	3B	HR	RBI	SB	G. by Pos
1966	6	.087	.217	23	2	0	0	1	2	0	1B-3, OF-3

Buster Mills

COLONEL BUSTER MILLS   BR TR
B. Sep. 16, 1908, Ranger, Tex.   5' 11½" 195 lbs.
D. Dec. 1, 1991, Arlington, Tex.

Year	Gms.	BA	SA	AB	H	2B	3B	HR	RBI	SB	G. by Pos
1940	34	.397	.587	63	25	3	1	0	15	0	OF-14

Mike Milosevich

MICHAEL MILOSEVICH   BR TR
B. Jan. 13, 1915, Zeigler, Ill.   5' 10½" 172 lbs.
D. Feb. 3, 1966, E. Chicago, Ind.

Year	Gms.	BA	SA	AB	H	2B	3B	HR	RBI	SB	G. by Pos
1944	94	.247	.308	312	77	11	4	0	32	1	SS-91
1945	30	.217	.246	69	15	2	0	0	7	0	SS-22, 2B-1
2 yrs.	124	.241	.297	381	92	13	4	0	39	1	SS-113, 2B-1

Willie Miranda

GUILLERMO MIRANDA   BB TR
B. May 24, 1926, Velasco, Cuba   5' 9½" 150 lbs.
D. Sep. 7, 1996, Baltimore, Md.

Year	Gms.	BA	SA	AB	H	2B	3B	HR	RBI	SB	G. by Pos
1953	48	.224	.276	58	13	0	0	1	5	1	SS-45

Year	Gms.	BA	SA	AB	H	2B	3B	HR	RBI	SB	G. by Pos

Willie Miranda *continued*

Year	Gms.	BA	SA	AB	H	2B	3B	HR	RBI	SB	G. by Pos
1954	92	.250	.345	116	29	4	2	1	12	0	SS-88, 2B-4, 3B-1
2 yrs.	140	.241	.322	174	42	4	2	2	17	1	SS-133, 2B-4, 3B-1

Bobby Mitchell

ROBERT VANCE MITCHELL BR TR
B. Oct. 22, 1943, Norristown, Pa. 6' 3" 185 lbs.

Year	Gms.	BA	SA	AB	H	2B	3B	HR	RBI	SB	G. by Pos
1970	10	.227	.318	22	5	2	0	0	4	0	OF-7

Fred Mitchell

FREDERICK FRANCIS MITCHELL BR TR
B. Jun. 5, 1878, Cambridge, Mass. 5' 9½" 185 lbs.
D. Oct. 13, 1970, Newton, Mass.

Year	Gms.	BA	SA	AB	H	2B	3B	HR	RBI	SB	G. by Pos
1910	68	.230	.286	196	45	7	2	0	18	6	C-68

Johnny Mitchell

JOHN FRANKLIN MITCHELL BB TR
B. Aug. 9, 1894, Detroit, Mich. 5' 8" 155 lbs.
D. Nov. 4, 1965, Birmingham, Mich.

Year	Gms.	BA	SA	AB	H	2B	3B	HR	RBI	SB	G. by Pos
1921	13	.262	.286	42	11	1	0	0	2	1	SS-7, 2B-5
1922	4	.000	.000	4	0	0	0	0	0	0	SS-4
2 yrs.	17	.239	.261	46	11	1	0	0	2	1	SS-11, 2B-5

Johnny Mize

JOHN ROBERT MIZE BL TR
B. Jan. 7, 1913, Demorest, Ga. 6' 2" 215 lbs.
D. Jun. 2, 1993, Demorest, Ga.
Hall of Fame 1981

Year	Gms.	BA	SA	AB	H	2B	3B	HR	RBI	SB	G. by Pos
1949	13	.261	.435	23	6	1	0	1	2	0	1B-6
1950	90	.277	.595	274	76	12	0	25	72	0	1B-72
1951	113	.259	.398	332	86	14	1	10	49	1	1B-93
1952	78	.263	.416	137	36	9	0	4	29	0	1B-27
1953	81	.250	.394	104	26	3	0	4	27	0	1B-15
5 yrs.	375	.264	.463	870	230	39	1	44	179	1	1B-213
World Series											
1949	2	1.000	1.000	2	2	0	0	0	2	0	
1950	4	.133	.133	15	2	0	0	0	0	0	1B-4
1951	4	.286	.429	7	2	1	0	0	1	0	1B-2
1952	5	.400	1.067	15	6	1	0	3	6	0	1B-4
1953	3	.000	.000	3	0	0	0	0	0	0	
5 yrs.	18	.286	.548	42	12	2	0	3	9	0	1B-10

Fenton Mole

FENTON LEROY MOLE BL TL
B. Jun. 14, 1925, San Leandro, Calif. 6' 1½" 200 lbs.

Year	Gms.	BA	SA	AB	H	2B	3B	HR	RBI	SB	G. by Pos
1949	10	.185	.333	27	5	2	1	0	2	0	1B-8

Archie Moore

ARCHIE FRANCIS MOORE BL TL
B. Aug. 30, 1941, Upper Darby, Pa. 6' 2" 190 lbs.

Year	Gms.	BA	SA	AB	H	2B	3B	HR	RBI	SB	G. by Pos
1964	31	.174	.261	23	4	2	0	0	1	0	OF-8, 1B-7
1965	9	.412	.706	17	7	2	0	1	4	0	OF-5
2 yrs.	40	.275	.450	40	11	4	0	1	5	0	OF-13, 1B-7

Ray Morehart

RAYMOND ANDERSON MOREHART BL TR
B. Dec. 2, 1899, Abner, Tex. 5' 9" 157 lbs.
D. Jan. 13, 1989, Dallas, Tex.

Year	Gms.	BA	SA	AB	H	2B	3B	HR	RBI	SB	G. by Pos
1927	73	.256	.328	195	50	7	2	1	20	4	2B-53

Omar Moreno

OMAR RENAN MORENO BL TL
B. Oct. 24, 1952, Puerto Armuelles, 6' 2" 180 lbs.
Panama

Year	Gms.	BA	SA	AB	H	2B	3B	HR	RBI	SB	G. by Pos
1983	48	.250	.342	152	38	9	1	1	17	7	OF-48
1984	117	.259	.361	355	92	12	6	4	38	20	OF-108, DH-1
1985	34	.197	.333	66	13	4	1	1	4	1	OF-26, DH-1
3 yrs.	199	.250	.353	573	143	25	8	6	59	28	OF-182, DH-2

George Moriarty

GEORGE JOSEPH MORIARTY BR TR
B. Jul. 7, 1884, Chicago, Ill. 6' 185 lbs.
D. Apr. 8, 1964, Miami, Fla.

Year	Gms.	BA	SA	AB	H	2B	3B	HR	RBI	SB	G. by Pos
1906	65	.234	.340	197	46	7	7	0	23	8	3B-39, OF-15, 1B-5, 2B-1

George Moriarty *continued*

Year	Gms.	BA	SA	AB	H	2B	3B	HR	RBI	SB	G. by Pos
1907	126	.277	.336	437	121	16	5	0	43	28	3B-91, 1B-22, OF-9, 2B-8, SS-1
1908	101	.236	.276	348	82	12	1	0	27	22	1B-52, 3B-28, OF-10, 2B-4
3 yrs.	292	.254	.316	982	249	35	13	0	93	58	3B-158, 1B-79, OF-34, 2B-13, SS-1

Jeff Moronko

JEFFREY ROBERT MORONKO BR TR
B. Aug. 17, 1959, Houston, Tex. 6' 2" 190 lbs.

Year	Gms.	BA	SA	AB	H	2B	3B	HR	RBI	SB	G. by Pos
1987	7	.091	.091	11	1	0	0	0	0	0	3B-3, SS-2, OF-2

Hal Morris

WILLIAM HAROLD MORRIS BL TL
B. Apr. 9, 1965, Fort Rucker, Ala. 6' 3" 200 lbs.

Year	Gms.	BA	SA	AB	H	2B	3B	HR	RBI	SB	G. by Pos
1988	15	.100	.100	20	2	0	0	0	0	0	OF-4, DH-1
1989	15	.278	.278	18	5	0	0	0	4	0	OF-5, 1B-2, DH-1
2 yrs.	30	.184	.184	38	7	0	0	0	4	0	OF-9, 1B-2, DH-2

Ross Moschitto

ROSAIRE ALLEN MOSCHITTO BR TR
B. Feb. 15, 1945, Fresno, Calif. 6' 2" 175 lbs.

Year	Gms.	BA	SA	AB	H	2B	3B	HR	RBI	SB	G. by Pos
1965	96	.185	.296	27	5	0	0	1	3	0	OF-89
1967	14	.111	.111	9	1	0	0	0	0	0	OF-8
2 yrs.	110	.167	.250	36	6	0	0	1	3	0	OF-97

Gerry Moses

GERALD BRAHEEN MOSES BR TR
B. Aug. 9, 1946, Yazoo City, Miss. 6' 3" 210 lbs.

Year	Gms.	BA	SA	AB	H	2B	3B	HR	RBI	SB	G. by Pos
1973	21	.254	.288	59	15	2	0	0	3	0	C-17, DH-1

Charlie Mullen

CHARLES GEORGE MULLEN BR TR
B. Mar. 15, 1889, Seattle, Wash. 5' 10½" 155 lbs.
D. Jun. 6, 1963, Seattle, Wash.

Year	Gms.	BA	SA	AB	H	2B	3B	HR	RBI	SB	G. by Pos
1914	93	.260	.285	323	84	8	0	0	44	11	1B-93
1915	40	.267	.278	90	24	1	0	0	7	5	1B-27
1916	59	.267	.342	146	39	9	1	0	18	7	2B-20, 1B-17, OF-6
3 yrs.	192	.263	.299	559	147	18	1	0	69	23	1B-137, 2B-20, OF-6

Jerry Mumphrey

JERRY WAYNE MUMPHREY BB TR
B. Sep. 9, 1952, Tyler, Tex. 6' 2" 185 lbs.

Year	Gms.	BA	SA	AB	H	2B	3B	HR	RBI	SB	G. by Pos
1981	80	.307	.429	319	98	11	5	6	32	14	OF-79
1982	123	.300	.449	477	143	24	10	9	68	11	OF-123
1983	83	.262	.412	267	70	11	4	7	36	2	OF-83
3 yrs.	286	.293	.434	1063	311	46	19	22	136	27	OF-285
Divisional Playoffs											
1981	5	.095	.095	21	2	0	0	0	0	1	OF-5
League Championship Series											
1981	3	.500	.583	12	6	1	0	0	0	0	OF-3
World Series											
1981	5	.200	.200	15	3	0	0	0	0	1	OF-5

Thurman Munson

THURMAN LEE MUNSON BR TR
B. Jun. 7, 1947, Akron, Ohio 5' 11" 190 lbs.
D. Aug. 2, 1979, Canton, Ohio

Year	Gms.	BA	SA	AB	H	2B	3B	HR	RBI	SB	G. by Pos
1969	26	.256	.349	86	22	1	2	1	9	0	C-25
1970	132	.302	.415	453	137	25	4	6	53	5	C-125
1971	125	.251	.368	451	113	15	4	10	42	6	C-117, OF-1
1972	140	.280	.364	511	143	16	3	7	46	6	C-132
1973	147	.301	.487	519	156	29	4	20	74	4	C-142
1974	144	.261	.381	517	135	19	2	13	60	2	C-130, DH-4
1975	157	.318	.429	597	190	24	3	12	102	3	C-130, DH-22, 1B-2, OF-2, 3B-1
1976	152	.302	.432	616	186	27	1	17	105	14	C-121, DH-21, OF-11
1977	149	.308	.462	595	183	28	5	18	100	5	C-136, DH-10
1978	154	.297	.373	617	183	27	1	6	71	2	C-125, DH-14, OF-13

Thurman Munson *continued*

Year	Gms.	BA	SA	AB	H	2B	3B	HR	RBI	SB	G. by Pos
1979	97	.288	.374	382	110	18	3	3	39	1	C-88, DH-5, 1B-3
11 yrs.	1423	.292	.410	5344	1558	229	32	113	701	48	C-1278, DH-76, OF-27, 1B-5, 3B-1
League Championship Series											
1976	5	.435	.522	23	10	2	0	0	3	0	C-5
1977	5	.286	.476	21	6	1	0	1	5	0	C-5
1978	4	.278	.500	18	5	1	0	1	2	0	C-4
3 yrs.	14	.339	.500	62	21	4	0	2	10	0	C-14
World Series											
1976	4	.529	.529	17	9	0	0	0	2	0	C-4
1977	6	.320	.520	25	8	2	0	1	3	0	C-6
1978	6	.320	.440	25	8	3	0	0	7	1	C-6
3 yrs.	16	.373	.493	67	25	5	0	1	12	1	C-16

Bobby Murcer

BOBBY RAY MURCER   BL TR
B. May 20, 1946, Oklahoma City, Okla.   5' 11" 160 lbs.

Year	Gms.	BA	SA	AB	H	2B	3B	HR	RBI	SB	G. by Pos
1965	11	.243	.378	37	9	0	1	1	4	0	SS-11
1966	21	.174	.217	69	12	1	1	0	5	2	SS-18
1969	152	.259	.454	564	146	24	4	26	82	7	OF-118, 3B-31
1970	159	.251	.420	581	146	23	3	23	78	15	OF-155
1971	146	.331	.543	529	175	25	6	25	94	14	OF-143
1972	153	.292	.537	585	171	30	7	33	96	11	OF-151
1973	160	.304	.464	616	187	29	2	22	95	6	OF-160
1974	156	.274	.378	606	166	25	4	10	88	14	OF-156
1979	74	.273	.409	264	72	12	0	8	33	1	OF-70
1980	100	.269	.438	297	80	9	1	13	57	2	OF-59, DH-33
1981	50	.265	.470	117	31	6	0	6	24	0	DH-33
1982	65	.227	.418	141	32	6	0	7	30	2	DH-47
1983	9	.182	.409	22	4	2	0	1	1	0	DH-5
13 yrs.	1256	.278	.453	4428	1231	192	29	175	687	74	OF-1012, DH-118, 3B-31, SS-29
Divisional Playoffs											
1981	2	.000	.000	1	0	0	0	0	0	0	
League Championship Series											
1980	1	.000	.000	4	0	0	0	0	0	0	DH-1
1981	1	.333	.333	3	1	0	0	0	0	0	DH-1
2 yrs.	2	.143	.143	7	1	0	0	0	0	0	DH-2
World Series											
1981	4	.000	.000	3	0	0	0	0	0	0	

Larry Murray

LARRY MURRAY   BB TR
B. Mar. 1, 1953, Chicago, Ill.   5' 11" 179 lbs.

Year	Gms.	BA	SA	AB	H	2B	3B	HR	RBI	SB	G. by Pos
1974	6	.000	.000	1	0	0	0	0	0	0	OF-3
1975	6	.000	.000	1	0	0	0	0	0	0	OF-4
1976	8	.100	.100	10	1	0	0	0	2	2	OF-7
3 yrs.	20	.083	.083	12	1	0	0	0	2	2	OF-14

Jerry Narron

JERRY AUSTIN NARRON   BL TR
B. Jan. 15, 1956, Goldsboro, N. C.   6' 3" 205 lbs.

Year	Gms.	BA	SA	AB	H	2B	3B	HR	RBI	SB	G. by Pos
1979	61	.171	.309	123	21	3	1	4	18	0	C-56, DH-1

Graig Nettles

GRAIG NETTLES   BL TR
B. Aug. 20, 1944, San Diego, Calif.   6' 180 lbs.

Year	Gms.	BA	SA	AB	H	2B	3B	HR	RBI	SB	G. by Pos
1973	160	.234	.386	552	129	18	0	22	81	0	3B-157, DH-2
1974	155	.246	.403	566	139	21	1	22	75	1	3B-154, SS-1
1975	157	.267	.430	581	155	24	4	21	91	1	3B-157
1976	158	.254	.475	583	148	29	2	32	93	11	3B-158, SS-1
1977	158	.255	.496	589	150	23	4	37	107	2	3B-156, DH-1
1978	159	.276	.460	587	162	23	2	27	93	1	3B-159, SS-2
1979	145	.253	.401	521	132	15	1	20	73	1	3B-144
1980	89	.244	.435	324	79	14	0	16	45	0	3B-88, SS-1
1981	103	.244	.398	349	85	7	1	15	46	0	3B-97, DH-4
1982	122	.232	.402	405	94	11	2	18	55	1	3B-113, DH-3
1983	129	.266	.446	462	123	17	3	20	75	0	3B-126, DH-3
11 yrs.	1535	.253	.433	5519	1396	202	20	250	834	18	3B-1509, DH-11, SS-5

Graig Nettles *continued*

Year	Gms.	BA	SA	AB	H	2B	3B	HR	RBI	SB	G. by Pos
Divisional Playoffs											
1981	5	.059	.059	17	1	0	0	0	1	0	3B-5
League Championship Series											
1976	5	.235	.647	17	4	1	0	2	4	0	3B-5
1977	5	.150	.150	20	3	0	0	0	1	0	3B-5
1978	4	.333	.667	15	5	0	1	1	2	0	3B-4
1980	2	.167	.667	6	1	0	0	1	1	0	3B-2
1981	3	.500	.917	12	6	2	0	1	9	0	3B-3
5 yrs.	19	.271	.557	70	19	3	1	5	17	0	3B-19
World Series											
1976	4	.250	.250	12	3	0	0	0	2	0	3B-4
1977	6	.190	.238	21	4	1	0	0	2	0	3B-6
1978	6	.160	.160	25	4	0	0	0	1	0	3B-6
1981	3	.400	.500	10	4	1	0	0	0	0	3B-3
4 yrs.	19	.221	.250	68	15	2	0	0	5	0	3B-19

Gus Niarhos

CONSTANTINE GREGORY NIARHOS   BR TR
B. Dec. 6, 1920, Birmingham, Ala.   6' 160 lbs.

Year	Gms.	BA	SA	AB	H	2B	3B	HR	RBI	SB	G. by Pos
1946	37	.225	.300	40	9	1	0	0	2	1	C-29
1948	83	.268	.338	228	61	12	2	0	19	1	C-82
1949	32	.279	.372	43	12	2	1	0	6	0	C-30
1950	1	—	—	0	0	0	0	0	0	0	
4 yrs.	153	.264	.338	311	82	15	4	0	27	2	C-141
World Series											
1949	1	—	—	0	0	0	0	0	0	0	C-1

Harry Niles

HERBERT CLYDE NILES   BR TR
B. Sep. 10, 1880, Buchanan, Mich.   5' 8" 175 lbs.
D. Apr. 18, 1953, Sturgis, Mich.

Year	Gms.	BA	SA	AB	H	2B	3B	HR	RBI	SB	G. by Pos
1908	96	.249	.355	361	90	14	6	4	24	18	2B-85, OF-7

Otis Nixon

OTIS JUNIOR NIXON   BB TR
B. Jan. 9, 1959, Evergreen, N. C.   6' 2" 175 lbs.

Year	Gms.	BA	SA	AB	H	2B	3B	HR	RBI	SB	G. by Pos
1983	13	.143	.143	14	2	0	0	0	0	2	OF-9

Matt Nokes

MATTHEW DODGE NOKES   BL TR
B. Oct. 31, 1963, San Diego, Calif.   6' 1" 180 lbs.

Year	Gms.	BA	SA	AB	H	2B	3B	HR	RBI	SB	G. by Pos
1990	92	.237	.354	240	57	4	0	8	32	2	C-46, DH-30, OF-2
1991	135	.268	.469	456	122	20	0	24	77	3	C-130, DH-3
1992	121	.224	.424	384	86	9	1	22	59	0	C-111
1993	76	.249	.424	217	54	8	0	10	35	0	C-56, DH-11
1994	28	.291	.595	79	23	3	0	7	19	0	C-17, DH-5, 1B-4
5 yrs.	452	.249	.437	1376	342	44	1	71	222	5	C-360, DH-49, 1B-4, OF-2

Irv Noren

IRVING ARNOLD NOREN   BL TL
B. Nov. 29, 1924, Jamestown, N. Y.   6' 190 lbs.

Year	Gms.	BA	SA	AB	H	2B	3B	HR	RBI	SB	G. by Pos
1952	93	.235	.353	272	64	13	2	5	21	4	OF-60, 1B-19
1953	109	.267	.388	345	92	12	6	6	46	3	OF-96
1954	125	.319	.481	426	136	21	6	12	66	4	OF-116, 1B-1
1955	132	.253	.375	371	94	19	1	8	59	5	OF-126
1956	29	.216	.243	37	8	1	0	0	6	0	OF-10, 1B-1
5 yrs.	488	.272	.402	1451	394	66	15	31	198	16	OF-408, 1B-21
World Series											
1952	4	.300	.300	10	3	0	0	0	1	0	OF-3
1953	2	.000	.000	1	0	0	0	0	0	0	
1955	5	.063	.063	16	1	0	0	0	1	0	OF-5
3 yrs.	11	.148	.148	27	4	0	0	0	2	0	OF-8

Les Nunamaker

LESLIE GRANT NUNAMAKER   BR TR
B. Jan. 25, 1889, Malcolm, Neb.   6' 2" 190 lbs.
D. Nov. 14, 1938, Hastings, Neb.

Year	Gms.	BA	SA	AB	H	2B	3B	HR	RBI	SB	G. by Pos
1914	87	.265	.350	257	68	10	3	2	29	11	C-70, 1B-5
1915	87	.225	.273	249	56	6	3	0	17	3	C-77, 1B-2

Year	Gms.	BA	SA	AB	H	2B	3B	HR	RBI	SB	G. by Pos

Les Nunamaker *continued*

Year	Gms.	BA	SA	AB	H	2B	3B	HR	RBI	SB	G. by Pos
1916	91	.296	.404	260	77	14	7	0	28	4	C-79
1917	104	.261	.303	310	81	9	2	0	33	5	C-91
4 yrs.	369	.262	.332	1076	282	39	15	2	107	23	C-317, 1B-7

Mike O'Berry

PRESTON MICHAEL O'BERRY   BR TR
B. Apr. 20, 1954, Birmingham, Ala.   6' 2" 190 lbs.

Year	Gms.	BA	SA	AB	H	2B	3B	HR	RBI	SB	G. by Pos
1984	13	.250	.313	32	8	2	0	0	5	0	C-12, 3B-1

Jack O'Connor

JOHN JOSEPH O'CONNOR   BR TR
B. Jun. 2, 1869, St. Louis, Mo.   5' 10" 170 lbs.
D. Nov. 14, 1937, St. Louis, Mo.

Year	Gms.	BA	SA	AB	H	2B	3B	HR	RBI	SB	G. by Pos
1903	64	.203	.231	212	43	4	1	0	12	4	C-63, 1B-1

Paddy O'Connor

PATRICK FRANCIS O'CONNOR   BR TR
B. Aug. 4, 1879, County Kerry,   5' 8" 168 lbs.
Ireland
D. Aug. 17, 1950, Springfield, Mass.

Year	Gms.	BA	SA	AB	H	2B	3B	HR	RBI	SB	G. by Pos
1918	1	.333	.333	3	1	0	0	0	0	0	C-1

Paul O'Neill

PAUL ANDREW O'NEILL   BL TL
B. Feb. 25, 1963, Columbus, Ohio   6' 4" 200 lbs.

Year	Gms.	BA	SA	AB	H	2B	3B	HR	RBI	SB	G. by Pos
1993	141	.311	.504	498	155	34	1	20	75	2	OF-138, DH-2
1994	103	.359	.603	368	132	25	1	21	83	5	OF-99, DH-4
1995	127	.300	.526	460	138	30	4	22	96	1	OF-121, DH-4
1996	150	.302	.474	546	165	35	1	19	91	0	OF-146, DH-3, 1B-1
4 yrs.	521	.315	.520	1872	590	124	7	82	345	8	OF-504, DH-13, 1B-1

Divisional Playoffs

Year	Gms.	BA	SA	AB	H	2B	3B	HR	RBI	SB	G. by Pos
1995	5	.333	.833	18	6	0	0	3	6	0	OF-5
1996	4	.133	.133	15	2	0	0	0	0	0	OF-4
2 yrs.	9	.242	.515	33	8	0	0	3	6	0	OF-9

League Championship Series

Year	Gms.	BA	SA	AB	H	2B	3B	HR	RBI	SB	G. by Pos
1996	4	.273	.545	11	3	0	1	0	2	0	OF-4

World Series

Year	Gms.	BA	SA	AB	H	2B	3B	HR	RBI	SB	G. by Pos
1996	5	.167	.333	12	2	2	0	0	0	0	OF-4

Steve O'Neill

STEPHEN FRANCIS O'NEILL   BR TR
B. Jul. 6, 1891, Minooka, Pa.   5' 10" 165 lbs.
D. Jan. 26, 1962, Cleveland, Ohio

Year	Gms.	BA	SA	AB	H	2B	3B	HR	RBI	SB	G. by Pos
1925	35	.286	.374	91	26	5	0	1	13	0	C-31

Queenie O'Rourke

JAMES STEPHEN O'ROURKE   BR TR
B. Dec. 26, 1883, Bridgeport, Conn.   5' 7" 150 lbs.
D. Dec. 22, 1955, Sparrows Point, Md.

Year	Gms.	BA	SA	AB	H	2B	3B	HR	RBI	SB	G. by Pos
1908	34	.231	.241	108	25	1	0	0	3	4	OF-14, SS-11, 2B-4, 3B-3

Johnny Oates

JOHNNY LANE OATES   BL TR
B. Jan. 21, 1946, Sylva, N. C.   5' 11" 188 lbs.

Year	Gms.	BA	SA	AB	H	2B	3B	HR	RBI	SB	G. by Pos
1980	39	.188	.281	64	12	3	0	1	3	1	C-39
1981	10	.192	.231	26	5	1	0	0	0	0	C-10
2 yrs.	49	.189	.267	90	17	4	0	1	3	1	C-49

Heinie Odom

HERMAN BOYD ODOM   BB TR
B. Oct. 13, 1900, Rusk, Tex.   6' 170 lbs.
D. Aug. 31, 1970, Rusk, Tex.

Year	Gms.	BA	SA	AB	H	2B	3B	HR	RBI	SB	G. by Pos
1925	1	1.000	1.000	1	1	0	0	0	0	0	3B-1

Rowland Office

ROWLAND JOHNIE OFFICE   BL TL
B. Oct. 25, 1952, Sacramento, Calif.   6' 170 lbs.

Year	Gms.	BA	SA	AB	H	2B	3B	HR	RBI	SB	G. by Pos
1983	2	.000	.000	2	0	0	0	0	1	0	OF-2

Rube Oldring

REUBEN HENRY OLDRING   BR TR
B. May 30, 1884, New York, N. Y.   5' 10" 186 lbs.
D. Sep. 9, 1961, Bridgeton, N. J.

Year	Gms.	BA	SA	AB	H	2B	3B	HR	RBI	SB	G. by Pos
1905	8	.300	.467	30	9	0	1	1	6	4	SS-8
1916	43	.234	.304	158	37	8	0	1	12	6	OF-43
2 yrs.	51	.245	.330	188	46	8	1	2	18	10	OF-43, SS-8

Bob Oliver

ROBERT LEE OLIVER   BR TR
B. Feb. 8, 1943, Shreveport, La.   6' 3" 205 lbs.

Year	Gms.	BA	SA	AB	H	2B	3B	HR	RBI	SB	G. by Pos
1975	18	.132	.158	38	5	1	0	0	1	0	1B-8, DH-3, 3B-1

Nate Oliver

NATHANIEL OLIVER   BR TR
B. Dec. 13, 1940, St. Petersburg, Fla.   5' 10" 160 lbs.

Year	Gms.	BA	SA	AB	H	2B	3B	HR	RBI	SB	G. by Pos
1969	1	.000	.000	1	0	0	0	0	0	0	

Al Orth

ALBERT LEWIS ORTH   BL TR
B. Sep. 5, 1872, Tipton, Ind.   6' 200 lbs.
D. Oct. 8, 1948, Lynchburg, Va.

Year	Gms.	BA	SA	AB	H	2B	3B	HR	RBI	SB	G. by Pos
1904	26	.297	.344	64	19	1	1	0	7	2	P-20, OF-2
1905	54	.183	.244	131	24	3	1	1	8	2	P-40, 1B-1, OF-1
1906	47	.274	.341	135	37	2	2	1	17	2	P-45, OF-1
1907	44	.324	.410	105	34	6	0	1	13	1	P-36, OF-1
1908	38	.290	.362	69	20	1	2	0	4	0	P-21
1909	22	.265	.324	34	9	0	1	0	5	1	2B-6, P-1
6 yrs.	231	.266	.333	538	143	13	7	3	54	8	P-163, 2B-6, OF-5, 1B-1

Champ Osteen

JAMES CHAMPLIN OSTEEN   BL TR
B. Feb. 24, 1877, Hendersonville, N. C.   5' 8" 150 lbs.
D. Dec. 14, 1962, Greenville, S. C.

Year	Gms.	BA	SA	AB	H	2B	3B	HR	RBI	SB	G. by Pos
1904	28	.196	.336	107	21	1	4	2	9	0	3B-17, SS-8, 1B-4

Bill Otis

PAUL FRANKLIN OTIS   BL TR
B. Dec. 24, 1889, Scituate, Mass.   5' 10½" 150 lbs.
D. Dec. 15, 1990, Duluth, Minn.

Year	Gms.	BA	SA	AB	H	2B	3B	HR	RBI	SB	G. by Pos
1912	4	.050	.050	20	1	0	0	0	2	0	OF-4

Spike Owen

SPIKE DEE OWEN   BB TR
B. Apr. 19, 1961, Cleburne, Tex.   5' 9" 160 lbs.

Year	Gms.	BA	SA	AB	H	2B	3B	HR	RBI	SB	G. by Pos
1993	103	.234	.311	334	78	16	2	2	20	3	SS-96, DH-1

Del Paddock

DELMAR. HAROLD PADDOCK   BL TR
B. Jun. 8, 1887, Volga, S. D.   5' 9" 165 lbs.
D. Feb. 6, 1952, Remer, Minn.

Year	Gms.	BA	SA	AB	H	2B	3B	HR	RBI	SB	G. by Pos
1912	45	.288	.378	156	45	5	3	1	14	9	3B-41, 2B-2, OF-1

Mike Pagliarulo

MICHAEL TIMOTHY PAGLIARULO   BL TR
B. Mar. 15, 1960, Medford, Mass.   6' 2" 195 lbs.

Year	Gms.	BA	SA	AB	H	2B	3B	HR	RBI	SB	G. by Pos
1984	67	.239	.448	201	48	15	3	7	34	0	3B-67
1985	138	.239	.442	380	91	16	2	19	62	0	3B-134
1986	149	.238	.464	504	120	24	3	28	71	4	3B-143, SS-2
1987	150	.234	.479	522	122	26	3	32	87	1	3B-147, 1B-1
1988	125	.216	.367	444	96	20	1	15	67	1	3B-124
1989	74	.197	.296	223	44	10	0	4	16	1	3B-69, DH-1
6 yrs.	703	.229	.427	2274	521	111	12	105	337	7	3B-684, SS-2, 1B-1, DH-1

Ben Paschal

BENJAMIN EDWIN PASCHAL   BR TR
B. Oct. 13, 1895, Enterprise, Ala.   5' 11" 185 lbs.
D. Nov. 10, 1974, Charlotte, N. C.

Year	Gms.	BA	SA	AB	H	2B	3B	HR	RBI	SB	G. by Pos
1924	4	.250	.333	12	3	1	0	0	3	0	OF-4
1925	89	.360	.611	247	89	16	5	12	56	14	OF-66
1926	96	.287	.438	258	74	12	3	7	33	7	OF-74
1927	50	.317	.549	82	26	9	2	2	16	0	OF-27

339

Year	Gms.	BA	SA	AB	H	2B	3B	HR	RBI	SB	G. by Pos

Ben Paschal *continued*

Year	Gms.	BA	SA	AB	H	2B	3B	HR	RBI	SB	G. by Pos
1928	65	.316	.456	79	25	6	1	1	15	1	OF-25
1929	42	.208	.333	72	15	3	0	2	11	1	OF-20
6 yrs.	346	.309	.497	750	232	47	11	24	134	23	OF-216
World Series											
1926	5	.250	.250	4	1	0	0	0	1	0	
1928	3	.200	.200	10	2	0	0	0	1	0	OF-3
2 yrs.	8	.214	.214	14	3	0	0	0	2	0	OF-3

Dan Pasqua

DANIEL ANTHONY PASQUA   BL TL
B. Oct. 17, 1961, Yonkers, N.Y.   6' 205 lbs.

Year	Gms.	BA	SA	AB	H	2B	3B	HR	RBI	SB	G. by Pos
1985	60	.209	.426	148	31	3	1	9	25	0	OF-37, DH-14
1986	102	.293	.525	280	82	17	0	16	45	2	OF-81, 1B-5, DH-3
1987	113	.233	.421	318	74	7	1	17	42	0	OF-74, DH-20, 1B-12
3 yrs.	275	.251	.461	746	187	27	2	42	112	2	OF-192, DH-37, 1B-17

Mike Patterson

MICHAEL LEE PATTERSON   BL TR
Jan. 26, 1958, Santa Monica, Calif.   5' 10" 170 lbs.

Year	Gms.	BA	SA	AB	H	2B	3B	HR	RBI	SB	G. by Pos
1981	4	.222	.667	9	2	0	2	0	0	0	OF-4
1982	11	.188	.438	16	3	1	0	1	1	1	OF-9, DH-1
2 yrs.	15	.200	.520	25	5	1	2	1	1	1	OF-13, DH-1

Roger Peckinpaugh

ROGER THORPE PECKINPAUGH   BR TR
B. Feb. 5, 1891, Wooster, Ohio   5' 10½" 165 lbs.
D. Nov. 17, 1977, Cleveland, Ohio

Year	Gms.	BA	SA	AB	H	2B	3B	HR	RBI	SB	G. by Pos
1913	95	.268	.347	340	91	10	7	1	32	19	SS-93
1914	157	.223	.284	570	127	14	6	3	51	38	SS-157
1915	142	.220	.307	540	119	18	7	5	44	19	SS-142
1916	146	.255	.346	552	141	22	8	4	58	18	SS-146
1917	148	.260	.330	543	141	24	7	0	41	17	SS-148
1918	122	.231	.278	446	103	15	3	0	43	12	SS-122
1919	122	.305	.404	453	138	20	2	7	33	10	SS-121
1920	139	.270	.386	534	144	26	6	8	54	8	SS-137
1921	149	.288	.397	577	166	25	7	8	71	2	SS-149
9 yrs.	1220	.257	.342	4555	1170	174	53	36	427	143	SS-1215
World Series											
1921	8	.179	.214	28	5	1	0	0	0	0	SS-8

Joe Pepitone

JOSEPH ANTHONY PEPITONE   BL TL
B. Oct. 9, 1940, Brooklyn, N.Y.   6' 2" 185 lbs.

Year	Gms.	BA	SA	AB	H	2B	3B	HR	RBI	SB	G. by Pos
1962	63	.239	.442	138	33	3	2	7	17	1	OF-32, 1B-16
1963	157	.271	.448	580	157	16	3	27	89	3	1B-143, OF-16
1964	160	.251	.418	613	154	12	3	28	100	2	1B-155, OF-30
1965	143	.247	.394	531	131	18	3	18	62	4	1B-115, OF-41
1966	152	.255	.463	585	149	21	4	31	83	4	1B-119, OF-55
1967	133	.251	.377	501	126	18	3	13	64	1	OF-123, 1B-6
1968	108	.245	.403	380	93	9	3	15	56	8	OF-92, 1B-12
1969	135	.242	.442	513	124	16	3	27	70	8	1B-132
8 yrs.	1051	.252	.423	3841	967	113	24	166	541	31	1B-698, OF-389
World Series											
1963	4	.154	.154	13	2	0	0	0	0	0	1B-4
1964	7	.154	.308	26	4	1	0	1	5	0	1B-7
2 yrs.	11	.154	.256	39	6	1	0	1	5	0	1B-11

Marty Perez

MARTIN ROMAN PEREZ   BR TR
B. Feb. 28, 1947, Visalia, Calif.   5' 11" 160 lbs.

Year	Gms.	BA	SA	AB	H	2B	3B	HR	RBI	SB	G. by Pos
1977	1	.500	.500	4	2	0	0	0	0	0	3B-1

Cy Perkins

RALPH FOSTER PERKINS   BR TR
B. Feb. 27, 1896, Gloucester, Mass.   5' 10½" 158 lbs.
D. Oct. 2, 1963, Philadelphia, Pa.

Year	Gms.	BA	SA	AB	H	2B	3B	HR	RBI	SB	G. by Pos
1931	16	.255	.277	47	12	1	0	0	7	0	C-16

Ken Phelps

KENNETH ALLEN PHELPS   BL TL
B. Aug. 6, 1954, Seattle, Wash.   6' 1" 209 lbs.

Year	Gms.	BA	SA	AB	H	2B	3B	HR	RBI	SB	G. by Pos
1988	45	.224	.551	107	24	5	0	10	22	0	DH-28, 1B-1
1989	86	.249	.378	185	46	3	0	7	29	0	DH-55, 1B-8
2 yrs.	131	.240	.442	292	70	8	0	17	51	0	DH-83, 1B-9

Eddie Phillips

EDWARD DAVID PHILLIPS   BR TR
B. Feb. 17, 1901, Worcester, Mass.   6' 178 lbs.
D. Jan. 26, 1968, Buffalo, N.Y.

Year	Gms.	BA	SA	AB	H	2B	3B	HR	RBI	SB	G. by Pos
1932	9	.290	.516	31	9	1	0	2	4	1	C-9

Jack Phillips

JACK DORN PHILLIPS   BR TR
B. Sep. 6, 1921, Clarence, N.Y.   6' 4" 193 lbs.

Year	Gms.	BA	SA	AB	H	2B	3B	HR	RBI	SB	G. by Pos
1947	16	.278	.417	36	10	0	1	1	2	0	1B-10
1948	1	.000	.000	2	0	0	0	0	0	0	1B-1
1949	45	.308	.407	91	28	4	1	1	10	1	1B-38
3 yrs.	62	.295	.403	129	38	4	2	2	12	1	1B-49
World Series											
1947	2	.000	.000	2	0	0	0	0	0	0	1B-1

Lou Piniella

LOUIS VICTOR PINIELLA   BR TR
B. Aug. 28, 1943, Tampa, Fla.   6' 182 lbs.

Year	Gms.	BA	SA	AB	H	2B	3B	HR	RBI	SB	G. by Pos
1974	140	.305	.407	518	158	26	0	9	70	1	OF-130, DH-6, 1B-1
1975	74	.196	.226	199	39	4	1	0	22	0	OF-46, DH-12
1976	100	.281	.394	327	92	16	6	3	38	0	OF-49, DH-38
1977	103	.330	.510	339	112	19	3	12	45	2	OF-51, DH-43, 1B-1
1978	130	.314	.445	472	148	34	5	6	69	3	OF-103, DH-23
1979	130	.297	.425	461	137	22	2	11	69	3	OF-112, DH-16
1980	116	.287	.361	321	92	18	0	2	27	0	OF-104, DH-7
1981	60	.277	.428	159	44	9	0	5	18	0	OF-36, DH-19
1982	102	.307	.448	261	80	17	1	6	37	0	DH-55, OF-40
1983	53	.291	.405	148	43	9	1	2	16	1	OF-43, DH-1
1984	29	.302	.407	86	26	4	1	1	6	0	OF-24, DH-2
11 yrs.	1037	.295	.413	3291	971	178	20	57	417	10	OF-738, DH-222, 1B-2
Divisional Playoffs											
1981	4	.200	.600	10	2	1	0	1	3	0	DH-4
League Championship Series											
1976	4	.273	.364	11	3	1	0	0	0	0	DH-3
1977	5	.333	.476	21	7	3	0	0	2	0	OF-4, DH-1
1978	4	.235	.235	17	4	0	0	0	0	0	OF-4
1980	2	.200	.800	5	1	0	0	1	1	0	OF-2
1981	3	.600	1.200	5	3	0	0	1	3	0	DH-2, OF-1
5 yrs.	18	.305	.475	59	18	4	0	2	6	0	OF-11, DH-6
World Series											
1976	4	.333	.444	9	3	1	0	0	0	0	DH-3, OF-2
1977	6	.273	.273	22	6	0	0	0	3	0	OF-6
1978	6	.280	.280	25	7	0	0	0	4	1	OF-6
1981	6	.438	.500	16	7	1	0	0	3	1	OF-3
4 yrs.	22	.319	.347	72	23	2	0	0	10	2	OF-17, DH-3

Wally Pipp

WALTER CLEMENT PIPP   BL TL
B. Feb. 17, 1893, Chicago, Ill.   6' 1" 180 lbs.
D. Jan. 11, 1965, Grand Rapids, Mich.

Year	Gms.	BA	SA	AB	H	2B	3B	HR	RBI	SB	G. by Pos
1915	136	.246	.367	479	118	20	13	4	60	18	1B-134
1916	151	.262	.417	545	143	20	14	12	93	18	1B-148
1917	155	.244	.380	587	143	29	12	9	70	11	1B-155
1918	91	.304	.415	349	106	15	9	2	44	11	1B-91
1919	138	.275	.398	523	144	23	10	7	50	9	1B-138
1920	153	.280	.430	610	171	30	14	11	76	4	1B-153
1921	153	.296	.427	588	174	35	9	8	97	17	1B-153
1922	152	.329	.466	577	190	32	10	9	90	7	1B-152
1923	144	.304	.397	569	173	19	8	6	108	6	1B-144
1924	153	.295	.457	589	174	30	19	9	113	12	1B-153
1925	62	.230	.348	178	41	6	3	3	24	3	1B-47
11 yrs.	1488	.282	.414	5594	1577	259	121	80	825	114	1B-1468
World Series											
1921	8	.154	.192	26	4	1	0	0	2	1	1B-8
1922	5	.286	.333	21	6	1	0	0	3	1	1B-5

Year	Gms.	BA	SA	AB	H	2B	3B	HR	RBI	SB	G. by Pos

Wally Pipp *continued*

Year	Gms.	BA	SA	AB	H	2B	3B	HR	RBI	SB	G. by Pos
1923	6	.250	.250	20	5	0	0	0	2	0	1B-6
3 yrs.	19	.224	.254	67	15	2	0	0	7	2	1B-19

Jim Pisoni

JAMES PETE PISONI   BR TR
B. Aug. 14, 1929, St. Louis, Mo.   5' 10" 169 lbs.

Year	Gms.	BA	SA	AB	H	2B	3B	HR	RBI	SB	G. by Pos
1959	17	.176	.294	17	3	0	1	0	1	0	OF-15
1960	20	.111	.111	9	1	0	0	0	1	0	OF-18
2 yrs.	37	.154	.231	26	4	0	1	0	2	0	OF-33

Luis Polonia

LUIS ANDREW POLONIA   BL TL
B. Oct. 12, 1964, Santiago City,   5' 8" 155 lbs.
Dominican Republic

Year	Gms.	BA	SA	AB	H	2B	3B	HR	RBI	SB	G. by Pos
1989	66	.313	.405	227	71	11	2	2	29	9	OF-53, DH-9
1990	11	.318	.318	22	7	0	0	0	3	1	DH-4
1994	95	.311	.414	350	109	21	6	1	36	20	OF-84, DH-2
1995	67	.261	.349	238	62	9	3	2	15	10	OF-64
4 yrs.	239	.297	.391	837	249	41	11	5	83	40	OF-201, DH-15

Jorge Posada

JORGE RAFAEL POSADA   BB TR
B. Aug. 17, 1971, Santurce,   6' 2" 190 lbs.
Puerto Rico

Year	Gms.	BA	SA	AB	H	2B	3B	HR	RBI	SB	G. by Pos
1995	1	.071	—	0	0	0	0	0	0	0	C-1
1996	8	.071	.071	14	1	0	0	0	0	0	C-4, DH-3
2 yrs.	9	.071	.071	14	1	0	0	0	0	0	C-5, DH-3
Divisional Playoffs											
1995	1	—	—	0	0	0	0	0	0	0	

Jake Powell

ALVIN JACOB POWELL   BR TR
B. Jul. 15, 1908, Silver Spring, Md.   5' 11½" 180 lbs.
D. Nov. 4, 1948, Washington, D. C.

Year	Gms.	BA	SA	AB	H	2B	3B	HR	RBI	SB	G. by Pos
1936	87	.306	.429	324	99	13	3	7	48	16	OF-84
1937	97	.263	.364	365	96	22	3	3	45	7	OF-94
1938	45	.256	.378	164	42	12	1	2	20	3	OF-43
1939	31	.244	.349	86	21	4	1	1	9	1	OF-23
1940	12	.185	.185	27	5	0	0	0	2	0	OF-7
5 yrs.	272	.272	.382	966	263	51	8	13	124	27	OF-251
World Series											
1936	6	.455	.636	22	10	1	0	1	5	1	OF-6
1937	1	.000	.000	1	0	0	0	0	0	0	
1938	1	—	—	0	0	0	0	0	0	0	OF-1
3 yrs.	8	.435	.609	23	10	1	0	1	5	1	OF-7

Mike Powers

MICHAEL RILEY POWERS   BR TR
B. Sep. 22, 1870, Pittsfield, Mass.
D. Apr. 26, 1909, Philadelphia, Pa.

Year	Gms.	BA	SA	AB	H	2B	3B	HR	RBI	SB	G. by Pos
1905	11	.182	.212	33	6	1	0	0	2	0	1B-7, C-4

Del Pratt

DERRILL BURNHAM PRATT   BR TR
B. Jan. 10, 1888, Walhalla, S. C.   5' 11" 175 lbs.
D. Sep. 30, 1977, Texas City, Tex.

Year	Gms.	BA	SA	AB	H	2B	3B	HR	RBI	SB	G. by Pos
1918	126	.275	.356	477	131	19	7	2	55	12	2B-126
1919	140	.292	.393	527	154	27	7	4	56	22	2B-140
1920	154	.314	.427	574	180	37	8	4	97	12	2B-154
3 yrs.	420	.295	.394	1578	465	83	22	10	208	46	2B-420

Gerry Priddy

GERALD EDWARD PRIDDY   BR TR
B. Nov. 9, 1919, Los Angeles, Calif.   5' 11½" 180 lbs.
D. Mar. 3, 1980, North Hollywood, Calif.

Year	Gms.	BA	SA	AB	H	2B	3B	HR	RBI	SB	G. by Pos
1941	56	.213	.270	174	37	7	0	1	26	4	2B-31, 3B-14, 1B-10
1942	59	.280	.381	189	53	9	2	2	28	0	3B-35, 1B-11, 2B-8, SS-3
2 yrs.	115	.248	.328	363	90	16	2	3	54	4	3B-49, 2B-39, 1B-21, SS-3

Gerry Priddy *continued*

Year	Gms.	BA	SA	AB	H	2B	3B	HR	RBI	SB	G. by Pos
World Series											
1942	3	.100	.200	10	1	1	0	0	1	0	1B-3, 3B-1

Johnnie Priest

JOHN GOODING PRIEST   BR TR
B. Jun. 23, 1886, St. Joseph, Mo.   5' 11" 170 lbs.
D. Nov. 4, 1979, Washington, D. C.

Year	Gms.	BA	SA	AB	H	2B	3B	HR	RBI	SB	G. by Pos
1911	7	.143	.143	21	3	0	0	0	2	3	2B-5, 3B-2
1912	2	.500	.500	2	1	0	0	0	1	0	
2 yrs.	9	.174	.174	23	4	0	0	0	3	3	2B-5, 3B-2

Jamie Quirk

JAMES PATRICK QUIRK   BL TR
B. Oct. 22, 1954, Whittier, Calif.   6' 4" 190 lbs.

Year	Gms.	BA	SA	AB	H	2B	3B	HR	RBI	SB	G. by Pos
1989	13	.083	.083	24	2	0	0	0	0	0	C-6, SS-1, DH-1

Tim Raines

TIMOTHY RAINES   BB TR
B. Sep. 16, 1959, Sanford, Fla.   5' 8" 160 lbs.

Year	Gms.	BA	SA	AB	H	2B	3B	HR	RBI	SB	G. by Pos
1996	59	.284	.468	201	57	10	0	9	33	10	OF-51, DH-2
Divisional Playoffs											
1996	4	.250	.250	16	4	0	0	0	0	0	OF-4
League Championship Series											
1996	5	.267	.333	15	4	1	0	0	0	0	OF-5
World Series											
1996	4	.214	.214	14	3	0	0	0	0	0	OF-4

Bobby Ramos

ROBERTO RAMOS   BR TR
B. Nov. 5, 1955, Calabazar de Sagua,   5' 11" 190 lbs.
Cuba

Year	Gms.	BA	SA	AB	H	2B	3B	HR	RBI	SB	G. by Pos
1982	4	.091	.364	11	1	0	0	1	2	0	C-4

Domingo Ramos

DOMINGO ANTONIO RAMOS   BR TR
B. Mar. 29, 1958, Santiago,   5' 10" 154 lbs.
Dominican Republic

Year	Gms.	BA	SA	AB	H	2B	3B	HR	RBI	SB	G. by Pos
1978	1	—	—	0	0	0	0	0	0	0	SS-1

John Ramos

JOHN JOSEPH RAMOS   BR TR
B. Aug. 6, 1965, Tampa, Fla.   6' 190 lbs.

Year	Gms.	BA	SA	AB	H	2B	3B	HR	RBI	SB	G. by Pos
1991	10	.308	.346	26	8	1	0	0	3	0	C-5, DH-4

Lenny Randle

LEONARD SHENOFF RANDLE   BB TR
B. Feb. 12, 1949, Long Beach, Calif.   5' 10" 169 lbs.

Year	Gms.	BA	SA	AB	H	2B	3B	HR	RBI	SB	G. by Pos
1979	20	.179	.179	39	7	0	0	0	3	0	OF-11, DH-2

Willie Randolph

WILLIE LARRY RANDOLPH   BR TR
B. Jul. 6, 1954, Holly Hill, S. C.   5' 11" 165 lbs.

Year	Gms.	BA	SA	AB	H	2B	3B	HR	RBI	SB	G. by Pos
1976	125	.267	.328	430	115	15	4	1	40	37	2B-124
1977	147	.274	.387	551	151	28	11	4	40	13	2B-147
1978	134	.279	.357	499	139	18	6	3	42	36	2B-134
1979	153	.270	.368	574	155	15	13	5	61	33	2B-153
1980	138	.294	.407	513	151	23	7	7	46	30	2B-138
1981	93	.232	.305	357	83	14	3	2	24	14	2B-93
1982	144	.280	.349	553	155	21	4	3	36	16	2B-142, DH-1
1983	104	.279	.348	420	117	21	1	2	38	12	2B-104
1984	142	.287	.348	564	162	24	2	2	31	10	2B-142
1985	143	.276	.356	497	137	21	2	5	40	16	2B-143
1986	141	.276	.346	492	136	15	2	5	50	15	2B-139, DH-1
1987	120	.305	.414	449	137	24	2	7	67	11	2B-119, DH-1
1988	110	.230	.300	404	93	20	1	2	34	8	2B-110
13 yrs.	1694	.275	.357	6303	1731	259	58	48	549	251	2B-1688, DH-3
Divisional Playoffs											
1981	5	.200	.200	20	4	0	0	0	1	0	2B-5
League Championship Series											
1976	5	.118	.118	17	2	0	0	0	1	1	2B-5
1977	5	.278	.333	18	5	1	0	0	2	0	2B-5

Willie Randolph *continued*

Year	Gms.	BA	SA	AB	H	2B	3B	HR	RBI	SB	G. by Pos
1980	3	.385	.538	13	5	2	0	0	1	0	2B-3
1981	3	.333	.583	12	4	0	0	1	2	0	2B-3
4 yrs.	16	.267	.367	60	16	3	0	1	6	1	2B-16
World Series
1976	4	.071	.071	14	1	0	0	0	0	0	2B-4
1977	6	.160	.360	25	4	2	0	1	1	0	2B-6
1981	6	.222	.722	18	4	1	1	2	3	1	2B-6
3 yrs.	16	.158	.404	57	9	3	1	3	4	1	2B-16

Jack Reed

JOHN BURWELL REED   BR TR
B. Feb. 2, 1933, Silver City, Miss.   6' 185 lbs.

Year	Gms.	BA	SA	AB	H	2B	3B	HR	RBI	SB	G. by Pos
1961	28	.154	.154	13	2	0	0	0	1	0	OF-27
1962	88	.302	.465	43	13	2	1	1	4	2	OF-75
1963	106	.205	.274	73	15	3	1	0	1	5	OF-89
3 yrs.	222	.233	.326	129	30	5	2	1	6	7	OF-191
World Series
1961	3	—	—	0	0	0	0	0	0	0	OF-3

Jimmy Reese

JAMES HERMAN REESE   BL TR
B. Oct. 1, 1901, New York, N. Y.   5' 11½" 165 lbs.
D. Jun. 13, 1994, Santa Ana, Calif.

Year	Gms.	BA	SA	AB	H	2B	3B	HR	RBI	SB	G. by Pos
1930	77	.346	.489	188	65	14	2	3	18	1	2B-48, 3B-5
1931	65	.241	.335	245	59	10	2	3	26	2	2B-61
2 yrs.	142	.286	.402	433	124	24	4	6	44	3	2B-109, 3B-5

Bill Renna

WILLIAM BENEDITTO RENNA   BR TR
B. Oct. 14, 1924, Hanford, Calif.   6' 3" 218 lbs.

Year	Gms.	BA	SA	AB	H	2B	3B	HR	RBI	SB	G. by Pos
1953	61	.314	.463	121	38	6	3	2	13	0	OF-40

Tony Rensa

GEORGE ANTHONY RENSA   BR TR
B. Sep. 29, 1901, Parsons, Pa.   5' 10" 180 lbs.
D. Jan. 4, 1987, Wilkes-Barre, Pa.

Year	Gms.	BA	SA	AB	H	2B	3B	HR	RBI	SB	G. by Pos
1933	8	.310	.448	29	9	2	1	0	3	0	C-8

Roger Repoz

ROGER ALLEN REPOZ   BL TL
B. Aug. 3, 1940, Bellingham, Wash.   6' 3" 190 lbs.

Year	Gms.	BA	SA	AB	H	2B	3B	HR	RBI	SB	G. by Pos
1964	11	.000	.000	1	0	0	0	0	0	0	OF-9
1965	79	.220	.454	218	48	7	4	12	28	1	OF-69
1966	37	.349	.488	43	15	4	1	0	9	0	OF-30
3 yrs.	127	.240	.458	262	63	11	5	12	37	1	OF-108

Dave Revering

DAVID ALLEN REVERING   BL TR
B. Feb. 12, 1953, Roseville, Calif.   6' 4" 210 lbs.

Year	Gms.	BA	SA	AB	H	2B	3B	HR	RBI	SB	G. by Pos
1981	45	.235	.336	119	28	4	1	2	7	0	1B-44
1982	14	.150	.200	40	6	2	0	0	2	0	1B-13, DH-1
2 yrs.	59	.214	.302	159	34	6	1	2	9	0	1B-57, DH-1
Divisional Playoffs
1981	2	—	—	0	0	0	0	0	0	0	1B-2
League Championship Series
1981	2	.500	.500	2	1	0	0	0	0	0	1B-2

Bill Reynolds

WILLIAM DEE REYNOLDS   BR TR
B. Aug. 14, 1884, Eastland, Tex.   6' 185 lbs.
D. Jun. 5, 1924, Carnegie, Okla.

Year	Gms.	BA	SA	AB	H	2B	3B	HR	RBI	SB	G. by Pos
1913	5	.000	.000	5	0	0	0	0	0	0	C-5
1914	4	.400	.400	5	2	0	0	0	0	0	C-1
2 yrs.	9	.200	.200	10	2	0	0	0	0	0	C-6

Harry Rice

HARRY FRANCIS RICE   BL TR
B. Nov. 22, 1901, Ware Station, Ill.   5' 9" 185 lbs.
D. Jan. 1, 1971, Portland, Ore.

Year	Gms.	BA	SA	AB	H	2B	3B	HR	RBI	SB	G. by Pos
1930	100	.298	.436	346	103	17	5	7	74	3	OF-87, 1B-6, 3B-1

Bobby Richardson

ROBERT CLINTON RICHARDSON   BR TR
B. Aug. 19, 1935, Sumter, S. C.   5' 9" 170 lbs.

Year	Gms.	BA	SA	AB	H	2B	3B	HR	RBI	SB	G. by Pos
1955	11	.154	.154	26	4	0	0	0	3	1	2B-6, SS-4
1956	5	.143	.143	7	1	0	0	0	0	0	2B-5
1957	97	.256	.298	305	78	11	1	0	19	1	2B-93
1958	73	.247	.302	182	45	6	2	0	14	1	2B-51, 3B-13, SS-2
1959	134	.301	.377	469	141	18	6	2	33	5	2B-109, SS-14, 3B-12
1960	150	.252	.298	460	116	12	3	1	26	6	2B-141, 3B-11
1961	162	.261	.316	662	173	17	5	3	49	9	2B-161
1962	161	.302	.406	692	209	38	5	8	59	11	2B-161
1963	151	.265	.330	630	167	20	6	3	48	15	2B-150
1964	159	.267	.333	679	181	25	4	4	50	11	2B-157, SS-1
1965	160	.247	.322	664	164	28	2	6	47	7	2B-158
1966	149	.251	.330	610	153	21	3	7	42	6	2B-147, 3B-2
12 yrs.	1412	.266	.335	5386	1432	196	37	34	390	73	2B-1339, 3B-38, SS-21
World Series
1957	2	—	—	0	0	0	0	0	0	0	2B-1
1958	4	.000	.000	5	0	0	0	0	0	0	3B-4
1960	7	.367	.667	30	11	2	2	1	12	0	2B-7
1961	5	.391	.435	23	9	1	0	0	0	1	2B-5
1962	7	.148	.148	27	4	0	0	0	0	0	2B-7
1963	4	.214	.286	14	3	1	0	0	0	0	2B-4
1964	7	.406	.469	32	13	2	0	0	3	1	2B-7
7 yrs.	36	.305	.405	131	40	6	2	1	15	2	2B-31, 3B-4

Nolen Richardson

CLIFFORD NOLEN RICHARDSON   BR TR
B. Jan. 18, 1903, Chattanooga, Tenn. 6' 1½" 170 lbs.
D. Sep. 25, 1951, Athens, Ga.

Year	Gms.	BA	SA	AB	H	2B	3B	HR	RBI	SB	G. by Pos
1935	12	.217	.283	46	10	1	1	0	5	0	SS-12

Branch Rickey

WESLEY BRANCH RICKEY   BL TR
B. Dec. 20, 1881, Flat, Ohio   5' 9" 175 lbs.
D. Dec. 9, 1965, Columbia, Mo.
Hall of Fame 1967

Year	Gms.	BA	SA	AB	H	2B	3B	HR	RBI	SB	G. by Pos
1907	52	.182	.241	137	25	2	3	0	15	4	OF-24, C-11, 1B-7

Ruben Rivera

RUBEN RIVERA   BR TR
B. Nov. 14, 1973, Chorrera, Panama   6' 3" 200 lbs.

Year	Gms.	BA	SA	AB	H	2B	3B	HR	RBI	SB	G. by Pos
1995	5	.000	.000	1	0	0	0	0	0	0	OF-4
1996	46	.284	.443	88	25	6	1	2	16	6	OF-45
2 yrs.	51	.281	.438	89	25	6	1	2	16	6	OF-49
Divisional Playoffs
1996	2	.000	.000	1	0	0	0	0	0	0	OF-2

Mickey Rivers

JOHN MILTON RIVERS   BL TL
B. Oct. 31, 1948, Miami, Fla.   5' 10" 165 lbs.

Year	Gms.	BA	SA	AB	H	2B	3B	HR	RBI	SB	G. by Pos
1976	137	.312	.432	590	184	31	8	8	67	43	OF-136
1977	138	.326	.439	565	184	18	5	12	69	22	OF-136, DH-1
1978	141	.265	.397	559	148	25	8	11	48	25	OF-138
1979	74	.287	.416	286	82	18	5	3	25	3	OF-69
4 yrs.	490	.299	.422	2000	598	92	26	34	209	93	OF-479, DH-1
League Championship Series
1976	5	.348	.435	23	8	0	1	0	0	0	OF-5
1977	5	.391	.478	23	9	2	0	0	2	1	OF-5
1978	4	.455	.455	11	5	0	0	0	0	0	OF-4
3 yrs.	14	.386	.456	57	22	2	1	0	2	1	OF-14
World Series
1976	4	.167	.167	18	3	0	0	0	0	1	OF-4
1977	6	.222	.296	27	6	2	0	0	1	1	OF-6
1978	5	.333	.333	18	6	0	0	0	1	1	OF-4
3 yrs.	15	.238	.270	63	15	2	0	0	2	3	OF-14

Phil Rizzuto

PHILIP FRANCIS RIZZUTO   BR TR
B. Sep. 25, 1917, New York, N. Y.   5' 6" 150 lbs.
Hall of Fame 1994

Year	Gms.	BA	SA	AB	H	2B	3B	HR	RBI	SB	G. by Pos
1941	133	.307	.398	515	158	20	9	3	46	14	SS-128

Phil Rizzuto *continued*

Year	Gms.	BA	SA	AB	H	2B	3B	HR	RBI	SB	G. by Pos
1942	144	.284	.374	553	157	24	7	4	68	22	SS-144
1946	126	.257	.310	471	121	17	1	2	38	14	SS-125
1947	153	.273	.364	549	150	26	9	2	60	11	SS-151
1948	128	.252	.328	464	117	13	2	6	50	6	SS-128
1949	153	.275	.358	614	169	22	7	5	64	18	SS-152
1950	155	.324	.439	617	200	36	7	7	66	12	SS-155
1951	144	.274	.346	540	148	21	6	2	43	18	SS-144
1952	152	.254	.341	578	147	24	10	2	43	17	SS-152
1953	134	.271	.351	413	112	21	3	2	54	4	SS-133
1954	127	.195	.251	307	60	11	0	2	15	3	SS-126, 2B-1
1955	81	.259	.322	143	37	4	1	1	9	7	SS-79, 2B-1
1956	31	.231	.231	52	12	0	0	0	6	3	SS-30
13 yrs.	1661	.273	.355	5816	1588	239	62	38	562	149	SS-1647, 2B-2
World Series											
1941	5	.111	.111	18	2	0	0	0	0	1	SS-5
1942	5	.381	.524	21	8	0	0	1	1	2	SS-5
1947	7	.308	.346	26	8	1	0	0	2	2	SS-7
1949	5	.167	.167	18	3	0	0	0	1	1	SS-5
1950	4	.143	.143	14	2	0	0	0	0	1	SS-4
1951	6	.320	.440	25	8	0	0	1	3	0	SS-6
1952	7	.148	.185	27	4	1	0	0	0	0	SS-7
1953	6	.316	.368	19	6	1	0	0	0	1	SS-6
1955	7	.267	.267	15	4	0	0	0	1	2	SS-7
9 yrs.	52	.246	.295	183	45	3	0	2	8	10	SS-52

Roxy Roach

WILBUR CHARLES ROACH BR TR
B. Nov. 28, 1882, Anita, Pa. 5' 11" 160 lbs.
D. Dec. 25, 1947, Bay City, Mich.

Year	Gms.	BA	SA	AB	H	2B	3B	HR	RBI	SB	G. by Pos
1910	70	.214	.273	220	47	9	2	0	20	15	SS-58, OF-9
1911	13	.250	.350	40	10	2	1	0	2	0	SS-8, 2B-5
2 yrs.	83	.219	.285	260	57	11	3	0	22	15	SS-66, OF-9, 2B-5

Andre Robertson

ANDRE LEVETT ROBERTSON BR TR
B. Oct. 2, 1957, Orange, Tex. 5' 10" 155 lbs.

Year	Gms.	BA	SA	AB	H	2B	3B	HR	RBI	SB	G. by Pos
1981	10	.263	.316	19	5	1	0	0	0	1	SS-8, 2B-3
1982	44	.220	.314	118	26	5	0	2	9	0	SS-27, 2B-15, 3B-2
1983	98	.248	.326	322	80	16	3	1	22	2	SS-78, 2B-29
1984	52	.214	.264	140	30	5	1	0	6	0	SS-49, 2B-6
1985	50	.328	.416	125	41	5	0	2	17	1	3B-33, SS-14, 2B-2
5 yrs.	254	.251	.327	724	182	32	4	5	54	4	SS-176, 2B-55, 3B-35
League Championship Series											
1981	1	.000	.000	1	0	0	0	0	0	0	SS-1
World Series											
1981	1	—	—	0	0	0	0	0	0	0	

Gene Robertson

EUGENE EDWARD ROBERTSON BL TR
B. Dec. 25, 1899, St. Louis, Mo. 5' 7" 152 lbs.
D. Oct. 21, 1981, Fallon, Nev.

Year	Gms.	BA	SA	AB	H	2B	3B	HR	RBI	SB	G. by Pos
1928	83	.291	.339	251	73	9	0	1	36	2	3B-70, 2B-3
1929	90	.298	.385	309	92	15	6	0	35	3	3B-77
2 yrs.	173	.295	.364	560	165	24	6	1	71	5	3B-147, 2B-3
World Series											
1928	3	.125	.125	8	1	0	0	0	2	0	3B-3

Aaron Robinson

AARON ANDREW ROBINSON BL TR
B. Jun. 23, 1915, Lancaster, S. C. 6' 2" 205 lbs.
D. Mar. 9, 1966, Lancaster, S. C.

Year	Gms.	BA	SA	AB	H	2B	3B	HR	RBI	SB	G. by Pos
1943	1	.000	.000	1	0	0	0	0	0	0	
1945	50	.281	.481	160	45	6	1	8	24	0	C-45
1946	100	.297	.506	330	98	17	2	16	64	0	C-95
1947	82	.270	.413	252	68	11	5	5	36	0	C-74
4 yrs.	233	.284	.468	743	211	34	8	29	124	0	C-214
World Series											
1947	3	.200	.200	10	2	0	0	0	1	0	C-3

Bill Robinson

WILLIAM HENRY ROBINSON BR TR
B. Jun. 26, 1943, McKeesport, Pa. 6' 2" 189 lbs.

Year	Gms.	BA	SA	AB	H	2B	3B	HR	RBI	SB	G. by Pos
1967	116	.196	.281	342	67	6	1	7	29	2	OF-102
1968	107	.240	.380	342	82	16	7	6	40	7	OF-98
1969	87	.171	.279	222	38	11	2	3	21	3	OF-62, 1B-1
3 yrs.	310	.206	.318	906	187	33	10	16	90	12	OF-262, 1B-1

Bruce Robinson

BRUCE PHILIP ROBINSON BL TR
B. Apr. 16, 1954, La Jolla, Calif. 6' 1" 185 lbs.

Year	Gms.	BA	SA	AB	H	2B	3B	HR	RBI	SB	G. by Pos
1979	6	.167	.167	12	2	0	0	0	2	0	C-6
1980	4	.000	.000	5	0	0	0	0	0	0	C-3
2 yrs.	10	.118	.118	17	2	0	0	0	2	0	C-9

Eddie Robinson

WILLIAM EDWARD ROBINSON BL TR
B. Dec. 15, 1920, Paris, Tex. 6' 2½" 210 lbs.

Year	Gms.	BA	SA	AB	H	2B	3B	HR	RBI	SB	G. by Pos
1954	85	.261	.387	142	37	9	0	3	27	0	1B-29
1955	88	.208	.491	173	36	1	0	16	42	0	1B-46
1956	26	.222	.519	54	12	1	0	5	11	0	1B-14
3 yrs.	199	.230	.455	369	85	11	0	24	80	0	1B-89
World Series											
1955	4	.667	.667	3	2	0	0	0	1	0	1B-1

Aurelio Rodriguez

AURELIO RODRIGUEZ BR TR
B. Dec. 28, 1947, Cananea, Mexico 5' 10" 180 lbs.

Year	Gms.	BA	SA	AB	H	2B	3B	HR	RBI	SB	G. by Pos
1980	52	.220	.323	164	36	6	1	3	14	0	3B-49, 2B-6
1981	27	.346	.500	52	18	2	0	2	8	0	3B-20, 2B-3, DH-2, 1B-1
2 yrs.	79	.250	.366	216	54	8	1	5	22	0	3B-69, 2B-9, DH-2, 1B-1
League Championship Series											
1980	2	.333	.500	6	2	1	0	0	0	0	3B-2
1981	1	—	—	0	0	0	0	0	0	0	3B-1
2 yrs.	3	.333	.500	6	2	1	0	0	0	0	3B-3
World Series											
1981	4	.417	.417	12	5	0	0	0	0	0	3B-3

Carlos Rodriguez

CARLOS RODRIGUEZ BB TR
B. Nov. 1, 1967, Mexico City, Mexico 5' 9" 160 lbs.

Year	Gms.	BA	SA	AB	H	2B	3B	HR	RBI	SB	G. by Pos
1991	15	.189	.189	37	7	0	0	0	2	0	SS-11, 2B-3

Edwin Rodriguez

EDWIN RODRIGUEZ BR TR
B. Aug. 14, 1960, Ponce, Puerto Rico 5' 11" 172 lbs.

Year	Gms.	BA	SA	AB	H	2B	3B	HR	RBI	SB	G. by Pos
1982	3	.333	.333	9	3	0	0	0	1	0	2B-3

Ellie Rodriguez

ELISEO RODRIGUEZ BR TR
B. May 24, 1946, Fajardo, Puerto Rico 5' 11" 185 lbs.

Year	Gms.	BA	SA	AB	H	2B	3B	HR	RBI	SB	G. by Pos
1968	9	.208	.208	24	5	0	0	0	1	0	C-9

Gary Roenicke

GARY STEVEN ROENICKE BR TR
B. Dec. 5, 1954, Covina, Calif. 6' 3" 205 lbs.

Year	Gms.	BA	SA	AB	H	2B	3B	HR	RBI	SB	G. by Pos
1986	69	.265	.368	136	36	5	0	3	18	1	OF-37, DH-15, 3B-3, 1B-2

Jay Rogers

JAY LEWIS ROGERS BR TR
B. Aug. 3, 1888, Sandusky, N. Y. 5' 11½" 178 lbs.
D. Jul. 1, 1964, Carlisle, Pa.

Year	Gms.	BA	SA	AB	H	2B	3B	HR	RBI	SB	G. by Pos
1914	5	.000	.000	8	0	0	0	0	0	0	C-4

Red Rolfe

ROBERT ABIAL ROLFE BL TR
B. Oct. 17, 1908, Penacook, N. H. 5' 11½" 170 lbs.
D. Jul. 8, 1969, Gifford, N. H.

Year	Gms.	BA	SA	AB	H	2B	3B	HR	RBI	SB	G. by Pos
1931	1	—	—	0	0	0	0	0	0	0	SS-1

Year	Gms.	BA	SA	AB	H	2B	3B	HR	RBI	SB	G. by Pos

Red Rolfe *continued*

Year	Gms.	BA	SA	AB	H	2B	3B	HR	RBI	SB	G. by Pos
1934	89	.287	.348	279	80	13	2	0	18	2	SS-46, 3B-26
1935	149	.300	.404	639	192	33	9	5	67	7	3B-136, SS-17
1936	135	.319	.493	568	181	39	15	10	70	3	3B-133
1937	154	.276	.378	648	179	34	10	4	62	4	3B-154
1938	151	.311	.441	631	196	36	8	10	80	13	3B-151
1939	152	.329	.495	648	213	46	10	14	80	7	3B-152
1940	139	.250	.366	588	147	26	6	10	53	4	3B-138
1941	136	.264	.364	561	148	22	5	8	42	3	3B-134
1942	69	.219	.355	265	58	8	2	8	25	1	3B-60
10 yrs.	1175	.289	.413	4827	1394	257	67	69	497	44	3B-1084, SS-64
World Series											
1936	6	.400	.400	25	10	0	0	0	4	0	3B-6
1937	5	.300	.500	20	6	2	1	0	1	0	3B-5
1938	4	.167	.167	18	3	0	0	0	1	1	3B-4
1939	4	.125	.125	16	2	0	0	0	0	0	3B-4
1941	5	.300	.300	20	6	0	0	0	0	0	3B-5
1942	4	.353	.471	17	6	2	0	0	0	0	3B-4
6 yrs.	28	.284	.336	116	33	4	1	0	6	1	3B-28

Buddy Rosar

WARREN VINCENT ROSAR BR TR
B. Jul. 3, 1914, Buffalo, N. Y. 5' 9" 190 lbs.
D. Mar. 13, 1994, Rochester, N. Y.

Year	Gms.	BA	SA	AB	H	2B	3B	HR	RBI	SB	G. by Pos
1939	43	.276	.343	105	29	5	1	0	12	4	C-35
1940	73	.298	.425	228	68	11	3	4	37	7	C-63
1941	67	.287	.402	209	60	17	2	1	36	0	C-60
1942	69	.230	.306	209	48	10	0	2	34	1	C-58
4 yrs.	252	.273	.374	751	205	43	6	7	119	12	C-216
World Series											
1941	1	—	—	0	0	0	0	0	0	0	C-1
1942	1	1.000	1.000	1	1	0	0	0	0	0	
2 yrs.	2	1.000	1.000	1	1	0	0	0	0	0	C-1

Larry Rosenthal

LAWRENCE JOHN ROSENTHAL BL TL
B. May 21, 1910, St. Paul, Minn. 6' ½" 190 lbs.
D. Mar. 4, 1992, Woodbury, Minn.

Year	Gms.	BA	SA	AB	H	2B	3B	HR	RBI	SB	G. by Pos
1944	36	.198	.228	101	20	3	0	0	9	1	OF-26

Braggo Roth

ROBERT FRANK ROTH BR TR
B. Aug. 28, 1892, Burlington, Wis. 5' 7½" 170 lbs.
D. Sep. 11, 1936, Chicago, Ill.

Year	Gms.	BA	SA	AB	H	2B	3B	HR	RBI	SB	G. by Pos
1921	43	.283	.408	152	43	9	2	2	10	1	OF-37

Jerry Royster

JERON KENNIS ROYSTER BR TR
B. Oct. 18, 1952, Sacramento, Calif. 6' 165 lbs.

Year	Gms.	BA	SA	AB	H	2B	3B	HR	RBI	SB	G. by Pos
1987	18	.357	.405	42	15	2	0	0	4	2	3B-13, 2B-1, SS-1, OF-1

Muddy Ruel

HEROLD DOMINIC RUEL BR TR
B. Feb. 20, 1896, St. Louis, Mo. 5' 9" 150 lbs.
D. Nov. 13, 1963, Palo Alto, Calif.

Year	Gms.	BA	SA	AB	H	2B	3B	HR	RBI	SB	G. by Pos
1917	6	.118	.118	17	2	0	0	0	1	1	C-6
1918	3	.333	.333	6	2	0	0	0	0	1	C-2
1919	81	.240	.266	233	56	6	0	0	31	4	C-81
1920	82	.268	.341	261	70	14	1	1	15	4	C-80
4 yrs.	172	.251	.300	517	130	20	1	1	47	10	C-169

Red Ruffing

CHARLES HERBERT RUFFING BR TR
B. May 3, 1904, Granville, Ill. 6' 1½" 205 lbs.
D. Feb. 17, 1986, Mayfield Heights, Ohio
Hall of Fame 1967

Year	Gms.	BA	SA	AB	H	2B	3B	HR	RBI	SB	G. by Pos
1930	52	.374	.596	99	37	6	2	4	21	0	P-34
1931	48	.330	.505	109	36	8	1	3	12	0	P-37, OF-1
1932	55	.306	.444	124	38	6	1	3	19	0	P-35
1933	55	.252	.348	115	29	3	1	2	13	0	P-35
1934	45	.248	.327	113	28	3	0	2	13	0	P-36
1935	50	.339	.486	109	37	10	0	2	18	0	P-30
1936	53	.291	.449	127	37	5	0	5	22	0	P-33

Red Ruffing *continued*

Year	Gms.	BA	SA	AB	H	2B	3B	HR	RBI	SB	G. by Pos
1937	54	.202	.248	129	26	3	0	1	10	0	P-31
1938	45	.224	.364	107	24	4	1	3	17	0	P-31
1939	44	.307	.342	114	35	1	0	1	20	1	P-28
1940	33	.124	.202	89	11	4	0	1	7	0	P-30
1941	38	.303	.483	89	27	8	1	2	22	0	P-23
1942	30	.250	.338	80	20	4	0	1	13	0	P-24
1945	21	.217	.326	46	10	0	1	1	5	0	P-11
1946	8	.120	.160	25	3	1	0	0	1	0	P-8
15 yrs.	631	.270	.388	1475	398	66	8	31	213	1	P-426, OF-1
World Series											
1932	2	.000	.000	4	0	0	0	0	0	0	P-1
1936	3	.000	.000	5	0	0	0	0	0	0	P-2
1937	1	.500	.750	4	2	1	0	0	3	0	P-1
1938	2	.167	.167	6	1	0	0	0	1	0	P-2
1939	1	.333	.333	3	1	0	0	0	0	0	P-1
1941	1	.000	.000	3	0	0	0	0	0	0	P-1
1942	4	.222	.222	9	2	0	0	0	0	0	P-2
7 yrs.	14	.176	.206	34	6	1	0	0	4	0	P-10

Babe Ruth

GEORGE HERMAN RUTH BL TL
B. Feb. 6, 1895, Baltimore, Md. 6' 2" 215 lbs.
D. Aug. 16, 1948, New York, N. Y.
Hall of Fame 1936

Year	Gms.	BA	SA	AB	H	2B	3B	HR	RBI	SB	G. by Pos
1920	142	.376	.847	458	172	36	9	54	137	14	OF-139, 1B-2, P-1
1921	152	.378	.846	540	204	44	16	59	171	17	OF-152, P-2, 1B-2
1922	110	.315	.672	406	128	24	8	35	99	2	OF-110, 1B-1
1923	152	.393	.764	522	205	45	13	41	131	17	OF-148, 1B-4
1924	153	.378	.739	529	200	39	7	46	121	9	OF-152
1925	98	.290	.543	359	104	12	2	25	66	2	OF-98
1926	152	.372	.737	495	184	30	5	47	145	11	OF-149, 1B-2
1927	151	.356	.772	540	192	29	8	60	164	7	OF-151
1928	154	.323	.709	536	173	29	8	54	142	4	OF-154
1929	135	.345	.697	499	172	26	6	46	154	5	OF-133
1930	145	.359	.732	518	186	28	9	49	153	10	OF-144, P-1
1931	145	.373	.700	534	199	31	3	46	163	5	OF-142, 1B-1
1932	133	.341	.661	457	156	13	5	41	137	2	OF-127, 1B-1
1933	137	.301	.582	459	138	21	3	34	103	4	OF-132, P-1, 1B-1
1934	125	.288	.537	365	105	17	4	22	84	1	OF-111
15 yrs.	2084	.349	.711	7217	2518	424	106	659	1970	110	OF-2042, 1B-14, P-5
World Series											
1921	6	.313	.500	16	5	0	0	1	4	2	OF-5
1922	5	.118	.176	17	2	1	0	0	1	0	OF-5
1923	6	.368	1.000	19	7	1	1	3	3	0	OF-6, 1B-1
1926	7	.300	.900	20	6	0	0	4	5	1	OF-7
1927	4	.400	.800	15	6	0	0	2	7	1	OF-4
1928	4	.625	1.375	16	10	3	0	3	4	0	OF-4
1932	4	.333	.733	15	5	0	0	2	6	0	OF-4
7 yrs.	36	.347	.788	118	41	5	1	15	30	4	OF-35, 1B-1

Blondy Ryan

JOHN COLLINS RYAN BR TR
B. Jan. 4, 1906, Lynn, Mass. 6' 1" 178 lbs.
D. Nov. 28, 1959, Swampscott, Mass.

Year	Gms.	BA	SA	AB	H	2B	3B	HR	RBI	SB	G. by Pos
1935	30	.238	.305	105	25	1	3	0	11	0	SS-30

Lenn Sakata

LENN HARUKI SAKATA BR TR
B. Jun. 8, 1954, Honolulu, Hawaii 5' 9" 160 lbs.

Year	Gms.	BA	SA	AB	H	2B	3B	HR	RBI	SB	G. by Pos
1987	19	.267	.444	45	12	0	1	2	4	0	3B-12, 2B-6

Mark Salas

MARK BRUCE SALAS BL TR
B. Mar. 8, 1961, Montebello, Calif. 6' 180 lbs.

Year	Gms.	BA	SA	AB	H	2B	3B	HR	RBI	SB	G. by Pos
1987	50	.200	.313	115	23	4	0	3	12	0	C-41, DH-4, OF-1

Jack Saltzgaver

OTTO HAMLIN SALTZGAVER BL TR
B. Jan. 23, 1903, Croton, Iowa 5' 11" 165 lbs.
D. Feb. 1, 1978, Keokuk, Iowa

Year	Gms.	BA	SA	AB	H	2B	3B	HR	RBI	SB	G. by Pos
1932	20	.128	.213	47	6	2	1	0	5	1	2B-16

Year	Gms.	BA	SA	AB	H	2B	3B	HR	RBI	SB	G. by Pos

Jack Saltzgaver *continued*

Year	Gms.	BA	SA	AB	H	2B	3B	HR	RBI	SB	G. by Pos
1934	94	.271	.351	350	95	8	1	6	36	8	3B-84, 1B-4
1935	61	.262	.362	149	39	6	0	3	18	0	2B-25, 3B-18, 1B-6
1936	34	.211	.300	90	19	5	0	1	13	0	3B-16, 2B-6, 1B-4
1937	17	.182	.182	11	2	0	0	0	0	0	1B-4
5 yrs.	226	.249	.334	647	161	21	2	10	72	9	3B-118, 2B-47, 1B-18

Billy Sample

WILLIAM AMOS SAMPLE   BR TR
B. Apr. 2, 1955, Roanoke, Va.   5' 9" 175 lbs.

Year	Gms.	BA	SA	AB	H	2B	3B	HR	RBI	SB	G. by Pos
1985	59	.288	.345	139	40	5	0	1	15	2	OF-55

Celerino Sanchez

CELERINO SANCHEZ   BR TR
B. Feb. 3, 1944, Veracruz, Mexico   5' 11" 160 lbs.
D. May. 1, 1992, Leon, Mexico

Year	Gms.	BA	SA	AB	H	2B	3B	HR	RBI	SB	G. by Pos
1972	71	.248	.304	250	62	8	3	0	22	0	3B-68
1973	34	.219	.313	64	14	3	0	1	9	1	3B-11, DH-11, SS-2, OF-2
2 yrs.	105	.242	.306	314	76	11	3	1	31	1	3B-79, DH-11, SS-2, OF-2

Deion Sanders

DEION LUWYNN SANDERS   BL TL
B. Aug. 9, 1967, Fort Myers, Fla.   6' 1" 195 lbs.

Year	Gms.	BA	SA	AB	H	2B	3B	HR	RBI	SB	G. by Pos
1989	14	.234	.404	47	11	2	0	2	7	1	OF-14
1990	57	.158	.271	133	21	2	2	3	9	8	OF-42, DH-4
2 yrs.	71	.178	.306	180	32	4	2	5	16	9	OF-56, DH-4

Charlie Sands

CHARLES DUANE SANDS   BL TR
B. Dec. 17, 1947, Newport News, Va.   6' 2" 200 lbs.

Year	Gms.	BA	SA	AB	H	2B	3B	HR	RBI	SB	G. by Pos
1967	1	.000	.000	1	0	0	0	0	0	0	

Rafael Santana

RAFAEL FRANCISCO SANTANA   BR TR
B. Jan. 31, 1958, La Romana,   6' 1" 156 lbs.
Dominican Republic

Year	Gms.	BA	SA	AB	H	2B	3B	HR	RBI	SB	G. by Pos
1988	148	.240	.294	480	115	12	1	4	38	1	SS-148

Don Savage

DONALD ANTHONY SAVAGE   BR TR
B. Mar. 5, 1919, Bloomfield, N. J.   6' 180 lbs.
D. Dec. 25, 1961, Montclair, N. J.

Year	Gms.	BA	SA	AB	H	2B	3B	HR	RBI	SB	G. by Pos
1944	71	.264	.385	239	63	7	5	4	24	1	3B-60
1945	34	.224	.241	58	13	1	0	0	3	1	3B-14, OF-2
2 yrs.	105	.256	.357	297	76	8	5	4	27	2	3B-74, OF-2

Steve Sax

STEPHEN LOUIS SAX   BR TR
B. Jan. 29, 1960, Sacramento, Calif.   5' 11" 185 lbs.

Year	Gms.	BA	SA	AB	H	2B	3B	HR	RBI	SB	G. by Pos
1989	158	.315	.387	651	205	26	3	5	63	43	2B-158
1990	155	.260	.325	615	160	24	2	4	42	43	2B-154
1991	158	.304	.414	652	198	38	2	10	56	31	2B-149, 3B-5, DH-4
3 yrs.	471	.294	.376	1918	563	88	7	19	161	117	2B-461, 3B-5, DH-4

Germany Schaefer

HERMAN A. SCHAEFER   BR TR
B. Feb. 4, 1877, Chicago, Ill.   5' 9" 175 lbs.
D. May 16, 1919, Saranac Lake, N. Y.

Year	Gms.	BA	SA	AB	H	2B	3B	HR	RBI	SB	G. by Pos
1916	1	—	—	0	0	0	0	0	0	0	OF-1

Roy Schalk

LEROY JOHN SCHALK   BR TR
B. Nov. 9, 1908, Chicago, Ill.   5' 10" 168 lbs.
D. Mar. 11, 1990, Gainesville, Tex.

Year	Gms.	BA	SA	AB	H	2B	3B	HR	RBI	SB	G. by Pos
1932	3	.250	.333	12	3	1	0	0	0	0	2B-3

Wally Schang

WALTER HENRY SCHANG   BB TR
B. Aug. 22, 1889, South Wales, N. Y.   5' 10" 180 lbs.
D. Mar. 6, 1965, St. Louis, Mo.

Year	Gms.	BA	SA	AB	H	2B	3B	HR	RBI	SB	G. by Pos
1921	134	.316	.453	424	134	30	5	6	55	7	C-132
1922	124	.319	.412	408	130	21	7	1	53	12	C-124

Wally Schang *continued*

Year	Gms.	BA	SA	AB	H	2B	3B	HR	RBI	SB	G. by Pos
1923	84	.276	.342	272	75	8	2	2	29	5	C-81
1924	114	.292	.427	356	104	19	7	5	52	2	C-109
1925	73	.240	.335	167	40	8	1	2	24	3	C-58
5 yrs.	529	.297	.406	1627	483	86	22	16	213	29	C-504
World Series											
1921	8	.286	.429	21	6	1	1	0	1	0	C-8
1922	5	.188	.250	16	3	1	0	0	0	0	C-5
1923	6	.318	.364	22	7	1	0	0	0	0	C-6
3 yrs.	19	.271	.356	59	16	3	1	0	1	0	C-19

Bob Schmidt

ROBERT BENJAMIN SCHMIDT   BR TR
B. Apr. 22, 1933, St. Louis, Mo.   6' 2" 205 lbs.

Year	Gms.	BA	SA	AB	H	2B	3B	HR	RBI	SB	G. by Pos
1965	20	.250	.350	40	10	1	0	1	3	0	C-20

Dick Schofield

JOHN RICHARD SCHOFIELD   BB TR
B. Jan. 7, 1935, Springfield, Ill.   5' 9" 163 lbs.

Year	Gms.	BA	SA	AB	H	2B	3B	HR	RBI	SB	G. by Pos
1966	25	.155	.190	58	9	2	0	0	2	0	SS-19

Art Schult

ARTHUR WILLIAM SCHULT   BR TR
B. Jun. 20, 1928, Brooklyn, N. Y.   6' 3" 210 lbs.

Year	Gms.	BA	SA	AB	H	2B	3B	HR	RBI	SB	G. by Pos
1953	7	—	—	0	0	0	0	0	0	0	

Bill Schwarz

WILLIAM DEWITT SCHWARZ   B TR
B. Jan. 30, 1891, Birmingham, Ala.
D. Jun. 24, 1949, Jacksonville, Fla.

Year	Gms.	BA	SA	AB	H	2B	3B	HR	RBI	SB	G. by Pos
1914	1	.000	.000	1	0	0	0	0	0	0	C-1

Pius Schwert

PIUS LOUIS SCHWERT   BR TR
B. Nov. 22, 1892, Angola, N. Y.   5' 10½" 160 lbs.
D. Mar. 11, 1941, Washington, D. C.

Year	Gms.	BA	SA	AB	H	2B	3B	HR	RBI	SB	G. by Pos
1914	2	.000	.000	5	0	0	0	0	0	0	C-2
1915	9	.278	.444	18	5	3	0	0	6	0	C-9
2 yrs.	11	.217	.348	23	5	3	0	0	6	0	C-11

Everett Scott

LEWIS EVERETT SCOTT   BR TR
B. Nov. 19, 1892, Bluffton, Ind.   5' 8" 148 lbs.
D. Nov. 2, 1960, Fort Wayne, Ind.

Year	Gms.	BA	SA	AB	H	2B	3B	HR	RBI	SB	G. by Pos
1922	154	.269	.345	557	150	23	5	3	45	2	SS-154
1923	152	.246	.325	533	131	16	4	6	60	1	SS-152
1924	153	.250	.316	548	137	12	6	4	64	3	SS-153
1925	22	.217	.217	60	13	0	0	0	4	0	SS-18
4 yrs.	481	.254	.324	1698	431	51	15	13	173	6	SS-477
World Series											
1922	5	.143	.143	14	2	0	0	0	1	0	SS-5
1923	6	.318	.318	22	7	0	0	0	3	0	SS-6
2 yrs.	11	.250	.250	36	9	0	0	0	4	0	SS-11

George Scott

GEORGE CHARLES SCOTT, JR.   BR TR
B. Mar. 23, 1944, Greenville, Miss.   6' 2" 200 lbs.

Year	Gms.	BA	SA	AB	H	2B	3B	HR	RBI	SB	G. by Pos
1979	16	.318	.500	44	14	3	1	1	6	1	DH-14, 1B-1

Rodney Scott

RODNEY DARRELL SCOTT   BB TR
B. Oct. 16, 1953, Indianapolis, Ind.   6' 160 lbs.

Year	Gms.	BA	SA	AB	H	2B	3B	HR	RBI	SB	G. by Pos
1982	10	.192	.192	26	5	0	0	0	0	2	SS-6, 2B-4

Ken Sears

KENNETH EUGENE SEARS   BL TR
B. Jul. 6, 1917, Streator, Ill.   6' 1" 200 lbs.
D. Jul. 17, 1968, Bridgeport, Tex.

Year	Gms.	BA	SA	AB	H	2B	3B	HR	RBI	SB	G. by Pos
1943	60	.278	.348	187	52	7	0	2	22	1	C-50

Bob Seeds

IRA ROBERT SEEDS   BR TR
B. Feb. 24, 1907, Ringgold, Tex.   6' 180 lbs.
D. Oct. 28, 1993, Erick, Okla.

Year	Gms.	BA	SA	AB	H	2B	3B	HR	RBI	SB	G. by Pos
1936	13	.262	.571	42	11	1	0	4	10	3	OF-9, 3B-3

345

Year	Gms.	BA	SA	AB	H	2B	3B	HR	RBI	SB	G. by Pos

Bob Seeds *continued*

World Series
| 1936 | 1 | — | — | 0 | 0 | 0 | 0 | 0 | 0 | 0 | |

Kal Segrist

KAL HILL SEGRIST BR TR
B. Apr. 14, 1931, Greenville, Tex. 6' 180 lbs.

| 1952 | 13 | .043 | .043 | 23 | 1 | 0 | 0 | 0 | 1 | 0 | 2B-11, 3B-1 |

George Selkirk

GEORGE ALEXANDER SELKIRK BL TR
B. Jan. 4, 1908, Huntsville, Ont., 6' 1" 182 lbs.
Canada
D. Jan. 19, 1987, Ft. Lauderdale, Fla.

1934	46	.313	.449	176	55	7	1	5	38	1	OF-46
1935	128	.312	.487	491	153	29	12	11	94	2	OF-127
1936	137	.308	.511	493	152	28	9	18	107	13	OF-135
1937	78	.328	.629	256	84	13	5	18	68	8	OF-69
1938	99	.254	.409	335	85	12	5	10	62	9	OF-95
1939	128	.306	.517	418	128	17	4	21	101	12	OF-124
1940	118	.269	.491	379	102	17	5	19	71	3	OF-111
1941	70	.220	.360	164	36	5	0	6	25	1	OF-47
1942	42	.192	.231	78	15	3	0	0	10	0	OF-19
9 yrs.	846	.290	.483	2790	810	131	41	108	576	49	OF-773

World Series
1936	6	.333	.667	24	8	0	1	2	3	0	OF-6
1937	5	.263	.316	19	5	1	0	0	6	0	OF-5
1938	3	.200	.200	10	2	0	0	0	1	0	OF-3
1939	4	.167	.250	12	2	1	0	0	0	0	OF-4
1941	2	.500	.500	2	1	0	0	0	0	0	
1942	1	.000	.000	1	0	0	0	0	0	0	
6 yrs.	21	.265	.412	68	18	2	1	2	10	0	OF-18

Ted Sepkowski

THEODORE WALTER SEPKOWSKI BL TR
B. Nov. 9, 1923, Baltimore, Md. 5' 11" 190 lbs.

| 1947 | 2 | — | — | 0 | 0 | 0 | 0 | 0 | 0 | 0 | |

Hank Severeid

HENRY LEVAI SEVEREID BR TR
B. Jun. 1, 1891, Story City, Iowa 6' 175 lbs.
D. Dec. 17, 1968, San Antonio, Tex.

| 1926 | 41 | .268 | .346 | 127 | 34 | 8 | 1 | 0 | 13 | 1 | C-40 |

World Series
| 1926 | 7 | .273 | .318 | 22 | 6 | 1 | 0 | 0 | 1 | 0 | C-7 |

Joe Sewell

JOSEPH WHEELER SEWELL BL TR
B. Oct. 9, 1898, Titus, Ala. 5' 6½" 155 lbs.
D. Mar. 6, 1990, Mobile, Ala.
Hall of Fame 1977

1931	130	.302	.388	484	146	22	1	6	64	1	3B-121, 2B-1
1932	124	.272	.392	503	137	21	3	11	68	0	3B-122
1933	135	.273	.323	524	143	18	1	2	54	2	3B-131
3 yrs.	389	.282	.367	1511	426	61	5	19	186	3	3B-374, 2B-1

World Series
| 1932 | 4 | .333 | .400 | 15 | 5 | 1 | 0 | 0 | 3 | 0 | 3B-4 |

Howard Shanks

HOWARD SAMUEL SHANKS BR TR
B. Jul. 21, 1890, Chicago, Ill. 5' 11" 170 lbs.
D. Jul. 30, 1941, Monaca, Pa.

| 1925 | 66 | .258 | .310 | 155 | 40 | 3 | 1 | 1 | 18 | 1 | 3B-26, 2B-21, OF-4 |

Billy Shantz

WILMER EBERT SHANTZ BR TR
B. Jul. 31, 1927, Pottstown, Pa. 6' 1" 160 lbs.
D. Dec. 13, 1993, Lauderhill, Fla.

| 1960 | 1 | — | — | 0 | 0 | 0 | 0 | 0 | 0 | 0 | C-1 |

Skeeter Shelton

ANDREW KEMPER SHELTON BR TR
B. Jun. 29, 1888, Huntington, W. Va. 5' 11" 175 lbs.
D. Jan. 9, 1954, Huntington, W. Va.

| 1915 | 10 | .025 | .025 | 40 | 1 | 0 | 0 | 0 | 0 | 0 | OF-10 |

Pat Sheridan

PATRICK ARTHUR SHERIDAN BL TR
B. Dec. 4, 1957, Ann Arbor, Mich. 6' 3" 175 lbs.

| 1991 | 62 | .204 | .336 | 113 | 23 | 3 | 0 | 4 | 7 | 1 | OF-34, DH-2 |

Dennis Sherrill

DENNIS LEE SHERRILL BR TR
B. May 3, 1956, Miami, Fla. 6' 165 lbs.

1978	2	.000	.000	1	0	0	0	0	0	0	3B-1, DH-1
1980	3	.250	.250	4	1	0	0	0	0	0	SS-2, 2B-1
2 yrs.	5	.200	.200	5	1	0	0	0	0	0	SS-2, 2B-1, 3B-1, DH-1

Tom Shopay

THOMAS MICHAEL SHOPAY BL TR
B. Feb. 21, 1945, Bristol, Conn. 5' 9½" 160 lbs.

1967	8	.296	.556	27	8	1	0	2	6	2	OF-7
1969	28	.083	.125	48	4	0	1	0	0	0	OF-11
2 yrs.	36	.160	.280	75	12	1	1	2	6	2	OF-18

Norm Siebern

NORMAN LEROY SIEBERN BL TR
B. Jul. 26, 1933, St. Louis, Mo. 6' 2" 200 lbs.

1956	54	.204	.333	162	33	1	4	4	21	1	OF-51
1958	136	.300	.454	460	138	19	5	14	55	5	OF-133
1959	120	.271	.403	380	103	17	0	11	53	3	OF-93, 1B-2
3 yrs.	310	.273	.415	1002	274	37	9	29	129	9	OF-277, 1B-2

World Series
1956	1	.000	.000	1	0	0	0	0	0	0	
1958	3	.125	.125	8	1	0	0	0	0	0	OF-3
2 yrs.	4	.111	.111	9	1	0	0	0	0	0	OF-3

Ruben Sierra

RUBEN ANGEL SIERRA BB TR
B. Oct. 6, 1965, Rio Piedras, 6' 1" 175 lbs.
Puerto Rico

1995	56	.260	.428	215	56	15	0	7	44	1	DH-46, OF-10
1996	96	.258	.403	360	93	17	1	11	52	1	DH-61, OF-33
2 yrs.	152	.259	.412	575	149	32	1	18	96	2	DH-107, OF-43

Divisional Playoffs
| 1995 | 5 | .174 | .522 | 23 | 4 | 2 | 0 | 2 | 5 | 0 | DH-5 |

Charlie Silvera

CHARLES ANTHONY RYAN SILVERA BR TR
B. Oct. 13, 1924, San Francisco, Calif. 5' 10" 175 lbs.

1948	4	.571	.714	14	8	1	0	0	1	0	C-4
1949	58	.315	.331	130	41	2	0	0	13	2	C-51
1950	18	.160	.160	25	4	0	0	0	1	0	C-15
1951	18	.275	.392	51	14	3	0	1	7	0	C-18
1952	20	.327	.382	55	18	3	0	0	11	0	C-20
1953	42	.280	.341	82	23	3	1	0	12	0	C-39, 3B-1
1954	20	.270	.297	37	10	1	0	0	4	0	C-18
1955	14	.192	.192	26	5	0	0	0	1	0	C-11
1956	7	.222	.222	9	2	0	0	0	0	0	C-7
9 yrs.	201	.291	.336	429	125	12	2	1	50	2	C-183, 3B-1

World Series
| 1949 | 1 | .000 | .000 | 2 | 0 | 0 | 0 | 0 | 0 | 0 | C-1 |

Dave Silvestri

DAVID JOSEPH SILVESTRI BR TR
B. Sep. 29, 1967, St. Louis, Mo. 6' 180 lbs.

1992	7	.308	.615	13	4	0	2	0	1	0	SS-6
1993	7	.286	.476	21	6	1	0	1	4	0	SS-4, 3B-3
1994	12	.111	.389	18	2	0	1	1	2	0	2B-9, 3B-2, SS-1
1995	17	.095	.238	21	2	0	0	1	4	0	2B-7, 1B-4, DH-4, SS-1
4 yrs.	43	.192	.411	73	14	1	3	3	11	0	2B-16, SS-12, 3B-5, 1B-4, DH-4

Ken Silvestri

KENNETH JOSEPH SILVESTRI BB TR
B. May 3, 1916, Chicago, Ill. 6' 1" 200 lbs.
D. Mar. 31, 1992, Tallahassee, Fla.

| 1941 | 17 | .250 | .450 | 40 | 10 | 5 | 0 | 1 | 4 | 0 | C-13 |
| 1946 | 13 | .286 | .333 | 21 | 6 | 1 | 0 | 0 | 1 | 0 | C-12 |

Year	Gms.	BA	SA	AB	H	2B	3B	HR	RBI	SB	G. by Pos

Ken Silvestri *continued*

Year	Gms.	BA	SA	AB	H	2B	3B	HR	RBI	SB	G. by Pos
1947	3	.200	.200	10	2	0	0	0	0	0	C-3
3 yrs.	33	.254	.380	71	18	6	0	1	5	0	C-28

Hack Simmons

GEORGE WASHINGTON SIMMONS BR TR
B. Jan. 29, 1885, Brooklyn, N. Y. 5' 8" 179 lbs.
D. Apr. 26, 1942, Arverne, N. Y.

Year	Gms.	BA	SA	AB	H	2B	3B	HR	RBI	SB	G. by Pos
1912	110	.239	.292	401	96	17	2	0	41	19	2B-88, 1B-13, SS-4

Dick Simpson

RICHARD CHARLES SIMPSON BR TR
B. Jul. 28, 1943, Washington, D. C. 6' 4" 176 lbs.

Year	Gms.	BA	SA	AB	H	2B	3B	HR	RBI	SB	G. by Pos
1969	6	.273	.455	11	3	2	0	0	4	0	OF-5

Harry Simpson

HARRY LEON SIMPSON BL TR
B. Dec. 3, 1925, Atlanta, Ga. 6' 1" 180 lbs.
D. Apr. 3, 1979, Akron, Ohio

Year	Gms.	BA	SA	AB	H	2B	3B	HR	RBI	SB	G. by Pos
1957	75	.250	.402	224	56	7	3	7	39	1	OF-42, 1B-21
1958	24	.216	.294	51	11	2	1	0	6	0	OF-15
2 yrs.	99	.244	.382	275	67	9	4	7	45	1	OF-57, 1B-21
World Series											
1957	5	.083	.083	12	1	0	0	0	1	0	1B-4

Duke Sims

DUANE B. SIMS BL TR
B. Jun. 5, 1941, Salt Lake City, Utah 6' 2" 197 lbs.

Year	Gms.	BA	SA	AB	H	2B	3B	HR	RBI	SB	G. by Pos
1973	4	.333	.667	9	3	0	0	1	1	0	DH-2, C-1
1974	5	.133	.200	15	2	1	0	0	2	0	C-1
2 yrs.	9	.208	.375	24	5	1	0	1	3	0	C-2, DH-2

Bill Skiff

WILLIAM FRANKLIN SKIFF BR TR
B. Oct. 16, 1895, New Rochelle, N. Y. 5' 10" 170 lbs.
D. Dec. 25, 1976, Bronxville, N. Y.

Year	Gms.	BA	SA	AB	H	2B	3B	HR	RBI	SB	G. by Pos
1926	6	.091	.091	11	1	0	0	0	0	0	C-6

Camp Skinner

ELISHA HARRISON SKINNER BL TR
B. Jun. 25, 1897, Douglasville, Ga. 5' 11" 165 lbs.
D. Aug. 4, 1944, Douglasville, Ga.

Year	Gms.	BA	SA	AB	H	2B	3B	HR	RBI	SB	G. by Pos
1922	27	.182	.182	33	6	0	0	0	2	1	OF-4

Joel Skinner

JOEL PATRICK SKINNER BR TR
B. Feb. 21, 1961, La Jolla, Calif. 6' 4" 195 lbs.

Year	Gms.	BA	SA	AB	H	2B	3B	HR	RBI	SB	G. by Pos
1986	54	.259	.301	166	43	4	0	1	17	0	C-54
1987	64	.137	.230	139	19	4	0	3	14	0	C-64
1988	88	.227	.335	251	57	15	0	4	23	0	C-85, OF-2, 1B-1
3 yrs.	206	.214	.299	556	119	23	0	8	54	0	C-203, OF-2, 1B-1

Lou Skizas

LOUIS PETER SKIZAS BR TR
B. Jun. 2, 1932, Chicago, Ill. 5' 11" 175 lbs.

Year	Gms.	BA	SA	AB	H	2B	3B	HR	RBI	SB	G. by Pos
1956	6	.167	.167	6	1	0	0	0	1	0	

Bill Skowron

WILLIAM JOSEPH SKOWRON BR TR
B. Dec. 18, 1930, Chicago, Ill. 5' 11" 195 lbs.

Year	Gms.	BA	SA	AB	H	2B	3B	HR	RBI	SB	G. by Pos
1954	87	.340	.577	215	73	12	9	7	41	2	1B-61, 3B-5, 2B-2
1955	108	.319	.524	288	92	17	3	12	61	1	1B-74, 3B-3
1956	134	.308	.528	464	143	21	6	23	90	4	1B-120, 3B-2
1957	122	.304	.470	457	139	15	5	17	88	3	1B-115
1958	126	.273	.424	465	127	22	3	14	73	1	1B-118, 3B-2
1959	74	.298	.539	282	84	13	5	15	59	1	1B-72
1960	146	.309	.528	538	166	34	3	26	91	2	1B-142
1961	150	.267	.472	561	150	23	4	28	89	0	1B-149
1962	140	.270	.473	478	129	16	6	23	80	0	1B-135
9 yrs.	1087	.294	.496	3748	1103	173	44	165	672	14	1B-986, 3B-12, 2B-2
World Series											
1955	5	.333	.750	12	4	2	0	1	3	0	1B-3

Bill Skowron *continued*

Year	Gms.	BA	SA	AB	H	2B	3B	HR	RBI	SB	G. by Pos
1956	3	.100	.400	10	1	0	0	1	4	0	1B-2
1957	2	.000	.000	4	0	0	0	0	0	0	1B-2
1958	7	.259	.481	27	7	0	0	2	7	0	1B-7
1960	7	.375	.625	32	12	2	0	2	6	0	1B-7
1961	5	.353	.529	17	6	0	0	1	5	0	1B-5
1962	6	.222	.333	18	4	0	1	0	1	0	1B-6
7 yrs.	35	.283	.508	120	34	4	1	7	26	0	1B-32

Don Slaught

DONALD MARTIN SLAUGHT BR TR
B. Sep. 11, 1958, Long Beach, Calif. 6' 1" 190 lbs.

Year	Gms.	BA	SA	AB	H	2B	3B	HR	RBI	SB	G. by Pos
1988	97	.283	.450	322	91	25	1	9	43	1	C-94, DH-1
1989	117	.251	.371	350	88	21	3	5	38	1	C-105, DH-3
2 yrs.	214	.266	.409	672	179	46	4	14	81	2	C-199, DH-4

Enos Slaughter

ENOS BRADSHER SLAUGHTER BL TR
B. Apr. 27, 1916, Roxboro, N. C. 5' 9½" 180 lbs.
Hall of Fame 1985

Year	Gms.	BA	SA	AB	H	2B	3B	HR	RBI	SB	G. by Pos
1954	69	.248	.336	125	31	4	2	1	19	0	OF-30
1955	10	.111	.111	9	1	0	0	0	1	0	
1956	24	.289	.386	83	24	4	2	0	4	1	OF-20
1957	96	.254	.368	209	53	7	1	5	34	0	OF-64
1958	77	.304	.435	138	42	4	1	4	19	2	OF-35
1959	74	.172	.374	99	17	2	0	6	21	1	OF-26
6 yrs.	350	.253	.376	663	168	21	6	16	98	4	OF-175
World Series											
1956	6	.350	.500	20	7	0	0	1	4	0	OF-6
1957	5	.250	.333	12	3	1	0	0	0	0	OF-5
1958	4	.000	.000	3	0	0	0	0	0	0	
3 yrs.	15	.286	.400	35	10	1	0	1	4	0	OF-11

Roy Smalley

ROY FREDERICK/III SMALLEY BB TR
B. Oct. 25, 1952, Los Angeles, Calif. 6' 1" 185 lbs.

Year	Gms.	BA	SA	AB	H	2B	3B	HR	RBI	SB	G. by Pos
1982	142	.257	.418	486	125	14	2	20	67	0	SS-89, 3B-53, DH-4, 2B-1
1983	130	.275	.452	451	124	24	1	18	62	3	SS-91, 3B-26, 1B-22
1984	67	.239	.388	209	50	8	1	7	26	2	3B-35, SS-13, 1B-5, DH-5
3 yrs.	339	.261	.426	1146	299	46	4	45	155	5	SS-193, 3B-114, 1B-27, DH-9, 2B-1

Charley Smith

CHARLES WILLIAM SMITH BR TR
B. Sep. 15, 1937, Charleston, S. C. 6' 1" 170 lbs.
D. Nov. 29, 1994, Reno, Nev.

Year	Gms.	BA	SA	AB	H	2B	3B	HR	RBI	SB	G. by Pos
1967	135	.224	.336	425	95	15	3	9	38	0	3B-115
1968	46	.229	.357	70	16	4	1	1	7	0	3B-13
2 yrs.	181	.224	.339	495	111	19	4	10	45	0	3B-128

Elmer Smith

ELMER JOHN SMITH BL TR
B. Sep. 21, 1892, Sandusky, Ohio 5' 10" 165 lbs.
D. Aug. 3, 1984, Columbia, Ky.

Year	Gms.	BA	SA	AB	H	2B	3B	HR	RBI	SB	G. by Pos
1922	21	.185	.296	27	5	0	0	1	5	0	OF-10
1923	70	.306	.475	183	56	6	2	7	35	3	OF-47
2 yrs.	91	.290	.452	210	61	6	2	8	40	3	OF-57
World Series											
1922	2	.000	.000	2	0	0	0	0	0	0	

Joe Smith

JOSEPH SMITH BR TR
B. Dec. 29, 1893, New York, N. Y. 5' 8" 190 lbs.
D. Jun. 12, 1974, Yonkers, N. Y.

Year	Gms.	BA	SA	AB	H	2B	3B	HR	RBI	SB	G. by Pos
1913	13	.156	.156	32	5	0	0	0	2	1	C-13

Keith Smith

PATRICK KEITH SMITH BB TR
B. Oct. 20, 1961, Los Angeles, Calif. 6' 1" 175 lbs.

Year	Gms.	BA	SA	AB	H	2B	3B	HR	RBI	SB	G. by Pos
1984	2	.000	.000	4	0	0	0	0	0	0	SS-2

347

Keith Smith *continued*

Year	Gms.	BA	SA	AB	H	2B	3B	HR	RBI	SB	G. by Pos
1985	4	—	—	0	0	0	0	0	0	0	SS-3
2 yrs.	6	.000	.000	4	0	0	0	0	0	0	SS-5

Klondike Smith

ARMSTRONG FREDERICK SMITH BL TL
B. Jan. 4, 1887, London, England 5' 9" 160 lbs.
D. Nov. 15, 1959, Springfield, Mass.

Year	Gms.	BA	SA	AB	H	2B	3B	HR	RBI	SB	G. by Pos
1912	7	.185	.222	27	5	1	0	0	0	1	OF-7

J. T. Snow

JACK THOMAS SNOW BB TL
B. Feb. 26, 1968, Long Beach, Calif. 6' 2" 200 lbs.

Year	Gms.	BA	SA	AB	H	2B	3B	HR	RBI	SB	G. by Pos
1992	7	.143	.214	14	2	1	0	0	2	0	1B-6

Eric Soderholm

ERIC THANE SODERHOLM BR TR
B. Sep. 24, 1948, Cortland, N. Y. 5' 11" 187 lbs.

Year	Gms.	BA	SA	AB	H	2B	3B	HR	RBI	SB	G. by Pos
1980	95	.287	.462	275	79	13	1	11	35	0	DH-51, 3B-37
League Championship Series											
1980	2	.167	.167	6	1	0	0	0	0	0	DH-2

Luis Sojo

LUIS BELTRAN SOJO BR TR
B. Jan. 3, 1966, Caracas, Venezuela 5' 11" 172 lbs.

Year	Gms.	BA	SA	AB	H	2B	3B	HR	RBI	SB	G. by Pos
1996	18	.275	.325	40	11	2	0	0	5	0	2B-14, SS-4, 3B-1
Divisional Playoffs											
1996	2	—	—	0	0	0	0	0	0	0	2B-2
League Championship Series											
1996	3	.200	.200	5	1	0	0	0	0	0	2B-3
World Series											
1996	5	.600	.800	5	3	1	0	1	0	0	2B-3

Tony Solaita

TOLIA SOLAITA BL TL
B. Jan. 15, 1947, Nuuuli,
American Samoa 6' 210 lbs.
D. Feb. 10, 1990, Tafuna, American Samoa

Year	Gms.	BA	SA	AB	H	2B	3B	HR	RBI	SB	G. by Pos
1968	1	.000	.000	1	0	0	0	0	0	0	1B-1

Steve Souchock

STEPHEN SOUCHOCK BR TR
B. Mar. 3, 1919, Yatesboro, Pa. 6' 2½" 203 lbs.

Year	Gms.	BA	SA	AB	H	2B	3B	HR	RBI	SB	G. by Pos
1946	47	.302	.477	86	26	3	2	10	0	0	1B-20
1948	44	.203	.322	118	24	3	1	3	11	3	1B-32
2 yrs.	91	.245	.387	204	50	6	4	5	21	3	1B-52

Jim Spencer

JAMES LLOYD SPENCER BL TL
B. Jul. 30, 1946, Hanover, Pa. 6' 2" 195 lbs.

Year	Gms.	BA	SA	AB	H	2B	3B	HR	RBI	SB	G. by Pos
1978	71	.227	.440	150	34	9	1	7	24	0	DH-35, 1B-15
1979	106	.288	.593	295	85	15	3	23	53	0	DH-71, 1B-26
1980	97	.236	.421	259	61	9	0	13	43	1	1B-75, DH-15
1981	25	.143	.270	63	9	2	0	2	4	0	1B-25
4 yrs.	299	.246	.478	767	189	35	4	45	124	1	1B-141, DH-121
League Championship Series											
1980	1	.000	.000	1	0	0	0	0	0	0	
World Series											
1978	4	.167	.167	12	2	0	0	0	0	0	1B-3

Charlie Spikes

LESLIE CHARLES SPIKES BR TR
B. Jan. 23, 1951, Bogalusa, La. 6' 3" 215 lbs.

Year	Gms.	BA	SA	AB	H	2B	3B	HR	RBI	SB	G. by Pos
1972	14	.147	.176	34	5	1	0	0	3	0	OF-9

Jake Stahl

GARLAND STAHL BR TR
B. Apr. 13, 1879, Elkhart, Ill. 6' 2" 195 lbs.
D. Sep. 18, 1922, Monrovia, Calif.

Year	Gms.	BA	SA	AB	H	2B	3B	HR	RBI	SB	G. by Pos
1908	74	.255	.380	274	70	18	5	2	42	16	OF-67, 1B-6

Roy Staiger

ROY JOSEPH STAIGER BR TR
B. Jan. 6, 1950, Tulsa, Okla. 6' 200 lbs.

Year	Gms.	BA	SA	AB	H	2B	3B	HR	RBI	SB	G. by Pos
1979	4	.273	.364	11	3	1	0	0	1	0	3B-4

Tuck Stainback

GEORGE TUCKER STAINBACK BR TR
B. Aug. 4, 1911, Los Angeles, Calif. 5' 11½" 175 lbs.
D. Nov. 29, 1992, Camarillo, Calif.

Year	Gms.	BA	SA	AB	H	2B	3B	HR	RBI	SB	G. by Pos
1942	15	.200	.200	10	2	0	0	0	0	0	OF-3
1943	71	.260	.325	231	60	11	2	0	10	3	OF-61
1944	30	.218	.256	78	17	3	0	0	5	1	OF-24
1945	95	.257	.352	327	84	12	2	5	32	0	OF-83
4 yrs.	211	.252	.328	646	163	26	4	5	47	4	OF-171
World Series											
1942	2	—	—	0	0	0	0	0	0	0	
1943	5	.176	.176	17	3	0	0	0	0	0	OF-5
2 yrs.	7	.176	.176	17	3	0	0	0	0	0	OF-5

Andy Stankiewicz

ANDREW NEAL STANKIEWICZ BR TR
B. Aug. 10, 1964, Inglewood, Calif. 5' 9" 165 lbs.

Year	Gms.	BA	SA	AB	H	2B	3B	HR	RBI	SB	G. by Pos
1992	116	.268	.347	400	107	22	2	2	25	9	SS-81, 2B-34, DH-1
1993	16	.000	.000	9	0	0	0	0	0	0	2B-6, 3B-4, SS-1, DH-1
2 yrs.	132	.262	.340	409	107	22	2	2	25	9	SS-82, 2B-40, 3B-4, DH-2

Fred Stanley

FREDERICK BLAIR STANLEY BR TR
B. Aug. 13, 1947, Farnhamville, Iowa 5' 10" 165 lbs.

Year	Gms.	BA	SA	AB	H	2B	3B	HR	RBI	SB	G. by Pos
1973	26	.212	.288	66	14	0	1	1	5	0	SS-21, 2B-3
1974	33	.184	.184	38	7	0	0	0	3	1	SS-19, 2B-15
1975	117	.222	.250	252	56	5	1	0	15	3	SS-83, 2B-33, 3B-1
1976	110	.238	.273	260	62	2	2	1	20	1	SS-110, 2B-3
1977	48	.261	.326	46	12	0	0	1	7	1	SS-42, 3B-3, 2B-2
1978	81	.219	.281	160	35	7	0	1	9	0	SS-71, 2B-11, 3B-4
1979	57	.200	.270	100	20	1	0	2	14	0	SS-31, 3B-16, 2B-8, 1B-1
1980	49	.209	.244	86	18	3	0	0	5	0	SS-19, 2B-17, 3B-12
8 yrs.	521	.222	.266	1008	224	18	4	6	78	6	SS-396, 2B-92, 3B-36, 1B-1
League Championship Series											
1976	5	.333	.467	15	5	2	0	0	0	0	SS-5
1977	2	—	—	0	0	0	0	0	0	0	SS-2
1978	2	.200	.200	5	1	0	0	0	0	0	2B-2
3 yrs.	9	.300	.400	20	6	2	0	0	0	0	SS-7, 2B-2
World Series											
1976	4	.167	.333	6	1	1	0	0	1	0	SS-4
1977	1	—	—	0	0	0	0	0	0	0	SS-1
1978	3	.200	.400	5	1	1	0	0	0	0	2B-3
3 yrs.	8	.182	.364	11	2	2	0	0	1	0	SS-5, 2B-3

Mike Stanley

ROBERT MICHAEL STANLEY BR TR
B. Jun. 25, 1963, Fort Lauderdale, Fla. 6' 1" 185 lbs.

Year	Gms.	BA	SA	AB	H	2B	3B	HR	RBI	SB	G. by Pos
1992	68	.249	.428	173	43	7	0	8	27	0	C-55, DH-6, 1B-4
1993	130	.305	.534	423	129	17	1	26	84	1	C-122, DH-2
1994	82	.300	.545	290	87	20	0	17	57	0	C-72, 1B-7, DH-3
1995	118	.268	.481	399	107	29	1	18	83	1	C-107, DH-10
4 yrs.	398	.285	.506	1285	366	73	2	69	251	2	C-356, DH-22, 1B-11
Divisional Playoffs											
1995	4	.313	.500	16	5	0	0	1	3	0	C-4

Dave Stegman

DAVID WILLIAM STEGMAN BR TR
B. Jan. 30, 1954, Inglewood, Calif. 5' 11" 190 lbs.

Year	Gms.	BA	SA	AB	H	2B	3B	HR	RBI	SB	G. by Pos
1982	2	—	—	0	0	0	0	0	0	0	

Dutch Sterrett

CHARLES HURLBUT STERRETT BR TR
B. Oct. 1, 1889, Milroy, Pa. 5' 11½" 165 lbs.
D. Dec. 9, 1965, Baltimore, Md.

Year	Gms.	BA	SA	AB	H	2B	3B	HR	RBI	SB	G. by Pos
1912	66	.265	.357	230	61	4	7	1	32	8	OF-38, 1B-17, C-10, 2B-1
1913	21	.171	.171	35	6	0	0	0	3	1	1B-6, C-1, OF-1
2 yrs.	87	.253	.332	265	67	4	7	1	35	9	OF-39, 1B-23, C-11, 2B-1

Bud Stewart
EDWARD PERRY STEWART   BL TR
B. Jun. 15, 1916, Sacramento, Calif.   5' 11" 160 lbs.

Year	Gms.	BA	SA	AB	H	2B	3B	HR	RBI	SB	G. by Pos
1948	6	.200	.400	5	1	1	0	0	0	0	

Snuffy Stirnweiss
GEORGE HENRY STIRNWEISS   BR TR
B. Oct. 26, 1918, New York, N. Y.   5' 8½" 175 lbs.
D. Sep. 15, 1958, Newark, N. J.

Year	Gms.	BA	SA	AB	H	2B	3B	HR	RBI	SB	G. by Pos
1943	83	.219	.288	274	60	8	4	1	25	11	SS-68, 2B-4
1944	154	.319	.460	643	205	35	16	8	43	55	2B-154
1945	152	.309	.476	632	195	32	22	10	64	33	2B-152
1946	129	.251	.318	487	122	19	7	0	37	18	3B-79, 2B-46, SS-4
1947	148	.256	.342	571	146	18	8	5	41	5	2B-148
1948	141	.252	.336	515	130	20	7	3	32	5	2B-141
1949	70	.261	.338	157	41	8	2	0	11	3	2B-51, 3B-4
1950	7	.000	.000	2	0	0	0	0	0	0	2B-4, 3B-1
8 yrs.	884	.274	.382	3281	899	140	66	27	253	130	2B-700, 3B-84, SS-72

World Series

Year	Gms.	BA	SA	AB	H	2B	3B	HR	RBI	SB	G. by Pos
1943	1	.000	.000	1	0	0	0	0	0	0	
1947	7	.259	.333	27	7	0	1	0	3	0	2B-7
1949	1	—	—	0	0	0	0	0	0	0	
3 yrs.	9	.250	.321	28	7	0	1	0	3	0	2B-7

Darryl Strawberry
DARRYL EUGENE STRAWBERRY   BL TL
B. Mar. 12, 1962, Los Angeles, Calif.   6' 6" 190 lbs.

Year	Gms.	BA	SA	AB	H	2B	3B	HR	RBI	SB	G. by Pos
1995	32	.276	.448	87	24	4	1	3	13	0	DH-15, OF-11
1996	63	.262	.490	202	53	13	0	11	36	6	OF-34, DH-26
2 yrs.	95	.266	.478	289	77	17	1	14	49	6	OF-45, DH-41

Divisional Playoffs

Year	Gms.	BA	SA	AB	H	2B	3B	HR	RBI	SB	G. by Pos
1995	2	.000	.000	2	0	0	0	0	0	0	
1996	2	.000	.000	5	0	0	0	0	0	0	DH-2
2 yrs.	4	.000	.000	7	0	0	0	0	0	0	DH-2

League Championship Series

Year	Gms.	BA	SA	AB	H	2B	3B	HR	RBI	SB	G. by Pos
1996	4	.417	1.167	12	5	0	0	3	5	0	OF-4

World Series

Year	Gms.	BA	SA	AB	H	2B	3B	HR	RBI	SB	G. by Pos
1996	5	.188	.188	16	3	0	0	0	1	0	OF-5

Gabby Street
CHARLES EVARD STREET   BR TR
B. Sep. 30, 1882, Huntsville, Ala.   5' 11" 180 lbs.
D. Feb. 6, 1951, Joplin, Mo.

Year	Gms.	BA	SA	AB	H	2B	3B	HR	RBI	SB	G. by Pos
1912	28	.182	.216	88	16	1	1	0	6	1	C-28

Bill Stumpf
WILLIAM FREDERICK STUMPF   BR TR
B. Mar. 21, 1892, Baltimore, Md.   6' ½" 175 lbs.
D. Feb. 14, 1966, Crownsville, Md.

Year	Gms.	BA	SA	AB	H	2B	3B	HR	RBI	SB	G. by Pos
1912	40	.240	.240	129	31	0	0	0	10	5	SS-27, 2B-8, 3B-4, 1B-1
1913	12	.207	.241	29	6	1	0	0	1	0	SS-6, 2B-5, OF-1
2 yrs.	52	.234	.241	158	37	1	0	0	11	5	SS-33, 2B-13, 3B-4, 1B-1, OF-1

Johnny Sturm
JOHN PETER JOSEPH STURM   BL TL
B. Jan. 23, 1916, St. Louis, Mo.   6' 1" 185 lbs.

Year	Gms.	BA	SA	AB	H	2B	3B	HR	RBI	SB	G. by Pos
1941	124	.239	.300	524	125	17	3	3	36	3	1B-124

World Series

Year	Gms.	BA	SA	AB	H	2B	3B	HR	RBI	SB	G. by Pos
1941	5	.286	.286	21	6	0	0	0	2	1	1B-5

Bill Sudakis
WILLIAM PAUL SUDAKIS   BB TR
B. Mar. 27, 1946, Joliet, Ill.   6' 1" 190 lbs.

Year	Gms.	BA	SA	AB	H	2B	3B	HR	RBI	SB	G. by Pos
1974	89	.232	.344	259	60	8	0	7	39	0	DH-39, 1B-33, 3B-3, C-1

Jeff Sweeney
EDWARD FRANCIS SWEENEY   BR TR
B. Jul. 19, 1888, Chicago, Ill.   6' 1" 200 lbs.
D. Jul. 4, 1947, Chicago, Ill.

Year	Gms.	BA	SA	AB	H	2B	3B	HR	RBI	SB	G. by Pos
1908	32	.146	.171	82	12	2	0	0	2	0	C-25, 1B-1, OF-1

Jeff Sweeney *continued*

Year	Gms.	BA	SA	AB	H	2B	3B	HR	RBI	SB	G. by Pos
1909	67	.267	.284	176	47	3	0	0	21	3	C-62, 1B-3
1910	78	.200	.256	215	43	4	4	0	13	12	C-78
1911	83	.231	.301	229	53	6	5	0	18	8	C-83
1912	110	.268	.308	351	94	12	1	0	30	6	C-108
1913	117	.265	.322	351	93	10	2	2	40	11	C-112, 1B-1
1914	87	.213	.264	258	55	8	1	1	22	19	C-78
1915	53	.190	.204	137	26	2	0	0	5	3	C-53
8 yrs.	627	.235	.281	1799	423	47	13	3	151	62	C-599, 1B-5, OF-1

Ron Swoboda
RONALD ALAN SWOBODA   BR TR
B. Jun. 30, 1944, Baltimore, Md.   6' 2" 195 lbs.

Year	Gms.	BA	SA	AB	H	2B	3B	HR	RBI	SB	G. by Pos
1971	54	.261	.333	138	36	2	1	2	20	0	OF-47
1972	63	.248	.345	113	28	8	0	1	12	0	OF-35, 1B-2
1973	35	.116	.186	43	5	0	0	1	2	0	OF-20, DH-4
3 yrs.	152	.235	.316	294	69	10	1	4	34	0	OF-102, DH-4, 1B-2

Danny Tartabull
DANILO TARTABULL   BR TR
B. Oct. 30, 1962, San Juan, Puerto Rico   6' 1" 185 lbs.

Year	Gms.	BA	SA	AB	H	2B	3B	HR	RBI	SB	G. by Pos
1992	123	.266	.489	421	112	19	0	25	85	2	OF-69, DH-53
1993	138	.250	.503	513	128	33	2	31	102	0	DH-88, OF-50
1994	104	.256	.464	399	102	24	1	19	67	1	DH-78, OF-26
1995	59	.224	.380	192	43	12	0	6	28	0	DH-39, OF-18
4 yrs.	424	.252	.473	1525	385	88	3	81	282	3	DH-258, OF-163

Zack Taylor
JAMES WREN TAYLOR   BR TR
B. Jul. 27, 1898, Yulee, Fla.   5' 11½" 180 lbs.
D. Sep. 19, 1974, Orlando, Fla.

Year	Gms.	BA	SA	AB	H	2B	3B	HR	RBI	SB	G. by Pos
1934	4	.143	.143	7	1	0	0	0	0	0	C-3

Frank Tepedino
FRANK RONALD TEPEDINO   BL TL
B. Nov. 23, 1947, Brooklyn, N.Y.   5' 11" 185 lbs.

Year	Gms.	BA	SA	AB	H	2B	3B	HR	RBI	SB	G. by Pos
1967	9	.400	.400	5	2	0	0	0	0	0	1B-1
1969	13	.231	.231	39	9	0	0	0	4	1	OF-13
1970	16	.316	.421	19	6	2	0	0	2	0	1B-1, OF-1
1971	6	.000	.000	6	0	0	0	0	0	0	OF-1
1972	8	.000	.000	8	0	0	0	0	0	0	
5 yrs.	52	.221	.247	77	17	2	0	0	6	1	OF-15, 1B-2

Dick Tettelbach
RICHARD MORLEY TETTELBACH   BR TR
B. Jun. 26, 1929, New Haven, Conn.   6' 195 lbs.
D. Jan. 26, 1995, East Harwich, Mass.

Year	Gms.	BA	SA	AB	H	2B	3B	HR	RBI	SB	G. by Pos
1955	2	.000	.000	5	0	0	0	0	0	0	OF-2

Ira Thomas
IRA FELIX THOMAS   BR TR
B. Jan. 22, 1881, Ballston Spa, N. Y.   6' 2" 200 lbs.
D. Oct. 11, 1958, Philadelphia, Pa.

Year	Gms.	BA	SA	AB	H	2B	3B	HR	RBI	SB	G. by Pos
1906	44	.200	.243	115	23	1	2	0	15	2	C-42
1907	80	.192	.269	208	40	5	4	1	24	5	C-66, 1B-2
2 yrs.	124	.195	.260	323	63	6	6	1	39	7	C-108, 1B-2

Lee Thomas
JAMES LEROY THOMAS   BL TL
B. Feb. 5, 1936, Peoria, Ill.   6' 2" 195 lbs.

Year	Gms.	BA	SA	AB	H	2B	3B	HR	RBI	SB	G. by Pos
1961	2	.500	.500	2	1	0	0	0	0	0	

Gary Thomasson
GARY LEAH THOMASSON   BL TL
B. Jul. 29, 1951, San Diego, Calif.   6' 1" 180 lbs.

Year	Gms.	BA	SA	AB	H	2B	3B	HR	RBI	SB	G. by Pos
1978	55	.276	.405	116	32	4	1	3	20	0	OF-50, DH-1

League Championship Series

Year	Gms.	BA	SA	AB	H	2B	3B	HR	RBI	SB	G. by Pos
1978	3	.000	.000	1	0	0	0	0	0	0	OF-3

World Series

Year	Gms.	BA	SA	AB	H	2B	3B	HR	RBI	SB	G. by Pos
1978	3	.250	.250	4	1	0	0	0	0	0	OF-3

Year	Gms.	BA	SA	AB	H	2B	3B	HR	RBI	SB	G. by Pos

Homer Thompson

HOMER THOMAS THOMPSON BR TR
B. Jun. 1, 1891, Spring City, Tenn.   5' 9" 160 lbs.
D. Sep. 12, 1957, Atlanta, Ga.

Year	Gms.	BA	SA	AB	H	2B	3B	HR	RBI	SB	G. by Pos
1912	1	—	—	0	0	0	0	0	0	0	C-1

Jack Thoney

JOHN THONEY BR TR
B. Dec. 8, 1879, Ft. Thomas, Ky.   5' 10" 175 lbs.
D. Oct. 24, 1948, Covington, Ky.

Year	Gms.	BA	SA	AB	H	2B	3B	HR	RBI	SB	G. by Pos
1904	36	.188	.250	128	24	4	2	0	12	9	3B-26, OF-10

Marv Throneberry

MARVIN EUGENE THRONEBERRY BL TL
B. Sep. 2, 1933, Collierville, Tenn.   6' 1" 190 lbs.
D. Jun. 23, 1994, Fisherville, Tenn.

Year	Gms.	BA	SA	AB	H	2B	3B	HR	RBI	SB	G. by Pos
1955	1	1.000	1.500	2	2	1	0	0	3	1	1B-1
1958	60	.227	.427	150	34	5	2	7	19	1	1B-40, OF-5
1959	80	.240	.391	192	46	5	0	8	22	0	1B-54, OF-13
3 yrs.	141	.238	.413	344	82	11	2	15	44	2	1B-95, OF-18
World Series											
1958	1	.000	.000	1	0	0	0	0	0	0	

Eddie Tiemeyer

EDWARD CARL TIEMEYER BR TR
B. May. 9, 1885, Cincinnati, Ohio   5' 11½" 185 lbs.
D. Sep. 27, 1946, Cincinnati, Ohio

Year	Gms.	BA	SA	AB	H	2B	3B	HR	RBI	SB	G. by Pos
1909	3	.375	.500	8	3	1	0	0	0	0	1B-3

Bob Tillman

JOHN ROBERT TILLMAN BR TR
B. Mar. 24, 1937, Nashville, Tenn.   6' 4" 205 lbs.

Year	Gms.	BA	SA	AB	H	2B	3B	HR	RBI	SB	G. by Pos
1967	22	.254	.365	63	16	1	0	2	9	0	C-15

Wayne Tolleson

JIMMY WAYNE TOLLESON BB TR
B. Nov. 22, 1955, Spartanburg, S. C.   5' 9" 160 lbs.

Year	Gms.	BA	SA	AB	H	2B	3B	HR	RBI	SB	G. by Pos
1986	60	.284	.344	215	61	9	2	0	14	4	SS-56, 3B-7, 2B-3
1987	121	.221	.241	349	77	4	0	1	22	5	SS-119, 3B-3
1988	21	.254	.288	59	15	2	0	0	5	1	2B-12, 3B-10, SS-1
1989	80	.164	.250	140	23	5	2	1	9	5	3B-28, SS-28, 2B-12, DH-10
1990	73	.149	.189	74	11	1	1	0	4	1	SS-45, 2B-13, DH-5, 3B-3
5 yrs.	355	.223	.268	837	187	21	5	2	54	16	SS-249, 3B-51, 2B-40, DH-15

Earl Torgeson

CLIFFORD EARL TORGESON BL TL
B. Jan. 1, 1924, Snohomish, Wash.   6' 3" 180 lbs.
D. Nov. 8, 1990, Everett, Wash.

Year	Gms.	BA	SA	AB	H	2B	3B	HR	RBI	SB	G. by Pos
1961	22	.111	.111	18	2	0	0	0	0	0	1B-8

Rusty Torres

ROSENDO TORRES BB TR
B. Sep. 30, 1948, Aguadilla, Puerto Rico   5' 10" 175 lbs.

Year	Gms.	BA	SA	AB	H	2B	3B	HR	RBI	SB	G. by Pos
1971	9	.385	.731	26	10	3	0	2	3	0	OF-5
1972	80	.211	.291	199	42	7	0	3	13	0	OF-62
2 yrs.	89	.231	.342	225	52	10	0	5	16	0	OF-67

Cesar Tovar

CESAR LEONARDO TOVAR BR TR
B. Jul. 3, 1940, Caracas, Venezuela   5' 9" 155 lbs.
D. Jul. 14, 1994, Caracas, Venezuela

Year	Gms.	BA	SA	AB	H	2B	3B	HR	RBI	SB	G. by Pos
1976	13	.154	.179	39	6	1	0	0	2	0	DH-9, 2B-3

Tom Tresh

THOMAS MICHAEL TRESH BB TR
B. Sep. 20, 1937, Detroit, Mich.   6' 1" 180 lbs.

Year	Gms.	BA	SA	AB	H	2B	3B	HR	RBI	SB	G. by Pos
1961	9	.250	.250	8	2	0	0	0	0	0	SS-3
1962	157	.286	.441	622	178	26	5	20	93	4	SS-111, OF-43
1963	145	.269	.487	520	140	28	5	25	71	3	OF-144
1964	153	.246	.402	533	131	25	5	16	73	13	OF-146
1965	156	.279	.477	602	168	29	6	26	74	5	OF-154

Tom Tresh *continued*

Year	Gms.	BA	SA	AB	H	2B	3B	HR	RBI	SB	G. by Pos
1966	151	.233	.421	537	125	12	4	27	68	5	OF-84, 3B-64
1967	130	.219	.377	448	98	23	3	14	53	1	OF-118
1968	152	.195	.308	507	99	18	3	11	52	10	SS-119, OF-27
1969	45	.182	.266	143	26	5	2	1	9	2	SS-41
9 yrs.	1098	.247	.413	3920	967	166	33	140	493	43	OF-716, SS-274, 3B-64
World Series											
1962	7	.321	.464	28	9	1	0	1	4	2	OF-7
1963	4	.200	.400	15	3	0	0	1	2	0	OF-4
1964	7	.273	.636	22	6	2	0	2	7	0	OF-7
3 yrs.	18	.277	.508	65	18	3	0	4	13	2	OF-18

Gus Triandos

GUS CONSTANTINE TRIANDOS BR TR
B. Jul. 30, 1930, San Francisco, Calif.   6' 3" 205 lbs.

Year	Gms.	BA	SA	AB	H	2B	3B	HR	RBI	SB	G. by Pos
1953	18	.157	.255	51	8	2	0	1	6	0	1B-12, C-5
1954	2	.000	.000	1	0	0	0	0	0	0	C-1
2 yrs.	20	.154	.250	52	8	2	0	1	6	0	1B-12, C-6

Frank Truesdale

FRANK DAY TRUESDALE BB TR
B. Mar. 31, 1884, St. Louis, Mo.   5' 8" 145 lbs.
D. Aug. 27, 1943, Albuquerque, N. M.

Year	Gms.	BA	SA	AB	H	2B	3B	HR	RBI	SB	G. by Pos
1914	77	.212	.230	217	46	4	0	0	13	11	2B-67, 3B-4

Bob Unglaub

ROBERT ALEXANDER UNGLAUB BR TR
B. Jul. 31, 1881, Baltimore, Md.   5' 11" 178 lbs.
D. Nov. 29, 1916, Baltimore, Md.

Year	Gms.	BA	SA	AB	H	2B	3B	HR	RBI	SB	G. by Pos
1904	6	.211	.211	19	4	0	0	0	2	0	3B-4, SS-1

Elmer Valo

ELMER WILLIAM VALO BL TR
B. Mar. 5, 1921, Ribnik, Czechoslovakia   5' 11" 190 lbs.

Year	Gms.	BA	SA	AB	H	2B	3B	HR	RBI	SB	G. by Pos
1960	8	.000	.000	5	0	0	0	0	0	0	OF-2

Bobby Vaughn

ROBERT VAUGHN BR TR
B. Jun. 4, 1885, Stamford, N. Y.   5' 9" 150 lbs.
D. Apr. 11, 1965, Seattle, Wash.

Year	Gms.	BA	SA	AB	H	2B	3B	HR	RBI	SB	G. by Pos
1909	5	.143	.143	14	2	0	0	0	0	1	2B-4, SS-1

Bobby Veach

ROBERT HAYES VEACH BL TR
B. Jun. 29, 1888, Island, Ky.   5' 11" 160 lbs.
D. Aug. 7, 1945, Detroit, Mich.

Year	Gms.	BA	SA	AB	H	2B	3B	HR	RBI	SB	G. by Pos
1925	56	.353	.474	116	41	10	2	0	15	1	OF-33

Randy Velarde

RANDY LEE VELARDE BR TR
B. Nov. 24, 1962, Midland, Tex.   6' 185 lbs.

Year	Gms.	BA	SA	AB	H	2B	3B	HR	RBI	SB	G. by Pos
1987	8	.182	.182	22	4	0	0	1	1	0	SS-8
1988	48	.174	.357	115	20	6	0	5	12	1	2B-24, SS-14, 3B-11
1989	33	.340	.480	100	34	4	2	2	11	0	3B-27, SS-9
1990	95	.210	.319	229	48	6	2	5	19	0	3B-74, SS-15, OF-5, 2B-3, DH-3
1991	80	.245	.332	184	45	11	1	1	15	3	3B-50, SS-31, OF-2
1992	121	.272	.386	412	112	24	1	7	46	7	SS-75, 3B-26, OF-23, 2B-3
1993	85	.301	.469	226	68	13	2	7	24	2	OF-50, SS-26, 3B-16, DH-1
1994	77	.279	.439	280	78	16	4	9	34	4	SS-49, 3B-27, OF-7, 2B-5
1995	111	.278	.392	367	102	19	1	7	46	5	2B-62, SS-28, OF-20, 3B-19
9 yrs.	658	.264	.392	1935	511	99	10	43	208	22	SS-255, 3B-250, OF-107, 2B-97, DH-4
Divisional Playoffs											
1995	5	.176	.176	17	3	0	0	0	1	0	2B-4, 3B-2, OF-2

Otto Velez

OTONIEL VELEZ   BR TR
B. Nov. 29, 1950, Ponce, Puerto Rico   6' 185 lbs.

Year	Gms.	BA	SA	AB	H	2B	3B	HR	RBI	SB	G. by Pos
1973	23	.195	.325	77	15	4	0	2	7	0	OF-23
1974	27	.209	.343	67	14	1	1	2	10	0	1B-21, OF-3, 3B-2
1975	6	.250	.250	8	2	0	0	0	1	0	1B-1, DH-1
1976	49	.266	.394	94	25	6	0	2	10	0	OF-24, 1B-8, DH-5, 3B-1
4 yrs.	105	.228	.354	246	56	11	1	6	28	0	OF-50, 1B-30, DH-6, 3B-3

League Championship Series

1976	1	.000	.000	1	0	0	0	0	0	0	

World Series

1976	3	.000	.000	3	0	0	0	0	0	0	

Frank Verdi

FRANK MICHAEL VERDI   BR TR
B. Jun. 2, 1926, Brooklyn, N. Y.   5' 10½" 170 lbs.

Year	Gms.	BA	SA	AB	H	2B	3B	HR	RBI	SB	G. by Pos
1953	1	—	—	0	0	0	0	0	0	0	SS-1

Sammy Vick

SAMUEL BRUCE VICK   BR TR
B. Apr. 12, 1895, Batesville, Miss.   5' 10½" 163 lbs.
D. Aug. 17, 1986, Memphis, Tenn.

Year	Gms.	BA	SA	AB	H	2B	3B	HR	RBI	SB	G. by Pos
1917	10	.278	.361	36	10	3	0	0	2	2	OF-10
1918	2	.667	.667	3	2	0	0	0	1	0	OF-1
1919	106	.248	.344	407	101	15	9	2	27	9	OF-100
1920	51	.220	.297	118	26	7	1	0	11	1	OF-33
4 yrs.	169	.246	.337	564	139	25	10	2	41	12	OF-144

Dick Wakefield

RICHARD CUMMINGS WAKEFIELD BL TR
B. May. 6, 1921, Chicago, Ill.   6' 4" 210 lbs.
D. Aug. 26, 1985, Redford, Mich.

Year	Gms.	BA	SA	AB	H	2B	3B	HR	RBI	SB	G. by Pos
1950	3	.500	.500	2	1	0	0	0	1	0	

Jim Walewander

JAMES WALEWANDER   BB TR
B. May. 2, 1961, Chicago, Ill.   5' 10" 160 lbs.

Year	Gms.	BA	SA	AB	H	2B	3B	HR	RBI	SB	G. by Pos
1990	9	.200	.400	5	1	1	0	0	1	1	2B-2, 3B-2, DH-2, SS-1

Curt Walker

WILLIAM CURTIS WALKER   BL TR
B. Jul. 3, 1896, Beeville, Tex.   5' 9½" 170 lbs.
D. Dec. 9, 1955, Beeville, Tex.

Year	Gms.	BA	SA	AB	H	2B	3B	HR	RBI	SB	G. by Pos
1919	1	.000	.000	1	0	0	0	0	0	0	

Dixie Walker

FRED WALKER   BL TR
B. Sep. 24, 1910, Villa Rica, Ga.   6' 1" 175 lbs.
D. May 17, 1982, Birmingham, Ala.

Year	Gms.	BA	SA	AB	H	2B	3B	HR	RBI	SB	G. by Pos
1931	2	.300	.500	10	3	2	0	0	1	0	OF-2
1933	98	.274	.500	328	90	15	7	15	51	2	OF-77
1934	17	.118	.118	17	2	0	0	0	0	0	OF-1
1935	8	.154	.231	13	2	1	0	0	1	0	OF-2
1936	6	.350	.700	20	7	0	2	1	5	1	OF-5
5 yrs.	131	.268	.485	388	104	18	9	16	58	3	OF-87

Jimmy Walsh

JAMES CHARLES WALSH   BL TR
B. Sep. 22, 1885, Killala, Ireland   5' 10½" 170 lbs.
D. Jul. 3, 1962, Syracuse, N. Y.

Year	Gms.	BA	SA	AB	H	2B	3B	HR	RBI	SB	G. by Pos
1914	43	.191	.265	136	26	1	3	1	11	6	OF-41

Joe Walsh

JOSEPH FRANCIS WALSH   BR TR
B. Oct. 14, 1886, Minersville, Pa.   6' 2" 170 lbs.
D. Jan. 6, 1967, Buffalo, N. Y.

Year	Gms.	BA	SA	AB	H	2B	3B	HR	RBI	SB	G. by Pos
1910	1	.000	.000	3	0	0	0	0	2	0	C-1
1911	4	.222	.333	9	2	1	0	0	0	0	C-3
2 yrs.	5	.167	.250	12	2	1	0	0	2	0	C-4

Roxy Walters

ALFRED JOHN WALTERS   BR TR
B. Nov. 5, 1892, San Francisco, Calif. 5' 8½" 160 lbs.
D. Jun. 3, 1956, Alameda, Calif.

Year	Gms.	BA	SA	AB	H	2B	3B	HR	RBI	SB	G. by Pos
1915	2	.333	.333	3	1	0	0	0	0	0	C-2
1916	66	.266	.340	203	54	9	3	0	23	2	C-65
1917	61	.263	.275	171	45	2	0	0	14	2	C-57
1918	64	.199	.236	191	38	5	1	0	12	3	C-50, OF-9
4 yrs.	193	.243	.285	568	138	16	4	0	49	7	C-174, OF-9

Danny Walton

DANIEL JAMES WALTON   BR TR
B. Jul. 14, 1947, Los Angeles, Calif.   6' 195 lbs.

Year	Gms.	BA	SA	AB	H	2B	3B	HR	RBI	SB	G. by Pos
1971	5	.143	.357	14	2	0	0	1	2	0	OF-4

Paul Waner

PAUL GLEE WANER   BL TL
B. Apr. 16, 1903, Harrah, Okla.   5' 8½" 153 lbs.
D. Aug. 29, 1965, Sarasota, Fla.
Hall of Fame 1952

Year	Gms.	BA	SA	AB	H	2B	3B	HR	RBI	SB	G. by Pos
1944	9	.143	.143	7	1	0	0	0	1	1	
1945	1	—	—	0	0	0	0	0	0	0	
2 yrs.	10	.143	.143	7	1	0	0	0	1	1	

Jack Wanner

CLARENCE CURTIS WANNER   BR TR
B. Nov. 29, 1885, Geneseo, Ill.   5' 11½" 190 lbs.
D. May 28, 1919, Geneseo, Ill.

Year	Gms.	BA	SA	AB	H	2B	3B	HR	RBI	SB	G. by Pos
1909	3	.125	.125	8	1	0	0	0	0	0	SS-2

Pee Wee Wanninger

PAUL LOUIS WANNINGER   BL TR
B. Dec. 12, 1902, Birmingham, Ala. 5' 7" 150 lbs.
D. Mar. 7, 1981, North Augusta, S. C.

Year	Gms.	BA	SA	AB	H	2B	3B	HR	RBI	SB	G. by Pos
1925	117	.236	.305	403	95	13	6	1	22	3	SS-111, 3B-3, 2B-1

Aaron Ward

AARON LEE WARD   BR TR
B. Aug. 28, 1896, Booneville, Ark.   5' 10½" 160 lbs.
D. Jan. 30, 1961, New Orleans, La.

Year	Gms.	BA	SA	AB	H	2B	3B	HR	RBI	SB	G. by Pos
1917	8	.115	.115	26	3	0	0	0	1	0	SS-7
1918	20	.125	.156	32	4	1	0	0	1	1	SS-11, 2B-4, OF-4
1919	27	.206	.265	34	7	2	0	0	2	0	1B-5, 3B-3, SS-2, 2B-1
1920	127	.256	.387	496	127	18	7	11	54	7	3B-114, SS-12
1921	153	.306	.423	556	170	30	10	5	75	6	2B-123, 3B-33
1922	154	.267	.357	558	149	19	5	7	68	7	2B-152, 3B-2
1923	152	.284	.422	567	161	26	11	10	82	8	2B-152
1924	120	.253	.395	400	101	13	10	8	66	1	2B-120, SS-1
1925	125	.246	.337	439	108	22	3	4	38	1	2B-113, 3B-10
1926	22	.323	.387	31	10	2	0	0	3	0	2B-4, 3B-1
10 yrs.	908	.268	.382	3139	840	133	46	45	390	31	2B-669, 3B-163, SS-33, 1B-5, OF-4

World Series

1921	8	.231	.231	26	6	0	0	0	4	0	2B-8
1922	5	.154	.615	13	2	0	0	2	3	0	2B-5
1923	6	.417	.542	24	10	0	0	1	2	1	2B-6
3 yrs.	19	.286	.429	63	18	0	0	3	9	1	2B-19

Gary Ward

GARY LAMELL WARD   BR TR
B. Dec. 6, 1953, Los Angeles, Calif.   6' 2" 195 lbs.

Year	Gms.	BA	SA	AB	H	2B	3B	HR	RBI	SB	G. by Pos
1987	146	.248	.384	529	131	22	1	16	78	9	OF-94, DH-36, 1B-15
1988	91	.225	.312	231	52	8	0	4	24	0	OF-54, 1B-11, 3B-2
1989	8	.294	.353	17	5	1	0	0	1	0	OF-6, DH-1
3 yrs.	245	.242	.362	777	188	31	1	20	103	9	OF-154, DH-37, 1B-26, 3B-2

Joe Ward

JOSEPH A. WARD   B TR
B. Sep. 2, 1884, Philadelphia, Pa.   ' " lbs.
D. Aug. 11, 1934, Philadelphia, Pa.

Year	Gms.	BA	SA	AB	H	2B	3B	HR	RBI	SB	G. by Pos
1909	9	.179	.179	28	5	0	0	0	0	2	2B-7, 1B-1

Year	Gms.	BA	SA	AB	H	2B	3B	HR	RBI	SB	G. by Pos

Pete Ward

PETER THOMAS WARD BL TR
B. Jul. 26, 1939, Montreal, Que.,
Canada 6' 1" 185 lbs.

Year	Gms.	BA	SA	AB	H	2B	3B	HR	RBI	SB	G. by Pos
1970	66	.260	.377	77	20	2	2	1	18	0	1B-13

Claudell Washington

CLAUDELL WASHINGTON BL TL
B. Aug. 31, 1954, Los Angeles, Calif. 6' 190 lbs.

Year	Gms.	BA	SA	AB	H	2B	3B	HR	RBI	SB	G. by Pos
1986	54	.237	.407	135	32	5	0	6	16	6	OF-38
1987	102	.279	.420	312	87	17	0	9	44	10	OF-72, DH-13
1988	126	.308	.442	455	140	22	3	11	64	15	OF-117
1990	33	.163	.200	80	13	1	1	0	6	3	OF-21, DH-2
4 yrs.	315	.277	.410	982	272	45	4	26	130	34	OF-248, DH-15

Bob Watson

ROBERT JOSE WATSON BR TR
B. Apr. 10, 1946, Los Angeles, Calif. 6' 1½" 201 lbs.

Year	Gms.	BA	SA	AB	H	2B	3B	HR	RBI	SB	G. by Pos
1980	130	.307	.456	469	144	25	3	13	68	2	1B-104, DH-21
1981	59	.212	.385	156	33	3	3	6	12	0	1B-50, DH-6
1982	7	.235	.412	17	4	3	0	0	3	0	1B-6, DH-1
3 yrs.	196	.282	.438	642	181	31	6	19	83	2	1B-160, DH-28
Divisional Playoffs											
1981	5	.438	.438	16	7	0	0	0	1	0	1B-5
League Championship Series											
1980	3	.500	.917	12	6	3	1	0	0	0	1B-3
1981	3	.250	.250	12	3	0	0	0	1	0	1B-3
2 yrs.	6	.375	.583	24	9	3	1	0	1	0	1B-6
World Series											
1981	6	.318	.636	22	7	1	0	2	7	0	1B-6

Roy Weatherly

CYRIL ROY WEATHERLY BL TR
B. Feb. 25, 1915, Warren, Tex. 5' 6½" 170 lbs.
D. Jan. 19, 1991, Woodville, Tex.

Year	Gms.	BA	SA	AB	H	2B	3B	HR	RBI	SB	G. by Pos
1943	77	.264	.389	280	74	8	3	7	28	4	OF-68
1946	2	.500	.500	2	1	0	0	0	0	0	
2 yrs.	79	.266	.390	282	75	8	3	7	28	4	OF-68
World Series											
1943	1	.000	.000	1	0	0	0	0	0	0	

Julie Wera

JULIAN VALENTINE WERA BR TR
B. Feb. 9, 1902, Winona, Minn. 5' 8" 164 lbs.
D. Dec. 12, 1975, Rochester, Minn.

Year	Gms.	BA	SA	AB	H	2B	3B	HR	RBI	SB	G. by Pos
1927	38	.238	.381	42	10	3	0	1	8	0	3B-19
1929	5	.417	.417	12	5	0	0	0	2	0	3B-4
2 yrs.	43	.278	.389	54	15	3	0	1	10	0	3B-23

Bill Werber

WILLIAM MURRAY WERBER BR TR
B. Jun. 20, 1908, Berwyn, Md. 5' 10" 170 lbs.

Year	Gms.	BA	SA	AB	H	2B	3B	HR	RBI	SB	G. by Pos
1930	4	.286	.286	14	4	0	0	0	2	0	SS-3, 3B-1
1933	3	.000	.000	2	0	0	0	0	0	0	3B-1
2 yrs.	7	.250	.250	16	4	0	0	0	2	0	SS-3, 3B-2

Dennis Werth

DENNIS DEAN WERTH BR TR
B. Dec. 29, 1952, Lincoln, Ill. 6' 1" 200 lbs.

Year	Gms.	BA	SA	AB	H	2B	3B	HR	RBI	SB	G. by Pos
1979	3	.250	.250	4	1	0	0	0	0	0	1B-1
1980	39	.308	.492	65	20	3	0	3	12	0	1B-12, OF-8, DH-8, C-1, 3B-1
1981	34	.109	.127	55	6	1	0	0	1	1	1B-19, OF-8, DH-4, C-3
3 yrs.	76	.218	.323	124	27	4	0	3	13	1	1B-32, OF-16, DH-12, C-4, 3B-1

Steve Whitaker

STEPHEN EDWARD WHITAKER BL TR
B. May. 7, 1943, Tacoma, Wash. 6' 180 lbs.

Year	Gms.	BA	SA	AB	H	2B	3B	HR	RBI	SB	G. by Pos
1966	31	.246	.491	114	28	3	2	7	15	0	OF-31
1967	122	.243	.358	441	107	12	3	11	50	2	OF-114
1968	28	.117	.150	60	7	2	0	0	3	0	OF-14
3 yrs.	181	.231	.363	615	142	17	5	18	68	2	OF-159

Roy White

ROY HILTON WHITE BB TR
B. Dec. 27, 1943, Los Angeles, Calif. 5' 10" 160 lbs.

Year	Gms.	BA	SA	AB	H	2B	3B	HR	RBI	SB	G. by Pos
1965	14	.333	.381	42	14	2	0	0	3	2	OF-10, 2B-1
1966	115	.225	.345	316	71	13	2	7	20	14	OF-82, 2B-2
1967	70	.224	.290	214	48	8	0	2	18	10	OF-36, 3B-17
1968	159	.267	.414	577	154	20	7	17	62	20	OF-154
1969	130	.290	.426	448	130	30	5	7	74	18	OF-126
1970	162	.296	.473	609	180	30	6	22	94	24	OF-161
1971	147	.292	.469	524	153	22	7	19	84	14	OF-145
1972	155	.270	.376	556	150	29	0	10	54	23	OF-155
1973	162	.246	.374	639	157	22	3	18	60	16	OF-162
1974	136	.275	.393	473	130	19	8	7	43	15	OF-67, DH-53
1975	148	.290	.430	556	161	32	5	12	59	16	OF-135, 1B-7, DH-2
1976	156	.286	.409	626	179	29	3	14	65	31	OF-156
1977	143	.268	.405	519	139	25	2	14	52	18	OF-135, DH-4
1978	103	.269	.393	346	93	13	3	8	43	10	OF-74, DH-23
1979	81	.215	.288	205	44	6	0	3	27	2	DH-29, OF-27
15 yrs.	1881	.271	.404	6650	1803	300	51	160	758	233	OF-1625, DH-111, 3B-17, 1B-7, 2B-3
League Championship Series											
1976	5	.294	.471	17	5	3	0	0	3	1	OF-5
1977	5	.400	.800	5	2	2	0	0	0	0	OF-1, DH-1
1978	4	.313	.563	16	5	1	0	1	1	0	OF-3, DH-1
3 yrs.	14	.316	.553	38	12	6	0	1	4	1	OF-9, DH-2
World Series											
1976	4	.133	.133	15	2	0	0	0	0	0	OF-4
1977	2	.000	.000	2	0	0	0	0	0	0	
1978	6	.333	.458	24	8	0	0	1	4	2	OF-6
3 yrs.	12	.244	.317	41	10	0	0	1	4	2	OF-10

George Whiteman

GEORGE WHITEMAN BR TR
B. Dec. 23, 1882, Peoria, Ill. 5' 7" 160 lbs.
D. Feb. 10, 1947, Houston, Tex.

Year	Gms.	BA	SA	AB	H	2B	3B	HR	RBI	SB	G. by Pos
1913	11	.344	.500	32	11	3	1	0	2	2	OF-11

Terry Whitfield

TERRY BERTLAND WHITFIELD BL TR
B. Jan. 12, 1953, Blythe, Calif. 6' 1½" 197 lbs.

Year	Gms.	BA	SA	AB	H	2B	3B	HR	RBI	SB	G. by Pos
1974	2	.200	.200	5	1	0	0	0	0	0	OF-1
1975	28	.272	.309	81	22	1	1	0	7	1	OF-25, DH-1
1976	1	—	—	0	0	0	0	0	0	0	OF-1
3 yrs.	31	.267	.302	86	23	1	1	0	7	1	OF-27, DH-1

Al Wickland

ALBERT WICKLAND BL TL
B. Jan. 27, 1888, Chicago, Ill. 5' 7" 155 lbs.
D. Mar. 14, 1980, Port Washington, Wis.

Year	Gms.	BA	SA	AB	H	2B	3B	HR	RBI	SB	G. by Pos
1919	26	.152	.174	46	7	1	0	0	1	0	OF-15

Ted Wilborn

THADDEAUS INGLEHART WILBORN BB TR
B. Dec. 16, 1958, Waco, Tex. 6' 165 lbs.

Year	Gms.	BA	SA	AB	H	2B	3B	HR	RBI	SB	G. by Pos
1980	8	.250	.250	8	2	0	0	0	1	0	OF-3

Ed Wilkinson

EDWARD HENRY WILKINSON BR TR
B. Jun. 20, 1890, Jacksonville, Ore. 6' 170 lbs.
D. Apr. 9, 1918, Tucson, Ariz.

Year	Gms.	BA	SA	AB	H	2B	3B	HR	RBI	SB	G. by Pos
1911	10	.231	.231	13	3	0	0	0	1	0	OF-3, 2B-1

Bernie Williams

BERNABE WILLIAMS BB TR
B. Sep. 13, 1968, San Juan, Puerto Rico 6' 2" 180 lbs.

Year	Gms.	BA	SA	AB	H	2B	3B	HR	RBI	SB	G. by Pos
1991	85	.237	.350	320	76	19	4	3	34	10	OF-85
1992	62	.280	.406	261	73	14	2	5	26	7	OF-62
1993	139	.268	.400	567	152	31	4	12	68	9	OF-139
1994	108	.289	.453	408	118	29	1	12	57	16	OF-107
1995	144	.307	.487	563	173	29	9	18	82	8	OF-144
1996	143	.305	.535	551	168	26	7	29	102	17	OF-140, DH-2
6 yrs.	681	.285	.449	2670	760	148	27	79	369	67	OF-677, DH-2
Divisional Playoffs											
1995	5	.429	.810	21	9	2	0	2	5	1	OF-5

Bernie Williams *continued*

Year	Gms.	BA	SA	AB	H	2B	3B	HR	RBI	SB	G. by Pos
1996	4	.467	1.067	15	7	0	0	3	5	1	OF-4
2 yrs.	9	.444	.917	36	16	2	0	5	10	2	OF-9
League Championship Series											
1996	5	.474	.947	19	9	3	0	2	6	1	OF-5
World Series											
1996	6	.167	.292	24	4	0	0	1	4	1	OF-6

Bob Williams

ROBERT ELIAS WILLIAMS   BR TR
B. Apr. 27, 1884, Monday, Ohio   6' 190 lbs.
D. Aug. 6, 1962, Nelsonville, Ohio

Year	Gms.	BA	SA	AB	H	2B	3B	HR	RBI	SB	G. by Pos
1911	20	.191	.234	47	9	2	0	0	8	1	C-20
1912	20	.136	.159	44	6	1	0	0	3	0	C-20
1913	6	.158	.158	19	3	0	0	0	0	0	C-6
3 yrs.	46	.164	.191	110	18	3	0	0	11	1	C-46

Gerald Williams

GERALD FLOYD WILLIAMS   BR TR
B. Aug. 10, 1966, New Orleans, La.   6' 2" 190 lbs.

Year	Gms.	BA	SA	AB	H	2B	3B	HR	RBI	SB	G. by Pos
1992	15	.296	.704	27	8	2	0	3	6	2	OF-12
1993	42	.149	.269	67	10	2	3	0	6	2	OF-37
1994	57	.291	.523	86	25	8	0	4	13	1	OF-43, DH-2
1995	100	.247	.467	182	45	18	2	6	28	4	OF-92, DH-1
1996	99	.270	.433	233	63	15	4	5	30	7	OF-93, DH-2
5 yrs.	313	.254	.450	595	151	45	9	18	83	16	OF-277, DH-5
Divisional Playoffs											
1995	5	.000	.000	5	0	0	0	0	0	0	OF-5

Harry Williams

HARRY PETER WILLIAMS   BR TR
B. Jun. 23, 1890, Omaha, Neb.   6' 1½" 200 lbs.
D. Dec. 21, 1963, Huntington Park, Calif.

Year	Gms.	BA	SA	AB	H	2B	3B	HR	RBI	SB	G. by Pos
1913	27	.256	.354	82	21	3	1	1	12	6	1B-27
1914	59	.163	.230	178	29	5	2	1	17	3	1B-58
2 yrs.	86	.192	.269	260	50	8	3	2	29	9	1B-85

Jimmy Williams

JAMES THOMAS WILLIAMS   BR TR
B. Dec. 20, 1876, St. Louis, Mo.   5' 9" 175 lbs.
D. Jan. 16, 1965, St. Petersburg, Fla.

Year	Gms.	BA	SA	AB	H	2B	3B	HR	RBI	SB	G. by Pos
1903	132	.267	.392	502	134	30	12	3	82	9	2B-132
1904	146	.263	.354	559	147	31	7	2	74	14	2B-146
1905	129	.228	.343	470	107	20	8	6	60	14	2B-129
1906	139	.277	.373	501	139	25	7	3	77	8	2B-139
1907	139	.270	.359	504	136	17	11	2	63	14	2B-139
5 yrs.	685	.261	.364	2536	663	123	45	16	356	59	2B-685

Walt Williams

WALTER ALLEN WILLIAMS   BR TR
B. Dec. 19, 1943, Brownwood, Tex.   5' 6" 165 lbs.

Year	Gms.	BA	SA	AB	H	2B	3B	HR	RBI	SB	G. by Pos
1974	43	.113	.113	53	6	0	0	0	3	1	OF-24, DH-3
1975	82	.281	.400	185	52	5	1	5	16	0	OF-31, DH-17, 2B-6
2 yrs.	125	.244	.336	238	58	5	1	5	19	1	OF-55, DH-20, 2B-6

Archie Wilson

ARCHIE CLIFTON WILSON   BR TR
B. Nov. 25, 1923, Los Angeles, Calif. 5' 11" 175 lbs.

Year	Gms.	BA	SA	AB	H	2B	3B	HR	RBI	SB	G. by Pos
1951	4	.000	.000	4	0	0	0	0	0	0	OF-2
1952	3	.500	.500	2	1	0	0	0	1	0	
2 yrs.	7	.167	.167	6	1	0	0	0	1	0	OF-2

Ted Wilson

GEORGE WASHINGTON WILSON   BL TR
B. Aug. 30, 1925, Cherryville, N. C.   6' 1½" 185 lbs.
D. Oct. 29, 1974, Gastonia, N. C.

Year	Gms.	BA	SA	AB	H	2B	3B	HR	RBI	SB	G. by Pos
1956	11	.167	.167	12	2	0	0	0	0	0	OF-6
World Series											
1956	1	.000	.000	1	0	0	0	0	0	0	

Gordie Windhorn

GORDON RAY WINDHORN   BR TR
B. Dec. 19, 1933, Watseka, Ill.   6' 1" 185 lbs.

Year	Gms.	BA	SA	AB	H	2B	3B	HR	RBI	SB	G. by Pos
1959	7	.000	.000	11	0	0	0	0	0	0	OF-4

Dave Winfield

DAVID MARK WINFIELD   BR TR
B. Oct. 3, 1951, St. Paul, Minn.   6' 6" 220 lbs.

Year	Gms.	BA	SA	AB	H	2B	3B	HR	RBI	SB	G. by Pos
1981	105	.294	.464	388	114	25	1	13	68	11	OF-102, DH-1
1982	140	.280	.560	539	151	24	8	37	106	5	OF-135, DH-4
1983	152	.283	.513	598	169	26	8	32	116	15	OF-151
1984	141	.340	.515	567	193	34	4	19	100	6	OF-140
1985	155	.275	.471	633	174	34	6	26	114	19	OF-152, DH-2
1986	154	.262	.462	565	148	31	5	24	104	6	OF-145, DH-6, 3B-2
1987	156	.275	.457	575	158	22	1	27	97	5	OF-145, DH-8
1988	149	.322	.530	559	180	37	2	25	107	9	OF-141, DH-6
1990	20	.213	.361	61	13	3	0	2	6	0	OF-12, DH-7
9 yrs.	1172	.290	.495	4485	1300	236	35	205	818	76	OF-1123, DH-32, 3B-2
Divisional Playoffs											
1981	5	.350	.500	20	7	3	0	0	0	0	OF-5
League Championship Series											
1981	3	.154	.231	13	2	1	0	0	2	1	OF-3
World Series											
1981	6	.045	.045	22	1	0	0	0	1	1	OF-6

Mickey Witek

NICHOLAS JOSEPH WITEK   BR TR
B. Dec. 19, 1915, Luzerne, Pa.   5' 10" 170 lbs.
D. Sep. 24, 1990, Kingston, Pa.

Year	Gms.	BA	SA	AB	H	2B	3B	HR	RBI	SB	G. by Pos
1949	1	1.000	1.000	1	1	0	0	0	0	0	

Whitey Witt

LAWTON WALTER WITT   BL TR
B. Sep. 28, 1895, Orange, Mass.   5' 7" 150 lbs.
D. Jul. 14, 1988, Salem County, N. J.

Year	Gms.	BA	SA	AB	H	2B	3B	HR	RBI	SB	G. by Pos
1922	140	.297	.364	528	157	11	6	4	40	5	OF-139
1923	146	.314	.408	596	187	18	10	6	56	2	OF-144
1924	147	.297	.362	600	178	26	5	1	36	9	OF-143
1925	31	.200	.300	40	8	2	1	0	0	1	OF-10
4 yrs.	464	.300	.376	1764	530	57	22	11	132	17	OF-436
World Series											
1922	5	.222	.389	18	4	1	1	0	0	0	OF-5
1923	6	.240	.320	25	6	2	0	0	4	0	OF-6
2 yrs.	11	.233	.349	43	10	3	1	0	4	0	OF-11

Harry Wolter

HARRY MEIGS WOLTER   BL TR
B. Jul. 11, 1884, Monterey, Calif.   5' 10" 175 lbs.
D. Jul. 7, 1970, Palo Alto, Calif.

Year	Gms.	BA	SA	AB	H	2B	3B	HR	RBI	SB	G. by Pos
1910	135	.267	.361	479	128	15	9	4	42	39	OF-130
1911	122	.304	.440	434	132	17	15	4	36	28	OF-113, 1B-2
1912	12	.344	.469	32	11	2	1	0	1	5	OF-9
1913	126	.254	.339	425	108	18	6	2	43	13	OF-121
4 yrs.	395	.277	.382	1370	379	52	31	10	122	85	OF-373, 1B-2

Harry Wolverton

HARRY STERLING WOLVERTON   BL TR
B. Dec. 6, 1873, Mt. Vernon, Ohio   5' 11" 205 lbs.
D. Feb. 4, 1937, Oakland, Calif.

Year	Gms.	BA	SA	AB	H	2B	3B	HR	RBI	SB	G. by Pos
1912	33	.300	.360	50	15	1	1	0	4	1	3B-7

Gene Woodling

EUGENE RICHARD WOODLING   BL TR
B. Aug. 16, 1922, Akron, Ohio   5' 9½" 195 lbs.

Year	Gms.	BA	SA	AB	H	2B	3B	HR	RBI	SB	G. by Pos
1949	112	.270	.412	296	80	13	7	5	44	2	OF-98
1950	122	.283	.412	449	127	20	10	6	60	5	OF-118
1951	120	.281	.462	420	118	15	8	15	71	0	OF-116
1952	122	.309	.473	408	126	19	6	12	63	1	OF-118
1953	125	.306	.468	395	121	26	4	10	58	2	OF-119
1954	97	.250	.352	304	76	12	5	3	40	3	OF-89
6 yrs.	698	.285	.434	2272	648	105	40	51	336	13	OF-658
World Series											
1949	3	.400	.700	10	4	3	0	0	0	0	OF-3
1950	4	.429	.429	14	6	0	0	0	0	0	OF-4
1951	6	.167	.500	18	3	1	1	1	1	0	OF-5
1952	7	.348	.609	23	8	1	1	1	1	0	OF-6
1953	6	.300	.450	20	6	0	0	1	3	0	OF-6
5 yrs.	26	.318	.529	85	27	5	2	3	6	0	OF-24

Ron Woods

RONALD LAWRENCE WOODS   BR TR
B. Feb. 1, 1943, Hamilton, Ohio   5' 10" 168 lbs.

Year	Gms.	BA	SA	AB	H	2B	3B	HR	RBI	SB	G. by Pos
1969	72	.175	.246	171	30	5	2	1	7	2	OF-67
1970	95	.227	.382	225	51	5	3	8	27	4	OF-78
1971	25	.250	.375	32	8	1	0	1	2	0	OF-9
3 yrs.	192	.208	.327	428	89	11	5	10	36	6	OF-154

Hank Workman

HENRY KILGARIFF WORKMAN   BL TR
B. Feb. 5, 1926, Los Angeles, Calif.   6' 1" 185 lbs.

Year	Gms.	BA	SA	AB	H	2B	3B	HR	RBI	SB	G. by Pos
1950	2	.200	.200	5	1	0	0	0	0	0	1B-1

Yats Wuestling

GEORGE WUESTLING   BR TR
B. Oct. 18, 1903, St. Louis, Mo.
D. Apr. 26, 1970, St. Louis, Mo.   5' 11" 167 lbs.

Year	Gms.	BA	SA	AB	H	2B	3B	HR	RBI	SB	G. by Pos
1930	25	.190	.224	58	11	0	1	0	3	0	SS-21, 3B-3

Butch Wynegar

HAROLD DELANO WYNEGAR   BB TR
B. Mar. 14, 1956, York, Pa.   6' 1" 190 lbs.

Year	Gms.	BA	SA	AB	H	2B	3B	HR	RBI	SB	G. by Pos
1982	63	.293	.393	191	56	8	1	3	20	0	C-62
1983	94	.296	.429	301	89	18	2	6	42	1	C-93
1984	129	.267	.342	442	118	13	1	6	45	1	C-126
1985	102	.223	.320	309	69	15	0	5	32	0	C-96
1986	61	.206	.345	194	40	4	1	7	29	0	C-57
5 yrs.	449	.259	.363	1437	372	58	5	27	168	2	C-434

Jimmy Wynn

JAMES SHERMAN WYNN   BR TR
B. Mar. 12, 1942, Hamilton, Ohio   5' 10" 160 lbs.

Year	Gms.	BA	SA	AB	H	2B	3B	HR	RBI	SB	G. by Pos
1977	30	.143	.234	77	11	2	1	1	3	1	DH-18, OF-8

Joe Yeager

JOSEPH F. YEAGER   BR TR
B. Aug. 28, 1875, Philadelphia, Pa.   5' 10" 160 lbs.
D. Jul. 2, 1937, Detroit, Mich.

Year	Gms.	BA	SA	AB	H	2B	3B	HR	RBI	SB	G. by Pos
1905	115	.267	.342	401	107	16	7	0	42	8	3B-90, SS-21
1906	57	.301	.366	123	37	6	1	0	12	3	SS-22, 2B-13, 3B-3
2 yrs.	172	.275	.347	524	144	22	8	0	54	11	3B-93, SS-43, 2B-13

Ralph Young

RALPH STUART YOUNG   BB TR
B. Sep. 19, 1889, Philadelphia, Pa.   5' 5" 165 lbs.
D. Jan. 24, 1965, Philadelphia, Pa.

Year	Gms.	BA	SA	AB	H	2B	3B	HR	RBI	SB	G. by Pos
1913	7	.067	.067	15	1	0	0	0	0	2	SS-7

Jack Zalusky

JOHN FRANCIS ZALUSKY   BR TR
B. Jun. 22, 1879, Minneapolis, Minn.   5' 11½" 172 lbs.
D. Aug. 11, 1935, Minneapolis, Minn.

Year	Gms.	BA	SA	AB	H	2B	3B	HR	RBI	SB	G. by Pos
1903	7	.313	.313	16	5	0	0	0	1	0	C-6, 1B-1

George Zeber

GEORGE WILLIAM ZEBER   BB TR
B. Aug. 29, 1950, Ellwood City, Pa.   5' 11" 170 lbs.

Year	Gms.	BA	SA	AB	H	2B	3B	HR	RBI	SB	G. by Pos
1977	25	.323	.508	65	21	3	0	3	10	0	2B-21, 3B-2, SS-2, DH-2
1978	3	.000	.000	6	0	0	0	0	0	0	2B-1
2 yrs.	28	.296	.465	71	21	3	0	3	10	0	2B-22, 3B-2, SS-2, DH-2

World Series
Year	Gms.	BA	SA	AB	H	2B	3B	HR	RBI	SB	G. by Pos
1977	2	.000	.000	2	0	0	0	0	0	0	

Rollie Zeider

ROLLIE HUBERT ZEIDER   BR TR
B. Nov. 16, 1883, Auburn, Ind.   5' 10" 162 lbs.
D. Sep. 12, 1967, Garrett, Ind.

Year	Gms.	BA	SA	AB	H	2B	3B	HR	RBI	SB	G. by Pos
1913	49	.233	.245	159	37	2	0	0	12	3	SS-23, 2B-19, 1B-4, 3B-2

Guy Zinn

GUY ZINN   BL TR
B. Feb. 13, 1887, Hallbrook, W. Va.   5' 10½" 170 lbs.
D. Oct. 6, 1949, Clarksburg, W. Va.

Year	Gms.	BA	SA	AB	H	2B	3B	HR	RBI	SB	G. by Pos
1911	9	.148	.296	27	4	0	2	0	1	0	OF-8
1912	106	.262	.394	401	105	15	10	6	55	17	OF-106
2 yrs.	115	.255	.388	428	109	15	12	6	56	17	OF-114

Paul Zuvella

PAUL ZUVELLA   BR TR
B. Oct. 31, 1958, San Mateo, Calif.   6' 173 lbs.

Year	Gms.	BA	SA	AB	H	2B	3B	HR	RBI	SB	G. by Pos
1986	21	.083	.104	48	4	1	0	0	2	0	SS-21
1987	14	.176	.176	34	6	0	0	0	0	0	2B-7, SS-6, 3B-1
2 yrs.	35	.122	.134	82	10	1	0	0	2	0	SS-27, 2B-7, 3B-1

Pitcher Register

The Pitcher Register is an alphabetical list of every man who pitched in the major leagues and played or managed for the New York Yankees from 1903 through today. Included are facts about the players and their year-by-year pitching records for the Yankees.

Year	W	L	PCT	ERA	G	IP	H	SO	BB	Sho	SV

Ron Guidry

RONALD AMES GUIDRY
B. Aug. 28, 1950, Lafayette, La.
BL TL
5' 11" 161 lbs.

Year	W	L	PCT	ERA	G	IP	H	SO	BB	Sho	SV
1975	0	1	.000	3.45	10	15.2	15	15	9	0	0
1976	0	0	—	5.63	7	16	20	12	4	0	0
1977	16	7	.696	2.82	31	211	174	176	65	5	1
1978	25	3	.893	1.74	35	273.2	187	248	72	9	0
1979	18	8	.692	2.78	33	236	203	201	71	2	2
1980	17	10	.630	3.56	37	220	215	166	80	3	1
1981	11	5	.688	2.76	23	127	100	104	26	0	0
1982	14	8	.636	3.81	34	222	216	162	69	1	0
1983	21	9	.700	3.42	31	250.1	232	156	60	3	0
1984	10	11	.476	4.51	29	195.2	223	127	44	1	0
1985	22	6	.786	3.27	34	259	243	143	42	2	0
1986	9	12	.429	3.98	30	192.1	202	140	38	0	0
1987	5	8	.385	3.67	22	117.2	111	96	38	0	0
1988	2	3	.400	4.18	12	56	57	32	15	0	0
14 yrs.	170	91	.651	3.29	368	2392.1	2198	1778	633	26	4
Divisional Playoffs											
1981	0	0	—	5.40	2	8.1	11	8	3	0	0
League Championship Series											
1977	1	0	1.000	3.97	2	11.1	9	8	3	0	0
1978	1	0	1.000	1.13	1	8	7	7	1	0	0
1980	0	1	.000	12.00	1	3	5	2	4	0	0
3 yrs.	2	1	.667	4.03	4	22.1	21	17	8	0	0
World Series											
1977	1	0	1.000	2.00	1	9	4	7	3	0	0
1978	1	0	1.000	1.00	1	9	8	4	7	0	0
1981	1	1	.500	1.93	2	14	8	15	4	0	0
3 yrs.	3	1	.750	1.69	4	32	20	26	14	0	0

Key

Year	Year Played
W	Games Won
L	Games Lost
PCT	Winning Percentage
ERA	Earned Run Average
G	Games Pitched
IP	Innings Pitched
H	Hits Allowed
SO	Strikeouts
BB	Bases on Balls
Sho	Stutouts
SV	Games Saved
BB	Bats Both
BL	Bats Left
BR	Bats Right
TL	Throws Left
TR	Throws Right

Jim Abbott
JAMES ANTHONY ABBOTT BL TL
B. Sep. 19, 1967, Flint, Mich. 6' 3" 200 lbs.

Year	W	L	PCT	ERA	G	IP	H	SO	BB	Sho	SV
1993	11	14	.440	4.37	32	214	221	95	73	1	0
1994	9	8	.529	4.55	24	160.1	167	90	64	0	0
2 yrs.	20	22	.476	4.45	56	374.1	388	185	137	1	0

Harry Ables
HARRY TERRELL ABLES BR TL
B. Oct. 4, 1884, Terrell, Tex. 6' 2½" 200 lbs.
D. Feb. 8, 1951, San Antonio, Tex.

Year	W	L	PCT	ERA	G	IP	H	SO	BB	Sho	SV
1911	0	1	.000	9.82	3	11	16	6	7	0	0

Doc Adkins
MERLE THERON ADKINS BR TR
B. Aug. 5, 1872, Troy, Wis. 5' 10½" 220 lbs.
D. Feb. 21, 1934, Durham, N. C.

Year	W	L	PCT	ERA	G	IP	H	SO	BB	Sho	SV
1903	0	0	—	7.71	2	7	10	0	5	0	1

Steve Adkins
STEVEN THOMAS ADKINS BR TL
B. Oct. 26, 1964, Chicago, Ill. 6' 6" 210 lbs.

Year	W	L	PCT	ERA	G	IP	H	SO	BB	Sho	SV
1990	1	2	.333	6.38	5	24	19	14	29	0	0

Jack Aker
JACK DELANE AKER BR TR
B. Jul. 13, 1940, Tulare, Calif. 6' 2" 190 lbs.

Year	W	L	PCT	ERA	G	IP	H	SO	BB	Sho	SV
1969	8	4	.667	2.06	38	65.2	51	40	22	0	11
1970	4	2	.667	2.06	41	70	57	36	20	0	16
1971	4	4	.500	2.57	41	56	48	24	26	0	4
1972	0	0	—	3.00	4	6	5	1	3	0	0
4 yrs.	16	10	.615	2.23	124	197.2	161	101	71	0	31

Doyle Alexander
DOYLE LAFAYETTE ALEXANDER BR TR
B. Sep. 4, 1950, Cordova, Ala. 6' 3" 190 lbs.

Year	W	L	PCT	ERA	G	IP	H	SO	BB	Sho	SV
1976	10	5	.667	3.29	19	136.2	114	41	39	2	0
1982	1	7	.125	6.08	16	66.2	81	26	14	0	0
1983	0	2	.000	6.35	8	28.1	31	17	7	0	0
3 yrs.	11	14	.440	4.47	43	231.2	226	84	60	2	0
World Series											
1976	0	1	.000	7.50	1	6	9	1	2	0	0

Johnny Allen
JOHN THOMAS ALLEN BR TR
B. Sep. 30, 1905, Lenoir, N. C. 6' 180 lbs.
D. Mar. 29, 1959, St. Petersburg, Fla.

Year	W	L	PCT	ERA	G	IP	H	SO	BB	Sho	SV
1932	17	4	.810	3.70	33	192	162	109	76	3	4
1933	15	7	.682	4.39	25	184.2	171	119	87	1	1
1934	5	2	.714	2.89	13	71.2	62	54	32	0	1
1935	13	6	.684	3.61	23	167	149	113	58	2	0
4 yrs.	50	19	.725	3.79	94	615.1	544	395	253	6	5
World Series											
1932	0	0	—	40.50	1	0.2	5	0	0	0	0

Neil Allen
NEIL PATRICK ALLEN BR TR
B. Jan. 24, 1958, Kansas City, Kans. 6' 3" 185 lbs.

Year	W	L	PCT	ERA	G	IP	H	SO	BB	Sho	SV
1985	1	0	1.000	2.76	17	29.1	26	16	13	0	1
1987	0	1	.000	3.65	8	24.2	23	16	10	0	0
1988	5	3	.625	3.84	41	117.1	121	61	37	1	0
3 yrs.	6	4	.600	3.62	66	171.1	170	93	60	1	1

Rick Anderson
RICHARD LEE ANDERSON BR TR
B. Dec. 25, 1953, Inglewood, Calif. 6' 2" 210 lbs.
D. Jun. 23, 1989, Wilmington, Calif.

Year	W	L	PCT	ERA	G	IP	H	SO	BB	Sho	SV
1979	0	0	—	4.50	1	2	1	0	4	0	0

Ivy Andrews
IVY PAUL ANDREWS BR TR
B. May 6, 1907, Dora, Ala. 6' 1" 200 lbs.
D. Nov. 24, 1970, Birmingham, Ala.

Year	W	L	PCT	ERA	G	IP	H	SO	BB	Sho	SV
1931	2	0	1.000	4.19	7	34.1	36	10	8	0	0
1932	2	1	.667	1.82	4	24.2	20	7	9	0	0

Ivy Andrews *continued*

Year	W	L	PCT	ERA	G	IP	H	SO	BB	Sho	SV
1937	3	2	.600	3.12	11	49	49	17	17	1	1
1938	1	3	.250	3.00	19	48	51	13	17	0	1
4 yrs.	8	6	.571	3.12	41	156	156	47	51	1	2
World Series											
1937	0	0	—	3.18	1	5.2	6	1	4	0	0

Pete Appleton
PETER WILLIAM APPLETON BR TR
B. May 20, 1904, Terryville, Conn. 5' 11" 180 lbs.
D. Jan. 18, 1974, Trenton, N. J.

Year	W	L	PCT	ERA	G	IP	H	SO	BB	Sho	SV
1933	0	0	—	0.00	1	2	3	0	1	0	0

Rugger Ardizoia
RINALDO JOSEPH ARDIZOIA BR TR
B. Nov. 20, 1919, Oleggio, Italy 5' 11" 180 lbs.

Year	W	L	PCT	ERA	G	IP	H	SO	BB	Sho	SV
1947	0	0	—	9.00	1	2	4	0	1	0	0

Mike Armstrong
MICHAEL DENNIS ARMSTRONG BR TR
B. Mar. 7, 1954, Glen Cove, N. Y. 6' 3" 193 lbs.

Year	W	L	PCT	ERA	G	IP	H	SO	BB	Sho	SV
1984	3	2	.600	3.48	36	54.1	47	43	26	0	1
1985	0	0	—	3.07	9	14.2	9	11	2	0	0
1986	0	1	.000	9.35	7	8.2	13	8	5	0	0
3 yrs.	3	3	.500	4.06	52	77.2	69	62	33	0	1

Brad Arnsberg
BRADLEY JAMES ARNSBERG BR TR
B. Aug. 20, 1963, Seattle, Wash. 6' 4" 205 lbs.

Year	W	L	PCT	ERA	G	IP	H	SO	BB	Sho	SV
1986	0	0	—	3.38	2	8	13	3	1	0	0
1987	1	3	.250	5.59	6	19.1	22	14	13	0	0
2 yrs.	1	3	.250	4.94	8	27.1	35	17	14	0	0

Luis Arroyo
LUIS ENRIQUE ARROYO BL TL
B. Feb. 18, 1927, Penuelas, Puerto Rico 5' 8½" 178 lbs.

Year	W	L	PCT	ERA	G	IP	H	SO	BB	Sho	SV
1960	5	1	.833	2.88	29	40.2	30	29	22	0	7
1961	15	5	.750	2.19	65	119	83	87	49	0	29
1962	1	3	.250	4.81	27	33.2	33	21	17	0	7
1963	0	1	.500	13.50	6	6	12	5	3	0	0
4 yrs.	22	10	.688	3.12	127	199.1	158	142	91	0	43
World Series											
1960	0	0	—	13.50	1	0.2	2	1	0	0	0
1961	1	0	1.000	2.25	2	4	4	3	2	0	0
2 yrs.	1	0	1.000	3.86	3	4.2	6	4	2	0	0

Paul Assenmacher
PAUL ANDRE ASSENMACHER BL TL
B. Dec. 10, 1960, Detroit, Mich. 6' 3" 195 lbs.

Year	W	L	PCT	ERA	G	IP	H	SO	BB	Sho	SV
1993	2	2	.500	3.12	26	17.1	10	11	9	0	0

Joe Ausanio
JOSEPH JOHN AUSANIO, JR. BR TR
B. Dec. 9, 1965, Kingston, N. Y. 6' 1" 205 lbs.

Year	W	L	PCT	ERA	G	IP	H	SO	BB	Sho	SV
1994	2	1	.667	5.17	13	15.2	16	15	6	0	0
1995	2	0	1.000	5.73	28	37.2	42	36	23	0	1
2 yrs.	4	1	.800	5.57	41	53.1	58	51	29	0	1

Stan Bahnsen
STANLEY RAYMOND BAHNSEN BR TR
B. Dec. 15, 1944, Council Bluffs, Iowa 6' 2" 185 lbs.

Year	W	L	PCT	ERA	G	IP	H	SO	BB	Sho	SV
1966	1	1	.500	3.52	4	23	15	16	7	0	1
1968	17	12	.586	2.05	37	267.1	216	162	68	1	0
1969	9	16	.360	3.83	40	220.2	222	130	90	2	1
1970	14	11	.560	3.32	36	233	227	116	75	2	0
1971	14	12	.538	3.35	36	242	221	110	72	3	0
5 yrs.	55	52	.514	3.10	153	986	901	534	312	8	2

Scott Bankhead
MICHAEL SCOTT BANKHEAD BR TR
B. Jul. 31, 1963, Raleigh, N. C. 5' 10" 175 lbs.

Year	W	L	PCT	ERA	G	IP	H	SO	BB	Sho	SV
1995	1	1	.500	6.00	20	39	44	20	16	0	0

Steve Barber

STEPHEN DAVID BARBER
B. Feb. 22, 1939, Takoma Park, Md.
BL TL — 6' 195 lbs.

Year	W	L	PCT	ERA	G	IP	H	SO	BB	Sho	SV
1967	6	9	.400	4.05	17	97.2	103	70	54	1	0
1968	6	5	.545	3.23	20	128.1	127	87	64	1	0
2 yrs.	12	14	.462	3.58	37	226	230	157	118	2	0

Cy Barger

EROS BOLIVAR BARGER
B. May 18, 1885, Jamestown, Ky.
D. Sep. 23, 1964, Columbia, Ky.
BL TR — 6' 160 lbs.

Year	W	L	PCT	ERA	G	IP	H	SO	BB	Sho	SV
1906	0	0	—	10.13	2	5.1	7	3	3	0	1
1907	0	0	—	3.00	1	6	10	0	1	0	0
2 yrs.	0	0	—	6.35	3	11.1	17	3	4	0	1

Frank Barnes

FRANK SAMUEL BARNES
B. Jan. 9, 1900, Dallas, Tex.
D. Sep. 27, 1967, Houston, Tex.
BL TL — 6' 2½" 195 lbs.

Year	W	L	PCT	ERA	G	IP	H	SO	BB	Sho	SV
1930	0	1	.000	8.03	2	12.1	13	2	13	0	0

Walter Beall

WALTER ESAU BEALL
B. Jul. 29, 1899, Washington, D. C.
D. Jan. 28, 1959, Suitland, Md.
BR TR — 5' 10" 178 lbs.

Year	W	L	PCT	ERA	G	IP	H	SO	BB	Sho	SV
1924	2	0	1.000	3.52	4	23	19	18	17	0	0
1925	0	1	1.000	12.71	8	11.1	11	8	19	0	0
1926	2	4	.333	3.53	20	81.2	71	56	68	0	0
1927	0	0	—	9.00	1	1	1	0	0	0	0
4 yrs.	4	5	.444	4.46	33	117	102	82	104	0	1

Jim Beattie

JAMES LOUIS BEATTIE
B. Jul. 4, 1954, Hampton, Va.
BR TR — 6' 5" 210 lbs.

Year	W	L	PCT	ERA	G	IP	H	SO	BB	Sho	SV
1978	6	9	.400	3.73	25	128	123	65	51	0	0
1979	3	6	.333	5.21	15	76	85	32	41	1	0
2 yrs.	9	15	.375	4.28	40	204	208	97	92	1	0
League Championship Series											
1978	1	0	1.000	1.69	1	5.1	2	3	5	0	0
World Series											
1978	1	0	1.000	2.00	1	9	9	8	4	0	0

Rich Beck

RICHARD HENRY BECK
B. Jan. 21, 1941, Pasco, Wash.
BB TR — 6' 3" 190 lbs.

Year	W	L	PCT	ERA	G	IP	H	SO	BB	Sho	SV
1965	2	1	.667	2.14	3	21	22	10	7	1	0

Fred Beene

FREDDY RAY BEENE
B. Nov. 24, 1942, Angleton, Tex.
BB TR — 5' 9" 155 lbs.

Year	W	L	PCT	ERA	G	IP	H	SO	BB	Sho	SV
1972	1	3	.250	2.33	29	58	55	37	24	0	3
1973	6	0	1.000	1.68	19	91	67	49	27	0	1
1974	0	0	—	2.70	6	10	9	10	2	0	1
3 yrs.	7	3	.700	1.98	54	159	131	96	53	0	5

Joe Beggs

JOSEPH STANLEY BEGGS
B. Nov. 4, 1910, Rankin, Pa.
D. Jul. 19, 1983, Indianapolis, Ind.
BR TR — 6' 1" 182 lbs.

Year	W	L	PCT	ERA	G	IP	H	SO	BB	Sho	SV
1938	3	2	.600	5.40	14	58.1	69	8	20	0	0

Walter Bernhardt

WALTER JACOB BERNHARDT
B. May 20, 1893, Pleasant Village, Pa.
D. Jul. 26, 1958, Watertown, N. Y.
BR TR — 6' 2" 195 lbs.

Year	W	L	PCT	ERA	G	IP	H	SO	BB	Sho	SV
1918	0	0	—	0.00	1	0.2	0	0	0	0	0

Bill Bevens

FLOYD CLIFFORD BEVENS
B. Oct. 21, 1916, Hubbard, Ore.
D. Oct. 26, 1991, Salem, Ore.
BR TR — 6' 3½" 210 lbs.

Year	W	L	PCT	ERA	G	IP	H	SO	BB	Sho	SV
1944	4	1	.800	2.68	8	43.2	44	16	13	0	0
1945	13	9	.591	3.67	29	184	174	76	68	2	0
1946	16	13	.552	2.23	31	249.2	213	120	78	3	0
1947	7	13	.350	3.82	28	165	167	77	77	1	0
4 yrs.	40	36	.526	3.08	96	642.1	598	289	236	6	0

Bill Bevens *continued*

World Series

Year	W	L	PCT	ERA	G	IP	H	SO	BB	Sho	SV
1947	0	1	.000	2.38	2	11.1	3	7	11	0	0

Harry Billiard

HARRY PREE BILLIARD
B. Nov. 11, 1883, Monroe, Ind.
D. Jun. 3, 1923, Wooster, Ohio
BR TR — 6' 190 lbs.

Year	W	L	PCT	ERA	G	IP	H	SO	BB	Sho	SV
1908	0	0	—	2.57	5	14	13	9	13	0	0

Doug Bird

JAMES DOUGLAS BIRD
B. Mar. 5, 1950, Corona, Calif.
BR TR — 6' 4" 180 lbs.

Year	W	L	PCT	ERA	G	IP	H	SO	BB	Sho	SV
1980	3	0	1.000	2.65	22	51	47	17	14	0	1
1981	5	1	.833	2.72	17	53	58	28	16	0	0
2 yrs.	8	1	.889	2.68	39	104	105	45	30	0	1

Ewell Blackwell

EWELL BLACKWELL
B. Oct. 23, 1922, Fresno, Calif.
D. Oct. 29, 1996, Hendersonville, N. C.
BR TR — 6' 6" 195 lbs.

Year	W	L	PCT	ERA	G	IP	H	SO	BB	Sho	SV
1952	1	0	1.000	0.56	5	16	12	7	12	0	1
1953	2	0	1.000	3.66	8	19.2	17	11	13	0	1
2 yrs.	3	0	1.000	2.27	13	35.2	29	18	25	0	2
World Series											
1952	0	0	—	7.20	1	5	4	4	3	0	0

Gil Blanco

GILBERT HENRY BLANCO
B. Dec. 15, 1945, Phoenix, Ariz.
BL TL — 6' 5" 205 lbs.

Year	W	L	PCT	ERA	G	IP	H	SO	BB	Sho	SV
1965	1	1	.500	3.98	17	20.1	16	14	12	0	0

Wade Blasingame

WADE ALLEN BLASINGAME
B. Nov. 22, 1943, Deming, N. M.
BL TL — 6' 1" 185 lbs.

Year	W	L	PCT	ERA	G	IP	H	SO	BB	Sho	SV
1972	0	1	.000	4.24	12	17	14	7	11	0	0

Steve Blateric

STEPHEN LAWRENCE BLATERIC
B. Mar. 20, 1944, Denver, Colo.
BR TR — 6' 3" 200 lbs.

Year	W	L	PCT	ERA	G	IP	H	SO	BB	Sho	SV
1972	0	0	—	0.00	1	4	2	4	0	0	0

Gary Blaylock

GARY NELSON BLAYLOCK
B. Oct. 11, 1931, Clarkton, Mo.
BR TR — 6' 196 lbs.

Year	W	L	PCT	ERA	G	IP	H	SO	BB	Sho	SV
1959	0	1	.000	3.51	15	25.2	30	20	15	0	0

Elmer Bliss

ELMER WARD BLISS
B. Mar. 9, 1875, Penfield, Pa.
D. Mar. 18, 1962, Bradford, Pa.
BL TR — 6' 180 lbs.

Year	W	L	PCT	ERA	G	IP	H	SO	BB	Sho	SV
1903	1	0	1.000	0.00	1	6	4	3	0	0	0

Brian Boehringer

BRIAN EDWARD BOEHRINGER
B. Jan. 8, 1969, St. Louis, Mo.
BB TR — 6' 2" 180 lbs.

Year	W	L	PCT	ERA	G	IP	H	SO	BB	Sho	SV
1995	0	3	.000	13.75	7	17.2	24	10	22	0	0
1996	2	4	.333	5.44	15	46.1	46	37	21	0	0
2 yrs.	2	7	.222	7.73	22	64	70	47	43	0	0
Divisional Playoffs											
1996	1	0	1.000	6.75	2	1.1	3	0	2	0	0
World Series											
1996	0	0	—	5.40	2	5	5	5	0	0	0

Ricky Bones

RICARDO BONES
B. Apr. 7, 1969, Salinas, Puerto Rico
BR TR — 5' 10" 175 lbs.

Year	W	L	PCT	ERA	G	IP	H	SO	BB	Sho	SV
1996	0	0	—	14.14	4	7	14	4	6	0	0

Ernie Bonham

ERNEST EDWARD BONHAM
B. Aug. 16, 1913, Ione, Calif.
D. Sep. 15, 1949, Pittsburgh, Pa.
BR TR — 6' 2" 215 lbs.

Year	W	L	PCT	ERA	G	IP	H	SO	BB	Sho	SV
1940	9	3	.750	1.90	12	99.1	83	37	13	3	0

Ernie Bonham *continued*

Year	W	L	PCT	ERA	G	IP	H	SO	BB	Sho	SV
1941	9	6	.600	2.98	23	126.2	118	43	31	1	2
1942	21	5	.808	2.27	28	226	199	71	24	6	0
1943	15	8	.652	2.27	28	225.2	197	71	52	4	1
1944	12	9	.571	2.99	26	213.2	228	54	41	1	0
1945	8	11	.421	3.29	23	180.2	186	42	22	0	0
1946	5	8	.385	3.70	18	104.2	97	30	23	2	3
7 yrs.	79	50	.612	2.73	158	1176.2	1108	348	206	17	6
World Series											
1941	1	0	1.000	1.00	1	9	4	2	2	0	0
1942	0	1	.000	4.09	2	11	9	3	3	0	0
1943	0	1	.000	4.50	1	8	6	9	3	0	0
3 yrs.	1	2	.333	3.21	4	28	19	14	8	0	0

Rich Bordi

RICHARD ALBERT BORDI BR TR
B. Apr. 18, 1959, San Francisco, Calif. 6' 7" 210 lbs.

Year	W	L	PCT	ERA	G	IP	H	SO	BB	Sho	SV
1985	6	8	.429	3.21	51	98	95	64	29	0	2
1987	3	1	.750	7.64	16	33	42	23	12	0	0
2 yrs.	9	9	.500	4.33	67	131	137	87	41	0	2

Hank Borowy

HENRY LUDWIG BOROWY BR TR
B. May 12, 1916, Bloomfield, N. J. 6' 175 lbs.

Year	W	L	PCT	ERA	G	IP	H	SO	BB	Sho	SV
1942	15	4	.789	2.52	25	178.1	157	85	66	4	1
1943	14	9	.609	2.82	29	217.1	195	113	72	3	0
1944	17	12	.586	2.64	35	252.2	224	107	88	3	2
1945	10	5	.667	3.13	18	132.1	107	35	58	1	0
4 yrs.	56	30	.651	2.74	107	780.2	683	340	284	11	3
World Series											
1942	0	0	—	18.00	1	3	6	1	3	0	0
1943	1	0	1.000	2.25	1	8	6	4	3	0	0
2 yrs.	1	0	1.000	6.55	2	11	12	5	6	0	0

Jim Bouton

JAMES ALAN BOUTON BR TR
B. Mar. 8, 1939, Newark, N. J. 6' 170 lbs.

Year	W	L	PCT	ERA	G	IP	H	SO	BB	Sho	SV
1962	7	7	.500	3.99	36	133	124	71	59	1	2
1963	21	7	.750	2.53	40	249.1	191	148	87	6	1
1964	18	13	.581	3.02	38	271.1	227	125	60	4	0
1965	4	15	.211	4.82	30	151.1	158	97	60	0	0
1966	3	8	.273	2.69	24	120.1	117	65	38	0	1
1967	1	0	1.000	4.67	17	44.1	47	31	18	0	0
1968	1	1	.500	3.68	12	44	49	24	9	0	0
7 yrs.	55	51	.519	3.36	197	1013.2	913	561	331	11	4
World Series											
1963	0	1	.000	1.29	1	7	4	4	5	0	0
1964	2	0	1.000	1.56	2	17.1	15	7	5	0	0
2 yrs.	2	1	.667	1.48	3	24.1	19	11	10	0	0

Neal Brady

CORNELIUS JOSEPH BRADY BR TR
B. Mar. 4, 1897, Covington, Ky. 6' ½" 197 lbs.
D. Jun. 19, 1947, Fort Mitchell, Ky.

Year	W	L	PCT	ERA	G	IP	H	SO	BB	Sho	SV
1915	0	0	—	3.12	2	8.2	9	6	7	0	0
1917	1	0	1.000	2.00	2	9	6	4	5	0	0
2 yrs.	1	0	1.000	2.55	4	17.2	15	10	12	0	0

Ralph Branca

RALPH THEODORE JOSEPH BRANCA BR TR
B. Jan. 6, 1926, Mt. Vernon, N. Y. 6' 3" 220 lbs.

Year	W	L	PCT	ERA	G	IP	H	SO	BB	Sho	SV
1954	1	0	1.000	2.84	5	12.2	9	7	13	0	0

Norm Branch

NORMAN DOWNS BRANCH BR TR
B. Mar. 22, 1915, Spokane, Wash. 6' 3" 200 lbs.
D. Nov. 21, 1971, Navasota, Tex.

Year	W	L	PCT	ERA	G	IP	H	SO	BB	Sho	SV
1941	5	1	.833	2.87	27	47	37	28	26	0	2
1942	0	1	.000	6.32	10	15.2	18	13	16	0	2
2 yrs.	5	2	.714	3.73	37	62.2	55	41	42	0	4

Garland Braxton

EDGAR GARLAND BRAXTON BB TL
B. Jun. 10, 1900, Snow Camp, N. C. 5' 11" 152 lbs.
D. Feb. 26, 1966, Norfolk, Va.

Year	W	L	PCT	ERA	G	IP	H	SO	BB	Sho	SV
1925	1	1	.500	6.52	3	19.1	26	11	5	0	0
1926	5	1	.833	2.67	37	67.1	71	30	19	0	2
2 yrs.	6	2	.750	3.53	40	86.2	97	41	24	0	2

Don Brennan

JAMES DONALD BRENNAN BR TR
B. Dec. 2, 1903, Augusta, Me. 6' 210 lbs.
D. Apr. 26, 1953, Boston, Mass.

Year	W	L	PCT	ERA	G	IP	H	SO	BB	Sho	SV
1933	5	1	.833	4.98	18	85	92	46	47	0	3

Jim Brenneman

JAMES LEROY BRENNEMAN BR TR
B. Feb. 13, 1941, San Diego, Calif. 6' 2" 180 lbs.

Year	W	L	PCT	ERA	G	IP	H	SO	BB	Sho	SV
1965	0	0	—	18.00	3	2	5	2	3	0	0

Ken Brett

KENNETH ALVEN BRETT BL TL
B. Sep. 18, 1948, Brooklyn, N. Y. 6' 190 lbs.

Year	W	L	PCT	ERA	G	IP	H	SO	BB	Sho	SV
1976	0	0	—	0.00	2	2.1	1	1	0	0	1

Marv Breuer

MARVIN HOWARD BREUER BR TR
B. Apr. 29, 1914, Rolla, Mo. 6' 2" 185 lbs.

Year	W	L	PCT	ERA	G	IP	H	SO	BB	Sho	SV
1939	0	0	—	9.00	1	1	2	0	1	0	0
1940	8	9	.471	4.55	27	164	175	71	61	0	0
1941	9	7	.563	4.09	26	141	131	77	49	1	2
1942	8	9	.471	3.07	27	164.1	157	72	37	0	1
1943	0	1	.000	8.36	5	14	22	6	6	0	0
5 yrs.	25	26	.490	4.03	86	484.1	487	226	154	1	3
World Series											
1941	0	0	—	0.00	1	3	3	2	1	0	0
1942	0	0	—	—	1	0	2	0	0	0	0
2 yrs.	0	0	—	0.00	2	3	5	2	1	0	0

Billy Brewer

WILLIAM ROBERT BREWER BL TL
B. Apr. 15, 1968, Fort Worth, Tex. 6' 1" 175 lbs.

Year	W	L	PCT	ERA	G	IP	H	SO	BB	Sho	SV
1996	1	0	1.000	9.53	4	5.2	7	8	8	0	0

Marshall Bridges

MARSHALL BRIDGES BB TL
B. Jun. 2, 1931, Jackson, Miss. 6' 1" 165 lbs.
D. Sep. 3, 1990, Jackson, Miss.

Year	W	L	PCT	ERA	G	IP	H	SO	BB	Sho	SV
1962	8	4	.667	3.14	52	71.2	49	66	48	0	18
1963	2	0	1.000	3.82	23	33	27	35	30	0	1
2 yrs.	10	4	.714	3.35	75	104.2	76	101	78	0	19
World Series											
1962	0	0	—	4.91	2	3.2	4	3	2	0	0

Johnny Broaca

JOHN JOSEPH BROACA BR TR
B. Oct. 3, 1909, Lawrence, Mass. 5' 11" 190 lbs.
D. May 16, 1985, Lawrence, Mass.

Year	W	L	PCT	ERA	G	IP	H	SO	BB	Sho	SV
1934	12	9	.571	4.16	26	177.1	203	74	65	1	0
1935	15	7	.682	3.58	29	201	199	78	79	2	0
1936	12	7	.632	4.24	37	206	235	84	66	1	3
1937	1	4	.200	4.70	7	44	58	9	17	0	0
4 yrs.	40	27	.597	4.04	99	628.1	695	245	227	4	3

Lew Brockett

LEWIS ALBERT BROCKETT BR TR
B. Jul. 23, 1880, Brownsville, Ill. 5' 10½" 168 lbs.
D. Sep. 19, 1960, Norris City, Ill.

Year	W	L	PCT	ERA	G	IP	H	SO	BB	Sho	SV
1907	1	2	.333	6.22	8	46.1	58	13	26	0	0
1909	10	8	.556	2.37	26	152	148	70	59	3	1
1911	2	4	.333	4.66	16	75.1	73	25	39	0	0
3 yrs.	13	14	.481	3.65	50	273.2	279	108	124	3	1

Jim Bronstad

JAMES WARREN BRONSTAD BR TR
B. Jun. 22, 1936, Fort Worth, Tex. 6' 3" 196 lbs.

Year	W	L	PCT	ERA	G	IP	H	SO	BB	Sho	SV
1959	0	3	.000	5.22	16	29.1	34	14	13	0	2

Year	W	L	PCT	ERA	G	IP	H	SO	BB	Sho	SV

Boardwalk Brown

CARROLL WILLIAM BROWN BR TR
B. Feb. 20, 1887, Woodbury, N. J. 6' 1½" 178 lbs.
D. Feb. 8, 1977, Burlington, N. J.

Year	W	L	PCT	ERA	G	IP	H	SO	BB	Sho	SV
1914	5	5	.500	3.24	20	122.1	123	57	42	0	1
1915	2	6	.250	4.10	19	96.2	95	34	47	0	1
2 yrs.	7	11	.389	3.62	39	219	218	91	89	0	2

Curt Brown

CURTIS STEVEN BROWN BR TR
B. Jan. 15, 1960, Ft. Lauderdale, Fla. 6' 5" 200 lbs.

Year	W	L	PCT	ERA	G	IP	H	SO	BB	Sho	SV
1984	1	1	.500	2.70	13	16.2	18	10	4	0	0

Hal Brown

HECTOR HAROLD BROWN BR TR
B. Dec. 11, 1924, Greensboro, N. C. 6' 2" 180 lbs.

Year	W	L	PCT	ERA	G	IP	H	SO	BB	Sho	SV
1962	0	1	.000	6.75	2	6.2	9	2	2	0	0

Jumbo Brown

WALTER GEORGE BROWN BR TR
B. Apr. 30, 1907, Greene, R. I. 6' 4" 295 lbs.
D. Oct. 2, 1966, Freeport, N. Y.

Year	W	L	PCT	ERA	G	IP	H	SO	BB	Sho	SV
1932	5	2	.714	4.45	19	56.2	58	31	30	1	1
1933	7	5	.583	5.23	21	74	78	55	52	0	0
1935	6	5	.545	3.61	20	87.1	94	41	37	0	0
1936	1	4	.200	5.91	20	64	93	19	29	0	1
4 yrs.	19	16	.543	4.72	80	282	323	146	148	1	2

Jess Buckles

JESSE ROBERT BUCKLES BL TL
B. May 20, 1890, LaVerne, Calif. 6' 2½" 205 lbs.
D. Aug. 2, 1975, Westminster, Calif.

Year	W	L	PCT	ERA	G	IP	H	SO	BB	Sho	SV
1916	0	0	—	2.25	2	4	3	2	1	0	0

Bill Burbach

WILLIAM DAVID BURBACH BR TR
B. Aug. 22, 1947, Dickeyville, Wis. 6' 4" 215 lbs.

Year	W	L	PCT	ERA	G	IP	H	SO	BB	Sho	SV
1969	6	8	.429	3.65	31	140.2	112	82	102	1	0
1970	0	2	.000	10.06	4	17	23	10	9	0	0
1971	0	1	.000	12.00	2	3	6	3	5	0	0
3 yrs.	6	11	.353	4.48	37	160.2	141	95	116	1	0

Lew Burdette

SELVA LEWIS BURDETTE BR TR
B. Nov. 22, 1926, Nitro, W. Va. 6' 2" 180 lbs.

Year	W	L	PCT	ERA	G	IP	H	SO	BB	Sho	SV
1950	0	0	—	6.75	2	1.1	3	0	0	0	0

Tim Burke

TIMOTHY PHILIP BURKE BR TR
B. Feb. 19, 1959, Omaha, Neb. 6' 3" 205 lbs.

Year	W	L	PCT	ERA	G	IP	H	SO	BB	Sho	SV
1992	2	2	.500	3.25	23	27.2	26	8	15	0	0

Ray Burris

BERTRAM RAY BURRIS BR TR
B. Aug. 22, 1950, Idabel, Okla. 6' 5" 200 lbs.

Year	W	L	PCT	ERA	G	IP	H	SO	BB	Sho	SV
1979	1	3	.250	6.11	15	28	40	19	10	0	0

Joe Bush

LESLIE AMBROSE BUSH BR TR
B. Nov. 27, 1892, Brainerd, Minn. 5' 9" 173 lbs.
D. Nov. 1, 1974, Ft. Lauderdale, Fla.

Year	W	L	PCT	ERA	G	IP	H	SO	BB	Sho	SV
1922	26	7	.788	3.31	39	255.1	240	92	85	0	3
1923	19	15	.559	3.43	37	275.2	263	125	117	3	0
1924	17	16	.515	3.57	39	252	262	80	109	3	1
3 yrs.	62	38	.620	3.44	115	783	765	297	311	6	4
World Series											
1922	0	2	.000	4.80	2	15	21	6	5	0	0
1923	1	1	.500	1.08	3	16.2	7	5	4	0	0
2 yrs.	1	3	.250	2.84	5	31.2	28	11	9	0	0

Tom Buskey

THOMAS WILLIAM BUSKEY BR TR
B. Feb. 20, 1947, Harrisburg, Pa. 6' 3" 200 lbs.

Year	W	L	PCT	ERA	G	IP	H	SO	BB	Sho	SV
1973	0	1	.000	5.40	8	16.2	18	8	4	0	1

Tom Buskey *continued*

Year	W	L	PCT	ERA	G	IP	H	SO	BB	Sho	SV
1974	0	1	.000	6.35	4	5.2	10	3	3	0	1
2 yrs.	0	2	.000	5.64	12	22.1	28	11	7	0	2

Ralph Buxton

RALPH STANLEY BUXTON BR TR
B. Jun. 7, 1911, Wayburn, Sask., Canada 5' 11½" 163 lbs.
D. Jan. 6, 1988, San Leandro, Calif.

Year	W	L	PCT	ERA	G	IP	H	SO	BB	Sho	SV
1949	0	1	.000	4.05	14	26.2	22	14	16	0	2

Harry Byrd

HARRY GLADWIN BYRD BR TR
B. Feb. 3, 1925, Darlington, S. C. 6' 1" 188 lbs.
D. May 14, 1985, Darlington, S. C.

Year	W	L	PCT	ERA	G	IP	H	SO	BB	Sho	SV
1954	9	7	.563	2.99	25	132.1	131	52	43	1	0

Tommy Byrne

THOMAS JOSEPH BYRNE BL TL
B. Dec. 31, 1919, Baltimore, Md. 6' 1" 182 lbs.

Year	W	L	PCT	ERA	G	IP	H	SO	BB	Sho	SV
1943	2	1	.667	6.54	11	31.2	28	22	35	0	0
1946	0	1	.000	5.79	4	9.1	7	5	8	0	0
1947	0	0	—	4.15	4	4.1	5	2	6	0	0
1948	8	5	.615	3.30	31	133.2	79	93	101	1	2
1949	15	7	.682	3.72	32	196	125	129	179	3	0
1950	15	9	.625	4.74	31	203.1	188	118	160	2	0
1951	2	1	.667	6.86	9	21	16	14	36	0	0
1954	3	2	.600	2.70	5	40	36	24	19	1	0
1955	16	5	.762	3.15	27	160	137	76	87	3	2
1956	7	3	.700	3.36	37	109.2	108	52	72	0	6
1957	4	6	.400	4.36	30	84.2	70	57	60	0	2
11 yrs.	72	40	.643	3.93	221	993.2	799	592	763	10	12
World Series											
1949	0	0	—	2.70	1	3.1	2	1	2	0	0
1955	1	1	.500	1.88	2	14.1	8	8	8	0	0
1956	0	0	—	0.00	1	0.1	1	1	0	0	0
1957	0	0	—	5.40	2	3.1	1	1	2	0	0
4 yrs.	1	1	.500	2.53	6	21.1	12	11	12	0	0

Marty Bystrom

MARTIN EUGENE BYSTROM BR TR
B. Jul. 26, 1958, Coral Gables, Fla. 6' 5" 200 lbs.

Year	W	L	PCT	ERA	G	IP	H	SO	BB	Sho	SV
1984	2	2	.500	2.97	7	39.1	34	24	13	0	0
1985	3	2	.600	5.71	8	41	44	16	19	0	0
2 yrs.	5	4	.556	4.37	15	80.1	78	40	32	0	0

Greg Cadaret

GREGORY JAMES CADARET BL TL
B. Feb. 27, 1962, Detroit, Mich. 6' 3" 200 lbs.

Year	W	L	PCT	ERA	G	IP	H	SO	BB	Sho	SV
1989	5	5	.500	4.58	20	92.1	109	66	38	1	0
1990	5	4	.556	4.15	54	121.1	120	80	64	0	3
1991	8	6	.571	3.62	68	121.2	110	105	59	0	3
1992	4	8	.333	4.25	46	103.2	104	73	74	1	1
4 yrs.	22	23	.489	4.12	188	439	443	324	235	2	7

Charlie Caldwell

CHARLES WILLIAM CALDWELL BR TR
B. Aug. 2, 1901, Bristol, Va. 5' 10" 180 lbs.
D. Nov. 1, 1957, Princeton, N. J.

Year	W	L	PCT	ERA	G	IP	H	SO	BB	Sho	SV
1925	0	0	—	16.88	3	2.2	7	1	3	0	0

Ray Caldwell

RAYMOND BENJAMIN CALDWELL BL TR
B. Apr. 26, 1888, Croydon, Pa. 6' 2" 190 lbs.
D. Aug. 17, 1967, Salamanca, N. Y.

Year	W	L	PCT	ERA	G	IP	H	SO	BB	Sho	SV
1910	1	0	1.000	3.72	6	19.1	19	17	9	0	1
1911	14	14	.500	3.35	41	255	240	145	79	1	1
1912	8	16	.333	4.47	30	183.1	196	95	67	3	0
1913	9	8	.529	2.41	27	164.1	131	87	60	2	1
1914	17	9	.654	1.94	31	213	153	92	51	5	1
1915	19	16	.543	2.89	36	305	266	130	107	3	0
1916	5	12	.294	2.99	21	165.2	142	76	65	1	0

Ray Caldwell *continued*

Year	W	L	PCT	ERA	G	IP	H	SO	BB	Sho	SV
1917	13	16	.448	2.86	32	236	199	102	76	1	0
1918	9	8	.529	3.06	24	176.2	173	59	62	1	1
9 yrs.	95	99	.490	3.00	248	1718.1	1519	803	576	17	5

Archie Campbell

ARCHIBALD STEWART CAMPBELL BR TR
B. Oct. 20, 1903, Maplewood, N. J.   6' 1" 180 lbs.
D. Dec. 22, 1989, Sparks, Nev.

Year	W	L	PCT	ERA	G	IP	H	SO	BB	Sho	SV
1928	0	1	.000	5.25	13	24	30	9	11	0	2

John Candelaria

JOHN ROBERT CANDELARIA BR TL
B. Nov. 6, 1953, New York, N. Y.   6' 7" 205 lbs.

Year	W	L	PCT	ERA	G	IP	H	SO	BB	Sho	SV
1988	13	7	.650	3.38	25	157	150	121	23	2	1
1989	3	3	.500	5.14	10	49	49	37	12	0	0
2 yrs.	16	10	.615	3.80	35	206	199	158	35	2	1

Mike Cantwell

MICHAEL JOSEPH CANTWELL BL TL
B. Jan. 15, 1896, Washington, D. C.   6' 160 lbs.
D. Jan. 5, 1953, Oteen, N. C.

Year	W	L	PCT	ERA	G	IP	H	SO	BB	Sho	SV
1916	0	0	—	0.00	1	2	0	2	0	0	0

Dick Carroll

RICHARD THOMAS CARROLL BR TR
B. Jul. 21, 1884, Cleveland, Ohio   6' 2" lbs.
D. Nov. 22, 1945, Cleveland, Ohio

Year	W	L	PCT	ERA	G	IP	H	SO	BB	Sho	SV
1909	0	0	—	3.60	2	5	7	1	1	0	0

Ownie Carroll

OWEN THOMAS CARROLL BR TR
B. Nov. 11, 1902, Kearny, N. J.   5' 10½" 165 lbs.
D. Jun. 8, 1975, Orange, N. J.

Year	W	L	PCT	ERA	G	IP	H	SO	BB	Sho	SV
1930	0	1	.000	6.61	10	32.2	49	8	18	0	0

Chuck Cary

CHARLES DOUGLAS CARY BL TL
B. Mar. 3, 1960, Whittier, Calif.   6' 4" 210 lbs.

Year	W	L	PCT	ERA	G	IP	H	SO	BB	Sho	SV
1989	4	4	.500	3.26	22	99.1	78	79	29	0	0
1990	6	12	.333	4.19	28	156.2	155	134	55	0	0
1991	1	6	.143	5.91	10	53.1	61	34	32	0	0
3 yrs.	11	22	.333	4.19	60	309.1	294	247	116	0	0

Hugh Casey

HUGH THOMAS CASEY BR TR
B. Oct. 14, 1913, Atlanta, Ga.   6' 1" 207 lbs.
D. Jul. 3, 1951, Atlanta, Ga.

Year	W	L	PCT	ERA	G	IP	H	SO	BB	Sho	SV
1949	1	0	1.000	8.22	4	7.2	11	5	8	0	0

Roy Castleton

ROYAL EUGENE CASTLETON BL TL
B. Jul. 26, 1885, Salt Lake City, Utah 5' 11" 167 lbs.
D. Jun. 24, 1967, Los Angeles, Calif.

Year	W	L	PCT	ERA	G	IP	H	SO	BB	Sho	SV
1907	1	1	.500	2.81	3	16	11	3	3	0	0

Bill Castro

WILLIAM RADHAMES CASTRO BR TR
B. Dec. 13, 1953, Santiago, Dominican Republic 5' 11" 170 lbs.

Year	W	L	PCT	ERA	G	IP	H	SO	BB	Sho	SV
1981	1	1	.500	3.79	11	19	26	4	5	0	0

Rick Cerone

RICHARD ALDO CERONE BR TR
B. May 19, 1954, Newark, N. J.   5' 11" 192 lbs.

Year	W	L	PCT	ERA	G	IP	H	SO	BB	Sho	SV
1987	0	0	—	0.00	2	2	0	1	1	0	0

Spud Chandler

SPURGEON FERDINAND CHANDLER BR TR
B. Sep. 12, 1907, Commerce, Ga.   6' 181 lbs.
D. Jan. 9, 1990, South Pasadena, Fla.

Year	W	L	PCT	ERA	G	IP	H	SO	BB	Sho	SV
1937	7	4	.636	2.84	12	82.1	79	31	20	2	0

Spud Chandler *continued*

Year	W	L	PCT	ERA	G	IP	H	SO	BB	Sho	SV
1938	14	5	.737	4.03	23	172	183	36	47	2	0
1939	3	0	1.000	2.84	11	19	26	4	9	0	0
1940	8	7	.533	4.60	27	172	184	56	60	1	0
1941	10	4	.714	3.19	28	163.2	146	60	60	4	4
1942	16	5	.762	2.38	24	200.2	176	74	74	3	0
1943	20	4	.833	1.64	30	253	197	134	54	5	0
1944	0	0		4.50	1	6	6	1	1	0	0
1945	2	1	.667	4.65	4	31	30	12	7	1	0
1946	20	8	.714	2.10	34	257.1	200	138	90	6	2
1947	9	5	.643	2.46	17	128	100	68	41	2	0
11 yrs.	109	43	.717	2.84	211	1485	1327	614	463	26	6
World Series											
1941	0	1	.000	3.60	1	5	4	2	2	0	0
1942	0	1	.000	1.08	2	8.1	5	3	1	0	1
1943	2	0	1.000	0.50	2	18	17	10	3	1	0
1947	0	0	—	9.00	1	2	2	1	3	0	0
4 yrs.	2	2	.500	1.62	6	33.1	28	16	9	1	1

Darrin Chapin

DARRIN JOHN CHAPIN BR TR
B. Feb. 1, 1966, Warren, Ohio   6' 170 lbs.

Year	W	L	PCT	ERA	G	IP	H	SO	BB	Sho	SV
1991	0	1	.000	5.06	3	5.1	3	5	6	0	0

Hal Chase

HAROLD HOMER CHASE BR TL
B. Feb. 13, 1883, Los Gatos, Calif.   6' 175 lbs.
D. May 18, 1947, Colusa, Calif.

Year	W	L	PCT	ERA	G	IP	H	SO	BB	Sho	SV
1908	0	0	—	0.00	1	0.1	0	0	0	0	0

Jack Chesbro

JOHN DWIGHT CHESBRO BR TR
B. Jun. 5, 1874, North Adams, Mass.   5' 9" 180 lbs.
D. Nov. 6, 1931, Conway, Mass.
Hall of Fame 1946

Year	W	L	PCT	ERA	G	IP	H	SO	BB	Sho	SV
1903	21	15	.583	2.77	40	324.2	300	147	74	1	0
1904	41	12	.774	1.82	55	454.2	338	239	88	6	0
1905	19	15	.559	2.20	41	303.1	262	156	71	3	0
1906	23	17	.575	2.96	49	325	314	152	75	4	1
1907	10	10	.500	2.53	30	206	192	78	46	1	0
1908	14	20	.412	2.93	45	289	271	124	67	3	1
1909	0	4	.000	6.34	9	49.2	70	17	13	0	0
7 yrs.	128	93	.579	2.58	269	1952.1	1747	913	434	18	2

Clay Christiansen

CLAY C. CHRISTIANSEN BR TR
B. Jun. 28, 1958, Wichita, Kans.   6' 5" 215 lbs.

Year	W	L	PCT	ERA	G	IP	H	SO	BB	Sho	SV
1984	2	4	.333	6.05	24	38.2	50	27	12	0	2

Al Cicotte

ALVA WARREN CICOTTE BR TR
B. Dec. 23, 1929, Melvindale, Mich.   6' 3" 185 lbs.
D. Nov. 29, 1982, Westland, Mich.

Year	W	L	PCT	ERA	G	IP	H	SO	BB	Sho	SV
1957	2	2	.500	3.03	20	65.1	57	36	30	0	2

George Clark

GEORGE MYRON CLARK BR TL
B. May 19, 1891, Smithland, Iowa   6' 190 lbs.
D. Nov. 14, 1940, Sioux City, Iowa

Year	W	L	PCT	ERA	G	IP	H	SO	BB	Sho	SV
1913	0	1	.000	9.00	11	19	22	5	19	0	0

Walter Clarkson

WALTER HAMILTON CLARKSON BR TR
B. Nov. 3, 1878, Cambridge, Mass.   5' 10" 150 lbs.
D. Oct. 10, 1946, Cambridge, Mass.

Year	W	L	PCT	ERA	G	IP	H	SO	BB	Sho	SV
1904	1	2	.333	5.02	13	66.1	63	43	25	0	1
1905	3	3	.500	3.91	9	46	40	35	13	0	0
1906	9	4	.692	2.32	32	151	135	64	55	3	0
1907	1	1	.500	6.23	5	17.1	19	3	8	0	0
4 yrs.	14	10	.583	3.46	59	280.2	257	145	101	3	1

Ken Clay

KENNETH EARL CLAY   BR TR
B. Apr. 6, 1954, Lynchburg, Va.   6' 3" 185 lbs.

Year	W	L	PCT	ERA	G	IP	H	SO	BB	Sho	SV
1977	2	3	.400	4.34	21	56	53	20	24	0	1
1978	3	4	.429	4.28	28	75.2	89	32	21	0	0
1979	1	7	.125	5.42	32	78	88	28	25	0	2
3 yrs.	6	14	.300	4.72	81	209.2	230	80	70	0	3
League Championship Series											
1978	0	0	—	0.00	1	3.2	0	2	3	0	1
World Series											
1977	0	0	—	2.45	2	3.2	2	0	1	0	0
1978	0	0	—	11.57	1	2.1	4	2	2	0	0
2 yrs.	0	0	—	6.00	3	6	6	2	3	0	0

Pat Clements

PATRICK BRIAN CLEMENTS   BR TL
B. Feb. 2, 1962, McCloud, Calif.   6' 175 lbs.

Year	W	L	PCT	ERA	G	IP	H	SO	BB	Sho	SV
1987	3	3	.500	4.95	55	80	91	36	30	0	7
1988	0	0	—	6.48	6	8.1	12	3	4	0	0
2 yrs.	3	3	.500	5.09	61	88.1	103	39	34	0	7

Tex Clevenger

TRUMAN EUGENE CLEVENGER   BR TR
B. Jul. 9, 1932, Visalia, Calif.   6' 1" 180 lbs.

Year	W	L	PCT	ERA	G	IP	H	SO	BB	Sho	SV
1961	1	1	.500	4.83	21	31.2	35	14	21	0	0
1962	2	0	1.000	2.84	21	38	36	11	17	0	0
2 yrs.	3	1	.750	3.75	42	69.2	71	25	38	0	0

Al Closter

ALAN EDWARD CLOSTER   BL TL
B. Jun. 15, 1943, Creighton, Neb.   6' 2" 190 lbs.

Year	W	L	PCT	ERA	G	IP	H	SO	BB	Sho	SV
1971	2	2	.500	5.14	14	28	33	22	13	0	0
1972	0	0	—	13.50	2	2	2	2	4	0	0
2 yrs.	2	2	.500	5.70	16	30	35	24	17	0	0

Andy Coakley

ANDREW JAMES COAKLEY   BL TR
B. Nov. 20, 1882, Providence, R. I.   6' 165 lbs.
D. Sep. 27, 1963, New York, N. Y.

Year	W	L	PCT	ERA	G	IP	H	SO	BB	Sho	SV
1911	0	1	.000	5.40	2	11.2	20	4	2	0	0

Jim Coates

JAMES ALTON COATES   BR TR
B. Aug. 4, 1932, Farnham, Va.   6' 4" 192 lbs.

Year	W	L	PCT	ERA	G	IP	H	SO	BB	Sho	SV
1956	0	0	—	13.50	2	2	1	0	4	0	0
1959	6	1	.857	2.87	37	100.1	89	64	36	0	3
1960	13	3	.813	4.28	35	149.1	139	73	66	2	1
1961	11	5	.688	3.44	43	141.1	128	80	53	1	5
1962	7	6	.538	4.44	50	117.2	119	67	50	0	6
5 yrs.	37	15	.712	3.84	167	510.2	476	284	209	3	15
World Series											
1960	0	0	—	5.68	3	6.1	6	3	1	0	0
1961	0	0	—	0.00	1	4	1	2	1	0	1
1962	0	1	.000	6.75	2	2.2	1	3	1	0	0
3 yrs.	0	1	.000	4.15	6	13	8	8	3	0	1

Rocky Colavito

ROCCO DOMENICO COLAVITO   BR TR
B. Aug. 10, 1933, New York, N. Y.   6' 3" 190 lbs.

Year	W	L	PCT	ERA	G	IP	H	SO	BB	Sho	SV
1968	1	0	1.000	0.00	1	2.2	1	1	2	0	0

King Cole

LEONARD LESLIE COLE   BR TR
B. Apr. 15, 1886, Toledo, Iowa   6' 1" 170 lbs.
D. Jan. 6, 1916, Bay City, Mich.

Year	W	L	PCT	ERA	G	IP	H	SO	BB	Sho	SV
1914	11	9	.550	3.30	33	141.2	151	43	51	2	0
1915	3	3	.500	3.18	10	51	41	19	22	0	1
2 yrs.	14	12	.538	3.27	43	192.2	192	62	73	2	1

Rip Coleman

WALTER GARY COLEMAN   BL TL
B. Jul. 31, 1931, Troy, N. Y.   6' 2" 185 lbs.

Year	W	L	PCT	ERA	G	IP	H	SO	BB	Sho	SV
1955	2	1	.667	5.28	10	29	40	15	16	0	1
1956	3	5	.375	3.67	29	88.1	97	42	42	0	2
2 yrs.	5	6	.455	4.07	39	117.1	137	57	58	0	3

Rip Coleman *continued*

Year	W	L	PCT	ERA	G	IP	H	SO	BB	Sho	SV
World Series											
1955	0	0	—	9.00	1	1	5	1	0	0	0

Rip Collins

HARRY WARREN COLLINS   BR TR
B. Feb. 26, 1896, Weatherford, Tex.   6' 1" 205 lbs.
D. May 27, 1968, Bryan, Tex.

Year	W	L	PCT	ERA	G	IP	H	SO	BB	Sho	SV
1920	14	8	.636	3.17	36	187.1	171	66	79	3	1
1921	11	5	.688	5.44	28	137.1	158	64	78	2	0
2 yrs.	25	13	.658	4.13	64	324.2	329	130	157	5	1
World Series											
1921	0	0	—	54.00	1	0.2	4	0	1	0	0

Loyd Colson

LOYD ALBERT COLSON   BR TR
B. Nov. 4, 1947, Wellington, Tex.   6' 1" 190 lbs.

Year	W	L	PCT	ERA	G	IP	H	SO	BB	Sho	SV
1970	0	0	—	4.50	1	2	3	3	0	0	0

David Cone

DAVID BRIAN CONE   BL TR
B. Jan. 2, 1963, Kansas City, Mo.   6' 1" 180 lbs.

Year	W	L	PCT	ERA	G	IP	H	SO	BB	Sho	SV
1995	9	2	.818	3.82	13	99	82	89	47	0	0
1996	7	2	.778	2.88	11	72	50	71	34	0	0
2 yrs.	16	4	.800	3.42	24	171	132	160	81	0	0
Divisional Playoffs											
1995	1	0	1.000	4.60	2	15.2	15	14	9	0	0
1996	0	1	.000	9.00	1	6	8	8	2	0	0
2 yrs.	1	1	.500	5.82	3	21.2	23	22	11	0	0
League Championship Series											
1996	0	0	—	3.00	1	6	5	5	5	0	0
World Series											
1996	1	0	1.000	1.50	1	6	4	3	4	0	0

Andy Cook

ANDREW BERNARD COOK   BR TR
B. Aug. 30, 1967, Memphis, Tenn.   6' 5" 205 lbs.

Year	W	L	PCT	ERA	G	IP	H	SO	BB	Sho	SV
1993	0	1	.000	5.06	4	5.1	4	4	7	0	0

Don Cooper

DONALD JAMES COOPER   BR TR
B. Feb. 15, 1956, New York, N. Y.   6' 1" 185 lbs.

Year	W	L	PCT	ERA	G	IP	H	SO	BB	Sho	SV
1985	0	0	—	5.40	7	10	12	4	3	0	0

Guy Cooper

GUY EVANS COOPER   BB TR
B. Jan. 28, 1893, Rome, Ga.   6' 1" 185 lbs.
D. Aug. 2, 1951, Santa Monica, Calif.

Year	W	L	PCT	ERA	G	IP	H	SO	BB	Sho	SV
1914	0	0	—	9.00	1	3	3	3	2	0	0

Ensign Cottrell

ENSIGN STOVER COTTRELL   BL TL
B. Aug. 29, 1888, Hoosick Falls, N. Y.   5' 9½" 173 lbs.
D. Feb. 27, 1947, Syracuse, N. Y.

Year	W	L	PCT	ERA	G	IP	H	SO	BB	Sho	SV
1915	0	1	.000	3.38	7	21.1	29	7	7	0	0

Stan Coveleski

STANLEY ANTHONY COVELESKI   BR TR
B. Jul. 13, 1889, Shamokin, Pa.   5' 11" 166 lbs.
D. Mar. 20, 1984, South Bend, Ind.
Hall of Fame 1969

Year	W	L	PCT	ERA	G	IP	H	SO	BB	Sho	SV
1928	5	1	.833	5.74	12	58	72	5	20	0	0

Joe Cowley

JOSEPH ALAN COWLEY   BR TR
B. Aug. 15, 1958, Lexington, Ky.   6' 5" 205 lbs.

Year	W	L	PCT	ERA	G	IP	H	SO	BB	Sho	SV
1984	9	2	.818	3.56	16	83.1	75	71	31	1	0
1985	12	6	.667	3.95	30	159.2	132	97	85	0	0
2 yrs.	21	8	.724	3.81	46	243	207	168	116	1	0

Casey Cox

JOSEPH CASEY COX   BR TR
B. Jul. 3, 1941, Long Beach, Calif.   6' 5" 200 lbs.

Year	W	L	PCT	ERA	G	IP	H	SO	BB	Sho	SV
1972	0	1	.000	4.63	5	11.2	13	4	3	0	0

Year	W	L	PCT	ERA	G	IP	H	SO	BB	Sho	SV

Casey Cox *continued*

Year	W	L	PCT	ERA	G	IP	H	SO	BB	Sho	SV
1973	0	0	—	6.00	1	3	5	0	1	0	0
2 yrs.	0	1	.000	4.91	6	14.2	18	4	4	0	0

Jack Cullen

JOHN PATRICK CULLEN BR TR
B. Oct. 6, 1939, Newark, N. J. 5' 11" 170 lbs.

Year	W	L	PCT	ERA	G	IP	H	SO	BB	Sho	SV
1962	0	0	—	0.00	2	3	2	2	2	0	1
1965	3	4	.429	3.05	12	59	59	25	21	1	0
1966	1	0	1.000	3.97	5	11.1	11	7	5	0	0
3 yrs.	4	4	.500	3.07	19	73.1	72	34	28	1	1

Nick Cullop

NORMAN ANDREW CULLOP BL TL
B. Sep. 17, 1887, Chilhowie, Va. 5' 11½" 172 lbs.
D. Apr. 15, 1961, Tazewell, Va.

Year	W	L	PCT	ERA	G	IP	H	SO	BB	Sho	SV
1916	13	6	.684	2.05	28	167	151	77	32	0	1
1917	5	9	.357	3.32	30	146.1	161	27	31	2	1
2 yrs.	18	15	.545	2.64	58	313.1	312	104	63	2	2

John Cumberland

JOHN SHELDON CUMBERLAND BR TL
B. May 10, 1947, Westbrook, Me. 6' 185 lbs.

Year	W	L	PCT	ERA	G	IP	H	SO	BB	Sho	SV
1968	0	0	—	9.00	1	2	3	1	1	0	0
1969	0	0	—	4.50	2	4	3	0	4	0	0
1970	3	4	.429	3.94	15	64	62	38	15	0	0
3 yrs.	3	4	.429	4.11	18	70	68	39	20	0	0

Bud Daley

LEAVITT LEO DALEY BL TL
B. Oct. 7, 1932, Orange, Calif. 6' 1" 185 lbs.

Year	W	L	PCT	ERA	G	IP	H	SO	BB	Sho	SV
1961	8	9	.471	3.96	23	129.2	127	83	51	0	0
1962	7	5	.583	3.59	43	105.1	105	55	21	0	4
1963	0	0	—	0.00	1	1	2	0	0	0	1
1964	3	2	.600	4.63	13	35	37	16	25	0	1
4 yrs.	18	16	.529	3.89	80	271	271	154	97	0	6
World Series											
1961	1	0	1.000	0.00	2	7	5	3	0	0	0
1962	0	0	—	0.00	1	1	1	0	1	0	0
2 yrs.	1	0	1.000	0.00	3	8	6	3	1	0	0

Bobby Davidson

ROBERT BANKS DAVIDSON BR TR
B. Jan. 6, 1963, Bad Kurznach, Germany 6' 185 lbs.

Year	W	L	PCT	ERA	G	IP	H	SO	BB	Sho	SV
1989	0	0	—	18.00	1	1	1	0	1	0	0

George Davis

GEORGE ALLEN DAVIS BB TR
B. Mar. 9, 1890, Lancaster, N. Y. 5' 10½" 175 lbs.
D. Jun. 4, 1961, Buffalo, N. Y.

Year	W	L	PCT	ERA	G	IP	H	SO	BB	Sho	SV
1912	1	4	.200	6.50	10	54	61	22	28	0	0

Ron Davis

RONALD GENE DAVIS BR TR
B. Aug. 6, 1955, Houston, Tex. 6' 4" 205 lbs.

Year	W	L	PCT	ERA	G	IP	H	SO	BB	Sho	SV
1978	0	0	—	11.57	4	2.1	3	0	3	0	0
1979	14	2	.875	2.86	44	85	84	43	28	0	9
1980	9	3	.750	2.95	53	131	121	65	32	0	7
1981	4	5	.444	2.71	43	73	47	83	25	0	6
4 yrs.	27	10	.730	2.93	144	291.1	255	191	88	0	22
Divisional Playoffs											
1981	1	0	1.000	0.00	3	6	1	6	2	0	0
League Championship Series											
1980	0	0	—	2.25	1	4	3	3	1	0	0
1981	0	0	—	0.00	2	3.1	0	4	2	0	0
2 yrs.	0	0	—	1.23	3	7.1	3	7	3	0	0
World Series											
1981	0	0	—	23.14	4	2.1	4	4	5	0	0

Jimmie DeShong

JAMES BROOKLYN DESHONG BR TR
B. Nov. 30, 1909, Harrisburg, Pa. 5' 11" 165 lbs.
D. Oct. 16, 1993, Dauphin County, Pa.

Year	W	L	PCT	ERA	G	IP	H	SO	BB	Sho	SV
1934	6	7	.462	4.11	31	133.2	126	40	56	0	3

Jimmie DeShong *continued*

Year	W	L	PCT	ERA	G	IP	H	SO	BB	Sho	SV
1935	4	1	.800	3.26	29	69	64	30	33	0	3
2 yrs.	10	8	.556	3.82	60	202.2	190	70	89	0	6

John Deering

JOHN THOMAS DEERING BR TR
B. Jun. 25, 1878, Lynn, Mass. 6' 180 lbs.
D. Feb. 15, 1943, Beverly, Mass.

Year	W	L	PCT	ERA	G	IP	H	SO	BB	Sho	SV
1903	3	3	.500	3.75	9	60	59	14	18	1	0

Jim Deshaies

JAMES JOSEPH DESHAIES BL TL
B. Jun. 23, 1960, Massena, N. Y. 6' 4" 222 lbs.

Year	W	L	PCT	ERA	G	IP	H	SO	BB	Sho	SV
1984	0	1	.000	11.57	2	7	14	5	7	0	0

Charlie Devens

CHARLES DEVENS BR TR
B. Jan. 1, 1910, Milton, Mass. 6' 1" 180 lbs.

Year	W	L	PCT	ERA	G	IP	H	SO	BB	Sho	SV
1932	1	0	1.000	2.00	1	9	6	4	7	0	0
1933	3	3	.500	4.35	14	62	59	23	50	0	0
1934	1	0	1.000	1.64	1	11	9	4	5	0	0
3 yrs.	5	3	.625	3.73	16	82	74	31	62	0	0

Murry Dickson

MURRY MONROE DICKSON BR TR
B. Aug. 21, 1916, Tracy, Mo. 5' 10½" 157 lbs.
D. Sep. 21, 1989, Kansas City, Kans.

Year	W	L	PCT	ERA	G	IP	H	SO	BB	Sho	SV
1958	1	2	.333	5.75	6	20.1	18	9	12	0	1
World Series											
1958	0	0	—	4.50	2	4	4	1	0	0	0

Art Ditmar

ARTHUR JOHN DITMAR BR TR
B. Apr. 3, 1929, Winthrop, Mass. 6' 2" 185 lbs.

Year	W	L	PCT	ERA	G	IP	H	SO	BB	Sho	SV
1957	8	3	.727	3.25	46	127.1	128	64	35	0	6
1958	9	8	.529	3.42	38	139.2	124	52	38	0	4
1959	13	9	.591	2.90	38	202	156	96	52	1	1
1960	15	9	.625	3.06	34	200	195	65	56	1	0
1961	2	3	.400	4.64	12	54.1	59	24	14	0	0
5 yrs.	47	32	.595	3.24	168	723.1	662	301	195	2	11
World Series											
1957	0	0	—	0.00	2	6	2	2	0	0	0
1958	0	0	—	0.00	1	3.2	2	2	0	0	0
1960	0	2	.000	21.60	2	1.2	6	0	1	0	0
3 yrs.	0	2	.000	3.18	5	11.1	10	4	1	0	0

Sonny Dixon

JOHN CRAIG DIXON BB TR
B. Nov. 5, 1924, Charlotte, N. C. 6' 2½" 205 lbs.

Year	W	L	PCT	ERA	G	IP	H	SO	BB	Sho	SV
1956	0	1	.000	2.08	3	4.1	5	1	5	0	0

Pat Dobson

PATRICK EDWARD DOBSON BR TR
B. Feb. 12, 1942, Depew, N. Y. 6' 3" 190 lbs.

Year	W	L	PCT	ERA	G	IP	H	SO	BB	Sho	SV
1973	9	8	.529	4.17	22	142.1	150	70	34	1	0
1974	19	15	.559	3.07	39	281	282	157	75	2	0
1975	11	14	.440	4.07	33	207.2	205	129	83	1	0
3 yrs.	39	37	.513	3.65	94	631	637	356	192	4	0

Atley Donald

RICHARD ATLEY DONALD BL TR
B. Aug. 19, 1910, Morton, Miss. 6' 1" 186 lbs.
D. Oct. 19, 1992, West Monroe, La.

Year	W	L	PCT	ERA	G	IP	H	SO	BB	Sho	SV
1938	0	1	.000	5.25	2	12	7	6	14	0	0
1939	13	3	.813	3.71	24	153	144	55	60	2	1
1940	8	3	.727	3.03	24	118.2	113	60	59	1	0
1941	9	5	.643	3.57	22	159	141	71	69	0	0
1942	11	3	.786	3.11	20	147.2	133	53	45	1	0
1943	6	4	.600	4.60	22	119.1	134	57	38	0	0
1944	13	10	.565	3.34	30	159	173	48	59	0	0
1945	5	4	.556	2.97	9	63.2	62	19	25	2	0
8 yrs.	65	33	.663	3.52	153	932.1	907	369	369	6	1

Year	W	L	PCT	ERA	G	IP	H	SO	BB	Sho	SV

Atley Donald continued

World Series

Year	W	L	PCT	ERA	G	IP	H	SO	BB	Sho	SV
1941	0	0	—	9.00	1	4	6	2	3	0	0
1942	0	1	.000	6.00	1	3	3	1	2	0	0
2 yrs.	0	1	.000	7.71	2	7	9	3	5	0	0

Wild Bill Donovan

WILLIAM EDWARD DONOVAN BB TR
B. Oct. 13, 1876, Lawrence, Mass. 5' 11" 190 lbs.
D. Dec. 9, 1923, Forsyth, N. Y.

Year	W	L	PCT	ERA	G	IP	H	SO	BB	Sho	SV
1915	0	3	.000	4.81	9	33.2	35	17	10	0	0
1916	0	0	—	0.00	1	1	1	0	1	0	0
2 yrs.	0	3	.000	4.67	10	34.2	36	17	11	0	0

Richard Dotson

RICHARD ELLIOTT DOTSON BR TR
B. Jan. 10, 1959, Cincinnati, Ohio 6' 1" 190 lbs.

Year	W	L	PCT	ERA	G	IP	H	SO	BB	Sho	SV
1988	12	9	.571	5.00	32	171	178	77	72	0	0
1989	2	5	.286	5.57	11	51.2	69	14	17	0	0
2 yrs.	14	14	.500	5.13	43	222.2	247	91	89	0	0

Al Downing

ALPHONSO ERWIN DOWNING BR TL
B. Jun. 28, 1941, Trenton, N. J. 5' 11" 175 lbs.

Year	W	L	PCT	ERA	G	IP	H	SO	BB	Sho	SV
1961	0	1	.000	8.00	5	9	7	12	12	0	0
1962	0	0	—	0.00	1	1	0	1	0	0	0
1963	13	5	.722	2.56	24	175.2	114	171	80	4	0
1964	13	8	.619	3.47	37	244	201	217	120	1	2
1965	12	14	.462	3.40	35	212	185	179	105	2	0
1966	10	11	.476	3.56	30	200	178	152	79	0	0
1967	14	10	.583	2.63	31	201.2	158	171	61	4	0
1968	3	3	.500	3.52	15	61.1	54	40	20	0	0
1969	7	5	.583	3.38	30	130.2	117	85	49	1	0
9 yrs.	72	57	.558	3.23	208	1235.1	1014	1028	526	12	2

World Series

Year	W	L	PCT	ERA	G	IP	H	SO	BB	Sho	SV
1963	0	1	.000	5.40	1	5	7	6	1	0	0
1964	0	1	.000	8.22	3	7.2	9	5	2	0	0
2 yrs.	0	2	.000	7.11	4	12.2	16	11	3	0	0

Slow Joe Doyle

JUDD BRUCE DOYLE BL TR
B. Sep. 15, 1881, Clay Center, Kans. 5' 8" 150 lbs.
D. Nov. 21, 1947, Tannersville, N. Y.

Year	W	L	PCT	ERA	G	IP	H	SO	BB	Sho	SV
1906	2	1	.667	2.38	9	45.1	34	28	13	2	0
1907	11	11	.500	2.65	29	193.2	169	94	67	1	1
1908	1	1	.500	2.63	12	48	42	20	14	1	0
1909	8	6	.571	2.58	17	125.2	103	57	37	3	0
1910	0	2	.000	8.03	3	12.1	19	6	5	0	0
5 yrs.	22	21	.512	2.75	70	425	367	205	136	7	1

Doug Drabek

DOUGLAS DEAN DRABEK BR TR
B. Jul. 25, 1962, Victoria, Tex. 6' 1" 185 lbs.

Year	W	L	PCT	ERA	G	IP	H	SO	BB	Sho	SV
1986	7	8	.467	4.10	27	131.2	126	76	50	0	0

Karl Drews

KARL AUGUST DREWS BR TR
B. Feb. 22, 1920, Staten Island, N. Y. 6' 4½" 192 lbs.
D. Aug. 13, 1963, Dania, Fla.

Year	W	L	PCT	ERA	G	IP	H	SO	BB	Sho	SV
1946	0	1	.000	8.53	3	6.1	6	4	6	0	0
1947	6	6	.500	4.91	30	91.2	92	45	55	0	1
1948	2	3	.400	3.79	19	38	35	11	31	0	1
3 yrs.	8	10	.444	4.76	52	136	133	60	92	0	2

World Series

Year	W	L	PCT	ERA	G	IP	H	SO	BB	Sho	SV
1947	0	0	—	3.00	2	3	2	0	1	0	0

Monk Dubiel

WALTER JOHN DUBIEL BR TR
B. Feb. 12, 1918, Hartford, Conn. 6' 190 lbs.
D. Oct. 23, 1969, Hartford, Conn.

Year	W	L	PCT	ERA	G	IP	H	SO	BB	Sho	SV
1944	13	13	.500	3.38	30	232	217	79	86	3	0
1945	10	9	.526	4.64	26	151.1	157	45	62	1	0
2 yrs.	23	22	.511	3.87	56	383.1	374	124	148	4	0

Ryne Duren

RINOLD GEORGE DUREN BR TR
B. Feb. 22, 1929, Cazenovia, Wis. 6' 2" 190 lbs.

Year	W	L	PCT	ERA	G	IP	H	SO	BB	Sho	SV
1958	6	4	.600	2.02	44	75.2	40	87	43	0	20
1959	3	6	.333	1.88	41	76.2	49	96	43	0	14
1960	3	4	.429	4.96	42	49	27	67	49	0	9
1961	0	1	.000	5.40	4	5	2	7	4	0	0
4 yrs.	12	15	.444	2.75	131	206.1	118	257	139	0	43

World Series

Year	W	L	PCT	ERA	G	IP	H	SO	BB	Sho	SV
1958	1	1	.500	1.93	3	9.1	7	14	6	0	1
1960	0	0	—	2.25	2	4	2	5	1	0	0
2 yrs.	1	1	.500	2.02	5	13.1	9	19	7	0	1

Rawly Eastwick

RAWLINS JACKSON EASTWICK III BR TR
B. Oct. 24, 1950, Camden, N. J. 6' 3" 180 lbs.

Year	W	L	PCT	ERA	G	IP	H	SO	BB	Sho	SV
1978	2	1	.667	3.28	8	24.2	22	13	4	0	0

Foster Edwards

FOSTER HAMILTON EDWARDS BR TR
B. Sep. 1, 1903, Holstein, Iowa 6' 3" 175 lbs.
D. Jan. 4, 1980, Orleans, Mass.

Year	W	L	PCT	ERA	G	IP	H	SO	BB	Sho	SV
1930	0	0	—	21.60	2	1.2	5	1	2	0	0

Dave Eiland

DAVID WILLIAM EILAND BR TR
B. Jul. 5, 1966, Dade City, Fla. 6' 3" 210 lbs.

Year	W	L	PCT	ERA	G	IP	H	SO	BB	Sho	SV
1988	0	0	—	6.39	3	12.2	15	7	4	0	0
1989	1	3	.250	5.77	6	34.1	44	11	13	0	0
1990	2	1	.667	3.56	5	30.1	31	16	5	0	0
1991	2	5	.286	5.33	18	72.2	87	18	23	0	0
1995	1	1	.500	6.30	4	10	16	6	3	0	0
5 yrs.	6	10	.375	5.23	36	160	193	58	48	0	0

Dock Ellis

DOCK PHILLIP ELLIS BB TR
B. Mar. 11, 1945, Los Angeles, Calif. 6' 3" 205 lbs.

Year	W	L	PCT	ERA	G	IP	H	SO	BB	Sho	SV
1976	17	8	.680	3.19	32	211.2	195	65	76	1	0
1977	1	1	.500	1.83	3	19.2	18	5	8	0	0
2 yrs.	18	9	.667	3.07	35	231.1	213	70	84	1	0

League Championship Series

Year	W	L	PCT	ERA	G	IP	H	SO	BB	Sho	SV
1976	1	0	1.000	3.38	1	8	6	5	2	0	0

World Series

Year	W	L	PCT	ERA	G	IP	H	SO	BB	Sho	SV
1976	0	1	.000	10.80	1	3.1	7	1	0	0	0

Red Embree

CHARLES WILLARD EMBREE BR TR
B. Aug. 30, 1917, El Monte, Calif. 6' 165 lbs.
D. Sep. 24, 1996, Eugene, Ore.

Year	W	L	PCT	ERA	G	IP	H	SO	BB	Sho	SV
1948	5	3	.625	3.76	20	76.2	77	25	30	0	0

Jack Enright

JACKSON PERCY ENRIGHT BR TR
B. Nov. 29, 1895, Fort Worth, Tex. 5' 11" 177 lbs.
D. Aug. 17, 1975, Pompano Beach, Fla.

Year	W	L	PCT	ERA	G	IP	H	SO	BB	Sho	SV
1917	0	1	.000	5.40	1	5	5	1	3	0	0

Roger Erickson

ROGER FARRELL ERICKSON BR TR
B. Aug. 30, 1956, Springfield, Ill. 6' 3" 180 lbs.

Year	W	L	PCT	ERA	G	IP	H	SO	BB	Sho	SV
1982	4	5	.444	4.46	16	70.2	86	37	17	0	1
1983	0	1	.000	4.32	5	16.2	13	7	8	0	0
2 yrs.	4	6	.400	4.43	21	87.1	99	44	25	0	1

Alvaro Espinoza

ALVARO ALBERTO ESPINOZA BR TR
B. Feb. 19, 1962, Valencia, Venezuela 6' 160 lbs.

Year	W	L	PCT	ERA	G	IP	H	SO	BB	Sho	SV
1991	0	0	—	0.00	1	0.2	0	0	0	0	0

Steve Farr

STEVEN MICHAEL FARR BR TR
B. Dec. 12, 1956, Cheverly, Md. 5' 10" 190 lbs.

Year	W	L	PCT	ERA	G	IP	H	SO	BB	Sho	SV
1991	5	5	.500	2.19	60	70	57	60	20	0	23
1992	2	2	.500	1.56	50	52	34	37	19	0	30
1993	2	2	.500	4.21	49	47	44	39	28	0	25
3 yrs.	9	9	.500	2.56	159	169	135	136	67	0	78

Year	W	L	PCT	ERA	G	IP	H	SO	BB	Sho	SV

Alex Ferguson

JAMES ALEXANDER FERGUSON   BR TR
B. Feb. 16, 1897, Montclair, N. J.   6' 180 lbs.
D. Apr. 26, 1976, Sepulveda, Calif.

Year	W	L	PCT	ERA	G	IP	H	SO	BB	Sho	SV
1918	0	0	—	0.00	1	1.2	2	1	2	0	0
1921	3	1	.750	5.91	17	56.1	64	9	27	0	1
1925	4	2	.667	7.79	21	54.1	83	20	42	0	1
3 yrs.	7	3	.700	6.73	39	112.1	149	30	71	0	2

Wes Ferrell

WESLEY CHEEK FERRELL   BR TR
B. Feb. 2, 1908, Greensboro, N. C.   6' 2" 195 lbs.
D. Dec. 9, 1976, Sarasota, Fla.

Year	W	L	PCT	ERA	G	IP	H	SO	BB	Sho	SV
1938	2	2	.500	8.10	5	30	52	7	18	0	0
1939	1	2	.333	4.66	3	19.1	14	6	17	0	0
2 yrs.	3	4	.429	6.75	8	49.1	66	13	35	0	0

Tom Ferrick

THOMAS JEROME FERRICK   BR TR
B. Jan. 6, 1915, New York, N. Y.   6' 2½" 220 lbs.
D. Oct. 15, 1996, Lima, Pa.

Year	W	L	PCT	ERA	G	IP	H	SO	BB	Sho	SV
1950	8	4	.667	3.65	30	56.2	49	20	22	0	9
1951	1	1	.500	7.50	9	12	21	3	7	0	1
2 yrs.	9	5	.643	4.33	39	68.2	70	23	29	0	10
World Series											
1950	1	0	1.000	0.00	1	1	1	0	1	0	0

Ed Figueroa

EDUARDO FIGUEROA   BR TR
B. Oct. 14, 1948, Ciales, Puerto Rico   6' 1" 190 lbs.

Year	W	L	PCT	ERA	G	IP	H	SO	BB	Sho	SV
1976	19	10	.655	3.02	34	256.2	237	119	94	4	0
1977	16	11	.593	3.58	32	239	228	104	75	2	0
1978	20	9	.690	2.99	35	253	233	92	77	2	0
1979	4	6	.400	4.11	16	105	109	42	35	1	0
1980	3	3	.500	6.98	15	58	90	16	24	0	1
5 yrs.	62	39	.614	3.53	132	911.2	897	373	305	9	1
League Championship Series											
1976	0	1	.000	5.84	2	12.1	14	5	2	0	0
1977	0	0	—	10.80	1	3.1	5	3	2	0	0
1978	0	1	.000	27.00	1	1	5	0	0	0	0
3 yrs.	0	2	.000	8.10	4	16.2	24	8	4	0	0
World Series											
1976	0	1	.000	5.63	1	8	6	2	5	0	0
1978	0	1	.000	8.10	2	6.2	9	2	5	0	0
2 yrs.	0	2	.000	6.75	3	14.2	15	4	10	0	0

Pete Filson

WILLIAM PETER FILSON   BB TL
B. Sep. 28, 1958, Darby, Pa.   6' 2" 195 lbs.

Year	W	L	PCT	ERA	G	IP	H	SO	BB	Sho	SV
1987	1	0	1.000	3.27	7	22	26	10	9	0	0

Happy Finneran

JOSEPH IGNATIUS FINNERAN   BR TR
B. Oct. 29, 1891, East Orange, N. J. 5' 10½" 169 lbs.
D. Feb. 3, 1942, Orange, N. J.

Year	W	L	PCT	ERA	G	IP	H	SO	BB	Sho	SV
1918	3	6	.333	3.78	23	114.1	134	34	35	0	0

Brian Fisher

BRIAN KEVIN FISHER   BR TR
B. Mar. 18, 1962, Honolulu, Hawaii   6' 4" 210 lbs.

Year	W	L	PCT	ERA	G	IP	H	SO	BB	Sho	SV
1985	4	4	.500	2.38	55	98.1	77	85	29	0	14
1986	9	5	.643	4.93	62	96.2	105	67	37	0	6
2 yrs.	13	9	.591	3.65	117	195	182	152	66	0	20

Ray Fisher

RAY LYLE FISHER   BR TR
B. Oct. 4, 1887, Middlebury, Vt.   5' 11½" 180 lbs.
D. Nov. 3, 1982, Ann Arbor, Mich.

Year	W	L	PCT	ERA	G	IP	H	SO	BB	Sho	SV
1910	5	3	.625	2.92	17	92.1	95	42	18	0	1
1911	10	11	.476	3.25	29	171.2	178	99	55	2	0
1912	2	8	.200	5.88	17	90.1	107	47	32	0	0
1913	12	16	.429	3.18	43	246.1	244	92	71	1	1
1914	10	12	.455	2.28	29	209	177	86	61	2	1
1915	18	11	.621	2.11	30	247.2	219	97	62	4	0
1916	11	8	.579	3.17	31	179	191	56	51	1	2

Ray Fisher *continued*

Year	W	L	PCT	ERA	G	IP	H	SO	BB	Sho	SV
1917	8	9	.471	2.19	23	144	126	64	43	3	0
8 yrs.	76	78	.494	2.91	219	1380.1	1337	583	393	13	5

Ray Fontenot

SILTON RAY FONTENOT   BL TL
B. Aug. 8, 1957, Lake Charles, La.   6' 175 lbs.

Year	W	L	PCT	ERA	G	IP	H	SO	BB	Sho	SV
1983	8	2	.800	3.33	15	97.1	101	27	25	1	0
1984	8	9	.471	3.61	33	169.1	189	85	58	0	0
2 yrs.	16	11	.593	3.51	48	266.2	290	112	83	1	0

Russ Ford

RUSSELL WILLIAM FORD   BR TR
B. Apr. 25, 1883, Brandon, Man.,
Canada   5' 11" 175 lbs.
D. Jan. 24, 1960, Rockingham, N. C.

Year	W	L	PCT	ERA	G	IP	H	SO	BB	Sho	SV
1909	0	0	—	9.00	1	3	4	2	4	0	0
1910	26	6	.813	1.65	36	299.2	194	209	70	8	1
1911	22	11	.667	2.27	37	281.1	251	158	76	1	0
1912	13	21	.382	3.55	36	291.2	317	112	79	0	0
1913	12	18	.400	2.66	33	237	244	72	58	1	2
5 yrs.	73	56	.566	2.54	143	1112.2	1010	553	287	10	3

Whitey Ford

EDWARD CHARLES FORD   BL TL
B. Oct. 21, 1926, New York, N. Y.   5' 10" 178 lbs.
Hall of Fame 1974

Year	W	L	PCT	ERA	G	IP	H	SO	BB	Sho	SV
1950	9	1	.900	2.81	20	112	87	59	52	2	1
1953	18	6	.750	3.00	32	207	187	110	110	3	0
1954	16	8	.667	2.82	34	210.2	170	125	101	3	1
1955	18	7	.720	2.63	39	253.2	188	137	113	5	2
1956	19	6	.760	2.47	31	225.2	187	141	84	2	1
1957	11	5	.688	2.57	24	129.1	114	84	53	0	0
1958	14	7	.667	2.01	30	219.1	174	145	62	7	1
1959	16	10	.615	3.04	35	204	194	114	89	2	1
1960	12	9	.571	3.08	33	192.2	168	85	65	4	0
1961	25	4	.862	3.21	39	283	242	209	92	3	0
1962	17	8	.680	2.90	38	257.2	243	160	69	0	0
1963	24	7	.774	2.74	38	269.1	240	189	56	3	1
1964	17	6	.739	2.13	39	244.2	212	172	57	8	1
1965	16	13	.552	3.24	37	244.1	241	162	50	2	1
1966	2	5	.286	2.47	22	73	79	43	24	0	0
1967	2	4	.333	1.64	7	44	40	21	9	1	0
16 yrs.	236	106	.690	2.75	498	3170.1	2766	1956	1086	45	10
World Series											
1950	1	0	1.000	0.00	1	8.2	7	7	1	0	0
1953	0	1	.000	4.50	2	8	9	7	2	0	0
1955	2	0	1.000	2.12	2	17	13	10	8	0	0
1956	1	1	.500	5.25	2	12	14	8	2	0	0
1957	1	1	.500	1.13	2	16	11	7	5	0	0
1958	0	1	.000	4.11	3	15.1	19	16	5	0	0
1960	2	0	1.000	0.00	2	18	11	8	2	2	0
1961	2	0	1.000	0.00	2	14	6	7	1	1	0
1962	1	1	.500	4.12	3	19.2	24	12	4	0	0
1963	0	2	.000	4.50	2	12	10	8	3	0	0
1964	0	1	.000	8.44	1	5.1	8	4	1	0	0
11 yrs.	10	8	.556	2.71	22	146	132	94	34	3	0

Ray Francis

RAY JAMES FRANCIS   BL TL
B. Mar. 8, 1893, Sherman, Tex.   6' 1½" 182 lbs.
D. Jul. 6, 1934, Atlanta, Ga.

Year	W	L	PCT	ERA	G	IP	H	SO	BB	Sho	SV
1925	0	0	—	7.71	4	4.2	5	1	3	0	0

George Frazier

GEORGE ALLEN FRAZIER   BR TR
B. Oct. 13, 1954, Oklahoma City, Okla.   6' 5" 205 lbs.

Year	W	L	PCT	ERA	G	IP	H	SO	BB	Sho	SV
1981	0	1	.000	1.61	16	28	26	17	11	0	3
1982	4	4	.500	3.47	63	111.2	103	69	39	0	1
1983	4	4	.500	3.43	61	115.1	94	78	45	0	8
3 yrs.	8	9	.471	3.25	140	255	223	164	95	0	12

George Frazier continued

Year	W	L	PCT	ERA	G	IP	H	SO	BB	Sho	SV
League Championship Series											
1981	1	0	1.000	0.00	1	5.2	5	5	1	0	0
World Series											
1981	0	3	.000	17.18	3	3.2	9	2	3	0	0

Mark Freeman

MARK PRICE FREEMAN   BR TR
B. Dec. 7, 1930, Memphis, Tenn.   6' 4" 220 lbs.

Year	W	L	PCT	ERA	G	IP	H	SO	BB	Sho	SV
1959	0	0	—	2.57	1	7	6	4	2	0	0

Bob Friend

ROBERT BARTMESS FRIEND   BR TR
B. Nov. 24, 1930, Lafayette, Ind.   6' 190 lbs.

Year	W	L	PCT	ERA	G	IP	H	SO	BB	Sho	SV
1966	1	4	.200	4.84	12	44.2	61	22	9	0	0

John Frill

JOHN EDMOND FRILL   BR TL
B. Apr. 3, 1879, Reading, Pa.   5' 10½" 170 lbs.
D. Sep. 28, 1918, Westerly, R. I.

Year	W	L	PCT	ERA	G	IP	H	SO	BB	Sho	SV
1910	2	2	.500	4.47	10	48.1	55	27	5	1	1

Bill Fulton

WILLIAM DAVID FULTON   BR TR
B. Oct. 22, 1963, Pittsburgh, Pa.   6' 3" 195 lbs.

Year	W	L	PCT	ERA	G	IP	H	SO	BB	Sho	SV
1987	1	0	1.000	11.57	3	4.2	9	2	1	0	0

John Gabler

JOHN RICHARD GABLER   BB TR
B. Oct. 2, 1930, Kansas City, Mo.   6' 2" 165 lbs.

Year	W	L	PCT	ERA	G	IP	H	SO	BB	Sho	SV
1959	1	1	.500	2.79	3	19.1	21	11	10	0	0
1960	3	3	.500	4.15	21	52	46	19	32	0	1
2 yrs.	4	4	.500	3.79	24	71.1	67	30	42	0	1

Rob Gardner

RICHARD FRANK GARDNER   BR TL
B. Dec. 19, 1944, Binghamton, N. Y.   6' 1" 176 lbs.

Year	W	L	PCT	ERA	G	IP	H	SO	BB	Sho	SV
1970	1	0	1.000	5.14	1	7	8	6	4	0	0
1971	0	0	—	3.00	2	3	3	2	2	0	0
1972	8	5	.615	3.06	20	97	91	58	28	0	0
3 yrs.	9	5	.643	3.20	23	107	102	66	34	0	0

Ned Garvin

VIRGIL LEE GARVIN   B TR
B. Jan. 1, 1874, Navasota, Tex.   6' 3½" 160 lbs.
D. Jun. 16, 1908, Fresno, Calif.

Year	W	L	PCT	ERA	G	IP	H	SO	BB	Sho	SV
1904	0	1	.000	2.25	2	12	14	8	2	0	0

Milt Gaston

NATHANIEL MILTON GASTON   BR TR
B. Jan. 27, 1896, Ridgefield Park, N. J.   6' 1" 185 lbs.
D. Apr. 26, 1996, Hyannis, Mass.

Year	W	L	PCT	ERA	G	IP	H	SO	BB	Sho	SV
1924	5	3	.625	4.50	29	86	92	24	44	0	1

Al Gettel

ALLEN JONES GETTEL   BR TR
B. Sep. 17, 1917, Norfolk, Va.   6' 3½" 200 lbs.

Year	W	L	PCT	ERA	G	IP	H	SO	BB	Sho	SV
1945	9	8	.529	3.90	27	154.2	141	67	53	0	3
1946	6	7	.462	2.97	26	103	89	54	40	2	0
2 yrs.	15	15	.500	3.53	53	257.2	230	121	93	2	3

Joe Giard

JOSEPH OSCAR GIARD   BL TL
B. Oct. 7, 1898, Ware, Mass.   5' 10½" 170 lbs.
D. Jul. 10, 1956, Worcester, Mass.

Year	W	L	PCT	ERA	G	IP	H	SO	BB	Sho	SV
1927	0	0	—	8.00	16	27	38	10	19	0	0

Paul Gibson

PAUL MARSHALL GIBSON   BR TL
B. Jan. 4, 1960, Southampton, N. Y.   6' 165 lbs.

Year	W	L	PCT	ERA	G	IP	H	SO	BB	Sho	SV
1993	2	0	1.000	3.06	20	35.1	31	25	9	0	0
1994	1	1	.500	4.97	30	29	26	21	17	0	0

Paul Gibson continued

Year	W	L	PCT	ERA	G	IP	H	SO	BB	Sho	SV
1996	0	0	—	6.23	4	4.1	6	3	0	0	0
3 yrs.	3	1	.750	4.06	54	68.2	63	49	26	0	0

Sam Gibson

SAMUEL BRAXTON GIBSON   BL TR
B. Aug. 5, 1899, King, N. C.   6' 2" 198 lbs.
D. Jan. 31, 1983, High Point, N. C.

Year	W	L	PCT	ERA	G	IP	H	SO	BB	Sho	SV
1930	0	1	.000	15.00	2	6	14	3	6	0	0

Fred Glade

FREDERICK MONROE GLADE   BR TR
B. Jan. 25, 1876, Dubuque, Iowa   5' 10" 175 lbs.
D. Nov. 21, 1934, Grand Island, Neb.

Year	W	L	PCT	ERA	G	IP	H	SO	BB	Sho	SV
1908	0	4	.000	4.22	5	32	30	11	14	0	0

Lefty Gomez

VERNON LOUIS GOMEZ   BL TL
B. Nov. 26, 1908, Rodeo, Calif.   6' 2" 173 lbs.
D. Feb. 17, 1989, Greenbrae, Calif.
Hall of Fame 1972

Year	W	L	PCT	ERA	G	IP	H	SO	BB	Sho	SV
1930	2	5	.286	5.55	15	60	66	22	28	0	1
1931	21	9	.700	2.63	40	243	206	150	85	1	3
1932	24	7	.774	4.21	37	265.1	266	176	105	1	1
1933	16	10	.615	3.18	35	234.2	218	163	106	4	2
1934	26	5	.839	2.33	38	281.2	223	158	96	6	1
1935	12	15	.444	3.18	34	246	223	138	86	2	1
1936	13	7	.650	4.39	31	188.2	184	105	122	0	0
1937	21	11	.656	2.33	34	278.1	233	194	93	6	0
1938	18	12	.600	3.35	32	239	239	129	99	4	0
1939	12	8	.600	3.41	26	198	173	102	84	2	0
1940	3	3	.500	6.59	9	27.1	37	14	18	0	0
1941	15	5	.750	3.74	23	156.1	151	76	103	2	0
1942	6	4	.600	4.28	13	80	67	41	65	0	0
13 yrs.	189	101	.652	3.34	367	2498.1	2286	1468	1090	28	9
World Series											
1932	1	0	1.000	1.00	1	9	9	8	1	0	0
1936	2	0	1.000	4.70	2	15.1	14	9	11	0	0
1937	2	0	1.000	1.50	2	18	16	8	2	0	0
1938	1	0	1.000	3.86	1	7	9	5	1	0	0
1939	0	0	—	9.00	1	1	3	1	0	0	0
5 yrs.	6	0	1.000	2.86	7	50.1	51	31	15	0	0

Wilbur Good

WILBUR DAVID GOOD   BL TL
B. Sep. 28, 1885, Punxsutawney, Pa.   5' 6" 165 lbs.
D. Dec. 30, 1963, Brooksville, Fla.

Year	W	L	PCT	ERA	G	IP	H	SO	BB	Sho	SV
1905	0	2	.000	4.74	5	19	18	13	14	0	0

Dwight Gooden

DWIGHT EUGENE GOODEN   BR TR
B. Nov. 16, 1964, Tampa, Fla.   6' 2" 190 lbs.

Year	W	L	PCT	ERA	G	IP	H	SO	BB	Sho	SV
1996	11	7	.611	5.01	29	170.2	169	126	88	1	0

Art Goodwin

ARTHUR INGRAM GOODWIN   B TR
B. Feb. 27, 1876, Greene County, Pa.   5' 8" 195 lbs.
D. Jun. 19, 1943, Greene County, Pa.

Year	W	L	PCT	ERA	G	IP	H	SO	BB	Sho	SV
1905	0	0	—	81.00	1	0.1	2	0	2	0	0

Tom Gorman

THOMAS ALOYSIUS GORMAN   BR TR
B. Jan. 4, 1925, New York, N. Y.   6' 1" 190 lbs.
D. Dec. 26, 1992, Valley Stream, N. Y.

Year	W	L	PCT	ERA	G	IP	H	SO	BB	Sho	SV
1952	6	2	.750	4.60	12	60.2	63	31	22	1	1
1953	4	5	.444	3.39	40	77	65	38	32	0	6
1954	0	0	—	2.21	23	36.2	30	31	14	0	2
3 yrs.	10	7	.588	3.56	75	174.1	158	100	68	1	9
World Series											
1952	0	0	—	0.00	1	0.2	1	0	0	0	0
1953	0	0	—	3.00	1	3	4	1	0	0	0
2 yrs.	0	0	—	2.45	2	3.2	5	1	0	0	0

Year	W	L	PCT	ERA	G	IP	H	SO	BB	Sho	SV

Goose Gossage
RICHARD MICHAEL GOSSAGE   BR TR
B. Jul. 5, 1951, Colorado Springs, Colo.   6' 3" 180 lbs.

Year	W	L	PCT	ERA	G	IP	H	SO	BB	Sho	SV
1978	10	11	.476	2.01	63	134.1	87	122	59	0	27
1979	5	3	.625	2.64	36	58	48	41	19	0	18
1980	6	2	.750	2.27	64	99	74	103	37	0	33
1981	3	2	.600	0.77	32	47	22	48	14	0	20
1982	4	5	.444	2.23	56	93	63	102	28	0	30
1983	13	5	.722	2.27	57	87.1	82	90	25	0	22
1989	1	0	1.000	3.77	11	14.1	14	6	3	0	1
7 yrs.	42	28	.600	2.14	319	533	390	512	185	0	151
Divisional Playoffs											
1981	0	0	—	0.00	3	6.2	3	8	2	0	3
League Championship Series											
1978	1	0	1.000	4.50	2	4	3	3	0	0	1
1980	0	1	.000	54.00	1	0.1	3	0	0	0	0
1981	0	0	—	0.00	2	2.2	1	2	0	0	1
3 yrs.	1	1	.500	5.14	5	7	7	5	0	0	2
World Series											
1978	1	0	1.000	0.00	3	6	1	4	1	0	0
1981	0	0	—	0.00	3	5	2	5	2	0	2
2 yrs.	1	0	1.000	0.00	6	11	3	9	3	0	2

Larry Gowell
LAWRENCE CLYDE GOWELL   BR TR
B. May 2, 1948, Lewiston, Me.   6' 2" 182 lbs.

Year	W	L	PCT	ERA	G	IP	H	SO	BB	Sho	SV
1972	0	1	.000	1.29	2	7	3	7	2	0	0

Wayne Granger
WAYNE ALLAN GRANGER   BR TR
B. Mar. 15, 1944, Springfield, Mass.   6' 2" 165 lbs.

Year	W	L	PCT	ERA	G	IP	H	SO	BB	Sho	SV
1973	0	1	.000	1.76	7	15.1	19	10	3	0	0

Ted Gray
TED GLENN GRAY   BB TL
B. Dec. 31, 1924, Detroit, Mich.   5' 11" 175 lbs.

Year	W	L	PCT	ERA	G	IP	H	SO	BB	Sho	SV
1955	0	0	—	3.00	1	3	3	1	0	0	0

Eli Grba
ELI GRBA   BR TR
B. Aug. 9, 1934, Chicago, Ill.   6' 2" 205 lbs.

Year	W	L	PCT	ERA	G	IP	H	SO	BB	Sho	SV
1959	2	5	.286	6.44	19	50.1	52	23	39	0	0
1960	6	4	.600	3.68	24	80.2	65	32	46	0	1
2 yrs.	8	9	.471	4.74	43	131	117	55	85	0	1

Mike Griffin
MICHAEL LEROY GRIFFIN   BR TR
B. Jun. 26, 1957, Colusa, Calif.   6' 4" 195 lbs.

Year	W	L	PCT	ERA	G	IP	H	SO	BB	Sho	SV
1979	0	0	—	4.50	3	4	5	5	2	0	1
1980	2	4	.333	4.83	13	54	64	25	23	0	0
1981	0	0	—	2.25	2	4	5	4	0	0	0
3 yrs.	2	4	.333	4.65	18	62	74	34	25	0	1

Clark Griffith
CLARK CALVIN GRIFFITH   BR TR
B. Nov. 20, 1869, Clear Creek, Mo.   5' 6½" 156 lbs.
D. Oct. 27, 1955, Washington, D. C.
Hall of Fame 1946

Year	W	L	PCT	ERA	G	IP	H	SO	BB	Sho	SV
1903	14	11	.560	2.70	25	213	201	69	33	3	0
1904	7	5	.583	2.87	16	100.1	91	36	16	1	0
1905	9	6	.600	1.67	25	102.2	82	46	15	2	1
1906	2	2	.500	3.02	17	59.2	58	16	15	0	2
1907	0	0	—	8.64	4	8.1	15	5	6	0	0
5 yrs.	32	24	.571	2.66	87	484	447	172	85	6	3

Bob Grim
ROBERT ANTON GRIM   BR TR
B. Mar. 8, 1930, New York, N. Y.   6' 1" 175 lbs.
D. Oct. 23, 1996, Shawnee, Kans.

Year	W	L	PCT	ERA	G	IP	H	SO	BB	Sho	SV
1954	20	6	.769	3.26	37	199	175	108	85	1	0
1955	7	5	.583	4.19	26	92.1	81	63	42	1	4
1956	6	1	.857	2.77	26	74.2	64	48	31	0	5
1957	12	8	.600	2.63	46	72	60	52	36	0	19

Bob Grim *continued*

Year	W	L	PCT	ERA	G	IP	H	SO	BB	Sho	SV
1958	0	1	.000	5.51	11	16.1	12	11	10	0	0
5 yrs.	45	21	.682	3.35	146	454.1	392	282	204	2	28
World Series											
1955	0	1	.000	4.15	3	8.2	8	8	5	0	1
1957	0	1	.000	7.71	2	2.1	3	2	0	0	0
2 yrs.	0	2	.000	4.91	5	11	11	10	5	0	1

Burleigh Grimes
BURLEIGH ARLAND GRIMES   BR TR
B. Aug. 18, 1893, Emerald, Wis.   5' 10" 175 lbs.
D. Dec. 6, 1985, Clear Lake, Wis.
Hall of Fame 1964

Year	W	L	PCT	ERA	G	IP	H	SO	BB	Sho	SV
1934	1	2	.333	5.50	10	18	22	5	14	0	1

Lee Grissom
LEE THEO GRISSOM   BB TL
B. Oct. 23, 1907, Sherman, Tex.   6' 3" 200 lbs.

Year	W	L	PCT	ERA	G	IP	H	SO	BB	Sho	SV
1940	0	0	—	0.00	5	4.2	4	1	2	0	0

Cecilio Guante
CECILIO GUANTE   BR TR
B. Feb. 1, 1960, Villa Mella, Dominican Republic 6' 3" 200 lbs.

Year	W	L	PCT	ERA	G	IP	H	SO	BB	Sho	SV
1987	3	2	.600	5.73	23	44	42	46	20	0	1
1988	5	6	.455	2.88	56	75	59	61	22	0	11
2 yrs.	8	8	.500	3.93	79	119	101	107	42	0	12

Lee Guetterman
ARTHUR LEE GUETTERMAN   BL TL
B. Nov. 22, 1958, Chattanooga, Tenn. 6' 8" 225 lbs.

Year	W	L	PCT	ERA	G	IP	H	SO	BB	Sho	SV
1988	1	2	.333	4.65	20	40.2	49	15	14	0	0
1989	5	5	.500	2.45	70	103	98	51	26	0	13
1990	11	7	.611	3.39	64	93	80	48	26	0	2
1991	3	4	.429	3.68	64	88	91	35	25	0	6
1992	1	1	.500	9.53	15	22.2	35	5	13	0	0
5 yrs.	21	19	.525	3.73	233	347.1	353	154	104	0	21

Ron Guidry
RONALD AMES GUIDRY   BL TL
B. Aug. 28, 1950, Lafayette, La.   5' 11" 161 lbs.

Year	W	L	PCT	ERA	G	IP	H	SO	BB	Sho	SV
1975	0	1	.000	3.45	10	15.2	15	15	9	0	0
1976	0	0	—	5.63	7	16	20	12	4	0	0
1977	16	7	.696	2.82	31	211	174	176	65	5	1
1978	25	3	.893	1.74	35	273.2	187	248	72	9	0
1979	18	8	.692	2.78	33	236	203	201	71	2	2
1980	17	10	.630	3.56	37	220	215	166	80	3	1
1981	11	5	.688	2.76	23	127	100	104	26	0	0
1982	14	8	.636	3.81	34	222	216	162	69	1	0
1983	21	9	.700	3.42	31	250.1	232	156	60	3	0
1984	10	11	.476	4.51	29	195.2	223	127	44	1	0
1985	22	6	.786	3.27	34	259	243	143	42	2	0
1986	9	12	.429	3.98	30	192.1	202	140	38	0	0
1987	5	8	.385	3.67	22	117.2	111	96	38	0	0
1988	2	3	.400	4.18	12	56	57	32	15	0	0
14 yrs.	170	91	.651	3.29	368	2392.1	2198	1778	633	26	4
Divisional Playoffs											
1981	0	0	—	5.40	2	8.1	11	8	3	0	0
League Championship Series											
1977	1	0	1.000	3.97	2	11.1	9	8	3	0	0
1978	1	0	1.000	1.13	1	8	7	7	1	0	0
1980	0	1	.000	12.00	1	3	5	2	4	0	0
3 yrs.	2	1	.667	4.03	4	22.1	21	17	8	0	0
World Series											
1977	1	0	1.000	2.00	1	9	4	7	3	0	0
1978	1	0	1.000	1.00	1	9	8	4	7	0	0
1981	1	1	.500	1.93	2	14	8	15	4	0	0
3 yrs.	3	1	.750	1.69	4	32	20	26	14	0	0

Don Gullett
DONALD EDWARD GULLETT   BR TL
B. Jan. 6, 1951, Lynn, Ky.   6' 190 lbs.

Year	W	L	PCT	ERA	G	IP	H	SO	BB	Sho	SV
1977	14	4	.778	3.59	22	158	137	116	69	1	0

Year	W	L	PCT	ERA	G	IP	H	SO	BB	Sho	SV

Don Gullett *continued*

Year	W	L	PCT	ERA	G	IP	H	SO	BB	Sho	SV
1978	4	2	.667	3.63	8	44.2	46	28	20	0	0
2 yrs.	18	6	.750	3.60	30	202.2	183	144	89	1	0

League Championship Series

1977	0	1	.000	18.00	1	2	4	0	2	0	0

World Series

1977	0	1	.000	6.39	2	12.2	13	10	7	0	0

Bill Gullickson

WILLIAM LEE GULLICKSON   BR TR
B. Feb. 20, 1959, Marshall, Minn.   6' 3" 200 lbs.

1987	4	2	.667	4.88	8	48	46	28	11	0	0

Randy Gumpert

RANDALL PENNINGTON GUMPERT   BR TR
B. Jan. 23, 1918, Monocacy, Pa.   6' 3" 185 lbs.

1946	11	3	.786	2.31	33	132.2	113	63	32	0	1
1947	4	1	.800	5.43	24	56.1	71	25	28	0	0
1948	1	0	1.000	2.88	15	25	27	12	6	0	0
3 yrs.	16	4	.800	3.20	72	214	211	100	66	0	1

Larry Gura

LAWRENCE CYRIL GURA   BB TL
B. Nov. 26, 1947, Joliet, Ill.   6' 170 lbs.

1974	5	1	.833	2.41	8	56	54	17	12	0	0
1975	7	8	.467	3.51	26	151.1	173	65	41	0	0
2 yrs.	12	9	.571	3.21	34	207.1	227	82	53	0	0

John Habyan

JOHN GABRIEL HABYAN   BR TR
B. Jan. 29, 1964, Bay Shore, N. Y.   6' 1" 195 lbs.

1990	0	0	—	2.08	6	8.2	10	4	2	0	0
1991	4	2	.667	2.30	66	90	73	70	20	0	2
1992	5	6	.455	3.84	56	72.2	84	44	21	0	7
1993	2	1	.667	4.04	36	42.1	45	29	16	0	1
4 yrs.	11	9	.550	3.16	164	213.2	212	147	59	0	10

Bump Hadley

IRVING DARIUS HADLEY   BR TR
B. Jul. 5, 1904, Lynn, Mass.   5' 11" 190 lbs.
D. Feb. 15, 1963, Lynn, Mass.

1936	14	4	.778	4.35	31	173.2	194	74	89	1	1
1937	11	8	.579	5.30	29	178.1	199	70	83	0	0
1938	9	8	.529	3.60	29	167.1	165	61	66	1	1
1939	12	6	.667	2.98	26	154	132	65	85	1	2
1940	3	5	.375	5.74	25	80	88	39	52	0	2
5 yrs.	49	31	.613	4.28	140	753.1	778	309	375	3	6

World Series

1936	1	0	1.000	1.13	1	8	10	2	1	0	0
1937	0	1	.000	33.75	1	1.1	6	0	0	0	0
1939	1	0	1.000	2.25	1	8	7	2	3	0	0
3 yrs.	2	1	.667	4.15	3	17.1	23	4	4	0	0

Noodles Hahn

FRANK GEORGE HAHN   BL TL
B. Apr. 29, 1879, Nashville, Tenn.   5' 9" 160 lbs.
D. Feb. 6, 1960, Candler, N. C.

1906	3	2	.600	3.86	6	42	38	17	6	1	0

Roger Hambright

ROGER DEE HAMBRIGHT   BR TR
B. Mar. 26, 1949, Sunnywise, Wash.   5' 10" 180 lbs.

1971	3	1	.750	4.33	18	27	22	14	10	0	2

Steve Hamilton

STEVE ABSHER HAMILTON   BL TL
B. Nov. 30, 1935, Columbia, Ky.   6' 6" 190 lbs.

1963	5	1	.833	2.60	34	62.1	49	63	24	0	5
1964	7	2	.778	3.28	30	60.1	55	49	15	0	3
1965	3	1	.750	1.39	46	58.1	47	51	16	0	5
1966	8	3	.727	3.00	44	90	69	57	22	1	3
1967	2	4	.333	3.48	44	62	57	55	23	0	4

Steve Hamilton *continued*

Year	W	L	PCT	ERA	G	IP	H	SO	BB	Sho	SV
1968	2	2	.500	2.13	40	50.2	37	42	13	0	11
1969	3	4	.429	3.32	38	57	39	39	21	0	2
1970	4	3	.571	2.78	35	45.1	36	33	16	0	3
8 yrs.	34	20	.630	2.78	311	486	389	389	150	1	36

World Series

1963	0	0	—	0.00	1	1	0	1	0	0	0
1964	0	0	—	4.50	2	2	3	2	0	0	1
2 yrs.	0	0	—	3.00	3	3	3	3	0	0	1

Jim Hanley

JAMES PATRICK HANLEY   BR TL
B. Oct. 13, 1885, Providence, R. I.   5' 11" 165 lbs.
D. May 1, 1961, Elmhurst, N. Y.

1913	0	0	—	6.75	1	4	5	2	4	0	0

Jim Hardin

JAMES WARREN HARDIN   BR TR
B. Aug. 6, 1943, Morris Chapel, Tenn.   6' 175 lbs.
D. Mar. 9, 1991, Key West, Fla.

1971	0	2	.000	5.08	12	28.1	35	14	9	0	0

Harry Harper

HARRY CLAYTON HARPER   BL TL
B. Apr. 24, 1895, Hackensack, N. J.   6' 2" 165 lbs.
D. Apr. 23, 1963, Layton, N. J.

1921	4	3	.571	3.76	8	52.2	52	22	25	0	0

World Series

1921	0	0	—	20.25	1	1.1	3	1	2	0	0

Greg Harris

GREG ALLEN HARRIS   BB TR
B. Nov. 2, 1955, Lynwood, Calif.   6' 165 lbs.

1994	0	1	.000	5.40	3	5	4	4	3	0	0

Andy Hawkins

MELTON ANDREW HAWKINS   BR TR
B. Jan. 21, 1960, Waco, Tex.   6' 4" 200 lbs.

1989	15	15	.500	4.80	34	208.1	238	98	76	2	0
1990	5	12	.294	5.37	28	157.2	156	74	82	1	0
1991	0	2	.000	9.95	4	12.2	23	5	6	0	0
3 yrs.	20	29	.408	5.21	66	378.2	417	177	164	3	0

Neal Heaton

NEAL HEATON   BL TL
B. Mar. 3, 1960, Jamaica, N. Y.   6' 2" 197 lbs.

1993	1	0	1.000	6.00	18	27	34	15	11	0	0

Fred Heimach

FREDERICK AMOS HEIMACH   BL TL
B. Jan. 27, 1901, Camden, N. J.   6' 175 lbs.
D. Jun. 1, 1973, Fort Myers, Fla.

1928	2	3	.400	3.31	13	68	66	25	16	0	0
1929	11	6	.647	4.01	35	134.2	141	26	29	3	4
2 yrs.	13	9	.591	3.77	48	202.2	207	51	45	3	4

Bill Henderson

WILLIAM MAXWELL HENDERSON   BR TR
B. Nov. 4, 1901, Pensacola, Fla.   6' 190 lbs.
D. Oct. 6, 1966, Pensacola, Fla.

1930	0	0	—	4.50	3	8	7	2	4	0	0

Bill Henry

WILLIAM FRANCIS HENRY   BL TL
B. Feb. 15, 1942, Long Beach, Calif.   6' 3" 195 lbs.

1966	0	0	—	0.00	2	3	3	2	1	0	0

Xavier Hernandez

FRANCIS XAVIER HERNANDEZ   BL TR
B. Aug. 16, 1965, Port Arthur, Tex.   6' 2" 185 lbs.

1994	4	4	.500	5.85	31	40	48	37	21	0	6

Year	W	L	PCT	ERA	G	IP	H	SO	BB	Sho	SV

Oral Hildebrand

ORAL CLYDE HILDEBRAND BR TR
B. Apr. 7, 1907, Indianapolis, Ind. 6' 3" 175 lbs.
D. Sep. 8, 1977, Southport, Ind.

Year	W	L	PCT	ERA	G	IP	H	SO	BB	Sho	SV
1939	10	4	.714	3.06	21	126.2	102	50	41	1	2
1940	1	1	.500	1.86	13	19.1	19	5	14	0	0
2 yrs.	11	5	.688	2.90	34	146	121	55	55	1	2

World Series

Year	W	L	PCT	ERA	G	IP	H	SO	BB	Sho	SV
1939	0	0	—	0.00	1	4	2	3	0	0	0

Shawn Hillegas

SHAWN PATRICK HILLEGAS BR TR
B. Aug. 21, 1964, Dos Palos, Calif. 6' 3" 205 lbs.

Year	W	L	PCT	ERA	G	IP	H	SO	BB	Sho	SV
1992	1	8	.111	5.51	21	78.1	96	46	33	1	0

Frank Hiller

FRANK WALTER HILLER BR TR
B. Jul. 13, 1920, Newark, N. J. 6' 200 lbs.
D. Jan. 8, 1987, West Chester, Pa.

Year	W	L	PCT	ERA	G	IP	H	SO	BB	Sho	SV
1946	0	2	.000	4.76	3	11.1	13	4	6	0	0
1948	5	2	.714	4.04	22	62.1	59	25	30	0	0
1949	0	2	.000	5.87	4	7.2	9	3	7	0	1
3 yrs.	5	6	.455	4.32	29	81.1	81	32	43	0	1

Rich Hinton

RICHARD MICHAEL HINTON BL TL
B. May 22, 1947, Tucson, Ariz. 6' 2" 185 lbs.

Year	W	L	PCT	ERA	G	IP	H	SO	BB	Sho	SV
1972	1	0	1.000	4.86	7	16.2	20	13	8	0	0

Sterling Hitchcock

STERLING ALEX HITCHCOCK BL TL
B. Apr. 29, 1971, Fayetteville, N. C. 6' 1" 200 lbs.

Year	W	L	PCT	ERA	G	IP	H	SO	BB	Sho	SV
1992	0	2	.000	8.31	3	13	23	6	6	0	0
1993	1	2	.333	4.65	6	31	32	26	14	0	0
1994	4	1	.800	4.20	23	49.1	48	37	29	0	2
1995	11	10	.524	4.70	27	168.1	155	121	68	1	0
4 yrs.	16	15	.516	4.78	59	261.2	258	190	117	1	2

Divisional Playoffs

Year	W	L	PCT	ERA	G	IP	H	SO	BB	Sho	SV
1995	0	0	—	5.40	2	1.2	2	1	2	0	0

Red Hoff

CHESTER CORNELIUS HOFF BL TL
B. May 8, 1891, Ossining, N. Y. 5' 9" 162 lbs.

Year	W	L	PCT	ERA	G	IP	H	SO	BB	Sho	SV
1911	0	1	.000	2.18	5	20.2	21	10	7	0	0
1912	0	1	.000	6.89	5	15.2	20	14	6	0	0
1913	0	0	—	0.00	2	3	0	2	1	0	0
3 yrs.	0	2	.000	3.89	12	39.1	41	26	14	0	0

Bill Hogg

WILLIAM JOHNSTON HOGG BR TR
B. Sep. 11, 1881, Port Huron, Mich. 6' 200 lbs.
D. Dec. 8, 1909, New Orleans, La.

Year	W	L	PCT	ERA	G	IP	H	SO	BB	Sho	SV
1905	9	13	.409	3.20	39	205	178	125	101	3	1
1906	14	13	.519	2.93	28	206	171	107	72	3	0
1907	10	8	.556	3.08	25	166.2	173	64	83	0	0
1908	4	16	.200	3.01	24	152.1	155	72	63	0	0
4 yrs.	37	50	.425	3.06	116	730	677	368	319	6	1

Bobby Hogue

ROBERT CLINTON HOGUE BR TR
B. Apr. 5, 1921, Miami, Fla. 5' 10" 195 lbs.
D. Dec. 22, 1987, Miami, Fla.

Year	W	L	PCT	ERA	G	IP	H	SO	BB	Sho	SV
1951	1	0	1.000	0.00	7	7.1	4	2	3	0	0
1952	3	5	.375	5.32	27	47.1	52	12	25	0	4
2 yrs.	4	5	.444	4.61	34	54.2	56	14	28	0	4

World Series

Year	W	L	PCT	ERA	G	IP	H	SO	BB	Sho	SV
1951	0	0	—	0.00	2	2.2	1	0	0	0	0

Ken Holcombe

KENNETH EDWARD HOLCOMBE BR TR
B. Aug. 23, 1918, Burnsville, N. C. 5' 11½" 169 lbs.

Year	W	L	PCT	ERA	G	IP	H	SO	BB	Sho	SV
1945	3	3	.500	1.79	23	55.1	43	20	27	0	0

Al Holland

ALFRED WILLIS HOLLAND BR TL
B. Aug. 16, 1952, Roanoke, Va. 5' 11" 207 lbs.

Year	W	L	PCT	ERA	G	IP	H	SO	BB	Sho	SV
1986	1	0	1.000	5.09	25	40.2	44	37	9	0	0
1987	0	0	—	14.21	3	6.1	9	5	9	0	0
2 yrs.	1	0	1.000	6.32	28	47	53	42	18	0	0

Ken Holloway

KENNETH EUGENE HOLLOWAY BR TR
B. Aug. 8, 1897, Thomas County, Ga. 6' 185 lbs.
D. Sep. 25, 1968, Thomasville, Ga.

Year	W	L	PCT	ERA	G	IP	H	SO	BB	Sho	SV
1930	0	0	—	5.24	16	34.1	52	11	8	0	0

Ken Holtzman

KENNETH DALE HOLTZMAN BR TL
B. Nov. 3, 1945, St. Louis, Mo. 6' 2" 175 lbs.

Year	W	L	PCT	ERA	G	IP	H	SO	BB	Sho	SV
1976	9	7	.563	4.17	21	149	165	41	35	2	0
1977	2	3	.400	5.75	18	72	105	14	24	0	0
1978	1	0	1.000	4.08	5	17.2	21	3	9	0	0
3 yrs.	12	10	.545	4.64	44	238.2	291	58	68	2	0

Rick Honeycutt

FREDERICK WAYNE HONEYCUTT BL TL
B. Jun. 29, 1952, Chattanooga, Tenn. 6' 1" 185 lbs.

Year	W	L	PCT	ERA	G	IP	H	SO	BB	Sho	SV
1995	0	0	—	27.00	3	1	2	0	1	0	0

Don Hood

DONALD HARRIS HOOD BL TL
B. Oct. 16, 1949, Florence, S. C. 6' 2" 180 lbs.

Year	W	L	PCT	ERA	G	IP	H	SO	BB	Sho	SV
1979	3	1	.750	3.09	27	67	62	22	30	0	1

Wally Hood

WALLACE JAMES HOOD, JR. BR TR
B. Sep. 24, 1925, Los Angeles, Calif. 6' 1" 190 lbs.

Year	W	L	PCT	ERA	G	IP	H	SO	BB	Sho	SV
1949	0	0	—	0.00	2	2.1	0	2	0	0	0

Steve Howe

STEVEN ROY HOWE BL TL
B. Mar. 10, 1958, Pontiac, Mich. 6' 1" 180 lbs.

Year	W	L	PCT	ERA	G	IP	H	SO	BB	Sho	SV
1991	3	1	.750	1.68	37	48.1	39	34	7	0	3
1992	3	0	1.000	2.45	20	22	9	12	3	0	6
1993	3	5	.375	4.97	51	50.2	58	19	10	0	4
1994	3	0	1.000	1.80	40	40	28	18	7	0	15
1995	6	3	.667	4.96	56	49	66	28	17	0	2
1996	0	1	.000	6.35	25	17	19	5	6	0	1
6 yrs.	18	10	.643	3.57	229	227	219	116	50	0	31

Divisional Playoffs

Year	W	L	PCT	ERA	G	IP	H	SO	BB	Sho	SV
1995	0	0	—	18.00	2	1	4	0	0	0	0

Harry Howell

HENRY HARRY HOWELL BR TR
B. Nov. 14, 1876, D. May 22, 1956 Spokane, Wash.

5' 9" lbs.

Year	W	L	PCT	ERA	G	IP	H	SO	BB	Sho	SV
1903	9	6	.600	3.53	25	155.2	140	62	44	0	0

Jay Howell

JAY CANFIELD HOWELL BR TR
B. Nov. 26, 1955, Miami, Fla. 6' 3" 200 lbs.

Year	W	L	PCT	ERA	G	IP	H	SO	BB	Sho	SV
1982	2	3	.400	7.71	6	28	42	21	13	0	0
1983	1	5	.167	5.38	19	82	89	61	35	0	0
1984	9	4	.692	2.69	61	103.2	86	109	34	0	7
3 yrs.	12	12	.500	4.38	86	213.2	217	191	82	0	7

Waite Hoyt

WAITE CHARLES HOYT BR TR
B. Sep. 9, 1899, Brooklyn, N. Y. 6' 180 lbs.
D. Aug. 25, 1984, Cincinnati, Ohio
Hall of Fame 1969

Year	W	L	PCT	ERA	G	IP	H	SO	BB	Sho	SV
1921	19	13	.594	3.09	43	282.1	301	102	81	1	3
1922	19	12	.613	3.43	37	265	271	95	76	3	0
1923	17	9	.654	3.02	37	238.2	227	60	66	1	1
1924	18	13	.581	3.79	46	247	295	71	76	2	4
1925	11	14	.440	4.00	46	243	283	86	78	1	6

Year	W	L	PCT	ERA	G	IP	H	SO	BB	Sho	SV

Waite Hoyt *continued*

Year	W	L	PCT	ERA	G	IP	H	SO	BB	Sho	SV
1926	16	12	.571	3.85	40	217.2	224	79	62	1	4
1927	22	7	.759	2.63	36	256.1	242	86	54	3	1
1928	23	7	.767	3.36	42	273	279	67	60	3	8
1929	10	9	.526	4.24	30	201.2	219	57	69	0	1
1930	2	2	.500	4.53	8	47.2	64	10	9	0	1
10 yrs.	157	98	.616	3.48	365	2272.1	2405	713	631	15	28
World Series											
1921	2	1	.667	0.00	3	27	18	18	11	1	0
1922	0	1	.000	1.13	2	8	11	4	2	0	0
1923	0	0	—	15.43	1	2.1	4	0	1	0	0
1926	1	1	.500	1.20	2	15	19	10	1	0	0
1927	1	0	1.000	4.91	1	7.1	8	2	1	0	0
1928	2	0	1.000	1.50	2	18	14	14	6	0	0
6 yrs.	6	3	.667	1.62	11	77.2	74	48	22	1	0

Charles Hudson

CHARLES LYNN HUDSON BB TR
B. Mar. 16, 1959, Ennis, Tex. 6' 3" 185 lbs.

Year	W	L	PCT	ERA	G	IP	H	SO	BB	Sho	SV
1987	11	7	.611	3.61	35	154.2	137	100	57	2	0
1988	6	6	.500	4.49	28	106.1	93	58	36	0	2
2 yrs.	17	13	.567	3.97	63	261	230	158	93	2	2

Long Tom Hughes

THOMAS JAMES HUGHES BR TR
B. Nov. 29, 1878, Chicago, Ill. 6' 1" 175 lbs.
D. Feb. 8, 1956, Chicago, Ill.

Year	W	L	PCT	ERA	G	IP	H	SO	BB	Sho	SV
1904	7	11	.389	3.70	19	136.1	141	75	48	1	0

Tom Hughes

THOMAS L. HUGHES BR TR
B. Jan. 28, 1884, Coal Creek, Colo. 6' 2" 175 lbs.
D. Nov. 1, 1961, Los Angeles, Calif.

Year	W	L	PCT	ERA	G	IP	H	SO	BB	Sho	SV
1906	1	0	1.000	4.20	3	15	11	5	1	0	0
1907	2	0	1.000	2.67	4	27	16	10	11	0	0
1909	7	8	.467	2.65	24	118.2	109	69	37	2	1
1910	7	9	.438	3.50	23	151.2	153	64	37	0	1
4 yrs.	17	17	.500	3.14	54	312.1	289	148	86	2	2

Catfish Hunter

JAMES AUGUSTUS HUNTER BR TR
B. Apr. 8, 1946, Hertford, N. C. 6' 190 lbs.
Hall of Fame 1987

Year	W	L	PCT	ERA	G	IP	H	SO	BB	Sho	SV
1975	23	14	.622	2.58	39	328	248	177	83	7	0
1976	17	15	.531	3.53	36	298.2	268	173	68	2	0
1977	9	9	.500	4.72	22	143	137	52	47	1	0
1978	12	6	.667	3.58	21	118	98	56	35	1	0
1979	2	9	.182	5.31	19	105	128	34	34	0	0
5 yrs.	63	53	.543	3.58	137	992.2	879	492	267	11	0
League Championship Series											
1976	1	1	.500	4.50	2	12	10	5	1	0	0
1978	0	0	—	4.50	1	6	7	5	3	0	0
2 yrs.	1	1	.500	4.50	3	18	17	10	4	0	0
World Series											
1976	0	1	.000	3.12	1	8.2	10	5	4	0	0
1977	0	1	.000	10.38	2	4.1	6	1	0	0	0
1978	1	1	.500	4.15	2	13	13	5	1	0	0
3 yrs.	1	3	.250	4.85	5	26	29	11	5	0	0

Mark Hutton

MARK STEVEN HUTTON BR TR
B. Feb. 6, 1970, South Adelaide, Australia 6' 6" 240 lbs.

Year	W	L	PCT	ERA	G	IP	H	SO	BB	Sho	SV
1993	1	1	.500	5.73	7	22	24	12	17	0	0
1994	0	0	—	4.91	2	3.2	4	1	0	0	0
1996	0	2	.000	5.04	12	30.1	32	25	18	0	0
3 yrs.	1	3	.250	5.30	21	56	60	38	35	0	0

Grant Jackson

GRANT DWIGHT JACKSON BB TL
B. Sep. 28, 1942, Fostoria, Ohio 6' 180 lbs.

Year	W	L	PCT	ERA	G	IP	H	SO	BB	Sho	SV
1976	6	0	1.000	1.69	21	58.2	38	25	16	1	1
League Championship Series											
1976	0	0	—	8.10	2	3.1	4	3	1	0	0

Grant Jackson *continued*

Year	W	L	PCT	ERA	G	IP	H	SO	BB	Sho	SV
World Series											
1976	0	0	—	4.91	1	3.2	4	3	0	0	0

Johnny James

JOHN PHILLIP JAMES BL TR
B. Jul. 23, 1933, Bonner's Ferry, Ida. 5' 10" 160 lbs.

Year	W	L	PCT	ERA	G	IP	H	SO	BB	Sho	SV
1958	0	0	—	0.00	1	3	2	1	4	0	0
1960	5	1	.833	4.36	28	43.1	38	29	26	0	2
1961	0	0	—	0.00	1	1.1	1	2	0	0	0
3 yrs.	5	1	.833	3.97	30	47.2	41	32	30	0	2

Domingo Jean

DOMINGO JEAN BR TR
B. Jan. 9, 1969, San Pedro de Macoris, Dominican
Republic 6' 2" 175 lbs.

Year	W	L	PCT	ERA	G	IP	H	SO	BB	Sho	SV
1993	1	1	.500	4.46	10	40.1	37	20	19	0	0

Tommy John

THOMAS EDWARD JOHN BR TL
B. May 22, 1943, Terre Haute, Ind. 6' 3" 180 lbs.

Year	W	L	PCT	ERA	G	IP	H	SO	BB	Sho	SV
1979	21	9	.700	2.97	37	276	268	111	65	3	0
1980	22	9	.710	3.43	36	265	270	78	56	6	0
1981	9	8	.529	2.64	20	140	135	50	39	0	0
1982	10	10	.500	3.66	30	186.2	190	54	34	2	0
1986	5	3	.625	2.93	13	70.2	73	28	15	0	0
1987	13	6	.684	4.03	33	187.2	212	63	47	1	0
1988	9	8	.529	4.49	35	176.1	221	81	46	0	0
1989	2	7	.222	5.80	10	63.2	87	18	22	0	0
8 yrs.	91	60	.603	3.59	214	1366	1456	483	324	12	0
Divisional Playoffs											
1981	0	1	.000	6.43	1	7	8	0	2	0	0
League Championship Series											
1980	0	0	—	2.70	1	6.2	8	3	1	0	0
1981	1	0	1.000	1.50	1	6	6	3	1	0	0
2 yrs.	1	0	1.000	2.13	2	12.2	14	6	2	0	0
World Series											
1981	1	0	1.000	0.69	3	13	11	8	0	0	0

Don Johnson

DONALD ROY JOHNSON BR TR
B. Nov. 12, 1926, Portland, Ore. 6' 3" 200 lbs.

Year	W	L	PCT	ERA	G	IP	H	SO	BB	Sho	SV
1947	4	3	.571	3.64	15	54.1	57	16	23	0	0
1950	1	0	1.000	10.00	8	18	35	9	12	0	0
2 yrs.	5	3	.625	5.23	23	72.1	92	25	35	0	0

Hank Johnson

HENRY WARD JOHNSON BR TR
B. May 21, 1906, Bradenton, Fla. 5' 11½" 175 lbs.
D. Aug. 20, 1982, Bradenton, Fla.

Year	W	L	PCT	ERA	G	IP	H	SO	BB	Sho	SV
1925	1	3	.250	6.85	24	67	88	25	37	1	0
1926	0	0	—	18.00	1	1	2	0	2	0	1
1928	14	9	.609	4.30	31	199	188	110	104	1	0
1929	3	3	.500	5.06	12	42.2	37	24	39	0	0
1930	14	11	.560	4.67	44	175.1	177	115	104	1	2
1931	13	8	.619	4.72	40	196.1	176	106	102	0	4
1932	2	2	.500	4.88	5	31.1	34	27	15	0	0
7 yrs.	47	36	.566	4.84	157	712.2	702	407	403	3	7

Jeff Johnson

WILLIAM JEFFREY JOHNSON BB TL
B. Aug. 4, 1966, Durham, N. C. 6' 3" 200 lbs.

Year	W	L	PCT	ERA	G	IP	H	SO	BB	Sho	SV
1991	6	11	.353	5.95	23	127	156	62	33	0	0
1992	2	3	.400	6.66	13	52.2	71	14	23	0	0
1993	0	2	.000	30.38	2	2.2	12	0	2	0	0
3 yrs.	8	16	.333	6.52	38	182.1	239	76	58	0	0

Johnny Johnson

JOHN CLIFFORD JOHNSON BL TL
B. Sep. 29, 1914, Belmore, Ohio 6' 182 lbs.
D. Jun. 26, 1991, Iron Mountain, Mich.

Year	W	L	PCT	ERA	G	IP	H	SO	BB	Sho	SV
1944	0	2	.000	4.05	22	26.2	25	11	24	0	3

Ken Johnson

KENNETH TRAVIS JOHNSON   BR TR
B. Jun. 16, 1933, West Palm Beach, Fla. 6' 4" 210 lbs.

Year	W	L	PCT	ERA	G	IP	H	SO	BB	Sho	SV
1969	1	2	.333	3.46	12	26	19	21	11	0	0

Gary Jones

GARETH HOWELL JONES   BL TL
B. Jun. 12, 1945, Huntington Park, Calif. 6' 191 lbs.

Year	W	L	PCT	ERA	G	IP	H	SO	BB	Sho	SV
1970	0	0	—	0.00	2	3	3	2	1	0	0
1971	0	0	—	9.00	12	14	19	10	7	0	0
2 yrs.	0	0	—	7.88	14	16	22	12	8	0	0

Jimmy Jones

JAMES CONDIA JONES   BR TR
B. Apr. 20, 1964, Dallas, Tex. 6' 2" 175 lbs.

Year	W	L	PCT	ERA	G	IP	H	SO	BB	Sho	SV
1989	2	1	.667	5.25	11	48	56	25	16	0	0
1990	1	2	.333	6.30	17	50	72	25	23	0	0
2 yrs.	3	3	.500	5.79	28	98	128	50	39	0	0

Sad Sam Jones

SAMUEL POND JONES   BR TR
B. Jul. 26, 1892, Woodsfield, Ohio   6' 170 lbs.
D. Jul. 6, 1966, Barnesville, Ohio

Year	W	L	PCT	ERA	G	IP	H	SO	BB	Sho	SV
1922	13	13	.500	3.67	45	260	270	81	76	0	8
1923	21	8	.724	3.63	39	243	239	68	69	3	4
1924	9	6	.600	3.63	36	178.2	187	53	76	3	3
1925	15	21	.417	4.63	43	246.2	267	92	104	1	2
1926	9	8	.529	4.98	39	161	186	69	80	1	5
5 yrs.	67	56	.545	4.06	202	1089.1	1149	363	405	8	22
World Series											
1922	0	0	—	0.00	2	2	1	0	1	0	0
1923	0	1	.000	0.90	2	10	5	3	2	0	1
1926	0	0	—	9.00	1	1	2	1	2	0	0
3 yrs.	0	1	.000	1.38	5	13	8	4	5	0	1

Mike Jurewicz

MICHAEL ALLEN JUREWICZ   BB TL
B. Sep. 20, 1945, Buffalo, N. Y.   6' 3" 205 lbs.

Year	W	L	PCT	ERA	G	IP	H	SO	BB	Sho	SV
1965	0	0	—	7.71	2	2.1	5	2	1	0	0

Jim Kaat

JAMES LEE KAAT   BL TL
B. Nov. 7, 1938, Zeeland, Mich.   6' 4½" 205 lbs.

Year	W	L	PCT	ERA	G	IP	H	SO	BB	Sho	SV
1979	2	3	.400	3.88	40	58	64	23	14	0	2
1980	0	1	.000	7.20	4	5	8	1	4	0	0
2 yrs.	2	4	.333	4.14	44	63	72	24	18	0	2

Scott Kamieniecki

SCOTT ANDREW KAMIENIECKI   BR TR
B. Apr. 19, 1964, Mt. Clemens, Mich.   6' 195 lbs.

Year	W	L	PCT	ERA	G	IP	H	SO	BB	Sho	SV
1991	4	4	.500	3.90	9	55.1	54	34	22	0	0
1992	6	14	.300	4.36	28	188	193	88	74	0	0
1993	10	7	.588	4.08	30	154.1	163	72	59	0	1
1994	8	6	.571	3.76	22	117.1	115	71	59	0	0
1995	7	6	.538	4.01	17	89.2	83	43	49	0	0
1996	1	2	.333	11.12	7	22.2	36	15	19	0	0
6 yrs.	36	39	.480	4.33	113	627.1	644	323	282	0	1
Divisional Playoffs											
1995	0	0	—	7.20	1	5	9	4	4	0	0

Bob Kammeyer

ROBERT LYNN KAMMEYER   BR TR
B. Dec. 2, 1950, Kansas City, Mo.   6' 4" 210 lbs.

Year	W	L	PCT	ERA	G	IP	H	SO	BB	Sho	SV
1978	0	0	—	5.82	7	21.2	24	11	6	0	0
1979	0	0	—	∞	1	0	7	0	0	0	0
2 yrs.	0	0	—	9.14	8	21.2	31	11	6	0	0

Herb Karpel

HERBERT KARPEL   BL TL
B. Dec. 27, 1917, Brooklyn, N. Y.   5' 9½" 180 lbs.

Year	W	L	PCT	ERA	G	IP	H	SO	BB	Sho	SV
1946	0	0	—	10.80	2	1.2	4	0	0	0	0

Curt Kaufman

CURT GERRARD KAUFMAN   BR TR
B. Jul. 19, 1957, Omaha, Neb.   6' 2" 175 lbs.

Year	W	L	PCT	ERA	G	IP	H	SO	BB	Sho	SV
1982	1	0	1.000	5.19	7	8.2	9	1	6	0	0

Curt Kaufman *continued*

Year	W	L	PCT	ERA	G	IP	H	SO	BB	Sho	SV
1983	0	0	—	3.12	4	8.2	10	8	4	0	0
2 yrs.	1	0	1.000	4.15	11	17.1	19	9	10	0	0

Ray Keating

RAYMOND HERBERT KEATING   BR TR
B. Jul. 21, 1891, Bridgeport, Conn.   5' 11" 185 lbs.
D. Nov. 28, 1963, Sacramento, Calif.

Year	W	L	PCT	ERA	G	IP	H	SO	BB	Sho	SV
1912	0	3	.000	5.80	6	35.2	36	21	18	0	0
1913	6	12	.333	3.21	28	151.1	146	83	51	2	0
1914	7	11	.389	2.96	34	210	198	109	67	0	1
1915	3	6	.333	3.63	11	79.1	66	37	45	1	0
1916	5	6	.455	3.07	14	91	91	35	37	0	0
1918	2	2	.500	3.91	15	48.1	39	16	30	0	0
6 yrs.	23	40	.365	3.36	108	615.2	576	301	248	3	1

Bob Keefe

ROBERT FRANCIS KEEFE   BR TR
B. Jun. 16, 1882, Folsom, Calif.   5' 11" 155 lbs.
D. Dec. 7, 1964, Sacramento, Calif.

Year	W	L	PCT	ERA	G	IP	H	SO	BB	Sho	SV
1907	3	5	.375	2.50	19	57.2	60	20	20	0	3

Mike Kekich

MICHAEL DENNIS KEKICH   BR TL
B. Apr. 2, 1945, San Diego, Calif.   6' 1" 196 lbs.

Year	W	L	PCT	ERA	G	IP	H	SO	BB	Sho	SV
1969	4	6	.400	4.54	28	105	91	66	49	0	1
1970	6	3	.667	4.82	26	99	103	63	55	0	0
1971	10	9	.526	4.08	37	170	167	93	82	0	0
1972	10	13	.435	3.70	29	175.1	172	78	76	0	0
1973	1	1	.500	9.20	5	14.2	20	4	14	0	0
5 yrs.	31	32	.492	4.31	125	564	553	304	276	0	1

Matt Keough

MATTHEW LON KEOUGH   BR TR
B. Jul. 3, 1955, Pomona, Calif.   6' 3" 190 lbs.

Year	W	L	PCT	ERA	G	IP	H	SO	BB	Sho	SV
1983	3	4	.429	5.17	12	55.2	59	26	20	0	0

Jimmy Key

JAMES EDWARD KEY   BR TL
B. Apr. 22, 1961, Huntsville, Ala.   6' 1" 180 lbs.

Year	W	L	PCT	ERA	G	IP	H	SO	BB	Sho	SV
1993	18	6	.750	3.00	34	236.2	219	173	43	2	0
1994	17	4	.810	3.27	25	168	177	97	52	0	0
1995	1	2	.333	5.64	5	30.1	40	14	6	0	0
1996	12	11	.522	4.68	30	169.1	171	116	58	0	0
4 yrs.	48	23	.676	3.68	94	604.1	607	400	159	2	0
Divisional Playoffs											
1996	0	0	—	3.60	1	5	5	3	1	0	0
League Championship Series											
1996	1	0	1.000	2.25	1	8	3	5	1	0	0
World Series											
1996	1	1	.500	3.97	2	11.1	15	1	5	0	0

Fred Kipp

FRED LEO KIPP   BL TL
B. Oct. 1, 1931, Piqua, Kans.   6' 4" 200 lbs.

Year	W	L	PCT	ERA	G	IP	H	SO	BB	Sho	SV
1960	0	1	.000	6.23	4	4.1	4	2	0	0	0

Frank Kitson

FRANK R. KITSON   BL TR
B. Sep. 11, 1869, Hopkins, Mich.   5' 11" 165 lbs.
D. Apr. 14, 1930, Allegan, Mich.

Year	W	L	PCT	ERA	G	IP	H	SO	BB	Sho	SV
1907	4	0	1.000	3.10	12	61	75	14	17	0	0

Ted Kleinhans

THEODORE OTTO KLEINHANS   BR TL
B. Apr. 8, 1899, Deer Park, Wis.   6' 170 lbs.
D. Jul. 24, 1985, Redington Beach, Fla.

Year	W	L	PCT	ERA	G	IP	H	SO	BB	Sho	SV
1936	1	1	.500	5.83	19	29.1	36	10	23	0	1

Ed Klepfer

EDWARD LLOYD KLEPFER   BR TR
B. Mar. 17, 1888, Summerville, Pa.   6' 185 lbs.
D. Aug. 9, 1950, Tulsa, Okla.

Year	W	L	PCT	ERA	G	IP	H	SO	BB	Sho	SV
1911	0	0	—	6.75	2	4	5	4	2	0	0

Ed Klepfer *continued*

Year	W	L	PCT	ERA	G	IP	H	SO	BB	Sho	SV
1913	0	1	.000	7.66	8	24.2	38	10	12	0	0
2 yrs.	0	1	.000	7.53	10	28.2	43	14	14	0	0

Ron Klimkowski

RONALD BERNARD KLIMKOWSKI BR TR
B. Mar. 1, 1944, Jersey City, N. J. 6' 2" 190 lbs.

Year	W	L	PCT	ERA	G	IP	H	SO	BB	Sho	SV
1969	0	0	—	0.64	3	14	6	3	5	0	0
1970	6	7	.462	2.66	45	98	80	40	33	1	1
1972	0	3	.000	4.06	16	31	32	11	15	0	1
3 yrs.	6	10	.375	2.77	64	143	118	54	53	1	2

Steve Kline

STEVEN JACK KLINE BR TR
B. Oct. 6, 1947, Wenatchee, Wash. 6' 3" 205 lbs.

Year	W	L	PCT	ERA	G	IP	H	SO	BB	Sho	SV
1970	6	6	.500	3.42	16	100	99	49	24	0	0
1971	12	13	.480	2.96	31	222	206	81	37	1	0
1972	16	9	.640	2.40	32	236	210	58	44	4	0
1973	4	7	.364	4.01	14	74	76	19	31	1	0
1974	2	2	.500	3.46	4	26	26	6	5	0	0
5 yrs.	40	37	.519	2.97	97	658	617	213	141	6	0

Jim Konstanty

CASIMIR JAMES KONSTANTY BR TR
B. Mar. 2, 1917, Strykersville, N. Y. 6' 1½" 202 lbs.
D. Jun. 11, 1976, Oneonta, N. Y.

Year	W	L	PCT	ERA	G	IP	H	SO	BB	Sho	SV
1954	1	1	.500	0.98	9	18.1	11	3	6	0	2
1955	7	2	.778	2.32	45	73.2	68	19	24	0	11
1956	0	0	—	4.91	8	11	15	6	6	0	2
3 yrs.	8	3	.727	2.36	62	103	94	28	36	0	15

Steve Kraly

STEVE CHARLES KRALY BL TL
B. Apr. 18, 1929, Whiting, Ind. 5' 10" 152 lbs.

Year	W	L	PCT	ERA	G	IP	H	SO	BB	Sho	SV
1953	0	2	.000	3.24	5	25	19	8	16	0	1

Jack Kramer

JOHN HENRY KRAMER BR TR
B. Jan. 5, 1918, New Orleans, La. 6' 2" 190 lbs.
D. May 18, 1995, Metairie, La.

Year	W	L	PCT	ERA	G	IP	H	SO	BB	Sho	SV
1951	1	3	.250	4.65	19	40.2	46	15	21	0	0

Johnny Kucks

JOHN CHARLES KUCKS BR TR
B. Jul. 27, 1933, Hoboken, N. J. 6' 3" 170 lbs.

Year	W	L	PCT	ERA	G	IP	H	SO	BB	Sho	SV
1955	8	7	.533	3.41	29	126.2	122	49	44	1	0
1956	18	9	.667	3.85	34	224.1	223	67	72	3	0
1957	8	10	.444	3.56	37	179.1	169	78	59	1	2
1958	8	8	.500	3.93	34	126	132	46	39	1	4
1959	0	1	.000	8.64	9	16.2	21	9	9	0	0
5 yrs.	42	35	.545	3.82	143	673	667	249	223	6	6
World Series											
1955	0	0	—	6.00	2	3	4	1	1	0	0
1956	1	0	1.000	0.82	3	11	6	2	3	1	0
1957	0	0	—	0.00	1	0.2	1	1	1	0	0
1958	0	0	—	2.08	2	4.1	4	0	1	0	0
4 yrs.	1	0	1.000	1.89	8	19	15	4	6	1	0

Bill Kunkel

WILLIAM GUSTAVE/JAMES KUNKEL BR TR
B. Jul. 7, 1936, Hoboken, N. J. 6' 1" 187 lbs.
D. May 4, 1985, Red Bank, N. J.

Year	W	L	PCT	ERA	G	IP	H	SO	BB	Sho	SV
1963	3	2	.600	2.72	22	46.1	42	31	13	0	0

Bob Kuzava

ROBERT LEROY KUZAVA BB TL
B. May 28, 1923, Wyandotte, Mich. 6' 2" 202 lbs.

Year	W	L	PCT	ERA	G	IP	H	SO	BB	Sho	SV
1951	8	4	.667	2.40	23	82.1	76	50	27	1	5
1952	8	8	.500	3.45	28	133	115	67	63	1	3
1953	6	5	.545	3.31	33	92.1	92	48	34	2	4
1954	1	3	.250	5.45	20	39.2	46	22	18	0	1
4 yrs.	23	20	.535	3.39	104	347.1	329	187	142	4	13

Bob Kuzava *continued*

Year	W	L	PCT	ERA	G	IP	H	SO	BB	Sho	SV
World Series											
1951	0	0	—	0.00	1	1	0	0	0	0	1
1952	0	0	—	0.00	1	2.2	0	2	0	0	1
1953	0	0	—	13.50	1	0.2	2	1	0	0	0
3 yrs.	0	0	—	2.08	3	4.1	2	3	0	0	2

Dave LaPoint

DAVID JEFFREY LAPOINT BL TL
B. Jul. 29, 1959, Glens Falls, N. Y. 6' 3" 205 lbs.

Year	W	L	PCT	ERA	G	IP	H	SO	BB	Sho	SV
1989	6	9	.400	5.62	20	113.2	146	51	45	0	0
1990	7	10	.412	4.11	28	157.2	180	67	57	0	0
2 yrs.	13	19	.406	4.74	48	271.1	326	118	102	0	0

Dave LaRoche

DAVID EUGENE LAROCHE BL TL
B. May 14, 1948, Colorado Springs, Colo. 6' 2" 200 lbs.

Year	W	L	PCT	ERA	G	IP	H	SO	BB	Sho	SV
1981	4	1	.800	2.49	26	47	38	24	16	0	0
1982	4	2	.667	3.42	25	50	54	31	11	0	0
1983	0	0	—	18.00	1	1	2	0	0	0	0
3 yrs.	8	3	.727	3.12	52	98	94	55	27	0	0
World Series											
1981	0	0	—	0.00	1	1	0	2	0	0	0

Joe Lake

JOSEPH HENRY LAKE BR TR
B. Jan. 6, 1881, Brooklyn, N. Y. 6' 185 lbs.
D. Jun. 30, 1950, Brooklyn, N. Y.

Year	W	L	PCT	ERA	G	IP	H	SO	BB	Sho	SV
1908	9	22	.290	3.17	38	269.1	252	118	77	2	0
1909	14	11	.560	1.88	31	215.1	180	117	59	3	1
2 yrs.	23	33	.411	2.60	69	484.2	432	235	136	5	1

Don Larsen

DON JAMES LARSEN BR TR
B. Aug. 7, 1929, Michigan City, Ind. 6' 4" 215 lbs.

Year	W	L	PCT	ERA	G	IP	H	SO	BB	Sho	SV
1955	9	2	.818	3.06	19	97	81	44	51	1	2
1956	11	5	.688	3.26	38	179.2	133	107	96	1	1
1957	10	4	.714	3.74	27	139.2	113	81	87	1	0
1958	9	6	.600	3.07	19	114.1	100	55	52	3	0
1959	6	7	.462	4.33	25	124.2	122	69	76	1	0
5 yrs.	45	24	.652	3.50	128	655.1	549	356	362	7	3
World Series											
1955	0	1	.000	11.25	1	4	5	2	2	0	0
1956	1	0	1.000	0.00	2	10.2	1	7	4	1	0
1957	1	1	.500	3.72	2	9.2	8	6	5	0	0
1958	1	0	1.000	0.96	2	9.1	9	9	6	0	0
4 yrs.	3	2	.600	2.67	7	33.2	23	24	17	1	0

Louis LeRoy

LOUIS PAUL LEROY BR TR
B. Feb. 18, 1879, Omro, Wis. 5' 10" 180 lbs.
D. Oct. 10, 1944, Shawano, Wis.

Year	W	L	PCT	ERA	G	IP	H	SO	BB	Sho	SV
1905	1	1	.500	3.75	3	24	26	8	1	0	0
1906	2	0	1.000	2.22	11	44.2	33	28	12	0	1
2 yrs.	3	1	.750	2.75	14	68.2	59	36	13	0	1

Tim Leary

TIMOTHY JAMES LEARY BR TR
B. Mar. 21, 1958, Santa Monica, Calif. 6' 3" 205 lbs.

Year	W	L	PCT	ERA	G	IP	H	SO	BB	Sho	SV
1990	9	19	.321	4.11	31	208	202	138	78	1	0
1991	4	10	.286	6.49	28	120.2	150	83	57	0	0
1992	5	6	.455	5.57	18	97	84	34	57	0	0
3 yrs.	18	35	.340	5.12	77	425.2	436	255	192	1	0

Al Leiter

ALOIS TERRY LEITER BL TL
B. Oct. 23, 1965, Toms River, N. J. 6' 2" 200 lbs.

Year	W	L	PCT	ERA	G	IP	H	SO	BB	Sho	SV
1987	2	2	.500	6.35	4	22.2	24	28	15	0	0
1988	4	4	.500	3.92	14	57.1	49	60	33	0	0
1989	1	2	.333	6.08	4	26.2	23	22	21	0	0
3 yrs.	7	8	.467	4.98	22	106.2	96	110	69	0	0

Mark Leiter

MARK EDWARD LEITER — BR TR
B. Apr. 13, 1963, Joliet, Ill. — 6' 3" 200 lbs.

Year	W	L	PCT	ERA	G	IP	H	SO	BB	Sho	SV
1990	1	1	.500	6.84	8	26.1	33	21	9	0	0

Jim Lewis

JAMES MARTIN LEWIS — BR TR
B. Oct. 12, 1955, Miami, Fla. — 6' 3" 190 lbs.

Year	W	L	PCT	ERA	G	IP	H	SO	BB	Sho	SV
1982	0	0	—	54.00	1	0.2	3	0	3	0	0

Terry Ley

TERRENCE RICHARD LEY — BL TL
B. Feb. 21, 1947, Portland, Ore. — 6' 190 lbs.

Year	W	L	PCT	ERA	G	IP	H	SO	BB	Sho	SV
1971	0	0	—	5.00	6	9	9	7	9	0	0

Paul Lindblad

PAUL AARON LINDBLAD — BL TL
B. Aug. 9, 1941, Chanute, Kans. — 6' 1" 185 lbs.

Year	W	L	PCT	ERA	G	IP	H	SO	BB	Sho	SV
1978	0	0	—	4.50	7	18	21	9	8	0	0
World Series											
1978	0	0	—	11.57	1	2.1	4	1	0	0	0

Johnny Lindell

JOHN HARLAN LINDELL — BR TR
B. Aug. 30, 1916, Greeley, Colo. — 6' 4½" 217 lbs.
D. Aug. 27, 1985, Newport Beach, Calif.

Year	W	L	PCT	ERA	G	IP	H	SO	BB	Sho	SV
1942	2	1	.667	3.76	23	52.2	52	28	22	0	1

Clem Llewellyn

CLEMENT MANLY LLEWELLYN — BL TR
B. Aug. 1, 1895, Dobson, N. C. — 6' 2" 195 lbs.
D. Nov. 26, 1969, Concord, N. C.

Year	W	L	PCT	ERA	G	IP	H	SO	BB	Sho	SV
1922	0	0	—	0.00	1	1	1	0	0	0	0

Graeme Lloyd

GRAEME JOHN LLOYD — BL TL
B. Apr. 9, 1967, Geelong, Australia — 6' 8" 225 lbs.

Year	W	L	PCT	ERA	G	IP	H	SO	BB	Sho	SV
1996	0	2	.000	17.47	13	5.2	12	6	5	0	0
Divisional Playoffs											
1996	0	0	—	0.00	2	1	1	0	0	0	0
League Championship Series											
1996	0	0	—	0.00	2	1.2	0	1	0	0	0
World Series											
1996	1	0	1.000	0.00	4	2.2	0	4	0	0	0

Tim Lollar

WILLIAM TIMOTHY LOLLAR — BL TL
B. Mar. 17, 1956, Poplar Bluff, Mo. — 6' 3" 200 lbs.

Year	W	L	PCT	ERA	G	IP	H	SO	BB	Sho	SV
1980	1	0	1.000	3.38	14	32	33	13	20	0	2

Ed Lopat

EDMUND WALTER LOPAT — BL TL
B. Jun. 21, 1918, New York, N. Y. — 5' 10" 185 lbs.
D. Jun. 15, 1992, Darien, Conn.

Year	W	L	PCT	ERA	G	IP	H	SO	BB	Sho	SV
1948	17	11	.607	3.65	33	226.2	246	83	66	3	0
1949	15	10	.600	3.26	31	215.1	222	70	69	4	1
1950	18	8	.692	3.47	35	236.1	244	72	65	3	1
1951	21	9	.700	2.91	31	234.2	209	93	71	5	0
1952	10	5	.667	2.53	20	149.1	127	56	53	2	0
1953	16	4	.800	2.42	25	178.1	169	50	32	3	0
1954	12	4	.750	3.55	26	170	189	54	33	0	0
1955	4	8	.333	3.74	16	86.2	101	24	16	1	0
8 yrs.	113	59	.657	3.19	217	1497.1	1507	502	405	21	2
World Series											
1949	1	0	1.000	6.35	1	5.2	9	4	1	0	0
1950	0	0	—	2.25	1	8	9	5	0	0	0
1951	2	0	1.000	0.50	2	18	10	4	3	0	0
1952	0	1	.000	4.76	2	11.1	14	3	4	0	0
1953	1	0	1.000	2.00	1	9	9	3	4	0	0
5 yrs.	4	1	.800	2.60	7	52	51	19	12	0	0

Slim Love

EDWARD HAUGHTON LOVE — BL TL
B. Aug. 1, 1890, Love, Miss. — 6' 7" 195 lbs.
D. Nov. 30, 1942, Memphis, Tenn.

Year	W	L	PCT	ERA	G	IP	H	SO	BB	Sho	SV
1916	2	0	1.000	4.91	20	47.2	46	21	23	0	0

Slim Love *continued*

Year	W	L	PCT	ERA	G	IP	H	SO	BB	Sho	SV
1917	6	5	.545	2.35	33	130.1	115	82	57	0	1
1918	13	12	.520	3.07	38	228.2	207	95	116	1	1
3 yrs.	21	17	.553	3.05	91	406.2	368	198	196	1	2

Sparky Lyle

ALBERT WALTER LYLE — BL TL
B. Jul. 22, 1944, Du Bois, Pa. — 6' 1" 182 lbs.

Year	W	L	PCT	ERA	G	IP	H	SO	BB	Sho	SV
1972	9	5	.643	1.91	59	108.1	84	75	29	0	35
1973	5	9	.357	2.51	51	82.1	66	63	18	0	27
1974	9	3	.750	1.66	66	114	93	89	43	0	15
1975	5	7	.417	3.12	49	89.1	94	65	36	0	6
1976	7	8	.467	2.26	64	103.2	82	61	42	0	23
1977	13	5	.722	2.17	72	137	131	68	33	0	26
1978	9	3	.750	3.47	59	111.2	116	33	33	0	9
7 yrs.	57	40	.588	2.41	420	746.1	666	454	234	0	141
League Championship Series											
1976	0	0	—	0.00	1	1	0	0	1	0	1
1977	2	0	1.000	0.96	4	9.1	7	3	0	0	0
1978	0	0	—	13.50	1	1.1	3	0	0	0	0
3 yrs.	2	0	1.000	2.31	6	11.2	10	3	1	0	1
World Series											
1976	0	0	—	0.00	2	2.2	1	3	0	0	0
1977	1	0	1.000	1.93	2	4.2	2	2	0	0	0
2 yrs.	1	0	1.000	1.23	4	7.1	3	5	0	0	0

Al Lyons

ALBERT HAROLD LYONS — BR TR
B. Jul. 18, 1918, St. Joseph, Mo. — 6' 2" 195 lbs.
D. Dec. 20, 1965, Inglewood, Calif.

Year	W	L	PCT	ERA	G	IP	H	SO	BB	Sho	SV
1944	0	0	—	4.54	11	39.2	43	14	24	0	0
1946	0	1	.000	5.40	2	8.1	11	4	6	0	0
1947	1	0	1.000	9.00	6	11	18	7	9	0	0
3 yrs.	1	1	.500	5.49	19	59	72	25	39	0	0

Duke Maas

DUANE FREDERICK MAAS — BR TR
B. Jan. 31, 1929, Utica, Mich. — 5' 10" 170 lbs.
D. Dec. 7, 1976, Mt. Clemens, Mich.

Year	W	L	PCT	ERA	G	IP	H	SO	BB	Sho	SV
1958	7	3	.700	3.82	22	101.1	93	50	36	1	0
1959	14	8	.636	4.43	38	138	149	67	53	1	4
1960	5	1	.833	4.09	35	70.1	70	28	35	0	4
1961	0	0	—	54.00	1	0.1	2	0	0	0	0
4 yrs.	26	12	.684	4.21	96	310	314	145	124	2	8
World Series											
1958	0	0	—	81.00	1	0.1	2	0	1	0	0
1960	0	0	—	4.50	1	2	2	1	0	0	0
2 yrs.	0	0	—	15.43	2	2.1	4	1	1	0	0

Bob MacDonald

ROBERT JOSEPH MACDONALD — BL TL
B. Apr. 27, 1965, East Orange, N. J. — 6' 3" 200 lbs.

Year	W	L	PCT	ERA	G	IP	H	SO	BB	Sho	SV
1995	1	1	.500	4.86	33	46.1	50	41	22	0	0

Danny MacFayden

DANIEL KNOWLES MACFAYDEN — BR TR
B. Jun. 10, 1905, North Truro, Mass. — 5' 11" 170 lbs.
D. Aug. 26, 1972, Brunswick, Me.

Year	W	L	PCT	ERA	G	IP	H	SO	BB	Sho	SV
1932	7	5	.583	3.93	17	121.1	137	33	37	0	1
1933	3	2	.600	5.88	25	90.1	120	28	37	0	0
1934	4	3	.571	4.50	22	96	110	41	31	0	0
3 yrs.	14	10	.583	4.68	64	307.2	367	102	105	0	1

Dave Madison

DAVID PLEDGER MADISON — BR TR
B. Feb. 1, 1921, Brooksville, Miss. — 6' 3" 190 lbs.
D. Dec. 8, 1985, Macon, Miss.

Year	W	L	PCT	ERA	G	IP	H	SO	BB	Sho	SV
1950	0	0	—	6.00	1	3	3	1	1	0	0

Sal Maglie

SALVATORE ANTHONY MAGLIE — BR TR
B. Apr. 26, 1917, Niagara Falls, N. Y. — 6' 2" 180 lbs.
D. Dec. 28, 1992, Niagara Falls, N. Y.

Year	W	L	PCT	ERA	G	IP	H	SO	BB	Sho	SV
1957	2	0	1.000	1.73	6	26	22	9	7	1	3

Sal Maglie *continued*

Year	W	L	PCT	ERA	G	IP	H	SO	BB	Sho	SV
1958	1	1	.500	4.63	7	23.1	27	7	9	0	0
2 yrs.	3	1	.750	3.10	13	49.1	49	16	16	1	3

Jim Magnuson

JAMES ROBERT MAGNUSON　BR TL
B. Aug. 18, 1946, Marinette, Wis.　6' 2" 190 lbs.
D. May 30, 1991, Green Bay, Wis.

Year	W	L	PCT	ERA	G	IP	H	SO	BB	Sho	SV
1973	0	1	.000	4.28	8	27.1	38	9	9	0	0

Frank Makosky

FRANK MAKOSKY　BR TR
B. Jan. 20, 1910, Boonton, N. J.　6' 1" 185 lbs.
D. Jan. 10, 1987, Stroudsburg, Pa.

Year	W	L	PCT	ERA	G	IP	H	SO	BB	Sho	SV
1937	5	2	.714	4.97	26	58	64	27	24	0	3

Pat Malone

PERCE LEIGH MALONE　BL TR
B. Sep. 25, 1902, Altoona, Pa.　6' 200 lbs.
D. May 13, 1943, Altoona, Pa.

Year	W	L	PCT	ERA	G	IP	H	SO	BB	Sho	SV
1935	3	5	.375	5.43	29	56.1	53	25	33	0	3
1936	12	4	.750	3.81	35	134.2	144	72	60	0	9
1937	4	4	.500	5.48	28	92	109	49	35	0	6
3 yrs.	19	13	.594	4.67	92	283	306	146	128	0	18
World Series											
1936	0	0	.000	1.80	2	5	2	2	1	0	1

Al Mamaux

ALBERT LEON MAMAUX　BR TR
B. May 30, 1894, Pittsburgh, Pa.　6' ½" 168 lbs.
D. Jan. 2, 1963, Santa Monica, Calif.

Year	W	L	PCT	ERA	G	IP	H	SO	BB	Sho	SV
1924	1	1	.500	5.68	14	38	44	12	20	0	0

Rube Manning

WALTER S. MANNING　BR TR
B. Apr. 29, 1883, Chambersburg, Pa.　6' 180 lbs.
D. Apr. 23, 1930, Williamsport, Pa.

Year	W	L	PCT	ERA	G	IP	H	SO	BB	Sho	SV
1907	0	1	.000	3.00	1	9	8	3	3	0	0
1908	13	16	.448	2.94	41	245	228	113	86	2	1
1909	7	11	.389	3.17	26	173	167	71	48	2	1
1910	2	4	.333	3.70	16	75.1	80	25	25	0	0
4 yrs.	22	32	.407	3.14	84	502.1	483	212	162	4	2

Josias Manzanillo

JOSIAS MANZANILLO　BR TR
B. Oct. 16, 1967, San Pedro de Macoris,
Dominican Republic　6' 190 lbs.

Year	W	L	PCT	ERA	G	IP	H	SO	BB	Sho	SV
1995	0	0	—	2.08	11	17.1	19	11	9	0	0

Cliff Markle

CLIFFORD MONROE MARKLE　BR TR
B. May 3, 1894, Dravosburg, Pa.　5' 8½" 160 lbs.
D. May 24, 1974, Temple City, Calif.

Year	W	L	PCT	ERA	G	IP	H	SO	BB	Sho	SV
1915	2	0	1.000	0.39	3	23	15	12	6	0	0
1916	4	3	.571	4.53	11	45.2	41	14	31	1	0
1924	0	3	.000	8.87	7	23.1	29	7	20	0	0
3 yrs.	6	6	.500	4.60	21	92	85	33	57	1	0

Jim Marquis

JAMES MILBURN MARQUIS　BR TR
B. Nov. 18, 1900, Yoakum, Tex.　5' 11" 174 lbs.
D. Aug. 5, 1992, Jackson, Calif.

Year	W	L	PCT	ERA	G	IP	H	SO	BB	Sho	SV
1925	0	0	—	9.82	2	7.1	12	0	6	0	0

Cuddles Marshall

CLARENCE WESTLY MARSHALL　BR TR
B. Apr. 28, 1925, Bellingham, Wash.　6' 3" 200 lbs.

Year	W	L	PCT	ERA	G	IP	H	SO	BB	Sho	SV
1946	3	4	.429	5.33	23	81	96	32	56	0	0
1948	0	0	—	0.00	1	1	0	0	3	0	0
1949	3	0	1.000	5.11	21	49.1	48	13	48	0	3
3 yrs.	6	4	.600	5.21	45	131.1	144	45	107	0	3

Tippy Martinez

FELIX ANTHONY MARTINEZ　BL TL
B. May 31, 1950, La Junta, Colo.　5' 10" 180 lbs.

Year	W	L	PCT	ERA	G	IP	H	SO	BB	Sho	SV
1974	0	0	—	4.15	10	13	14	10	9	0	0
1975	1	2	.333	2.68	23	37	27	20	32	0	8
1976	2	0	1.000	1.93	11	28	18	14	14	0	2
3 yrs.	3	2	.600	2.65	44	78	59	44	55	0	10

Rudy May

RUDOLPH MAY　BL TL
B. Jul. 18, 1944, Coffeyville, Kans.　6' 2" 205 lbs.

Year	W	L	PCT	ERA	G	IP	H	SO	BB	Sho	SV
1974	8	4	.667	2.29	17	114	75	90	48	2	0
1975	14	12	.538	3.06	32	212	179	145	99	1	0
1976	4	3	.571	3.57	11	68	49	38	28	1	0
1980	15	5	.750	2.47	41	175	144	133	39	1	3
1981	6	11	.353	4.14	27	148	137	79	41	0	1
1982	6	6	.500	2.89	41	106	109	85	14	0	3
1983	1	5	.167	6.87	15	18.1	22	16	12	0	0
7 yrs.	54	46	.540	3.12	184	841.1	715	586	281	5	7
Divisional Playoffs											
1981	0	0	—	0.00	1	2	1	1	0	0	0
League Championship Series											
1980	0	1	.000	3.38	1	8	6	4	3	0	0
1981	0	0	—	8.10	1	3.1	6	5	0	0	0
2 yrs.	0	1	.000	4.76	2	11.1	12	9	3	0	0
World Series											
1981	0	0	—	2.84	3	6.1	5	5	1	0	0

Carl Mays

CARL WILLIAM MAYS　BL TR
B. Nov. 12, 1891, Liberty, Ky.　5' 11½" 195 lbs.
D. Apr. 4, 1971, El Cajon, Calif.

Year	W	L	PCT	ERA	G	IP	H	SO	BB	Sho	SV
1919	9	3	.750	1.65	13	120	96	54	37	1	0
1920	26	11	.703	3.06	45	312	310	92	84	6	2
1921	27	9	.750	3.05	49	336.2	332	70	76	1	7
1922	12	14	.462	3.60	34	240	257	41	50	1	2
1923	5	2	.714	6.20	23	81.1	119	16	32	0	0
5 yrs.	79	39	.669	3.25	164	1090	1114	273	279	9	11
World Series											
1921	1	2	.333	1.73	3	26	20	9	0	1	0
1922	0	1	.000	4.50	1	8	9	1	2	0	0
2 yrs.	1	3	.250	2.38	4	34	29	10	2	1	0

Larry McCall

LARRY STEPHEN McCALL　BL TR
B. Sep. 8, 1952, Asheville, N. C.　6' 2" 195 lbs.

Year	W	L	PCT	ERA	G	IP	H	SO	BB	Sho	SV
1977	0	1	.000	7.50	2	6	12	0	1	0	0
1978	1	1	.500	5.63	5	16	20	7	6	0	0
2 yrs.	1	2	.333	6.14	7	22	32	7	7	0	0

George McConnell

GEORGE NEELY McCONNELL　BR TR
B. Sep. 16, 1877, Shelbyville, Tenn.　6' 3" 190 lbs.
D. May 10, 1964, Chattanooga, Tenn.

Year	W	L	PCT	ERA	G	IP	H	SO	BB	Sho	SV
1909	0	1	.000	2.25	2	4	3	4	3	0	0
1912	8	12	.400	2.75	23	176.2	172	91	52	0	0
1913	4	15	.211	3.20	35	180	162	72	60	0	3
3 yrs.	12	28	.300	2.97	60	360.2	337	167	115	0	3

Mike McCormick

MICHAEL FRANCIS McCORMICK　BL TL
B. Sep. 29, 1938, Pasadena, Calif.　6' 2" 195 lbs.

Year	W	L	PCT	ERA	G	IP	H	SO	BB	Sho	SV
1970	2	0	1.000	6.00	9	21	26	12	13	0	0

Lance McCullers

LANCE GRAYE McCULLERS　BB TR
B. Mar. 8, 1964, Tampa, Fla.　6' 1" 185 lbs.

Year	W	L	PCT	ERA	G	IP	H	SO	BB	Sho	SV
1989	4	3	.571	4.57	52	84.2	83	82	37	0	3
1990	1	0	1.000	3.60	11	15	14	11	6	0	0
2 yrs.	5	3	.625	4.42	63	99.2	97	93	43	0	3

Lindy McDaniel

LYNDALL DALE McDANIEL　BR TR
B. Dec. 13, 1935, Hollis, Okla.　6' 3" 195 lbs.

Year	W	L	PCT	ERA	G	IP	H	SO	BB	Sho	SV
1968	4	1	.800	1.75	24	51.1	30	43	12	0	10

Year	W	L	PCT	ERA	G	IP	H	SO	BB	Sho	SV

Lindy McDaniel *continued*

Year	W	L	PCT	ERA	G	IP	H	SO	BB	Sho	SV
1969	5	6	.455	3.55	51	83.2	84	60	23	0	5
1970	9	5	.643	2.01	62	112	88	81	23	0	29
1971	5	10	.333	5.01	44	70	82	39	24	0	4
1972	3	1	.750	2.25	37	68	54	47	25	0	0
1973	12	6	.667	2.86	47	160.1	148	93	49	0	10
6 yrs.	38	29	.567	2.89	265	545.1	486	363	156	0	58

Mickey McDermott
MAURICE JOSEPH MCDERMOTT BL TL
B. Aug. 29, 1928, Poughkeepsie, N.Y. 6' 2" 170 lbs.

Year	W	L	PCT	ERA	G	IP	H	SO	BB	Sho	SV
1956	2	6	.250	4.24	23	87	85	38	47	0	0
World Series											
1956	0	0	—	3.00	1	3	2	3	3	0	0

Danny McDevitt
DANIEL EUGENE MCDEVITT BL TL
B. Nov. 18, 1932, New York, N.Y. 5' 10" 175 lbs.

Year	W	L	PCT	ERA	G	IP	H	SO	BB	Sho	SV
1961	1	2	.333	7.62	8	13	18	8	8	0	1

Jim McDonald
JIMMIE LEROY MCDONALD BR TR
B. May 17, 1927, Grant's Pass, Ore. 5' 10½" 185 lbs.

Year	W	L	PCT	ERA	G	IP	H	SO	BB	Sho	SV
1952	3	4	.429	3.50	26	69.1	71	20	40	0	0
1953	9	7	.563	3.82	27	129.2	128	43	39	2	0
1954	4	1	.800	3.17	16	71	54	20	45	1	0
3 yrs.	16	12	.571	3.57	69	270	253	83	124	3	0
World Series											
1953	1	0	1.000	5.87		7.2	12	3	0	0	0

Jack McDowell
JACK BURNS MCDOWELL BR TR
B. Jan. 16, 1966, Van Nuys, Calif. 6' 5" 180 lbs.

Year	W	L	PCT	ERA	G	IP	H	SO	BB	Sho	SV
1995	15	10	.600	3.93	30	217.2	211	157	78	2	0
Divisional Playoffs											
1995	0	2	.000	9.00	2	7	8	6	4	0	0

Sam McDowell
SAMUEL EDWARD MCDOWELL BL TL
B. Sep. 21, 1942, Pittsburgh, Pa. 6' 5" 190 lbs.

Year	W	L	PCT	ERA	G	IP	H	SO	BB	Sho	SV
1973	5	8	.385	3.95	16	95.2	73	75	64	1	0
1974	1	6	.143	4.69	13	48	42	33	41	0	0
2 yrs.	6	14	.300	4.20	29	143.2	115	108	105	1	0

Lou McEvoy
LOUIS ANTHONY MCEVOY BR TR
B. May 30, 1902, Williamsburg, Kans. 6' 2½" 203 lbs.
D. Dec. 17, 1953, Webster Groves, Mo.

Year	W	L	PCT	ERA	G	IP	H	SO	BB	Sho	SV
1930	1	3	.250	6.71	28	52.1	64	14	29	0	3
1931	0	0	—	12.41	6	12.1	19	3	12	0	1
2 yrs.	1	3	.250	7.79	34	64.2	83	17	41	0	4

Andy McGaffigan
ANDREW JOSEPH MCGAFFIGAN BR TR
B. Oct. 25, 1956, West Palm Beach, Fla. 6' 3" 185 lbs.

Year	W	L	PCT	ERA	G	IP	H	SO	BB	Sho	SV
1981	0	0	—	2.57	2	7	5	2	3	0	0

Lynn McGlothen
LYNN EVERETT MCGLOTHEN BL TR
B. Mar. 27, 1950, Monroe, La. 6' 2" 185 lbs.
D. Aug. 14, 1984, Dubach, La.

Year	W	L	PCT	ERA	G	IP	H	SO	BB	Sho	SV
1982	0	0		10.80	4	5	9	2	2	0	0

Bob McGraw
ROBERT EMMETT MCGRAW BR TR
B. Apr. 10, 1895, La Veta, Colo. 6' 2" 160 lbs.
D. Jun. 2, 1978, Seal Beach, Calif.

Year	W	L	PCT	ERA	G	IP	H	SO	BB	Sho	SV
1917	0	1	.000	0.82	2	11	9	3	3	0	0
1918	0	1	.000	∞	1	0	0	0	4	0	0
1919	1	0	1.000	3.31	6	16.1	11	3	10	0	0

Year	W	L	PCT	ERA	G	IP	H	SO	BB	Sho	SV

Bob McGraw *continued*

Year	W	L	PCT	ERA	G	IP	H	SO	BB	Sho	SV
1920	0	0	—	4.67	15	27	24	11	20	0	0
4 yrs.	1	2	.333	4.14	24	54.1	44	17	37	0	0

Marty McHale
MARTIN JOSEPH MCHALE BR TR
B. Oct. 30, 1888, Stoneham, Mass. 5' 11½" 174 lbs.
D. May 7, 1979, Hempstead, N.Y.

Year	W	L	PCT	ERA	G	IP	H	SO	BB	Sho	SV
1913	2	4	.333	2.96	7	48.2	49	11	10	1	0
1914	7	16	.304	2.97	31	191	195	75	33	0	1
1915	3	7	.300	4.25	13	78.1	86	25	19	0	0
3 yrs.	12	27	.308	3.28	51	318	330	111	62	1	1

Herb McQuaid
HERBERT GEORGE MCQUAID BR TR
B. Mar. 29, 1899, San Francisco, Calif. 6' 2" 185 lbs.
D. Apr. 4, 1966, Richmond, Calif.

Year	W	L	PCT	ERA	G	IP	H	SO	BB	Sho	SV
1926	1	0	1.000	6.10	17	38.1	48	6	13	0	0

Jim Mecir
JAMES JASON MECIR BB TR
B. May 16, 1970, Bayside, N.Y. 6' 1" 195 lbs.

Year	W	L	PCT	ERA	G	IP	H	SO	BB	Sho	SV
1996	1	1	.500	5.13	26	40.1	42	38	23	0	0

Doc Medich
GEORGE FRANCIS MEDICH BR TR
B. Dec. 9, 1948, Aliquippa, Pa. 6' 5" 225 lbs.

Year	W	L	PCT	ERA	G	IP	H	SO	BB	Sho	SV
1972	0	0	—	∞	1	0	2	0	2	0	0
1973	14	9	.609	2.95	34	235	217	145	74	3	0
1974	19	15	.559	3.60	38	280	275	154	91	4	0
1975	16	16	.500	3.50	38	272.1	271	132	72	2	0
4 yrs.	49	40	.551	3.40	111	787.1	765	431	239	9	0

Andy Messersmith
JOHN ALEXANDER MESSERSMITH BR TR
B. Aug. 6, 1945, Toms River, N.J. 6' 1" 200 lbs.

Year	W	L	PCT	ERA	G	IP	H	SO	BB	Sho	SV
1978	0	3	.000	5.64	6	22.1	24	16	15	0	0

Tom Metcalf
THOMAS JOHN METCALF BR TR
B. Jul. 16, 1940, Amherst, Wis. 6' 2½" 174 lbs.

Year	W	L	PCT	ERA	G	IP	H	SO	BB	Sho	SV
1963	1	0	1.000	2.77	8	13	12	3	3	0	0

Bob Meyer
ROBERT BERNARD MEYER BR TL
B. Aug. 4, 1939, Toledo, Ohio 6' 2" 185 lbs.

Year	W	L	PCT	ERA	G	IP	H	SO	BB	Sho	SV
1964	0	3	.000	4.91	7	18.1	16	12	12	0	0

Gene Michael
EUGENE RICHARD MICHAEL BB TR
B. Jun. 2, 1938, Kent, Ohio 6' 2" 183 lbs.

Year	W	L	PCT	ERA	G	IP	H	SO	BB	Sho	SV
1968	0	0	—	0.00	1	3	5	3	0	0	0

Pete Mikkelsen
PETER JAMES MIKKELSEN BR TR
B. Oct. 25, 1939, Staten Island, N.Y. 6' 2" 210 lbs.

Year	W	L	PCT	ERA	G	IP	H	SO	BB	Sho	SV
1964	7	4	.636	3.56	50	86	79	63	41	0	12
1965	4	9	.308	3.28	41	82.1	78	69	36	0	1
2 yrs.	11	13	.458	3.42	91	168.1	157	132	77	0	13
World Series											
1964	0	1	.000	5.79	4	4.2	4	2	4	0	0

Sam Militello
SAM SALVATORE MILITELLO BR TR
B. Nov. 26, 1969, Tampa, Fla. 6' 3" 200 lbs.

Year	W	L	PCT	ERA	G	IP	H	SO	BB	Sho	SV
1992	3	3	.500	3.45	9	60	43	42	32	0	0
1993	1	1	.500	6.75	3	9.1	10	5	7	0	0
2 yrs.	4	4	.500	3.89	12	69.1	53	47	39	0	0

Bill Miller
WILLIAM PAUL MILLER BL TL
B. Jul. 26, 1927, Minersville, Pa. 6' 175 lbs.

Year	W	L	PCT	ERA	G	IP	H	SO	BB	Sho	SV
1952	4	6	.400	3.48	21	88	78	45	49	2	0

Year	W	L	PCT	ERA	G	IP	H	SO	BB	Sho	SV

Bill Miller *continued*

Year	W	L	PCT	ERA	G	IP	H	SO	BB	Sho	SV
1953	2	1	.667	4.76	13	34	46	17	19	0	1
1954	0	1	.000	6.35	2	5.2	9	6	1	0	0
3 yrs.	6	8	.429	3.95	36	127.2	133	68	69	2	1

Alan Mills

ALAN BERNARD MILLS BR TR
B. Oct. 18, 1966, Lakeland, Fla. 6' 1" 190 lbs.

Year	W	L	PCT	ERA	G	IP	H	SO	BB	Sho	SV
1990	1	5	.167	4.10	36	41.2	48	24	33	0	0
1991	1	1	.500	4.41	6	16.1	16	11	8	0	0
2 yrs.	2	6	.250	4.19	42	58	64	35	41	0	0

Paul Mirabella

PAUL THOMAS MIRABELLA BL TL
B. Mar. 20, 1954, Belleville, N. J. 6' 1" 190 lbs.

Year	W	L	PCT	ERA	G	IP	H	SO	BB	Sho	SV
1979	0	4	.000	9.00	10	14	16	4	10	0	0

Kevin Mmahat

KEVIN PAUL MMAHAT BL TL
B. Nov. 9, 1964, Memphis, Tenn. 6' 5" 220 lbs.

Year	W	L	PCT	ERA	G	IP	H	SO	BB	Sho	SV
1989	0	2	.000	12.91	4	7.2	13	3	8	0	0

George Mogridge

GEORGE ANTHONY MOGRIDGE BL TL
B. Feb. 18, 1889, Rochester, N. Y. 6' 2" 165 lbs.
D. Mar. 4, 1962, Rochester, N. Y.

Year	W	L	PCT	ERA	G	IP	H	SO	BB	Sho	SV
1915	2	3	.400	1.76	6	41	33	11	11	1	0
1916	6	12	.333	2.31	30	194.2	174	66	45	2	0
1917	9	11	.450	2.98	29	196.1	185	46	39	1	0
1918	16	13	.552	2.27	45	230.1	232	62	43	1	7
1919	10	7	.588	2.50	35	187	159	58	46	3	0
1920	5	9	.357	4.31	26	125.1	146	35	36	0	1
6 yrs.	48	55	.466	2.71	171	974.2	929	278	220	8	8

Dale Mohorcic

DALE ROBERT MOHORCIC BR TR
B. Jan. 25, 1956, Cleveland, Ohio 6' 3" 220 lbs.

Year	W	L	PCT	ERA	G	IP	H	SO	BB	Sho	SV
1988	2	2	.500	2.78	13	22.2	21	19	9	0	1
1989	2	1	.667	4.99	32	57.2	65	24	18	0	2
2 yrs.	4	3	.571	4.37	45	80.1	86	43	27	0	3

Bill Monbouquette

WILLIAM CHARLES MONBOUQUETTE BR TR
B. Aug. 11, 1936, Medford, Mass. 5' 11" 190 lbs.

Year	W	L	PCT	ERA	G	IP	H	SO	BB	Sho	SV
1967	6	5	.545	2.36	33	133.1	122	53	17	1	1
1968	5	7	.417	4.43	17	89.1	92	32	13	0	0
2 yrs.	11	12	.478	3.19	50	222.2	214	85	30	1	1

Ed Monroe

EDWARD OLIVER MONROE BR TR
B. Feb. 22, 1895, Louisville, Ky. 6' 5" 187 lbs.
D. Apr. 29, 1969, Louisville, Ky.

Year	W	L	PCT	ERA	G	IP	H	SO	BB	Sho	SV
1917	1	0	1.000	3.45	9	28.2	31	12	6	0	1
1918	0	0	—	4.50	1	2	1	1	2	0	0
2 yrs.	1	0	1.000	3.52	10	30.2	36	13	8	0	1

Zack Monroe

ZACHARY CHARLES MONROE BR TR
B. Jul. 8, 1931, Peoria, Ill. 6' 198 lbs.

Year	W	L	PCT	ERA	G	IP	H	SO	BB	Sho	SV
1958	4	2	.667	3.26	21	58	57	18	27	0	1
1959	0	0	—	5.40	3	3.1	3	1	2	0	0
2 yrs.	4	2	.667	3.38	24	61.1	60	19	29	0	1
World Series											
1958	0	0	—	27.00	1	1	3	1	1	0	0

John Montefusco

JOHN JOSEPH MONTEFUSCO BR TR
B. May 25, 1950, Long Branch, N. J. 6' 1" 180 lbs.

Year	W	L	PCT	ERA	G	IP	H	SO	BB	Sho	SV
1983	5	0	1.000	3.32	6	38	39	15	10	0	0
1984	5	3	.625	3.58	11	55.1	55	23	13	0	0
1985	0	0	—	10.29	3	7	12	2	2	0	0

John Montefusco *continued*

Year	W	L	PCT	ERA	G	IP	H	SO	BB	Sho	SV
1986	0	0	—	2.19	4	12.1	9	3	5	0	0
4 yrs.	10	3	.769	3.75	24	112.2	115	43	30	0	0

Rich Monteleone

RICHARD MONTELEONE BR TR
B. Mar. 22, 1963, Tampa, Fla. 6' 2" 205 lbs.

Year	W	L	PCT	ERA	G	IP	H	SO	BB	Sho	SV
1990	0	1	.000	6.14	5	7.1	8	8	2	0	0
1991	3	1	.750	3.64	26	47	42	34	19	0	0
1992	7	3	.700	3.30	47	92.2	82	62	27	0	0
1993	7	4	.636	4.94	42	85.2	85	50	35	0	0
4 yrs.	17	9	.654	4.06	120	232.2	217	154	83	0	0

Earl Moore

EARL ALONZO MOORE BR TR
B. Jul. 29, 1879, Pickerington, Ohio 6' 195 lbs.
D. Nov. 28, 1961, Columbus, Ohio

Year	W	L	PCT	ERA	G	IP	H	SO	BB	Sho	SV
1907	2	6	.250	3.94	12	64	72	28	30	0	1

Wilcy Moore

WILLIAM WILCY MOORE BR TR
B. May 20, 1897, Bonita, Tex. 6' 195 lbs.
D. Mar. 29, 1963, Hollis, Okla.

Year	W	L	PCT	ERA	G	IP	H	SO	BB	Sho	SV
1927	19	7	.731	2.28	50	213	185	75	59	1	13
1928	4	4	.500	4.18	35	60.1	71	18	31	0	2
1929	6	4	.600	4.06	41	62	64	21	19	0	8
1932	2	0	1.000	2.52	10	25	27	8	6	0	4
1933	5	6	.455	5.52	35	62	92	17	20	0	8
5 yrs.	36	21	.632	3.30	171	422.1	439	139	135	1	35
World Series											
1927	1	0	1.000	0.84	2	10.2	11	2	2	0	1
1932	1	0	1.000	0.00	1	5.1	2	1	0	0	0
2 yrs.	2	0	1.000	0.56	3	16	13	3	2	0	1

Mike Morgan

MICHAEL THOMAS MORGAN BR TR
B. Oct. 8, 1959, Tulare, Calif. 6' 3" 195 lbs.

Year	W	L	PCT	ERA	G	IP	H	SO	BB	Sho	SV
1982	7	11	.389	4.37	30	150.1	167	71	67	0	0

Tom Morgan

TOM STEPHEN MORGAN BR TR
B. May 20, 1930, El Monte, Calif. 6' 1" 180 lbs.
D. Jan. 13, 1987, Anaheim, Calif.

Year	W	L	PCT	ERA	G	IP	H	SO	BB	Sho	SV
1951	9	3	.750	3.68	27	124.2	119	57	36	2	2
1952	5	4	.556	3.07	16	93.2	86	35	33	1	2
1954	11	5	.688	3.34	32	143	149	34	40	4	1
1955	7	3	.700	3.25	40	72	72	17	24	0	10
1956	6	7	.462	4.16	41	71.1	74	20	27	0	11
5 yrs.	38	22	.633	3.48	156	504.2	500	163	160	7	26
World Series											
1951	0	0	—	0.00	1	2	2	3	1	0	0
1955	0	0	—	4.91	2	3.2	3	1	3	0	0
1956	0	1	.000	9.00	2	4	6	3	4	0	0
3 yrs.	0	1	.000	5.59	5	9.2	11	7	8	0	0

Terry Mulholland

TERENCE JOHN MULHOLLAND BR TL
B. Mar. 9, 1963, Uniontown, Pa. 6' 3" 200 lbs.

Year	W	L	PCT	ERA	G	IP	H	SO	BB	Sho	SV
1994	6	7	.462	6.49	24	120.2	150	72	37	0	0

Bob Muncrief

ROBERT CLEVELAND MUNCRIEF BR TR
B. Jan. 28, 1916, Madill, Okla. 6' 2" 190 lbs.
D. Feb. 6, 1996, Duncanville, Tex.

Year	W	L	PCT	ERA	G	IP	H	SO	BB	Sho	SV
1951	0	0	—	9.00	2	3	5	2	4	0	0

Bobby Munoz

ROBERTO MUNOZ BR TR
B. Mar. 3, 1968, Rio Piedras,
Puerto Rico 6' 7" 237 lbs.

Year	W	L	PCT	ERA	G	IP	H	SO	BB	Sho	SV
1993	3	3	.500	5.32	38	45.2	48	33	26	0	0

Year	W	L	PCT	ERA	G	IP	H	SO	BB	Sho	SV

Johnny Murphy

JOHN JOSEPH MURPHY
B. Jul. 14, 1908, New York, N. Y.
D. Jan. 14, 1970, New York, N. Y.
BR TR
6' 2" 190 lbs.

Year	W	L	PCT	ERA	G	IP	H	SO	BB	Sho	SV
1932	0	0	—	16.20	2	3.1	7	2	3	0	0
1934	14	10	.583	3.12	40	207.2	193	70	76	0	4
1935	10	5	.667	4.08	40	117	110	28	55	0	5
1936	9	3	.750	3.38	27	88	90	34	36	0	5
1937	13	4	.765	4.17	39	110	121	36	50	0	10
1938	8	2	.800	4.24	32	91.1	90	43	41	0	11
1939	3	6	.333	4.40	38	61.1	57	30	28	0	19
1940	8	4	.667	3.69	35	63.1	58	23	15	0	9
1941	8	3	.727	1.98	35	77.1	68	29	40	0	15
1942	4	10	.286	3.41	31	58	66	24	23	0	11
1943	12	4	.750	2.51	37	68	44	31	30	0	8
1946	4	2	.667	3.40	27	45	40	19	19	0	7
12 yrs.	93	53	.637	3.54	383	990.1	944	369	416	0	104
World Series											
1936	0	0	—	3.38	1	2.2	1	1	1	0	1
1937	0	0	—	0.00	1	0.1	0	0	0	0	1
1938	0	0	—	0.00	1	2	2	1	1	0	1
1939	1	0	1.000	2.70	1	3.1	5	2	0	0	0
1941	1	0	1.000	0.00	2	6	2	3	1	0	0
1943	0	0	—	0.00	2	2	1	1	1	0	1
6 yrs.	2	0	1.000	1.10	8	16.1	11	8	4	0	4

Rob Murphy

ROBERT ALBERT MURPHY, JR.
B. May 26, 1960, Miami, Fla.
BL TL
6' 2" 200 lbs.

Year	W	L	PCT	ERA	G	IP	H	SO	BB	Sho	SV
1994	0	0	—	16.20	3	1.2	3	0	0	0	0

Dale Murray

DALE ALBERT MURRAY
B. Feb. 2, 1950, Cuero, Tex.
BR TR
6' 4" 205 lbs.

Year	W	L	PCT	ERA	G	IP	H	SO	BB	Sho	SV
1983	2	4	.333	4.48	40	94.1	113	45	22	0	1
1984	1	2	.333	4.94	19	23.2	30	13	5	0	0
1985	0	0	—	13.50	3	2	4	0	0	0	0
3 yrs.	3	6	.333	4.72	62	120	147	58	27	0	1

George Murray

GEORGE KING MURRAY
B. Sep. 23, 1898, Charlotte, N. C.
D. Oct. 18, 1955, Memphis, Tenn.
BR TR
6' 2" 200 lbs.

Year	W	L	PCT	ERA	G	IP	H	SO	BB	Sho	SV
1922	4	2	.667	3.97	22	56.2	53	14	26	0	0

Bots Nekola

FRANCIS JOSEPH NEKOLA
B. Dec. 10, 1906, New York, N. Y.
D. Mar. 11, 1987, Rockville Centre, N. Y.
BL TL
5' 11½" 175 lbs.

Year	W	L	PCT	ERA	G	IP	H	SO	BB	Sho	SV
1929	0	0	—	4.34	9	18.2	21	2	15	0	0

Gene Nelson

WAYLAND EUGENE NELSON
B. Dec. 3, 1960, Tampa, Fla.
BR TR
6' 172 lbs.

Year	W	L	PCT	ERA	G	IP	H	SO	BB	Sho	SV
1981	3	1	.750	4.85	8	39	40	16	23	0	0

Jeff Nelson

JEFFREY ALLAN NELSON
B. Nov. 17, 1966, Baltimore, Md.
BR TR
6' 8" 225 lbs.

Year	W	L	PCT	ERA	G	IP	H	SO	BB	Sho	SV
1996	4	4	.500	4.36	73	74.1	75	91	36	0	2
Divisional Playoffs											
1996	1	0	1.000	0.00	2	3.2	2	5	2	0	0
League Championship Series											
1996	0	1	.000	11.57	2	2.1	5	2	0	0	0
World Series											
1996	0	0	—	0.00	3	4.1	1	5	1	0	0

Luke Nelson

LUTHER MARTIN NELSON
B. Dec. 4, 1893, Cable, Ill.
D. Nov. 14, 1985, Moline, Ill.
BR TR
6' 180 lbs.

Year	W	L	PCT	ERA	G	IP	H	SO	BB	Sho	SV
1919	3	0	1.000	2.96	9	24.1	22	11	11	0	0

Tex Neuer

JOHN S. NEUER
B. Jun. 8, 1877, Fremont, Ohio
D. Jan. 14, 1966, Northumberland, Pa.
B TL
' " lbs.

Year	W	L	PCT	ERA	G	IP	H	SO	BB	Sho	SV
1907	4	2	.667	2.17	7	54	40	22	19	3	0

Ernie Nevel

ERNIE WYRE NEVEL
B. Aug. 17, 1919, Charleston, Mo.
D. Jul. 10, 1988, Springfield, Mo.
BR TR
5' 11" 190 lbs.

Year	W	L	PCT	ERA	G	IP	H	SO	BB	Sho	SV
1950	0	1	.000	9.95	3	6.1	10	3	6	0	0
1951	0	0	—	0.00	1	4	1	1	1	0	1
2 yrs.	0	1	.000	6.10	4	10.1	11	4	7	0	1

Floyd Newkirk

FLOYD ELMO NEWKIRK
B. Jul. 16, 1908, Norris City, Ill.
D. Apr. 15, 1976, Clayton, Mo.
BR TR
5' 11" 178 lbs.

Year	W	L	PCT	ERA	G	IP	H	SO	BB	Sho	SV
1934	0	0	—	0.00	1	1	1	0	1	0	0

Bobo Newsom

LOUIS NORMAN NEWSOM
B. Aug. 11, 1907, Hartsville, S. C.
D. Dec. 7, 1962, Orlando, Fla.
BR TR
6' 3" 200 lbs.

Year	W	L	PCT	ERA	G	IP	H	SO	BB	Sho	SV
1947	7	5	.583	2.80	17	115.2	109	42	30	2	0
World Series											
1947	0	1	.000	19.29	2	2.1	6	0	2	0	0

Doc Newton

EUSTACE JAMES NEWTON
B. Oct. 26, 1877, Indianapolis, Ind.
D. May 14, 1931, Memphis, Tenn.
BL TL
6' 185 lbs.

Year	W	L	PCT	ERA	G	IP	H	SO	BB	Sho	SV
1905	2	2	.500	2.11	11	59.2	61	15	24	0	0
1906	7	5	.583	3.17	21	125	118	52	33	2	0
1907	7	10	.412	3.18	19	133	132	70	31	0	0
1908	4	5	.444	2.95	23	88.1	78	49	41	1	1
1909	0	3	.000	2.82	4	22.1	27	11	11	0	0
5 yrs.	20	25	.444	2.96	78	428.1	416	197	140	3	1

Joe Niekro

JOSEPH FRANKLIN NIEKRO
B. Nov. 7, 1944, Martins Ferry, Ohio
BR TR
6' 1" 185 lbs.

Year	W	L	PCT	ERA	G	IP	H	SO	BB	Sho	SV
1985	2	1	.667	5.84	3	12.1	14	4	8	0	0
1986	9	10	.474	4.87	25	125.2	139	59	63	0	0
1987	3	4	.429	3.55	8	50.2	40	30	19	0	0
3 yrs.	14	15	.483	4.58	36	188.2	193	93	90	0	0

Phil Niekro

PHILIP HENRY NIEKRO
B. Apr. 1, 1939, Blaine, Ohio
Hall of Fame 1997
BR TR
6' 1" 180 lbs.

Year	W	L	PCT	ERA	G	IP	H	SO	BB	Sho	SV
1984	16	8	.667	3.09	32	215.2	219	136	76	1	0
1985	16	12	.571	4.09	33	220	203	149	120	1	0
2 yrs.	32	20	.615	3.59	65	435.2	422	285	196	2	0

Jerry Nielsen

GERALD ARTHUR NIELSEN
B. Aug. 5, 1966, Sacramento, Calif.
BL TL
6' 3" 185 lbs.

Year	W	L	PCT	ERA	G	IP	H	SO	BB	Sho	SV
1992	1	0	1.000	4.58	20	19.2	17	12	18	0	0

Scott Nielsen

JEFFREY SCOTT NIELSEN
B. Dec. 18, 1958, Salt Lake City, Utah
BR TR
6' 1" 190 lbs.

Year	W	L	PCT	ERA	G	IP	H	SO	BB	Sho	SV
1986	4	4	.500	4.02	10	56	66	20	12	2	0
1988	1	2	.333	6.86	7	19.2	27	4	13	0	0
1989	1	0	1.000	13.50	2	0.2	2	0	1	0	0
3 yrs.	6	6	.500	4.83	19	76.1	95	24	26	2	0

Don Nottebart

DONALD EDWARD NOTTEBART
B. Jan. 23, 1936, West Newton, Mass.
BR TR
6' 1" 190 lbs.

Year	W	L	PCT	ERA	G	IP	H	SO	BB	Sho	SV
1969	0	0	—	4.50	4	6	6	5	0	0	0

Year	W	L	PCT	ERA	G	IP	H	SO	BB	Sho	SV

Andy O'Connor

ANDREW JAMES O'CONNOR BR TR
B. Sep. 14, 1884, Roxbury, Mass. 6' 160 lbs.
D. Sep. 26, 1980, Norwood, Mass.

Year	W	L	PCT	ERA	G	IP	H	SO	BB	Sho	SV
1908	0	1	.000	10.13	1	8	15	5	7	0	0

Lefty O'Doul

FRANCIS JOSEPH O'DOUL BL TL
B. Mar. 4, 1897, San Francisco, Calif. 6' 180 lbs.
D. Dec. 7, 1969, San Francisco, Calif.

Year	W	L	PCT	ERA	G	IP	H	SO	BB	Sho	SV
1919	0	0	—	3.60	3	5	7	2	4	0	0
1920	0	0	—	4.91	2	3.2	4	2	2	0	0
1922	0	0	—	3.38	6	16	24	5	12	0	0
3 yrs.	0	0	—	3.65	11	24.2	35	9	18	0	0

Bob Ojeda

ROBERT MICHAEL OJEDA BL TL
B. Dec. 17, 1957, Los Angeles, Calif. 6' 1" 185 lbs.

Year	W	L	PCT	ERA	G	IP	H	SO	BB	Sho	SV
1994	0	0	—	24.00	2	3	11	3	6	0	0

Al Orth

ALBERT LEWIS ORTH BL TR
B. Sep. 5, 1872, Tipton, Ind. 6' 200 lbs.
D. Oct. 8, 1948, Lynchburg, Va.

Year	W	L	PCT	ERA	G	IP	H	SO	BB	Sho	SV
1904	11	6	.647	2.68	20	137.2	122	47	19	2	0
1905	18	16	.529	2.86	40	305.1	273	121	61	6	0
1906	27	17	.614	2.34	45	338.2	317	133	66	3	0
1907	14	21	.400	2.61	36	248.2	244	78	53	2	0
1908	2	13	.133	3.42	21	139.1	134	22	30	1	0
1909	0	0	—	12.00	1	3	6	1	1	0	0
6 yrs.	72	73	.497	2.72	163	1172.2	1096	402	230	14	0

Joe Ostrowski

JOSEPH PAUL OSTROWSKI BL TL
B. Nov. 15, 1916, West Wyoming, Pa. 6' 180 lbs.

Year	W	L	PCT	ERA	G	IP	H	SO	BB	Sho	SV
1950	1	1	.500	5.15	21	43.2	50	15	15	0	3
1951	6	4	.600	3.49	34	95.1	103	30	18	0	5
1952	2	2	.500	5.63	20	40	56	17	14	0	2
3 yrs.	9	7	.563	4.37	75	179	209	62	47	0	10

World Series

Year	W	L	PCT	ERA	G	IP	H	SO	BB	Sho	SV
1951	0	0	—	0.00	1	2	1	1	0	0	0

Stubby Overmire

FRANK W. OVERMIRE BR TL
B. May 16, 1919, Moline, Mich. 5' 7" 170 lbs.
D. Mar. 3, 1977, Lakeland, Fla.

Year	W	L	PCT	ERA	G	IP	H	SO	BB	Sho	SV
1951	1	1	.500	4.63	15	44.2	50	14	18	0	0

John Pacella

JOHN LEWIS PACELLA BR TR
B. Sep. 15, 1956, Brooklyn, N.Y. 6' 3" 195 lbs.

Year	W	L	PCT	ERA	G	IP	H	SO	BB	Sho	SV
1982	0	1	.000	7.20	3	10	13	2	9	0	0

Dave Pagan

DAVID PERCY PAGAN BR TR
B. Sep. 15, 1949, Nipawin, Sask., Canada 6' 2" 175 lbs.

Year	W	L	PCT	ERA	G	IP	H	SO	BB	Sho	SV
1973	0	0	—	2.84	4	12.2	16	9	1	0	0
1974	1	3	.250	5.14	16	49	49	39	28	0	0
1975	0	0	—	4.06	13	31	30	18	13	0	1
1976	1	1	.500	2.28	7	23.2	18	13	4	0	0
4 yrs.	2	4	.333	4.02	40	116.1	113	79	46	0	1

Joe Page

JOSEPH FRANCIS PAGE BL TL
B. Oct. 28, 1917, Cherry Valley, Pa. 6' 3" 200 lbs.
D. Apr. 21, 1980, Latrobe, Pa.

Year	W	L	PCT	ERA	G	IP	H	SO	BB	Sho	SV
1944	5	7	.417	4.56	19	102.2	100	63	52	0	0
1945	6	3	.667	2.82	20	102	95	50	46	0	0
1946	9	8	.529	3.57	31	136	126	77	72	1	3
1947	14	8	.636	2.48	56	141.1	105	116	72	0	17
1948	7	8	.467	4.26	55	107.2	116	77	66	0	16
1949	13	8	.619	2.59	60	135.1	103	99	75	0	27
1950	3	7	.300	5.04	37	55.1	66	33	31	0	13
7 yrs.	57	49	.538	3.44	278	780.1	711	515	414	1	76

Joe Page *continued*

World Series

Year	W	L	PCT	ERA	G	IP	H	SO	BB	Sho	SV
1947	1	1	.500	4.15	4	13	12	7	2	0	1
1949	1	0	1.000	2.00	3	9	6	8	3	0	1
2 yrs.	2	1	.667	3.27	7	22	18	15	5	0	2

Donn Pall

DONN STEVEN PALL BR TR
B. Jan. 11, 1962, Chicago, Ill. 6' 2" 185 lbs.

Year	W	L	PCT	ERA	G	IP	H	SO	BB	Sho	SV
1994	1	2	.333	3.60	26	35	43	21	9	0	0

Clay Parker

JAMES CLAYTON PARKER BR TR
B. Dec. 19, 1962, Columbia, La. 6' 1" 185 lbs.

Year	W	L	PCT	ERA	G	IP	H	SO	BB	Sho	SV
1989	4	5	.444	3.67	22	120	123	53	31	0	0
1990	1	1	.500	4.50	5	22	19	20	7	0	0
2 yrs.	5	6	.455	3.80	27	142	142	73	38	0	0

Gil Patterson

GILBERT THOMAS PATTERSON BR TR
B. Sep. 5, 1955, Philadelphia, Pa. 6' 1" 185 lbs.

Year	W	L	PCT	ERA	G	IP	H	SO	BB	Sho	SV
1977	1	2	.333	5.45	10	33	38	29	20	0	1

Jeff Patterson

JEFFREY SIMMONS PATTERSON BR TR
B. Oct. 1, 1968, Anaheim, Calif. 6' 2" 200 lbs.

Year	W	L	PCT	ERA	G	IP	H	SO	BB	Sho	SV
1995	0	0	—	2.70	3	3.1	3	3	3	0	0

Dave Pavlas

DAVID LEE PAVLAS BR TR
B. Aug. 12, 1962, Frankfurt, Germany 6' 7" 180 lbs.

Year	W	L	PCT	ERA	G	IP	H	SO	BB	Sho	SV
1995	0	0	—	3.18	4	5.2	8	3	0	0	0
1996	0	0	—	2.35	16	23	23	18	7	0	1
2 yrs.	0	0	—	2.51	20	28.2	31	21	7	0	1

Monte Pearson

MONTGOMERY MARCELLUS PEARSON BR TR
B. Sep. 2, 1909, Oakland, Calif. 6' 175 lbs.
D. Jan. 27, 1978, Fresno, Calif.

Year	W	L	PCT	ERA	G	IP	H	SO	BB	Sho	SV
1936	19	7	.731	3.71	33	223	191	118	135	1	1
1937	9	3	.750	3.17	22	144.2	145	71	64	1	1
1938	16	7	.696	3.97	28	202	198	98	113	1	0
1939	12	5	.706	4.49	22	146.1	151	76	70	0	0
1940	7	5	.583	3.69	16	109.2	108	43	44	1	0
5 yrs.	63	27	.700	3.82	121	825.2	793	406	426	4	2

World Series

Year	W	L	PCT	ERA	G	IP	H	SO	BB	Sho	SV
1936	1	0	1.000	2.00	1	9	7	7	2	0	0
1937	1	0	1.000	1.04	1	8.2	5	4	2	0	0
1938	1	0	1.000	1.00	1	9	5	9	2	0	0
1939	1	0	1.000	0.00	1	9	2	8	1	1	0
4 yrs.	4	0	1.000	1.01	4	35.2	19	28	7	1	0

Steve Peek

STEPHEN GEORGE PEEK BB TR
B. Jul. 30, 1914, Springfield, Mass. 6' 2" 195 lbs.
D. Sep. 20, 1991, Syracuse, N.Y.

Year	W	L	PCT	ERA	G	IP	H	SO	BB	Sho	SV
1941	4	2	.667	5.06	17	80	85	18	39	0	0

Hipolito Pena

HIPOLITO PENA BL TL
B. Jan. 30, 1964, Fantino, Dominican Republic 6' 3" 168 lbs.

Year	W	L	PCT	ERA	G	IP	H	SO	BB	Sho	SV
1988	1	1	.500	3.14	16	14.1	10	10	9	0	0

Herb Pennock

HERBERT JEFFERIS PENNOCK BB TL
B. Feb. 10, 1894, Kennett Square, Pa. 6' 160 lbs.
D. Jan. 30, 1948, New York, N.Y.
Hall of Fame 1948

Year	W	L	PCT	ERA	G	IP	H	SO	BB	Sho	SV
1923	19	6	.760	3.33	35	224.1	235	93	68	1	3
1924	21	9	.700	2.83	40	286.1	302	101	64	4	3
1925	16	17	.485	2.96	47	277	267	88	71	2	2
1926	23	11	.676	3.62	40	266.1	294	78	43	1	2

Herb Pennock continued

Year	W	L	PCT	ERA	G	IP	H	SO	BB	Sho	SV
1927	19	8	.704	3.00	34	209.2	225	51	48	1	2
1928	17	6	.739	2.56	28	211	215	53	40	5	3
1929	9	11	.450	4.90	27	158	205	49	28	1	2
1930	11	7	.611	4.32	25	156.1	194	46	20	1	0
1931	11	6	.647	4.28	25	189.1	247	65	30	1	0
1932	9	5	.643	4.60	22	146.2	191	54	38	1	0
1933	7	4	.636	5.54	23	65	96	22	21	1	4
11 yrs.	162	90	.643	3.56	346	2190	2471	700	471	19	21
World Series											
1923	2	0	1.000	3.63	3	17.1	19	8	1	0	1
1926	2	0	1.000	1.23	3	22	13	8	4	0	0
1927	1	0	1.000	1.00	1	9	3	1	0	0	0
1932	0	0	—	2.25	2	4	2	4	1	0	2
4 yrs.	5	0	1.000	2.06	9	52.1	37	21	6	0	3

Melido Perez

MELIDO TURPEN PEREZ BR TR
B. Feb. 15, 1966, San Cristobal, Dominican Republic 6' 4" 180 lbs.

Year	W	L	PCT	ERA	G	IP	H	SO	BB	Sho	SV
1992	13	16	.448	2.87	33	247.2	212	218	93	1	0
1993	6	14	.300	5.19	25	163	173	148	64	0	0
1994	9	4	.692	4.10	22	151.1	134	109	58	0	0
1995	5	5	.500	5.58	13	69.1	70	44	31	0	0
4 yrs.	33	39	.458	4.06	93	631.1	589	519	246	1	0

Pascual Perez

PASCUAL PEREZ BR TR
B. May 17, 1957, San Cristobal, Dominican Republic 6' 2" 162 lbs.

Year	W	L	PCT	ERA	G	IP	H	SO	BB	Sho	SV
1990	1	2	.333	1.29	3	14	8	12	3	0	0
1991	2	4	.333	3.18	14	73.2	68	41	24	0	0
2 yrs.	3	6	.333	2.87	17	87.2	76	53	27	0	0

Cecil Perkins

CECIL BOYCE PERKINS BR TR
B. Dec. 1, 1940, Baltimore, Md. 6' 175 lbs.

Year	W	L	PCT	ERA	G	IP	H	SO	BB	Sho	SV
1967	0	1	.000	9.00	2	5	6	1	2	0	0

Gaylord Perry

GAYLORD JACKSON PERRY BR TR
B. Sep. 15, 1938, Williamston, N. C. 6' 4" 205 lbs.
Hall of Fame 1991

Year	W	L	PCT	ERA	G	IP	H	SO	BB	Sho	SV
1980	4	4	.500	4.41	10	51	65	28	18	0	0

Fritz Peterson

FRED INGLES PETERSON BB TL
B. Feb. 8, 1942, Chicago, Ill. 6' 185 lbs.

Year	W	L	PCT	ERA	G	IP	H	SO	BB	Sho	SV
1966	12	11	.522	3.31	34	215	196	96	40	2	0
1967	8	14	.364	3.47	36	181.1	179	102	43	1	0
1968	12	11	.522	2.63	36	212.1	187	115	29	2	0
1969	17	16	.515	2.55	37	272	228	150	43	4	0
1970	20	11	.645	2.91	39	260	247	127	40	2	0
1971	15	13	.536	3.05	37	274	269	139	42	4	1
1972	17	15	.531	3.24	35	250	270	100	44	3	0
1973	8	15	.348	3.95	31	184.1	207	59	49	0	0
1974	0	0	—	4.50	3	8	13	5	2	0	0
9 yrs.	109	106	.507	3.10	288	1857	1796	893	332	18	1

Andy Pettitte

ANDREW EUGENE PETTITTE BL TL
B. Jun. 15, 1972, Baton Rouge, La. 6' 5" 235 lbs.

Year	W	L	PCT	ERA	G	IP	H	SO	BB	Sho	SV
1995	12	9	.571	4.17	31	175	183	114	63	0	0
1996	21	8	.724	3.87	35	221	229	162	72	0	0
2 yrs.	33	17	.660	4.00	66	396	412	276	135	0	0
Divisional Playoffs											
1995	0	0	—	5.14	1	7	9	0	3	0	0
1996	0	0	—	5.68	1	6.1	4	3	6	0	0
2 yrs.	0	0	—	5.40	2	13.1	13	3	9	0	0
League Championship Series											
1996	1	0	1.000	3.60	2	15	10	7	5	0	0
World Series											
1996	1	1	.500	5.91	2	10.2	11	5	4	0	0

Cy Pieh

EDWIN JOHN PIEH BR TR
B. Sep. 29, 1886, Waunakee, Wis. 6' 2" 190 lbs.
D. Sep. 12, 1945, Jacksonville, Fla.

Year	W	L	PCT	ERA	G	IP	H	SO	BB	Sho	SV
1913	1	0	1.000	4.35	4	10.1	10	6	7	0	0
1914	4	4	.500	5.05	18	62.1	68	24	29	0	0
1915	4	5	.444	2.87	21	94	78	46	39	2	0
3 yrs.	9	9	.500	3.78	43	166.2	156	76	75	2	0

Bill Piercy

WILLIAM BENTON PIERCY BR TR
B. May 2, 1896, El Monte, Calif. 6' 1½" 170 lbs.
D. Aug. 28, 1951, Long Beach, Calif.

Year	W	L	PCT	ERA	G	IP	H	SO	BB	Sho	SV
1917	0	1	.000	3.00	1	9	9	4	2	0	0
1921	5	4	.556	2.98	14	81.2	82	35	28	1	0
2 yrs.	5	5	.500	2.98	15	90.2	91	39	30	1	0
World Series											
1921	0	0	—	0.00	1	1	2	2	0	0	0

Duane Pillette

DUANE XAVIER PILLETTE BR TR
B. Jul. 24, 1922, Detroit, Mich. 6' 3" 195 lbs.

Year	W	L	PCT	ERA	G	IP	H	SO	BB	Sho	SV
1949	2	4	.333	4.34	12	37.1	43	9	19	0	0
1950	0	0	—	1.29	4	7	9	4	3	0	0
2 yrs.	2	4	.333	3.86	16	44.1	52	13	22	0	0

George Pipgras

GEORGE WILLIAM PIPGRAS BR TR
B. Dec. 20, 1899, Ida Grove, Iowa 6' 1½" 185 lbs.
D. Oct. 19, 1986, Gainesville, Fla.

Year	W	L	PCT	ERA	G	IP	H	SO	BB	Sho	SV
1923	1	3	.250	5.94	8	33.1	34	12	25	0	0
1924	0	1	.000	9.98	9	15.1	20	4	18	0	1
1927	10	3	.769	4.11	29	166.1	148	81	77	1	0
1928	24	13	.649	3.38	46	300.2	314	139	103	4	3
1929	18	12	.600	4.23	39	225.1	229	125	95	3	0
1930	15	15	.500	4.11	44	221	230	111	70	3	4
1931	7	6	.538	3.79	36	137.2	134	59	58	0	3
1932	16	9	.640	4.19	32	219	235	111	87	2	0
1933	2	2	.500	3.27	4	33	32	14	12	0	0
9 yrs.	93	64	.592	4.04	247	1351.2	1376	656	545	13	11
World Series											
1927	1	0	1.000	2.00	1	9	7	2	1	0	0
1928	1	0	1.000	2.00	1	9	4	8	4	0	0
1932	1	0	1.000	4.50	1	8	9	1	3	0	0
3 yrs.	3	0	1.000	2.77	3	26	20	11	8	0	0

Eric Plunk

ERIC VAUGHN PLUNK BR TR
B. Sep. 3, 1963, Wilmington, Calif. 6' 5" 210 lbs.

Year	W	L	PCT	ERA	G	IP	H	SO	BB	Sho	SV
1989	7	5	.583	3.69	27	75.2	65	61	52	0	0
1990	6	3	.667	2.72	47	72.2	58	67	43	0	0
1991	2	5	.286	4.76	43	111.2	128	103	62	0	0
3 yrs.	15	13	.536	3.88	117	260	251	231	157	0	0

Bob Porterfield

ERWIN COOLEDGE PORTERFIELD BR TR
B. Aug. 10, 1923, Newport, Va. 6' 190 lbs.
D. Apr. 28, 1980, Charlotte, N. C.

Year	W	L	PCT	ERA	G	IP	H	SO	BB	Sho	SV
1948	5	3	.625	4.50	16	78	85	30	34	1	0
1949	2	5	.286	4.06	12	57.2	53	25	29	0	0
1950	1	1	.500	8.69	10	19.2	28	9	8	0	1
1951	0	0	—	15.00	2	3	5	2	3	0	0
4 yrs.	8	9	.471	5.06	40	158.1	171	66	74	1	1

Jack Powell

JOHN JOSEPH POWELL BR TR
B. Jul. 9, 1874, Bloomington, Ill. 5' 11" 195 lbs.
D. Oct. 17, 1944, Chicago, Ill.

Year	W	L	PCT	ERA	G	IP	H	SO	BB	Sho	SV
1904	23	19	.548	2.44	47	390.1	340	202	92	3	0
1905	8	13	.381	3.52	37	202	214	84	57	1	1
2 yrs.	31	32	.492	2.81	84	592.1	554	286	149	4	1

Alfonso Pulido

ALFONSO PULIDO BL TL
B. Jan. 23, 1957, Veracruz, Mexico 5' 11" 170 lbs.

Year	W	L	PCT	ERA	G	IP	H	SO	BB	Sho	SV
1986	1	1	.500	4.70	10	30.2	38	13	9	0	1

Ambrose Puttmann

AMBROSE NICHOLAS PUTTMANN B TL
B. Sep. 9, 1880, Cincinnati, Ohio 6' 4" 185 lbs.
D. Jun. 21, 1936, Jamaica, N. Y.

Year	W	L	PCT	ERA	G	IP	H	SO	BB	Sho	SV
1903	2	0	1.000	0.95	3	19	16	8	4	0	0
1904	2	0	1.000	2.74	9	49.1	40	26	17	1	0
1905	2	7	.222	4.27	17	86.1	79	39	37	1	1
3 yrs.	6	7	.462	3.38	29	154.2	135	73	58	2	1

Mel Queen

MELVIN JOSEPH QUEEN BR TR
B. Mar. 4, 1918, Maxwell, Pa. 6' ½" 204 lbs.
D. Apr. 4, 1982, Fort Smith, Ark.

Year	W	L	PCT	ERA	G	IP	H	SO	BB	Sho	SV
1942	1	0	1.000	0.00	4	5.2	6	0	3	0	0
1944	6	3	.667	3.31	10	81.2	68	30	34	1	0
1946	1	1	.500	6.53	14	30.1	40	26	21	0	0
1947	0	0	—	9.45	5	6.2	9	2	4	0	0
4 yrs.	8	4	.667	4.27	33	124.1	123	58	62	1	0

Ed Quick

EDWIN S. QUICK B TR
B. Dec, 1881, Baltimore, Md. 5' 11" lbs.
D. Jun. 19, 1913, Rocky Ford, Colo.

Year	W	L	PCT	ERA	G	IP	H	SO	BB	Sho	SV
1903	0	0	—	9.00	1	2	5	0	1	0	0

Jack Quinn

JOHN PICUS QUINN BR TR
B. Jul. 5, 1883, Jeanesville, Pa. 6' 196 lbs.
D. Apr. 17, 1946, Pottsville, Pa.

Year	W	L	PCT	ERA	G	IP	H	SO	BB	Sho	SV
1909	9	5	.643	1.97	23	118.2	110	36	24	0	1
1910	18	12	.600	2.36	35	236.2	214	82	58	0	0
1911	8	10	.444	3.76	40	174.2	203	71	41	0	2
1912	5	7	.417	5.79	18	102.2	139	47	23	0	0
1919	15	14	.517	2.63	38	264	242	97	65	4	0
1920	18	10	.643	3.20	41	253.1	271	101	48	2	3
1921	8	7	.533	3.48	33	129.1	158	44	32	0	0
7 yrs.	81	65	.555	3.12	228	1279.1	1337	478	291	6	6

World Series

Year	W	L	PCT	ERA	G	IP	H	SO	BB	Sho	SV
1921	0	1	.000	9.82	3	3.2	8	2	1	0	0

Dave Rajsich

DAVID CHRISTOPHER RAJSICH BL TL
B. Sep. 28, 1951, Youngstown, Ohio 6' 5" 175 lbs.

Year	W	L	PCT	ERA	G	IP	H	SO	BB	Sho	SV
1978	0	0	—	4.05	4	13.1	16	9	6	0	0

Pedro Ramos

PEDRO RAMOS BB TR
B. Apr. 28, 1935, Pinar del Rio, Cuba 6' 175 lbs.

Year	W	L	PCT	ERA	G	IP	H	SO	BB	Sho	SV
1964	1	0	1.000	1.25	13	21.2	13	21	0	0	8
1965	5	5	.500	2.92	65	92.1	80	68	27	0	19
1966	3	9	.250	3.61	52	89.2	98	58	18	0	13
3 yrs.	9	14	.391	3.05	130	203.2	191	147	45	0	40

Vic Raschi

VICTOR JOHN ANGELO RASCHI BR TR
B. Mar. 28, 1919, West Springfield, Mass. 6' 1" 205 lbs.
D. Oct. 14, 1988, Groveland, N. Y.

Year	W	L	PCT	ERA	G	IP	H	SO	BB	Sho	SV
1946	2	0	1.000	3.94	2	16	14	11	5	0	0
1947	7	2	.778	3.87	15	104.2	89	51	38	1	0
1948	19	8	.704	3.84	36	222.2	208	124	74	6	1
1949	21	10	.677	3.34	38	274.2	247	124	138	3	0
1950	21	8	.724	4.00	33	256.2	232	155	116	2	1
1951	21	10	.677	3.27	35	258.1	233	164	103	4	0
1952	16	6	.727	2.78	31	223	174	127	91	4	0
1953	13	6	.684	3.33	28	181	150	76	55	4	1
8 yrs.	120	50	.706	3.47	218	1537	1347	832	620	24	3

World Series

Year	W	L	PCT	ERA	G	IP	H	SO	BB	Sho	SV
1947	0	0	—	6.75	2	1.1	2	1	0	0	0
1949	1	1	.500	4.30	2	14.2	15	11	5	0	0
1950	1	0	1.000	0.00	1	9	2	5	1	1	0
1951	1	1	.500	0.87	2	10.1	12	4	8	0	0
1952	2	0	1.000	1.59	3	17	12	18	8	0	0
1953	0	1	.000	3.38	1	8	9	4	3	0	0
6 yrs.	5	3	.625	2.24	11	60.1	52	43	25	1	0

Dennis Rasmussen

DENNIS LEE RASMUSSEN BL TL
B. Apr. 18, 1959, Los Angeles, Calif. 6' 7" 230 lbs.

Year	W	L	PCT	ERA	G	IP	H	SO	BB	Sho	SV
1984	9	6	.600	4.57	24	147.2	127	110	60	0	0
1985	3	5	.375	3.98	22	101.2	97	63	42	0	0
1986	18	6	.750	3.88	31	202	160	131	74	1	0
1987	9	7	.563	4.75	26	146	145	89	55	0	0
4 yrs.	39	24	.619	4.28	103	597.1	529	393	231	1	0

Shane Rawley

SHANE WILLIAM RAWLEY BR TL
B. Jul. 27, 1955, Racine, Wis. 6' 170 lbs.

Year	W	L	PCT	ERA	G	IP	H	SO	BB	Sho	SV
1982	11	10	.524	4.06	47	164	165	111	54	0	3
1983	14	14	.500	3.78	34	238.1	246	124	79	2	1
1984	2	3	.400	6.21	11	42	46	24	27	0	0
3 yrs.	27	27	.500	4.11	92	444.1	457	259	160	2	4

Jeff Reardon

JEFFREY JAMES REARDON BR TR
B. Oct. 1, 1955, Pittsfield, Mass. 6' 190 lbs.

Year	W	L	PCT	ERA	G	IP	H	SO	BB	Sho	SV
1994	1	0	1.000	8.38	11	9.2	17	4	3	0	2

Hal Reniff

HAROLD EUGENE RENIFF BR TR
B. Jul. 2, 1938, Warren, Ohio 6' 215 lbs.

Year	W	L	PCT	ERA	G	IP	H	SO	BB	Sho	SV
1961	2	0	1.000	2.58	25	45.1	31	21	31	0	2
1962	0	0	—	7.36	2	3.2	6	1	5	0	0
1963	4	3	.571	2.62	48	89.1	63	56	42	0	18
1964	6	4	.600	3.12	41	69.1	47	38	30	0	9
1965	3	4	.429	3.80	51	85.1	74	74	48	0	3
1966	3	7	.300	3.21	56	95.1	80	79	49	0	9
1967	0	2	.000	4.28	24	40	40	24	14	0	0
7 yrs.	18	20	.474	3.26	247	428.1	341	293	219	0	41

World Series

Year	W	L	PCT	ERA	G	IP	H	SO	BB	Sho	SV
1963	0	0	—	0.00	3	3	0	1	1	0	0
1964	0	0	—	0.00	1	0.1	2	0	0	0	0
2 yrs.	0	0	—	0.00	4	3.1	2	1	1	0	0

Rick Reuschel

RICKEY EUGENE REUSCHEL BR TR
B. May 16, 1949, Quincy, Ill. 6' 3" 215 lbs.

Year	W	L	PCT	ERA	G	IP	H	SO	BB	Sho	SV
1981	4	4	.500	2.66	12	71	75	22	10	0	0

Divisional Playoffs

Year	W	L	PCT	ERA	G	IP	H	SO	BB	Sho	SV
1981	0	1	.000	3.00	1	6	4	3	1	0	0

World Series

Year	W	L	PCT	ERA	G	IP	H	SO	BB	Sho	SV
1981	0	0	—	4.91	2	3.2	7	2	3	0	0

Allie Reynolds

ALLIE PIERCE REYNOLDS BR TR
B. Feb. 10, 1915, Bethany, Okla. 6' 195 lbs.
D. Dec. 26, 1994, Oklahoma City, Okla.

Year	W	L	PCT	ERA	G	IP	H	SO	BB	Sho	SV
1947	19	8	.704	3.20	34	241.2	207	129	123	4	2
1948	16	7	.696	3.77	39	236.1	240	101	111	1	3
1949	17	6	.739	4.00	35	213.2	200	105	123	2	1
1950	16	12	.571	3.74	35	240.2	215	160	138	2	2
1951	17	8	.680	3.05	40	221	171	126	100	7	7
1952	20	8	.714	2.06	35	244.1	194	160	97	6	6
1953	13	7	.650	3.41	41	145	140	86	61	1	13
1954	13	4	.765	3.32	36	157.1	133	100	66	4	7
8 yrs.	131	60	.686	3.30	295	1700	1500	967	819	27	41

World Series

Year	W	L	PCT	ERA	G	IP	H	SO	BB	Sho	SV
1947	1	0	1.000	4.76	2	11.1	15	6	3	0	0
1949	1	0	1.000	0.00	2	12.1	2	14	4	1	1
1950	1	0	1.000	0.87	2	10.1	7	7	4	0	1
1951	1	1	.500	4.20	2	15	16	8	11	0	1
1952	2	1	.667	1.77	4	20.1	12	18	6	1	1
1953	1	0	1.000	6.75	3	8	9	9	4	0	1
6 yrs.	7	2	.778	2.79	15	77.1	61	62	32	2	4

Rick Rhoden

RICHARD ALAN RHODEN BR TR
B. May 16, 1953, Boynton Beach, Fla. 6' 3" 195 lbs.

Year	W	L	PCT	ERA	G	IP	H	SO	BB	Sho	SV
1987	16	10	.615	3.86	30	181.2	184	107	61	1	0
1988	12	12	.500	4.29	30	197	206	94	56	1	0
2 yrs.	28	22	.560	4.09	60	378.2	390	201	117	1	0

Gordon Rhodes

JOHN GORDON RHODES BR TR
B. Aug. 11, 1907, Winnemucca, Nev.
D. Mar. 24, 1960, Long Beach, Calif. 6' 187 lbs.

Year	W	L	PCT	ERA	G	IP	H	SO	BB	Sho	SV
1929	0	4	.000	4.85	10	42.2	57	13	16	0	0
1930	0	0	—	9.00	3	2	3	1	4	0	0
1931	6	3	.667	3.41	18	87	82	36	52	0	0
1932	1	2	.333	7.88	10	24	25	15	21	0	0
4 yrs.	7	9	.438	4.57	41	155.2	167	65	93	0	0

Dave Righetti

DAVID ALLAN RIGHETTI BL TL
B. Nov. 28, 1958, San Jose, Calif. 6' 4" 195 lbs.

Year	W	L	PCT	ERA	G	IP	H	SO	BB	Sho	SV
1979	0	1	.000	3.71	3	17	10	13	10	0	0
1981	8	4	.667	2.06	15	105	75	89	38	0	0
1982	11	10	.524	3.79	33	183	155	163	108	0	1
1983	14	8	.636	3.44	31	217	194	169	67	2	0
1984	5	6	.455	2.34	64	96.1	79	90	37	0	31
1985	12	7	.632	2.78	74	107	96	92	45	0	29
1986	8	8	.500	2.45	74	106.2	88	83	35	0	46
1987	8	6	.571	3.51	60	95	95	77	44	0	31
1988	5	4	.556	3.52	60	87	86	70	37	0	25
1989	2	6	.250	3.00	55	69	73	51	26	0	25
1990	1	1	.500	3.57	53	53	48	43	26	0	36
11 yrs.	74	61	.548	3.11	522	1136	999	940	473	2	224
Divisional Playoffs											
1981	2	0	1.000	1.00	2	9	8	13	3	0	0
League Championship Series											
1981	1	0	1.000	0.00	1	6	4	4	2	0	0
World Series											
1981	0	0	—	13.50	1	2	5	1	2	0	0

Jose Rijo

JOSE ANTONIO RIJO BR TR
B. May 13, 1965, San Cristobal, Dominican
Republic 6' 1" 200 lbs.

Year	W	L	PCT	ERA	G	IP	H	SO	BB	Sho	SV
1984	2	8	.200	4.76	24	62.1	74	47	33	0	2

Mariano Rivera

MARIANO RIVERA BR TR
B. Nov. 29, 1969, Panama City, Panama 6' 4" 168 lbs.

Year	W	L	PCT	ERA	G	IP	H	SO	BB	Sho	SV
1995	5	3	.625	5.51	19	67	71	51	30	0	0
1996	8	3	.727	2.09	61	107.2	73	130	34	0	5
2 yrs.	13	6	.684	3.40	80	174.2	144	181	64	0	5
Divisional Playoffs											
1995	1	0	1.000	0.00	3	5.1	3	8	1	0	0
1996	0	0	—	0.00	2	4.2	0	1	1	0	0
2 yrs.	1	0	1.000	0.00	5	10	3	9	2	0	0
League Championship Series											
1996	1	0	1.000	0.00	2	4	6	5	1	0	0
World Series											
1996	0	0	—	1.59	4	5.2	4	4	3	0	0

Dale Roberts

DALE ROBERTS BR TL
B. Apr. 12, 1942, Owenton, Ky. 6' 4" 180 lbs.

Year	W	L	PCT	ERA	G	IP	H	SO	BB	Sho	SV
1967	0	0	—	9.00	2	2	3	0	2	0	0

Hank Robinson

JOHN HENRY ROBINSON BR TL
B. Aug. 16, 1889, Floyd, Ark.
D. Jul. 3, 1965, North Little Rock, Ark. 5' 11½" 160 lbs.

Year	W	L	PCT	ERA	G	IP	H	SO	BB	Sho	SV
1918	2	4	.333	3.00	11	48	47	14	16	0	0

Jeff Robinson

JEFFREY DANIEL ROBINSON BR TR
B. Dec. 13, 1960, Santa Ana, Calif. 6' 4" 195 lbs.

Year	W	L	PCT	ERA	G	IP	H	SO	BB	Sho	SV
1990	3	6	.333	3.45	54	88.2	82	43	34	0	0

Oscar Roettger

OSCAR FREDERICK LOUIS ROETTGER BR TR
B. Feb. 19, 1900, St. Louis, Mo. 6' 170 lbs.
D. Jul. 4, 1986, St. Louis, Mo.

Year	W	L	PCT	ERA	G	IP	H	SO	BB	Sho	SV
1923	0	0	—	8.49	5	11.2	16	7	12	0	1

Oscar Roettger *continued*

Year	W	L	PCT	ERA	G	IP	H	SO	BB	Sho	SV
1924	0	0	—	—	1	0	1	0	2	0	0
2 yrs.	0	0	—	8.49	6	11.2	17	7	14	0	1

Kenny Rogers

KENNETH SCOTT ROGERS BL TL
B. Nov. 10, 1964, Savannah, Ga. 6' 1" 200 lbs.

Year	W	L	PCT	ERA	G	IP	H	SO	BB	Sho	SV
1996	12	8	.600	4.68	30	179	179	92	83	1	0
Divisional Playoffs											
1996	0	0	—	9.00	2	5	5	1	2	0	0
League Championship Series											
1996	0	0	—	12.00	1	3	5	3	2	0	0
World Series											
1996	0	0	—	22.50	1	2	5	0	2	0	0

Tom Rogers

THOMAS ANDREW ROGERS BR TR
B. Feb. 12, 1892, Sparta, Tenn. 6' ½" 180 lbs.
D. Mar. 7, 1936, Nashville, Tenn.

Year	W	L	PCT	ERA	G	IP	H	SO	BB	Sho	SV
1921	0	1	.000	7.36	5	11	12	0	9	0	1
World Series											
1921	0	0	—	6.75	1	1.1	3	1	0	0	0

Jim Roland

JAMES IVAN ROLAND BR TL
B. Dec. 14, 1942, Franklin, N. C. 6' 3" 175 lbs.

Year	W	L	PCT	ERA	G	IP	H	SO	BB	Sho	SV
1972	0	1	.000	5.04	16	25	27	13	16	0	0

Steve Roser

EMERSON COREY ROSER BR TR
B. Jan. 25, 1918, Rome, N. Y. 6' 4" 220 lbs.

Year	W	L	PCT	ERA	G	IP	H	SO	BB	Sho	SV
1944	4	3	.571	3.86	16	84	80	34	34	0	1
1945	0	0	—	3.67	11	27	27	11	8	0	0
1946	1	1	.500	16.20	4	3.1	7	1	4	0	0
3 yrs.	5	4	.556	4.17	31	114.1	114	46	46	0	1

Dutch Ruether

WALTER HENRY RUETHER BL TL
B. Sep. 13, 1893, Alameda, Calif. 6' 1½" 180 lbs.
D. May 16, 1970, Phoenix, Ariz.

Year	W	L	PCT	ERA	G	IP	H	SO	BB	Sho	SV
1926	2	3	.400	3.50	5	36	32	8	18	0	0
1927	13	6	.684	3.38	27	184	202	45	52	3	0
2 yrs.	15	9	.625	3.40	32	220	234	53	70	3	0
World Series											
1926	0	1	.000	8.31	1	4.1	7	1	2	0	0

Red Ruffing

CHARLES HERBERT RUFFING BR TR
B. May 3, 1904, Granville, Ill. 6' 1½" 205 lbs.
D. Feb. 17, 1986, Mayfield Heights, Ohio
Hall of Fame 1967

Year	W	L	PCT	ERA	G	IP	H	SO	BB	Sho	SV
1930	15	5	.750	4.14	34	197.2	220	117	62	2	1
1931	16	14	.533	4.41	37	237	240	132	87	1	2
1932	18	7	.720	3.09	35	259	219	190	115	3	2
1933	9	14	.391	3.91	35	235	230	122	93	0	3
1934	19	11	.633	3.93	36	256.1	232	149	104	5	0
1935	16	11	.593	3.12	30	222	201	81	76	2	0
1936	20	12	.625	3.85	33	271	274	102	90	3	0
1937	20	7	.741	2.98	31	256.1	242	131	68	5	0
1938	21	7	.750	3.31	31	247.1	246	127	82	4	0
1939	21	7	.750	2.93	28	233.1	211	95	75	5	0
1940	15	12	.556	3.38	30	226	218	97	76	3	0
1941	15	6	.714	3.54	23	185.2	177	60	54	2	0
1942	14	7	.667	3.21	24	193.2	183	80	41	4	0
1945	7	3	.700	2.89	11	87.1	85	24	20	1	0
1946	5	1	.833	1.77	8	61	37	19	23	2	0
15 yrs.	231	124	.651	3.47	426	3168.2	3015	1526	1066	42	8
World Series											
1932	1	0	1.000	4.00	1	9	10	10	6	0	0
1936	0	1	.000	4.50	2	14	16	12	5	0	0
1937	1	0	1.000	1.00	1	9	7	8	3	0	0
1938	2	0	1.000	1.50	2	18	17	11	2	0	0
1939	1	0	1.000	1.00	1	9	4	4	1	0	0
1941	1	0	1.000	1.00	1	9	6	5	3	0	0

Year	W	L	PCT	ERA	G	IP	H	SO	BB	Sho	SV

Red Ruffing *continued*

Year	W	L	PCT	ERA	G	IP	H	SO	BB	Sho	SV
1942	1	1	.500	4.08	2	17.2	14	11	7	0	0
7 yrs.	7	2	.778	2.63	10	85.2	74	61	27	0	0

Allan Russell

ALLAN E. RUSSELL BB TR
B. Jul. 31, 1893, Baltimore, Md. 5' 11" 165 lbs.
D. Oct. 20, 1972, Baltimore, Md.

Year	W	L	PCT	ERA	G	IP	H	SO	BB	Sho	SV
1915	1	2	.333	2.67	5	27	21	21	21	0	0
1916	6	10	.375	3.20	34	171.1	138	104	75	1	6
1917	7	8	.467	2.24	25	104.1	89	55	39	0	2
1918	7	11	.389	3.26	27	141	139	54	73	2	4
1919	5	5	.500	3.47	23	90.2	89	50	32	1	1
5 yrs.	26	36	.419	3.05	114	534.1	476	284	240	4	13

Marius Russo

MARIUS UGO RUSSO BR TL
B. Jul. 19, 1914, Brooklyn, N. Y. 6' 1" 190 lbs.

Year	W	L	PCT	ERA	G	IP	H	SO	BB	Sho	SV
1939	8	3	.727	2.41	21	116	86	55	41	2	2
1940	14	8	.636	3.28	30	189.1	181	87	55	0	1
1941	14	10	.583	3.09	28	209.2	195	105	87	3	1
1942	4	1	.800	2.78	9	45.1	41	15	14	0	0
1943	5	10	.333	3.72	24	101.2	89	42	45	1	1
1946	0	2	.000	4.34	8	18.2	26	7	11	0	0
6 yrs.	45	34	.570	3.13	120	680.2	618	311	253	6	5
World Series											
1941	1	0	1.000	1.00	1	9	4	5	2	0	0
1943	1	0	1.000	0.00	1	9	7	2	1	0	0
2 yrs.	2	0	1.000	0.50	2	18	11	7	3	0	0

Babe Ruth

GEORGE HERMAN RUTH BL TL
B. Feb. 6, 1895, Baltimore, Md. 6' 2" 215 lbs.
D. Aug. 16, 1948, New York, N. Y.
Hall of Fame 1936

Year	W	L	PCT	ERA	G	IP	H	SO	BB	Sho	SV
1920	1	0	1.000	4.50	1	4	3	0	2	0	0
1921	2	0	1.000	9.00	2	9	14	2	9	0	0
1930	1	0	1.000	3.00	1	9	11	3	2	0	0
1933	1	0	1.000	5.00	1	9	12	0	3	0	0
4 yrs.	5	0	1.000	5.52	5	31	40	5	16	0	0

Rosy Ryan

WILFRED PATRICK DOLAN RYAN BL TR
B. Mar. 15, 1898, Worcester, Mass. 6' 185 lbs.
D. Dec. 10, 1980, Scottsdale, Ariz.

Year	W	L	PCT	ERA	G	IP	H	SO	BB	Sho	SV
1928	0	0	—	16.50	3	6	17	5	1	0	0

Johnny Sain

JOHN FRANKLIN SAIN BR TR
B. Sep. 25, 1917, Havana, Ark. 6' 2" 185 lbs.

Year	W	L	PCT	ERA	G	IP	H	SO	BB	Sho	SV
1951	2	1	.667	4.14	7	37	41	21	8	0	1
1952	11	6	.647	3.46	35	148.1	149	57	38	0	7
1953	14	7	.667	3.00	40	189	189	84	45	1	9
1954	6	6	.500	3.16	45	77	66	33	15	0	22
1955	0	0	—	6.75	3	5.1	6	5	1	0	0
5 yrs.	33	20	.623	3.31	130	456.2	451	200	107	1	39
World Series											
1951	0	0	—	9.00	1	2	4	2	2	0	0
1952	0	1	.000	3.00	1	6	6	3	3	0	0
1953	1	0	1.000	4.76	2	5.2	8	1	1	0	0
3 yrs.	1	1	.500	4.61	4	13.2	18	6	6	0	0

Roy Sanders

ROY LEE SANDERS BR TR
B. Jun. 10, 1894 6' 185 lbs.
D. Jul. 8, 1963, Louisville, Ky.

Year	W	L	PCT	ERA	G	IP	H	SO	BB	Sho	SV
1918	0	2	.000	4.21	6	25.2	28	8	16	0	0

Scott Sanderson

SCOTT DOUGLAS SANDERSON BR TR
B. Jul. 22, 1956, Dearborn, Mich. 6' 5" 195 lbs.

Year	W	L	PCT	ERA	G	IP	H	SO	BB	Sho	SV
1991	16	10	.615	3.81	34	208	200	130	29	2	0
1992	12	11	.522	4.93	33	193.1	220	104	64	1	0
2 yrs.	28	21	.571	4.35	67	401.1	420	234	93	3	0

Fred Sanford

JOHN FREDERICK SANFORD BB TR
B. Aug. 9, 1919, Garfield, Utah 6' 1" 200 lbs.

Year	W	L	PCT	ERA	G	IP	H	SO	BB	Sho	SV
1949	7	3	.700	3.87	29	95.1	100	51	57	0	0
1950	5	4	.556	4.55	26	112.2	103	54	79	0	0
1951	0	3	.000	3.71	11	26.2	15	10	25	0	0
3 yrs.	12	10	.545	4.18	66	234.2	218	115	161	0	0

Rick Sawyer

RICHARD CLYDE SAWYER BR TR
B. Apr. 7, 1948, Bakersfield, Calif. 6' 2" 205 lbs.

Year	W	L	PCT	ERA	G	IP	H	SO	BB	Sho	SV
1974	0	0	—	13.50	1	2	2	1	1	0	0
1975	0	0	—	3.00	4	6	7	3	2	0	0
2 yrs.	0	0	—	5.63	5	8	9	4	3	0	0

Ray Scarborough

RAE WILSON SCARBOROUGH BR TR
B. Jul. 23, 1917, Mt. Gilead, N. C. 6' 185 lbs.
D. Jul. 1, 1982, Mount Olive, N. C.

Year	W	L	PCT	ERA	G	IP	H	SO	BB	Sho	SV
1952	5	1	.833	2.91	9	34	27	13	15	0	0
1953	2	2	.500	3.29	25	54.2	52	20	26	0	2
2 yrs.	7	3	.700	3.15	34	88.2	79	33	41	0	2
World Series											
1952	0	0	—	9.00	1	1	1	1	0	0	0

Harry Schaeffer

HARRY EDWARD SCHAEFFER BL TL
B. Jun. 23, 1924, Reading, Pa. 6' 2½" 175 lbs.

Year	W	L	PCT	ERA	G	IP	H	SO	BB	Sho	SV
1952	0	1	.000	5.29	5	17	18	15	18	0	0

Art Schallock

ARTHUR LAWRENCE SCHALLOCK BL TL
B. Apr. 25, 1924, Mill Valley, Calif. 5' 9" 160 lbs.

Year	W	L	PCT	ERA	G	IP	H	SO	BB	Sho	SV
1951	3	1	.750	3.88	11	46.1	50	19	20	0	0
1952	0	0	—	9.00	2	3	3	1	2	0	0
1953	0	0	—	2.95	7	21.1	30	13	15	0	1
1954	0	1	.000	4.15	6	17.1	20	9	11	0	0
1955	0	0	—	6.00	2	3	4	2	1	0	0
5 yrs.	3	2	.600	3.90	28	90	107	44	49	0	1
World Series											
1953	0	0	—	4.50	1	2	2	1	1	0	0

Butch Schmidt

CHARLES JOHN SCHMIDT BL TL
B. Jul. 19, 1886, Baltimore, Md. 6' 1½" 200 lbs.
D. Sep. 4, 1952, Baltimore, Md.

Year	W	L	PCT	ERA	G	IP	H	SO	BB	Sho	SV
1909	0	0	—	7.20	1	5	10	2	1	0	0

Johnny Schmitz

JOHN ALBERT SCHMITZ BR TL
B. Nov. 27, 1920, Wausau, Wis. 6' 170 lbs.

Year	W	L	PCT	ERA	G	IP	H	SO	BB	Sho	SV
1952	1	1	.500	3.60	5	15	15	3	9	0	1
1953	0	0	—	2.08	3	4.1	2	0	3	0	0
2 yrs.	1	1	.500	3.26	8	19.1	17	3	12	0	1

Pete Schneider

PETER JOSEPH SCHNEIDER BR TR
B. Aug. 20, 1895, Los Angeles, Calif. 6' 1" 194 lbs.
D. Jun. 1, 1957, Los Angeles, Calif.

Year	W	L	PCT	ERA	G	IP	H	SO	BB	Sho	SV
1919	0	1	.000	3.41	7	29	19	11	22	0	0

Paul Schreiber

PAUL FREDERICK SCHREIBER BR TR
B. Oct. 8, 1902, Jacksonville, Fla. 6' 2" 180 lbs.
D. Jan. 28, 1982, Sarasota, Fla.

Year	W	L	PCT	ERA	G	IP	H	SO	BB	Sho	SV
1945	0	0	—	4.15	2	4.1	4	1	2	0	0

Al Schulz

ALBERT CHRISTOPHER SCHULZ BR TL
B. May 12, 1889, Toledo, Ohio 6' 182 lbs.
D. Dec. 13, 1931, Gallipolis, Ohio

Year	W	L	PCT	ERA	G	IP	H	SO	BB	Sho	SV
1912	1	1	.500	2.20	3	16.1	11	8	11	0	0
1913	7	13	.350	3.73	38	193	197	77	69	0	0
1914	1	3	.250	4.76	6	28.1	27	18	10	0	0
3 yrs.	9	17	.346	3.75	47	237.2	235	103	90	0	0

Don Schulze

DONALD ARTHUR SCHULZE
B. Sep. 27, 1962, Roselle, Ill.
BR TR 6' 3" 215 lbs.

Year	W	L	PCT	ERA	G	IP	H	SO	BB	Sho	SV
1989	1	1	.500	4.09	2	11	12	5	5	0	0

Rod Scurry

RODNEY GRANT SCURRY
B. Mar. 17, 1956, Sacramento, Calif.
D. Nov. 5, 1992, Reno, Nev.
BL TL 6' 2" 180 lbs.

Year	W	L	PCT	ERA	G	IP	H	SO	BB	Sho	SV
1985	1	0	1.000	2.84	5	12.2	5	17	10	0	1
1986	1	2	.333	3.66	31	39.1	38	36	22	0	2
2 yrs.	2	2	.500	3.46	36	52	43	53	32	0	3

Bobby Shantz

ROBERT CLAYTON SHANTZ
B. Sep. 26, 1925, Pottstown, Pa.
BR TL 5' 6" 139 lbs.

Year	W	L	PCT	ERA	G	IP	H	SO	BB	Sho	SV
1957	11	5	.688	2.45	30	173	157	72	40	1	5
1958	7	6	.538	3.36	33	126	127	80	35	0	0
1959	7	3	.700	2.38	33	94.2	64	66	33	2	3
1960	5	4	.556	2.79	42	67.2	57	54	24	0	11
4 yrs.	30	18	.625	2.73	138	461.1	405	272	132	3	19
World Series											
1957	0	1	.000	4.05	3	6.2	8	7	2	0	0
1960	0	0	—	4.26	3	6.1	4	1	1	0	1
2 yrs.	0	1	.000	4.15	6	13	12	8	3	0	1

Bob Shawkey

JAMES ROBERT SHAWKEY
B. Dec. 4, 1890, Sigel, Pa.
D. Dec. 31, 1980, Syracuse, N. Y.
BR TR 5' 11" 168 lbs.

Year	W	L	PCT	ERA	G	IP	H	SO	BB	Sho	SV
1915	4	7	.364	3.26	16	85.2	78	31	35	1	0
1916	24	14	.632	2.21	53	276.2	204	122	81	4	8
1917	13	15	.464	2.44	37	236.1	207	97	72	2	0
1918	1	1	.500	1.13	3	16	7	3	10	1	0
1919	20	11	.645	2.72	41	261.1	218	122	92	3	4
1920	20	13	.606	2.45	38	267.2	246	126	85	5	2
1921	18	12	.600	4.08	38	245	245	126	86	3	2
1922	20	12	.625	2.91	39	299.2	286	130	98	3	1
1923	16	11	.593	3.51	36	258.2	232	125	102	1	1
1924	16	11	.593	4.12	38	207.2	226	114	74	1	0
1925	6	14	.300	4.11	33	186	209	81	67	1	0
1926	8	7	.533	3.62	29	104.1	102	63	37	1	3
1927	2	3	.400	2.89	19	43.2	44	23	16	0	4
13 yrs.	168	131	.562	3.12	415	2488.2	2304	1163	855	26	25
World Series											
1921	0	1	.000	7.00	2	9	13	5	6	0	0
1922	0	0	—	2.70	1	10	8	4	2	0	0
1923	1	0	1.000	3.52	1	7.2	12	2	4	0	0
1926	0	1	.000	5.40	3	10	8	7	2	0	0
4 yrs.	1	2	.333	4.66	7	36.2	41	18	14	0	0

Spec Shea

FRANCIS JOSEPH SHEA
B. Oct. 2, 1920, Naugatuck, Conn.
BR TR 6' 195 lbs.

Year	W	L	PCT	ERA	G	IP	H	SO	BB	Sho	SV
1947	14	5	.737	3.07	27	178.2	127	89	89	3	1
1948	9	10	.474	3.41	28	155.2	117	71	87	3	1
1949	1	1	.500	5.33	20	52.1	48	22	43	0	1
1951	5	5	.500	4.33	25	95.2	112	38	50	2	0
4 yrs.	29	21	.580	3.68	100	482.1	404	220	269	8	3
World Series											
1947	2	0	1.000	2.35	3	15.1	10	10	8	0	0

Al Shealy

ALBERT BERLY SHEALY
B. May 20, 1900, Chapin, S. C.
D. Mar. 7, 1967, Hagerstown, Md.
BR TR 5' 11" 175 lbs.

Year	W	L	PCT	ERA	G	IP	H	SO	BB	Sho	SV
1928	8	6	.571	5.06	23	96	124	39	42	0	2

George Shears

GEORGE PENFIELD SHEARS
B. Apr. 13, 1890, Marshall, Mo.
D. Nov. 12, 1978, Loveland, Colo.
BR TL 6' 3" 180 lbs.

Year	W	L	PCT	ERA	G	IP	H	SO	BB	Sho	SV
1912	0	0	—	5.40	4	15	24	9	11	0	0

Tom Sheehan

THOMAS CLANCY SHEEHAN
B. Mar. 31, 1894, Grand Ridge, Ill.
D. Oct. 29, 1982, Chillicothe, Ohio
BR TR 6' 2½" 190 lbs.

Year	W	L	PCT	ERA	G	IP	H	SO	BB	Sho	SV
1921	1	0	1.000	5.45	12	33	43	7	19	0	1

Rollie Sheldon

ROLAND FRANK SHELDON
B. Dec. 17, 1936, Putnam, Conn.
BR TR 6' 4" 185 lbs.

Year	W	L	PCT	ERA	G	IP	H	SO	BB	Sho	SV
1961	11	5	.688	3.60	35	162.2	149	84	55	2	0
1962	7	8	.467	5.49	34	118	136	54	28	0	1
1964	5	2	.714	3.61	19	102.1	92	57	18	0	1
1965	0	0	—	1.42	3	6.1	5	7	1	0	0
4 yrs.	23	15	.605	4.14	91	389.1	382	202	102	2	2
World Series											
1964	0	0	—	0.00	2	2.2	0	2	0	0	0

Roy Sherid

ROYDEN RICHARD SHERID
B. Jan. 25, 1907, Norristown, Pa.
D. Feb. 28, 1982, Parker Ford, Pa.
BR TR 6' 2" 185 lbs.

Year	W	L	PCT	ERA	G	IP	H	SO	BB	Sho	SV
1929	6	6	.500	3.49	33	159.2	165	51	55	0	1
1930	12	13	.480	5.23	37	184	214	59	87	0	4
1931	5	5	.500	5.69	17	74.1	94	39	24	0	2
3 yrs.	23	24	.489	4.65	87	418	473	149	166	0	7

Ben Shields

BENJAMIN COWAN SHIELDS
B. Jun. 17, 1903, Huntersville, N. C.
D. Jan. 24, 1982, Woodruff, S. C.
BR TL 6' 1½" 195 lbs.

Year	W	L	PCT	ERA	G	IP	H	SO	BB	Sho	SV
1924	0	0	—	27.00	2	2	6	3	2	0	0
1925	3	0	1.000	4.88	4	24	24	5	12	0	0
2 yrs.	3	0	1.000	6.58	6	26	30	8	14	0	0

Steve Shields

STEPHEN MACK SHIELDS
B. Nov. 30, 1958, Gadsden, Ala.
BR TR 6' 5" 220 lbs.

Year	W	L	PCT	ERA	G	IP	H	SO	BB	Sho	SV
1988	5	5	.500	4.37	39	82.1	96	55	30	0	0

Bob Shirley

ROBERT CHARLES SHIRLEY
B. Jun. 25, 1954, Cushing, Okla.
BR TL 5' 11" 180 lbs.

Year	W	L	PCT	ERA	G	IP	H	SO	BB	Sho	SV
1983	5	8	.385	5.08	25	108	122	53	36	1	0
1984	3	3	.500	3.38	41	114.1	119	48	38	0	0
1985	5	5	.500	2.64	48	109	103	55	26	0	2
1986	0	4	.000	5.04	39	105.1	108	64	40	0	3
1987	1	0	1.000	4.50	12	34	36	12	16	0	0
5 yrs.	14	20	.412	4.05	165	470.2	488	232	156	1	5

Urban Shocker

URBAN JAMES SHOCKER
B. Aug. 22, 1890, Cleveland, Ohio
D. Sep. 9, 1928, Denver, Colo.
BR TR 5' 10" 170 lbs.

Year	W	L	PCT	ERA	G	IP	H	SO	BB	Sho	SV
1916	4	3	.571	2.62	12	82.1	67	43	32	1	0
1917	8	5	.615	2.61	26	145	124	68	46	0	1
1925	12	12	.500	3.65	41	244.1	278	74	58	2	2
1926	19	11	.633	3.38	41	258.1	272	59	71	2	2
1927	18	6	.750	2.84	31	200	207	35	41	2	0
1928	0	0	—	0.00	1	2	3	0	0	0	0
6 yrs.	61	37	.622	3.14	152	932	951	279	248	5	5
World Series											
1926	0	1	.000	5.87	2	7.2	13	3	0	0	0

Ernie Shore

ERNEST GRADY SHORE
B. Mar. 24, 1891, East Bend, N. C.
D. Sep. 24, 1980, Winston-Salem, N. C.
BR TR 6' 4" 220 lbs.

Year	W	L	PCT	ERA	G	IP	H	SO	BB	Sho	SV
1919	5	8	.385	4.17	20	95	105	24	44	0	0
1920	2	2	.500	4.87	14	44.1	61	12	21	0	1
2 yrs.	7	10	.412	4.39	34	139.1	166	36	65	0	1

Bill Short

WILLIAM ROSS SHORT
B. Nov. 27, 1937, Kingston, N. Y.
BL TL 5' 9" 170 lbs.

Year	W	L	PCT	ERA	G	IP	H	SO	BB	Sho	SV
1960	3	5	.375	4.79	10	47	49	14	30	0	0

Roger Slagle
ROGER LEE SLAGLE — BR TR
B. Nov. 4, 1953, Wichita., Kans. — 6' 3" 190 lbs.

Year	W	L	PCT	ERA	G	IP	H	SO	BB	Sho	SV
1979	0	0	—	0.00	1	2	0	2	0	0	0

Walt Smallwood
WALTER CLAYTON SMALLWOOD — BR TR
B. Apr. 24, 1893, Dayton, Md. — 6' 2" 190 lbs.
D. Apr. 29, 1967, Baltimore, Md.

Year	W	L	PCT	ERA	G	IP	H	SO	BB	Sho	SV
1917	0	0	—	0.00	2	2	1	1	1	0	0
1919	0	0	—	4.98	6	21.2	20	6	9	0	0
2 yrs.	0	0	—	4.56	8	23.2	21	7	10	0	0

Lee Smith
LEE ARTHUR SMITH, JR. — BR TR
B. Dec. 4, 1957, Jamestown, La. — 6' 5" 220 lbs.

Year	W	L	PCT	ERA	G	IP	H	SO	BB	Sho	SV
1993	0	0	—	0.00	8	8	4	11	5	0	3

Harry Smythe
WILLIAM HENRY SMYTHE — BL TL
B. Oct. 24, 1904, Augusta, Ga. — 5' 10½" 179 lbs.
D. Aug. 28, 1980, Augusta, Ga.

Year	W	L	PCT	ERA	G	IP	H	SO	BB	Sho	SV
1934	0	2	.000	7.80	8	15	24	7	8	0	1

Russ Springer
RUSSELL PAUL SPRINGER — BR TR
B. Nov. 7, 1968, Alexandria, La. — 6' 4" 195 lbs.

Year	W	L	PCT	ERA	G	IP	H	SO	BB	Sho	SV
1992	0	0	—	6.19	14	16	18	12	10	0	0

Bill Stafford
WILLIAM CHARLES STAFFORD — BR TR
B. Aug. 13, 1939, Catskill, N. Y. — 6' 1" 188 lbs.

Year	W	L	PCT	ERA	G	IP	H	SO	BB	Sho	SV
1960	3	1	.750	2.25	11	60	50	36	18	1	0
1961	14	9	.609	2.68	36	195	168	101	59	3	2
1962	14	9	.609	3.67	35	213.1	188	109	77	2	0
1963	4	8	.333	6.02	28	89.2	104	52	42	0	3
1964	5	0	1.000	2.67	31	60.2	50	39	22	0	4
1965	3	8	.273	3.56	22	111.1	93	71	31	0	0
6 yrs.	43	35	.551	3.48	163	730	653	408	249	6	9
World Series										
1960	0	0	—	1.50	2	6	5	2	1	0	0
1961	0	0	—	2.70	1	6.2	7	5	2	0	0
1962	1	0	1.000	2.00	1	9	4	5	2	0	0
3 yrs.	1	0	1.000	2.08	4	21.2	16	12	5	0	0

Gerry Staley
GERALD LEE STALEY — BR TR
B. Aug. 21, 1920, Brush Prairie, Wash. — 6' 195 lbs.

Year	W	L	PCT	ERA	G	IP	H	SO	BB	Sho	SV
1955	0	0	—	13.50	2	2	5	0	1	0	0
1956	0	0	—	108.00	1	0.1	4	1	0	0	0
2 yrs.	0	0	—	27.00	3	2.1	9	1	1	0	0

Charley Stanceu
CHARLES STANCEU — BR TR
B. Jan. 9, 1916, Canton, Ohio — 6' 2" 190 lbs.
D. Apr. 3, 1969, Canton, Ohio

Year	W	L	PCT	ERA	G	IP	H	SO	BB	Sho	SV
1941	3	3	.500	5.63	22	48	58	21	35	0	0
1946	0	0	—	9.00	3	4	6	3	5	0	0
2 yrs.	3	3	.500	5.88	25	52	64	24	40	0	0

Dick Starr
RICHARD EUGENE STARR — BR TR
B. Mar. 2, 1921, Kittanning, Pa. — 6' 3" 190 lbs.

Year	W	L	PCT	ERA	G	IP	H	SO	BB	Sho	SV
1947	1	0	1.000	1.46	4	12.1	12	1	8	0	0
1948	0	0	—	4.50	1	2	0	2	2	0	0
2 yrs.	1	0	1.000	1.88	5	14.1	12	3	10	0	0

Lee Stine
LEE ELBERT STINE — BR TR
B. Nov. 17, 1913, Stillwater, Okla. — 5' 11" 185 lbs.

Year	W	L	PCT	ERA	G	IP	H	SO	BB	Sho	SV
1938	0	0	—	1.04	4	8.2	9	4	1	0	0

Tim Stoddard
TIMOTHY PAUL STODDARD — BR TR
B. Jan. 24, 1953, East Chicago, Ind. — 6' 7" 230 lbs.

Year	W	L	PCT	ERA	G	IP	H	SO	BB	Sho	SV
1986	4	1	.800	3.83	24	49.1	41	34	23	0	0
1987	4	3	.571	3.50	57	92.2	83	78	30	0	8
1988	2	2	.500	6.38	28	55	62	33	27	0	3
3 yrs.	10	6	.625	4.39	109	197	186	145	80	0	11

Mel Stottlemyre
MELVIN LEON STOTTLEMYRE, SR. — BR TR
B. Nov. 13, 1941, Hazelton, Mo. — 6' 1" 178 lbs.

Year	W	L	PCT	ERA	G	IP	H	SO	BB	Sho	SV
1964	9	3	.750	2.06	13	96	77	49	35	2	0
1965	20	9	.690	2.63	37	291	250	155	88	4	0
1966	12	20	.375	3.80	37	251	239	146	82	3	1
1967	15	15	.500	2.96	36	255	235	151	88	4	0
1968	21	12	.636	2.45	36	278.2	243	140	65	6	0
1969	20	14	.588	2.82	39	303	267	113	97	3	0
1970	15	13	.536	3.09	37	271	262	126	84	0	0
1971	16	12	.571	2.87	35	270	234	132	69	7	0
1972	14	18	.438	3.22	36	260	250	110	85	7	0
1973	16	16	.500	3.07	38	273	259	95	79	4	0
1974	6	7	.462	3.58	16	113	119	40	37	0	0
11 yrs.	164	139	.541	2.97	360	2661.2	2435	1257	809	40	1
World Series										
1964	1	1	.500	3.15	3	20	18	12	6	0	0

Hal Stowe
HAROLD RUDOLPH STOWE — BL TL
B. Aug. 29, 1937, Gastonia, N. C. — 6' 170 lbs.

Year	W	L	PCT	ERA	G	IP	H	SO	BB	Sho	SV
1960	0	0	—	9.00	1	1	0	0	1	0	0

Marlin Stuart
MARLIN HENRY STUART — BL TR
B. Aug. 8, 1918, Paragould, Ark. — 6' 2" 185 lbs.
D. Jun. 16, 1994, Paragould, Ark.

Year	W	L	PCT	ERA	G	IP	H	SO	BB	Sho	SV
1954	3	0	1.000	5.40	10	18.1	28	2	12	0	1

Tom Sturdivant
THOMAS VIRGIL STURDIVANT — BL TR
B. Apr. 28, 1930, Gordon, Kans. — 6' ½" 170 lbs.

Year	W	L	PCT	ERA	G	IP	H	SO	BB	Sho	SV
1955	1	3	.250	3.16	33	68.1	48	48	42	0	0
1956	16	8	.667	3.30	32	158.1	134	110	52	2	5
1957	16	6	.727	2.54	28	201.2	170	118	80	2	0
1958	3	6	.333	4.20	15	70.2	77	41	38	0	0
1959	0	2	.000	4.97	7	25.1	20	16	9	0	0
5 yrs.	36	25	.590	3.19	115	524.1	449	333	221	4	5
World Series										
1955	0	0	—	6.00	2	3	5	0	2	0	0
1956	1	0	1.000	2.79	2	9.2	8	9	8	0	0
1957	0	0	—	6.00	2	6	6	2	1	0	0
3 yrs.	1	0	1.000	4.34	6	18.2	19	11	11	0	0

Steve Sundra
STEPHEN RICHARD SUNDRA — BR TR
B. Mar. 27, 1910, Luxor, Pa. — 6' 2" 190 lbs.
D. Mar. 23, 1952, Cleveland, Ohio

Year	W	L	PCT	ERA	G	IP	H	SO	BB	Sho	SV
1936	0	0	—	0.00	1	2	2	1	2	0	0
1938	6	4	.600	4.80	25	93.2	107	33	43	0	0
1939	11	1	.917	2.76	24	120.2	110	27	56	1	0
1940	4	6	.400	5.53	27	99.1	121	26	42	0	2
4 yrs.	21	11	.656	4.22	77	315.2	340	87	143	1	2
World Series										
1939	0	0	—	0.00	1	2.2	4	2	1	0	0

Fred Talbot
FREDERICK LEALAND TALBOT — BR TR
B. Jun. 28, 1941, Washington, D. C. — 6' 2" 195 lbs.

Year	W	L	PCT	ERA	G	IP	H	SO	BB	Sho	SV
1966	7	7	.500	4.15	23	123.2	123	48	45	0	0
1967	6	8	.429	4.22	29	138.2	132	61	54	0	0
1968	1	9	.100	3.36	29	99	89	67	42	0	0
1969	0	0	—	5.11	8	12.1	13	7	6	0	0
4 yrs.	14	24	.368	4.00	89	373.2	357	183	147	0	0

Year	W	L	PCT	ERA	G	IP	H	SO	BB	Sho	SV

Vito Tamulis

VITAUTRIS CASIMIRUS TAMULIS   BL TL
B. Jul. 11, 1911, Cambridge, Mass.   5' 9" 170 lbs.
D. May 5, 1974, Nashville, Tenn.

Year	W	L	PCT	ERA	G	IP	H	SO	BB	Sho	SV
1934	1	0	1.000	0.00	1	9	7	5	1	1	0
1935	10	5	.667	4.09	30	160.2	178	57	55	3	1
2 yrs.	11	5	.688	3.87	31	169.2	185	62	56	4	1

Frank Tanana

FRANK DARYL TANANA   BL TL
B. Jul. 3, 1953, Detroit, Mich.   6' 2" 180 lbs.

Year	W	L	PCT	ERA	G	IP	H	SO	BB	Sho	SV
1993	0	2	.000	3.20	3	19.2	18	12	7	0	0

Jesse Tannehill

JESSE NILES TANNEHILL   BB TL
B. Jul. 14, 1874, Dayton, Ky.   5' 8" 150 lbs.
D. Sep. 22, 1956, Dayton, Ky.

Year	W	L	PCT	ERA	G	IP	H	SO	BB	Sho	SV
1903	15	15	.500	3.27	32	239.2	258	106	34	2	0

Wade Taylor

WADE ERIC TAYLOR   BR TR
B. Oct. 19, 1965, Mobile, Ala.   6' 1" 185 lbs.

Year	W	L	PCT	ERA	G	IP	H	SO	BB	Sho	SV
1991	7	12	.368	6.27	23	116.1	144	72	53	0	0

Walt Terrell

CHARLES WALTER TERRELL   BL TR
B. May 11, 1958, Jeffersonville, Ind.   6' 2" 205 lbs.

Year	W	L	PCT	ERA	G	IP	H	SO	BB	Sho	SV
1989	6	5	.545	5.20	13	83	102	30	24	1	0

Ralph Terry

RALPH WILLARD TERRY   BR TR
B. Jan. 9, 1936, Big Cabin, Okla.   6' 3" 195 lbs.

Year	W	L	PCT	ERA	G	IP	H	SO	BB	Sho	SV
1956	1	2	.333	9.45	3	13.1	17	8	11	0	0
1957	1	1	.500	3.05	7	20.2	18	7	8	1	0
1959	3	7	.300	3.39	24	127.1	130	55	30	1	0
1960	10	8	.556	3.40	35	166.2	149	92	52	3	1
1961	16	3	.842	3.15	31	188.1	162	86	42	2	0
1962	23	12	.657	3.19	43	298.2	257	176	57	3	2
1963	17	15	.531	3.22	40	268	246	114	39	3	1
1964	7	11	.389	4.54	27	115	130	77	31	1	4
8 yrs.	78	59	.569	3.44	210	1198	1109	615	270	14	8

World Series

Year	W	L	PCT	ERA	G	IP	H	SO	BB	Sho	SV
1960	0	2	.000	5.40	2	6.2	7	5	1	0	0
1961	0	1	.000	4.82	2	9.1	12	7	2	0	0
1962	2	1	.667	1.80	3	25	17	16	2	1	0
1963	0	0	—	3.00	1	3	3	0	1	0	0
1964	0	0	—	0.00	1	2	2	3	0	0	0
5 yrs.	2	4	.333	2.93	9	46	41	31	6	1	0

Bob Tewksbury

ROBERT ALAN TEWKSBURY   BR TR
B. Nov. 30, 1960, Concord, N. H.   6' 4" 200 lbs.

Year	W	L	PCT	ERA	G	IP	H	SO	BB	Sho	SV
1986	9	5	.643	3.31	23	130.1	144	49	31	0	0
1987	1	4	.200	6.75	8	33.1	47	12	7	0	0
2 yrs.	10	9	.526	4.01	31	163.2	191	61	38	0	0

Myles Thomas

MYLES LEWIS THOMAS   BR TR
B. Oct. 22, 1897, State College, Pa.   5' 9½" 170 lbs.
D. Dec. 12, 1963, Toledo, Ohio

Year	W	L	PCT	ERA	G	IP	H	SO	BB	Sho	SV
1926	6	6	.500	4.23	33	140.1	140	38	65	0	0
1927	7	4	.636	4.87	21	88.2	111	25	43	0	0
1928	1	0	1.000	3.41	12	31.2	33	10	9	0	0
1929	0	2	.000	10.80	5	15	27	3	9	0	0
4 yrs.	14	12	.538	4.70	71	275.2	311	76	126	0	0

World Series

Year	W	L	PCT	ERA	G	IP	H	SO	BB	Sho	SV
1926	0	0	—	3.00	2	3	3	0	0	0	0

Stan Thomas

STANLEY BROWN THOMAS   BR TR
B. Jul. 11, 1949, Rumford, Me.   6' 2" 185 lbs.

Year	W	L	PCT	ERA	G	IP	H	SO	BB	Sho	SV
1977	1	0	1.000	7.11	3	6.1	7	1	4	0	0

Tommy Thompson

THOMAS CARL THOMPSON   BR TR
B. Nov. 7, 1889, Spring City, Tenn.   5' 9½" 170 lbs.
D. Jan. 16, 1963, La Jolla, Calif.

Year	W	L	PCT	ERA	G	IP	H	SO	BB	Sho	SV
1912	0	2	.000	6.06	7	32.2	43	15	13	0	0

Hank Thormahlen

HERBERT EHLER THORMAHLEN   BL TL
B. Jul. 5, 1896, Jersey City, N. J.   6' 180 lbs.
D. Feb. 6, 1955, Los Angeles, Calif.

Year	W	L	PCT	ERA	G	IP	H	SO	BB	Sho	SV
1917	0	1	.000	2.25	1	8	9	5	4	0	0
1918	7	3	.700	2.48	16	112.2	85	22	52	2	0
1919	12	10	.545	2.62	30	188.2	155	62	61	2	1
1920	9	6	.600	4.14	29	143.1	178	35	43	0	1
4 yrs.	28	20	.583	3.06	76	452.2	427	124	160	4	2

Luis Tiant

LUIS CLEMENTE TIANT   BR TR
B. Nov. 23, 1940, Marianao, Cuba   6' 180 lbs.

Year	W	L	PCT	ERA	G	IP	H	SO	BB	Sho	SV
1979	13	8	.619	3.90	30	196	190	104	53	1	0
1980	8	9	.471	4.90	25	136	139	84	50	0	0
2 yrs.	21	17	.553	4.31	55	332	329	188	103	1	0

Dick Tidrow

RICHARD WILLIAM TIDROW   BR TR
B. May 14, 1947, San Francisco, Calif.   6' 4" 210 lbs.

Year	W	L	PCT	ERA	G	IP	H	SO	BB	Sho	SV
1974	11	9	.550	3.86	33	191	205	100	53	0	1
1975	6	3	.667	3.13	37	69	65	38	31	0	5
1976	4	5	.444	2.63	47	92.1	80	65	24	0	10
1977	11	4	.733	3.16	49	151	143	83	41	0	5
1978	7	11	.389	3.84	31	185.1	191	73	53	0	0
1979	2	1	.667	7.83	14	23	38	7	4	0	2
6 yrs.	41	33	.554	3.60	211	711.2	722	366	206	0	23

League Championship Series

Year	W	L	PCT	ERA	G	IP	H	SO	BB	Sho	SV
1976	1	0	1.000	3.68	3	7.1	6	0	4	0	0
1977	0	0	—	3.86	2	7	6	3	3	0	0
1978	0	0	—	4.76	1	5.2	8	1	2	0	0
3 yrs.	1	0	1.000	4.05	6	20	20	4	9	0	0

World Series

Year	W	L	PCT	ERA	G	IP	H	SO	BB	Sho	SV
1976	0	0	—	7.71	2	2.1	5	1	1	0	0
1977	0	0	—	4.91	2	3.2	5	1	0	0	0
1978	0	0	—	1.93	2	4.2	4	5	0	0	0
3 yrs.	0	0	—	4.22	6	10.2	14	7	1	0	0

Bobby Tiefenauer

BOBBY GENE TIEFENAUER   BR TR
B. Oct. 10, 1929, Desloge, Mo.   6' 2" 185 lbs.

Year	W	L	PCT	ERA	G	IP	H	SO	BB	Sho	SV
1965	1	1	.500	3.54	10	20.1	19	15	5	0	2

Ray Tift

RAYMOND FRANK TIFT   B TR
B. Jun. 21, 1884, Fitchburg, Mass.   ' " lbs.
D. Mar. 29, 1945, Verona, N. J.

Year	W	L	PCT	ERA	G	IP	H	SO	BB	Sho	SV
1907	0	0	—	4.74	4	19	33	6	4	0	0

Thad Tillotson

THADDEUS ASA TILLOTSON   BR TR
B. Dec. 20, 1940, Merced, Calif.   6' 2½" 195 lbs.

Year	W	L	PCT	ERA	G	IP	H	SO	BB	Sho	SV
1967	3	9	.250	4.03	43	98.1	99	62	39	0	2
1968	1	0	1.000	4.35	7	10.1	11	1	7	0	0
2 yrs.	4	9	.308	4.06	50	108.2	110	63	46	0	2

Dan Tipple

DANIEL E. TIPPLE   BR TR
B. Feb. 13, 1890, Rockford, Ill.   6' 176 lbs.
D. Mar. 26, 1960, Omaha, Neb.

Year	W	L	PCT	ERA	G	IP	H	SO	BB	Sho	SV
1915	1	1	.500	2.84	3	19	14	14	11	0	0

Mike Torrez

MICHAEL AUGUSTINE TORREZ   BR TR
B. Aug. 28, 1946, Topeka, Kans.   6' 5" 220 lbs.

Year	W	L	PCT	ERA	G	IP	H	SO	BB	Sho	SV
1977	14	12	.538	3.86	31	217	212	90	75	2	0

League Championship Series

Year	W	L	PCT	ERA	G	IP	H	SO	BB	Sho	SV
1977	0	1	.000	4.09	2	11	11	5	5	0	0

Year	W	L	PCT	ERA	G	IP	H	SO	BB	Sho	SV

Mike Torrez *continued*

World Series
Year	W	L	PCT	ERA	G	IP	H	SO	BB	Sho	SV
1977	2	0	1.000	2.50	2	18	16	15	5	0	0

Steve Trout

STEVEN RUSSELL TROUT   BL TL
B. Jul. 30, 1957, Detroit, Mich.   6' 4" 195 lbs.

Year	W	L	PCT	ERA	G	IP	H	SO	BB	Sho	SV
1987	0	4	.000	6.60	14	46.1	51	27	37	0	0

Virgil Trucks

VIRGIL OLIVER TRUCKS   BR TR
B. Apr. 26, 1917, Birmingham, Ala.   5' 11" 198 lbs.

Year	W	L	PCT	ERA	G	IP	H	SO	BB	Sho	SV
1958	2	1	.667	4.54	25	39.2	40	26	24	0	1

Bob Turley

ROBERT LEE TURLEY   BR TR
B. Sep. 19, 1930, Troy, Ill.   6' 2" 215 lbs.

Year	W	L	PCT	ERA	G	IP	H	SO	BB	Sho	SV
1955	17	13	.567	3.06	36	246.2	168	210	177	6	1
1956	8	4	.667	5.05	27	132	138	91	103	1	1
1957	13	6	.684	2.71	32	176.1	120	152	85	4	3
1958	21	7	.750	2.97	33	245.1	178	168	128	6	1
1959	8	11	.421	4.32	33	154.1	141	111	83	3	0
1960	9	3	.750	3.27	34	173.1	138	87	87	1	5
1961	3	5	.375	5.75	15	72	74	48	51	0	0
1962	3	3	.500	4.57	24	69	68	42	47	0	1
8 yrs.	82	52	.612	3.62	234	1269	1025	909	761	21	12

World Series
Year	W	L	PCT	ERA	G	IP	H	SO	BB	Sho	SV
1955	0	1	.000	8.44	3	5.1	7	7	4	0	0
1956	0	1	.000	0.82	3	11	4	14	8	0	0
1957	1	0	1.000	2.31	3	11.2	7	12	6	0	0
1958	2	1	.667	2.76	4	16.1	10	13	7	1	1
1960	1	0	1.000	4.82	2	9.1	15	0	4	0	0
5 yrs.	4	3	.571	3.19	15	53.2	43	46	29	1	1

Jim Turner

JAMES RILEY TURNER   BL TR
B. Aug. 6, 1903, Antioch, Tenn.   6' 185 lbs.

Year	W	L	PCT	ERA	G	IP	H	SO	BB	Sho	SV
1942	1	1	.500	1.29	5	7	4	2	1	0	1
1943	3	0	1.000	3.53	18	43.1	44	15	13	0	1
1944	4	4	.500	3.46	35	41.2	42	13	22	0	7
1945	3	4	.429	3.64	30	54.1	45	22	31	0	10
4 yrs.	11	9	.550	3.44	88	146.1	135	52	67	0	19

World Series
Year	W	L	PCT	ERA	G	IP	H	SO	BB	Sho	SV
1942	0	0	—	0.00	1	1	0	0	1	0	0

George Uhle

GEORGE ERNEST UHLE   BR TR
B. Sep. 18, 1898, Cleveland, Ohio   6' 190 lbs.
D. Feb. 26, 1985, Lakewood, Ohio

Year	W	L	PCT	ERA	G	IP	H	SO	BB	Sho	SV
1933	6	1	.857	5.16	12	61	63	26	20	0	0
1934	2	4	.333	9.92	10	16.1	30	10	7	0	0
2 yrs.	8	5	.615	6.17	22	77.1	93	36	27	0	0

Tom Underwood

THOMAS GERALD UNDERWOOD   BR TL
B. Dec. 22, 1953, Kokomo, Ind.   5' 11" 170 lbs.

Year	W	L	PCT	ERA	G	IP	H	SO	BB	Sho	SV
1980	13	9	.591	3.66	38	187	163	116	66	2	2
1981	1	4	.200	4.36	9	33	32	29	13	0	0
2 yrs.	14	13	.519	3.76	47	220	195	145	79	2	2

League Championship Series
Year	W	L	PCT	ERA	G	IP	H	SO	BB	Sho	SV
1980	0	0	—	0.00	2	3	3	3	0	0	0

Cecil Upshaw

CECIL LEE UPSHAW   BR TR
B. Oct. 22, 1942, Spearsville, La.   6' 6" 205 lbs.
D. Feb. 7, 1995, Lawrenceville, Ga.

Year	W	L	PCT	ERA	G	IP	H	SO	BB	Sho	SV
1974	1	5	.167	3.00	36	60	53	27	24	0	6

Russ Van Atta

RUSSELL VAN ATTA   BL TL
B. Jun. 21, 1906, Augusta, N. J.   6' 184 lbs.
D. Oct. 10, 1986, Andover, N. J.

Year	W	L	PCT	ERA	G	IP	H	SO	BB	Sho	SV
1933	12	4	.750	4.18	26	157	160	76	63	2	1

Russ Van Atta *continued*

Year	W	L	PCT	ERA	G	IP	H	SO	BB	Sho	SV
1934	3	5	.375	6.34	28	88	107	39	46	0	0
1935	0	0	—	3.86	5	4.2	5	3	4	0	0
3 yrs.	15	9	.625	4.94	59	249.2	272	118	113	2	1

Dazzy Vance

CLARENCE ARTHUR VANCE   BR TR
B. Mar. 4, 1891, Orient, Iowa   6' 2" 200 lbs.
D. Feb. 16, 1961, Homosassa Springs, Fla.
Hall of Fame 1955

Year	W	L	PCT	ERA	G	IP	H	SO	BB	Sho	SV
1915	0	3	.000	3.54	8	28	23	18	16	0	0
1918	0	0	—	15.43	2	2.1	9	0	2	0	0
2 yrs.	0	3	.000	4.45	10	30.1	32	18	18	0	0

Joe Vance

JOSEPH ALBERT VANCE   BR TR
B. Sep. 16, 1905, Devine, Tex.   6' 1½" 190 lbs.
D. Jul. 4, 1978, Devine, Tex.

Year	W	L	PCT	ERA	G	IP	H	SO	BB	Sho	SV
1937	1	0	1.000	3.00	2	15	11	3	9	0	0
1938	0	0	—	7.15	3	11.1	20	2	4	0	0
2 yrs.	1	0	1.000	4.78	5	26.1	31	5	13	0	0

Hippo Vaughn

JAMES LESLIE VAUGHN   BB TL
B. Apr. 9, 1888, Weatherford, Tex.   6' 4" 215 lbs.
D. May 29, 1966, Chicago, Ill.

Year	W	L	PCT	ERA	G	IP	H	SO	BB	Sho	SV
1908	0	0	—	3.86	2	2.1	1	4	0	0	0
1910	13	11	.542	1.83	30	221.2	190	107	58	5	1
1911	8	10	.444	4.39	26	145.2	158	74	54	0	0
1912	2	8	.200	5.14	15	63	66	46	37	1	0
4 yrs.	23	29	.442	3.18	73	432.2	415	229	153	6	1

Joe Verbanic

JOSEPH MICHAEL VERBANIC   BR TR
B. Apr. 24, 1943, Washington, Pa.   6' 155 lbs.

Year	W	L	PCT	ERA	G	IP	H	SO	BB	Sho	SV
1967	4	3	.571	2.80	28	80.1	74	39	21	1	2
1968	6	7	.462	3.15	40	97	104	40	41	1	4
1970	1	0	1.000	4.50	7	16	20	8	12	0	0
3 yrs.	11	10	.524	3.12	75	193.1	198	87	74	2	6

Jake Wade

JACOB FIELDS WADE   BL TL
B. Apr. 1, 1912, Morehead City, N. C.   6' 2" 175 lbs.

Year	W	L	PCT	ERA	G	IP	H	SO	BB	Sho	SV
1946	2	1	.667	2.29	13	35.1	33	22	14	0	1

Mike Wallace

MICHAEL SHERMAN WALLACE   BL TL
B. Feb. 3, 1951, Gastonia, N. C.   6' 2" 190 lbs.

Year	W	L	PCT	ERA	G	IP	H	SO	BB	Sho	SV
1974	6	0	1.000	2.42	23	52	42	34	35	0	0
1975	0	0	—	15.75	3	4	11	2	1	0	0
2 yrs.	6	0	1.000	3.38	26	56	53	36	36	0	0

Jack Warhop

JOHN MILTON WARHOP   BR TR
B. Jul. 4, 1884, Hinton, W. Va.   5' 9½" 168 lbs.
D. Oct. 4, 1960, Freeport, Ill.

Year	W	L	PCT	ERA	G	IP	H	SO	BB	Sho	SV
1908	1	2	.333	4.46	5	36.1	40	11	8	0	0
1909	13	15	.464	2.40	36	243.1	197	95	81	3	2
1910	14	14	.500	2.87	37	254	219	75	79	0	2
1911	12	13	.480	4.16	31	209.2	239	71	44	1	0
1912	10	19	.345	2.86	39	258	256	110	59	0	3
1913	4	6	.400	3.75	15	62.1	69	11	33	0	0
1914	8	15	.348	2.37	37	216.2	182	56	44	0	0
1915	7	9	.438	3.96	21	143.1	164	34	52	0	0
8 yrs.	69	93	.426	3.09	221	1423.2	1366	463	400	4	7

George Washburn

GEORGE EDWARD WASHBURN   BL TR
B. Oct. 6, 1914, Solon, Me.   6' 1" 175 lbs.
D. Jan. 5, 1979, Baton Rouge, La.

Year	W	L	PCT	ERA	G	IP	H	SO	BB	Sho	SV
1941	0	1	.000	13.50	1	2	2	1	5	0	0

Gary Waslewski
GARY LEE WASLEWSKI BR TR
B. Jul. 21, 1941, Meriden, Conn. 6' 4" 190 lbs.

Year	W	L	PCT	ERA	G	IP	H	SO	BB	Sho	SV
1970	2	2	.500	3.11	26	55	42	27	27	0	0
1971	0	1	.000	3.25	24	36	28	17	16	0	1
2 yrs.	2	3	.400	3.16	50	91	70	44	43	0	1

Dave Weathers
JOHN DAVID WEATHERS BR TR
B. Sep. 25, 1969, Lawrenceburg, Tenn. 6' 3" 205 lbs.

Year	W	L	PCT	ERA	G	IP	H	SO	BB	Sho	SV
1996	0	2	.000	9.35	11	17.1	23	13	14	0	0

Divisional Playoffs

| 1996 | 1 | 0 | 1.000 | 0.00 | 2 | 5 | 1 | 5 | 0 | 0 | 0 |

League Championship Series

| 1996 | 1 | 0 | 1.000 | 0.00 | 2 | 3 | 3 | 0 | 0 | 0 | 0 |

World Series

| 1996 | 0 | 0 | — | 3.00 | 3 | 3 | 2 | 3 | 3 | 0 | 0 |

Jim Weaver
JAMES DEMENT WEAVER BR TR
B. Nov. 25, 1903, Obion County, Tenn. 6' 6" 230 lbs.
D. Dec. 12, 1983, Lakeland, Fla.

Year	W	L	PCT	ERA	G	IP	H	SO	BB	Sho	SV
1931	2	1	.667	5.31	17	57.2	66	28	29	0	0

Dave Wehrmeister
DAVID THOMAS WEHRMEISTER BR TR
B. Nov. 9, 1952, Berwyn, Ill. 6' 4" 195 lbs.

Year	W	L	PCT	ERA	G	IP	H	SO	BB	Sho	SV
1981	0	0	—	5.14	5	7	6	7	7	0	0

Lefty Weinert
PHILIP WALTER WEINERT BL TL
B. Apr. 21, 1902, Philadelphia, Pa. 6' 1" 195 lbs.
D. Apr. 17, 1973, Rockledge, Fla.

Year	W	L	PCT	ERA	G	IP	H	SO	BB	Sho	SV
1931	2	2	.500	6.20	17	24.2	31	24	19	0	0

Ed Wells
EDWIN LEE WELLS BL TL
B. Jun. 7, 1900, Ashland, Ohio 6' 1½" 183 lbs.
D. May 1, 1986, Montgomery, Ala.

Year	W	L	PCT	ERA	G	IP	H	SO	BB	Sho	SV
1929	13	9	.591	4.33	31	193.1	179	78	81	3	0
1930	12	3	.800	5.20	27	150.2	185	46	49	0	0
1931	9	5	.643	4.32	27	116.2	130	34	37	0	2
1932	3	3	.500	4.26	22	31.2	38	13	12	0	2
4 yrs.	37	20	.649	4.59	107	492.1	532	171	179	3	4

Butch Wensloff
CHARLES WILLIAM WENSLOFF BR TR
B. Dec. 3, 1915, Sausalito, Calif. 5' 11" 185 lbs.

Year	W	L	PCT	ERA	G	IP	H	SO	BB	Sho	SV
1943	13	11	.542	2.54	29	223.1	179	105	70	1	1
1947	3	1	.750	2.61	11	51.2	41	18	22	0	0
2 yrs.	16	12	.571	2.55	40	275	220	123	92	1	1

World Series

| 1947 | 0 | 0 | — | 0.00 | 1 | 2 | 0 | 0 | 0 | 0 | 0 |

John Wetteland
JOHN KARL WETTELAND BR TR
B. Aug. 21, 1966, San Mateo, Calif. 6' 2" 195 lbs.

Year	W	L	PCT	ERA	G	IP	H	SO	BB	Sho	SV
1995	1	5	.167	2.93	60	61.1	40	66	14	0	31
1996	2	3	.400	2.83	62	63.2	54	69	21	0	43
2 yrs.	3	8	.273	2.88	122	125	94	135	35	0	74

Divisional Playoffs

1995	0	1	.000	14.54	3	4.1	8	5	2	0	0
1996	0	0	—	0.00	3	4	2	4	4	0	2
2 yrs.	0	1	.000	7.56	6	8.1	10	9	6	0	2

League Championship Series

| 1996 | 0 | 0 | — | 4.50 | 4 | 4 | 2 | 5 | 1 | 0 | 1 |

World Series

| 1996 | 0 | 0 | — | 2.08 | 5 | 4.1 | 4 | 6 | 1 | 0 | 4 |

Stefan Wever
STEFAN MATTHEW WEVER BR TR
B. Apr. 22, 1958, Marburg, Germany 6' 8" 245 lbs.

Year	W	L	PCT	ERA	G	IP	H	SO	BB	Sho	SV
1982	0	1	.000	27.00	1	2.2	6	2	3	0	0

Wally Whitehurst
WALTER RICHARD WHITEHURST BR TR
B. Apr. 11, 1964, Shreveport, La. 6' 3" 180 lbs.

Year	W	L	PCT	ERA	G	IP	H	SO	BB	Sho	SV
1996	1	1	.500	6.75	2	8	11	1	2	0	0

Ed Whitson
EDDIE LEE WHITSON BR TR
B. May 19, 1955, Johnson City, Tenn. 6' 3" 195 lbs.

Year	W	L	PCT	ERA	G	IP	H	SO	BB	Sho	SV
1985	10	8	.556	4.88	30	158.2	201	89	43	2	0
1986	5	2	.714	7.54	14	37	54	27	23	0	0
2 yrs.	15	10	.600	5.38	44	195.2	255	116	66	2	0

Kemp Wicker
KEMP CASWELL WICKER BR TL
B. Aug. 13, 1906, Kernersville, N. C. 5' 11" 182 lbs.
D. Jun. 11, 1973, Kernersville, N. C.

Year	W	L	PCT	ERA	G	IP	H	SO	BB	Sho	SV
1936	1	2	.333	7.65	7	20	31	5	11	0	0
1937	7	3	.700	4.40	16	88	107	14	26	1	0
1938	1	0	1.000	0.00	1	1	0	0	1	0	0
3 yrs.	9	5	.643	4.95	24	109	138	19	38	1	0

World Series

| 1937 | 0 | 0 | — | 0.00 | 1 | 1 | 0 | 0 | 0 | 0 | 0 |

Bob Wickman
ROBERT JOE WICKMAN BR TR
B. Feb. 6, 1969, Green Bay, Wis. 6' 1" 207 lbs.

Year	W	L	PCT	ERA	G	IP	H	SO	BB	Sho	SV
1992	6	1	.857	4.11	8	50.1	51	21	20	0	0
1993	14	4	.778	4.63	41	140	156	70	69	1	4
1994	5	4	.556	3.09	53	70	54	56	27	0	6
1995	2	4	.333	4.05	63	80	77	51	33	0	1
1996	4	1	.800	4.67	58	79	94	61	34	0	0
5 yrs.	31	14	.689	4.21	223	419.1	432	259	183	1	11

Divisional Playoffs

| 1995 | 0 | 0 | — | 0.00 | 3 | 3 | 5 | 3 | 0 | 0 | 0 |

Bob Wiesler
ROBERT GEORGE WIESLER BB TL
B. Aug. 13, 1930, St. Louis, Mo. 6' 3" 188 lbs.

Year	W	L	PCT	ERA	G	IP	H	SO	BB	Sho	SV
1951	0	2	.000	13.50	4	9.1	13	3	11	0	0
1954	3	2	.600	4.15	6	30.1	28	25	30	0	0
1955	0	2	.000	3.91	16	53	39	22	49	0	0
3 yrs.	3	6	.333	4.95	26	92.2	80	50	90	0	0

Bill Wight
WILLIAM ROBERT WIGHT BL TL
B. Apr. 12, 1922, Rio Vista, Calif. 6' 1" 180 lbs.

Year	W	L	PCT	ERA	G	IP	H	SO	BB	Sho	SV
1946	2	2	.500	4.46	14	40.1	44	11	30	0	0
1947	1	0	1.000	1.00	1	9	8	3	2	0	0
2 yrs.	3	2	.600	3.83	15	49.1	52	14	32	0	0

Stan Williams
STANLEY WILSON WILLIAMS BR TR
B. Sep. 14, 1936, Enfield, N. H. 6' 5" 230 lbs.

Year	W	L	PCT	ERA	G	IP	H	SO	BB	Sho	SV
1963	9	8	.529	3.20	29	146.1	137	98	57	1	0
1964	1	5	.167	3.84	21	82	76	54	38	0	0
2 yrs.	10	13	.435	3.43	50	228.1	213	152	95	1	0

World Series

| 1963 | 0 | 0 | — | 0.00 | 1 | 3 | 1 | 5 | 0 | 0 | 0 |

Pete Wilson
PETER ALEX WILSON B TL
B. Oct. 9, 1885, Springfield, Mass. ' " lbs.
D. Jun. 5, 1957, St. Petersburg, Fla.

Year	W	L	PCT	ERA	G	IP	H	SO	BB	Sho	SV
1908	3	3	.500	3.46	6	39	27	28	33	1	0
1909	6	5	.545	3.17	14	93.2	82	44	43	1	0
2 yrs.	9	8	.529	3.26	20	132.2	109	72	76	2	0

Snake Wiltse
LEWIS DEWITT WILTSE BR TL
B. Dec. 5, 1871, Bouckville, N. Y. ' " lbs.
D. Aug. 25, 1928, Harrisburg, Pa.

Year	W	L	PCT	ERA	G	IP	H	SO	BB	Sho	SV
1903	1	3	.250	5.40	4	25	35	6	6	0	1

387

Year	W	L	PCT	ERA	G	IP	H	SO	BB	Sho	SV

Mike Witt

MICHAEL ATWATER WITT BR TR
B. Jul. 20, 1960, Fullerton, Calif. 6' 7" 185 lbs.

Year	W	L	PCT	ERA	G	IP	H	SO	BB	Sho	SV
1990	5	6	.455	4.47	16	96.2	87	60	34	1	0
1991	0	1	.000	10.13	2	5.1	8	0	1	0	0
1993	3	2	.600	5.27	9	41	39	30	22	0	0
3 yrs.	8	9	.471	4.91	27	143	134	90	57	1	0

Bill Wolfe

WILBERT OTTO WOLFE BR TR
B. Jun. 7, 1876, Independence, Pa. 6' 1" lbs.
D. Feb. 27, 1953, Gibsontown, Pa.

Year	W	L	PCT	ERA	G	IP	H	SO	BB	Sho	SV
1903	6	9	.400	2.97	20	148.1	143	48	26	1	0
1904	0	3	.000	3.21	7	33.2	31	8	4	0	0
2 yrs.	6	12	.333	3.02	27	182	174	56	30	1	0

Dooley Womack

HORACE GUY WOMACK BL TR
B. Aug. 25, 1939, Columbia, S. C. 6' 170 lbs.

Year	W	L	PCT	ERA	G	IP	H	SO	BB	Sho	SV
1966	7	3	.700	2.64	42	75	52	50	23	0	4
1967	5	6	.455	2.41	65	97	80	57	35	0	18
1968	3	7	.300	3.21	45	61.2	53	27	29	0	2
3 yrs.	15	16	.484	2.70	152	233.2	185	134	87	0	24

Dick Woodson

RICHARD LEE WOODSON BR TR
B. Mar. 30, 1945, Oelwein, Iowa 6' 5" 205 lbs.

Year	W	L	PCT	ERA	G	IP	H	SO	BB	Sho	SV
1974	1	2	.333	5.79	8	28	34	12	12	0	0

Ken Wright

KENNETH WARREN WRIGHT BR TR
B. Sep. 4, 1946, Pensacola, Fla. 6' 2" 210 lbs.

Year	W	L	PCT	ERA	G	IP	H	SO	BB	Sho	SV
1974	0	0	—	3.00	3	6	5	2	7	0	0

John Wyatt

JOHN THOMAS WYATT BR TR
B. Apr. 19, 1935, Chicago, Ill. 5' 11½" 200 lbs.

Year	W	L	PCT	ERA	G	IP	H	SO	BB	Sho	SV
1968	0	2	.000	2.16	7	8.1	7	6	9	0	0

Jim York

JAMES HARLAN YORK BR TR
B. Aug. 27, 1947, Maywood, Calif. 6' 3" 200 lbs.

Year	W	L	PCT	ERA	G	IP	H	SO	BB	Sho	SV
1976	1	0	1.000	5.59	3	9.2	14	6	4	0	0

Curt Young

CURTIS ALLEN YOUNG BR TL
B. Apr. 16, 1960, Saginaw, Mich. 6' 175 lbs.

Year	W	L	PCT	ERA	G	IP	H	SO	BB	Sho	SV
1992	3	0	1.000	3.32	13	43.1	51	13	10	0	0

Tom Zachary

JONATHAN THOMPSON WALTON ZACHARY BL TL
B. May 7, 1896, Graham, N. C. 6' 1" 187 lbs.
D. Jan. 24, 1969, Burlington, N. C.

Year	W	L	PCT	ERA	G	IP	H	SO	BB	Sho	SV
1928	3	3	.500	3.94	7	45.2	54	7	15	0	1
1929	12	0	1.000	2.48	26	119.2	131	35	30	2	2
1930	1	1	.500	6.48	3	16.2	18	1	9	0	0
3 yrs.	16	4	.800	3.21	36	182	203	43	54	2	3
World Series											
1928	1	0	1.000	3.00	1	9	9	7	1	0	0

Bill Zuber

WILLIAM HENRY ZUBER BR TR
B. Mar. 26, 1913, Middle Amana, Iowa 6' 2" 195 lbs.
D. Nov. 2, 1982, Cedar Rapids, Iowa

Year	W	L	PCT	ERA	G	IP	H	SO	BB	Sho	SV
1943	8	4	.667	3.89	20	118	100	57	74	0	1
1944	5	7	.417	4.21	22	107	101	59	54	1	0
1945	5	11	.313	3.19	21	127	121	50	56	0	1
1946	0	1	.000	12.71	3	5.2	10	3	3	0	0
4 yrs.	18	23	.439	3.88	66	357.2	332	169	187	1	2

Manager Register

The Manager Register is an alphabetical listing of every man who has managed the New York Yankees. Included are facts about the managers and their year-by-year managerial records for the Yankees.

Year	G	W	L	T	N	Pct.	Standing

Joe McCarthy

JOSEPH VINCENT MCCARTHY
B. Apr. 21, 1887, Philadelphia, Pa.
D. Jan. 13, 1978, Buffalo, N. Y.
Hall of Fame 1957

Year	G	W	L	T	N	Pct.	Standing
1931	155	94	59	2	0	.614	**2**
1932	156	107	47	1	1	.695	**1**
1933	152	91	59	2	0	.607	**2**
1934	154	94	60	0	0	.610	**2**
1935	149	89	60	0	0	.597	**2**
1936	155	102	51	2	0	.667	**1**
1937	157	102	52	2	1	.662	**1**
1938	157	99	53	5	0	.651	**1**
1939	152	106	45	1	0	.702	**1**
1940	155	88	66	0	1	.571	**3**
1941	156	101	53	2	0	.656	**1**
1942	154	103	51	0	0	.669	**1**
1943	155	98	56	1	0	.636	**1**
1944	154	83	71	0	0	.539	**3**
1945	152	81	71	0	0	.533	**4**
1946	35	22	13	0	0	.629	**2** 3
16 yrs.	2348	1460	867	18	3	.627	

World Series

Year	G	W	L	T	N	Pct.	Standing
1932	4	4	0	0	0	1.000	
1936	6	4	2	0	0	.667	
1937	5	4	1	0	0	.800	
1938	4	4	0	0	0	1.000	
1939	4	4	0	0	0	1.000	
1941	5	4	1	0	0	.800	
1942	5	1	4	0	0	.200	
1943	5	4	1	0	0	.800	
8 yrs.	38	29	9	0	0	.763	

Key

Year	Year Managed
G	Games Managed
W	Games Won
L	Games Lost
T	Games Tied
N	No Decision Games
PCT	Winning Percentage
Standing*	Finishing Position

*The figures in this column indicate the standing of the team at the end of the season and when there was a managerial change. The four possible cases are:

Only Manager For The Team That Year—Indicated by a single boldfaced figure in the extreme left-hand column that shows the final standing of the team.

Manager Started Season, But Did Not Finish—Indicated by two figures: the first is boldfaced and shows the standing of the team when this manager left; the second shows the final standing of the team.

Manager Finished Season, But Did Not Start—Indicated by two figures: the first shows the standing of the team when this manager started; the second is boldfaced and shows the final standing of the team.

Manager Did Not Start or Finish Season—Indicated by three figures: the first shows the standing when this manager started; the second is boldfaced and shows the standing when this manager left; the third shows the final standing of the team.

Yogi Berra
LAWRENCE PETER BERRA
B. May 12, 1925, St. Louis, Mo.
Hall of Fame 1972

Year	G	W	L	T	N	Pct.	Standing
1964	164	99	63	2	0	.611	1
1984	162	87	75	0	0	.537	3
1985	16	6	10	0	0	.375	7 2
3 yrs.	342	192	148	2	0	.565	

World Series

Year	G	W	L	T	N	Pct.	Standing
1964	7	3	4	0	0	.429	

Frank Chance
FRANK LEROY CHANCE
B. Sep. 9, 1877, Fresno, Calif.
D. Sep. 15, 1924, Los Angeles, Calif.
Hall of Fame 1946

Year	G	W	L	T	N	Pct.	Standing
1913	153	57	94	2	0	.377	7
1914	137	60	74	3	0	.448	7 6
2 yrs.	290	117	168	5	0	.411	

Hal Chase
HAROLD HOMER CHASE
B. Feb. 13, 1883, Los Gatos, Calif.
D. May 18, 1947, Colusa, Calif.

Year	G	W	L	T	N	Pct.	Standing
1910	14	10	4	0	0	.714	3 2
1911	153	76	76	1	0	.500	6
2 yrs.	167	86	80	1	0	.518	

Bucky Dent
RUSSELL EARL DENT
B. Nov. 25, 1951, Savannah, Ga.

Year	G	W	L	T	N	Pct.	Standing
1989	40	18	22	0	0	.450	6 5
1990	49	18	31	0	0	.367	7 7
2 yrs.	89	36	53	0	0	.404	

Bill Dickey
WILLIAM MALCOLM DICKEY
B. Jun. 6, 1907, Bastrop, La.
D. Nov. 12, 1993, Little Rock, Ark.
Hall of Fame 1954

Year	G	W	L	T	N	Pct.	Standing
1946	105	57	48	0	0	.543	2 3 3

Wild Bill Donovan
WILLIAM EDWARD DONOVAN
B. Oct. 13, 1876, Lawrence, Mass.
D. Dec. 9, 1923, Forsyth, N. Y.

Year	G	W	L	T	N	Pct.	Standing
1915	154	69	83	2	0	.454	5
1916	156	80	74	2	0	.519	4
1917	155	71	82	2	0	.464	6
3 yrs.	465	220	239	6	0	.479	

Kid Elberfeld
NORMAN ARTHUR ELBERFELD
B. Apr. 13, 1875, Pomeroy, Ohio
D. Jan. 13, 1944, Chattanooga, Tenn.

Year	G	W	L	T	N	Pct.	Standing
1908	98	27	71	0	0	.276	6 8

Art Fletcher
ARTHUR FLETCHER
B. Jan. 5, 1885, Collinsville, Ill.
D. Feb. 6, 1950, Los Angeles, Calif.

Year	G	W	L	T	N	Pct.	Standing
1929	11	6	5	0	0	.545	2 2

Dallas Green
GEORGE DALLAS GREEN
B. Aug. 4, 1934, Newport, Del.

Year	G	W	L	T	N	Pct.	Standing
1989	121	56	65	0	0	.463	6 5

Clark Griffith
CLARK CALVIN GRIFFITH
B. Nov. 20, 1869, Clear Creek, Mo.
D. Oct. 27, 1955, Washington, D. C.
Hall of Fame 1946

Year	G	W	L	T	N	Pct.	Standing
1903	136	72	62	2	0	.537	4

Clark Griffith continued

Year	G	W	L	T	N	Pct.	Standing
1904	155	92	59	4	0	.609	2
1905	152	71	78	3	0	.477	6
1906	155	90	61	4	0	.596	2
1907	152	70	78	4	0	.473	5
1908	57	24	32	1	0	.429	6 8
6 yrs.	807	419	370	18	0	.531	

Bucky Harris
STANLEY RAYMOND HARRIS
B. Nov. 8, 1896, Port Jervis, N. Y.
D. Nov. 8, 1977, Bethesda, Md.
Hall of Fame 1975

Year	G	W	L	T	N	Pct.	Standing
1947	155	97	57	1	0	.630	1
1948	154	94	60	0	0	.610	3
2 yrs.	309	191	117	1	0	.620	

World Series

Year	G	W	L	T	N	Pct.	Standing
1947	7	4	3	0	0	.571	

Ralph Houk
RALPH GEORGE HOUK
B. Aug. 9, 1919, Lawrence, Kans.

Year	G	W	L	T	N	Pct.	Standing
1961	163	109	53	1	0	.673	1
1962	162	96	66	0	0	.593	1
1963	161	104	57	0	0	.646	1
1966	140	66	73	1	0	.475	10 10
1967	163	72	90	1	0	.444	9
1968	164	83	79	2	0	.512	5
1969	162	80	81	1	0	.497	5
1970	163	93	69	1	0	.574	2
1971	162	82	80	0	0	.506	4
1972	155	79	76	0	0	.510	4
1973	162	80	82	0	0	.494	4
11 yrs.	1757	944	806	7	0	.539	

World Series

Year	G	W	L	T	N	Pct.	Standing
1961	5	4	1	0	0	.800	
1962	7	4	3	0	0	.571	
1963	4	0	4	0	0	.000	
3 yrs.	16	8	8	0	0	.500	

Dick Howser
RICHARD DALTON HOWSER
B. May 14, 1936, Miami, Fla.
D. Jun. 17, 1987, Kansas City, Mo.

Year	G	W	L	T	N	Pct.	Standing
1978	1	0	1	0	0	.000	3 3 1
1980	162	103	59	0	0	.636	1
2 yrs.	163	103	60	0	0	.632	

League Championship Series

Year	G	W	L	T	N	Pct.	Standing
1980	3	0	3	0	0	.000	

Miller Huggins
MILLER JAMES HUGGINS
B. Mar. 27, 1879, Cincinnati, Ohio
D. Sep. 25, 1929, New York, N. Y.
Hall of Fame 1964

Year	G	W	L	T	N	Pct.	Standing
1918	126	60	63	3	0	.488	4
1919	141	80	59	2	0	.576	3
1920	154	95	59	0	0	.617	3
1921	153	98	55	0	0	.641	1
1922	154	94	60	0	0	.610	1
1923	152	98	54	0	0	.645	1
1924	153	89	63	1	0	.586	2
1925	156	69	85	2	0	.448	7
1926	155	91	63	1	0	.591	1
1927	155	110	44	1	0	.714	1
1928	154	101	53	0	0	.656	1
1929	143	82	61	0	0	.573	2 2
12 yrs.	1796	1067	719	10	0	.597	

World Series

Year	G	W	L	T	N	Pct.	Standing
1921	8	3	5	0	0	.375	
1922	5	0	4	1	0	.000	

Miller Huggins continued

Year	G	W	L	T	N	Pct.	Standing
1923	6	4	2	0	0	.667	
1926	7	3	4	0	0	.429	
1927	4	4	0	0	0	1.000	
1928	4	4	0	0	0	1.000	
6 yrs.	34	18	15	1	0	.545	

Johnny Keane
JOHN JOSEPH KEANE
B. Nov. 3, 1911, St. Louis, Mo.
D. Jan. 6, 1967, Houston, Tex.

Year	G	W	L	T	N	Pct.	Standing
1965	162	77	85	0	0	.475	6
1966	20	4	16	0	0	.200	10 10
2 yrs.	182	81	101	0	0	.445	

Clyde King
CLYDE EDWARD KING
B. May 23, 1925, Goldsboro, N. C.

Year	G	W	L	T	N	Pct.	Standing
1982	62	29	33	0	0	.468	5 5

Bob Lemon
ROBERT GRANVILLE LEMON
B. Sep. 22, 1920, San Bernardino, Calif.
Hall of Fame 1976

Year	G	W	L	T	N	Pct.	Standing
1978	68	48	20	0	0	.706	3 1
1979	65	34	31	0	0	.523	4 4
1981	25	11	14	0	0	.440	5 6 (2nd)
1982	14	6	8	0	0	.429	4 5
4 yrs.	172	99	73	0	0	.576	

Divisional Playoffs

Year	G	W	L	T	N	Pct.	Standing
1981	5	3	2	0	0	.600	

League Championship Series

Year	G	W	L	T	N	Pct.	Standing
1978	4	3	1	0	0	.750	
1981	3	3	0	0	0	1.000	
2 yrs.	7	6	1	0	0	.857	

World Series

Year	G	W	L	T	N	Pct.	Standing
1978	6	4	2	0	0	.667	
1981	6	2	4	0	0	.333	
2 yrs.	12	6	6	0	0	.500	

Billy Martin
ALFRED MANUEL MARTIN
B. May 16, 1928, Berkeley, Calif.
D. Dec. 25, 1989, Johnson City, N. Y.

Year	G	W	L	T	N	Pct.	Standing
1975	56	30	26	0	0	.536	3 3
1976	159	97	62	0	0	.610	1
1977	162	100	62	0	0	.617	1
1978	94	52	42	0	0	.553	3 1
1979	96	55	40	0	0	.579	4 4
1983	162	91	71	0	0	.562	3
1985	145	91	54	0	0	.628	7 2
1988	68	40	28	0	0	.588	2 5
8 yrs.	941	556	385	0	0	.591	

League Championship Series

Year	G	W	L	T	N	Pct.	Standing
1976	5	2	3	0	0	.600	
1977	5	3	2	0	0	.600	
2 yrs.	10	6	4	0	0	.600	

World Series

Year	G	W	L	T	N	Pct.	Standing
1976	4	0	4	0	0	.000	
1977	6	4	2	0	0	.667	
2 yrs.	10	4	6	0	0	.400	

Joe McCarthy
JOSEPH VINCENT MCCARTHY
B. Apr. 21, 1887, Philadelphia, Pa.
D. Jan. 13, 1978, Buffalo, N. Y.
Hall of Fame 1957

Year	G	W	L	T	N	Pct.	Standing
1931	155	94	59	2	0	.614	2
1932	156	107	47	1	1	.695	1
1933	152	91	59	2	0	.607	2
1934	154	94	60	0	0	.610	2

Year	G	W	L	T	N	Pct.	Standing

Joe McCarthy *continued*

Year	G	W	L	T	N	Pct.	Standing
1935	149	89	60	0	0	.597	2
1936	155	102	51	2	0	.667	1
1937	157	102	52	2	1	.662	1
1938	157	99	53	5	0	.651	1
1939	152	106	45	1	0	.702	1
1940	155	88	66	0	1	.571	3
1941	156	101	53	2	0	.656	1
1942	154	103	51	0	0	.669	1
1943	155	98	56	1	0	.636	1
1944	154	83	71	0	0	.539	3
1945	152	81	71	0	0	.533	4
1946	35	22	13	0	0	.629	2 3
16 yrs.	2348	1460	867	18	3	.627	

World Series

Year	G	W	L	T	N	Pct.	Standing
1932	4	4	0	0	0	1.000	
1936	6	4	2	0	0	.667	
1937	5	4	1	0	0	.800	
1938	4	4	0	0	0	1.000	
1939	4	4	0	0	0	1.000	
1941	5	4	1	0	0	.800	
1942	5	1	4	0	0	.200	
1943	5	4	1	0	0	.800	
8 yrs.	38	29	9	0	0	.763	

Stump Merrill
CARL HARRISON MERRILL
B. Feb. 25, 1944, Brunswick, Me.

Year	G	W	L	T	N	Pct.	Standing
1990	113	49	64	0	0	.434	7 7
1991	162	71	91	0	0	.438	5
2 yrs.	275	120	155	0	0	.436	

Gene Michael
EUGENE RICHARD MICHAEL
B. Jun. 2, 1938, Kent, Ohio

Year	G	W	L	T	N	Pct.	Standing	
1981	56	34	22	0	0	.607	1	(1st)
1981	26	14	12	0	0	.538	5 6	(2nd)
1982	86	44	42	0	0	.512	4 5 5	
2 yrs.	168	92	76	0	0	.548		

Johnny Neun
JOHN HENRY NEUN
B. Oct. 28, 1900, Baltimore, Md.
D. Mar. 28, 1990, Baltimore, Md.

Year	G	W	L	T	N	Pct.	Standing
1946	14	8	6	0	0	.571	3 3

Roger Peckinpaugh
ROGER THORPE PECKINPAUGH
B. Feb. 5, 1891, Wooster, Ohio
D. Nov. 17, 1977, Cleveland, Ohio

Year	G	W	L	T	N	Pct.	Standing
1914	20	10	10	0	0	.500	7 6

Lou Piniella
LOUIS VICTOR PINIELLA
B. Aug. 28, 1943, Tampa, Fla.

Year	G	W	L	T	N	Pct.	Standing
1986	162	90	72	0	0	.556	2
1987	162	89	73	0	0	.549	4
1988	93	45	48	0	0	.484	2 5
3 yrs.	417	224	193	0	0	.537	

Bob Shawkey
JAMES ROBERT SHAWKEY
B. Dec. 4, 1890, Sigel, Pa.
D. Dec. 31, 1980, Syracuse, N. Y.

Year	G	W	L	T	N	Pct.	Standing
1930	154	86	68	0	0	.558	3

Buck Showalter
WILLIAM NATHANIEL SHOWALTER III
B. May 23, 1956, DeFuniak, Fla.

Year	G	W	L	T	N	Pct.	Standing
1992	162	76	86	0	0	.469	4
1993	162	88	74	0	0	.543	2
1994	113	70	43	0	0	.619	1
1995	144	79	65	0	0	.549	2
4 yrs.	581	313	268	0	0	.539	

Divisional Playoffs

Year	G	W	L	T	N	Pct.	Standing
1995	5	2	3	0	0	.400	

George Stallings
GEORGE TWEEDY STALLINGS
B. Nov. 17, 1867, Augusta, Ga.
D. May 13, 1929, Haddock, Ga.

Year	G	W	L	T	N	Pct.	Standing
1909	153	74	77	2	0	.490	5
1910	142	78	59	5	0	.569	3 2
2 yrs.	295	152	136	7	0	.528	

Casey Stengel
CHARLES DILLON STENGEL
B. Jul. 30, 1890, Kansas City, Mo.
D. Sep. 29, 1975, Glendale, Calif.
Hall of Fame 1966

Year	G	W	L	T	N	Pct.	Standing
1949	155	97	57	1	0	.630	1
1950	155	98	56	1	0	.636	1
1951	154	98	56	0	0	.636	1
1952	154	95	59	0	0	.617	1

Casey Stengel *continued*

Year	G	W	L	T	N	Pct.	Standing
1953	151	99	52	0	0	.656	1
1954	155	103	51	1	0	.669	2
1955	154	96	58	0	0	.623	1
1956	154	97	57	0	0	.630	1
1957	154	98	56	0	0	.636	1
1958	155	92	62	1	0	.597	1
1959	155	79	75	1	0	.513	3
1960	155	97	57	1	0	.630	1
12 yrs.	1851	1149	696	6	0	.623	

World Series

Year	G	W	L	T	N	Pct.	Standing
1949	5	4	1	0	0	.800	
1950	4	4	0	0	0	1.000	
1951	6	4	2	0	0	.667	
1952	7	4	3	0	0	.571	
1953	6	4	2	0	0	.667	
1955	7	3	4	0	0	.429	
1956	7	4	3	0	0	.571	
1957	7	3	4	0	0	.429	
1958	7	4	3	0	0	.571	
1960	7	3	4	0	0	.429	
10 yrs.	63	37	26	0	0	.587	

Joe Torre
JOSEPH PAUL TORRE
B. Jul. 18, 1940, Brooklyn, N. Y.

Year	G	W	L	T	N	Pct.	Standing
1996	162	92	70	0	0	.568	1

Divisional Playoffs

Year	G	W	L	T	N	Pct.	Standing
1996	4	3	1	0	0	.750	

League Championship Series

Year	G	W	L	T	N	Pct.	Standing
1996	5	4	1	0	0	.800	

World Series

Year	G	W	L	T	N	Pct.	Standing
1996	6	4	2	0	0	.667	

Bill Virdon
WILLIAM CHARLES VIRDON
B. Jun. 9, 1931, Hazel Park, Mich.

Year	G	W	L	T	N	Pct.	Standing
1974	162	89	73	0	0	.549	2
1975	104	53	51	0	0	.510	3 3
2 yrs.	266	142	124	0	0	.534	

Harry Wolverton
HARRY STERLING WOLVERTON
B. Dec. 6, 1873, Mt. Vernon, Ohio
D. Feb. 4, 1937, Oakland, Calif.

Year	G	W	L	T	N	Pct.	Standing
1912	153	50	102	1	0	.329	8

Year-by-Year Record

Key

Year	Year Managed
W	Games Won
L	Games Lost
Pct.	Winning Percentage
Finish	Games Tied
Manager	Finishing Position

Year	W	L	Pct.	Finish	Manager
1903	72	62	.537	4	Clark Griffith
1904	92	59	.609	2	"
1905	71	78	.477	6	"
1906	90	61	.596	2	"
1907	70	78	.473	5	"
1908	51	103	.331	8	Clark Griffith, Kid Elberfield
1909	74	77	.490	5	George Stallings
1910	88	63	.583	2	George Stallings, Hal Chase
1911	76	76	.500	6	Hal Chase
1912	50	102	.329	8	Harry Wolverton
1913	57	94	.377	7	Frank Chance
1914	70	84	.455	7	Frank Chance, Roger Peckinpaugh
1915	69	83	.454	5	Wild Bill Donovan
1916	80	74	.519	4	"
1917	71	82	.464	6	"
1918	60	63	.488	4	Miller Huggins
1919	80	59	.576	3	"
1920	95	59	.617	3	"
1921	98	55	.641	1	"
1922	94	60	.610	1	"
1923	98	54	.645	1	"
1924	89	63	.586	2	"
1925	69	85	.448	7	"
1926	91	63	.591	1	"
1927	110	44	.714	1	"
1928	101	53	.656	1	"
1929	88	66	.571	2	Miller Huggins, Art Fletcher
1930	86	68	.558	3	Bob Shawkey
1931	94	59	.614	2	Joe McCarthy
1932	107	47	.695	1	"
1933	91	59	.607	1	"
1934	94	60	.610	2	"
1935	89	60	.597	2	"
1936	102	51	.667	1	"
1937	102	52	.662	1	"
1938	99	53	.651	1	"
1939	106	45	.702	1	"
1940	88	66	.571	3	"
1941	101	53	.656	1	"
1942	103	51	.669	1	"
1943	98	56	.636	1	"
1944	83	71	.539	3	"
1945	81	71	.533	4	"
1946	87	67	.565	3	Joe McCarthy, Bill Dickey, Johnny Neun
1947	97	57	.630	1	Bucky Harris
1948	94	60	.610	3	"
1949	97	57	.630	1	Casey Stengel
1950	98	56	.636	1	"
1951	98	56	.636	1	"
1952	95	59	.617	1	"
1953	99	52	.656	1	"
1954	103	51	.669	2	"
1955	96	58	.623	1	"
1956	97	57	.630	1	"
1957	98	56	.636	1	"
1958	92	62	.597	1	"
1959	79	75	.513	3	"
1960	97	57	.630	1	"
1961	109	53	.673	1	Ralph Houk
1962	96	66	.593	1	"
1963	104	57	.646	1	"
1964	99	63	.611	1	Yogi Berra
1965	77	85	.475	6	Johnny Keane
1966	70	89	.440	10	Johnny Keane, Ralph Houk
1967	72	90	.444	9	Ralph Houk
1968	83	79	.512	5	"
1969	80	81	.497	5	"
1970	93	69	.574	2	"
1971	82	80	.506	4	"
1972	79	76	.510	4	"
1973	80	82	.494	4	"
1974	89	73	.549	2	Bill Virdon
1975	83	77	.519	3	Bill Virdon, Billy Martin
1976	97	62	.610	1	Billy Martin
1977	100	62	.617	1	"
1978	100	63	.613	1	Billy Martin, Dick Howser, Bob Lemon
1979	89	71	.556	4	Bob Lemon, Billy Martin
1980	103	59	.636	1	Dick Howser
1981	59	48	.551	3	Gene Michael, Bob Lemon
1982	79	83	.488	5	Bob Lemon, Gene Michael, Clyde King
1983	91	71	.562	3	Billy Martin
1984	87	75	.537	3	Yogi Berra
1985	97	64	.602	2	Yogi Berra, Billy Martin
1986	90	72	.556	2	Lou Piniella
1987	89	73	.549	4	"
1988	85	76	.528	5	Billy Martin, Lou Piniella
1989	74	87	.460	5	Dallas Green, Bucky Dent
1990	67	95	.414	7	Bucky Dent, Stump Merrill
1991	71	91	.438	5	Stump Merrill
1992	76	86	.469	5	Buck Showalter
1993	88	74	.543	2	"
1994	70	43	.619	1	"
1995	79	65	.549	2	"
1996	92	70	.568	1	Joe Torre

Index

Numbers in *italics* refer to photos.